D0002478

GREAT LIVES
FROM
HISTORY

GREAT LIVES FROM HISTORY

Renaissance
to 1900
Series

Volume 1
A-Cov

Edited by
FRANK N. MAGILL

SALEM PRESS

Pasadena, California   Englewood Cliffs, New Jersey

1/90

REF
920.009
GRE
V. I

Library of Congress Cataloging-in-Publication Data
Great lives from history. Renaissance to 1900 series /
edited by Frank N. Magill.
    p.   cm.
Includes bibliographical references.
Summary: This five-volume work examines the lives
of 495 individuals whose contributions greatly influenced the world's cultures that flourished from the Renaissance through 1900. An annotated bibliography accompanies each entry.
    1. Biography. 2. World history [1. Biography. 2. World
history.] I. Magill, Frank Northen, 1907-
CT104.G68   1989
920′.009′03—dc20
[B]
[920]   89-24039
ISBN 0-89356-551-2 (set)   CIP
ISBN 0-89356-552-0 (volume 1)   AC

PUBLISHER'S NOTE

Great Lives from History, Renaissance to 1900, is the fourth set in a series which, when completed by the forthcoming Twentieth Century series, will offer broad yet accessible coverage of the lives, careers, and achievements of historically significant individuals from ancient times to the twentieth century. Previously published sets include the American series (1987), covering 456 individuals who played key roles in the history of the United States from the time of the explorers to the late twentieth century; the British and Commonwealth series (1987), covering 483 individuals from the British Isles and Commonwealth nations, from earliest times to the late twentieth century; and the Ancient and Medieval series (1988), whose worldwide coverage of figures not previously treated ranges from the earliest known Egyptian king to the late medieval inventor Johann Gutenberg. The final five volumes, the Twentieth Century series, are scheduled to appear in 1990 and will examine major figures not considered in any of the other sets. Similarly, the current set does not duplicate coverage of individuals who appear in the American and British sets, but rather extends the coverage to other, worldwide figures who flourished during the period encompassing the mid-fifteenth century through 1900.

The Renaissance to 1900 series includes 481 articles on 495 individuals. Areas of achievement for the individuals covered include the sciences (both "hard" and social), the military, government, politics, patronage of the arts, art, architecture, philosophy, religion, music, literature, education, and theater and drama, among others. Thus, the set provides, for example, coverage of personages such as the Renaissance artist Leonardo da Vinci, the seventeenth century musician Johann Sebastian Bach, the eighteenth century religious figure Ba'al Shem Tov, and the nineteenth century philosopher Friedrich Nietzsche.

The format of the articles, which average two thousand words in length, is standard, beginning with a ready-reference listing, including birth and death dates and places, areas of achievement, and a short statement on the individual's overall contribution to his discipline and to the world. The remainder of the article is divided into four parts. The Early Life section covers the figure's life up to the point at which his or her major work began. The Life's Work section chronologically follows the figure, relating major events and achievements. The Summary section constitutes an evaluation of the figure's contribution to or impact on history and places the individual in context within his or her particular field. The final section is an annotated, evaluative bibliography, which is intended to serve as a starting point for further research. Works are chosen for their accessibility and availability to the student through most libraries.

Citations of works appearing in the text include, on first mention, the date of the work's first publication and, if the work was originally written in a language other than English, its English title in publication and the translation's publication date; where no published translation exists, a literal translation (appearing in lowercase letters and roman typeface) has been added where deemed valuable to the reader. Names of famous personages appearing for the first time in the text of an article identify the individual by first and last name or the equivalent thereof. All efforts have been made to verify essential facts: birth and death dates and places, name spellings, titles and dates of literary and other works, chronology, bibliographical information, and the like.

Volume V contains three indexes designed to aid the student: A Biographical Index lists the figures covered in the set, including cross-references of other names by which the individual may be known. An index by Areas of Achievement allows the user to access historical personages covered by their fields of endeavor (art, astronomy, and so on). Finally, a Geographical Index places these individuals by nation or region most familiar to the modern reader.

Thanks are extended to our contributors, experts from fields as various as the broad array of personages covered: general historians, intellectual historians, historians of art, literature, science, and numerous other disciplines. Their names appear at the ends of the articles as well as in a roster of contributors and their academic affiliations in the front matter of Volume I. To them we extend our appreciation for their dedication to making historical scholarship available to the general reader.

CONTRIBUTING REVIEWERS

Michael Adams
Wagner College

Patrick Adcock
Henderson State University

C. D. Akerley
United States Naval Academy

Arthur L. Alt
College of Great Falls

J. Stewart Alverson
University of Tennessee at Chattanooga

Nancy Fix Anderson
Loyola University, New Orleans

Kathy Saranpa Anstine
Yale University

Madeline Cirillo Archer
Duquesne University

Stanley Archer
Texas A&M University

James A. Arieti
Hampden-Sydney College

Stephen M. Ashby
Bowling Green State University

Dorothy B. Aspinwall
University of Hawaii at Manoa

Bryan Aubrey
Maharishi International University

Theodore P. Aufdemberge
Concordia College

Tom L. Auffenberg
Ouachita Baptist University

Ehrhard Bahr
University of California, Los Angeles

Brian S. Baigrie
University of Calgary

Barbara Ann Barbato
Webster University

Jeffrey G. Barlow
Lewis and Clark College

Dan Barnett
California State University, Chico

Thomas F. Barry
University of Southern California

Iraj Bashiri
University of Minnesota at Minneapolis St. Paul

Christopher Bassford
Purdue University, West Lafayette

Michael Bauman
Northeastern Bible College

Dorathea K. Beard
Northern Illinois University

Erving E. Beauregard
University of Dayton

Alice H. R. H. Beckwith
Providence College

Graydon Beeks
Pomona College

S. Carol Berg
College of Saint Benedict

Martin Berger
Youngstown State University

Cynthia A. Bily
Adrian College

Wayne M. Bledsoe
University of Missouri at Rolla

Julia B. Boken
State University of New York College at Oneonta

John Braeman
University of Nebraska at Lincoln

Harold Branam
Temple University

Gerhard Brand
California State University, Los Angeles

J. R. Broadus
University of North Carolina at Chapel Hill

Celeste Williams Brockington
Independent Scholar

William S. Brockington, Jr.
University of South Carolina

Judit Brody
Independent Scholar

vii

Alan Brown
Livingston University

Philip C. Brown
University of North Carolina at Charlotte

David D. Buck
University of Wisconsin—Milwaukee

David L. Bullock
Kansas State University

William H. Burnside
John Brown University

Linnea Goodwin Burwood
State University of New York at Binghamton

John A. Calabrese
Texas Woman's University

Edmund J. Campion
University of Tennessee at Knoxville

Byron D. Cannon
University of Utah

Joan E. Carr
Washington University

Allan D. Charles
University of South Carolina

Nan K. Chase
Independent Scholar

Victor W. Chen
Chabot College

Walter Aaron Clark
University of California, Los Angeles

Bernard A. Cook
Loyola University, New Orleans

Patricia Cook
Emory University, Atlanta

Randolf G. S. Cooper
Florida State University

Dennis Costanzo
State University of New York College at Plattsburgh

Loren W. Crabtree
Colorado State University

Frederic M. Crawford
Middle Tennessee State University

Daniel A. Crews
Central Missouri State University

Lee B. Croft
Arizona State University

LouAnn Faris Culley
Kansas State University

Victoria Hennessey Cummins
Austin College

Abraham A. Davidson
Temple University

Ronald W. Davis
Western Michigan University

Thomas Derdak
University of Chicago

Charles A. Desnoyers
Temple University
Villanova University

Tom Dewey II
University of Mississippi

Reidar Dittmann
Saint Olaf College

Ian Duffy
Lehigh University

Surjit S. Dulai
Michigan State University

Frederick Dumin
Washington State University

Burton L. Dunbar III
University of Missouri at Kansas City

Wilton Eckley
Colorado School of Mines

Lester Eckman
Touro College

Bruce L. Edwards
Bowling Green State University

David G. Egler
Western Illinois University

Mary Sweeney Ellett
Randolph-Macon Woman's College

Robert P. Ellis
Worcester State College

Thomas L. Erskine
Salisbury State University

Paul F. Erwin
University of Cincinnati

CONTRIBUTING REVIEWERS

Clara Estow
University of Massachusetts, Boston

Peter R. Faber
United States Air Force Academy

Barbara M. Fahy
Albright College

James J. Farsolas
University of South Carolina
Coastal Carolina Community College

Gary B. Ferngren
Oregon State University

Patricia A. Finch
College of the Albemarle

Edward Fiorelli
Saint John's University, New York

David Marc Fischer
Independent Scholar

Michael S. Fitzgerald
Purdue University, West Lafayette

Robert J. Frail
Centenary College

Margot K. Frank
Randolph-Macon Woman's College

Shirley F. Fredricks
Metropolitan State College

Ronald Fritze
Lamar University

C. George Fry
Saint Francis College

John G. Gallaher
Southern Illinois University at Edwardsville

John Gardner
Delaware State College

Keith Garebian
Independent Scholar

Leonardas V. Gerulaitis
Oakland University

Paul E. Gill
Shippensburg University

K. Fred Gillum
Colby College

William C. Griffin
Appalachian State University

Gil L. Gunderson
Monterey Institute of International Studies

Surendra K. Gupta
Pittsburg State University

Gavin R. G. Hambly
University of Texas at Dallas

William S. Haney II
Maharishi International University

Fred R. van Hartesveldt
Fort Valley State College

Paul B. Harvey, Jr.
Pennsylvania State University

John A. Heitmann
University of Dayton

Michael F. Hembree
Florida State University

Carlanna Hendrick
Governors School for Science and Mathematics

Sharon Hill
Virginia Commonwealth University

Richard L. Hillard
University of Arkansas, Pine Bluff

Michael Craig Hillmann
University of Texas at Austin

James R. Hofmann
California State University, Fullerton

Arthur B. Holmes
West Virginia Wesleyan College

Edelma Huntley
Appalachian State University

George Javor
Northern Michigan University

Shakuntala Jayaswal
University of New Haven

Loretta Turner Johnson
Mankato State University

Philip Dwight Jones
Bradley University

Anand Karnad
Boston City Hospital

Cynthia Lee Katona
Ohlone College

Donald R. Kelm
Northern Kentucky University

Karen A. Kildahl
South Dakota State University

Kenneth F. Kitchell, Jr.
Louisiana State University

Ann Klefstad
Sun and Moon Press

Wm. Laird Kleine-Ahlbrandt
Purdue University, West Lafayette

Dwight A. Klett
Rutgers University, New Brunswick

James Kline
Independent Scholar

Gregory C. Kozlowski
De Paul University

Charles Kraszewski
Pennsylvania State University

Jane Kristof
Portland State University

Lynn C. Kronzek
Independent Scholar

Paul E. Kuhl
Winston-Salem State University

David Z. Kushner
University of Florida, Gainesville

Pavlin Lange
Independent Scholar

Eugene S. Larson
Los Angeles Pierce College

Jack M. Lauber
University of Wisconsin—Eau Claire

J. David Lawrence
David Lipscomb University

Harry Lawton
University of California, Santa Barbara

Douglas A. Lee
Vanderbilt University

Leon Lewis
Appalachian State University

James Livingston
Northern Michigan University

Rey M. Longyear
University of Kentucky, Lexington

Karl Lunde
William Paterson College of New Jersey

Reinhart Lutz
University of California, Santa Barbara

David S. Lux
Virginia Polytechnic Institute and State University

Garrett L. McAinsh
Hendrix College

C. S. McConnell
University of Calgary

Philip McDermott
Independent Scholar

James Edward McGoldrick
Cedarville College

David K. McQuilkin
Bridgewater College

Paul Madden
Hardin Simmons University

Claudette R. Mainzer
University of Georgia, Athens

William C. Marceau
Saint John Fisher College

Charles E. May
California State University, Long Beach

Patrick Meanor
State University of New York College at Oneonta

Sara Joan Miles
Wheaton College

Mary-Emily Miller
Salem State College

Robert A. Morace
Daemen College

Gordon R. Mork
Purdue University, West Lafayette

Robert E. Morsberger
California State Polytechnic University, Pomona

Barbara Mujica
Georgetown University

Terence R. Murphy
American University

CONTRIBUTING REVIEWERS

John W. Myers
University of North Carolina at Wilmington

D. Gosselin Nakeeb
Pace University

William Nelles
Northwestern State University

Edwin L. Neville, Jr.
Canisius College

Brian J. Nichelson
United States Air Force Academy

Frank Nickell
Southeast Missouri State University

Charles H. O'Brien
Western Illinois University

Robert H. O'Connor
North Dakota State University

Lisa Paddock
Independent Scholar

Robert J. Paradowski
Rochester Institute of Technology

Mark Pestana
University of Chicago

R. Craig Philips
Michigan State University

Susan L. Piepke
Bridgewater College

Marjorie J. Podolsky
*Behrend College of Pennsylvania State
  University*

Richard H. Popkin
*University of California, Los Angeles
  Washington University*

Clifton W. Potter, Jr.
Lynchburg College

Dorothy Turner Potter
Lynchburg College

Victoria Price
Lamar University

Charles Pullen
Queen's University

Edna B. Quinn
Salisbury State University

William G. Ratliff
Georgia Southern College

John D. Raymer
*Indiana University at South Bend
  Indiana Vocational Technical College*

Dennis Reinhartz
University of Texas at Arlington

Rosemary M. Canfield Reisman
Troy State University

Ann E. Reynolds
Independent Scholar

Victoria Reynolds
*Southeastern Louisiana University
  Mandeville High School*

Vicki Robinson
State University of New York at Farmingdale

John O. Robison
University of South Florida

Carl Rollyson
*Bernard M. Baruch College
  City University of New York*

Paul Rosefeldt
University of New Orleans

Joseph Rosenblum
University of North Carolina at Greensboro

Emanuel D. Rudolph
Ohio State University

Victor Anthony Rudowski
Clemson University

Joyce E. Salisbury
University of Wisconsin—Green Bay

Hilel B. Salomon
University of South Carolina

Victor A. Santi
University of New Orleans

Stephen P. Sayles
University of La Verne

Daniel C. Scavone
University of Southern Indiana

Per Schelde
York College

William C. Schrader
Tennessee Technological University

Thomas C. Schunk
Bellevue College

Roger Sensenbaugh
Indiana University at Bloomington

Richard M. Shaw
North Dakota State University

John C. Sherwood
University of Oregon

J. Lee Shneidman
Adelphi University

Steven W. Shrader
University of the South

R. Baird Shuman
University of Illinois, Urbana-Champaign

Anne W. Sienkewicz
Independent Scholar

Genevieve Slomski
Independent Scholar

Ronald F. Smith
Massachusetts Maritime Academy

Ira Smolensky
Monmouth College

James E. Southerland
Brenan College

Robert M. Spector
Worcester State College

Joseph L. Spradley
Wheaton College

C. Fitzhugh Spragins
Arkansas College

Diane Prenatt Stevens
Indiana University at Bloomington

John Knox Stevens
Indiana University at Bloomington

David R. Stevenson
Kearney State College

Paul Stewart
Southern Connecticut State University

Martha Bennett Stiles
Independent Scholar

Donald D. Sullivan
University of New Mexico

James Sullivan
California State University, Los Angeles

Roy Arthur Swanson
University of Wisconsin—Milwaukee

Glenn L. Swygart
Tennessee Temple University

Daniel Taylor
Bethel College

Thomas J. Taylor
Purdue University, West Lafayette

J. A. Thompson
University of Kentucky, Lexington

Ralph Troll
Augustana College

Eileen Tess Tyler
United States Naval Academy

Ronald D. Tyler
Independent Scholar

William Urban
Monmouth College

Larry W. Usilton
University of North Carolina at Wilmington

George W. Van Devender
Hardin Simmons University

Eric Van Schaack
Colgate University

Abraham Verghese
East Tennessee State University

Charles L. Vigue
University of New Haven

Paul R. Waibel
Trinity College

Eric L. Wake
Cumberland College

Brent Waters
University of Redlands

Donald V. Weatherman
Arkansas College

Martha Ellen Webb
University of Nebraska at Lincoln

Allen Wells
Bowdoin College

CONTRIBUTING REVIEWERS

John D. Windhausen
Saint Anselm College

Michael Witkoski
South Carolina House of Representatives

Diane Wolfthal
Brooklyn Museum

Byron A. Wolverton
Southwest Texas State University

William Ross Woofenden
Swedenborg School of Religion

Clifton K. Yearley
State University of New York College at Buffalo

Robert Zaller
Drexel University

William M. Zanella
Hawaii Loa College

LIST OF BIOGRAPHIES IN VOLUME ONE

LIST OF BIOGRAPHIES IN VOLUME ONE

ABAHAI

Born: November 28, 1592; Hetu Ala
Died: September 21, 1643; Sheng-ching, Manchuria
Areas of Achievement: Government and the military
Contribution: Abahai consolidated and then expanded the empire begun by his father, Nurhachi, and established the foundations for Manchu rule over China during the Ch'ing Dynasty (1644-1911).

Early Life

Abahai (also known as Hung Taiji) was the eighth son of Nurhachi (1559-1626). Little is known about his early youth, but apparently as a teen he impressed his father with his fierce courage and intelligence. By the beginning of the 1600's, Nurhachi had created a unified Juchen political state and originally intended that his son Cuyen succeed him. In 1613, however, when Abahai and several of his other sons swore that Cuyen had tried to recruit them in a conspiracy against their father, Nurhachi had Cuyen killed.

In 1616, Nurhachi reorganized his government, calling it the Later Chin, in reference to his ancestors' rule over North China during the Chin Dynasty (1116-1234). Apparently stung by the earlier ambitions of his eldest son, Nurhachi determined to leave a council form of government to rule after his death. Accordingly, in 1616, he created the Four Senior Beile, which were to assist him in the administration of his growing kingdom. The Four Beile consisted of his three sons, Daisan, Manggultai, and Abahai, and a nephew, Amin. In 1621, members of the Four Beile began to take monthly turns in the administration of national affairs.

Nurhachi warned his sons against choosing a strong, vigorous leader, predicting that such a man's only goal would be to satisfy his own ambition. Upon Nurhachi's death, in September of 1626, the Four Beile nominated Abahai to become the second khan of the Later Chin. Clearly out of deference to their father's wishes, but also in keeping with their own ambitions, they expected Abahai to be merely *primus inter pares*. In the beginning, during all state functions, the Four Beile sat at the same level. The youngest of them, however, having secured the title khan, had no intention of sharing his power. Sensing the group's fear of their other brother, Dorgon, Abahai convinced them to force the suicide of Dorgon's mother, the Empress Hsiao-lieh. In doing so, however, Abahai was able to gain control over another banner (a military administrative unit which Nurhachi had created) and thereby end the equality among the senior Beile. He thereupon used his military advantage and political skills to consolidate his rule and expand the empire which his father had begun.

Life's Work

In 1629, Abahai abolished the monthly rotation of beile. One year later, he imprisoned Amin for a variety of offenses, and Daisan and Manggultai "voluntarily" swore allegiance to the khan. Upon Manggultai's death, Abahai declared his brother to have been a traitor and gained control of still another banner. In consolidating his power, Abahai relied on two separate sources of support: Chinese military and civilian officials serving the khan and younger Juchen military officers who opposed the strictly hereditary power of the princes.

Abahai's relationship with the Chinese provides an interesting reflection of both his political cunning and his historical acumen. He listened carefully to the advice of Chinese officials on political and administrative policies and acted on their suggestions to centralize his government. Moreover, he cautiously paid heed to their exhortation to fight the Ming Dynasty (1368-1644) and plan the conquest of China. On May 14, 1636, he proclaimed himself emperor, changing the name of his dynasty to Ch'ing, and his reign title to Ch'ung-te. (In the Chinese dynastic chronicles, his temple name would be Ch'ing T'ai-tsung.) Nevertheless, Abahai was exceptionally fearful of his people's being Sinicized, and he embarked on a series of measures to keep the Chinese and Manchus (a term he adopted for the Juchen in 1636) separate forever.

Abahai's special handling of the Chinese was militarily astute and politically brilliant. Although Nurhachi had also employed Chinese, his son developed a comprehensive program for recruiting Chinese military, technical, and political experts. In warring against the Ming Dynasty, Abahai took special pains to lure the Chinese military commanders to his side. He offered them substantial rewards for abandoning the Ming Dynasty and defecting to the Manchus. Moreover, Abahai was careful to insist that his own troops refrain from looting or any conduct which would alienate the Chinese population. Chinese officers who had previously submitted to the Manchus often appeared in Chinese towns or garrisons to relate their own good fortunes and recruit people to the Manchu side. In this manner, countless Chinese not only submitted to the Manchus but also came to serve Abahai loyally.

The Chinese served not only as allies in Abahai's struggles against his brothers but also frequently were masterful at cannonry and therefore instrumental in Manchu victories over fortified Ming towns. Equally important, however, was the fact that Abahai was preparing for the possible conquest of China. To this end, he needed knowledgeable officials to serve him and his successors. Undoubtedly, he was aware of the ancient Chinese adage that "one may conquer China on horseback, but one needs learned officials to rule it." Under Chinese guidance, he established a chancellery or literary office, which he gradually developed into a secretariat. He also borrowed from China the concept of six boards and a censorate. All these measures were intended to facilitate the eventual transfer of power from Ming China to the Manchus.

Abahai understood that many of his younger officers sought a more accessible route of advancement. He promoted young men on the basis of their courage, service, and loyalty, and created a network of capable and trustworthy officers. In 1637, Abahai created the Council of Deliberative Officials, composed of lieutenant and deputy-lieutenant generals. Princes and generals were excluded on the grounds that they were too often absent and lived too far from the capital.

Abahai also sought to attract non-Chinese people into his burgeoning empire. Accordingly, he created in 1638, the Li Fan Yuan (board of colonial affairs), which would oversee the management of relations between Manchus and those Mongolians who submitted to the Ch'ing. Eventually, it came to include Tibetans and Uighurs as well. Although not personally given to religious beliefs, Abahai sponspored Lamaism, the form of Buddhism prevalent among the Mongolians and Tibetans, and established an excellent relationship with the Dalai and Panchen Lamas. Understanding the value of symbolism, he secured the great seal of the Mongol Khan and began to style himself as the successor of Genghis Khan. The seal accorded Abahai enormous prestige in inner Asia and enhanced his potential claim to China.

A masterful politician and an insightful statesman, Abahai was also capable of great personal courage and strategic brilliance on the battlefield. Immediately after his ascendancy to the Later Chin throne, he had embarked on a program to defeat or at least neutralize his father's Chinese nemesis, General Yuan Ch'ung-huan. Failing the first approach, Abahai moved, in November, 1629, through the territory of the Karacin and Tumed Mongolians, around Yuan's forces, and into China proper through the Hsi-feng k'ou passes. Yuan was forced to hurry his troops to Peking to defend against the invaders, who were at the capital's gates. Yuan's success in driving off the enemy did not mitigate his failure to have prevented the invasion, and the Ming court ordered him arrested and dismembered. Among the reasons for the Chinese general's demise were the rumors, planted by Abahai's spies, that Yuan was planning to defect to the Manchus.

With his Chinese adversary removed, Abahai began, in the fall of 1631, an attack upon the heavily fortified garrison complex at Ta-ling Ho. During the complicated seige, Abahai himself led a contingent of about two hundred men and successfully routed a rescue army of seven thousand. In the end, Abahai's diplomacy and military skill secured the Chinese commander's surrender. Subsequently, many of Abahai's military maneuvers in China proper were actually designed and executed by Chinese officers in the service of the Manchus.

From 1631 to 1636, in addition to successful forays into China, Abahai's forces succeeded in subjugating the Chahar Mongolians and gained valuable horse-breeding grounds. During the closing days of 1638, the Ch'ing emperor personally led an army into Korea, and within one month secured the submission of the Korean king. In subsequent years, most of northeast Asia fell under Manchu control.

On March 18, 1642, the Manchus captured Sung-shan and, shortly thereafter, Chin-chou, two strategic Chinese towns. With these victories, the fall of Peking and the Ming Dynasty seemed inevitable. The first emperor of the Ch'ing Dynasty, however, did not live long enough to see this transpire. On September 21, 1643, Abahai died of natural causes at Sheng-ching. His brother Dorgon would complete the conquest of the Ming, and his oldest son Fu-lin (1644-1661) would become the first emperor of the unified Ch'ing Dynasty.

Summary

Abahai was a rare man in the annals of history. Skillful at the politics of survival, he was equally at home on the battlefields. In the ultimate analysis, however, his genius lay in attracting capable men, earning and maintaining their loyalty, and effecting the best of their suggestions into policy. In these matters, he was even more successful than his father, Nurhachi. Not since Genghis Khan had there been such a talented leader in the steppes of northeast Asia. Though perhaps lacking the overall military genius of Genghis, Abahai was particularly strong in areas where even the "khan of khans" had been lacking. Abahai was an educated man who valued the lessons of history and had a sense of the future that bordered on prescience.

Having used Chinese advisers and military men to his advantage, he nevertheless determined to keep the Manchus racially and culturally distinct from the Chinese. He repeatedly exhorted his Manchu followers to read the history of the Chin and profit from earlier mistakes. His decision to forbid further use of the terms *Juchen* or *Chien-chou* may have been an effort to disavow the assimilation and political demise of his ancestors. Abahai predicted that the ultimate penalty for Sinicization would be the disappearance of the Manchus as a people. Having essentially guaranteed the Manchu conquest of China, he perhaps foresaw that his people might someday vanish. In a sense, the life of Abahai, as it relates to the history of the Manchus, constitutes an epilogue to a classical tragedy. Destined to create an empire which included China, the Manchus were destined to fulfill Abahai's ominous prophesy and disappear as a people.

Bibliography
Hummel, Arthur W., ed. *Eminent Chinese of the Ch'ing Period (1644-1912)*. 2 vols. Washington, D.C.: Government Printing Office, 1943-1944. Volume 1 contains an excellent biography of Abahai.
Kessler, Lawrence D. *K'ang-hsi and the Consolidation of Ch'ing Rule, 1661-1684*. Chicago: University of Chicago Press, 1976. Although concentrating on the achievements of Abahai's grandson, the K'ang Hsi em-

peror, the author provides an analysis of the administrative beginnings of the Ch'ing under Abahai's direction.

Michael, Franz. *The Origin of Manchu Rule in China: Frontier and Bureaucracy as Interacting Forces in the Chinese Empire.* Baltimore: Johns Hopkins University Press, 1942. A somewhat controversial, but still incisive discussion of the frontier state and the processes undertaken by Nurhachi and Abahai to prepare for the conquest of China.

Oxnam, Robert B. *Ruling from Horseback: Manchu Politics in the Oboi Regency, 1661-1669.* Chicago: University of Chicago Press, 1975. In searching for the origins of the concept of regency and the nature of Oboi's policies, the author devotes considerable attention to Abahai.

Roth, Gertraude. "The Manchu-Chinese Relationship, 1618-1636." In *From Ming to Ch'ing: Conquest, Region, and Continuity in Seventeenth-Century China,* edited by Jonathan D. Spence and John E. Wills, Jr. New Haven, Conn.: Yale University Press, 1979. This article explores the role of Chinese advisers in Abahai's consolidation of power and his establishment of the Ch'ing.

Wakeman, Frederic, Jr. *The Great Enterprise: The Manchu Reconstruction of Imperial Order in Seventeenth-Century China.* 2 vols. Berkeley: University of California Press, 1985. This work is destined to be a classic in the study of Chinese history. Wakeman presents a comprehensive study of the Manchu conquest and rule over China. Volume 1 devotes much attention to Abahai's political and military activities.

Hilel B. Salomon

'ABBĀS THE GREAT

Born: January 27, 1571; Iran
Died: January 19, 1629; Ashraf, Mazandaran, Iran
Areas of Achievement: Government and politics
Contribution: The most famous of all Islamic era monarchs of Iran, 'Abbās
the Great was the chief architect of the modern Iranian state. His legacy
also includes great achievements in architecture, literature, textiles, and
painting.

Early Life

In 1501, an Iranian dynasty named for their Sufi ancestor Safī od-Dīn
established control over the region which constitutes modern Iran. These
Safavids were the first native dynasty to do so since the Arab Muslims had
overthrown the Sasanian Empire (224-651) nearly nine centuries earlier.
Reigning for more than two hundred years, the Safavids developed and
expanded a middle Islamic empire between the Ottomans, centered in Turkey to the west, and the Moguls, in the Indian subcontinent to the East.
Modern Iran owes to the Safavids the territorial configuration of the country
and its national religion, Twelver Shi'i Islam, which they established as the
official religion, thus enhancing Iranian distinctiveness and separateness
from their Sunni Muslim neighbors and contributing later to their sense of
cultural and political nationalism.

In all, eleven Safavid monarchs ruled over Iran, the last two in name only,
from 1722, when a successful invasion and occupation by the Afghans took
place, until 1736, when Nāder Shāh (ruled 1736-1747) established his own
short-lived dynasty. Among the Safavid monarchs, the most famous and
important was Shāh 'Abbās I, who ruled for more than forty years and on
whom Iranians have bestowed the title "the Great."

The second son of the relatively weak and incompetent Soltān Mohammad
Shāh (ruled 1578-1587), 'Abbās spent his youth in Mashhad and Herat under
the tutelage of a regional governor. Royal intrigue and strife between the
royal family and Iranian tribal military leaders led to the assassination of his
mother, the ambitious Queen Khayronnesa Begum, and his older brother, the
crown prince Hamzeh. 'Abbās himself at the age of sixteen, led by a second
guardian and tutor, deposed his father after a successful march on the royal
capital at Qazvīn.

At his accession, 'Abbās faced three serious tasks. First was the internal
need to establish control and authority over local dynasties which had reas-
serted themselves during his father's reign and the tribal leaders, mostly
Turkoman, who constituted a Safavid military aristocracy which had developed from the dynasty's early days. Second was another internal issue,
that of securing the throne against other claimants or threats from within the

royal family. Third was the monumental chore of defending Iran against perennial incursions by the powerful Ottomans to the West and the troublesome Uzbeks to the East.

Life's Work

From the beginning of his reign, 'Abbās focused his attention on the organization of the military and the Ottoman and Uzbek threats. In 1590, ending a war that had begun early in his father's reign, 'Abbās signed the unfavorable Treaty of Istanbul with the Ottomans so as to avoid having to deal simultaneously with two military fronts. He was now in a position to challenge the Uzbeks, who had occupied Mashhad and Herat for a decade. He regained those two important cities.

At the same time, 'Abbās began a long-term reorganization of the corps of musketeers and the artillery corps and formed a new cavalry corps paid directly out of the royal treasury and composed of former slaves, prisoners of war, and others, many of them Georgians and Circassians, who would be loyal to the Crown rather than to regional tribal affiliations. Subsequently, he was able to quell revolts by tribal leaders and groups, to dispose of the governor-tutor who had helped him attain the throne, and to proceed to pacify various Iranian provinces. In effect, he had permanently tipped the scales in favor of the Iranian city and settled life as opposed to earlier rural and nomadic ways. He was effecting a centralized governmental administration that would be his legacy in Iran in succeeding centuries. His annexation of vassal states and his incorporation of vast amounts of territory into crown lands were other dimensions of this policy.

By 1603, however, 'Abbās was ready to confront the Ottomans again on his own terms. In 1605, the Safavid army inflicted a great defeat on them near Tabriz, regaining that important city and former Iranian capital in the process. A new treaty in 1612 reestablished old borders more favorable to Iran. In the meantime, 'Abbās had annexed the island of Bahrein in 1601-1602. Later, in 1622, with British assistance, he took Hormoz Island from the Portuguese. In 1623-1624, 'Abbās broke the peace he had made with the Ottomans and reclaimed Kurdish territory to the West. In short, as of the first quarter of the seventeenth century, 'Abbās had made the Safavid empire as large territorially as Iran would ever later be.

When 'Abbās ascended the throne, the Iranian population was suffering from wretched living conditions. By the end of his reign, the economic lot of ordinary Iranians was better than it had ever been in history. One of the reasons for the improvement was the stability his military and centralizing policies achieved. Another reason has to do with the energy and resources he invested into improving communication and transportation in Iran by numerous construction projects of roads, bridges, and caravansaries. Other factors are apparent in the king's development of Ispahan.

In 1598, 'Abbās had moved the Safavid capital from Qazvīn to Ispahan. He then undertook great projects of construction in his new capital, building avenues, palaces, mosques, and gardens. He established commercial and diplomatic ties with the Portuguese, the Dutch, and the British. The already-cited multiracial composition of his military corps and his relocation of several thousand Armenian families from Azerbaijan to a new Jolfa in Ispahan reflected a tolerant attitude on 'Abbās' part in general toward races and creeds. This led to the presence of foreign merchants and orders of Christian missionaries. He hoped, through good relations with Europe, to form an alliance against the Ottomans, which never happened. What did happen was economic growth, to which his interest in the arts also contributed. For example, 'Abbās established textile workshops for export production which were the ancestors of contemporary Iranian carpet-weaving firms.

On the negative side of the ledger, it was in dealing with the problem of royal sucession and protection of his throne that 'Abbās exhibited uncharacteristic shortsightedness and instituted policies which contributed in the long run to the decline of the Safavids. Plagued no doubt by the memory of the assassinations of his mother and brother, 'Abbās was suspicious to the point of paranoia about the aims of members of the royal family and tribal leaders and princes who might rally around them or use them. After deposing his father, 'Abbās had him blinded and apparently imprisoned. He ordered the executions of many tribal princes. He had two of his brothers blinded as well. In 1615, he ordered his eldest son, the Crown Prince Safi Mīrzā, assassinated, and later ordered the blinding of another son and two grandsons. (According to Islamic tradition, a blind person cannot succeed to a throne.) Further, he confined potential heirs to the harem, preventing them from receiving any training necessary for future leadership roles. At 'Abbās' death, because none of his brothers or sons was alive or able to ascend the throne, his grandson Sam Mīrzā became the sixth Safavid monarch with the title Shāh Safi I.

Summary

Without falling into the popular error of assuming that subsequent Safavid rulers added no luster to the Iranian empire and without minimizing the accomplishments of 'Abbās the Great's Safavid predecessors, one can hardly overemphasize the achievements of this astute ruler. To be sure, 'Abbās had his shortcomings, among them his paranoia with respect to threats to the throne and a tendency toward superstitiousness (an astrologer's warning had contributed to his decision to order the assassination of Prince Safi Mīrzā). In addition, he was a despot and hardly enlightened with respect to the rights of his subjects.

Yet 'Abbās had uncommon vision and sense of purpose. He saw the need for secure borders, a centralized state and administrative system, and a standing army loyal to the Crown. He understood the significance of Twelver Shi'i Islam as the cultural core to Iranian life and paid special attention to Shi'i Muslim shrines, particularly those at Ardabīl and Mashhad, and to his role as a Sufi leader in the Safavid order. He had a sense of the grandeur of Iranian traditions, which he expressed most forcefully in making Ispahan one of the world's great capitals, leading to its hyperbolic epithet as "Half the World." Yet he accomplished much more, especially in terms of his legacy to Iran. Accordingly, he stands in many Iranian minds alongside Cyrus the Great, Darius, Shāpūr I, and others as one of the greatest Iranian monarchs.

'Abbās' manifold legacy played a significant part in the imperial government of Iran of the short-lived Pahlavi dynasty (1926-1979) and in the Islamic Republic of Iran instituted by Ruhollah Khomeini in 1979. In the former era, Reza Shah Pahlavi and Mohammad Reza Shah Pahlavi strove both to carry forward 'Abbās' policies of centralizing power and to instill in the Iranian population loyalty based primarily on obedience and respect toward the traditional institution of Iranian monarchy. They modeled their behavior as absolute monarchs on such historical forebears as 'Abbās the Great. 'Abbās' particular devotion to the Twelver Shi'i faith, which the Safavids promulgated as an official religion, became the theocratic basis for the Iranian state.

Of equal significance is the fact that Iran survived to inherit such legacies from 'Abbās. His strengthening of the Safavid state and provision of a model for Safavid, Afshar, Zand, and Qajar successor monarchs were efficacious in giving Iran the means to avoid becoming directly subject to colonial powers in the nineteenth and early twentieth centuries in contrast to the experience of most of Iran's Near Eastern, Central Asian, and South Asian neighbors.

Bibliography
Dimand, M. S. "Safavid Textiles and Rugs." In *Highlights of Persian Art*, edited by Richard Ettinghausen and Ehsan Yarshater. New York: Wittenborn Art Books, 1981. Surveys sixteenth and seventeenth century production with emphasis on achievements during the reigns of Shāh Tahmasp (1524-1576) and 'Abbās.
Eskandar Beg Monshi. *The History of Shah 'Abbās the Great*. 2 vols. Translated by Roger M. Savory. Boulder, Colo.: Westview Press, 1978. A compendious history by the chief secretary of 'Abbās' court and the most important source of Safavid history in general. Ends with 'Abbās' death and funeral.
Jackson, Peter, and Laurence Lockhart, eds. *The Cambridge History of Iran*. Vol. 6, *The Timurid and Safavid Periods*. Cambridge, England: Cambridge University Press, 1986. Includes four chapters dealing with 'Abbās the Great: "The Safavid Period," a chronological treatment of the period with a biographical sketch of his life and a characterization and

assessment of his reign; "Carpets and Textiles"; "Safavid Architecture"; and "The Arts in the Safavid Period."

Savory, Roger M. *Iran Under the Safavids*. Cambridge, England: Cambridge University Press, 1980. A treatment which emphasizes the monarchy and the royal court by the leading Western authority on Safavid history.

Welch, Anthony. *Artists for the Shah: Late Sixteenth Century Painting at the Imperial Court of Iran*. New Haven, Conn.: Yale University Press, 1976. Describes the transitional nature of Safavid painting of the period. Includes political and historical contexts.

_____. *Shah 'Abbās and the Arts of Isfahan*. New York: Asia Society, 1973. A catalog of an important exhibition at the Asia House Gallery in New York City and Harvard University's Fogg Art Museum in Cambridge, Massachusetts.

Michael Craig Hillmann

ABDELKADER
'Abd al-Qādir

Born: September 26, 1807; Guetna, Ottoman Empire
Died: May 26, 1883; Damascus, Ottoman Empire
Areas of Achievement: Government, politics, and the military
Contribution: After the French landed in Algiers in 1830, Abdelkader carved a semiautonomous state out of the remnants of the former Turkish possessions in Algeria. He achieved lasting fame for his various campaigns against the French, whom he fought until his surrender in 1847.

Early Life
The first son of Zurah, the second wife of the Islamic holy man Muhi al-Din, who traced his ancestry as far back as the prophet Muhammad, Abdelkader was born on September 26, 1807, in the small town of Guetna, near Mascara in modern Algeria. There his grandfather had founded a religious school of the Sufi Order, and Muhi al-Din had followed him as leader and himself taught his son reading, writing, and the Koran. Abdelkader's mother was learned and venerated by the people as a marabout, or holy person, as well; for a woman to accomplish this was quite extraordinary and could have helped Abdelkader to surpass his half brother, the son of his father's first wife, in the affection of his father.

As a boy, Abdelkader's handsome features and his remarkable intellectual gifts endeared him to his parents and to the people of Guetna. Throughout his life, Abdelkader would be quite aware of the potential impressiveness of his well-made body and keep himself in condition so as to command maximum respect. His dark eyes, together with the clear features of his well-formed face and full beard, conveyed an image of Oriental nobility that would prove to affect friend and foe alike.

A fine horseman and a quick learner, Abdelkader soon developed the qualities of a leader. When his father sent him to the coastal city of Oran as a student of religion in 1821, the boy became a classmate of the scions of the ruling Turks. He observed at first hand how even while the country suffered from famine and plague its Turkish masters continued to levy taxes and luxuriate in a life of debauchery and neglect of Islamic moral principles. In reaction, Arabs gathered around their holy men and led several unsuccessful revolts in the 1820's against the Turks, who repressed upheaval and summarily executed suspicious subjects. As a marabout, Muhi al-din was spared execution and placed under house arrest with his son in Oran for two years, before the two set out on a pilgrimage to Mecca in 1826. Traveling further widened Abdelkader's experience.

Two years after Abdelkader's return to Guetna, the French captured Algiers on July 5, 1830, thus ending three hundred years of Turkish rule.

When the neighboring Moroccans tried to assume power in Algeria, Muhi al-Din accepted their mandate and became the leader of a jihad, or holy war, against the French infidels. The Moroccans withdrew, but Abdelkader commanded a force of ten thousand men for his father and, in the Battle of Oran from May 3 to 8, 1832, fought courageously but was defeated.

Life's Work

On November 22, 1832, tribes of the Oran Province gathered to witness the proclamation of Abdelkader as emir al-mu'minin, or commander of the believers, on the plain of Eghris. Thus, the twenty-five-year-old man was made leader of a movement to scourge the land of the French. Rather than fighting in open attacks, which his weak forces were sure to lose, Abdelkader began his jihad with a boycott against French-held Oran; Arabs who traded with the infidels were mutilated or hanged. In his dealings with Muslim tribes, Abdelkader soon strove for political recognition as emir and even tried to win the support of the Sultan of Morocco. As emir, Abdelkader wielded a power that was legitimated by religion and used it to the fullest. From the believers, he collected both new and traditional taxes to finance the jihad and used these monies to build a strong force of his own. Thus, from 1832 to 1834, he was able to subjugate most people in the Oran Province, and the sporadic French attacks were too limited to threaten seriously his nascent power; further, French blunders such as the humiliation of Turks and local leaders played into his hands.

In January, 1834, the French general Louis Alexis Desmichels, whose troops had defeated Abdelkader's without achieving a lasting effect, negotiated a bilingual treaty, complete with a secret codicil. Officially, Abdelkader would rule the Oran Province under the French, with the exception of three coastal cities; however, both Desmichels and Abdelkader told their people that the other had completely submitted to him.

For more than a year, Abdelkader enjoyed the valuable support of Desmichels, who helped him to build an army with which to defeat his indigenous enemies. The replacement of the general brought new fighting with the French, who prevented Abdelkader from forcefully relocating two tribes who had placed themselves under French protection. At the onset of his second jihad in June, 1835, Abdelkader ambushed a French force at Macta and killed 210 of their men; however, the French were able to occupy temporarily two of his cities.

While the blockade of Oran continued, General Thomas Robert Bugeaud organized a mobile French force and delivered Abdelkader a stinging blow at the Battle of Sikkak on July 6, 1836. Yet Bugeaud knew that he could not occupy the whole country. In the Treaty of Tafna, ratified on June 21, 1837, Bugeaud conceded and placed most of Algeria under Abdelkader's immediate rule. In return, Abdelkader promised peace, free trade, and, secretly,

180,000 gold francs for Bugeaud; however, only twenty-five thousand francs were delivered, as the clause was discovered. Now, Abdelkader could even buy rifles through the French, and he established a firm rule over two thirds of Algeria. There, he established an Islamic government and consolidated his rule by placing strong emphasis on the one factor that united his subjects against the Europeans: the Muslim religion.

In the summer of 1839, it became clear that France and Abdelkader would soon clash over Algeria. On July 3, Abdelkader declared a conditional jihad, which became fully effective November 3, after the French crown prince had marched through Abdelkader's territory. The warriors of the jihad scored a first victory when they attacked a European settlement on the Mitidja plains near Algiers on November 20 and succeeded in massacring or chasing away its colonists. Until the return of Bugeaud, Abdelkader maintained the military initiative.

In May, 1841, however, Tagdempt, Abdelkader's capital, fell to Bugeaud, whose forces had razed most of his cities by October 12. In turn, Abdelkader moved to a tent city, the Zmalah, and continued to harass the enemy throughout the next year. Yet on May 16, 1843, a surprise attack on the Zmalah led to its destruction, the capture of three thousand of Abdelkader's people, and the loss of his treasury. With the French following on his heels and devastating the land of his tribes after the fashion of local warfare, Abdelkader was forced to flee into Morocco late in 1843.

From his exile, Abdelkader saw Bugeaud's defeat of the Moroccan army at the Battle of Isly in August, 1844, and the French military begin to control Algeria. Yet the harshness of their rule led to a popular uprising and agitation for a new jihad. Until he returned in September, 1845, Abdelkader had wielded no influence, but now people followed him. Yet his renewed campaign culminated in a failed attempt at capturing Algiers in January, 1846; thereafter, Abdelkader was again chased into Morocco. While the war wound down with heavy civilian casualties, Morocco grew hostile to Abdelkader. On December 21, 1847, he surrendered himself to General Christophe de Lamoricière, who had promised that he could stay in Africa. Instead, the French government kept the rebel leader under arrest in France for four years before Napoleon III released him in 1852.

From 1855 on, Abdelkader stayed in Damascus as a philosopher and religious man. During an uprising there in 1860, he saved the lives of thousands of Christians, and, when unrest returned to Algeria in 1871, he disowned one of his sons who took sides with the rebels. Abdelkader died in Damascus on May 26, 1883; in 1968, his remains were transferred to Algeria.

Summary
As an exile in Damascus, Abdelkader was seen by the French as a prime

example of the beneficial effects of their rule, which had transformed a fiery Muslim fanatic and hero of desert warfare into an elder statesman of the French empire; the French government even had plans to establish a throne for him somewhere in the Middle East. With the coming of another bitter war in Algeria after 1945, Algerian interest turned to Abdelkader, who was idolized as an early protagonist of independence; the French quickly discovered that his legend had been kept alive. In 1962, after independence, Abdelkader was declared a national hero, and in Algiers his statue soon replaced the toppled one of Bugeaud.

A final historical assessment can only stress the charisma of Abdelkader and his profound impact on the history of two countries. Abdelkader's qualities as a leader of men who venerated him for his religious conviction enabled him to build an indigenous state in defiance of the French-controlled cities on the coast. When open warfare erupted, Abdelkader achieved lasting fame through his never-ending zeal and military prowess, a combination that led him into battle as long as there was a chance to reverse fortunes and prevent French rule over Algeria.

Bibliography

Abun-Nasr, Jamil N. "The Emergence of French Algeria." In *A History of the Maghrib*. Cambridge, England: Cambridge University Press, 1971. Briefly describes Abdelkader's accomplishments and places him in the context of the overall history of the region. Presents an Arab point of view. Contains only brief information on Abdelkader but is an interesting complement to European and American historiography.

Alby, François Antoine. *The Prisoners of Abd-el-Kader: Or, Five Month's Captivity Among the Arabs in the Autumn of 1836.* Translated by R. F. Porter. London: Smith, Elder, 1838. An account of the ordeal of a French sailor who was captured in Algeria in 1836, delivered to Abdelkader, and released five months later. An intimate description of Abdelkader, his people, and their actions; shows what the common man in Paris or London believed about them.

Blunt, Wilfrid. *Desert Hawk: Abd el Kader and the French Conquest of Algeria.* London: Methuen, 1947. A descriptive account of Abdelkader's life and his campaigns. Takes a great interest in his military strategies, tactics, and triumphs, and in his adversaries. Admires Abdelkader's position against the French. A readable and interesting work.

Churchill, Charles Henry. *The Life of AbdelKader: Ex-Sultan of the Arabs of Algeria.* London: Chapman and Hall, 1867. This is the oldest biography of Abdelkader in English. Invaluable because it exemplifies the popular European reaction to Abdelkader during his lifetime.

Clayton, Vista. *The Phantom: Or, Abd el Kader, Emir of Algeria (1808-1883).* Hicksville, N.Y.: Exposition Press, 1975. An analysis of the life and warfare strategies of Abdelkader. Examines French and indigenous military, logistics, and politics. Presents Abdelkader's life against the background of his region. Emphasizes the charisma of Abdelkader and gives a detailed account of his military exploits.

Danziger, Raphael. *Abd al-Qadir and the Algerians: Resistance to the French and Internal Consolidation.* New York: Holmes & Meier, 1977. A detailed account of Abdelkader's struggle for power and consolidation of his rule, and his dealings with the French. Deals primarily with the time period before 1839. This is a sympathetic view, written for both a scholarly and a general audience; useful exploitation of French sources. Contains a fine bibliography and a rare reproduction of pages of treaties in Arabic.

Sullivan, Antony Thrall. *Thomas-Robert Bugeaud, France and Algeria 1784-1849: Politics, Power, and the Good Society.* Hamden, Conn.: Archon Books, 1983. A fascinating portrait of Abdelkader's great adversary; room is given to a description of their relationship. Illuminates the historical background of the actions of Abdelkader's enemies by providing an explanation for the French interest in Algeria and the methods of warfare employed. For a general audience.

Reinhart Lutz

MUHAMMAD 'ABDUH

Born: c. 1849; Mahallat Nasr, Gharbiyyah Province, Egypt
Died: July 11, 1905; Alexandria, Egypt
Areas of Achievement: Education, journalism, and government
Contribution: 'Abduh was a major figure in the articulation of modern political, ethical, and social values in an Islamic context. His writings were a major stimulus to the development of Egyptian nationalism and, in a wider sense, to the elaboration of social and political thought throughout Islam.

Early Life

Muhammad 'Abduh was the child of Egyptian peasants of the Nile delta. His family life appears to have been serene and his father highly respected in his village. Although without formal education themselves, 'Abduh's parents went to considerable effort, and no doubt sacrificed much, to ensure his receiving educational opportunities. 'Abduh was trained in basic literary skills and, when ten years of age, went to learn recitation of the Koran with a professional. Few other educational opportunities were available to Egyptian peasants at the time.

'Abduh shortly became restless with Koranic memorization and Arabic grammar. Instead, he became enamored of the teachings of a number of Sufi mystics. From them, 'Abduh first perceived the relationship between the true practice of and devotion to Islam, and the pursuit of morality and ethical conduct. He gravitated toward Cairo and the great theological center of Al Azhar, where he continued his education and increasingly rigorous Sufi practices.

'Abduh's mentor at Al Azhar was the famed Jamāl al-Dīn al-Afghānī, perhaps the most important Muslim intellectual figure in the nineteenth century. Although equally devoted to Sufism, Jamāl, a dynamic reformer and pan-Islamic advocate, turned 'Abduh from the internal contemplation that had absorbed nearly all of his energies to more worldly avenues of learning and social involvement. With Jamāl's encouragement, many of his students, 'Abduh included, began writing articles for newspapers on a host of subjects related to the state of Egypt at the time and the challenge of modernization.

Despite his outstanding academic work, 'Abduh's outspoken opinions on Egyptian society and the suspicion that he meant to revive the skeptical philosophical movements characteristic of earlier periods in Islam drew the wrath of conservative clerics at Al Azhar. It required the intervention of the more liberal rector for 'Abduh to receive passing marks on his examinations and his teaching certificate in 1877.

Life's Work

Although he held numerous positions throughout his life in addition to his explicitly educational ones, 'Abduh always regarded himself as a teacher. The essence of his teachings is first a concern for the state of Egypt. He and fellow intellectuals deplored their country's drift in the 1870's toward financial chaos and foreign intervention. They understood that only internal reforms could change Egypt's fortunes. 'Abduh's experience at Al Azhar convinced him that the most essential reform must come in education. At a time when European economic and technological forces were closing in on Egypt, its greatest academic institution was still under the control of rigidly conservative theologians who resisted curricular innovation. ('Abduh had been obliged to seek instruction in mathematics and natural sciences in the streets, among unofficial, black market classes held outside the walls of Al Azhar.)

Yet it was not merely these additions to curriculum that concerned 'Abduh. He also argued that the study of religion itself must be subject to the same rigor and philosophical scrutiny that attended the sciences and other secular studies. Further, he believed that leading institutions such as Al Azhar must, in their own reforms, assume leadership in rebuilding and expanding the entire Egyptian educational system. 'Abduh's ideas and teaching methods generated much controversy at Al Azhar but also earned for him support from the reform-minded prime minister Riad Pasha, who in 1878 appointed him to the experimental school Dar al-'Ulum, founded as a pilot institution for educational reform.

In 1879, the Egyptian ruler Khedive Ismail, who had been intent on modernizing Egypt but unfortunately went far beyond the country's limited financial means, under European pressure abdicated in favor of his son, Tawfiq. The new khedive expelled Jamāl from the country and fired 'Abduh, placing him under virtual house arrest. 'Abduh was rescued from potential oblivion by Riad Pasha, who appointed him to the editorial staff of the official Egyptian government gazette *Al-Waka'i' al-Misriyyah.* 'Abduh quickly turned this rather stodgy publication into a vibrant, reformist organ, with contributions from many Egyptian intellectuals and government critics. In his own editorials, 'Abduh continually returned to the need for educational reform and his campaign to cast Egyptian national consciousness in a new Islamic mold. Islam, he argued, should return to its basic simplicity and revive the spirit of inquiry and pursuit of knowledge characteristic of its early history.

In 1881, Egyptian army officers, led by the nationalist firebrand Colonel Ahmed 'Arabi, mutinied. The uprising sparked a general confrontation between the government and its critics. Alarmed at the prospect of violence against Europeans, British troops landed in Egypt in May, 1882. 'Abduh, though opposed to 'Arabi's methods, spoke out as usual in favor of national revival and reform. In September, a government tribunal ordered him expelled from Egypt.

'Abduh went first to Syria and later to Paris, where he was reunited with Jamāl. In exile, he continued to speak and publish actively. The wide venue of his travels led 'Abduh to perceive the potential vitality of a unified Islam and the cultural renaissance of all Muslims. Increasingly he drew on the early history of Islam as a source of inspiration. On the other hand, his experiences in Syria, a country rife with ethnic and religious factionalism, led him to question whether Islam was a suitable rubric for the expression of modern Arab national aspirations. 'Abduh's reservations about pan-Islamic agitation caused him to part ways with Jamāl, who was disposed to intrigue and political maneuvering. 'Abduh insisted that his role should be educational and instructive rather than activist.

In 1886, having received a government pardon, 'Abduh returned to Egypt a national hero. He was now able to use this influence to implement his earlier ideas of curricular and institutional reform at Al Azhar, in order to make it a model of education in Islam. In 1895, the new khedive, Abbas II, at 'Abduh's instigation created an administrative committee for Al Azhar, dominated by 'Abduh and other reformists.

In an effort to enlist faculty support for curriculum changes, the government provided significant new sums for salaries, to be distributed according to a merit system rather than at the discretion of the rector. Students, many of whom lived under appalling conditions, received double their previous board allowance. New dormitories with running water and suitable furniture appeared. The committee significantly lengthened the academic year, organized it according to European standards, and eliminated many disruptive holidays. It also established modern administrative systems for the university's finances and organized its library collections.

Fears that these changes would turn students away from theology and ancient history disappeared when the student success rate on examinations increased by nearly an order of magnitude in the first two years of reform. 'Abduh himself produced statistics that he claimed proved that students who studied modern subjects along with the traditional ones performed better in both areas on examinations.

The climax of 'Abduh's career came with his appointment as Mufti of Egypt in 1899, from which post he was the final arbiter of questions of shari'a, or Muslim canon law. In this position 'Abduh had to confront, more than ever before, his own ambivalence about the relationship between Islam and modern nationalism. His arguments with respect to interpretation of shari'a generated more controversy than anything else in his career. Like many other Muslim scholars, particularly in Egypt, 'Abduh regarded shari'a as possessing a divinely inspired core of behavior and values to which all Muslims are expected to adhere. The community, however, by consensus might accept amendations to shari'a pertinent to its own experience and circumstances.

'Abduh perceived the emerging Egyptian nation as the logical outgrowth of this sense of community in Islam. Yet he believed that the nation, because it contained citizens who were Christian or Jewish rather than Muslim, and because it aspired to a role in a secular world not anticipated by shari'a, should exercise a consensus of its own. Thus 'Abduh decided that Muslims could eat animal flesh killed by Christians or Jews. Despite the ban on usury, in shari'a Egyptians could, and should, make use of modern postal savings and banking systems opposed by traditional clergy on the grounds that their strength contributed to the welfare of the nation. These positions 'Abduh regarded not as a repudiation of Islam but as an act of defense of Islam, in that they reconstituted Islam as an open and tolerant culture capable of meeting the demands of a changing world.

Summary
   When Muhammad 'Abduh died in July, 1905, he received the equivalent of a state funeral. The public demonstration of respect and reverence from all political factions and religious communities was unprecedented in Egypt. The country sensed that it had lost a singular patriot and scholar, and one of the most important figures in Egypt's transformation. Later generations have borne out this assessment. Because of 'Abduh's reforms and the new intellectual environment they created, Al Azhar, and other large Egyptian universities, remain in the forefront of higher education in Islam and are recognized as among the world's major institutions of higher learning.
   In all of his teachings, 'Abduh struggled to articulate an Egyptian sense of identity that reconciled the inconsistencies and often conflicting perceptions of Islam, the Islamic community, the modern nation and its role in a European-dominated world, and the tensions between modernity and tradition.
   'Abduh is most fairly regarded, perhaps, as one who, rather than answering the multitude of questions arising from these issues, helped to air the issues and suggest ways in which they could be addressed satisfactorily. 'Abduh is a symbol, rather than a model, for the contemporary, educated Egyptian. His intellectual journey represents what each Egyptian individually—and the nation as a whole—must consider in the process of finding satisfying and rewarding identity in the modern world.

Bibliography
Adams, Charles C. *Islam and Modernism in Egypt: A Study of the Modern Reform Movement Inaugurated by Muhammad 'Abduh*. Reprint. New York: Russell & Russell, 1968. Includes one of the most extensive biographical accounts of 'Abduh and attempts to analyze his personality and ideas in the light of his life experience.
Ahmed, Jamal Mohammed. *The Intellectual Origins of Egyptian Nationalism*. New York: Oxford University Press, 1960. A survey of the varied sources of inspiration for Egyptian nationalism. Stresses how this variety

contributes to the often conflicting roles of issues such as Egyptian ethnic identity, pan-Arabism, Ottomanism, and Islamic and pan-Islamic values.

Badawi, Muhammad Zaki. *The Reformers of Egypt*. London: Croom Helm, 1978. Treats 'Abduh as a product of the same circumstances that produced other Egyptian nationalists and intellectuals, and attempts to draw comparisons among the careers of these figures.

Jankowski, James. "Ottomanism and Arabism in Egypt, 1860-1914." *Muslim World* 70 (1980): 226-259. In the late nineteenth century, many Egyptians regarded the Ottoman Empire—to the extent that it stood for Islam as a whole—as a more legitimate outlet than identifying with the Arabs. This article shows how Ottomanism provided a more vigorous environment for the growth of Egyptian ethnic nationalism.

Kedourie, Elie. *Afghani and 'Abduh: An Essay on Religious Unbelief and Political Activism in Modern Islam*. London: Frank Cass, 1966. A brief but very controversial essay when it appeared. Argues that 'Abduh was an atheist and subverter of Islam, and a Machiavellian who behaved as a Muslim only to advance his career.

Kerr, Malcolm. *Islamic Reform: The Political and Legal Theories of Muhammad 'Abduh and Rashīd Ridā*. Berkeley: University of California Press, 1966. Considers the impact of the many influences acting on 'Abduh and his generation in the matter of articulating the nature of the state and the rationale required for a legitimate legal system supported by the citizenry.

Ronald W. Davis

NIELS HENRIK ABEL

Born: August 5, 1802; Finnøy, Norway
Died: April 6, 1829; Froland, Norway
Area of Achievement: Mathematics
Contribution: Abel was instrumental in the evolution of modern mathematics, especially in the field of algebra. Regarded as one of the foremost analysts of his time, he insisted on a rigorous approach to mathematical proof which was critical for the further development of abstract mathematics.

Early Life
Niels Henrik Abel was the second child of Søren Georg Abel, a second-generation Lutheran minister, and Anne Marie Simonsen, a daughter of a successful merchant and shipowner. Soon after his birth in Finnöy, his father was transferred to the parish of Gjerstad, in southeastern Norway, about 250 kilometers from Oslo, where Abel spent his childhood with his five brothers and sisters. Abel was an attractive youth, with light ash-brown hair and blue eyes.

Although his father's earnings were never adequate to provide for the large family, the emphasis on educational stimulation in the Abel household was an important formative influence on the young boy. Although his early education was conducted at home, it was sufficient to allow him to attend the Cathedral School at Oslo when he was thirteen years old. It was there that his talent in mathematics was discovered, although his initial efforts were somewhat unpromising.

The Cathedral School had once been quite good, but many positions had been filled by inexperienced or inadequate teachers because their predecessors had been recruited to join the faculty of the newly formed University of Oslo. Indeed, Abel's first mathematics instructor was dismissed abruptly after beating a student to death. Fortunately, the replacement in that position was Bernt Michael Holmboe, who was the first to recognize Abel's talent and who later edited the first edition of his work. Holmboe also assisted Christopher Hansteen, a professor at the university; this connection would prove valuable to Abel.

When Holmboe first arrived at the school, he noticed Abel's ability in mathematics and suggested that the two of them study some of the contemporary mathematics works together. Abel soon outpaced Holmboe and began developing a general solution for the quintic equation, that is, an equation of the fifth degree $(ax^5 + bx^4 + cx^3 + dx^2 + ex + f = 0)$. When Abel believed that the work was complete, Holmboe and Hansteen sensed that no one in Norway, including themselves, could review the work capably. They forwarded the paper to Ferdinand Degen of the Danish Academy, who carefully reviewed the work. Before publication, Degen helped Abel discover that his solution was flawed, but he steered Abel into the field of elliptic functions, which Degen believed would be more fruitful.

At about this time, Abel discovered that several of his predecessors, particularly Leonhard Euler and Joseph-Louis Lagrange, had not completed the reasoning required to prove some of their work. Abel diligently supplied rigorous proofs where they were missing; a noted case is his proof of the general binomial theorem, which had been stated previously in part by Sir Isaac Newton and Euler. The mathematics community later was to find his meticulous treatment of the works he studied invaluable. Unfortunately for his personal life and his financial situation, Abel's father, who had served two terms in the *Storting* (congress), was impeached and disgraced. His father died in 1829, leaving his family in even more desperate financial straits than ever before.

Life's Work

The nineteen-year-old Abel entered the University of Oslo in 1821. While this entering age would not normally denote a prodigy, the fact that the university granted him a free room and that several professors donated funds for his support does. Abel completed the preliminary requirements for a degree in a single year. He was then free to study mathematics on his own, as he had no peers among the faculty. He developed a love for the theater at this time, which lasted throughout his short life. A modest person, he made many lasting friendships.

In addition to studying all available work, he began writing papers, the first of which were published in the journal *Magazin for Naturvidenskaberne* begun by Hansteen. In 1823, Abel's first important paper, "Opläsning afet Par Opgaver ved bjoelp af bestemte Integraler" ("Solution of Some Problems by Means of Definite Integrals"), was published, containing the first published solutions of integral equations. During 1822 and 1823, he also developed a longer paper discussing the integration of functions. This work is recognized as very significant in the evolution of that field of study.

At this time, Abel's work was largely ignored by the international mathematics community because Abel was from Norway and wrote in Norwegian, and the focal point of the mathematics community of the day was Paris, with the language of the learned being French. By applying himself diligently, Abel learned French and began to publish work in that language. The quintic equation still held his attention, and, as he thought of possibilities for its solution, he also considered that there might be no solution that could be found for all such equations. In time, he was able to prove this result. Yet still the mathematicians whose approval he desired so fervently, those in Paris, ignored his work.

He began to press for the opportunity to go to Paris, but penniless as he was he was forced to rely on grants. After his first application, it was decided that he needed to study more foreign languages before going abroad. Although it meant delaying his dream for nearly two years, Abel applied himself to learning various languages. Meanwhile, he became engaged to Christine (Krelly) Kemp before he finally received a royal grant to travel abroad in 1825.

This trip was unsuccessful in many ways. When he arrived at Copenhagen, he discovered that Degen had died. Instead of going on to Paris, Abel decided to go to Berlin because several of his friends were there. The time in Berlin was invaluable, for he met and befriended August Leopold Crelle, who became his strongest supporter and mentor. When Abel met him, Crelle was preparing to begin publication of a new journal, *Journal für die reine und angewandte Mathematik*. Crelle was so taken by Abel's ability that much of the first few issues was devoted to Abel's work in an attempt to win recognition for the young mathematician.

For a variety of reasons, Abel did not proceed to Paris until the spring of 1826. By this time, he had spent most of his grant and was physically tired, and the Parisian mathematicians he had hoped to convince were nearly all on holiday. Yet his masterwork, *Mémoire sur une propriété générale d'une classe très-étendue de fonctions transcendantes* (memoir on a general property of a very extensive class of transcendental functions), was presented to the Academy of Sciences on October 30, 1826. The paper was left in the keeping of Augustin-Louis Cauchy, a prominent mathematician, and Cauchy and Adrien-Marie Legendre were to be the referees. Whether the paper was illegible, as Cauchy claimed, or was misplaced, as most historians believe, no judgment was issued until after Abel's death.

Abel felt a great sense of failure, for many young mathematicians had been established by recognition from the academy. He returned first to Berlin and finally to Oslo in May, 1827. His prospects were bleak: He had contracted tuberculosis, there was no prospect for a mathematical position in Norway, and he was in debt. Abel began tutoring and lecturing at the university on a substitute basis in order to support himself.

Another young mathematician, Carl Gustav Jacob Jacobi, soon began publishing work in Abel's foremost field, the theory of elliptic functions and integrals. The rivalry created between them dominated the rest of Abel's life. He worked furiously to prove his ideas, and his efforts were spurred by his correspondence with Legendre. As he finally began to be recognized in Europe, many mathematicians, led by Crelle, attempted to secure a patronage for him. He succumbed, however, to tuberculosis on April 6, 1829, two days before Crelle wrote to inform him that such financial support had been found. In June, 1830, he and Jacobi were awarded the Grand Prix of the French Academy of Sciences for their work in elliptic integrals. Abel's original manuscript was found and finally published in 1841.

Summary

Although Niels Henrik Abel's life was short and his work was unrecognized for most of his life, he has exercised a great influence on modern mathematics. His primary work with elliptic functions and integrals led to interest in what became one of the great research topics of his century. Without his preliminary findings, many of the developments in mathematics and, consequently, science, may not have been made. One example of this is his theory of elliptic functions, much of which was developed very quickly during his race with Jacobi. In addition, his proof that there is no general solution to the quintic equation is quite important, as are his other findings in equation theory.

His theory of solutions using definite integrals, including what is now called Abel's theorem, is also widely used in engineering and the physical sciences and provided a foundation for the later work of others. Abelian (commutative) groups, Abelian functions, and Abelian equations are but three of the ideas which commonly carry his name. Given Abel's short life span and his living in Norway, a definite academic backwater at the time, his prolific achievements are amazing.

Abel is also significant because his writing and mathematical styles, which were easily comprehended, made his discoveries available to his contemporaries and successors. Abel's insistence that ideas should be demonstrated in such a way that the conclusions would be supported by clear and easily comprehended arguments, that is, proved rigorously, is the cornerstone of modern mathematics. It is in this regard that Abel is most often remembered.

Bibliography

Abel, Niels Henrik. "From a Memoir on Algebraic Equations, Proving the Impossibility of a Solution of the General Equation of the Fifth Degree." In *Classics of Mathematics*, edited by Ronald Calinger. Oak Park, Ill.: Moore, 1982. This extract of Abel's paper on the general quintic equation demonstrates Abel's style. Although it is too technical for the casual reader, it is of interest to mathematicians. The excerpt is preceded by a brief biography. This work also demonstrates how Abel fits into the overall development of mathematics.

Bell, Eric T. "Genius and Poverty: Abel." In *Men of Mathematics*. New York: Simon & Schuster, 1937. This book is a compilation of brief biographies of the most famous mathematicians throughout recorded history. The emphasis is more on the subject's life than the mathematics produced.

Boyer, Carl B. *A History of Mathematics*. New York: John Wiley & Sons, 1968. This general history of mathematics will aid the reader in placing Abel within the general development of mathematics.

Kline, Morris. *Mathematical Thought from Ancient to Modern Times*. New York: Oxford University Press, 1972. Kline includes both a brief biography of Abel and discussions of his most important work in this history of mathematics.

Ore, Øystein. *Niels Henrik Abel: Mathematician Extraordinary.* Minneapolis: University of Minnesota Press, 1957. This standard English-language biography gives a detailed account of Abel's life without requiring specialized knowledge of mathematics.

Celeste Williams Brockington

GEORGIUS AGRICOLA
Georg Bauer

Born: March 24, 1494; Glauchau, Saxony
Died: November 21, 1555; Chemnitz, Saxony
Area of Achievement: Geology
Contribution: Agricola was the forerunner of the new period of scientific investigation involving study and description of natural phenomena (especially geological in nature), preparation of metals from ores, and the development of mechanical procedures. He is regarded as the father of modern mineralogy.

Early Life

Born the son of a draper and named Georg Bauer, the young man Latinized his name, in the fashion of the time, to Georgius Agricola. Little of his life before 1514 is known, at which point he entered the University of Leipzig. In 1518, he was graduated, then went to Italy to continue his studies at the Universities of Bologna and Padua. His subsequent career began as a philologist, an expert in classical languages and the works of the classical writers. He then turned to medicine, took his degree at the University of Ferrare, and adopted medicine as a profession. While in Venice, he was employed for two years in the printing and publishing house of Aldus Manutius. At the Aldine Press, Agricola collaborated with John Clement, secretary to Thomas More. During this period, he also met and became friends with Desiderius Erasmus, who encouraged him to write and later published a number of his books. Coming home, Agricola began his medical practice in 1527 in Joachimsthal, in Bohemia, as city physician until 1533. In 1534, he moved to Chemnitz, another mining town, where he stayed for the rest of his life. In 1545, he was appointed Burgermeister.

Life's Work

As with his contemporary Paracelsus, Agricola's interest in mineralogy grew out of its possible connections with medicine and the diseases of the miners he treated. For more than two centuries, this combination of physician-mineralogist was to be prominent in the development of chemistry and geology. Agricola spent much time with the miners, in the mines and smelters, thus gaining an intimate knowledge of mining, mineralogy, and allied sciences. Most of his writings dealt with the geological sciences, although he wrote on many aspects of human endeavor. The beauty of his works lies in his use of illustrations, the woodcuts clear enough to let a modern builder re-create models of the ancient machines. His works were extremely difficult to decipher, particularly as they are written in Latin, a language ill equipped with appropriate terms for the mining trades. Since his ideas were based on German sources, he had to invent an entire new Latin vocabulary. As a result, some parts of the texts were difficult to understand even by contemporary readers. Only centuries after his death did Agricola get the credit he so richly deserved.

At Chemnitz, Agricola first became court historian, then city physician. Beginning in 1546, he published six works on mining and geology, a small work on the plague, and works on medical, religious, political, and historical subjects. It was a measure of his liberalism that, as a staunch Catholic, he served two Protestant dukes and worked diligently with other men of the Reformation. He served his dukes on many diplomatic and military missions, and he dedicated his major work, *De re metallica libri XII* (1556; English translation, 1912), to them.

Abandoning inductive speculation as he had learned it through his classical studies, Agricola disregarded biblical beliefs about the nature of the world, expressed his impatience with the alchemists, and concentrated on exploring the structure of the world on the basis of scientific observation. Such observation led him to the first adequate description of the part played by erosion in the shaping of mountain ranges, the origin of ores, the filling of rock interstices by circulating solutions, and the classifying of minerals on the basis of special physical characteristics, such as solubility and hardness.

Working with the miners in the two cities in which he had settled, Agricola began accumulating a massive amount of information on mining, smelting, the characteristics of ore deposits, and chemical analysis. *Bermannus sive de re metallica dialogus* (1530) was his first contribution to geology. It covered the rise of the mining industry in Germany and the early development of the great mining centers in the region of the Erzgebirge. Agricola discussed topics in mineralogy and mining, and various ores, such as silver, copper, and other metals. He showed some of the prejudices of his time, however, by dealing with the demons that supposedly haunted many of the mines. This was really an introduction to his greater work.

In 1546, he published *De ortu et causis subterraneorum*, treating the origin of ore deposits. After critically reviewing the opinions of early writers, particularly Aristotle, he rejected them, specifically the notion that metals are formed from watery vapors, and the alchemic view that all metals are composed of mercury and sulfur. He also criticized the astrological belief that the stars influence the earth's interior. Two major ideas came from this work: the origins of mountains and the origins of ore deposits. For mountains, Agricola found five means of formation: the eroding action of water, the heaping of sands by winds, subterranean winds, the actions of earthquakes, and volcanic fires. For ores, he presented the theory of lapidifying juices, solutions carrying dissolved minerals that, when cooled, left the deposits in the cracks of the rocks, thus giving rise to mineral veins. Here he predates two of the modern theories of ore deposits, the theory of ascension and the theory of lateral secretion.

Agricola's next important work, published in 1546, was *De natura fossilium* (English translation, 1955), in which he introduced a new basis for the classification of minerals (called "fossils" at that time). Agricola reviewed and rejected the systems of Aristotle, Avicenna, and others. His system was based on physical properties such as color, weight, transparency, taste, odor, texture, solubility, and combustibility. He carefully defined and explained the terms he developed. He also discussed the medicinal properties of the minerals.

Agricola's problem was understanding what he called "mista," composed of two or more fossils so intermingled as to be inseparable except by fire. His problem was a result of the alchemy of the time, the lack of a microscope, and the lack of real chemical analysis. Even without that knowledge, however, Agricola managed to remove the tales of supernatural forces in minerals and the theories of thunderstones and rocks with crystal power.

Agricola wrote three other works before his great opus: *De natura eorum quae effluent ex Terra* (1546), on subsurface waters and gases; *De veteribus et novis metallis* (1546), dealing with creatures that lived underground; and *De animantibus subterraneis* (1549), sketching the history and geographical distribution of the various metals as far as they had been known to the ancients.

De re metallica, his greatest work, concentrated on mining and metallurgy and contained an abundance of information on the conditions of the time, such as mine management, machinery used, and processes employed. The book is still in print, having the unique distinction of being translated and edited (1912) by President Herbert Hoover and his wife, Lou Henry Hoover. Indeed, it was the leading textbook for miners and metallurgists for two centuries. At a time when it was customary to hold industrial processes secret, Agricola published every practice and improvement he could find.

In *De re metallica*, Agricola's interests are all-consuming. Tracing the history of mineralogy and mining, Agricola addressed the earliest Greek and Roman sources, using them as a springboard for a major study in the locating of mines and a classification of the types of liquids emanating from them. In part of his opus, Agricola covered the specific working of metallic veins and ores in mines. Original contributions by him include the idea that rocks containing ores are older than the ores themselves and that the ores are deposited from solutions passing through fissures in the rocks—revolutionary ideas. He also suggested the procedure of using a magnetic compass for exploring and charting underground tunnels and provided the first real assessment of the wealth available for the three richest mines of the area. The work also includes hundreds of informative drawings showing the mechanical aspects of mining.

Agricola benefited greatly from the period of tolerance during which he worked. The religious wars of the period eroded this tolerance. Well regarded by his contemporaries, Agricola died in Chemnitz on November 21, 1555.

Summary

   Georgius Agricola has been considered one of the most outstanding figures in the history of geological sciences. Johann Wolfgang von Goethe compared him to Roger Bacon. Alfred Werner called him the "father of mineralogy," and Karl von Vogelsang addressed him as the "forefather of geology." His works became the most comprehensive source on mining and metallurgy, acknowledged as the true beginning of geological sciences. Equally important, however, was that, in publishing that which tradition had retained as family and guild secrets, such as the process of smelting, he brought alert and innovative minds into the field of geology. Among those contemporaries were Conrad Gesner, who classified minerals on the basis of the form of the stone, gem, or fossil, avoiding all references to magic and miraculous properties of minerals, and Lazarus Ercker, who amplified Agricola's descriptions for separating precious metals through smelting. The instructions and descriptions that Agricola, Gesner, and Ercker prepared were so accurate that they would be used as handbooks for the next two centuries.
   Agricola's works also helped establish, at Freiberg, a central source of mining and metallurgy knowledge, leading to a formalized, definite curriculum emphasizing observation and information-sharing. Agricola's work and his determination to use observation as the basis of science led to the use of scientific theories based on observation and experimentation.

Bibliography
Adams, Frank Dawson. *The Birth and Development of the Geological Sciences*. Reprint. New York: Dover, 1954. Traces the history of ideas and people contributing to the science of geology. Topics covered include the origins of metals, mountains, rivers, and oceans, and the nature of earthquakes.
Dibner, Bern. *Agricola on Metals*. Norwalk, Conn.: Burndy Library, 1958. Concise treatment of Agricola's life, with special emphasis on his major work *De re metallica*. Contains a book-by-book explanation of topics of interest. Excellent reproductions of original woodcuts.
Faul, Henry. *It Began with a Stone*. New York: John Wiley & Sons, 1983. A comprehensive work on the history of geology. Emphasizes people and their ideas, particularly as to how they arrived at their discoveries. Providing some of the original writings, the author shows how people such as Agricola thought.
Fenton, Carroll Lane, and Mildred Adams Fenton. *Giants of Geology*. New York: Doubleday, 1952. Details the thinking of the pioneers of geology,

concentrating on the men who nurtured geological knowledge in exploring new areas of the world. Shows how ideas have altered over time, based on explorations and exquisite observations used to overthrow prejudices. Excellent references.

Geikie, Archibald. *The Founders of Geology.* New York: Doubleday, 1905. Tracing the slow growth of geology from ancient to modern cultures, the book deals with the controversies surrounding such geological ideas as volcanism, fossils, earth's origin, and geological succession.

Kranzberg, Melvin, and Carroll W. Pursell, Jr., eds. *Technology in Western Civilization.* Vol. 1, *The Emergence of Modern Industrial Society.* New York: Oxford University Press, 1967. This work portrays technology as one of the major determinants in the overall development of Western civilization. Attempting to integrate technological development with other aspects of society affected by it, the book deals nicely with the people and machines giving rise to modern society.

Singer, Charles, E. J. Holmyard, A. R. Hell, and Trevor Williams, eds. *A History of Technology.* Vol. 3, *From the Renaissance to the Industrial Revolution, c.1500-c.1750.* New York: Oxford University Press, 1957. A superb overview of the development and emergence of modern science during the Renaissance and later periods. Chronicles the development of technology and the people involved.

Arthur L. Alt

SIR SAYYID AHMAD KHAN

Born: October 17, 1817; Delhi, India
Died: March 27, 1898; Alīgarh, India
Areas of Achievement: Education, literature, and religion
Contribution: Sayyid Ahmad's theological writings summarized a number of important trends within Islamic thought and attempted to redirect religious thinking to meet the challenges of the modern, European-dominated, world. His religious views were, however, too controversial to be widely influential. Yet in the field of education he founded the Muhammadan Anglo-Oriental College, and in literature he created modern Urdu prose.

Early Life

Sir Sayyid Ahmad Khan was an exceptional man born into an exceptional family. While custom in well-to-do families dictated that a bride moved in with her husband's parents, Sayyid Ahmad's mother was the favorite daughter of a wealthy and distinguished man who wanted her to remain in his home. Sayyid Ahmad's father enjoyed high status as a descendant of the prophet Muhammad, a sayyid, but he was relatively poor. Moving into his wife's home gave him the leisure to pursue his interest in archery and swimming. In that way Sayyid Ahmad came to be reared in his maternal grandfather's house.

The careers of grandfather and grandson resembled each other in many ways. The grandfather, Khwajah Farid ud-din Ahmad, not only held the post of chief minister in the much reduced Mughal court but also had the trust of the British, who sent him on a number of diplomatic missions. During an extended stay in Calcutta, he acted as superintendent of that city's premier Muslim educational establishment, the Calcutta Madrasah. He enjoyed a reputation as a mathematician and astronomer.

Sayyid Ahmad's early education took place in Khwajah Farid's home. It involved learning the Koran and the rudiments of Persian grammar. One of his maternal uncles instructed him in mathematics. He then went to study Greek medicine (*Yunani Tibb*) with one of Delhi's prominent physicians. Apart from this training, Sayyid Ahmad educated himself prodigiously in theology and history, while retaining a lifelong interest in the sciences. In addition to that small amount of formal learning, Sayyid Ahmad absorbed a deep religious seriousness. Both his mother's and his father's families were connected to the noted spiritual reformers of the seventeenth and eighteenth centuries: Ahmad Sirhindī and Shah Walliullah. These men and their disciples stressed a rational approach to Islam that avoided miracle-mongering and criticized the lax behavior of the Muslim masses. They also emphasized a moral earnestness that especially affected Sayyid Ahmad's mother. He saw dedication to high moral values as her chief legacy to him.

Life's Work

In 1838, the year of his father's death, Sayyid Ahmad began attending the office of an uncle who worked as a subordinate judge for the British. Before the latter instituted examinations and educational qualifications for government employees, this was the most common way of securing appointment as an official. Sayyid Ahmad soon began ascending through the ranks of the East India Company's judiciary. He served as a magistrate in a number of north Indian district towns before retiring in 1876.

Sayyid Ahmad's literary career began in the 1840's. He wrote a number of religious tracts encouraging the reform of Muslim social customs. He contributed to a newspaper published by his brother and edited a number of Persian works, such as the memoirs of the Mughal emperor Jahāngīr. In 1846, he published a unique book, *Āthār assanadīd* (*Asar-oos-sunnadeed: A History of Old and New Rules, or Governments and of Old and New Buildings, in the District of Delhi*, 1854), which described some of the famous buildings and personalities of Old Delhi. Though his early style of Urdu imitated the flowery diction and indirect discourse of Persian, throughout his life his writing became more vigorous and straightforward. Later writers considered him a model of clarity and acknowledged him as the creator of Urdu political rhetoric. His collected writings and speeches occupied nineteen volumes.

The Mutiny of 1857 had a lasting impact on Sayyid Ahmad's activity and thought. During the conflict, he remained loyal to the British, even risking his own life to save a number of Englishmen as well as the Bijnor district's cash box. After the uprising, a number of British officials blamed Muslims for fomenting the rebellion. Sayyid Ahmad spent the rest of his life refuting that notion, constantly reminding the government that many of India's Muslims stood firmly for the Empire. To his fellow Muslims, he repeated the message that the failure of the revolt proved that England's way was the way of the future and that Muslims need not abandon their religion in order to adapt to the new order. He argued that in following the "new light," they were being faithful to Islam's highest ideals. After all, Islam's advanced civilization had influenced that of Europe and made the Renaissance possible. The decline of his own day Sayyid Ahmad attributed to superstitions that had become commonplace only in the century or so before. Until then, Islam had been in the vanguard of human progress.

Sayyid Ahmad's loyalty to the British and his liberal opinions about Islam brought him honors from the imperial government. In 1869, he became a commander in the Order of the Star of India and in 1888 received a knighthood in that fraternity. He became a member of the Viceroy's Legislative Council in 1878 and sat on this largely advisory body until 1883. When he visited England in 1869-1870, he was presented to Queen Victoria and the Prince of Wales while mixing with London's literary notables.

More tangible support came from a number of Sayyid Ahmad's British friends. They encouraged his educational projects both in spirit and in various forms of government aid. When he founded a translation society to render English books, especially mathematics and science texts, into Urdu, the provincial education bureau supported the effort by buying most of the books published. At this stage of his career, Sayyid Ahmad's efforts were not solely devoted to India's Muslims. The Mughal gentry of his youth had many non-Muslim members. Hindus counted in their number masters of Persian and Urdu whose talents were equal or even superior to those of Muslims. Sayyid Ahmad was concerned that this entire class, the north Indian Urdu-speaking elite, was in danger of annihilation.

With the founding of the Muhammadan Anglo-Oriental College at Aligarh in 1875, Sayyid Ahmad labored increasingly for Muslims. He envisioned the Muhammadan Anglo-Oriental College to be a residential school on the model of Eton. He thought it essential that young boys be removed from the easy discipline of their homes and taught the virtues of diligence. In place of the intensely personal, but seemingly slipshod, educational methods of his own youth, Sayyid Ahmad installed the classroom and the fixed daily schedule of study, prayer, and sport, and regular academic examinations.

Many of the school's first students came from families that combined landowning and government service. By the 1870's, posts in the imperial bureaucracy increasingly required modern educational qualifications. The Muhammadan Anglo-Oriental College provided the training in English, history, and the sciences that helped in obtaining those appointments. The majority of the school's earliest graduates became officials or lawyers.

Throughout the latter years of his life, Sayyid Ahmad spent countless hours requesting contributions to the Muhammadan Anglo-Oriental College. Often his political stands were influenced by his belief that he should utter the sentiments most likely to ensure continued government support for the college. On the surface at least, his thinking became increasingly communal, urging Muslims to develop a separate political agenda. At the same time, Sayyid Ahmad was responding to an ever more assertive Hindu nationalism. When these groups demanded democracy, Sayyid Ahmad became fearful since the Muslim minority was bound to be overwhelmed by the majority community in any strictly representative system.

While pursuing his educational and political work, Sayyid Ahmad remained a social critic and theological controversialist. As publisher of the Urdu journal *Tahzib ul-Akhlaq* (moral reform), he had a forum in which to publicize his views on religious and moral subjects. Many religious scholars hotly opposed him, finding his thought dangerously close to pure rationalism. Many of the gentry attached to the accustomed ways in religion considered him too rational. Sayyid Ahmad held on tenaciously to his approach, but his opinions did not receive a hearing even in his own college. Many of his financial backers insisted that Sayyid Ahmad have no influence over religious instruction at the Muhammadan Anglo-Oriental College. Less controversial men took charge of introducing the young to their faith.

The affairs of the college on which he lavished such great care made the last years of Sayyid Ahmad's life miserable. In 1895, his chief clerk was caught embezzling considerable sums from the college's funds. This led to confrontations between Sayyid Ahmad and one of his sons, who wanted to acquire more control over the college. On two occasions, the son ordered Sayyid Ahmad out of his own home. For a short period, he stayed in a dormitory but finally moved to the house of a longtime friend, where he died a discouraged and embittered man.

Summary

Within Sir Sayyid Ahmad Khan's lifetime, the last shadows of Mughal glory disappeared and India became the brightest diamond in Great Britain's imperial diadem. While his family had been attached to the Mughal court, Sayyid Ahmad's achievements depended, in part, on his close association with the British. While his early education had been conducted along traditional lines, he founded a college with a curriculum and discipline modeled on Great Britain's public schools. He somehow found time to write extensively on religious and social matters, presenting a bold theological program that incorporated elements from Islam's classical tradition and European sources. In the realm of politics, he encouraged Muslims to develop a renewed self-confidence. The Muhammadan Anglo-Oriental College went on to become a university that would attract thousands of students not only from India but also from Africa and the Middle East. This university, with its many buildings clustered around Sayyid Ahmad's grave, is his most obvious and fitting memorial.

Bibliography

Ahmad, Aziz. *Islamic Modernism in India and Pakistan, 1857-1964.* New York: Oxford University Press, 1967. This work provides an important discussion of Sayyid Ahmad and his critics. Tends to concentrate on Sayyid Ahmad's political thought and work to the exclusion of his theology.
Ahmad, Aziz, and G. E. von Grunebaum, eds. *Muslim Self-Statement in India and Pakistan.* Weisbaden, Germany: Otto Harrassowitz, 1970. Since very little of the writings of India's Muslims has been translated into English, this is a valuable anthology of their work. It contains selections from the writings of Sayyid Ahmad and a number of his contemporaries.
Hardy, Peter. *The Muslims of British India.* Cambridge, England: Cambridge University Press, 1972. This is a fine overview of the political, social, and religious history of Muslims in the British period. Readers will find all the basic interpretive themes employed by contemporary scholars—both

Euro-Americans and South Asians—introduced here. The chapter "The Medieval Legacy" is a good summary of the governmental style of the Mughals.

Lelyveld, David. *Aligarh's First Generation: Muslim Solidarity in British India*. Princeton, N.J.: Princeton University Press, 1977. This brilliantly written book evokes the lives of Muslims from the period of Sayyid Ahmad's birth to the early years of the college. Not only is its scholarship first rate, but also it is written with a literary flair that makes it easily accessible to the nonspecialist.

Metcalf, Barbara D. *Islamic Revival in British India*. Princeton, N.J.: Princeton University Press, 1982. While focusing on the school of theology founded at the town of Deoband in the 1860's, Metcalf does a masterful job of describing the various groups of Muslim scholars and their divergent opinions. Covers the intellectual atmosphere of the period of Sayyid Ahmad's maturity and provides accounts of a number of debates between him and theologians connected with the Deoband movement.

Robinson, Francis. *Separatism Among Indian Muslims: The Politics of the United Provinces' Muslims, 1860-1923*. Cambridge, England: Cambridge University Press, 1974. An encyclopedic treatment of individual Muslims, including Sayyid Ahmad, and the issues that concerned them in the nineteenth and twentieth centuries. Contains a good description of the interplay between British imperial policy and Muslim politics.

Troll, Christian. *Sayyid Ahmad Khan: A Reinterpretation of Muslim Theology*. Atlantic Highlands, N.J.: Humanities Press, 1978. Written by a trained theologian, this book reemphasizes the importance of Sayyid Ahmad's theology. The author has a fund of knowledge of classical Islamic thought, and he connects Sayyid Ahmad's views with it. He frequently refers to Sayyid Ahmad's writings and provides in an appendix a translation of one of his most important works.

Gregory C. Kozlowski

AKBAR

Born: October 15, 1542; Umarkot, Sind
Died: October 17, 1605; Āgra, India
Area of Achievement: Monarchy
Contribution: As one of India's greatest Mughal emperors, Akbar conquered and unified northern India under his rule. In addition to military conquest, his most significant achievements include the development of an efficient bureaucratic structure, patronage of the arts, and enlightened policies of religious toleration.

Early Life

Abū-ul-Fath Jahāl-ud-Dīn Muhammad Akbar was born in the Kingdom of Sind, in what would become modern Pakistan. Of mixed Turkish, Persian, and Mongol ancestry, Akbar was a descendant of both Tamerlane and Genghis Khan. His grandfather, Bābur "the Tiger," a Muslim chieftain of a small state in Turkestan, invaded India in 1526 and within four years conquered Hindustan in northern India and Afghanistan. The Mughal (from the Persian word for Mongol) Dynasty, founded by Bābur, ruled northern India until the British took over in the eighteenth and nineteenth centuries.

Bābur was succeeded in 1530 by his weak son Humayun, who was unable to prevent the conquest of the empire by the Afghan chieftain Sher Khan Sur. Driven from his throne at Delhi, Humayun fled to Persia to seek support. During this flight, his Persian wife, Hamida, in 1542 gave birth to Akbar while in the Kingdom of Sind. In 1555, with the aid of Persian troops, Humayun reconquered the area around Delhi and reclaimed his throne. He died the next year, in January, 1556, as a result of an accident caused by the effects of opium.

Akbar was thirteen when he succeeded his father as the third Mughal emperor of India. He had been reared in the rough wilds of Afghanistan, where he developed a love of hunting and riding. Throughout his life, he sought reckless, dangerous activities, such as riding wild elephants and spearing tigers. Such risk-taking was probably the result of his recurrent bouts of depression, which caused him to take extreme chances in order, he said, to see whether he should die. A kindly person, he was also high-strung and had a violent temper.

Of only moderate height, Akbar was muscular and broad-shouldered. He had narrow eyes (reflecting his Mongolian ancestry), a dark complexion, a thin mustache, and long hair. Although his head drooped slightly toward the right and he suffered from epilepsy, he had an impressive commanding presence. He had a keen intelligence but never learned to read or write, even though he had been provided with a tutor from age five. He had, however, a deep love and knowledge of literature, which he learned through oral readings. He also enjoyed inventions and was skilled in mechanical arts.

When he became emperor, Akbar, despite his youth, was already serving as governor of the Punjab and had military experience. His claim to the throne, however, was immediately challenged by ambitious rivals, the most threatening of whom was a Hindu named Hemu. Akbar's rule was secured when his father's loyal and capable general Bayram Khan, on November 5, 1556, defeated Hemu's large army at Panipat, north of Delhi. Bayram Khan then ruled as the young emperor's regent for five years, until Akbar's ambitious nurse Maham Anaga had the regent deposed so that she could run the empire herself. In 1562, at age twenty, Akbar took personal control of his empire.

Life's Work

At the beginning of Akbar's rule, only a portion of the territory originally conquered by Bābur was under Mughal control. His reign characterized by successful military conquests, Akbar regained that territory and much more. With a large, efficient standing army that he himself often led, he extended Mughal authority over Afghanistan and all of India except the Deccan, in the south. The greatest resistance to his rule came from the fiercely independent Hindu Rajputs, who controlled the area west of Delhi known as Rajastan. The Rajputs were eventually subdued through both conciliatory and ruthless policies. In 1562, Akbar married the daughter of Raja Bihari Mal of Amber, one of the leading Rajput rulers. Although Akbar had a large harem, this Hindu princess was his favorite wife and mother of his heir Salim (later known as Jahangir). As a result of the marriage alliance, many Rajputs came to serve in the Mughal administration and army. The princes could continue to rule, but they had to acknowledge Akbar's suzerainty and supply him with money and soldiers. To facilitate Indian acceptance of Mughal rule, Akbar abolished the enslavement of prisoners of war and no longer forced those he conquered to convert to Islam. If rulers nevertheless resisted, they were mercilessly crushed. When the Rajput ruler of Mewar refused to follow his orders, Akbar, in 1568, captured the fortress of Chitor and ordered the massacre of thirty thousand prisoners.

Despite some episodes of draconian cruelty, Akbar's reign was generally marked by enlightened reforms promoting social peace. Most notably, he instituted a policy of religious toleration. In addition to his own sense of fairness and interest in unrestricted religious dialogue, Akbar believed that the conquering Mughals, who were Muslim, had to have the support of the native Hindu populace. Akbar therefore removed many of the penalties that had burdened Indian Hindus. In 1563, he abolished a tax, which dated back well before Bābur's invasion, on Hindu pilgrims who traveled to holy places. In 1564, he abolished the *jizya*, a tax on non-Muslims. He ended the destruction of Hindu temples and allowed new ones to be built. He encouraged Muslim acceptance of Hindu traditions, although he did try to eliminate the Hindu practices of child marriage and widow burning (suttee). Schools were founded under government sponsorship for Hindus as well as Muslims. Hindus served and advanced equally with the Muslims in the government and the army.

Akbar's economic policies were also fair and effective. Taxation was based on landed property, and one-third of the value of the harvest went to the royal treasury. (This was a lower taxation than before or after Akbar.) In times of poor harvest, taxation was reduced or suspended. Efficient tax collection, coupled with a sound currency and flourishing trade, created great prosperity. Most of the hundred million people under Akbar's rule were still very poor, but historians have suggested that peasants were probably better off then than in more modern times.

Akbar maintained centralized control over his empire by instituting an effective bureaucratic hierarchy based on standardized ranks and salaries. The higher administration was divided into thirty-three ranks, classified according to the number of cavalry the officeholder was expected to raise for the emperor. There was no distinction between civil and military ranks, and all were theoretically appointed by and responsible to the emperor. The empire was territorially divided into twelve provinces and further subdivided into systematic administrative units. The civil code was based on Muslim law, but local disputes that took place between Hindus could be decided according to Hindu law.

The prosperity of the empire allowed Akbar to amass a huge fortune, making him the richest king in the world. He had an elaborate court, which for many years he held at a magnificent new palace-city, Fatehpur Sikri (city of victory). Despite the grandeur of his public life, in which he assumed an almost godlike persona, Akbar in his personal life had simple, even austere habits. He maintained a very moderate diet, with usually only one main meal a day. Near the end of his life, under Jain influence, he almost entirely gave up eating meat. He did, however, drink liquor excessively and, like his father, was a regular user of opium. He slept very little, no more than about three hours a night.

During Akbar's reign, Mughal culture flowered, characterized by a distinctive, elegant blend of Persian and Hindu styles, with some European influence. Akbar employed more than one hundred painters at court who exhibited their work regularly to him. He himself was a gifted artist. He was also a musician, performing on a kind of kettle drum, and was skilled in Hindu singing. Although illiterate, he collected a large library and encouraged literary production. He created the post of poet laureate for Hindi, the northern Indian vernacular that became India's national language, and had Sanskrit works translated into Persian for his courtiers.

Akbar's primary interest was religion. He built at Fatehpur Sikri a house of worship in which to discuss theological questions. At first limited to Muslims, the debates were soon opened to Hindus and other faiths. He invited Jesuits from the Portuguese colony at Goa to come to his court, and he listened so intently to them that they thought he was about to convert to Christianity. He did reject orthodox Islam, but, instead of becoming a Christian, he sponsored his own religion, known as the Divine Faith, a mystical blend of Hinduism and Islam. Akbar claimed that he was God's vice-regent, with authority to rule over spiritual as well as temporal matters. This new religion had little influence and disappeared after his death.

Akbar's last years were marred by his son Salim's attempts to usurp his throne. Salim may have caused his father's death in 1605 by poisoning him. When he succeeded Akbar, Salim took the Persian name Jahangir, meaning "world seizer." Akbar is buried in a mausoleum at Sicandra, near Āgra.

Summary

Known as "the Great Mughal," Akbar created an imperial government that lasted until the nineteenth century. His administrative system, efficient and open to the promotion of talent, was adopted by the British when they later conquered India. Although there were enormous disparities of income between the Mughal elite and the impoverished peasants, his reign was characterized by a level of general prosperity unmatched in later years. The contemporary of Elizabeth I of England and Philip II of Spain, Akbar surpassed both of them in wealth, power, and majesty. He enjoyed a semidivine status but nevertheless had a personal concern for the well-being of his subjects. He was humble enough to disguise himself sometimes in order to mix with his subjects and listen to their views.

Akbar succeeded in establishing internal peace within his empire, because he combined a realistic assessment of the limits of power with a humanistic concern and just administration. His system of taxation, for example, which brought great wealth into his treasury, was flexible enough to encourage rather than crush those suffering economic hardship. The glory of Akbar's reign included a cultural blending that produced the beautiful, distinctive Mughal style. This creativity was stimulated by the toleration for cultural and religious differences, a toleration which was perhaps Akbar's greatest achievement. With India later to be so torn apart by conflict between Hindu and Muslim, Akbar's policy of religious toleration and mixing makes him a model of enlightened rule.

Bibliography

Binyon, Laurence. *Akbar.* New York: D. Appleton, 1932. A brief, readable biography of Akbar with emphasis on his personality rather than on his rule.
Burn, Richard, ed. *The Cambridge History of India.* Vol. 4, *The Mughal*

Period. New York: Macmillan, 1937. This history of the Mughal Empire from the conquest of Bābur to the eighteenth century includes a detailed account of Akbar's rule, with emphasis on his military conquests and religious thought.

Du Jarric, Pierre. *Akbar and the Jesuits: An Account of the Jesuit Missions to the Court of Akbar*. Translated with an introduction and notes by C. H. Payne. London: George Routledge & Sons, 1926. A translation and reprint of an early seventeenth century French account of Akbar and his rule, based on reports and letters by Jesuits in Akbar's court.

Malleson, G. B. *Akbar*. Oxford, England: Clarendon Press, 1891. An outdated, overly laudatory, but engaging short biography.

Moreland, W. H. *India at the Death of Akbar: An Economic Study*. London: Macmillan, 1920. A very critical account of Indian economy and administration under Akbar. Written to justify British rule in India. Contains very little information on Akbar himself.

Smith, Vincent A. *Akbar, the Great Mogul, 1542-1605*. Oxford, England: Clarendon Press, 1917. Still the most complete biography of Akbar. A balanced account that assesses the strengths and weaknesses of Akbar's personality and rule. Contains a lengthy annotated bibliography.

Wellesz, Emmy. *Akbar's Religious Thought, Reflected in Mogul Painting*. London: Allen & Unwin, 1952. A lucid account of how Akbar's eclectic religious interests and policy of religious toleration influenced the creation of Mughal painting. Includes forty black-and-white art plates.

Wolpert, Stanley. *A New History of India*. 2d ed. New York: Oxford University Press, 1982. The chapter on Akbar in this general history, written by one of the leading historians of India, provides an accessible introduction.

Nancy Fix Anderson

LEON BATTISTA ALBERTI

Born: February 18, 1404; Genoa
Died: April, 1472; Rome
Areas of Achievement: Architecture and philosophy
Contribution: Alberti is identified by Renaissance historians as an archetype of the universal man. He established a leading reputation as a theorist and practitioner of the visual arts, notably in the field of architecture. As a Humanist, he was the author of numerous moral dialogues.

Early Life

The prominent Albertis were known as textile merchants and bankers. In Florence they were associated with the Popular Party. Their decline began with the exile of Leon Battista Alberti's grandfather Benedetto, who left Florence with his son Lorenzo in 1387. Leon Battista was born in Genoa, the second natural son of Lorenzo and Bianca Fieschi, widow of a prominent Genoese family. On her death from the plague in 1406, Lorenzo moved to Venice, where he joined another brother, Ricciardo, in trade, shortly thereafter marrying a Florentine woman in 1408.

Leon Battista and his brother Carlo received the best Humanist education available. At Gasparino, Barzizza's academy in Padua, he studied with many who were to become major scholars in the world of Renaissance learning, such as Panormita and Francesco Filelfo. In 1421, Alberti went to Bologna, where he deepened his knowledge of Greek and Latin literature and began his studies of mathematics. Following the death of his father (1421) and his uncle Ricciardo a year later, the brothers were deprived of their legitimate inheritance by the machinations of their cousins, Ricciardo's sons. A combination of grief and academic pressure led to a serious deterioration of Leon Battista's health, in particular his eyesight. During his recuperation, he turned from the study of ancient texts to that of mathematics, an interest that profoundly affected his future researches. Alberti's friendship in Bologna with Tommaso Parentucelli da Sarzana—the future Pope Nicholas V—led to an appointment as secretary to a cardinal of Bologna. In 1428, the Florentine ban on the Albertis was lifted. It is most likely that Leon Battista made a brief visit to the city of his father that year, or early in 1429. These years coincide with the climax of the struggle between the Albizzi faction and the Popular Party, resulting in the eventual consolidation in Florence of Medici power under Cosimo de' Medici: Historically the Albertis had been closely allied to the Medicis.

Life's Work

As a papal secretary in the service of Eugenius IV, Alberti followed the pope to Florence, where he had been invited on the expulsion of the Papacy from Rome. Here he came into contact with all the major personalities responsible for the explosion of the new art and architecture of the Renaissance. In Florence, he established strong ties of friendship with the sculptor Donatello, the architects Filippo Brunelleschi, who had completed the dome of the cathedral, Michelozzo, who was to design the Palazzo Medici, and Lorenzo Ghiberti, who was working on the doors of the baptistery. The first fruits of this experience are the *De pictura* (1435; *Of Painting*, 1726) and *De statua* (possibly pre-1435; *Of Sculpture*, 1726), in both of which Alberti displays the fundamental principles of Renaissance art, in particular the relationship between mathematics and composition, the consequent rules of perspective, and the use of nature as a model. Alberti wrote both Latin and Italian versions of these treatises.

While the majority of his moral dialogues are in Latin, Alberti also turned to the vernacular in a conscious attempt to reach a wider audience and to restore to Tuscan the literary prestige it had enjoyed in the previous century as the result of the works of Dante, Petrarch, and Giovanni Boccaccio. *Theogenius* (c. 1440) and *Della tranquillità dell'anima* (c. 1442; of peace of mind) mark moments of deep reflection in Alberti's career: an internal debate on the relative merits of the active and contemplative life. The high point of these years came earlier, with the completion of the first three books of Alberti's most popular work, *Della famiglia* (1434; *The Family in Renaissance Florence*, 1969). In dialogue form, he details the moral basis of the family and its role in civic life, offering to the coming generation, in spite of the reverses he himself suffered at the hands of certain relatives, the example of the contributions made by their ancestors to the commercial expansion and intellectual vigor of Renaissance Florence.

Alberti's career as an architect was launched in Ferrara in 1442, when he was asked to judge the designs for an equestrian statue in honor of Nicolò d'Este. Alberti designed the minitriumphal arch for the statue's base. With the elevation of Parentucelli to the Papacy as Nicholas V, Alberti was named the pope's principal architectural adviser: the man he depended on more than any other in an ambitious program of restoration, street widening, and building projects designed to return to Rome the dignity it deserved as the seat of the Catholic church. The years that followed were to be the most productive of his career, and the achievements recorded between 1450 and 1470 were to give him his greatest satisfaction and ensure Alberti enduring fame. The buildings completed and designed were all the fruit of an experience that had ripened in the light of extensive theoretical meditation. Alberti's principles of architecture are detailed in the ten volumes of *De re aedificatoria* (1452; *The Architecture*, 1726), dedicated to his patron Nicholas V. In it Alberti acknowledges the contribution of the Roman theorist Vetruvius. His intention was to take the principles of harmony and proportion and apply them to the aesthetic and practical requirements of his own age.

Passing from theory to practice, he accepted a commission from Sigismondo Malatesta (1450) to transform the Gothic Church of San Francesco into the Tempio Malatestano, with its bold classical façade divided into three triumphal arches. Also around 1450, he was called by the merchant Giovanni Rucellai to redesign the façade of his family's palazzo in Florence which, with its elegant pillars and flat beveled masonry, makes the building rather more inviting than the more fortresslike structures such as the Palazzo Medici-Ricciardi. During the reign of Pius II, one of the foremost Renaissance Humanists, Alberti accepted the invitation of Ludovico Gonzaga of Mantua to build the Church of San Sebastiano in that city. The same princely patron gave Alberti his final commission: to design the Church of Sant'Andrea in Mantua. The latter was only completed in the eighteenth century, following modified Albertian concepts. He did live to see the completion of a major project: the façade of Santa Maria Novella in Florence, again commissioned by his patron Rucellai. Here the addition of classical forms harmonizes with existing Gothic elements of the basilica, and the use of the characteristic black-and-white marble blends Santa Maria Novella with other major Florentine churches, including Santa Maria del Fiore. Alberti, who served popes and princes, also remained in touch with his allies the Medicis; in the tradition of the scholar advising civic leaders, he dedicated a small treatise on rhetoric (*Trivia senatoria*, c. 1460) to Lorenzo de'Medici, who was still in his teens. Alberti died in Rome in April, 1472.

Summary

Leon Battista Alberti's writings in Italian, both on art and on social behavior, explore all the major themes of Renaissance Humanism. Scholars and editors of his works have asserted that he shaped and defined this movement in the history of ideas and that the Renaissance would not have made the intellectual advances it did without his contributions and prodding. In the introduction to *The Family in Renaissance Florence*, he expounds on the themes of virtue and fortune that so exercised the speculative curiosity of fifteenth century thinkers. In the decline of glory of his own family, he sees a parallel with the rise and fall of states. Against the thesis of inevitability and the stoic acceptance of a fate governing human affairs, Alberti juxtaposes the Renaissance idea of free will that allows men to shape an independent life for themselves in defiance of even the direst circumstances. This is what he means by virtue, which must never allow fortune to serve as an alibi for failure or incompetence. Virtue is also dedicated hard work and the determination to cultivate all the seeds of natural talents and curiosity with which one is endowed. The proclamation of these ideals makes Alberti a principal spokesman of the spirit of the active life that animates the mercantile ethic of civic Humanism in the first half of Quattrocento Florence. Man was born, he says, to be useful to other men.

44 *Great Lives from History*

While the impact of Alberti the moralist needs emphasizing, his dominant role as art theorist and architectural mentor is his most enduring achievement. Architecture in fact could be taken as a metaphor for the highest ideals of Renaissance culture, for it involves the most detailed knowledge of an infinite variety of activities, skills, and materials that must ultimately be synthesized into a harmonious whole. Granted his major achievements in so many fields, it is amazing to observe that Alberti's final significance was nearly overlooked. His original insights into art theory had been so integrated into practice and elaborated on by Leonardo da Vinci and others that the originator of the ideas had been largely forgotten.

Bibliography

Alberti, Leon Battista. *The Family in Renaissance Florence.* Translated by Renee Neu Watkins. Columbia: University of South Carolina Press, 1969. This modern translation includes a good introduction and bibliography of writings on civic Humanism in English.

Gadol, Joan. *Leon Battista Alberti: Universal Man of the Early Renaissance.* Chicago: University of Chicago Press, 1969. A very useful study detailing Alberti's contributions to the theory and practice of art and the development of architecture in the fifteenth century. Although mostly directed to his work in the visual arts (with reference to optics and perspective), the book places its subject firmly in the context of Humanism. The first chapter is biographical and includes a critical survey of views on Alberti's ultimate significance.

Garin, Eugenio. *Italian Humanism: Philosophy and Civic Life in the Renaissance.* Translated by Peter Munz. New York: Harper & Row, 1965. This extremely lucid intellectual history of Renaissance Humanism includes some indispensable pages on Alberti in chapter 2 on the subject of civic life. Garin presents him as a major representative of the spirt of *negotium* (the active life) and thus a key figure in the intellectual life of the first half of the Quattrocento.

Grayson, Cecil. "The Humanism of Alberti." *Italian Studies* 12 (1957): 37-56. An essential synopsis of Alberti's thought and moral imperatives by the writer's most distinguished commentator and the major editor of his works. Grayson succinctly relates Alberti's thought to his family's commercial activity and the intellectual atmosphere of fifteenth century Florence.

Mancini, Girolamo. *Vita di Leon Battista Alberti.* Florence: G. C. Sansoni, 1882. The definitive life in Italian by the nineteenth century's most distinguished Albertian scholar and editor of his Italian and Latin works. Mancini has added his authoritative voice to questions about Alberti's life.

Harry Lawton

AFONSO DE ALBUQUERQUE

Born: 1453; Alhandra, near Lisbon, Portugal
Died: December 15, 1515; at sea, near Goa Harbor
Areas of Achievement: Government and the military
Contribution: Albuquerque, called "the Great" and "the Portuguese Mars," conquered Goa in India (1510) and Malacca on the Malay Peninsula (1511), ended the Arabian trade monopoly in Asia, made Goa a center of the Portuguese colonial government and commerce in that area, and developed colonial administration using native officials. He served as the second Portuguese governor of India. His most lasting contribution was the foundation of the Portuguese colonial empire in the East.

Early Life

Afonso de Albuquerque was born the second son of Gonzalvo de Albuquerque, Lord of Villaverde. Through his father, he was related to the royal house of Portugal (through illegitimate descent), the males in the family having for several generations been confidential secretaries to Portuguese kings. On the maternal side, his grandfather had served as an admiral of Portugal. With these connections, it is not unexpected that Afonso's early education was at the court of King Afonso V. He served in the army of Portugal in North Africa, gaining military experience crusading against the Muslims. He fought in the conquest of Arzila and Tangier (1471), participated in the invasion of Spain (1476), and served in the expedition led by King Afonso against the Turks and in the Battle of Otranto (1480-1481).

On the death of King Afonso, Albuquerque returned to Lisbon and the court, where he was appointed chief equerry (master of the horse) under John II. He served again in military expeditions against the Muslims in North Africa (at the defense of Graciosa) and under King Manuel I in Morocco. During this period of Portuguese history, the court was continually concerned at home with the struggle of the king for dominance over the nobles. Albuquerque was little engaged in these affairs but did seemingly establish jealousy and make enemies among the nobles at court. He later fell victim to intrigues at court against him.

Life's Work

While his education had been at the Portuguese court and his military service for the most part crusading against the Muslims in Northern Africa and Europe, Albuquerque's fame was made in the East during the reign of Manuel. Here, again, he was engaged in battles against the Muslims, this time for trade dominance and empire. In a relatively short period of time (1503-1515), he secured Portuguese hegemony of the Deccan in India, Portuguese control of the spice trade through conquest and fortification of the Malay Peninsula and Sunda Isles, and the dominance of the waters through the Malaccan Strait. He governed the eastern empire of Portugal (though he never received the title of viceroy).

After the history making voyage of Vasco da Gama, in which he rounded the Cape of Good Hope to India (1499), the way was opened to the Portuguese to challenge the monopoly held by the Venetians and Muslims of the spice-trade routes between Europe and the East. Albuquerque, with his kinsman, Francisco de Albuquerque, sailed under Pedro Álvars Cabral (1503) to open relations and trade with the rulers of the East (India). During this first of his voyages to Asia, Albuquerque assisted in establishing the Hindu ruler of Cochin in a bid for power against the native ruler, who was friendly to the Arabs, at Calicut. In return, the Portuguese were able to build a fortress at Cochin and establish a trading post at Quilon; thus began the Portuguese empire in the East.

Albuquerque returned in July, 1504, to Lisbon, where Manuel received him with honor. For a time, Albuquerque assisted in the formulation of policy at court. When Tristão da Cunha sailed from Portugal in April, 1506, with a fleet of sixteen ships, Albuquerque sailed with him as an officer in command of five of the ships. The object of the voyage was to explore the east coast of Africa and to build a fortress at the mouth of the Red Sea to block Arab trade with India. Admiral da Cunha's fleet successfully attacked several Arab cities on the African east coast, explored the coasts of Madagascar and Mozambique, and built a fortress on Socotra Island, effectively blocking the mouth of the Red Sea. On September 27, 1507, Albuquerque led his squadron in a successful siege of the island of Hormuz, which commands the Strait of Hormuz between the Persian Gulf and Gulf of Oman. Hormuz was one of the trade centers of the Arab monopoly. His ships' captains desired more to ply their trade on the seas than to be engaged in fortifying Hormuz, and Albuquerque temporarily was forced to abandon the project.

In 1505, Dom Francisco de Almeida was appointed the first governor in India with the rank of viceroy. In 1508, Manuel appointed Albuquerque to succeed Almeida at the end of his term. This commission did not, however, include the rank of viceroy though the distinction seemed never to have been made in the colonies or by Albuquerque.

Albuquerque proceeded to the Malabar Coast and arrived in December, 1508, at Cannanore, India, where Almeida refused to honor the commission and jailed Albuquerque. In previous skirmishes which Almeida had had with Arab forces from Egypt, his son had been killed and Almeida determined to remain in command in India until he had avenged his son's death. Almeida defeated the Muslims near Diu in February, 1509, and the Portuguese fleet arrived in November, 1509, confirming Albuquerque's commission. Albuquerque was then released from jail and subsequently assumed his position as governor. Almeida returned to Lisbon.

Albuquerque set out to control all the major sea-trade routes to the East and to establish permanent colonial posts with fortresses and settled populations. He destroyed Calicut, which had continued hostilities, in January, 1510. He moved next to secure a permanent center for commerce and government on the Indian coast. Rather than moving to displace the Hindu rulers to the south, he attacked and captured Goa from the Muslims in March, 1510, with a fleet of twenty-three ships but was driven back by the Muslim army two months later; he regained the city permanently for the Portuguese in November. He executed the Muslim defenders of the city. This hard won victory also established Portuguese acceptance by the Hindu rulers on the eastern coast of India.

Albuquerque was able then for a short time to turn his attention to administration. Using the government of Lisbon as a model, he established a senate for Goa, the first such senate in Asia, and gave financial and judicial responsibilities to native officials. He encouraged the intermarriage of his men with the population of Goa. He also developed a network of supply from interior villages for the coastal city.

In 1511, Albuquerque resumed his expeditions to break the trade monopoly of the Muslims to the Spice Islands (Moluccas). He established the Portuguese in Ceylon and the Sunda Isles. He attacked and sacked Malacca in July, 1511. He built a Portuguese fortress there, established control of the straits between the Malay Peninsula and the Island of Sumatra, and by these means guaranteed for Portugal the domination of the maritime route to the Spice Islands. While in Malacca, he established a colonial government with native officials (as in Goa) and developed trade relations with Pegu, Cochin (in what is now South Vietnam), China, Siam (modern Thailand), and Java.

Once more, in February, 1515, Albuquerque undertook a military expedition, this time with twenty-six ships, to the Red Sea. This early commission, from his first coming to the East, to establish Portuguese trade over the Persian Gulf region was yet unaccomplished. He laid seige to Aden (1513) unsuccessfully, led what is probably the first modern European voyage in the Red Sea, and retook Hormuz (1515). The retaking of Hormuz effectively established Portuguese dominance over the Persian Gulf trade. In September, 1515, Albuquerque became ill and set sail for Goa.

Whether his enemies at court succeeded in their jealous intrigues against him or whether Manuel was concerned about the state of Albuquerque's health, a successor to Albuquerque was appointed to govern the Portuguese holdings in the East. Albuquerque met the vessel from Europe carrying news of the appointment and learned, as he approached the harbor of Goa, that the post had been given to his enemy, Lope Soares. Manuel had recommended that Soares pay special deference to Albuquerque; weakened by illness and embittered by what he considered betrayal, Albuquerque died on December 15, 1515, while still at sea. Before his death, he wrote to the king giving an account of his service in the East and claiming for his natural son, Brás (later called Afonso the Younger), the reward and honor that he claimed as his own.

Albuquerque was buried in Goa in the Church of Our Lady, which he had built. For many years, Muslims and Hindus visited his grave to solicit his intercession against the injustices of their later rulers. A superstition held that the Portuguese dominion would be safe as long as Albuquerque's bones lay in Goa. These were, however, moved to Portugal in 1566. His natural son (Albuquerque was never married) was later honored by Manuel as befitted the accomplishments of his father.

Summary

Afonso de Albuquerque was one of those men distinguished in leadership, military achievements, and administration of which southern Europe seemed to have a bounteous supply at the end of the fifteenth century and through the mid-sixteenth. Facing long lines of supply and communication around the Cape of Good Hope, facing enemies by sea and by land, his enemies often as accomplished as the Europeans of the time in military organization and technology, Albuquerque was able to establish the basis for a Portuguese empire in the East. He was able to organize in the area colonial administration and trade practices that endured to times past Portuguese domination. He did not amass vast fortunes (that which he did have he lost through shipwreck early in his adventures in the East). He did not obtain enormous landholdings or accrue glorious titles. A loyal son of Portugal, his ambition was tied to its glory, wealth, and position; in Portugal's name, he gained control of all the main sea trade routes of the East and built permanent fortresses which, with their settled populations, were the foundation of Portuguese hegemony in the East.

Bibliography

Albuquerque, Afonso de. *The Commentaries of the Great Alfonso Dalboquerque, Second Viceroy of India.* Edited and translated by Walter de Gray Birch. 4 vols. London: Hakluyt Society, 1875-1884. This resource includes Albuquerque's reports and letters compiled originally by his son Brás. It was first published by the Lisbon Academy of Sciences in 1576.

Armstrong, Richard. *A History of Seafaring.* Vol. 2, *Discoverers.* Westport, Conn.: Praeger, 1969. The work is general in scope, designed for the general reader, and well illustrated with diagrams, maps, and reproductions. The short and vivid sketch of Albuquerque presents the major accomplishments of his career within the context of the history of discovery. Includes a good index and bibliography.

Boxer, C. R. *The Portuguese Seaborne Empire, 1415-1825.* London: Hutchinson, 1969. A social history by one of Great Britain's leading Portuguese scholars. These tales of Portuguese sailing and trading and the transplantation of their social institutions to India are easy to read. Basing his research on original sources, Boxer contradicts the Portuguese myth of "no color bar" as the secret of successful governing of an empire vaster than its base. Good maps are included.

Neilson, J. B. *Great Men of the East*. London: Longmans, Green, 1947. Neilson gives a glowing portrait of Albuquerque and his achievements.

Sanceau, Elaine. *Indies Adventure*. Hamden, Conn.: Archon Books, 1938. Albuquerque's voyages and achievements in the East are vividly chronicled with emphasis on what made them remarkable.

Stephens, Henry Morse. *Albuquerque*. Oxford, England: Clarendon Press, 1892. In the Rulers of India series. This is a standard biography of Albuquerque and is one of the most complete available in English. It is the one found in most libraries of the United States and is a scholarly chronicle of and commentary on Albuquerque's achievements.

Barbara Ann Barbato

JEAN LE ROND D'ALEMBERT

Born: November 17, 1717; Paris, France
Died: October 29, 1783; Paris, France
Areas of Achievement: Mathematics, physics, philosophy, and music
Contribution: A pioneer in the use of differential calculus, d'Alembert applied his mathematical genius to solve problems in mechanics. He provided valuable assistance with the *Encyclopédie* and wrote a number of treatises on musical theory.

Early Life

On the night of November 17, 1717, Mme Claudine-Alexandrine Guérin, Marquise de Tencin, gave birth to a son whom she promptly abandoned on the steps of the Church of Saint-Jean-Le-Rond. There, he was baptized with the name of the church; he was then sent to the Maison de la Coucher, from which he went to a foster home in Picardy. When his father, Louis-Camus Destouches, a military officer, returned to Paris, he sought his son and arranged for the child to be cared for by Mme Rousseau, the wife of a glazier. D'Alembert would always regard Mme Rousseau as his real mother and would continue to live with her until 1765, when illness compelled him to seek new quarters in the home of Julie de Lespinasse.

Destouches continued to watch over his illegitimate child, sending him to private schools; when Destouches died in 1726, he left the boy a legacy of twelve hundred livres a year. The sum, though not luxurious, guaranteed him an independence he cherished throughout his life. Through the interest of the Destouches family, the young man entered the Jansenist Collège des Quatre-Nations, where he took the name Jean-Baptiste Daremberg, later changing it, perhaps for euphony, to d'Alembert. Although he, like many other Enlightenment figures, abandoned the religious training he received there, he never shed the Cartesian influence that dominated the school.

After receiving his *baccalauréat* in 1735, he spent two years studying law, receiving a license to practice in 1738. Neither jurisprudence nor medicine, to which he devoted a year, held his interest. He turned to mathematics, for which he had a natural talent. At the age of twenty-two, he submitted his first paper to the Académie des Sciences; in that piece, he corrected a number of errors in Father Charles Reyneau's *Analyse demontrée* (1714). A second paper, on refraction and fluid mechanics, followed the next year, and in May, 1741, he was made an adjunct member of the Académie des Sciences.

Life's Work

Two years later, d'Alembert published a major contribution to mechanics, *Traité de dynamique* (1743), which includes his famous principle stating that the force which acts on a body in a system is the sum of the forces within the system restraining it and the external forces acting on that system. Although Isaac Newton and Johann Bernoulli had already offered similar observations, neither had expressed the matter so simply. The effect of d'Alembert's principle was to convert a problem of dynamics to one of statics, making it easier to solve. The treatise is characteristic of d'Alembert's work in several ways: It illustrates his exceptional facility with mathematics; it reveals a desire to find universal laws in a discipline; and it indicates his ability to reduce complex matters to simple components. Over the next several years, he wrote a number of other innovative works in both mathematics and fluid mechanics.

At the same time that d'Alembert was establishing himself as one of Europe's leading mathematicians—in 1752 Frederick the Great offered him the presidency of the Berlin Academy—he emerged as a leading figure of the Parisian salons. In 1743, he was introduced to the influential Mme du Deffand, who would secure his election to the Académie Française in 1754. He remained a fixture of her assemblies until Julie de Lespinasse, whom he met there, established her own salon following a quarrel with the older woman. Later in the 1740's, he also joined the gatherings at the homes of Mme Marie-Thérèse Rodet Geoffrin and Anne-Louise Bénédicte de Bourbon, Duchesse du Maine. Not striking in appearance—he was short and, according to a contemporary, "of rather undistinguished features, with a fresh complexion that tends to ruddiness," his eyes small and his mouth large—he compensated for his looks with his excellent ability with mimicry and his lively conversation.

While enjoying the female-dominated world of the salons, d'Alembert was also meeting a number of important male intellectuals, with whom he dined weekly at the Hôtel du Panier Fleuri—Denis Diderot, Jean-Jacques Rousseau (no relation to his stepmother), and Étienne Bonnot de Condillac. He probably also knew Gua de Malves, a fellow mathematician and member of the Académie des Sciences, who was chosen as the first editor of the *Encyclopédie* (1751-1772), and Malves may have been the one who introduced d'Alembert to the project; after Malves resigned, d'Alembert was named coeditor with Diderot.

D'Alembert did not plan to assume as much responsibility for the work as his coeditor. He wrote to Samuel Formey in September, 1749:

> I never intended to have a hand in [the *Encyclopédie*] except for what has to do with mathematics and physical astronomy. I am in a position to do only that, and besides, I do not intend to condemn myself for ten years to the tedium of seven or eight folios.

It was Diderot who conceived of the work as a summation of human knowledge, but d'Alembert's involvement extended well beyond the mathematical articles that the title page credits to him.

His contributions took many forms. He used his scientific contacts to solicit articles, and his connection with the world of the salons, which Diderot did not frequent, permitted him to enlist support among the aristocracy and upper middle class. Not only was such backing politically important, given the controversial nature of the enterprise, but also the financial assistance d'Alembert secured may well have prevented its collapse. Mme Geoffrin alone is reported to have donated more than 100,000 livres.

Also significant are the fifteen hundred articles that d'Alembert wrote, including the important *Discours préliminaire* (1751; *Preliminary Discourse to the Encyclopedia of Diderot*, 1963). Praised by all the great French intellectuals as well as Frederick the Great, it seeks to explain the purpose and plan of the *Encyclopédie* by showing the links between disciplines and tracing the progress of knowledge from the Renaissance to 1750. In its view of the Enlightenment as the culmination of progress in thought, it reflects the philosophes' optimistic, humanistic attitude. D'Alembert's own understanding of the role of the philosopher and the nature of learning also emerges clearly in this essay. For him, "The universe is but a vast ocean, on the surface of which we perceive certain islands more or less large, whose link with the continent is hidden from us." The goal of the scientist is to discover, not invent, these concealed links, and mathematics would provide the means for establishing these connections. Just as physicists of the twentieth century seek the one force that impels all nature, so d'Alembert sought the single principle that underlies all knowledge.

In 1756, d'Alembert went to Geneva to visit Voltaire, his closest friend among the philosophes, and to gather information for an article on this center of Calvinism. Already in "Collège" d'Alembert had antagonized the Church by criticizing ecclesiastical control of education. "Genève," with its intended praise of Protestant ministers, provoked sharp protests from the Catholic establishment in France, and Calvinists were upset as well by d'Alembert's portrait of them as virtual agnostics. Opposition to the *Encyclopédie* was growing in court circles; in March, 1759, permission to publish would be withdrawn. Never as daring as Voltaire or Diderot, d'Alembert resigned as coeditor in 1758, despite protests from his friends and associates. He did, however, continue to write articles on mathematics and science.

While the controversy surrounding the enterprise, especially "Genève," was the primary reason for d'Alembert's distancing himself from the *Encyclopédie*, another important factor was his growing disagreement with Diderot over the direction the work was taking. By 1758, Diderot, who had himself published a treatise on mathematics—*Mémoires sur différens sujets de mathématiques* (1748)—had come to believe that no further progress was possible in that field, so he rejected his coeditor's emphasis on mathematics as the key to knowledge, stating that "the reign of mathematics is over." D'Alembert's Cartesian theories also troubled Diderot. Like René Descartes, d'Alembert believed that matter is inert; Diderot disagreed. While d'Alembert maintained that the most precise sciences were those like geometry that relied on abstract principles derived from reason, Diderot regarded experimentation and observation—empiricism—as the best guarantees of reliability. For d'Alembert, the more abstruse the science the better, for he sought to solve problems. Diderot preferred knowledge that directly affected life. In later years, Diderot continued to praise d'Alembert's mathematical abilities, and d'Alembert unsuccessfully tried to secure Diderot's election to the Académie Française, but the two remained only distant friends.

Withdrawing from the *Encyclopédie* did not signal d'Alembert's rejection of the Enlightenment. Instead, he sought to use the Académie Française as a forum to promulgate the views of the philosophes. His first speech before the Académie Française urged toleration and freedom of expression, and in 1769 he nearly succeeded in having the body offer a prize for the best poem on the subject of "The Progress of Reason Under Louis XIV," the notion of such progress being a fundamental tenet of the Enlightenment. In 1768, when the King of Denmark, Christian VII, visited the Académie Française, and again in March, 1771, when Gustavus III of Sweden attended a session, d'Alembert spoke of the benefits of enlightened policies. Through his influence in the salons, he arranged for the election of nine philosophes to the Académie Française between 1760 and 1770, and a number of others sympathetic to their cause also entered because of d'Alembert. Elected permanent secretary of the body in 1772, he thereafter used his official eulogies to attack the enemies of the Enlightenment and to encourage advanced ideas.

D'Alembert also continued to publish. The first three volumes of *Opuscules mathématiques* (1761-1780) contain much original work on hydrodynamics, lenses, and astronomy. His anonymous *Sur la destruction des Jésuites en France* (1765; *An Account of the Destruction of the Jesuits in France*, 1766), occasioned by the suppression of the order, discusses the danger of linking civil and ecclesiastical power because theological disputes then disturb domestic peace. In addition to attacking the Jesuits, d'Alembert urged the suppression of their rivals, the Jansenists.

Active as he was in the Académie Française, d'Alembert's last years were marked by physical and emotional pain. Devoted to Julie de Lespinasse, he was doubly distressed by her death in 1776 and the discovery of love letters to her from the Comte de Guibert and the Marquis de Mora. As permanent secretary of the Académie Française, he was entitled to a small apartment in the Louvre, and there he spent the final seven years of his life, which ended on October 29, 1783. Although he produced little original work of his own during this period, he remained an important correspondent of Voltaire and Frederick the Great, urging the monarch to grant asylum to those persecuted for their views. He also encouraged young mathematicians such as Joseph-Louis Lagrange, Pierre-Simon Laplace, and the Marquis de Condorcet.

Summary

Voltaire sometimes doubted Jean Le Rond d'Alembert's zeal for the cause of Enlightenment, and d'Alembert's distancing himself from the *encyclopédistes* reveals that he was not one to take great risks. He observed that "honest men can no longer fight except by hiding behind the hedges, but from that position they can fire some good shots at the wild beasts infesting the country." From his post in the salons and the Académie Française, he worked, as he told Voltaire, "to gain esteem for the little flock" of philosophes.

If Voltaire could accuse d'Alembert of excessive caution, d'Alembert could in turn charge Voltaire with toadying to the powerful. In his 1753 *Essai sur les gens de lettres*, d'Alembert urged writers to rely solely on their talents, and he reminded the nobility that intellectuals were their equals. "I am determined never to put myself in the service of anyone and to die as free as I have lived," he wrote Voltaire. Neither Frederick the Great's repeated invitations to assume the presidency of the Berlin Academy nor Catherine the Great's offer of 100,000 livres a year to tutor her son Grand Duke Paul could lure him away from France and independence.

In both his life and thought he was loyal to the ideals of the philosophes, so it is fitting that Ernst Cassirer should choose him as the representative of the Enlightenment and call him "one of the most important scholars of the age and one of its intellectual spokesmen." His belief in the ability of reason to solve any problem epitomizes the view of eighteenth century intellectuals, but he also recognized the role of experimentation and imagination. In his *Eléméns de musique théorique et practique suivant les principes de M. Rameau* (1752), d'Alembert dissented from Jean-Philippe Rameau's view that one can devise mathematical rules for composition. As in his article on elocution in the *Encyclopédie*, he argued that rules are necessary, but only genius can elevate a work beyond mediocrity. Excellent scientist though he was, he ranked the artist above the philosopher.

Bibliography

Cassirer, Ernst. *The Philosophy of the Enlightenment.* Princeton, N.J.: Princeton University Press, 1951. A translation of Cassirer's 1932 book in German, this work explores the way the Enlightenment looked at nature, psychology, religion, history, society, and aesthetics. Much, *inter alia*, about d'Alembert.

Essar, Dennis F. *The Language Theory, Epistemology, and Aesthetics of Jean Lerond d'Alembert.* Oxford, England: Voltaire Foundation at the Taylor Institution, 1976. A study of d'Alembert's philosophy. Argues that d'Alembert's "position in the Enlightenment remains of central, pivotal importance." Also treats d'Alembert's mathematical and scientific contributions.

Grimsley, Ronald. *Jean d'Alembert, 1717-83*. Oxford, England: Clarendon Press, 1963. A topical study of d'Alembert's contributions to the *Encyclopédie*, his relations with other philosophers, and his own views. Largely ignores the scientific and mathematical aspects of d'Alembert's career.

Hankins, Thomas L. *Jean d'Alembert: Science and the Enlightenment*. Oxford, England: Clarendon Press, 1970. An ideal complement to Grimsley's book, for it concentrates on the science and the mathematics. Relates d'Alembert's achievements to those of other scientists and the role of science to that of philosophy in the eighteenth century.

Pappas, John Nicholas. *Voltaire and d'Alembert*. Bloomington: Indiana University Press, 1962. Drawing heavily on the correspondence between the two, this study seeks to rectify the view, fostered in large part by Voltaire, that d'Alembert was a hesitant follower of the older intellectual. Notes that the influence was mutual and shows where the two differed.

Van Treese, Glen Joseph. *D'Alembert and Frederick the Great: A Study of Their Relationship*. New York: Learned Publications, 1974. Treats the origin, nature, and consequences of the friendship between d'Alembert and the Prussian ruler. Offers a portrait of the two men and of their age.

Joseph Rosenblum

ALEXANDER I

Born: December 23, 1777; St. Petersburg, Russia
Died: December 1, 1825; Taganrog, Russia
Areas of Achievement: Government and politics
Contribution: As czar of Russia, Alexander I initiated a series of educational, social, and political reforms early in his reign. He was instrumental in forming the coalition that defeated Napoleon I and played a major role in the Congress of Vienna following the Napoleonic Wars.

Early Life

Alexander's birth in the Winter Palace of St. Petersburg marked his destiny to occupy the Russian throne. He was the first child of Grand Duke Pavel Petrovich (later Paul I) and Grand Duchess Maria Fyodorovna. Shortly after his birth, Alexander was taken from his parents by his grandmother, Empress Catherine II (Catherine the Great), to be reared under her careful supervision. It was Catherine's intent to disinherit her son, Pavel, because she believed that he was mentally unstable and unfit to inherit her throne. Alexander would be trained to succeed her directly. A number of outstanding tutors were brought to the imperial court by Catherine to provide an education that would prepare her grandson to be czar. The most notable tutor was Frédéric-César de La Harpe, a Swiss republican, who used classical and Enlightenment texts to inspire many of the future czar's liberal ideals. In his adolescence, Alexander was also allowed an extended visit with his father at Gatchina, where he received his military training. Alexander's formal education ended at the age of sixteen, when his grandmother arranged his marriage to Princess Louise of Baden-Durlach (later Grand Duchess and Empress Elizabeth) in 1793.

Three years later, Catherine died suddenly on November 17. She had written a manifesto disinheriting her son and naming Alexander her heir. Since the document had not been released, however, her son assumed the title of Czar Paul I. His reign was characterized by a fanatical tyranny and an irrational foreign policy. A small group of nobles and military officers formed a conspiracy to remove Paul from the throne. Alexander reluctantly agreed to the plot on the condition that his father's life be spared. Paul, however, was assassinated on the night of March 23, 1801. The next day, Alexander was proclaimed the new czar.

At the age of twenty-three, Alexander became the leader of the most populous as well as one of the most backward and troubled nations of Europe. He was a handsome young man known for his intelligence and charm, but some worried that he did not have the necessary courage to fulfill his new duties. On the night that his father was murdered, he reportedly sobbed: "I cannot go on with it. I have no strength to reign. Let someone else take my place." To which Count Peter von der Pahlen, the chief conspirator, replied: "You have played the child long enough; go reign."

Life's Work

Upon assuming his new responsibilities, Alexander I rescinded Paul's tyrannical laws. He also formed a private committee composed of four liberal friends from noble families to advise him on a variety of domestic issues. They urged him to pursue a series of educational, social, and political reforms. A comprehensive educational system was proposed by Alexander's private committee. Public and parish schools were opened to all Russians. In addition, a number of specialized and college preparatory schools were established. Existing universities received increased support, and three new ones were built during Alexander's reign.

The social institution of serfdom had long been a problem. Nearly three-quarters of the population was owned by the nobility. Alexander detested this widespread slavery among his subjects, but he moved cautiously to avoid alienating the nobility whose wealth and support depended upon this slave labor. In 1803, however, the Free Cultivator's Law was enacted which permitted the nobility to free their serfs under certain highly restricted conditions. Although its success was extremely limited—only thirty-seven thousand serfs out of ten million were freed during Alexander's reign—the new law did prompt a national debate on serfdom leading to its abolition in 1861.

Alexander also reformed the corrupt and inept bureaucracy he inherited from Catherine and Paul. The senate and state council were relieved of administrative duties, and their role was limited to offering advice and comment on proposed legislation. Administration of the czar's laws would be the responsibility of a "collegium," or cabinet, of eight ministers who reported directly to Alexander. Measures to ensure greater control over the imperial treasury and to limit expenditures by the court were also implemented. The most ambitious proposal was for a constitution that would limit the czar's autocracy. Although Alexander supported a constitution in principle—he granted constitutions to the Ionian Islands in 1803, to Finland in 1809, and to Poland in 1815—the document was never made public for fear that such rapid change would be opposed by reactionary elements in the nobility.

At the height of his reforming zeal, however, Alexander suddenly and unexpectedly turned his attention to foreign affairs. Initially his foreign policy was based on his hope for a peaceful and unified Europe. He reestablished an alliance with England that had been broken by his father, while at the same time he pursued good relations with France. A treaty of friendship was signed with Prussia, and relations with Austria were improved. Alexander believed that these alliances and overtures not only would moderate Napoleon I's aggressive ambitions but also would eventually lead to a European federation of nations.

Alexander's idealistic hopes were shattered with Napoleon's conquests and with his coronation as Emperor of France, forcing Russia to declare war in 1804. The czar assumed the role of field commander, and, along with the Austrians, suffered a bitter defeat at the Battle of Austerlitz in 1805. The following year, Napoleon invaded Prussia. Against the advice of his ministers, Alexander again intervened against the French, losing a series of battles in eastern Prussia.

Following these defeats, Alexander and Napoleon met at the village of Tilsit (now Sovetsk) on June 25, 1807. The czar used his charm to flatter the French emperor and to gain a favorable peace treaty. Russia agreed to break all relations with England and to recognize the newly created Grand Duchy of Warsaw. In exchange, Alexander would be allowed to expand his empire at the expense of Persia, Sweden, and Turkey. Napoleon left Tilsit believing that in Alexander he had a new friend and ally, and that they would conquer and divide Europe between them. The czar, however, was deceptive; his flattery and acceptance of the peace treaty were designed to buy time.

When Alexander returned to St. Petersburg, his popularity quickly declined. The Tilsit Alliance was perceived as a humiliation, and the trade restrictions with England hurt the economy. Partly in response to this criticism, Alexander backed away from any of his earlier reforms and increasingly aligned himself with reactionary forces among the nobility. He imposed his autocratic prerogatives to ensure domestic stability in order to reorganize the army and to devise a strategy that once again would challenge the French emperor.

Alexander's public break with Napoleon came slowly. Trade with England was secretly resumed, and Russia failed to aid France in its war with Austria in 1809. Napoleon retaliated by annexing the Grand Duchy of Oldenburg (territory controlled by the czar's brother-in-law) and threatened to establish an independent kingdom of Poland. Relations between the two nations steadily deteriorated as both sides prepared for war.

On June 24, 1812, Napoleon's grand army invaded Russia. Although Alexander had been rebuilding his army for a number of years, the Russians were still outnumbered by nearly three to one. Given these odds, the Russian army quickly retreated until it faced the French at the Battle of Borodino. The two armies fought to a stalemate, but, as a result of their inferior strength, the Russians were again forced to retreat. Napoleon entered a burning Moscow that had already been torched by its citizens. The French pitched their winter camp in a burned-out city. Disease and lack of supplies took their toll forcing a retreat. Constant raids by Russian soldiers and partisans during the retreat inflicted heavy casualties. Napoleon escaped from Russia with a decimated army.

Throughout the invasion Alexander provided forceful and inspirational leadership. Even in the darkest days of the campaign, the Russian people rallied behind their czar and vowed never to surrender. The burning of Moscow had reportedly "illuminated his soul," and Alexander swore that he would defeat Napoleon. Alexander's resolve was contagious. He rallied the leaders of Europe to join his crusade against Napoleon. Along with the Prussians and Austrians, he won the decisive Battle of Nations, near Leipzig, in October, 1813. Five months later, Alexander triumphantly entered Paris, forcing Napoleon's abdication and restoring Louis XVIII to the French throne.

Alexander was now the most powerful monarch in Europe. He annexed Poland over the objections of other leaders, but none could challenge his strength. He helped convene and was a dominant figure at the Congress of Vienna, which restored European political stability following the unrest of the Napoleonic era. Even with Napoleon's brief return from exile in 1815, Alexander was still the premier monarch in establishing a new era of European peace that lasted until 1871. With the defeat of his archenemy, Alexander had achieved his dream of becoming the arbiter of Europe.

Summary

Alexander I never exploited his position of power. During the last ten years of his life, he largely withdrew from public life both in terms of foreign affairs and in terms of domestic reforms. His last foray into international politics was an unsuccessful attempt to form the Holy Alliance. The purpose of this alliance was to unite European leaders by using the principles of Christian love, peace, and justice as a common basis for their political activities. In practice, it was used to justify reactionary policies against revolutionaries. Alexander's domestic policies became increasingly autocratic and repressive because of his fear of conspiracies and revolts. The czar retreated into a private religious mysticism and piety, and, shortly before his death, he indicated a desire to abdicate.

Alexander displayed contradictory attitudes that helped shape the future of Russia and Europe. He was deeply influenced by liberal ideals, yet at crucial moments he backed away from specific reforms. Had he resolved the serfdom issue and enacted a constitution, the numerous Russian revolts of the nineteenth century and the Revolution of 1917 perhaps could have been avoided. With the defeat of Napoleon, Alexander reached the pinnacle of political power only to retreat into a private world of religious devotion, leaving the future of Europe primarily in the hands of Austria's Prince Metternich. Despite this inconsistent behavior, Alexander was both a progressive, though paternalistic, reformer and the driving force that rid Europe of Napoleon's tyranny.

Bibliography
Almedingen, Edith M. *The Emperor Alexander I.* New York: Vanguard

Press, 1964. A sympathetic biography of Alexander and his court. Provides much personal information about the czar and his relations with family, friends, and colleagues.

Glover, Michael. *The Napoleonic Wars: An Illustrated History, 1792-1815.* New York: Hippocrene Books, 1978. A general summary of the major military battles and campaigns during the Napoleonic era. Its principal value is the numerous illustrations reproduced from the nineteenth century.

Grimstead, Patricia Kennedy. *The Foreign Ministers of Alexander I: Political Attitudes and the Conduct of Russian Diplomacy, 1801-1825.* Berkeley: University of California Press, 1969. An in-depth study of the various foreign ministers who served during Alexander's reign. Provides some insight on the development of Russia's foreign policy as well as on the influence of liberal and reactionary ideas on Alexander's thinking.

Holt, Lucius Hudson, and Alexander Wheeler Chilton. *A Brief History of Europe from 1789 to 1815.* New York: Macmillan, 1919. This text offers a general historical summary of major Europeans events during this period. Provides good background material for placing Alexander in a larger context during the time of his greatest achievements.

McConnell, Allen. *Tsar Alexander I: Paternalistic Reformer.* New York: Thomas Y. Crowell, 1970. Provides a critical review of Alexander's foreign and domestic policies. The author's interest is primarily to evaluate the czar's political career and to influence rather than to provide biographical information.

Nicolson, Harold. *The Congress of Vienna: A Study in Allied Unity, 1812-1822.* New York: Harcourt Brace Jovanovich, 1946. Beginning with Napoleon's retreat from Moscow, this book offers a detailed overview of European politics from 1812 to 1822.

Tarle, Eugene. *Napoleon's Invasion of Russia, 1812.* New York: Oxford University Press, 1942. A detailed account of Napoleon's invasion, campaign, and retreat from Russia.

Brent Waters

ALEXANDER II

Born: April 29, 1818; Moscow, Russia
Died: March 13, 1881; St. Petersburg, Russia
Area of Achievement: Government
Contribution: Called the czar liberator, Alexander emancipated the serfs in 1861, the first of political and legal reforms designed to quicken the pace of modernization in Russia. Despite the reforms, rising expectations caused dissidents to become radicalized. Hence, Alexander's life was ended by political assassins, and reforms were suspended by his successor.

Early Life

Born in the Chudov Monastery in the Moscow kremlin on April 29, 1818, during Easter week, Alexander Nikolayevich Romanov was the oldest son of Czar Nicholas I (reigned 1825-1855), then Grand Duke, and Charlotte, daughter of King Frederick William III of Prussia and sister of future German emperor Wilhelm I. Alexander had five siblings: Nicholas, Michael, Maria, Olga, and Alexandra. After their father became czar in 1825 they lived in the royal Russian residence, the Winter Palace, and in a royal palace at Tsarskoe Selo.

The heir to the throne was given two tutors: Captain Karl Karlovich Merder and the poet Vasily Andreyevich Zhukovsky. The former was hired when Alexander was six years old, and he stressed martial values and discipline; the latter emphasized history, letters, and the cultivation of humane sentiments. Both teachers believed in autocracy. A model soldier, throughout his life Alexander expressed excitement at watching and participating in military drills and parades. In 1837, after completing his formal education, Alexander was sent on a seven-month tour through thirty provinces of the empire. Accompanied by Zhukovsky, he received his first acquaintance with poverty. A year later Alexander took his grand tour of Western Europe, where he fell in love with fourteen-year-old Princess Wilhelmina of Hesse-Darmstadt. His father reluctantly accepted the proposed match, and the girl arrived in Russia in 1840 to be rebaptized in the Orthodox church as Maria Alexandrovna. They were married on April 16, 1841. Among their eight children the first two, Alexandra and Nicholas, died in 1849 and 1865, respectively; the third child, the future Alexander III, was born in 1845.

Czar Nicholas I carefully prepared his son for governance by appointing him to numerous positions such as chancellor of Alexander University in Finland, member of the Holy Synod and several imperial councils, and, in his father's absence, chairman of the state council. Several times Alexander participated in diplomatic missions, including one to Vienna in 1849 to persuade the Austrian Emperor Franz Joseph to pardon the Hungarian rebel generals. Although frightened by the European revolutions in 1849 and reminded by Zhukovsky about the irresponsibility of rapid reforms, Alexander would launch a movement for widespread changes after his accession.

Life's Work

Alexander came to power on February 19, 1855, during the Crimean War before the fall of Sebastopol to the French and English. Although he reminded his generals of the victory after the fall of Moscow in 1812, he was soon persuaded to negotiate for peace. The czar was compelled to accept defeat and sign the Treaty of Paris on March 30, 1856. His coronation did not occur until the 26th of August. It is unclear to what extent Russia's weak performance in the war led him to embark upon reforms. Since his background did not portend such a reign, historians are divided by what occurred. Furthermore, since his policies were not uniformly progressive, his goals are difficult to assess. Less dictatorial than his predecessors, he freely accepted advice.

In matters of foreign affairs, he relied upon his chief aide, General Aleksandr Mikhailovich Gorchakov, who agreed with the czar that foreign affairs must be subordinated to domestic developments. Together they forged a rapprochement with Napoleon III of France, only to see it fail when the French extended sympathy to the Polish rebels in 1863. Thereafter, Alexander II drew closer to his German relatives, whom he supported during the creation of the German Empire in 1871. By that year Alexander dared to violate the terms of the Treaty of Paris by sailing warships on the Black Sea. Russia also joined with Germany and Austria-Hungary in the Three Emperors' League, but it fell apart when Alexander succumbed to Pan-Slavic pressures and to a war with the Ottoman Empire on April 24, 1877. Victorious Russian armies forced the sultan to sign a peace at San Stephano the following year, allowing Russia significant gains in Bessarabia and the lower Caucasus. Western powers compelled the Russians to scale back their gains at a congress in Berlin later that year. That event damaged Russian-German ties, but Otto von Bismarck managed to assuage the czar's feelings somewhat. The end of German-Russian cooperation came in the following reign.

Meanwhile, Russian expansion in the Far East and Central Asia was impressive. Although Alaska was sold to the United States in 1867, and Gorchakov tried to restrain commanders from conquests in Asia, the czar was pleased with their acquisitions. From 1859 to 1861 China ceded territory to Russia in the Amur-Ussuri district, and Japan yielded Sakhalin Island for the remaining Kurile Islands in 1875. Between 1865 and 1876, Alexander's empire reached Kokand, Bokhara, and Khiva in Central Asia; in 1881, other lands east of the Caspian Sea were added. Such gains in the East, however, were little appreciated.

The centerpiece of the reign was the emancipation of about twenty-five million serfs on February 19, 1861. Not only did this measure fulfill a goal which had baffled previous rulers such as Alexander I, it also made possible free labor that was so indispensable for later industrial programs and a free citizenry that was a precondition for further reforms. Alexander opened discussions for serf reform in his state council after the Crimean War and urged that the deliberations of the matter be removed from secret negotiations. He indicated that he wanted the obstacles to solution of this question overcome. Hence, the gentry accepted its inevitability and joined the czar in realizing the edict. The decree gave peasants immediate legal freedoms with lands to buy from the state. Although the terms allowed concessions to the gentry, many people agreed with Aleksandr Ivanovich Herzen that official society had moved in a progressive direction. Much of the credit was attributed to Alexander. Peasants, however, were bewildered by the requirement to purchase their lands.

Despite the uprising in Poland in 1863, Alexander forged ahead with decrees in 1864 to reform the legal administration. Reforms that were introduced were trial by jury in civil cases, equal access to the courts for all, life tenure for judges, and measures to protect due process. Also that year, local government was reorganized and newly elected assemblies called zemstvos were given wide control over local education, fire fighting, veterinary medicine, road and bridge construction, hospital care, and other matters in the thirty-four provinces of the empire. Members were elected on the all-class principle, removing the monopoly of local authority from the gentry. Alexander eased censorship in 1865 and disbanded the secret police. Similar elective bodies were introduced in 1870 in urban administration. In the 1870's, military reforms drawn up by D. A. Miliutin incorporated many principles of civil law into military law, and the penal environment of the soldier was changed to a dignified profession for national defense. Hence the brutality of military training was largely eliminated, and terms of active service were reduced from fifteen to six years.

Alexander's reforming zeal was tempered by firm measures to protect his regime. In 1862 he ordered the arrest of radical journalist Nikolay Guvrilovich Chernyshevsky for inciting violence, and he ordered Russification of the Poles after 1863. On April 4, 1866, while Alexander was walking through the Summer Gardens, an inept attempt on his life was made by a deranged nihilist, Dmitry V. Karakazov. Although the attempt failed, Alexander was shaken by the incident and appointed reactionary minister Dmitry Andreyevich Tolstoy to preside over the ministry of education. When the populist intelligentsia failed to arouse the peasantry by talking about socialism in the earlier 1870's, some turned to violence. Alexander responded with strong measures of his own, and the nation witnessed several treason trials which gave exposure to the radical cause and undermined respect for the czar. Eventually, a faction of radicals decided upon the ultimate act of terrorism—the killing of the czar.

Members of the People's Will Party believed that the assassination of the czar would bring peasants to the point of national rebellion. Their single-minded devotion to this end was realized on the morning of March 13, 1881, as Alexander was riding through the streets of the capital after addressing a meeting. When a bomb was thrown at this coach, wounding his coachmen, the czar alighted from the carriage to attend to the victims; a second bomb then killed him. On that spot was constructed the Church of the Spilt Blood.

Summary

Despite relapses into conservative policies, Alexander II authored the most significant reforms in czarist history. Designed to modernize Russian life so that the nation could better compete internationally, the reforms also fulfilled Alexander's own desires for the improvement of the common-wealth. Unfortunately, they were not effective in stemming the tide of radical politics. Some regard the reforms as too little, too late; others believe that they were meant simply to strengthen the old structures in order to make additional reforms unnecessary; and yet others believe that they were too much, too soon. The most radical intelligentsia feared that the reforms might defuse the public's desire for revolution.

The czar's popularity waned in his last years, partly through his own doing. The moving of his second family into the Winter Palace under the same roof as the empress, his hasty marriage to Princess Catherine E. Dol-goruka on the fortieth day after his wife died in 1880, and his replacement of progressive ministers with conservative ministers obscured the fact that he was, at the end, considering a major step toward representative government, having commissioned Count Mikhail Tariyelovich Loris-Melikov to draw up a plan for a national consultative assembly. Alexander's assassination came just before the plan was unveiled; the new czar dismissed the proposal and began measures to undo the work of his father.

Bibliography

Almedingen, E. M. *The Emperor Alexander II*. London: Bodley Head, 1962. This work, by a writer who specializes in biographies of Russian figures, contains the most extensive account of Alexander's personal life. Despite Alexander's vacillations, the author laments that what his reign began was not pursued by his successors.

Billington, James H. *The Icon and the Axe: An Interpretive History of Russian Culture*. New York: Vintage Books, 1970. The author divides Alexander's reign into a period of reform followed by a period of reaction, while brilliantly exploring the sociopolitical dimensions of art and literature in this era.

Kornilov, Alexander. *Modern Russian History from the Age of Catherine the Great to the End of the Nineteenth Century*. New York: Alfred A. Knopf,

1952. This classic view of the age demonstrates with keen insight the political machinations of the czar and his court.

Mosse, W. E. *Alexander II and the Modernization of Russia*. London: English Universities Press, 1958. A short but scholarly synopsis of the reign that traces much of the czar's troubles to his alienation of society and even of the police in the 1870's.

Pereira, N. G. O. *Tsar-Liberator: Alexander II of Russia, 1818-1881*. Newtonville, Mass.: Oriental Research Partners, 1983. Despite modest claims to the contrary by the author, this is the best biographical study of the czar's reign. Pereira, an academic historian, clearly lauds Alexander's imperial policies in the East.

Pushkarev, Sergei. *The Emergence of Modern Russia, 1801-1917*. Translated by Robert H. McNeal and Tova Yedlin. New York: Holt, Rinehart and Winston, 1963. Herein are the views of a modern liberal historian who maximizes the changes at the beginning of the century and minimizes those in the 1860's.

Seton-Watson, Hugh. *The Decline of Imperial Russia, 1855-1914*. New York: Praeger, 1952. In part 1, "The Tsar Liberator 1855-1881," the author discovers the roots of the collapse of the old regime in this era.

John D. Windhausen

ALEXANDER VI
Rodrigo de Borja y Doms

Born: 1431; Játiva, Valencia
Died: August 18, 1503; Rome
Areas of Achievement: Politics, government, and religion
Contribution: Alexander VI's policies contributed to the growth of papal temporal power in the Papal States. A discriminating patron of the arts, he employed a number of noteworthy artists, including Pinturicchio and Michelangelo.

Early Life

Born Rodrigo de Borja y Doms (Borgia) in Játiva, Valencia, the boy who was to become Pope Alexander VI was the nephew of Pope Calixtus III, who adopted him, showered him with church benefices, and sent him to the University of Bologna to study law. In 1456, Rodrigo was appointed a cardinal-deacon, and the following year he was made the vice-chancellor of the Church, a lucrative post that he held until his own elevation to the papacy in 1492.

Rodrigo's many benefices enabled him to live in great magnificence and to indulge himself in such pastimes as cardplaying and merrymaking. His youthful indiscretions prompted Pope Pius II to send a scathing letter of reproof in 1460 for his alleged scandalous misconduct at Siena sometime earlier. His ordination to the priesthood in 1468 did not cause him to change his immoral behavior. Sometime in the early 1470's, Rodrigo entered into an illicit relationship with the beautiful Vannozza dei Cattanei, who was to be the mother of four of his children, Juan, Cesare, Lucrezia, and Jofré. In spite of these moral failings, Rodrigo was appointed Bishop of Pôrto in 1476 and made dean of the Sacred College in Rome. On August 11, 1492, he was elected pope by a bare two-thirds majority, amid charges, never substantiated, that he had bribed several cardinals to switch their votes in his favor. So worldly had the office of pope become by his time that there was little public criticism of his elevation to the See of Saint Peter, despite his reputation for moral irregularity. In fact, the Roman people held torchlight processions and erected triumphal arches to commemorate his election.

Life's Work

Described as a handsome and imposing figure, Pope Alexander brought considerable talent to his office. Francesco Guicciardini, a contemporary historian, noted that "in him were combined rare prudence and vigilance, mature reflection, marvellous power of persuasion, skill and capacity for the conduct of the most difficult affairs."

He began his pontificate by restoring order to Rome, which had been the scene of considerable violence, including more than two hundred assassinations, in the several years before Alexander's elevation. He divided the city into four districts, over each of which he placed a magistrate who was given plenary powers to maintain order. In the course of his pontificate, he subjugated the fractious Orsini and Colonna families, who had been troublesome elements in Roman politics for generations. In addition, he designated Tuesday of each week as a time for any man or woman in Rome to come before him personally to present his or her grievances.

As pope, Alexander advanced the interests of his own children, not only for their sakes but also as a means of strengthening papal political power. He betrothed his daughter Lucrezia to Giovanni Sforza in order to link the Borgia family with the powerful Sforza rulers of Milan. When this union ceased to be politically useful, Alexander annulled it and married Lucrezia to the son of the King of Naples. When Lucrezia's second husband was killed in 1501, Alexander arranged her marriage to Duke Alfonso I of Ferrara in the hope that it would further papal schemes in the Romagna. Favorite among his children, however, was his eldest son, Juan, the Duke of Gandía, and Alexander provided richly for him until Juan was murdered in 1497, whereupon the pope then placed his fondest hopes in Cesare. Alexander encouraged Cesare to establish a powerful principality in the Romagna, the most troublesome part of the Papal States.

Italy was subjected to two French invasions during the reign of Alexander. While the French kings had hereditary claims to both the Duchy of Milan and the kingdom of Naples, as long as the Triple Alliance powers of Naples, Florence, and Milan had been united, a French effort to make good these claims seemed remote. By January of 1494, however, the Triple Alliance had collapsed. Ludovico Sforza, the Duke of Milan, finding himself politically isolated in Italy, attempted to ingratiate himself to the French king, Charles VIII, by encouraging him to invade Italy and claim the kingdom of Naples. Pope Alexander joined King Alfonso II of Naples, and Neapolitan troops were sent northward to block Charles's advance through the Papal States. Alexander's position worsened when two of his enemies, Cardinals Giuliano della Rovere (the future Pope Julius II) and Ascanio Sforza secretly went to the advancing Charles and tried to persuade him to call a council that would put Alexander on trial and depose him. Alexander met with King Charles, and an agreement was reached whereby Charles was allowed to enter Rome on December 31. A month later, Charles set out for Naples. In March of 1495, with Charles in possession of Naples, Pope Alexander formed the League of Venice, consisting of the Empire, Spain, and all the major Italian states except Florence. Its main purpose was to drive the French from Italian soil, a goal achieved by the end of the year.

When Louis XII succeeded Charles VIII as King of France in 1498, he quickly began planning an invasion of Italy to lay claim to the Duchy of

Milan. Before executing this invasion, however, he dissolved the League of Venice by negotiating with Alexander, who agreed to remain neutral in return for Louis' assistance to Alexander's son Cesare in his efforts to conquer the Romagna. Louis invaded Milan in August of 1499, and by April of the following year he was firmly entrenched there. Louis then prepared for the conquest of Naples. King Ferdinand II also had claims to Naples, and Alexander arranged a settlement in November of 1500, whereby Naples would be partitioned between them, with Louis in control of the northern provinces and Ferdinand, the southern.

Meanwhile, Cesare, encouraged by the promise of the French king's friendship and assistance, waged vigorous war against the petty tyrants of the Romagna. His masterful and unscrupulous resourcefulness, coupled with his father's unstinting support, made Cesare remarkably successful. In April of 1501, Alexander made his son Duke of the Romagna, and it appeared that a powerful state would soon be his. The death of Alexander in August, 1503, however, ended Cesare's successful course. Cesare was defeated by the forces of Pope Julius II, a bitter enemy of the Borgia family, and his lands were added to those of the Papacy. Julius would eventually make a modern Renaissance state of the papal holdings.

In 1495, Alexander first took official notice of the Dominican friar Girolamo Savonarola, when he ordered the latter to cease preaching in Florence. Savonarola's fiery sermons, in which he spared neither prince nor pope, had led to the expulsion of the Medicis from Florence, and he had begun to denounce the political machinations of Alexander. Savonarola had defied the pope, asserting: "You err; you are not the Roman Church, you are a man and a sinner." Pope Alexander excommunicated Savonarola in May of 1497 and again ordered him to cease preaching. While Savonarola had many supporters in Florence, and the pope had many enemies, in order to restore public order to the city the magistrates arrested the monk in April of 1498; after papal commissioners officially pronounced him guilty of heresy, Savonarola was ordered hanged and burned in May of that year.

Among the more positive acts of Pope Alexander were his efforts to preserve peace between Spain and Portugal by proclaiming the Line of Demarcation in 1493, whereby he allocated the New World to Spain, and Africa and India to Portugal for the purposes of exploration. Though he was generally preoccupied with worldly affairs, Alexander did, on occasion, assert religious leadership. He was the first pope to give strong support to missionary activity in the New World. The beginnings of *Index Librorum Prohibitorum*, or the Index, can be traced to his pontificate. The Sapienza was considerably augmented under his direction. He proclaimed the year 1500 a jubilee year, and pilgrims flocked to Rome. That same year, Alexander preached a crusade against the Turks, and, in a period of remorse and reflection after the death of his favorite son Juan, Alexander appointed a commission of cardinals that was charged with establishing proposals for extensive reform within the Church.

Despite the "moral miseries of the reign of Alexander VI," he was a splendid patron of the arts. Alexander employed architects and painters who beautified the region around the Vatican called the Borgo Nuovo. The artist Pinturicchio decorated many of the rebuilt and new Borgia apartments in the Vatican. His work included a famous portrait of Alexander kneeling in adoration of the miracle of the Resurrection. Churches and buildings were renovated, and new ones, such as the Tempietto, designed by Donato Bramante, were erected. It was under the patronage of Alexander that Michelangelo's *Pietà* was completed in 1499.

Pope Alexander and his son Cesare both became seriously ill at a banquet that they were attending in August of 1503. Although Cesare recovered, the pope died on August 18. While there were rumors that Alexander was the victim of poison that he had intended for certain of his enemies at the banquet, it is generally believed that he died as a result of a plague.

Summary

Nineteenth and twentieth century scholarship has tended to reject many of the more vicious moral crimes charged to Alexander VI. While few scholars have attempted and none has succeeded in exonerating him of corruption, immorality, and Machiavellian statecraft, it has been noted that many of the Renaissance popes were guilty of similar behavior. Although he did use the power and wealth of his office to advance the interests of his children, he was able to enhance papal power as well. The petty tyrannies in the Romagna that were destroyed by Cesare Borgia were never reestablished, and Julius II would be able to build a strong papal government in the Papal States on the foundation laid by Alexander's son. Although the political machinations practiced by Alexander hardly seem appropriate for the Vicar of Christ, the necessity to protect papal lands in Italy from encroachments by the Empire, France, and Spain led many medieval and early modern popes to practice a diplomacy characterized by capriciousness and deceit.

While some scholars might be willing to acknowledge that Alexander's failure as pope was in a measure counterbalanced by his patronage of the arts or that his encouragement of missions to the Americas more than compensated for his unwholesome example as a spiritual leader, most will not. Catholic scholars generally conclude, however, that "the dignity of Peter suffers no diminution even in an unworthy successor."

Bibliography

De la Bedoyere, Michael. *The Meddlesome Friar: The Story of the Conflict Between Savonarola and Alexander VI*. London: Collins, 1957. A good discussion of the early lives of the two men, with an explanation of the political events that led to the conflict. Dispels many of the legends that have surrounded both men. A well-balanced reassessment of the much-maligned Alexander. This book is based on extensive documentary research, although there are no footnotes and no bibliography.

Ferrara, Orestes. *The Borgia Pope, Alexander the Sixth.* New York: Sheed & Ward, 1940. An attempt by a practicing lawyer to rehabilitate the character of Alexander and to refute the legends of his misdeeds and evil influence on the Church and the secular history of his time. While based on extensive research, the author's interpretation of evidence is often questionable. Must be read in conjunction with other works on Alexander.

Mallett, Michael. *The Borgias: The Rise and Fall of a Renaissance Dynasty.* New York: Barnes & Noble Books, 1969. Hailed as the best treatment of the Borgia family in any language. Presents Alexander as a representative personality of the Renaissance and places his achievements as well as his vices into a sound historical perspective. Discredits many of the legends concerning the Borgias. Includes extensive footnoting, an annotated bibliography, genealogies, and maps.

Pastor, Ludwig. *The History of the Popes from the Close of the Middle Ages.* 4th ed. Vols. 5 and 6. London: Kegan Paul, Trench, Trubner, 1923. Much of both of these volumes of this classic, monumental history of the modern papacy is devoted to the pontificate of Alexander. In part based on archival material not available to earlier scholars, Pastor's account is well balanced and strongly documented. While acknowledging the merits of Alexander's cultural patronage, this account is critical of Alexander's failure as a spiritual leader. Includes an extensive bibliography, much of which is not in English.

Portigliotti, Giuseppe. *The Borgias: Alexander VI, Caesar, Lucrezia.* Translated by Bernard Miall. New York: Alfred A. Knopf, 1928. Purports to be a historical and psychological study of the Borgias, their ancestry, characters, and crimes. Relies too much on gossip and suspicions and ignores the historical background of events and ideas. Also ignores the positive achievements of Alexander as statesman and pope. Should be read only in conjunction with more balanced accounts. Includes illustrations of Borgia family members.

Paul E. Gill

ANDREA DEL SARTO
Andrea d'Agnolo

Born: July 16, 1486; Florence
Died: September 28, 1530; Florence
Area of Achievement: Art
Contribution: Andrea del Sarto is considered to be one of the most important Florentine painters of the early sixteenth century and is also a figure of great historical importance. In his own work, he was clearly inspired by the classical ideals of the central Italian High Renaissance, particularly by Raphael and Leonardo da Vinci, but his pupils were to become the creators of the anticlassical style later known as mannerism, which dominated Italian art from about 1520 until 1600.

Early Life

Andrea d'Agnolo, the son of Agnolo di Francesco Lanfranchi and Constanza, was born in Florence in 1486, probably one of twins, for the surviving documents indicate that Agnolo di Francesco's two sons, Andrea and Domenico, were both baptized on July 17, 1486, the day after their birth. Andrea's great-grandfather had been an agricultural laborer, his grandfather a linen weaver, and his father a tailor (*un sarto*), and for that reason Andrea was given the nickname of Andrea del Sarto. Andrea left school at the age of seven to work for a goldsmith before beginning his training as a painter, first in the studio of the little-known Andrea di Salvi Barile and later with Piero di Cosimo. It has also been persuasively argued by modern critics that Andrea must have studied with the technically accomplished Raffaellino del Garbo, or at least been strongly influenced by his work.

On December 11, 1508, Andrea was matriculated in the guild of Florentine painters. About two years earlier, he had entered into a partnership with Francesco di Cristoforo Bigi, known as Franciabigio. The two artists shared a studio and were later joined by the young sculptor Jacopo Sansovino, who had come from Rome.

Life's Work

Two fresco cycles in Florence are the major works of the collaboration of Andrea and Franciabigio. In the forecourt of the Church of Santissima Annunziata in Florence, they continued the fresco cycle which had been begun in the fifteenth century and which illustrated the life of Saint Filippo Benizzi and scenes from the life of the Virgin. The scenes from the life of Saint Filippo Benizzi, the chief saint of the Servite Order (of which the Santissima Annunziata is the mother church), were Andrea's first fresco commissions and show him experimenting with a variety of compositions. Two of the scenes are loosely organized and recall the pictorial ideals of the preceding century, but in the *Saint Curing the Possessed Woman*, *The Death of the Saint*, and the *Miracles Performed by the Relics of the Saint*, dated 1510, Andrea introduced rigidly organized, symmetrical compositions which reveal his debt to Leonardo da Vinci, while his handling of color, light, and shade shows how much he admired the work of Raphael. The finest work in this cycle is the last one that Andrea painted, the *Birth of the Virgin* (1514). In this remarkable work, which marks the beginning of his artistic maturity, the severity of the earlier scenes has given way to a more flexible and subtly harmonious type of composition. One can see in this work how completely Andrea had absorbed the pictorial ideals of the High Renaissance.

The two artists also collaborated in a commission which they received from the Florentine Compagnia dello Scalzo, a secular confraternity. The oratory of the compagnia was located not far from the Church of San Marco, and the frescoes by Andrea del Sarto and Franciabigio, which are still extant, are in what was once the cloister. The subjects are scenes from the life of Saint John the Baptist and the Cardinal Virtues. These frescoes are executed in girisaille, that is, in varying shades of gray. Although they were probably begun as early as 1511, Andrea continued to work on them from time to time until 1526. Ten of the scenes are by Andrea, who also painted *The Cardinal Virtues*, while two are by Franciabigio. The Scalzo frescoes are among the finest examples of the High Renaissance style in Florence. Each scene is elegantly composed, but with a naturalism of attitude and gesture that makes it completely plausible, a reality that is convincing but one that has become a realm of grace and beauty.

While he was working on these commissions, Andrea also had a hand in the preparation of the civic decorations in celebration of the return of the Medici family from their exile (February, 1513) and for the ceremonial entrance of the Medici Pope Leo X into Florence in 1515. In 1517, he completed one of his most impressive paintings, the *Madonna of the Harpies*. In this, the characteristic elegance of composition and pose is enriched by startling innovations in color, intermittent passages of light and shadow, and a softness of modeling which create a richly atmospheric effect.

The work at the cloister of the Scalzo was interrupted by Andrea's departure from Florence to enter the service of Francis I of France. He accepted the invitation to go to Fontainbleau in the late spring or early summer of 1516 and remained there until 1519. Only a few paintings can be identified as having been painted in France, but one of these, the *Charity* (signed and dated 1518), is a masterpiece, one of his most completely realized works. Like the *Madonna of the Harpies*, it fuses the discipline of classical composition with a richly pictorial palette. The *Charity*, however, is enriched by a beautifully painted landscape background in which the idealistic transformation of nature echoes the visionary grace of the figures.

Andrea probably returned to Florence because he did not want to remain separated from his wife, Lucrezia del Fede, whom he had married shortly after her husband died in 1516. She was about four years younger than Andrea and, at the time of their marriage, was already the mother of a small child. Andrea's biographer Giorgio Vasari states that the French king gave him money to purchase paintings and sculptures for the royal collection after Andrea had solemnly promised that he would come back to France within a few months. Instead, he remained in Florence. While Vasari's account has been doubted, it is known that Andrea arrived in Florence with a large sum of money and that in October, 1520, he bought a plot of land on which he later built a large house and studio. He visited Rome about 1520 and in 1523 left Florence because of an outbreak of the plague. He went to the Mugello, north of Florence, where he worked for the nuns of San Piero a Luco for about a year before he returned to his native city. In November of 1524, he was back in Florence; very little is known about his activities from this point until his death in 1530 at the age of forty-four.

Andrea continued to work in the Scalzo until 1526 and produced a number of altarpieces for churches in and around Florence. The *Madonna and Child with Saints* of 1525-1526 is typical of his work during this period, with its soft modeling, strong color harmonies, and strong, simple grouping. Paintings such as this one made a great impression on the younger painters in Florence. Two artists who had studied with Andrea earlier, Jacopo Carucci da Pontormo and Giovanni Battista di Jacopo, called Rosso Fiorentino, had by this time evolved their striking anticlassical or early mannerist styles, but between 1520 and 1530 a new generation of painters turned to Andrea for inspiration. He strongly influenced the subsequent development of Florentine painting.

One of the finest of his late works is *The Last Supper* in the refectory of the former convent of San Salvi in Florence (1526-1527), a work of great pictorial interest that comes close to the dramatic intensity of Leonardo da Vinci's rendering of the subject. The *Madonna del Sacco* of 1525 in the Chiostro dei Morti of the Santissima Annunziata is another impressive example of his mature style, which shows the lack of emotional content seen in many of his last works.

Summary

Andrea del Sarto was an artist of great virtuosity. His surviving drawings, most of which are studies from life, are superb examples of draftmanship. He is equally skillful as a colorist and as a composer. He was also proficient at fresco painting and panel painting. Modern critics have noted that his work not only directly inspired a number of younger artists but also laid the foundations for some of the most exciting developments of Italian art during the seventeenth century. For Vasari, however, Andrea was an artist whose work was flawed because he lacked the moral strength to make the exertions required to achieve the highest results. There is a certain justice to this criticism, particularly in Andrea's late works, many of which are interesting for the virtuosity of their pictorial effects but are lacking in strong emotional content.

His frescoes in the Scalzo and the Santissima Annunziata, however, are some of the finest achievements of Florentine art. It is to Andrea's credit that while many of his contemporaries were able to imitate certain aspects of the style of Leonardo and Raphael, he was one of the few who were able to assimilate their styles without losing individuality.

Bibliography

Borsook, Eve. *The Mural Painters of Tuscany: From Cimabue to Andrea del Sarto*. 2d ed. Oxford, England: Clarendon Press, 1980. A detailed analysis of Andrea del Sarto's frescoes in the oratory of the Compagnia dello Scalzo in Florence. Includes much information on the relationship of the murals to the site and on the technique.

Freedberg, Sydney J. *Andrea del Sarto*. 2 vols. Cambridge, Mass.: Harvard University Press, 1963. A comprehensive study of all aspects of the artist's career. This book and the one by Shearman (see below) are the standard monographs on the artist. While Freedberg traces Andrea's development within the context of the classical style of the High Renaissance, Shearman shows the importance of Andrea's work, particularly his use of color, for subsequent developments in Italian art of the seventeenth century.

McKillop, Susan Regan. *Franciabigio*. Berkeley: University of California Press, 1974. The author publishes a number of new documents and includes a careful evaluation of the collaboration between Andrea del Sarto and Franciabigio.

Neufeld, Gunther. "On the Genesis of the *Madonna del Sacco*." *The Art Bulletin* 47 (1965): 117-118. A study of the preparatory drawings for Andrea del Sarto's *Madonna del Sacco* (1525) in the Cloister of the SS. Annunziata, Florence, and its derivation from a work by the Venetian artist Titian.

O'Gorman, James F. "An Interpretation of Andrea del Sarto, *Borgheriri Holy Family*." *The Art Bulletin* 48 (1965): 502-504. A study of the religious significance of Andrea del Sarto's painting of *Mary, Joseph, the Christ Child, and Young Saint John the Baptist* and its relationship to Florentine religious and political ideals of the late fifteenth and early sixteenth centuries.

Shearman, John. *Andrea del Sarto*. 2 vols. New York: Oxford University Press, 1965. One of the two standard monographs on the artist.

Vasari, Giorgio. *Lives of the Most Eminent Painters, Sculptors, and Architects*. Vol. 5. Translated by Gaston du C. de Vere. London: Macmillan and the Medici Society, 1913. The standard translation of the second edition (1568) of the only contemporary biography of the artist. Although Vasari was only nineteen when Andrea died, he had access to reliable information about the artist when he was preparing his biography.

Eric Van Schaack

FRA ANGELICO
Guido di Pietro

Born: c. 1400; Vicchio, Tuscany
Died: February 18, 1455; Rome
Area of Achievement: Art
Contribution: Fra Angelico is best known for adapting the most advanced artistic techniques of his time (perspective and brilliant use of color and line) to extraordinary evocations of purely spiritual subjects.

Early Life
Not much is known about Fra Angelico's early life. His baptismal name was Guido or Guidolino di Pietro, but he was also named Giovanni da Fiesole. Il Beato Fra Giovanni Angelico is the name he was given after his death, even though he was never actually beatified. He was apparently an extremely devout man who, in or about 1425, took his vows in the Dominican Order. The first painting of his that can be confidently dated is the *Madonna Linaivoli Altarpiece* (1433), which is in St. Mark's Convent in Florence, Italy. It is speculated that he began painting perhaps ten years earlier, working on small pictures and miniatures, such as *Saint Jerome Penitent*, which is in the collection of Princeton University.

As Giulio Carlo Argon puts it, Fra Angelico was a man of "saintly habits, a learned and zealous friar." He seems to have turned to art not only as a way of glorifying God but also as a way of demonstrating the sacred contents of His world. This meant painting angels and holy figures in vivid color and specific detail; there is nothing abstract or stilted about Fra Angelico's human and divine figures. They are a recognizable part of the viewer's world, set off only by their brilliance and repose.

Fra Angelico may have achieved a significant place of authority among the Dominicans. One unverified account claims that the pope wished him to be Archbishop of Florence. What is certain is that Fra Angelico enjoyed the respect of the Vatican and worked for many years on papal commissions. From 1449 to 1452, he was prior of the convent of San Marco. Still, his fame as a painter far exceeded his accomplishments in the Church. His paintings reveal such skill, clarity, and intensity that many critics have presumed that the artist's aim was to combine Renaissance Humanism with an exalted portrayal of Christian doctrine.

Life's Work
Fra Angelico's main purpose was to give depth, resonance, and substance to his spiritual conception of existence. What separates his work from earlier medieval religious painting is his use of perspective, the portrayal of objects or people on a flat surface so as to give the illusion of three dimensions. In

other words, Fra Angelico learned the technique of making his religious figures stand out, as though what he painted had an objective, concrete existence in the world of the senses. Perspective was a fifteenth century invention, and it is likely that Fra Angelico learned it from his contemporaries in Florence. At about 1420, the Florentine architects Filippo Brunelleschi and Leon Battista Alberti designed two panels depicting architectural views of Florence. For the first time, viewers of these panels could get a sense of the space in and around objects rather than having each object or image appear flattened out along the same plane. It was as if the viewer could look into a painting and not simply at it.

In *The Annunciation*, painted sometime in the 1430's, the Virgin Mary and the archangel Gabriel are framed by two arches that curve over them and create a coherent, concrete space which they can be seen to inhabit. This architectural detail is not merely decorative; it serves the function of creating a scene, a small drama that draws the viewer's attention to the entrance of the angel into the human realm. Gabriel is depicted leaning forward, with the tail ends of his golden wings and of his heavily ornamented pink-and-gold gown bisected by one of the pillars of an arch. Mary, on the other hand, is completely separate in her own panel, save for a small piece of her royal blue gown edged with gold that extends slightly into Gabriel's space. The Annunciation, Gabriel's announcement that Mary will bear the Son of God, is rendered in three streams of gold lines that penetrate the pillar that separates Mary's panel from Gabriel's. Visually, the two archways are linked by the representation of the Annunciation, yet their very solidity and the openness to the viewer suggests the simultaneous separation and unity of the human and divine worlds. Gabriel's index finger on his right hand points at Mary while his left hand is slightly raised, his fingers pointing upward. Mary, with her head inclining slightly toward him and her hands crossed on her breast, assumes the pose appropriate to receiving the Word of God. As Argon observes, "every line in the Virgin's figure is galvanized and taut, as she starts from her absorption in the prayer book on her knee." The delicacy with which these figures are profiled within the archways makes them intriguing, integral parts of a spiritual allegory.

In 1436, the Dominicans of Fiesole took up residence in St. Mark's Convent in Florence. Their protector, Cosimo de' Medici (1389-1464), the first of his noble family to rule Florence, made it possible for Fra Angelico to supervise the preparation of the frescoes of the building. One of the most ambitious projects was *The Presentation in the Temple*, a work renowned for its deeply receding perspective and its portrayal of interior lighting. As many critics have pointed out, the color schemes and lighting of Fra Angelico's paintings and frescoes account for much of his success, for they reveal his intense concern with natural and artificial environments, and the contrast between nature and architecture. The presentation of the Christ child, for example, is depicted in a scene of semidarkness. In three panels—the largest of which is set off by two archways with pillars—the artist assembles three figures in the foreground that emit the most light and that are naturally set apart from the dim interior. Slightly behind Jesus, Joseph and Mary are two votaries, a male and female, emerging from the archways and entering the center panel in prayerful and respectful poses. This arrangement of space was at the service of Fra Angelico's effort to show how God had proportioned the world, with the sight lines of the painting converging on the Christ child.

Other works, such as *Christ on the Cross Adored by Saint Dominic*, *The Crucifixion*, *Christ Scorned*, and *The Transfiguration*, all of which were completed after 1437, suggest the artist's growing concern with spiritual insight. They evince the effort of a devout man bent on creating objects of meditation. These paintings appeared in the Dominicans' cells, and they represent (much more than Fra Angelico's earlier work) an intimate concern with the relation of the individual soul to its Maker. There is, for example, Saint Dominic's contracted brows and the tightness of his jaw and pursed lips as he devoutly gazes upward at Christ, whose blood streams down the Cross. Saint Dominic is kneeling at the base of the Cross, his hands gripping it as though to steady himself or to look directly at Jesus. This is the study of a man undergoing the agony of his own faith.

In painting after painting in the last ten years of his life, Fra Angelico concentrated on Christ as the very light of human life. In *The Transfiguration*, Jesus is depicted in his threefold aspect as martyr, creator, and savior. Enclosed in an oval light, with his arms outstretched and level with his shoulders, his hands, palms open, emerge from the light in benediction of the prophets and saints encircling him with expressions of supplication, yearning, thanksgiving, and contemplation. In *The Transfiguration*, the artist invokes the whole community of faith.

Summary

In 1445, Pope Eugenius IV called Fra Angelico to Rome to design the Cappella del Sacramento in the Vatican. Although he accepted other commissions in the late 1440's, his greatest work was accomplished in Rome during his final years with his rendering of episodes from the lives of Saints Stephen and Lawrence, some of which was undoubtedly completed by his pupils. In 1449, Nicholas V was finally successful in healing the breach in the Catholic church known as the Schism, and that probably accounts, in part, for the themes of Fra Angelico's frescoes, which emphasized the unity of the religious community and the renewal of the faithful.

Although Fra Angelico continued to paint after his years in Rome, his return to Florence in 1449 as the Prior of San Marco evidently meant that he had much less time for his art. None of the works from his very last period of creativity amplifies in any significant respect the achievement of his mature years. He never painted a subject that was not religious. All of his work was suffused with the Humanism of the Renaissance. His religious figures are vibrantly alive with his age's growing interest in the human personality. An innovator in art, Fra Angelico sought to adapt the latest advances in painting to a depiction of the greatest spiritual subjects. The faith he professed had to be palpable and demonstrable, in vivid color and in space that had a sculptural clarity of form and depth. His Christianity took the shape of an art that made a union of seeing and believing and put religion in a realm of the senses that every human being could experience.

Bibliography

Argon, Giulio Carlo. *Fra Angelico and His Times*. Lausanne, Switzerland: Skira, 1955. A biographical and critical study that skillfully places the artist not only in his times but also in the aesthetic traditions that influenced his work. Includes close analysis of several paintings, color plates, bibliography, index, and biographical notices for historical figures mentioned in the text. Somewhat difficult to follow for students not familiar with art terms.

Douglas, Langton. *Fra Angelico*. London: G. Bell & Sons, 1902. Still informative as a general treatment of the artist's life and career. Douglas examines Fra Angelico's work, his influence on subsequent painting and his use of architectural forms. The critic maintains a careful discussion of the differences between Fra Angelico's early and late work. Seventy-three plates, a bibliography, and an index of the artist's work, as well as a general index, make this a study worth consulting.

Hausenstein, Wilhelm. *Fra Angelico*. London: Methuen, 1928. Useful primarily for discussions of individual paintings, although the criticism is sometimes marred by an excessively impressionistic and speculative style. Hausenstein often writes as an enthusiast, not a discerning commentator. A list of sixty-four plates is included but no table of contents.

LeClerc, André. *Fra Angelico*. New York: Hyperion Press, 1949. Concise introduction to the artist's importance, including a brief biography and a survey of his work. There is not much critical analysis of the painting, but the color plates present a comprehensive view of Fra Angelico's opus. Should be consulted for a clear, quick, summary of the artist's significance.

Phillemore, Catherine Mary. *Fra Angelico*. London: Sampson, Law, Marston, Searle and Rivington, 1881. Draws directly on late nineteenth century Italian scholarship on the early period of the Italian Renaissance. The study begins with a discussion of the precursors of Fra Angelico, then treats him in the context of Florentine oil painters and goldsmiths and Florentine artists in Rome. Useful index; illustrations in black and white.

Pope-Hennessy, John. *Fra Angelico*. Ithaca, N.Y.: Cornell University Press, 1974. A systematic study of the artist's life, early works, panel painting and frescoes, period in Rome, and late works. Includes a catalog of works attributed to Fra Angelico. The index and black-and-white and color plates are presented with impeccable scholarship drawing on sources from both the artist's period and this century.

Schottmüller, Frida. *The Work of Fra Angelico Da Fiesole*. New York: Brentanos, 1913. A biographical introduction situates the artist's life and work in the context of the Middle Ages, the Renaissance, and Western art generally. Especially valuable for a discussion of Fra Angelico's contemporaries. Contains 327 black-and-white plates.

Carl Rollyson
Lisa Paddock

LUDOVICO ARIOSTO

Born: September 8, 1474; Reggio Emilia
Died: July 6, 1533; Ferrara
Area of Achievement: Literature
Contribution: Ariosto, although an accomplished Latin poet, made vernacu-
lar Italian the established language for serious poetry from lyrics and
satires to drama and the epic.

Early Life

The life and works of Ludovico Ariosto, like those of his administrator-
soldier father, are closely bound to the house of Este, the Dukes of Ferrara.
In spite of the instability created by the almost-constant struggles between
this city-kingdom and other rival city-states, the Estensi court in Ferrara was
one of the finest in Renaissance Europe. It supported an army, a university,
jousts and hunts, and many artists. Architects, painters, sculptors, musicians, and poets were an everyday presence in the life of this court, which
was located on the main pilgrimage and trade routes of Spain, France, and
Italian city-states such as Venice and Bologna. The young Ariosto was introduced to this center of gracious living in 1485, when his father, Niccolò,
after commanding citadels surrounding Ferrara for twelve years, was recalled. Ariosto had been born in Reggio, one such vast citadel, in 1474, the
first of ten children.

Ariosto's love of literature only became a problem when Count Niccolò,
his father, enrolled him in the five-year law curriculum at the university
about 1489. He completed slightly more than two uncongenial years toward
his doctorate of law, while working with the court theater in his spare time,
before his father relented and allowed him to study classical poetry in about
1494. His teacher, Gregorio da Spoleto, who also taught the sons of the
Strozzi and Este families, was a gifted and devoted teacher. Within one
and a half years, Ludovico was the prize student, giving recitations at court
and composing humorous poems about student life as well as lyrics and ec-
logues in Latin. It was not until 1503-1505, under Pietro Bembo, that Ariosto started composing serious poetry in the vernacular.

Ariosto's devotion to such work, however, was interrupted by family financial problems in 1498. That year, to lessen problems occasioned by his
father's fall from ducal grace, Ariosto entered the service of Ercole I d'Este.
Two years later, Niccolò died, leaving Ariosto head of the family, with four
younger brothers to educate and five sisters to support until their marriages,
with only meager income from properties surrounding Ferrara. Duke Ercole
appointed him to a more lucrative position as captain of a garrison in 1502.
The next year, however, the last of his uncles died and Ariosto was forced to
return to Ferrara to look after his family. He was then given a position in the

household of Ercole's son, Cardinal Ippolito d'Este, which he kept until 1517. Ippolito's household, rather than being churchly, rivaled his father's and his brother Alfonso's in all aspects—art, women, hunting, feasting, and battling. Services demanded by a courtier might range from overseeing feasts to accompanying Ippolito on diplomatic or military missions. Ariosto's health declined, and stomach disorders, which would plague him all of his life, began.

Life's Work

The first written evidence of an inner conflict between Ariosto's art and his courtier occupation is found in two poems written at about the same time. One was in praise of Ippolito's purity and chastity, and the second was an epithalamium for Lucrezia Borgia, already twice married. These poems helped establish his position as the court poet and are, perhaps, the first evidence of what was to become his dominant tone as a poet—irony. His burdens were not lightened by the birth of his first illegitimate son, Giambattista, after a brief liaison, probably with a servant. It is also possible that during this time, in order to increase his income, he took minor Holy Orders, but he steadfastly refused the hypocrisy of the lucrative benefices of full priesthood. By 1507, his growing reputation as a poet relieved him from some of the least congenial aspects of his service. That year, he was sent to Ippolito's sister's court in Mantua to convey a poem celebrating the birth of Princess Isabella's first son. Isabella and her court welcomed him and especially admired a work in progress he read to them, a work all scholars agree must have been the first draft of the *Orlando furioso* (1516, 1521, 1532; English translation, 1591).

During the time between this visit and the poem's publication, Ariosto's time was doubly occupied. At court, he was in charge of many theatrical productions. In 1508, his own comedy, *La cassaria* (*The Coffer*, 1975), was elaborately produced and popularly received for *Carnivale*. He followed with another success, *I suppositi* (*The Pretenders*, 1566), in 1509, and prepared *Il negromante* (*The Necromancer*, 1975) for *Carnivale* in 1510, although its production was stopped because of the precarious political and military concerns of the city. Violence plagued Ferrara. In 1508, Ariosto's best friend, Ercole Strozzi, was assassinated, supposedly by Alfonso's men. Ariosto himself was mediating between Ferrara and the Papacy in Rome and France, with whom Ferrara had allied itself between 1507 and 1509, attempting to reassure each faction. He was on such a mission when Pope Julius' troops attacked Ferrara, and Alfonso was excommunicated. He rejoined Ippolito the next year, in time to witness the sacking of Ravenna in 1512. Later that year, when an attempted reconciliation between Alfonso and the pope suddenly failed, he accompanied Alfonso in a dangerous escape from Rome to Florence. In between, he worked on *Orlando furioso*. Probably in Florence, in 1513, he fell in love with a married woman, Alessandra Strozzi-Benucci.

Ariosto continued to travel on diplomatic missions for Ippolito and Alfonso, finding time to write between the assignments. Somehow, the first forty cantos of *Orlando furioso* were completed in 1515, the same year that Alessandra's husband died. Still, the couple did not marry. *Orlando furioso* was published in 1516, and all two thousand copies of the first edition sold within five years, making it the first best-seller of the Renaissance. Ariosto became famous throughout Europe.

His means of support still came primarily from his service at court. When Ippolito, who was also Primate of Hungary and Bishop of Buda, decided to move his court to Hungary in 1517, Ariosto chose to stay in Ferrara. Ippolito agreed but dismissed Ariosto from his services. Yet Alfonso almost immediately took Ariosto into service at his court in Ferrara at a better salary.

For the next three years, Ariosto's life was quite pleasant. He had time to finish and rewrite one of his earlier dramas, *The Necromancer*. He wrote his first three satires and started revising *Orlando furioso*. Its second edition was published in 1521, to be followed by multiple editions in the next seven years. By 1519, however, Ferrara was again rumored to be the target of a papal invasion.

Renewal of warfare drained Ferrara's resources and forced Alfonso to suspend pay to the professors and to many artists, including Ariosto. By 1522, Ariosto was forced to accept a post as commissioner of the Garfagnana district, which was controlled by Alfonso. He found himself temperamentally unsuited to deliver the severe punishment perhaps needed to establish peace and law in the area. Ariosto found the post beyond his powers and felt exiled rather than rewarded. When offered an ambassadorship to the court of Clement VII, he refused it and returned to his beloved Ferrara and Alessandra in June, 1525.

Finally, Ariosto had the leisure and enough money to live as he wished. Between 1526 and 1528, he composed *Cinque canti*, which was published posthumously in 1545. In 1528, the people of Ferrara elected him to be Judge of the Twelve Sages. Also in 1528, he was appointed to be director of the court theater, which Alfonso wanted restored to its former glory after the disruptions of the wars. Not only did Ariosto supervise construction of sets and productions but also he had a chance to revise his own dramatic works to fit his newer ideas of dramatic style. *La Lena* (1529; *Lena*, 1975) and a new version of *The Coffer* were both performed. His prestige as a diplomat was the highest, and he was asked to make a few visits to Florence, Venice, and Mantua for Alfonso. Meanwhile, he worked on his final version of *Orlando furioso*, which was published in October, 1532. Weeks later, he was in Mantua with Alfonso to welcome Charles V, the Holy Roman Emperor, and give him a presentation copy. Most biographers also believe that Ariosto and

Alessandra were secretly married between 1526 and 1530, but that they continued to live separately, perhaps to keep income from minor benefices conferred by Ippolito. By December, 1532, his lifelong stomach problems and later chest pains had taken their toll. Ariosto fell severely ill and died on July 6, 1533. Alessandra and his second son, Virginio, were by his bedside. He was buried by the monks of San Benedetto at their church, quietly, as he desired. His body was later entombed in the Biblioteca Ariostea of Ferrara beneath a marble tomb supplied by Napoleon.

Summary

Ludovico Ariosto is a prime example of the Renaissance man. An outstanding poet in all forms—lyrical, satirical, dramatic, and epic—he also was always involved in the active life of the courts of Ferrara as administrator and diplomat. He was always conscientious and loyal to family, friends, and patrons. He never sought great riches or titles but only enough to support himself and his family comfortably while he pursued his writing. Ariosto became the poet for whom Dante had called, one who would embody the greatest of Italian culture in a new form fit for the greatest of Italian vernacular poetry. *Orlando furioso* was a best-seller not only in Italy but also in France and in England, where Elizabeth I ordered an English translation. The almost picaresque structure of simultaneous multiple plots, the mixture of comic and tragic material, and the persona of a semidetached narrator were inventive strokes that allowed Ariosto to examine the form and values of the dying chivalric romance tradition while deeply investigating the problems of society in general and those of human nature. The *Orlando furioso* is great poetry, great fun for the reader, and full of great wisdom about man and his world. Because of a lack of readable translations, its American readership almost disappeared. Two translations, Barbara Reynolds' (Penguin, 1977) and Guido Waldman's (Oxford University Press, 1983) have again made the text widely accessible.

Bibliography

Brand, C. P. *Ludovico Ariosto: A Preface to the Orlando Furioso.* Edinburgh, Scotland: Edinburgh University Press, 1974. An excellent overview of Ariosto's life and works. Contains full chapters on life, lyrics, satires, and dramas while concentrating on a thematic study of the *Orlando furioso*. Emphasizes the opposition of love and war. Contains brief bibliographies for each chapter and two indexes.

Croce, Benedetto. *Ariosto, Shakespeare, and Corneille.* Translated by Douglas Ainslie. New York: Holt, Rinehart and Winston, 1920. Reprint. New York: Russell & Russell, 1966. An extremely influential early modern essay on *Orlando furioso*. Rebutting the traditional criticism, Croce argues that the work achieves unity through the artist's control of point of view and style, a unity which ultimately reflects the rhythm and harmony of God's creation.

Gardner, Edmund G. *The King of Court Poets: Ariosto.* New York: E. P. Dutton, 1906. Reprint. New York: Haskell House, 1968. Gardner's full-length biography contains a wealth of material and is easy to read. He includes a social, cultural, and political background of Ariosto's life and work. Contains a dated bibliography, a useful index, and three foldout genealogies of the houses of Ariosto, Este, and Pio.

Griffin, Robert. *Ludovico Ariosto.* Boston: Twayne, 1974. Good introductory work on Ariosto, beginning with a chapter on his life and ending with a survey of criticism. Also contains chapters on lyrics, satires, dramas, and a thematic analysis of *Orlando furioso.* Argues that the unity of the poem rests on man's inability to accept the will of fortune in a world beyond his limited comprehension. Contains chronology, notes, selected bibliography with brief annotations, and two indexes.

Rodini, Robert J., and Salvatore Di Maria. *Ludovico Ariosto: An Annotated Bibliography of Criticism, 1956-1980.* Columbia: University of Missouri Press, 1984. Contains 930 entries from journals, monographs, essays in books, North American dissertations, and books. Although meant primarily for scholars, the entry synopses are excellent and can easily be skimmed. Arranged by author but also contains detailed subject index and an index by works treated.

Wiggins, Peter De Sa. *Figures in Ariosto's Tapestry: Character and Design in the "Orlando Furioso."* Baltimore: Johns Hopkins University Press, 1986. Agreeing with Galileo's early comments on the psychological consistency of Ariosto's characters and his exact knowledge of human nature, Wiggins suggests that their complex inner lives are universal human types. This invisible interior world, at odds with an exterior world of folly and depravity, is a major theme of the work. Excellent index and notes for each chapter.

——————. *The Satires of Ludovico Ariosto: A Renaissance Autobiography.* Athens: Ohio University Press, 1976. A bilingual text, using the Italian original edited by Cesare Segre with Wiggins' clear prose translations on the facing page. Each satire is placed in biographical and historical context with its own separate preface and notes. Argues that the narrator of the satires is an idealized poet courtier in typical situations rather than a factual mirror of Ariosto himself. Suggests that the satires share similarities with *Orlando furioso*: the theme of illusion and reality, the ironic humor, and the use of a dramatic persona as narrator.

Ann E. Reynolds

AURANGZEB
Muhī-ud-Dīn Muhammad

Born: November 3, 1618; Dohad, India
Died: March 3, 1707; Ahmadnagar, India
Areas of Achievement: Government and politics
Contribution: Aurangzeb was the last of the great Mughal emperors who ruled north and central India after 1526. The most pious and ruthless of these rulers, he was a great conqueror, a brilliant administrator, and an extraordinarily cunning statesman.

Early Life

Muhī-ud-Dīn Muhammad Aurangzeb was born in the city of Dohad, about three hundred miles north of Bombay, on November 3, 1618. He was the third of the four sons of the Mughal Emperor Shāh Jahān and his wife, Mumtāz Mahal, for whom the Tāj Mahal was built. The Mughals, a Muslim people descended from the Turkish and Mongol conquerors of central Asia, had ruled much of India since 1526. Aurangzeb was reared in a rich and powerful home destined to be torn by imperial intrigue and violence.

As youths, Aurangzeb and his three brothers (Dārā Shukōh, Shujah, and Murad) were taught the Koran, standard works of Persian poetry, calligraphy, and the history of their great ancestors. Prince Dārā, the favorite of his father, Shāh Jahān, was a liberal-minded, aesthetically inclined Muslim, who believed that truth resided in a variety of traditions and could not be contained in a single religion. Aurangzeb, in contrast, from his youth displayed narrow, literalistic religious and ethnic propensities. He memorized most of the Koran, became expert in Muslim law, and largely ignored poetry, music, and painting. Unlike his predecessors, he took little interest in monumental architecture and seldom patronized the arts. In the eventual struggle to succeed Shāh Jahān as emperor, the two protagonists were Dārā and Aurangzeb—mystic versus puritan, unorthodox versus orthodox.

As a young man, Aurangzeb was ambitious, aggressive, and ruthless, but he was hardly more cruel than others of his time. Rather, he was more successful because of his superior skill in statecraft and intrigue. Recognizing Aurangzeb's ambitions, Shāh Jahān appointed him viceroy (*nabob*) of the Deccan (central India) in July, 1636. He spent eight years there, isolated most of the time from the center of power at the Mughal court in Āgra. When he returned to Āgra in 1644, it became apparent to him that his father was discriminating against him in favor of Dārā. This conviction caused him to misbehave at the court, which resulted in his temporary banishment. Soon restored to favor, however, he served as the Governor of Gujarat province (1645-1647) and of the northwestern Multan and Sind provinces (1648-1652). It was there that he honed his military and command skills, as his armies were sent out to fight Afghan hill tribes and Persian soldiers. He suffered crushing defeats in central Asia against the Persians, however, and found himself reassigned to the Deccan in August, 1652, once again isolated from the center of power.

Aurangzeb's second viceroyalty in the Deccan (1652-1658) allowed him the opportunity to develop further his considerable administrative and military talents. His relations with his father and with Dārā continued to be contentious, however, and both of his major military campaigns in the Deccan—against two rich Muslim principalities, Golconda and Bijapur—were halted just short of victory by orders from Shāh Jahān, who was influenced by anti-Aurangzeb factions at his court. In effect, Aurangzeb's attempts to expand Mughal influence in central India were nullified by the court intrigues of Dārā's supporters. It was thus a frustrated Aurangzeb who received word in September, 1657, that Shāh Jahān had fallen seriously ill. This illness precipitated a struggle for succession that eventually brought Aurangzeb to the throne.

Life's Work

At the time Shāh Jahān fell ill with strangury, the four brothers were widely separated. Aurangzeb was in the Deccan, Shujah was in Bengal, Murad was in Gujarat, and Dārā was at Shāh Jāhān's side in Delhi. Shāh Jahān's illness took him to death's door and threw his court into panic over the inevitable succession struggle.

Aurangzeb began his campaign for the throne by luring his inept brother, Murad, into an alliance against Dārā, denying at first that he had any regal ambitions and then promising Murad the provinces of Punjab and Sind for his support. In the meantime, both Shujah and Murad publicly announced their own claims to the Mughal throne.

By early 1658, Shāh Jahān had recovered from his illness and tried to help Dārā cope with his brother's conspiracy against him. Yet Dārā, who was always more interested in mysticism than in imperial politics, was no match for the aggressive, battle-hardened Aurangzeb. In April, 1658, the combined forces of Aurangzeb and Murad defeated a formidable imperial force and on May 29, 1658, confronted Dārā's main army several miles east of Āgra on the plain of Samugarh. Under his superior generalship, Aurangzeb's army overwhelmed Dārā's troops, and Dārā fled toward Āgra, leaving ten thousand of his men dead on the battlefield. On May 30, Dārā gathered about five thousand of his remaining troops and embarked for Delhi. On June 8, Āgra fell to Aurangzeb and Shāh Jahān was placed under house arrest, where he would remain until his death in 1666.

Moving quickly to consolidate his power, Aurangzeb arrested his erstwhile ally, Murad, imprisoned him for the next three years, and then had him executed. Shortly after taking Āgra, his troops set out in pursuit of Dārā, but it was not until August 30, 1659, that Aurangzeb was able to capture his brother and have him executed. In the interim, he also eliminated Shujah, who eventually died a fugitive in Burma. Aurangzeb thus cemented his ascendance to the peacock throne as Ālamgīr ("world conqueror") I in July, 1658. He reigned until his death in March, 1707.

Aurangzeb's nearly fifty-year reign aroused passionate support from orthodox Muslims and equally fervent opposition from some of his Hindu subjects, upon whom his policies inflicted enormous suffering. Noted mostly for his single-minded pursuit of power and territory, he brought monumental construction to an end, ceased to patronize nonreligious celebrations, and enforced Muslim puritanism in his court and realm.

His strict adherence to orthodox Islam led him to abandon the religious tolerance and preferred treatment of Hindus, which had been the hallmark of Mughal rule since the time of his grandfather Akbar. The Mughals had attempted to be rulers of all Indians, irrespective of creed and ethnicity, and had welcomed Rajput warriors into the highest ranks of their armies and administration. They had also abolished the hated *jizya*, a head tax imposed on all non-Muslims. Such policies had created a large reservoir of Hindu support for the Mughal Empire.

Aurangzeb reversed these policies, despite warnings from his advisers that such action would likely result in widespread rebellions. He began by appointing "censors of public morals" (*muhtasibs*) in every large city, ordering these censors to enforce Islamic laws and customs strictly. He outlawed some Hindu festivals, prohibited repairs to Hindu temples, and in 1679 reimposed the poll tax. By refusing to treat Hindus as equals, he broke the Hindu-Mughal alliance and ensured the emergence of rebellion in 1669 in the Punjab and thereafter throughout much of the empire.

The fiercest and most persistent Hindu opposition to Aurangzeb arose in the western Indian province of Maharashtra under the leadership of Śivajī, who is popularly regarded as the founder of Hindu nationalism, but whom the Mughals reviled as a "mountain rat" because of the guerrilla tactics he employed. Śivajī was a ferocious Marāthā warrior, who was reared by his mother to love Hinduism and hate all varieties of Muslim rule in India. He sought self-rule and full freedom to practice his own religion. He took to the Maharashtran hills at the age of twenty to fight a guerrilla war against the Mughals and other Muslims. He soon developed a number of fortresses on mountain plateaus and gained control of much of Maharashtra. His rising power alarmed Aurangzeb, who sent a huge army against him in 1665. Śivajī was soundly defeated, but he managed to escape from the Mughals in time and by 1670 recaptured most of the ground he had lost in 1665. He remained independent of the Mughals until his death in 1680, and his sons and followers continued the battle against the Mughals thereafter.

It was the Deccan, in combination with Maharashtra, that attracted most of Aurangzeb's attention after 1680. In that year, Aurangzeb's son, Akbar, rose in rebellion against his father in alliance with two Rajput princes and Śivajī's elder son, Sambhājī, who had succeeded his father. Aurangzeb invaded the Deccan in 1681 to try to quell this potentially dangerous rebellion. Akbar's anti-Aurangzeb alliance never operated effcctively, and Akbar eventually fled in 1686 to Iran, where he died in exile. In 1689, Aurangzeb captured and executed Sambhājī, who had effectively employed guerrilla tactics to frustrate Aurangzeb's completion of the Deccan conquest. In spite of Sambhājī's death, the Marāthās continued to defy the Mughals. They were the only power remaining outside Aurangzeb's control, however, as he brought Mughal power to its pinnacle. Never before or since did a single ruler control so much of India.

Yet the costs of Aurangzeb's conquest of the Deccan were enormous. At least 100,000 lives were lost and much of the Deccan's surplus wealth was consumed by military expenditures. The military slaughter was accompanied by famine and bubonic plague, which killed countless thousands more before Aurangzeb eventually quit the Deccan and returned to the north in 1705. By then, even he seems to have regretted the carnage he had inflicted on the Deccan.

Summary

Scholars disagree about Aurangzeb's character and accomplishments. His life was so dramatic and forceful that it seems to compel extreme assessments. His critics point to his bigotry against non-Muslims and his excessive military adventures as marks of monumental failure. Forgotten is that he ruled India for more than forty-eight years and that he took the empire to its greatest territorial extent. Moreover, while he was cruel and shed much blood trying to conquer all of India, ruthless ambition was hardly unique to him in the India of that time. His archrivals, the Marāthās, matched him in their pursuit of wealth and power. Although he lacked the charisma of his father, Shāh Jahān, and his grandfather, Akbar, he was a firm and capable administrator.

Although the Deccan struggles severely weakened the Mughal Empire, Aurangzeb's successor, Bahādur Shāh, was able to restore the empire's vigor within five years of Aurangzeb's death, suggesting that Aurangzeb's misgovernment may not have been as severe as some contend. It is clear to most historians that Aurangzeb was, at the least, a complex personality and an able statesman who united more of India under his personal rule than any other sovereign in history.

Bibliography
Gascoigne, Bamber. *The Great Moghuls*. New York: Harper & Row, 1971. This well-written, general history of the Mughals chronicles the rise and

fall of the empire from the founder, Bābur, through Aurangzeb. It is profusely illustrated and provides a handy guide to the complex history of the major emperors. Presents a balanced view of Aurangzeb's reign.

Hallissey, Robert C. *The Rajput Rebellion Against Aurangzeb: A Study of the Mughal Empire in Seventeenth Century India.* Columbia: University of Missouri Press, 1977. This slender scholarly volume examines the Rajput rebellion against Aurangzeb in the light of the internal dynamics of the Rajput state and the religious differences between the Hindus and the Muslims. It reveals how complex the Mughal-Rajput relationship was.

Hansen, Waldemar. *The Peacock Throne.* New York: Holt, Rinehart and Winston, 1972. A detailed history of the Mughal period. Provides many insights into Aurangzeb's character and style of rule. His account of the succession struggle is particularly helpful, as is his explication of the relationship between Aurangzeb and his enemies, especially Śivajī.

Majumdar, R. C., et al. *An Advanced History of India.* London: Macmillan, 1961. One of the most detailed histories of India by Indian scholars readily available in the West. Majumdar's thick volume strikes a balanced view of Aurangzeb's leadership style and explains both his successes and his failures. Some of his interpretations, especially of the Rajputs, are not supported by more modern scholarship.

Pearson, M. N. "Shivaji and the Decline of the Mughal Empire." *Journal of Asian Studies* 35 (February, 1976): 221-236. Focuses on the relationship between Aurangzeb's nemesis, Śivajī, and the decline of Mughal power. Although Aurangzeb's expeditions into the Deccan weakened his empire, other causes also were at work.

Sarkar, Jadunath. *A Short History of Aurangzeb, 1618-1707.* London: Longmans, Green, 1930. Sarkar's work is the most detailed and scholarly on Aurangzeb and Śivajī. This book is a distillation of his extensive studies of the Aurangzeb era.

Loren W. Crabtree

BA'AL SHEM TOV
Israel ben Eliezer

Born: c. 1700; Okup, Polish Ukraine
Died: 1760; probably near Medzhibozh, Polish Ukraine
Area of Achievement: Religion
Contribution: Ba'al Shem Tov brought Eastern European Jewry out of a long period of decay and spread a rejuvenated religious outlook through society. He founded the modern Hasidic branch of Judaism.

Early Life

The man known as Ba'al Shem Tov, which means "master of the good name," was born Israel ben Eliezer in the village of Okup in the Polish Ukraine, one of the strongholds of Judaism from the Middle Ages, with Jewish schools, community organizations, and businesses active throughout. Israel's parents were poor and elderly, and they died when he was a young child. Some sources report that Israel was an infant when his parents died, but at least one scholar has him as being old enough to be influenced by his father's dying words: "Fear nothing because God will take care of all."

The boy had a strikingly exuberant spirit, and even though he was taken under the wing of community leaders, he made his own way from an early age. Israel sporadically attended elementary school and spent many hours wandering in the nearby forests and studying nature; by night, he studied the mystical texts of the Cabala. At age twelve, Israel was made an assistant to the schoolmaster and later became a synagogue attendant. Even as a boy he was known for his warm, magnetic personality and for his study of Judaism.

Although Israel was married at eighteen, his bride died almost immediately after the ceremony, and the young widower commenced a life of wandering. He worked in Galicia as a school assistant before settling in the Ukrainian village of Blust, near Brody, as a teacher. In his personal habits, Israel showed the utmost simplicity.

His second marriage was fraught with conflict before it began. Israel was betrothed to Hannah, the daughter of a leading citizen in a nearby town, but her father died before the wedding. Hannah's brother, who disliked Israel's rough appearance and seemingly limited prospects, opposed the marriage. By now, however, Hannah had fallen in love with her fiancé, and the couple were married and left Brody, taking only a few belongings. Later, as Hannah's brother understood Ba'al Shem Tov's powers of healing and spirituality, he repented his harsh treatment and helped the couple financially.

In their early married life, Israel and Hannah settled in the Carpathian Mountains, where she helped support him as he performed menial labor and returned to the forest to learn everything he could about plants, the themes of nature, and the relationship between God and the mind.

Life's Work

The work of Ba'al Shem Tov evolved from his study of nature and what he perceived as God's relationships to the natural world and to man. Yet the troubled times in which he lived did much to direct his studies toward helping the masses of peasants and ultimately to sparking a popular revival of Judaism.

During the sixteenth and seventeenth centuries Judaism flourished in Eastern Europe, especially in Poland. The Jewish population in the region grew tenfold, from fifty thousand to a half million, between 1500 and 1650. Jews enjoyed vibrant educational and social institutions, and had some measure of self-government. In the mid-1600's, however, came anti-Jewish violence that killed one hundred thousand people and destroyed seven hundred communities.

After this devastating blow, Jewish institutions were crippled and mystical strains of the religion gained popularity over the more formal and structured Talmud study. The asceticism of the earlier scholar Isaac Luria, emphasizing self-mortification as the way to know God, took hold. There was little in formal Talmudic Judaism to appeal to the needs of the dispirited masses. This was a time of deep pessimism and superstition for the Jews of Eastern Europe.

During this period there was widespread use of amulets to ward off evil spirits and to invite beneficent ones. Someone who produced these amulets was called a ba'al shem, meaning that he manipulated the letters of God's name to produce potent phrases. Israel was a ba'al shem with such renown that the adjective tov, or "good," was added. Yet he was more than this.

As Ba'al Shem Tov took to the forests in his twenties, he became a skilled herbalist and was known throughout the area as a sort of homeopathic doctor. His wit and charm, combined with his healing ways, drew throngs of people to him for help. Not only could he cure their physical ailments, but also he offered psychological counseling. His followers included Jewish and gentile peasants, members of the nobility, and some religious leaders.

While wandering by himself in the Carpathian Mountains, Ba'al Shem Tov had formulated a pantheistic outlook: God was present in all living things; even the struggle with Satan could be found in the godliness of the natural world. From this he discerned that in the close relation between God's creations and the actions of everyday human life could spring a communion with God. Here was a valuable and sincere form of prayer. This kind of communion, in observing the minutiae of Jewish law and in performing necessary tasks, was the basis of modern Hasidism.

Ba'al Shem Tov wanted this kind of modest yet constant religious observance to be joyful, which meant an end to asceticism and unhealthy self-denial as ways to know God, and the beginning of dancing and singing in prayerful practice. He wanted Jews' spiritual ardor to be buttressed with good health habits. A sound body and a rested soul would be ready to begin again each day a new cycle of observance and communion with God. Since he wanted those who had gone astray to have an easy path to repentance, he was considerably more lenient than many Jewish leaders in treating human frailties.

At age thirty-six, Ba'al Shem Tov had emerged from his long period of solitary study to share his wisdom. By 1740, he had established his home and spiritual community in Medzhibozh, a town in the frontier region of Poland, Ukrainia, and Lithuania, where he was to live the rest of his life. Ba'al Shem Tov made a good living providing amulets and advice, and his inspirational stories and parables were the treasured source of a rich oral legacy. His voluminous correspondence required the help of two secretaries. Among the adherents who came to his new spiritual community were some of the rabbis who spread Hasidism: Rabbi Jacob Joseph, Rabbi Dov Baer of Merzeritz, and Rabbi Pinchas.

Hasidim, by definition, were pious disciples, and Ba'al Shem Tov was the *zaddik*, their master. Through his ordination of visiting cantors, prayer leaders, rabbis, and lay followers, Hasidism spread like a wave through Jewish society. The religion was now accessible to everyone, unlike the rigid and rationalist system of Talmudic study that heretofore had been held up as the pinnacle of Jewish observance. Ba'al Shem Tov did not oppose formal Talmud study himself but said that he had no time for that luxury.

The teachings of Ba'al Shem Tov were not met with universal approval. The Hasidic communities that had spread through the region were opposed by some orthodox scholars. During a journey to a theological debate in 1759, Ba'al Shem Tov fell ill, and he died a short time later. The Hasidic movement, however, gained strength after his death, and by 1780 Hasidism so threatened the orthodox leaders that the movement was excommunicated by Jewish civil authority.

Ba'al Shem Tov left little written record, no more than a few letters, and his legacy was based on oral tales passed down among his disciples. It was not until 1814-1815 that *Shivhei ha-Besht* (*In Praise of the Ba'al Shem Tov*, 1970) was published by his followers. After this came a wider body of literature that further propelled Hasidism.

Summary

Ba'al Shem Tov's most important contribution was the revitalization of Polish Jewry in a populist movement lasting two hundred years, from the waning days of the Polish kingdom until the Holocaust of World War II forced its remnants to the New World. The large, vibrant Hasidic community in Brooklyn, New York, for example, is a sign that the underlying themes of joyful daily observance still hold great appeal among Jews. Despite the brutal dislocation of the Polish Jews in the twentieth century, the oral legacy begun by Ba'al Shem Tov's first disciples has remained unbroken to the present. The pattern of early Hasidism, with a local spiritual leader surrounded by a community of disciples, has endured.

Some of the herbal remedies discovered by Ba'al Shem Tov have survived in modern medicine; his treatment of insanity and melancholy relied on influencing the mind rather than inflicting punishment. The patterns of song and dance that formed in Hasidism are discerned in popular culture, although some of the earlier gesticulation and conjuring have faded.

Although he lived simply, Ba'al Shem Tov did not despise riches. In one of his tales, he takes into account the sad family history of a rich man for whom eating was a form of revenge against anti-Semitic violence. Ba'al Shem Tov explains that sincere prayers from such a man may be more pleasing to God that the supplications of a man prideful of his own poverty and asceticism. In the same vein, Ba'al Shem Tov was not reluctant to proclaim the importance of a *zaddik*, or righteous master, in spreading his message. He was mindful of his critics and supplied ample justification to protect his appeal.

Bibliography
Blumenthal, David R. *Understanding Jewish Mysticism.* Vol. 2. New York: Ktav Publishing House, 1982. The book explores the evolution of Hasidism in the daily rituals, stories, prayer life, community relations, and modern Hasidic lore. Contains unusual instructions for mystic spells. The text of a short tale about Ba'al Shem Tov is included with comments.
Heschel, Abraham J. *The Circle of the Baal Shem Tov: Studies in Hasidism.* Chicago: University of Chicago Press, 1985. A testament to the growth of Hasidic studies, this historical work explores the beginnings of Hasidism through the lives of Ba'al Shem Tov's philosophical circle.
Klepfisz, Herszel. *Culture and Compassion: The Spirit of Polish Jewry from Hasidism to the Holocaust.* New York: Ktav Publishing House, 1983. Written by one of the foremost scholars of Hasidism. Klepfisz traces his descent from the original disciples. A warm, personal look at the spiritual life of the Polish Jews.
Noveck, Simon. *Creators of the Jewish Experience.* Washington, D.C.: B'nai B'rith Books, 1985. The chapter on seminal Jewish theologians places the life of Ba'al Shem Tov in the relatively modern role in guiding the religion in new directions. Succinct biographical selections.
Seltzer, Robert M. *Jewish People, Jewish Thought: The Jewish Experience in History.* New York: Macmillan, 1980. A major reference work on the roots of Judaism from earliest times. Illustrated, with numerous clear maps and a detailed bibliography. Charts compare timelines of Judaism and other civilizations. Contains concise definition of Hasidism and is valuable in explaining the early fractures in the movement.

Weiss, Joseph. *Studies in Eastern European Jewish Mysticism.* Edited by David Goldstein. New York: Oxford University Press, 1985. Detailed analysis of Hasidic teachings as well as the lives of the early followers. A tightly woven vessel for some of the historical riches of Hasidism.

Nan K. Chase

BĀBUR
Zahīr-ud-Dīn Muhammad

Born: February 14, 1483; Fergana
Died: December 26, 1530; Āgra, India
Areas of Achievement: The military and government
Contribution: Bābur, the first of the Mughal rulers in India, spread the Mughal Empire over most of northern India. He was a wise and kind king whose memoirs have revealed much about his life.

Early Life

Bābur, whose name is a Mongol word meaning tiger, was born in Fergana (modern Afghanistan), on February 14, 1483. A descendant of Genghis Khan and Tamerlane, Bābur became King of Fergana in 1494 at the age of eleven, when his father, 'Umar Shaykh Mīrzā, died. Along with the kingdom, Bābur inherited his father's struggles with his cousins for the kingdom of Transoxiana with its capital Samarkand. Bābur spent the first three years of his reign fighting his cousin Faisunqur, from whom he captured Samarkand in 1497 after a siege of seven months; yet he was soon forced to relinquish the city. Between 1498 and 1499, Bābur married, and he divided Fergana with his brother. In 1501, Bābur once again attempted to conquer Samarkand. Between April and May of 1501, Bābur suffered a defeat at Sari-Pul and retreated to Samarkand. After taking the city by surprise, Bābur and the inhabitants of Samarkand tried to repel the forces of Shaybānī Khān, chief of the Uzbeks, who had agreed to help Baisunqur Mīrzā fight his cousin, Bābur. Bābur was able to hold off Shaybānī Khān's men for four months but was finally forced to surrender the city. Bābur was released from his captivity, but only after he had agreed to give his sister's hand in marriage to Uzbek Khan.

Once free, Bābur spent the next three years in hiding at Tashkent, which had been given to him by his uncle, Sultan Mahmud Khan. Even though Bābur's uncle furnished him with a command of one thousand men, Bābur was defeated in 1503 at Arciyan by Tanbal, who had appealed to Shaybānī Khān for assistance. Having lost Fergana, Bābur spent the next year as a nomad in the remote territories of Sukh and Hushyar. In June, 1504, Bābur and his brother formed another army, composed of refugees from the Uzbeks, and secured Kabul, from which he would maintain himself until 1525. While at Kabul, Bābur came under the influence of Persian culture, traces of which can be found in his poetry.

From Kabul, Bābur conducted unsuccessful raids in central Asia and northwestern India. In January, 1505, Bābur made his expedition to Hindustan in search of badly needed supplies. Bābur, at the invitation of Husain Baiqara, who died soon afterward, marched on Herāt against Shaybānī Khān but returned to Kabul, because he was not prepared for the fierce winter. In June, 1507, Herāt surrendered to Shaybānī Khān. Meanwhile, Bābur's uncle, Muhammad Hussayn, had proclaimed Bābur's cousin Khan Mīrzā lord of Kabul in Bābur's absence.

After suppressing this rebellion by attacking the rebels without warning in the streets of Kabul, Bābur decided to gain possession of Qandahār, which was strategically important. Thus, when the Arghun princes in Qandahār asked Bābur for military assistance, he rushed to their aid. He had not traveled very far, though, before the Arghun princes changed their minds and decided to oppose Bābur. After defeating them in combat, Bābur learned that Shaybānī Khān was preparing to attack Qandahār. Instead of meeting Shaybānī Khān in combat, Bābur took a more prudent though admittedly less courageous course: He undertook his second invasion of India in 1507. During his return to Kabul, Bābur decided to change his title from *mīrzā* (prince) to *padishah* (emperor).

Three years later, Bābur conquered Samarkand for the third time by taking advantage of the political situation at the time. Shaybānī Khān's dispute with the Persian Shah Esmā'īl erupted into warfare. In 1510, Esmā'īl lured Shaybānī Khān from his refuge at Marv and slew him. As a result, the Uzbeks withdrew to Transoxiana. Elated by Esmā'īl's victory, Bābur sent Khan Mīrzā to thank him. Esmā'īl responded by returning Bābur's sister whom Bābur had given in marriage to Shaybānī Khān years before.

As a client of Esmā'īl, Bābur lost much of his popular support among the Mughals. Because Esmā'īl would not allow Bābur to break his pact, Bābur believed that the most expedient thing to do was to give lip service to the Shī'ite creed while remaining faithful to the Sunni doctrine. Years later, he was to prove the sincerity of his beliefs by writing a lengthy religious poem.

In 1511, Bābur once again invaded Samarkand and was pronounced king in 1511. Yet Bābur's reign as ruler of Samarkand proved to be short-lived. The Uzbeks, who were determined to remain in Transoxiana, encountered and defeated Bābur's forces at Kul-i-Malik. Bābur retreated to Hisar. He managed to solidify his hold on Badakhshān by placing his cousin, Khan Mīrzā, on the throne, but he relinquished all hope of reascending the throne of Samarkand. Instead, he occupied himself between 1515 and 1518 by waging wars in every direction in order to force the mountain dwellers of Kabul and Ghazni to fear and respect him.

Life's Work

The second phase of Bābur's career—his invasion and conquest of Hindustan—began only after he had finally relinquished his boyhood dream of conquering Samarkand. In a sense, Bābur decided to assimilate into his empire people who were not of Indo-Aryan stock because he considered the Hindu Kush to be his lawful heritage, passed down to him from his ancestor

Tamerlane, who had established his rule in all the country between the Oxus and the Indus on his passage to India. One could also say that Bābur compensated for his failure to conquer Samarkand by turning his attention toward India. While it is true that Bābur prepared the way for the Mughal Empire in India, his forays into India were really nothing more than a military preparation for the more permanent rule that would be established years later by his grandson.

Before Bābur could become lord of India, he had to dethrone the five Muslim and two pagan rulers who governed Hindustan. Bābur initiated this campaign in 1519, when he cemented an alliance with the Yusufzais by marrying the daughter of one of their chiefs. He concluded what he considered to be his first expedition into Hindustan by conquering Bhera but winning the hearts of its occupants by sparing their lives.

Owing to the dearth of details in Bābur's memoirs concerning the second, third, and fourth expeditions, it is with his fifth expedition that the history of Bābur's Hindustani campaigns continues. Bābur agreed to assist Dawlat Khān Lodī in deposing Lodī's kinsman, who ruled most of northern Hindustan. In return for Dawlat Khān Lodī's promise to regard Bābur as his sovereign, Bābur utterly defeated the army of Ibrāhīm Lodī near Lahore, which Bābur claimed for his own. This impetuous decision on Bābur's part brought his alliance with Dawlat Khān Lodī to an abrupt end. Bābur quickly formed another alliance with 'Ālam Khān, the uncle of Ibrāhīm Lodī, who offered to cede Lahore to Bābur if Bābur helped him conquer Delhi. Bābur hoped that by substituting 'Ālam Khān for Ibrāhīm Lodī, he would not only be given the legitimate right to Lahore but also have control over 'Ālam Khān, who was old and feeble. Thus, Bābur ordered his soldiers to assist 'Ālam Khān in the assault on Delhi, but he decided that his presence was more sorely needed at Balkh, which Esmā'īl was defending against the Uzbeks. Dawlat Khān Lodī then seized the opportunity to recover Lahore by offering to help 'Ālam Khān conquer Delhi. After failing to take Delhi, Dawlat Khān Lodī's army scattered in disorder, so he and his son retreated to the fortress of Milwat, where they surrendered. Dawlat Khān Lodī died while being taken to the prison at Bhera.

Having secured Lahore, Bābur began his campaign to conquer Delhi. Aware of the political advantages of having the loyalty of an Afghan prince, Bābur gave 'Ālam Khān a command at Panipat and Khanua. Bābur then marched on Delhi with his eighteen-year-old son, Humāyūn, who led the forces that defeated the armies of one of Ibrāhīm Lodī's emirs. Taking a defensive position at Panipat, Bābur's Mughals utterly defeated the vastly superior numbers of Afghan forces by flanking them with arrows and bombarding them with gunfire from the front. At the battle's end, Ibrāhīm Lodī was dead, and Bābur had reached his greatest goal: the conquest of northern India. As soon as he made his grand entrance into Delhi, he won the favor of the people by preventing his soldiers from looting and by taking the wives and children of the Rajah of Gwalior under his protection. On April 27, 1526, a week after his arrival at Delhi, Bābur was proclaimed Emperor of Hindustan in the Grand Mosque.

The founding of Bābur's vast empire in Hindustan, which began with the capture of Lahore in 1524, was completed in six years. With his victory at Panipat, most of the Afghan chiefs united under Bābur's rule. Bābur most likely restricted his conquests to northern India because of his reluctance to offend Esmā'īl by attacking Persian territory.

Bābur's death cannot be attributed to only one cause. From boyhood, he had suffered from a troublesome lesion, and throughout his adult life he was stricken with bouts of marsh fever. His body was further weakened by his intemperate ways, particularly his fondness for wine. He also became seriously ill as the result of an attempted poisoning by the mother of Ibrāhīm Lodī. His eventual death is enshrouded in mystery and legend. In the year 1530, when Bābur's son Humāyūn was attacked with fever, Bābur prayed that God would accept his life in exchange for that of his son. Coincidentally, Bābur was taken ill as his son slowly recovered, and he died three months later in Āgra on December 26, 1530. Several years later, his body was moved to its present location at Kabul.

Summary

Bābur is a prime example of a class of political entrepreneurs who vied with other seminomadic rulers from central Asia for revenues from the herdsmen and territory. Like his rivals and enemies, Bābur's kingdom was linked and sometimes divided by the loyalties of clan and family, not by treaties of national states. He was also typical of the rulers of that time in the savagery he displayed during battle.

Even though Bābur was born to the ruling class, he maintained and increased his kingdom as a result of his own adaptability and courage. He was a resourceful general who learned about musketry and artillery from the Uzbeks; he then applied these methods with great success against the lords of Hindustan. Thus, he became one of the first military commanders in Asia to realize the full potential of artillery. Bābur was a skillful diplomat, who prepared Hindustan for conquest by playing the emirs of Ibrāhīm Lodī against one other. He also performed the seemingly impossible task of molding an array of fiercely independent and competitive bands of Mongols into a nation by employing a prudent blend of force and kindness. In addition, he displayed moral courage as he risked the disapproval of other Sunni Muslims in his decision to appease Esmā'īl by adopting the Qizilbash headdress for himself and his soldiers. In addition, Bābur's custom of showing mercy to his defeated enemies endeared him to the people he conquered. While Bābur inherited some of the barbaric ways of the descendants of Tamerlane, he differed from most of the Mongol rulers of the sixteenth century in his love of beauty. An accomplished poet and diarist, Bābur composed works which rank with the best literature written at that time.

Bibliography

Bābur. *The Bāburnāma*. Translated by Annette Susannah Beveridge. 2 vols. London: Luzac, 1921. An exciting and revealing first hand history of Bābur's life and times in his own words. This is the primary source for most of the biographies that have followed.

Brown, F. Yeats. *Pageant of India*. Philadelphia: Macrae Smith, 1942. A brief biographical sketch of Bābur's life, heavily laced with quotations from Bābur's memoirs. Provides interesting anecdotes, especially regarding the assassination attempt by the mother of Ibrāhām Lodī.

Burn, Richard, ed. *The Cambridge History of India*. Vol. 4, *The Mughal Period*. New York: Macmillan, 1937. Chapter 1 is an excellent summation of Bābur's life. Although the chapter emphasizes his military campaigns, it also provides historical background, sketching the personalities who had an important influence on Bābur's life.

Grenard, Fernand. *Baber: First of the Moguls*. New York: Robert McBride, 1930. Based entirely on Bābur's memoirs, this is a biased but highly readable account of his life. The fanciful story line is enhanced by the reproduction of sixteenth century paintings.

Lewis, B. "Bābur." In *Encyclopaedia of Islam*, edited by B. Lewis, Ch. Pellat, and J. Schacht. Leiden, the Netherlands: Brill, 1959. This concise treatment of Bābur's life concentrates almost exclusively on his military conquests, paying little attention to his personal life.

Williams, L. F. Rushbrook. *An Empire Builder of the Sixteenth Century*. London: Longmans, Green, 1918. A standard biography covering Bābur's entire life. Beautifully illustrated with paintings from the period. The book refrains from romanticizing Bābur's life, opting for the objective approach instead. Recommended for the serious student of Bābur's life and of this period of Mughal history.

Alan Brown

JOHANN SEBASTIAN BACH

Born: March 21, 1685; Eisenach, Germany
Died: July 28, 1750; Leipzig, Germany
Area of Achievement: Music
Contribution: For three hundred years, Bach has brought joyful, profound, and uplifting music to millions of people the world over. So significant was his contribution to musical composition that some historians classify music history as "before Bach" and "after Bach."

Early Life

Johann Sebastian Bach was born in the shadow of Wartburg Castle, in the spring of 1685 in Eisenach, a few miles from where his great fellow composer, George Frideric Handel, was born in the same year. Bach came from seven generations of musically talented Bachs and so was born into an extended family of competent musicians. Bach's father was a court musician for the Duke of Eisenach and several of his close relatives were organists in the larger nearby churches. His eldest brother was apprenticed to the famous Johann Pachelbel.

Bach was only nine years old when his mother died, and his father died the following year. Consequently, in 1695, he moved thirty miles to Ohrdruf to live with his brother, the organist at St. Michael's Church. He continued his musical education and began studying New Testament Greek and other basic subjects at the cloister school. His brother, an excellent musician, taught him keyboard techniques and worked with him on the construction of a new organ. Very early, Bach became interested in the harmonic structure underlying the melodies he copied from manuscripts.

In March of 1700, Bach, at the age of fifteen, walked two hundred miles with a fellow student to the ancient northern German city of Lüneburg to attend the Knights' Academy, a school of practical education for young noblemen. The curriculum included courtly dancing, fencing and riding, and the study of feudal law, politics, and history. Young Bach had the ability to read music at first sight and supported himself largely by singing and playing the organ.

Bach broadened his experiences while at Lüneburg. More than once he walked the thirty miles to Hamburg to hear two of the largest organs in the world. The great organist Johann Reincken was in Hamburg, and Dietrich Buxtehude in Lübeck. Bach also observed a French community of Huguenot exiles; music was a focal point of their lives, and Bach heard French instrumental music performed by French orchestras, which enhanced his knowledge of German and Italian musical forms.

Life's Work

In 1703, Bach was ready for his first career appointment; he found it with the installation of a new organ in the old church at Arnstadt, a small city of lovely, tree-lined streets some twenty-five miles from Eisenach. His salary was substantial enough to enable him to purchase a harpsichord, several books, and clothing that befitted his new position. His duties as church organist were light, but his choir, he said, consisted of "a band of ruffians."

Bach's early compositions, as might be expected, were marked by immaturity. Perhaps his best organ work of this period was the serene *Pastorale in F Major*, characterized by its "free flow and logical unfolding of melody." At Arnstadt, Bach also wrote his first cantata, later revised, *For Thou Wilt Not Leave My Soul in Hell*. His continuous melody creates a musical soliloquy of the text.

Needing greater depth to his musical experience, Bach, in the autumn of 1705, received a one-month leave of absence to observe and listen to the great Dietrich Buxtehude in Lübeck. Bach was impressed with Buxtehude's arrangement of cantatas in his Vesper Concerts, sung as dialogues between soloists and the chorus. When, after four months, Bach finally returned to Arnstadt, he brought fresh ideas with him and began ornamenting his organ playing with coloratura and countermelodies.

In 1707, Bach left Arnstadt to become organist at St. Blaise Church in Mühlhausen. That same year, at twenty-three years of age, he married his second cousin, Maria Barbara. At Mühlhausen Bach gained valuable technical experience in overseeing the repair of the aged organ in the church. He was also called upon to write music for various civic occasions, such as the cantata *God Is My King*, calling for a brass ensemble, two woodwind ensembles, a string section, and two separate choirs.

The Duke of Saxe-Weimar, Wilhelm Ernst, appointed Bach chamber musician and court organist in 1708 and, later, his concertmaster. The duke doubled Bach's salary as he entered a completely different social world. Bach loved the melodic warmth and intensity of Italian music and moved more into that style. His cousin, Johann Gottfried Walther (1684-1748), was his close companion, and he and Bach developed musical theory together. Both were particularly interested in the philosophical values underlying music, believing music a gift from God and of great spiritual importance. Bach wrote many dances and loved joyful music.

During the Weimar years, Bach composed some of the greatest organ music ever written. He perfected his technique of counterpoint and mastered the relation between melodic and harmonic considerations in his writing of counterpoint. The Bachs had six children born to them at Weimar, two of whom (twins) died at birth.

Bach's fame spread throughout Germany, more as a performing musician than as a composer. In 1717, Prince Leopold of Köthen appointed Bach his court conductor, and Bach entered a creative, relaxed period of his life. As *Kapellmeister*, Bach was left alone to create as he saw fit. The twenty-three-year-old Prince Leopold loved music and understood it well. Unfortunately, most of his work from the Köthen years is lost, but Bach captured the vitality of that pleasant place in the *Brandenburg Concertos* and in *The Well-Tempered Clavier*, both written in Köthen.

Bach's relaxed, joyful life-style was marred by two tragedies. In 1719 his young son, one-year-old Leopold Augustus, died, and the next year while he was traveling with the prince in northern Germany, his wife suddenly died. In December, 1721, Bach, age thirty-six, married Anna Magdalena Wilcken, age twenty. Anna had a lovely soprano voice and Bach often wrote music for her to sing. They were devoted to each other and often worked together, since they both earned their living as musicians at the Köthen court. Of the thirteen children that Anna bore, seven died as infants. Altogether Bach had twenty children, ten of whom survived to adulthood.

Bach spent the last twenty-seven years of his life in Leipzig, Germany, writing church music of such quality that it continues to be performed. Bach did not want to leave Köthen, but his main purpose in life was not yet complete. Years before, he had written that his chief goal in life was to write "well-conceived and well-regulated church music to the glory of God." To realize his creative ideas for church music and to provide a better education for his sons at St. Thomas School, Bach took a 75 percent reduction in salary and relinquished his post of court musician to take up one of the most famous cantorships in Germany.

Bach's principal responsibilities revolved around St. Thomas Church and the St. Thomas School. Leipzig was an imperial free city, so it had no princely court and, thus, no court orchestra. The town musicians were used at both church and civic events. Since the Lutheran church was the established church, the government officials on the city council of Leipzig had the responsibility of securing a music director for all musical activities in the four churches of Leipzig. Bach had to compose or select the music and plan the musical part of the liturgy. He personally directed his music on alternate Sundays at St. Thomas Church and at St. Nicholas Church.

As director of music, Bach also composed cantatas for festive civic occasions such as the visit of royalty or the birthdays of leading citizens of the town. His office also made him cantor of St. Thomas School, in charge of teenage boys. He called the boys for the opening of classes at 6:00 A.M., taught several classes, and had prayers with them at 8:00 P.M. He also visited the sick in the school hospital next to the church.

Weak-sighted for years, partly because of overwork and poor lighting, Bach was almost blind by 1749. The next year, after two strokes, Bach died in Leipzig at the age of sixty-five. In a most fitting culmination of his life and calling, his final work was the chorale *Before Thy Throne I Now Appear*. Bach's joyful legacy continues to inspire and refresh countless thousands three hundred years later.

Summary

Portraits of Johann Sebastian Bach from young man to old all reveal the same serious demeanor, intelligent eyes, cheerful disposition, determined lips, and kindly face. He loved life, his family, his music, and his God, and his works demonstrate as much. He wrote cheerful dances as well as joyful church music, because he separated neither his life nor his music into sacred and secular categories, but saw the purpose of all music as for "the glory of God and the re-creation of the human spirit."

Bach enjoyed life. His wives and children loved him, and he helped them develop their varied musical talents. All of his children, he believed, were born musicians and he could put on a vocal and instrumental concert with his own family alone. He wrote many songs of love for his wives. Bach was "temperate, industrious, devout, a home lover and a family man; genuine, hospitable, and jovial. Frugality and discipline ruled in the Bach home, also unity, laughter, loyalty, and love."

Three categories of musical performance were common in Bach's time: church music, theatrical, and chamber. Bach's eleven hundred compositions fall into the first and last categories. His instrumental concertos, suites, and overtures were mostly for drawing-room performance. His three hundred church cantatas were his "musical sermons" and consciously sought to complement the spoken word and illumine the liturgy. Bach composed five entire yearly sets of cantatas. His passions and oratorios are musical dramas full of action and events, more dramatic than much that was written for the theater.

Although Bach lived his entire life in Germany, he quickly learned other national styles of music and incorporated them into his compositions: from France, delicate dance suites and restrained instrumental music; from Germany, particularly the fugue; from Italy, melodic and dramatic operatic music and the vocal motets of the Renaissance.

Bach's library reveals something of his thinking and attitude toward life. The eighty-one volumes that Bach owned all dealt with theological and religious subjects, and Bach used them in finding the precise wording he wanted for his lyrics. He personally selected the 141 Scripture verses in *The Saint Matthew Passion* and took equal care in planning the musical composition.

Many appreciate and love *Jesu, Joy of Man's Desiring*, *Sheep May Safely Graze*, and Bach's glorious *Christmas Oratorio* as great art, but to understand them one must realize the spiritual view of life that motivated Johann Sebastian Bach. His belief in the reality of eternity caused his music to be timeless.

Bibliography

Chiapusso, Jan. *Bach's World*. Bloomington: Indiana University Press, 1968. A readable, thorough biography of Johann Sebastian Bach with attention given to the cultural and historical setting in which Bach composed his music. Both topically and chronologically arranged. The author obviously understands musical philosophy underlying musical composition, and his knowledge is applied to Bach's work.

David, Hans T., and Arthur Mendel, eds. *The Bach Reader: A Life of Johann Sebastian Bach in Letters and Documents*. New York: W. W. Norton, 1945, rev. ed. 1966. Following a twenty-four-page "Portrait in Outline," many of the letters and other documents written by Bach are available. A lengthy section is entitled "Bach as Seen by His Contemporaries."

Dowley, Tim. *Bach: His Life and Times*. Neptune City, N.J.: Paganiniana Publications, 1981. A large, profusely illustrated book of less than 150 pages. Arranged chronologically. Tells the story of Bach's life in a succinct, interesting manner. The many well-chosen illustrations help make an absorbing tale. A fascinating introduction to the subject.

Heckscher, Martin A., et al. *The Universal Bach: Lectures Celebrating the Tercentenary of Bach's Birthday*. Philadelphia: American Philosophical Society, 1986. An interesting collection of essays written for the three hundredth birthday of Bach under the auspices of the Basically Bach Festival of Philadelphia. The five essays examine such topics as Bach's musical symbolism, Bach as a musical scholar, and Bach as biblical interpreter.

Schweitzer, Albert. *J. S. Bach*. 2 vols. New York: Macmillan, 1950. A profoundly intellectual but sensitive biography by an eminent Bach scholar. Bach's techniques of composition are examined in an erudite fashion.

Terry, Charles Sanford. *Bach: A Biography*. 2d ed. London: Oxford University Press, 1933. One of the oldest "modern" biographies of Bach. Tends to be dry and somewhat wordy, but carefully accurate. An interesting feature is its section of seventy-six photographs of places where Bach lived and worked. Taken in the early twentieth century, they are themselves an important historical record.

William H. Burnside

KARL ERNST VON BAER

Born: February 29, 1792; Piep, near Jerwen, Estonia
Died: November 28, 1876; Dorpat, Estonia
Areas of Achievement: Biology, anthropology, and geology
Contribution: Baer gained his greatest fame early in his career through his discovery of the mammalian egg and his contributions to the understanding of embryological development. In his later years, Baer would turn his attention to anthropological investigations, including the state of primitiveness of various races, and to geological studies, especially in Russia.

Early Life

In the mid-sixteenth century, an ancestor of Karl Ernst von Baer emigrated from Prussia to Livonia, and one of that ancestor's descendants bought an estate in Estonia during the mid-seventeenth century. He was made a member of the Prussian nobility, and by the time of Karl's father, Magnus Johann von Baer, the estate at Piep was of modest size. Karl's father was trained in law and served as a public official. Karl's parents were first cousins, and they had seven daughters and three sons. Because of the large size of the family, Karl was sent to live with his father's childless brother and wife on a nearby estate. It was there that Karl began to cultivate his love of botany and natural history.

He entered medical school at the University of Dorpat in 1810 but apparently never planned on a medical career. Instead, upon graduation, he continued his studies in Berlin, Vienna, and finally Würzburg. There he studied under the anatomist Ignaz Döllinger, a disciple of the German Romantic Friedrich Schelling, and was inspired to devote himself to the study of comparative embryology. In 1819, Baer finally received an appointment as an anatomy professor at Königsberg, where he stayed until 1834. That allowed him to marry Auguste von Medem, a resident of Königsberg, on January 1, 1820. They had five sons, of whom one died in childhood and a second of typhus at the age of twenty-one, and one daughter.

During Baer's tenure at Königsberg, he established himself as a brilliant embryologist and made his initial discoveries of the mammalian egg. His initial contributions are found in the first two volumes of Karl Friedrich Burdach's *Die Physiologie als Erfahrungswissenschaft* (1826-1828; physiology as empirical science). A small brochure entitled *De ovi mammalium et hominis genesis epistola* (1827; *The Discovery of the Mammalian Egg*, 1956) appeared at about the same time. In 1834, he left Königsberg for the Academy of Sciences in St. Petersburg, and in 1837 the still-unfinished second volume of his animal embryology was published, with the two volumes now entitled *Über Entwickelungsgeschichte der Thiere* (1828-1837; on the developmental history of animals). A portion of the missing material for this volume was published posthumously in 1888.

Life's Work

While at the University of Würzburg, Baer was encouraged by Döllinger and Christian Heinrich Pander to continue the largely unknown work of Caspar Friedrich Wolff concerning the detailed development of the hen's egg. Baer expanded that research to include a wide range of organisms, and the results of his studies virtually assured the epigeneticists of victory in their battle with the preformationists. He was the first to discover and describe the mammalian egg (first found in Burdach's house dog), and he concluded that "every animal which springs from the coition of male and female is developed from an ovum, and none from a simple formative liquid." This important theoretical statement, although based on German *Naturphilosophie* and rejected by later embryologists in the vitalistic terms understood by Baer, allowed for reproductive and embryological studies to continue on a doctrinally unified basis and hence permitted the development of comparative embryology as a discipline.

In addition to describing mammalian and other vertebrate ova, Baer described the developing embryo. One of his major conceptual innovations was that he could see the individual organism as a historical entity which underwent a developmental process. He thus examined organisms at various stages of development, and he was one of the first to describe the process in terms of the formation of germ layers and the gradual production of organs and body parts. Conducting research for the second volume of his monumental work, he examined and compared the developmental processes of different organisms. In the process, he discovered the notochord (the flexible supportive rod ventral to the nerve chord, which is characteristic of all chordates) in the chicken embryo, explained the significance of the gill slits and gill arches, which Martin Rathke had earlier discovered in the embryo, and then explained the cause of the amnion formation. Finally, he described the development of the urogenital system, the formation of the lungs, the development of the digestive canal, and the formation of the nervous system. These findings are detailed and commented on in his pioneering *Über Entwickelungsgeschichte der Thiere*.

Baer is best known for his remarks in the fifth scholium of this work, in which he argued against a single *scala naturae* (chain of being), presented a parody of Jean-Baptiste de Monet, chevalier de Lamarck, rejected evolution in any form as well as the idea that embryos of higher animals pass through the adult forms of the lower animals, and proposed his own laws of individual development. His comparative embryology had led him to the same conclusions that Georges Cuvier's comparative anatomy had produced, that is, that instead of a single chain of being, there were essentially four animal types. He further argued that comparative embryology actually provided better data than did comparative anatomy for classifying animals. Baer's method for classifying organisms was based on the fact that all animal embryos begin as a single fertilized egg. According to Baer, they diverged immediately into one of four types of development. Vertebrate embryos can be distinguished from the annulate embryos (essentially worms), which in turn are different from the embryos of the mollusks, and all of which differ from the radiata (echinoderms).

In addition, Baer argued that the more general traits of the group of animals to which an embryo belongs appear earlier in individual development than the specialized characteristics, that the more general form always precedes a more specialized form, that every embryo of a given form, rather than passing through the stages of other forms, instead diverges more and more from them, and that, as a result, the embryo of a higher form never resembles the adult of lower animals but only the embryonic form of those animals. He concluded that development takes place from homogeneous and general to heterogeneous and special and that ontological development reflects divergence from other forms rather than parallelism or recapitulation. With this latter conclusion, he thus argued against Johann Meckel's law of parallel development and against Ernst Haeckel's biogenetic law of ontogeny recapitulating phylogeny.

With the publication of the second volume of *Über Entwickelungsgeschichte der Thiere* in 1837, Baer had transformed embryology into a modern laboratory science. Moreover, he had produced a theoretical framework that would greatly influence evolutionary thought even though he would strongly maintain a lifelong antievolutionary position. Charles Darwin, for example, used embryological evidence to support his theory and noted that he agreed with Baer's view of divergence rather than the competing doctrine of recapitulation. Darwin also used Baer's standard for judging an organism to be "higher" than another as being related to the degree of differentiation of parts and specialization of function.

By the time the second volume of his great embryological work was published, Baer had left Königsberg for reasons that are not well understood and had settled in St. Petersburg, working at the Academy of Sciences. In 1846, he took a position with the academy in comparative anatomy and physiology, a decision that was related to his long-term interest in anthropology. Under the academy's auspices, he made a number of expeditions to such places as Novaya Zemlya, Lapland, the North Cape, and other regions of Russia as well as England and continental Europe. He collected specimens and made a number of geological discoveries. Although none of his work in these areas was as significant as his embryological achievements, he was instrumental in the founding of the Society of Geography and Ethnology of St. Petersburg and became a cofounder of the German Anthropological Society.

Baer retired from the academy in St. Petersburg in 1862 because of increasing problems with his vision and hearing. In 1867, he went to Dorpat, where he continued his studies and writing until 1876, when he died at the age of eighty-four.

Summary

Karl Ernst von Baer's contributions to the fledgling science of embryology in the nineteenth century were immeasurable. Methodologically and conceptually he provided the basis for further research. Yet apart from his empirical findings, little remains in modern biology of Baer's embryology. His adherence to German Idealism and *Naturphilosophie*, including the use of vitalistic explanations in embryological development, and his fervent anti-evolutionary position caused many scientists in the latter part of the century to ignore him. Nevertheless, his contributions were viewed as monumental during his time. He published more than three hundred papers on topics ranging from embryology and entomology to anthropology, Russian fisheries, and the routes of Odysseus' voyage. He was honored and respected by scientists throughout the world, and admired and loved for his loyalty and wit by his Estonian neighbors.

Bibliography

Baer, Karl Ernst von. *Autobiography of Karl Ernst von Baer.* Edited by Jane Oppenheimer. Translated by H. Schneider. Canton, Mass.: Science History, 1986. This relatively long autobiography was first published by the Estonian Knights in 1864 on the golden jubilee of Baer's doctorate. Oppenheimer provides a very helpful preface. An extensive bibliography and an index make this work a valuable tool for the serious student.
Coleman, William. *Biology in the Nineteenth Century: Problems of Form, Function, and Transformation.* New York: Cambridge University Press, 1977. Chapter 3 provides an excellent context for Baer's embryological work as it details the advances in cytology, explains the arguments between preformationists and epigeneticists, and describes the contributions that Baer made to the understanding of ontogeny.
Lovejoy, Arthur O. "Recent Criticism of the Darwinian Theory of Recapitulation: Its Grounds and Its Initiator." In *Forerunners of Darwin, 1745-1859*, edited by Bentley Glass et al. Baltimore: Johns Hopkins University Press, 1968. Lovejoy tries to explain why so many misread Baer. Explains Baer's four embryological laws, including what is and what is not affirmed. Examines Darwin's misreading of Baer and Baer's fallacies in his criticism of Darwin's theory. The notes provide helpful explanations.
Oppenheimer, Jane. "An Embryological Enigma in the *Origin of Species.*" In *Forerunners of Darwin, 1745-1859*, edited by Bentley Glass et al.

Baltimore: Johns Hopkins University Press, 1968. Oppenheimer explores the professional relationship between Darwin and Baer. She examines the various ideas that each developed independently of the other and the diverse ways in which each incorporated these ideas into a total system. As a result, one understands how Darwin can use many of Baer's findings while rejecting his conclusion, and why Baer is unable to support Darwin's evolutionary position.

Ospovat, Dov. "The Influence of Karl Ernst von Baer's Embryology, 1828-1859." *Journal of the History of Biology* 9 (Spring, 1976): 1-28. This article discusses the degree of influence that Baer's embryological explanations had during his own life, especially in terms of their ability to dislodge the earlier theory of recapitulation. In the process, it clarifies the content of Baer's theories and shows the similarities to other theories then available as well as describes the essential points of difference between them. Ospovat also explains why he disagrees with some of the Baerean scholarship, including the articles by Oppenheimer and Lovejoy cited above.

Winsor, Mary P. *Starfish, Jellyfish, and the Order of Life: Issues in Nineteenth Century Science.* New Haven, Conn.: Yale University Press, 1976. While this book is not specifically about Baer, it is concerned with the issues and debates which surrounded his work and the work of other embryologists, comparative anatomists, taxonomists, and proponents of evolution. For that reason, it provides the scientific and philosophical context for understanding Baer.

Sara Joan Miles

MIKHAIL BAKUNIN

Born: May 30, 1814; Premukhino, Russia
Died: July 1, 1876; Bern, Switzerland
Areas of Achievement: Philosophy and social reform
Contribution: Bakunin was the foremost anarchist of his time. A relentless revolutionary agitator, he wrote prolifically and inspired a political movement which survived well into the twentieth century.

Early Life

Mikhail Aleksandrovich Bakunin was born into a noble Russian family in 1814. The oldest male child in a large family, Bakunin enjoyed an especially close relationship with his four sisters, born between 1811 and 1816. His parents' marriage seems to have been a good one, and Bakunin's childhood, by all accounts, was outwardly happy. A small landowner, Bakunin's father had become a doctor of philosophy at the University of Padua in Italy. He instilled in Bakunin an appreciation of the encyclopedists and the ideas of Jean-Jacques Rousseau. Ultimately, Bakunin would retain traces of both of these influences, elevating reason over faith and advocating a social philosophy which carried Rousseau's emphasis on individual consent to radical lengths.

Bakunin was sent to artillery school in St. Petersburg at the age of fourteen. He eventually was granted a commission and was posted to a military unit on the Polish frontier. The military life was not for Bakunin, and in 1835, he bolted from his unit, narrowly avoiding arrest and certain disgrace for desertion. His disdain for authority now established, Bakunin began the study of German philosophers such as Johann Gottlieb Fichte and Georg Wilhelm Friedrich Hegel and spent time in Moscow, where he became acquainted with Vissarion Grigoryevich Belinsky, advocate of the poor, and Aleksandr Herzen, a reform-minded journalist. In 1840, Bakunin journeyed to Berlin to continue his education. There, he was further influenced toward political radicalism by his contact with some of the Young Hegelians.

This atmosphere of unlimited potential for change fastened Bakunin into a career of revolutionary activism. In 1842, having moved to Dresden, Bakunin published his first theoretical work in a radical journal, concluding it with what remains his most famous aphorism: "The passion for destruction is also a creative passion." A vigorous young man with a charismatic presence, Bakunin had come of age. His education continued as he journeyed to Paris, where he met Pierre-Joseph Proudhon and Karl Marx. Bakunin's concerns would expand to include everything from national liberation for the Slavic peoples to social revolution on a global scale.

Life's Work

Bakunin began his revolutionary career in earnest during the Revolution of

1848, a series of uprisings by workers which took place in a number of European cities. Bakunin took part in street fighting during the Paris uprising, which began in February. He then traveled to Germany and Poland in an effort to aid the Revolution's spread. In June of 1848, he was present at the Slav congress in Prague, which was brought to an unceremonious end by Austrian troops. Later that year, Bakunin produced his first major manifesto, *An Appeal to the Slavs*. In it, Bakunin cited the tradition of peasant insurrections in Russia as the model for more far-reaching social revolution throughout Europe.

In May, 1849, Bakunin took part in the Dresden insurrection. He was arrested by German authorities and imprisoned until 1851, when he was sent back to Russia. There, after six more years of imprisonment, Bakunin was released to live in Siberia. Prison life had weakened his health and perhaps even dampened his revolutionary spirit temporarily. In 1857, Bakunin married Antonia Kwiatkowski, the daughter of a Polish merchant. The marriage was curious in a number of ways. Antonia was in her teens, Bakunin in his mid-forties at the time of the marriage. Troubled by impotence, Bakunin reportedly never consummated the marriage. Antonia displayed no interest in politics and disliked Bakunin's revolutionary associates. She also appears to have been unfaithful to Bakunin. Yet the marriage lasted nearly twenty years. During that time, Antonia endured embarrassing financial straits, dislocation, and a variety of other disappointments, apparently serving as a comfort to her husband until his death.

In 1861, Bakunin managed to escape his exile in Siberia and traveled to London via Japan and the United States. In London, he renewed his acquaintance with Herzen. Herzen, however, was alienated both by Bakunin's political extremism and by his nearly complete disregard for the dictates of financial responsibility. In 1863, Bakunin tried to take part in the Polish insurrection, but got only as far as Sweden. The next year, Bakunin established himself in Italy, surrounding himself with a band of disciples and organizing a largely illusory network of secret revolutionary societies across Europe. In 1868, Bakunin relocated to Geneva, where he joined the First International, a federation of various working-class parties for world socialism. It was during this period that Bakunin quarreled with Marx, also a powerful member of the International. Though ideological disparities were undoubtedly a factor, much of the conflict was personal, with neither Marx nor Bakunin inclined to share power or the spotlight. In 1872, Marx managed to have Bakunin and his followers expelled from the International. The move ultimately destroyed the International and divided the revolutionary movement in Europe for decades.

Prior to this split, the Paris Commune was formed as a result of the Revolution of 1870. Bakunin played no direct role in bringing the Commune into existence, and its success was brief. Nevertheless, the Paris Commune constituted the peak of revolutionary achievement during the nineteenth century. In its rejection of conventional political organization, the Commune lent credibility to Bakunin's ideal of an anarchistic order based on voluntary compliance rather than obedience to laws, no matter how democratically they might be derived.

The last years of Bakunin's life, spent in Switzerland, were marred by his brief association with Sergey Gennadiyevich Nechayev, an unscrupulous opportunist and nihilist, who gained Bakunin's favor. This association did little to improve the image of anarchists, and common usage often finds the words anarchist and nihilist treated as synonyms. Otherwise, Bakunin continued to work on a variety of projects, attracted disciples, and wrote. His health and financial situation grew worse, but Bakunin continued working, convinced that the Revolution, though it must wait a decade or two, would triumph eventually.

At the time of his death, Bakunin had written enough to fill volumes, but he never finished a single major work. The fragments that he left behind were ill organized and often unfocused. Thus, where Bakunin far surpassed his rival Marx in terms of direct political action, Marx clearly won the battle of theory, leaving an unfinished but nevertheless impressive body of written work that would inspire successful revolutionary movements as well as a broad array of scholars. Bakuninism also survived but was based more on legend than on the written word.

For Bakunin, the very essence of humanity lay in thought and rebellion. Thought, or science, allowed human beings to understand the world around them in a way that other animals could never approach. Rebellion, or freedom, allowed human beings to exercise thought rather than blindly follow external authorities. To accept religious or political authority was, for Bakunin, to be less than fully human. The full development of humanity, in turn, demanded thoroughgoing social revolution, which would erase all manner of legal tyranny, class domination, and privilege, opening the way for true community.

This mandated not only exposing the bogus foundations of religion and the state but also using mass violence to overthrow established governments once they had been discredited. Bakunin disagreed with Marx on the use of political power to consolidate the gains of revolution. Marx believed that a dictatorship of the proletariat would be needed temporarily (though just how temporarily he did not say) in order to avoid counterrevolution. Bakunin's principled anarchism would not allow this compromise: All political power was tyrannical in Bakunin's eyes, even that exercised in the name of the working class. Bakunin's was a social or communitarian anarchism: Freedom and authority would no longer be at odds with each other. The result, according to Bakunin, would be a splendid harmony, featuring spontaneous cooperation rather than coercion.

Summary

During his lifetime, Mikhail Bakunin established himself as a charismatic and energetic figure, one who can truly be said to have devoted himself to social revolution. This involved extraordinary hardships. Bakunin risked his life repeatedly, spent years in prison, and, except for his highly sporadic efforts to please Antonia, disregarded material possessions. He was thoroughly impoverished at the end of his life, dependent on friends for his survival. In addition to this life of direct revolutionary action and the sacrifices it entailed, Bakunin wrote tirelessly, producing thousands of pages of treatises, polemics, and letters.

Yet, for all of this, Bakunin has left behind a rather small footprint. Though anarchist movements remained a force in Italy and Spain through the 1930's, they rarely achieved major status and never achieved victory. Bakuninism never came to rival Marxism. Both have been overshadowed by nationalism, the greatest anathema of all to Bakunin's prescriptions regarding political authority.

Why has Bakunin's influence faded so completely? One reason is that he never achieved the theoretical depth or clarity that Marx did. Marx raised questions, in a systematic way, about history, economics, sociology, and politics which have remained vitally interesting to ideologues as well as to scholars. Bakunin's fragmentary and undisciplined writings could not do the same.

Still, Bakunin's accomplishments were considerable. He transformed a polite, drawing-room philosophy into a notable historical movement, raised pertinent questions about the unlimited power of revolutionary parties and regimes that have come to haunt twentieth century Marxists, and produced written work rich in imagery and ideas. Though they may strike many people as bizarre, these images and ideas reflect commonly held values extrapolated to uncommon lengths. Bakunin valued personal freedom, and he carried this value to a logical extreme. He also tried to honor his beliefs with a life devoted to unflinching action. In this respect, too, Bakunin was uncommon.

Bibliography

Avrich, Paul. *The Russian Anarchists*. Princeton, N.J.: Princeton University Press, 1967. Focuses on the fate of the Russian anarchists, Bakunin's closest political heirs, from the Revolution of 1905 to the movement's dissolution shortly after the triumph of Bolshevism in 1917.

Bakunin, Mikhail A. *The Political Philosophy of Bakunin: Scientific Anarchism*. Edited by G. P. Maximoff. New York: Free Press, 1953. Maximoff has carefully assembled a selection of Bakunin's written work, organizing sections according to topic. The result is more coherent and comprehensive than anything produced by Bakunin during his lifetime. Includes a helpful preface, an introduction, and a biographical sketch by three different Bakunin scholars.

Carr, E. H. *Michael Bakunin*. London: Macmillan, 1937. A straightforward biography, innocent of any discernible ideological agenda. Provides a balanced account of the conflict between Bakunin and Marx. Carr does not examine Bakunin's political philosophy in any detail.

Kelly, Aileen. *Mikhail Bakunin: A Study in the Psychology and Politics of Utopianism*. Oxford, England: Clarendon Press, 1982. Kelly tries to reconcile the polar images of Bakunin as champion of liberty, on one hand, and dictatorial confederate of the cynical and despotic Nechayev, on the other. She does so by showing the psychological link between absolute liberty and absolute dictatorship.

Masters, Anthony. *Bakunin: The Father of Anarchism*. New York: Saturday Review Press, 1974. A sympathetic view of Bakunin's life and work. Includes a chapter on the fate of Bakuninism in the hundred years or so following Bakunin's death.

Mendel, Arthur P. *Michael Bakunin: Roots of Apocalypse*. New York: Praeger, 1981. A haunting psychohistory, which reveals the dark side of Bakunin's revolutionary zeal, linking it to some very personal details in his life as well as the notion of Christian Apocalypse. Impassioned and controversial.

Pyziur, Eugene. *The Doctrine of Anarchism of Michael A. Bakunin*. Milwaukee: Gateway Press, 1955. Provides a clear and undoctrinaire exposition of Bakunin's political and social philosophy.

Wolff, Robert Paul. *In Defense of Anarchism*. New York: Harper & Row, 1970. Coming from a perspective far different from that of Bakunin, Wolff contends that, philosophically speaking, anarchism is defensible, since the authority of even a democratic state must come at the expense of individual autonomy. Most critics have considered the book subversively clever rather than profound, partly because Wolff lacks Bakunin's commitment to action.

Ira Smolensky

VASCO NÚÑEZ DE BALBOA

Born: 1475; Jeres de los Caballeros, Estremadura Province, Spain
Died: January, 1519; Acla, Castillo de Oro, Panama
Area of Achievement: Exploration
Contribution: Balboa was a Spanish conquistador who participated in the exploration and conquest of the Caribbean and the Central American mainland during the early sixteenth century. In 1513, he discovered the Pacific Ocean.

Early Life

Vasco Núñez de Balboa was born in 1475 in Jeres de los Caballeros in the Spanish province of Estremadura. Although part of the *hidalgo* class, Balboa's family was very poor. Thrilled by the reports of Christopher Columbus' voyages to the New World in 1492 and 1493, he drifted toward the vibrant atmosphere of Spain's port cities. He served eight years under Don Pedro Puertocarrero, Lord of Moguer, and acquired a reputation as an excellent fighter. In 1501, Balboa sailed to the New World under Don Pedro de Bastides, who discovered Barbados and sailed along the north coast of Tierra Firme (northern South America). The Bastides expedition terminated disastrously when his ships became infested with shipworms and eventually sank off the coast of Hispaniola (Haiti).

Balboa remained on Hispaniola to farm near Salvatierra, to mine for gold, and to fight Indians. He fell deeply into debt, and his creditors constantly harassed him for payments. As an Indian fighter, however, Balboa acquired great renown for his spirit and skill. Equally famous was Balboa's dog, the great "Leoncico" (little lion), that was noted for his ferocity in combat. Indeed, Leoncico was said to have been paid the equivalent of a captain's pay for his services.

Life's Work

At this time of his life (1510), Balboa was thirty-five years old, tall and well built, with red hair and blue eyes. He was charming and blessed with great energy and stamina. His presence on Hispaniola, however, had become untenable because of his creditors. Thus, in September, 1510, learning of an expedition bound for Tierra Firme under Martín Fernández de Enciso, Balboa arranged to have both himself and Leoncico smuggled on board in a large barrel. Once safely beyond Hispaniola, Balboa presented himself to an astonished and angry Enciso, who reluctantly allowed him to remain with the expedition.

Balboa became the key member of an extraordinary adventure in Latin American colonial history. In 1507, King Ferdinand V of Spain had given grants and powers to Diego de Nicuesa and Alonzo de Ojeda to explore and settle areas of Tierra Firme. Enciso was a lawyer and Ojeda's second-in-command, and he was expected to meet Ojeda at San Sebastian with supplies and reinforcements. At San Sebastian, Enciso learned that Ojeda, mortally wounded, had returned to Hispaniola, leaving behind forty-one near-starved survivors under Franciso Pizarro, later of Peruvian fame. San Sebastian was too difficult to hold in the face of Indian hostility, and Balboa suggested that they move to a more defensible site across the Bay of Urabá. Here, on the bank of the Darién River, Enciso established Santa María la Antigua del Darién, the first permanent settlement on the mainland.

Thereafter, Balboa's life was mired in political intrigue at Darién and the royal court. Enciso proved to be an arbitrary and unpopular leader, and settlers rallied behind the charismatic Balboa, who overthrew the petty tyrant. By spring, 1511, a three-way power struggle was under way. The Balboa-Enciso fight was complicated by the claims of Diego de Nicuesa, in whose grant Darién was mistakenly located. Nicuesa, however, was stranded and starving at Nombre de Dios. When supplies and news of the Darién colony arrived, he recovered and sought to impose his authority over the trespassers. Balboa led the resistance and sent Nicuesa away on a worm-infested vessel. Nicuesa was never seen alive again.

Balboa now moved aggressively on many fronts. He consolidated his authority over Darién and banished Enciso. He rescued the remaining survivors at Nombre de Dios, compelled settlers to grow crops and build homes, and pushed Spanish power into the interior. During these *entradas*, Balboa heard rumors of a great ocean to the south and of a great civilization in Peru. He also brought Franciscan priests to convert and baptize the Indians and to make them loyal subjects of the king.

Balboa discussed these events and other matters in an extraordinary letter to Ferdinand V in January, 1513. He provided a detailed description of the land and climate, and he defended himself against charges of usurpation of power and mistreatment of Indians. He noted the discoveries that he made, particularly gold mines, and rumors that a vast sea existed to the south. If he had only one thousand men, he wrote, he would bring the South Sea and all the gold mines under the dominion of the king.

In June, 1513, Balboa received contradictory news from Spain. He was made captain and interim governor of Tierra Firme, but he received stunning news that a new governor would soon replace him and that he would face arrest and trial for Nicuesa's death. Also, unknown to Balboa, Ferdinand sent a secret agent, Don Pedro de Arbolancha, to investigate affairs in Darién. Balboa's successor proved to be Don Pedro Arias Dávila (Pedrarias), an elderly, but iron-willed and cruel, military man. He left Apin in April, 1514, carrying *el requerimiento* (the requirement), a document designed to justify war with—and hegemony over—the natives.

To save himself, Balboa decided to find the South Sea. He left Darién on

September 1, 1513, with 190 men. It was a grueling and arduous ordeal. On September 25 or 27, 1513, however, Balboa reached the crest of a mountain and sighted the South Sea. He promptly made a formal act of possession in the name of Ferdinand V. On September 29, 1513, he reached the ocean's shore at the Gulf of San Miguel. The party remained in the area for several weeks, found pearl beds, and learned more about the Inca civilization to the south. On November 3, 1513, they began their return to Darién, which was accomplished without major incident on January 19, 1514. Among the cheering throng was the secret agent, Arbolancha, who determined that he would endorse Balboa's continued rule over the settlement.

Events occurred too rapidly, however, for Balboa to rescue himself from his enemies. Pedrarias arrived at Darién with the crushing news that he was governor of the province, now called Castillo de Oro (golden castle). Balboa, bitterly disappointed, nevertheless sought to make the transition in leadership successful. Matters, however, soured almost immediately. Pedrarias quickly implemented his instructions to hold a two-month-long *residencia* (investigation) of Balboa's conduct. Then Darién was hit with a devastating plague, and Pedrarias' men made savage and bloody forays among nearby Indian tribes, killing, enslaving, and stealing gold, silver, and food. Pedrarias allowed these activities to continue well into 1515, undoing Balboa's earlier work to secure these tribes' friendship and loyalty.

Meanwhile, Arbolancha's report induced Ferdinand to appoint Balboa Adelantado of the coast of the South Sea and of Panama and Coiba. Although Balboa remained under Pedrarias' authority, the latter became embittered and alarmed over the former's restored reputation. Accordingly, Balboa was arrested on a charge of conspiracy to rebel against Pedrarias and was kept in a cage in the latter's home. Finally, Balboa was released on the condition that he marry Pedrarias' daughter in Spain by proxy; once Pedrarias had consolidated his position with the marriage, he allowed Balboa to go to the Pacific coast and erect a shipbuilding yard.

Summary

During subsequent years, Vasco Núñez de Balboa and Pedrarias were wary of each other. Balboa was far the more popular of the two leaders. He took the nearby Pearl Islands and seemed intent in moving south against Peru. By late 1518, Pedrarias had had enough of Balboa and ordered him to Acla, where he arrested Balboa on a charge of treason. In January, 1519, Balboa and several of his associates were beheaded, and Balboa's head was placed on a pike and put on display in Acla's plaza.

Thus died Balboa, one of the greatest conquistadores for *los reyes católicos*, a man of humble origins who possessed attributes of greatness: bravery, valor, humility, and a sense of fairness. He provided the inspired leadership that placed Spain on the mainland of Central America, setting the stage for the great conquests to the north and south. His greatest achievement was the discovery of the Pacific Ocean, which reinforced the growing realization that Columbus had discovered a great barrier to the Asian market. The temporal and spiritual power of the Spanish Crown was rarely served better in the New World.

Bibliography

Anderson, Charles G. *Vida y cartas de Vasco Núñez de Balboa*. Buenos Aires: Emece Editoriales, 1944. A biographical account and a collection of correspondence relative to Balboa's life and career. Oriented toward the specialist. No English translation accompanies the text.

Méndez Pereira, Octavio. *El Tesoro del Dabaibe*. Panama: Talleres Gráficos "Benedetti," 1934. Presents Balboa as having been fair in his treatment of the Indians. Méndez Pereira was a Panamanian diplomat and educator.

Ober, Frederick A. *Vasco Núñez de Balboa*. New York: Hayes & Brothers, 1906. A volume of the Heroes of American History series; a popular account of Balboa's life.

Romoli, Kathleen. *Balboa of Darién: Discoverer of the Pacific*. Garden City, N.Y.: Doubleday, 1953. The best account of the life and career of Balboa. Very readable and scholarly. Sympathetic toward Balboa while giving an objective analysis of the men who served with and under him.

Strawn, Arthur. *The Golden Adventure of Balboa: Discoverer of the Pacific*. London: John Lane, 1929. Another useful though dated account of Balboa. Like Romoli, Strawn was a great admirer of Balboa as a warrior and as a diplomat.

Stephen P. Sayles

HONORÉ DE BALZAC

Born: May 20, 1799; Tours, France
Died: August 18, 1850; Paris, France
Area of Achievement: Literature
Contribution: Balzac's novels, assembled under the collective title *The Human Comedy*, form a literary monument composed of some ninety-five works, with more than two thousand characters, which provides a comprehensive survey and analysis of French society and culture at all levels during the first half of the nineteenth century.

Early Life

The son of a peasant, Bernard-François Balzac had risen in society to become the head of the hospital administration and deputy mayor of the town of Tours. His wife, Anne Laure Sallambier, was the daughter of an affluent merchant. At the time of their arranged marriage, he was fifty-one and she was nineteen. Perhaps understandably, the eccentric elderly husband and romantic (but soon bitter) young wife both engaged in extramarital affairs and were not always devoted parents. When their son Honoré was born in 1799, he was sent to a wet nurse and was joined two years later by his sister Laure. After spending the first four years of his life away from his mother, he lived at home until he was seven (though even during this period he attended boarding school and was only brought home on Sundays). At the age of eight, he was sent to the Collège de Vendôme for five years, partly to get him out of the way while his mother had a child by another man, during which time he later claimed never to have been visited by his parents. Many of his biographers see his perception of this early neglect, especially on the part of his mother, as one of the reasons that several of his early love affairs were with older women. These relationships, many of which developed into friendships that lasted for decades, may in turn account for the many portraits of strong, intelligent women in his novels.

Balzac studied law for three years, a knowledge of which later became useful to him as a novelist, but after passing his law examinations in 1819 he announced to his family his determination to become a writer. Despite their apparent coldness, his parents generously agreed to support him for a two-year trial period, during which he lived in a fifth-floor attic in Paris and wrote a five-act verse tragedy on Oliver Cromwell. The experiment was a failure, never produced or even published during his lifetime, but Balzac was committed to his new vocation and merely resolved to turn from the theater to journalism and novel writing to support himself.

He produced a series of novels under various pseudonyms over the next several years, all written in haste and many in collaboration with other hack writers. During this time he also borrowed large sums of money, much of it from his mother and mistress, to establish himself in business, first as a printer, then as a publisher, and eventually as a typefounder, the beginning of a life-long series of business failures. As a result of these speculative ventures as well as of an always extravagant life-style, he was heavily in debt throughout his life, despite a considerable income from his writing in later years.

Life's Work

In 1829, Balzac published *Les Chouans* (English translation, 1890), the first of his novels to have lasting merit and, significantly, the first published under his own name. Indeed, for his next novel, *La Peau de chagrin* (1831; *The Magic Skin*, 1888), the first of his masterpieces, he even embellished his name by the addition, before his surname, of the particle "de," a sign of nobility to which he was not entitled by law or birth. It is a sign of the esteem of posterity that his name has since been written invariably, if technically inaccurately, as "Honoré de Balzac."

As a result of the pressure to earn money created by his constant condition of indebtedness, Balzac's literary output reached staggering proportions. In the twenty years between 1830 and 1850, the period of his maturity as a writer, he produced some ninety-five novels, featuring more than two thousand characters, as well as several hundred short stories, essays, reviews, and plays. Even more remarkable than the sheer quantity of his work is its remarkably high quality. All but a handful of his novels are of the first rank. Balzac was able to produce so much good work only by virtue of his tremendous physical and mental vitality.

Balzac would begin a typical working day at midnight, when his servant would knock on his door to wake him. He always worked in a long white robe, similar to a monk's, at a table with candles, blank paper (of a slightly blue tinge—so as to tire his eyes less rapidly—and with an especially smooth surface that would allow him to write as quickly and effortlessly as possible), an inkwell, and several raven's quill pens. He never used any notes or books, having already fixed everything in his mind before writing. Balzac would then write for eight hours with no interruptions except for preparing and drinking large quantities of strong black coffee. At eight, he would have a light breakfast and a bath and send the night's work to the printer.

The composition of a novel had only just begun for Balzac at this stage. At about nine o'clock he would begin revising the proofs of the pages he had written the night before. His emendations and additions were often much longer than the text he was correcting, and he therefore required that his galleys be printed on large sheets, with the text occupying only a small square in the middle. After he had completely filled all the margins with scribbled changes, he would send them back to be reset. Even experienced compositors had difficulty deciphering these corrections, and even at double wages they would refuse to work more than an hour at a time on his proof sheets. When Balzac received the second revised galleys he would repeat the process, sometimes entirely rewriting a book in this manner fifteen or twenty times. Often the exorbitant cost of these typesetting charges would come out of his own fees, but his effort to make all of his work as nearly perfect as possible could never be compromised. He kept a copy of each of his books together with all the successive revisions, and these would often total two thousand pages for a two-hundred-page novel. Finally, toward five in the afternoon, he would finish the day's writing. He would then eat, perhaps see a friend, and plan the next night's writing. At eight he would go to bed, to be awakened again at midnight for another sixteen to eighteen hours of continuous labor.

Only a powerful constitution allowed him to carry out such a demanding work schedule, and Balzac was not the stereotypical delicate poet. Though only five feet, two or three inches tall, he was very strongly built, with a thick, muscular neck, broad shoulders, and a huge chest. His bulk made him an easy target for caricaturists, and most of the likenesses of Balzac that remain are caricatures, not only because of his build but also because he always insisted on attempting to dress in the latest, and invariably the least flattering, fashions, frequently carrying one of his famous gem-studded walking sticks. Despite his lack of what would normally be thought good looks and his absurd manner of dressing, Balzac was quite attractive to women because of his depth of understanding and the intensity of his personality, which immediately dominated any gathering at which he was present, an intensity that even his enemies admitted.

Balzac's workload certainly played a part in shortening his life—he died at the age of fifty-one—but in any given year or two he produced more lasting work than many of his contemporaries did in their entire careers. The huge scale of his achievement makes it impossible to represent or judge his work on the basis of one or two, or even a dozen, examples. Although *Le Père Goriot* (1835; *Father Goriot*, 1844) and *Eugénie Grandet* (1833; English translation, 1859) might be singled out as his best-known works, there are literally dozens of others of the same caliber. It is doubtful that any other writer has produced so much work of such consistent quality, a consistency that extends over the full twenty years of his maturity. Early novels such as *La Peau de chagrin* and late novels such as *La Cousine Bette* (1846; *Cousin Bette*, 1888) are equally likely to be chosen as examples of his best work. Whereas some critics have noticed certain types of development over this period, for example a tendency toward greater realism, exceptions can be found to every rule. Balzac seems to have reached his full development almost at one stroke, at age thirty, and to have continued at full power until a year or two before his death, with few pauses between masterpieces.

When Balzac began the program for *La Comédie humaine* (1829-1848;

The Comedy of Human Life, 1885-1893, 1896; also known as *The Human Comedy*), he set himself the task of writing the gigantic work in three sections: the "Studies of Manners," which would depict every kind of character and every way of living for every stratum of society; the "Philosophical Studies," which would analyze the motivating causes behind all of this social behavior; and the "Analytical Studies," which would outline the principles behind these various effects and causes. While his project was never to be finished (at his death he left some fifty titles of works to be written in order to complete the structure of the whole), the novels he did write are usually grouped according to these categories, with the "Studies of Manners" further subdivided into scenes of private, provincial, Parisian, political, military, and country life.

In 1842, Balzac signed a contract to issue a collected edition of his works, a massive undertaking requiring the collaboration of three publishers. Believing that "Collected Works" was too commonplace a title for the edition, they asked Balzac to find another title. He chose *The Human Comedy* by way of contrasting his work with Dante's *La divina commedia* (c. 1320; *The Divine Comedy*, 1802) and also to suggest its comprehensive scope, announcing in his preface to the edition his intention to present a history and criticism of the whole of society.

Summary

Although Honoré de Balzac lived to write "only" ninety-five of the 144 novels he had planned for the structure of *The Human Comedy*, the completed sections constitute one of the greatest achievements ever produced by the literary imagination, a series of explorations not only of French society of the first half of the nineteenth century but also of an unparalleled range of human types. Balzac was, in his time, France's most popular writer and, internationally, France's most respected author. Since that time, his prestige has steadily grown. As André Maurois has asserted, "It has been said that the works of Balzac, of Shakespeare, and of Tolstoy constitute the three great monuments raised by humanity to humanity. That is true and moreover *The Human Comedy* is the vastest and most complete of the three."

Bibliography
Bertault, Philippe. *Balzac and the Human Comedy.* Translated by Richard Monges. New York: New York University Press, 1963. Primarily a study of *The Human Comedy* rather than of its author, but it does include analysis of the effects of Balzac's life on his work, and features a convenient ten-page biographical sketch at the beginning of the text.

Gerson, Noel B. *The Prodigal Genius: The Life and Times of Honoré de Balzac.* Garden City, N.Y.: Doubleday, 1972. Written by a best-selling author for a general audience. Despite occasional sensationalism, an absorbing and well-researched account and a very good introduction for the nonspecialist.

Hunt, Herbert J. *Honoré de Balzac: A Biography.* London: Athlone Press, 1957. A straightforward historical narration of the major events of Balzac's life, competent and concise, though superseded by more recent works. Hunt's running commentary on the literary works is often still interesting. Many passages quoted in French are not translated.

Marceau, Félicien. *Balzac and His World.* Translated by Derek Coltman. New York: Orion Press, 1966. More a study of Balzac's characters than of his life, but interspersed with much relevant biographical information.

Maurois, André. *Prometheus: The Life of Balzac.* Translated by Norman Denny. New York: Harper & Row, 1965. The definitive biography by France's premier literary biographer. Primarily aimed at an audience already knowledgeable about the subject. A thorough and usually objective account of the facts of Balzac's life, clarifying many previously obscure details. Despite its close attention to specifics, however, Maurois' book is also a highly readable and entertaining narrative.

Oliver, E. J. *Balzac, the European.* London: Sheed & Ward, 1959. An overview of both the life and the novels, organized around a variety of thematic emphases such as "Women of Letters," "Religion," and "The Absolute." Provides a usefully condensed survey.

Pritchett, V. S. *Balzac.* New York: Alfred A. Knopf, 1973. Includes more than two hundred valuable illustrations of Balzac, his contemporaries, and his environment, among them forty high-quality color plates. Extremely valuable for orienting the reader unfamiliar with Balzac and his time and place.

Zweig, Stefan. *Balzac.* Edited by Richard Friedenthal. Translated by William Rose and Dorothy Rose. New York: Viking Press, 1946. After Maurois, Zweig is the best biographer of Balzac. Although slightly dated, this fascinating book reads almost like a novel about his life. Zweig's tendency to offer his own interpretations of events makes his work more subjective than Maurois', and perhaps less reliable in some particulars, but it remains the best introduction for the nonspecialist.

William Nelles

JOHANN BERNHARD BASEDOW

Born: September 11, 1723; Hamburg
Died: July 25, 1790; Magdeburg, Prussia
Area of Achievement: Education
Contribution: A charismatic teacher, Basedow believed that children should be permitted their childhood, and he taught them accordingly, encouraging them to learn through observation and experience more than through books. He insisted on a secular approach to an education that included nature study, physical education, and manual training.

Early Life

Johann Bernhard Basedow was born in the northeastern German seaport of Hamburg, the son of an unhappy, alcoholic wig maker, a man of dark moods, whose wife lapsed into madness and died shortly after the birth of her son. As a youth, Basedow exhibited erratic behavior. He was given to practical jokes, which annoyed his father. The boy, who learned Latin from his father by the time he was eight, ran away from home but soon returned and applied himself to his studies.

By the time he was twenty, Basedow had entered the University of Leipzig as a student in theology. His unconventional, though brilliant, thinking and his extreme egotism soon put him at odds with important faculty members, and he decided not to prepare for the priesthood. Rather, in 1749, he became a tutor in Holstein, and during his three years of tutoring he discovered that teaching was his real vocation. His views were unique for his time in that he eschewed book learning and was convinced that people learn best from observation and experience. Basedow taught Latin as though he were a Roman citizen, chatting informally in Latin with his students, who began to learn by what modern theorists have termed the audiolingual approach. By 1752, Basedow had taken a doctorate in foreign languages at the University of Kiel, where his dissertation explored some of the new methods of teaching he had developed as a tutor.

Soon afterward, Basedow accepted his first regular teaching job, in a Danish academy attended by the children of affluent, influential Danes. A gifted teacher, Basedow drew attention to himself by his unorthodox religious views and by his heterodox teaching methods. He advocated nonsectarian teaching, a shocking idea in his day. By 1761, he was no longer welcome among the Danes and moved to a classical *Gymnasium* in Altona, near his birthplace. Long a philosophical rationalist, Basedow issued broadsides so shocking to the people of Altona that the Church barred him and his family from taking Holy Communion and they were placed under an ecclesiastical ban. Anyone who read his work was threatened with exile, but these restraints did not stifle Basedow, who issued vituperation after vituperation.

Life's Work

Basedow was forty-five and had lost several teaching jobs when he published his *Vorstellung an Menschenfreunde und vermögende Männer über Schulen, Studien, und ihren Enfluss in die öffentliche Wohlfahrt* (1768). His tract, in part a direct appeal for funds from the affluent readers at whom the book was directed, called for nonsectarian schools, noninvolvement of the clergy in schools, the establishment of a state school board, and educational reform based on the philosophies and methodologies expounded by John Amos Comenius in *Orbis sensualium pictus* (1658; *The Visible World in Pictures*, 1659), by John Locke in *Some Thoughts Concerning Education* (1693), and by Jean-Jacques Rousseau in *Émile: Ou, De l'éducation* (1762; *Emilius and Sophia: Or, A New System of Education*, 1762-1763). Basedow's book received wide attention and, remarkably, brought to its author a flood of contributions sufficient to assure his family's future for some years and to allow him the leisure to work on two other books he had promised his supporters. Contributions came to him from every sector—from Catholics, Protestants, Jews, and, quite particularly, Freemasons, to whom the secularization of education was especially appealing.

Two years afterward, Basedow published the books he had promised, *Des Methodenbuchs für Väter und Mütter der Familien und Völker* (1770; *Book of Methods for Fathers and Mothers of Families and Nations*, 1913) and *Des Elementarbuchs für die Jugend und für ihre Lehrer und Freunde in gesitteten ständen* (1770), both of which were reissued four years later as a single, four-volume work, *Des Elementarwerks erster Band* (1774), richly illustrated for pedagogical purposes as Comenius' *The Visible World in Pictures* had been. The aim of *Des Elementarwerks erster Band* was to entice children into reading while keeping them completely captivated by what they were doing. The four volumes covered much of what was then known about the world, including commerce, manners, virtue, science, and how to adapt to situations.

The book was received enthusiastically, and its publication encouraged Prince Leopold of Anhalt-Dessau to subsidize a school in which Basedow could practice his unique teaching methods. The prince offered Basedow eight hundred dollars a year for his efforts, a comfortable sum at that time. In December, 1774, Basedow, aided by three assistants, opened his quite expensive boarding school, the Philanthropinum (later named the Institute), to which the affluent, many of them daunted by the novelty of the operation, sent their children only in small numbers and often reluctantly, attracted usually because Basedow was eager to work with children who experienced difficulties in more conventional schools. At no time did the school's total enrollment exceed fifty, including Basedow's two children.

Basedow expected to enroll three kinds of students: those who planned to attend the university; those preparing to become teachers themselves; and those who would enter service occupations when they left school. He encouraged impoverished students to enroll by offering them subventions, but attracting students to a school of this kind was a continuing problem, as were the financial struggles that continued to plague Basedow.

The school, which distributed a twenty-item list of rules and regulations, forbade its students to powder their hair and to rouge their cheeks, as was then the custom among many upper-class children. The school day was divided into segments for studying (five hours), for manual work and play (six hours), and for physical activities such as fencing, dancing, or singing (three hours). Although a religious attitude was encouraged among students, no time was devoted to the discussion of minor points of theological disagreement, as was the custom in many religiously oriented schools of that period.

Among its other departures from conventional educational practices, Basedow's school was coeducational. It emphasized play over study, consistent with the theory that real learning takes place from informal activities. Even the foreign languages the school offered, Latin and French, were approached by emphasizing the spoken languages rather than by the rote learning of vocabulary and of paradigms for the conjugation of verbs or the declension of nouns. Perhaps the most controversial element in Basedow's new pedagogy, however, was its insistence that students receive sex education and that this education be provided in a straightforward and honest manner. Simple anatomical terms were to be used, along with charts and drawings that would amplify the instruction.

Basedow aimed to prepare students for the real world. So far did his means of achieving this end depart from expected norms that the public became indignant. Basedow, a tall person, unprepossessing in appearance, had a monumental ego that stood in the way of his communicating meaningfully with those who questioned his educational procedures. When challenged, he became defensive, so that his opponents usually wanted to defeat him rather than understand him.

Perhaps the greatest influence upon Basedow's educational philosophy, greater even than his reading of Rousseau's *Emilius and Sophia*, was John Locke's concept of the *tabula rasa*, the blank slate Locke considered the mind of every newborn infant to be, and his strident calls in *Some Thoughts Concerning Education* for an emphasis on physical education. Locke's conception of the human mind joined with his recognition of the need to develop a sound body justified Basedow's notion that observation, experience, and play are quintessential ingredients of any effective education.

Not surprisingly, Basedow lasted for only two years as director of his school before he turned to regular teaching. He continued teaching for eight more years, and in 1784 resigned from the school altogether. The institution continued until 1793, when, burdened by debt and low enrollments, it was forced to close. The closing of the school did not mark the end of Basedow's educational influence. Joachim Heinrich Campe, who succeeded Basedow as director, opened a school of his own, based on Basedow's principles, in Hamburg and ran it for several years until he became director of education for the state of Brunswick. In his later years, in collaboration with others who admired Basedow's ideas, Campe published a sixteen-volume work that called for school reform of the kind Basedow had earlier promulgated.

Another educator who taught under Basedow's influence, Christian Saltzmann, founded his own school in Schnepfenthal in Coxe-Saxony in 1784, and ran it until his death, following Basedow's general pedagogical theories but adapting them wisely to his immediate situation. Saltzmann's school, on falling into the hands of his assistants, prospered and continued to flourish for more than one hundred years after its founding.

Summary

Johann Bernhard Basedow is a striking example of a man far ahead of his time. Educational ideas that sounded extreme to people at the beginning of the eighteenth century are taken quite for granted by twentieth century Western society. Basedow, flourishing in a time of educational reform marked by such eminent thinkers as Rousseau, Johann Heinrich Pestalozzi, Johann Friedrich Herbart, and Friedrich Froebel, has not received the celebrity they commanded. Nevertheless, his educational writings and practices directly affected the history of Western education.

His idea of secularizing schools is widely accepted in most Western countries today. Basedow's support of coeducation, at a time when such an idea was virtually unthinkable and when the education of women was severely limited, was courageous. That notion not only has come of age in the twentieth century but also has finally been generally accepted, as has the establishment of central governing bodies for education as suggested by Basedow.

As society has grown more open, frank, and honest, sex education has pervaded the schools. As society has grown increasingly diverse and as the age for leaving school has increased in most countries, manual training, now extended to include sophisticated levels of vocational education, has become a significant element of education, having exceeded by far anything Basedow could have envisioned. Even though such an eminent figure as Immanuel Kant lauded Basedow's Philanthropinum publicly, most people were not yet ready for Basedow's proposals during his lifetime. His cause was undoubtedly damaged by his unattractive demeanor and by his enormous ego, both of which stood in the way of many who could not separate the man from his farsighted pedagogy.

Bibliography
Good, Harry, and James D. Teller. *A History of American Education.* 3d ed.

New York: Macmillan, 1973. This brief profile of Basedow relates his pedagogical theories to the development of education in the United States and comments on Kant's admiration of the Philanthropinum. The section tends sometimes to be irritatingly didactic.

_____. *A History of Western Education*. 3d ed. New York: Macmillan, 1969. This treatment, although brief, is fuller than that in the authors' *A History of American Education*. Offers good commentary on Basedow's most important books and considers contemporary criticism of those books.

Lucas, Christopher J. *Our Western Educational Heritage*. New York: Macmillan, 1971. Although brief, Lucas' treatment relates Basedow well to those who influenced him most substantially—Comenius, Locke, Rousseau—and presents a clear exposition on the establishment of the Philanthropinum.

Meyer, Adolphe E. *An Educational History of the Western World*. 2d ed. New York: McGraw-Hill, 1972. Meyer's presentation of Basedow, although limited, is in many ways the most complete one available. Overwritten but well researched and accurate, it gives valuable insights into the early influences that shaped Basedow's personality.

Randall, John Herman. *The Making of the Modern Mind*. Rev. ed. Boston: Houghton Mifflin, 1940. A brilliant overall cultural history that relates Basedow to the philosophical movement of rationalism. Badly dated, but the book's shrewd observations make it worthwhile for modern readers.

R. Baird Shuman

CHARLES BAUDELAIRE

Born: April 9, 1821; Paris, France
Died: August 31, 1867; Paris, France
Area of Achievement: Literature
Contribution: Baudelaire was instrumental in the transformation from a classical conception of poetry, which concentrated on the subject, to the Romantic focus on the self and presented in his own poetry a heightened sensitivity to the dark dimensions of the beautiful, which served as a consolation for his own awareness of the human inclination toward self-destruction.

Early Life

Charles Baudelaire was born in Paris in 1821. His father, a member of the senate during the reign of Napoleon I, died in 1827 at the age of sixty-eight, and his mother was married to a successful career officer twenty months later. In 1830, Baudelaire entered the Collège Royal, a boarding school in Lyons, where his stepfather was stationed, and remained there until his family returned to Paris in 1836. He loathed the routine and the excessively strict code of discipline at the Collège Louis-le-Grand and was expelled in 1839. To satisfy his stepfather, who hoped that he would follow a career in law, Baudelaire continued his studies at the Collège Saint-Louis and passed the examination for his baccalaureate later that year.

Between 1839 and 1841, Baudelaire lived as a sort of idle protodandy in the Latin Quarter while he tried to pursue a literary career. One of his closest friends, Ernest Praround, described him:

> . . . coming down a staircase in the Baily house, slim, a low collar, an extremely long waistcoat, detached cuffs, carrying a light cane with a small gold head, walking with a supple, almost rhythmic step . . . Baudelaire had a somewhat yellow and even complexion, which had a little color on the cheekbones, a delicate beard which he didn't clip, and which did not smother his face.
> His expression, sharpened sometimes by genuine malice, sometimes by irony, would relax when he stopped talking or listening to withdraw into himself.

Théodore de Banville remarked on his "long, dense, and silk-black hair," while others noted that he presented himself with a painterly regard for appearance, a reflection of his growing commitment to art as a means of enhancing every aspect of life. His stepfather believed that he could find "better sources of inspiration" than "the sewers of Paris," and, to separate him from his "abominable friends," convinced him to sail to India. The trip lasted eight months, giving Baudelaire a taste for the exotic.

In 1842, having returned to France, Baudelaire took possession of his inheritance, a small fortune equivalent to $100,000. He settled in the expensive Quai de Bethune area, the first of fourteen addresses he maintained in Paris during the next fourteen years, and with the resources to cultivate his public presentation of himself, he moved with a crowd that valued the shocking remark and the outrageous gesture. His experiments with hashish began at about this time, as did his liaison with Jeanne Duval, a beautiful actress of mixed racial descent—the "Black Venus" of *Les Fleurs du Mal* (1857, 1861, 1868; *Flowers of Evil*, 1909). His stepfather was so alarmed by Baudelaire's style of living that he appointed a guardian to handle his monetary affairs, an act which irritated Baudelaire for the remainder of his life and may have contributed to a halfhearted attempt at suicide in 1845.

Baudelaire's spirits were revived by his first real success as a writer, his review of the 1845 exhibition at the Louvre, which blended the emotional responsiveness of the poet with the critical acuity of the trained art critic. His "Salon de 1846" ("Salon of 1846," 1964) was similarly successful, and on its last pages there was an announcement for a book of poems to be titled "Les Lesbiennes"—a title designed for its effect. This was the first public reference to *Flowers of Evil*, which in fact would not be published for another decade. In 1847, Baudelaire published *La Fanfarlo*, an extended short story with a protagonist who served as a semisatiric reflection on his inclinations toward the sensational and began to suffer from the periodic onslaughts of syphilis, which eventually led to his death. His gradually declining health caused a radical change in his appearance, the dandy now transposed into a prematurely aged flaneur with an almost-grim visage, high forehead, and piercing eyes.

Life's Work

In 1846 or 1847, Baudelaire read Edgar Allan Poe and remarked, "The first time I opened a book of his, I saw, with horror and delight, not just subjects I had dreamt of, but *sentences* I had thought of." He began to publish translations of Poe in 1848 and was also placing some poetry in *Revue de Paris*, a journal edited by Théophile Gautier and other friends. In 1857, the first edition of *Flowers of Evil* appeared. The title was proposed by Hippolyte Babou; Baudelaire liked its suggestion that beauty could be born of evil and that the seemingly perverse could be recast into poetic grace. Baudelaire knew that the book might be considered obscene, but a critic in *Le Figaro* may have exceeded his expectations by saying, "The book is a hospital open to all forms of mental derangements and emotional putrefaction." The government agreed and brought an indictment which compelled the confiscation of the book on July 17, three weeks after it had gone on sale. Baudelaire was found not guilty of blasphemy at the resulting hearing, but the charge of offending public morality stood, and six poems were banned. When asked if he expected to be acquitted, Baudelaire replied, "Acquitted! I was hoping for a public apology."

The prosecution of his masterwork diminished whatever remained of an optimistic outlook, and in 1860 he published *Les Paradis artificiels: Opium et haschisch* (partial translation as *Artificial Paradises: On Hashish and Wine as a Means of Expanding Individuality,* 1971). The book condemned hallucinogenic agents as providers of an illusion of the paradisiacal and described opium as a sapper of the will, which made it impossible to work. The essay, however, was misread as a celebration of decadence. Baudelaire knew that this was likely, but his imp of the perverse compelled him to continue. In 1861, he completed his definitive edition of *Flowers of Evil* (although an uncensored version did not appear in France until the twentieth century) and briefly considered applying for election to the French Academy. From 1862 to 1864, the twin plagues of poor health and poverty continued to unsettle him, but he was able to focus his mood into his final collection of poetry, *Le Spleen de Paris* (1869; *Paris Spleen, 1869,* 1905), a volume that dealt with the unreal city of T. S. Eliot's vision. He attempted to capitalize on his notoriety by scheduling a lecture tour of Belgium, and when this failed he remained in Europe until July, 1866, suffering from the effects of a stroke. His health worsened steadily, and he died in Paris in 1867.

Summary

Along with his transoceanic double, his brother in letters Edgar Allan Poe, Charles Baudelaire was the model for the nineteenth century archetype of the doomed artist, driven by an implacable destiny while struggling against his own self-destructive tendencies, an ignorant public, and a reactionary literary establishment. Underrated and misunderstood in his own time, Baudelaire—like Poe—had mythic aspects of his life that have a perverse allure that captures the imagination; but—like Poe—the perfected originality of his art, and the intensity and seriousness of his approach to his profession (which he listed as "lyric poet" on a passport application), have ultimately been recognized as the real attributes of his genius.

Baudelaire was one of the inventors of the Romantic attitude which has shaped and influenced the manner in which artists see themselves in relation to their work to this day. As Victor Brombert notes, Baudelaire's poetry defined Romantic sensibility in some of its most crucial aspects. The obsessive fascination with "erotic exoticism"; the urge to escape from the world while, in turn, being lured into its debauchery; the urge to follow the imagination to the furthest ranges of the conceivable; the sense of the artist as simultaneous victim and tyrant; the inclination toward prophetic affirmation of poetic destiny; a pervasive sense of sadness leading to strange beauty and an expression of the artist's awareness that he is damned by a kind of hyperconsciousness are some of the elements of the Romantic vision which Baudelaire fashioned.

On the other hand, as T. S. Eliot's well-known essay "Tradition and the

Individual Talent" argues, Baudelaire had other attributes that are ordinarily included under the rubric of classical constraint. Baudelaire's background and early formal education enabled him to use the French language with subtlety, elegance, and precision. His command of traditional poetic technique permitted him to employ a philosophy of composition that called for the accumulation of effect through a mastery of poetic means that would overcome or transform the ugly into the beautiful, the evil into the potentially divine. Even as Baudelaire's life and work projected a counterstrain to classical aesthetics which has become a permanent part of modern artistic thinking, his ability to use the resources of language with a meticulous awareness of linguistic traditions demonstrates that placing the self at the center of experience does not mean that a refinement of craft is obsolete. The power of art, he believed, could enable mankind to transcend the limits of an inherently evil world and a fundamentally sinful human condition. This belief was based on his Catholic background, but Baudelaire's real religion was poetry, and his own work was its truest sacrament.

As Peter Quennel observes, Baudelaire was "the chief accuser of the modern world, yet he is also its most patriotic citizen." Baudelaire never felt really comfortable in his world, but he knew how to make the most of his life there. "One must always be drunk," he advised. "To escape being the martyred slaves of time, be continually drunk. On wine, poetry, or virtue, whatever you fancy." For Baudelaire himself, an intoxication with art was the only form of addiction that provided true satisfaction.

Bibliography
Baudelaire, Charles. *The Flowers of Evil.* New York: New Directions, 1955. A complete bilingual edition which includes the work of many translators. The best single source for Baudelaire's poetry in English.

_____. *Selected Poems of Charles Baudelaire.* New York: Grove Press, 1974. A collection of translations by Geoffrey Wagner which concentrate chiefly on the erotic poetry, including some of the poems banned from the 1857 edition of *Flowers of Evil.* Includes an excellent introduction by Enid Starkie, which covers Baudelaire's life and work.

Brombert, Victor. *The Hidden Reader.* Cambridge, Mass.: Harvard University Press, 1988. Described as "a close reading of a high order," Brombert places Baudelaire within the context of Romanticism in "an uncommonly thoughtful commentary on the greatest of all ages of French literature."

Butor, Michel. *Histoire Extraordinaire: Essay on a Dream of Baudelaire.* Translated by Richard Howard. London: Jonathan Cape, 1969. An approach to Baudelaire from the underside. Written in a very contemporary, somewhat fragmented style, this is a most perceptive psychoanalytic study. Speculative, daring, and sympathetic, it covers Baudelaire's life and his relationship with Poe, and captures the spirit of Baudelaire's work.

de Jonge, Alex. *Baudelaire: Prince of Clouds*. New York: Paddington Press, 1976. Probably the best biography of Baudelaire in English. De Jonge is an intelligent and understanding biographer and translator, who has utilized the best biographical work prior to his own book and included many of Baudelaire's own letters to substantiate his observations.

Poulet, Georges. *Exploding Poetry: Baudelaire/Rimbaud*. Translated by Françoise Meltzer. Chicago: University of Chicago Press, 1984. A study of the affinities between two poets from the perspective of a critic who is firmly located in the cerebral realm of contemporary French literary criticism. Much arcane terminology combined with much critical insight. Tends toward the philosophical but offers some quite worthwhile conjectures for the advanced student.

Ruff, Marcel A. *Baudelaire*. Translated by Agnes Kertesz. New York: New York University Press, 1966. An extremely thorough but very readable biography, based on sound scholarship, sympathetic understanding, and an appealing basic decency. A good companion to de Jonge's more dramatic presentation, with a list of all Baudelaire's publications, including dates and other important annotations.

Sartre, Jean-Paul. *Baudelaire*. Translated by Martin Turnell. London: Horizon, 1949. One brilliant, quirky, singular genius regarding another. Sometimes incisive, sometimes wrongheaded, almost always fascinating if not always reliable.

Starkie, Enid. *Baudelaire*. New York: G. P. Putnam's Sons, 1933. Accurately described as the "foremost modern English authority on Baudelaire's life and work," Starkie writes a groundbreaking work which has provided an essential foundation for all Baudelaire studies in the United States and the United Kingdom. Still unsurpassed for breadth of coverage and intelligent commentary on the poetry and its sources in Baudelaire's life.

Leon Lewis

BAYEZID II

Born: December, 1447 or January, 1448; Demotika, Ottoman Empire
Died: May 26, 1512; en route to Demotika, Ottoman Empire
Areas of Achievement: Government and the military
Contribution: Without being among the great sultans of the Ottoman Empire, Bayezid II filled an important transitional role. The fame of his father, Mehmed II, as well as the symbolic memory of his namesake Bayezid I, would have made it difficult for Bayezid to earn a reputation for strong rule or aggressive foreign policy. That much of Bayezid's time was spent trying unsuccessfully to respond to conflicts toward the East is probably the main historical significance of his reign.

Early Life

Little or nothing is known about Bayezid II's early life or education prior to his first official appointment to a key government training post. This appointment occurred a few years before the death of his father, Mehmed II, the more famous sultan who conquered the capital İstanbul in 1453, at about the time of Bayezid's birth. As governor of Amasya province (between Ankara and the Black Sea), Bayezid received important military experience, particularly at the distant Battle of Otluk Beli in 1473. This encounter marked a turning point in the long Ottoman struggle to subdue the Turcoman populations in the zone spanning western Iran and eastern Anatolia that had rallied around the famous tribal chief Uzun Hasan.

The most significant chapter of Bayezid's early life came when his father died in 1481. His younger brother Cem, Governor of Karaman, with its influential religious capital Konya, challenged Bayezid's right to succeed. This succession struggle would go on, in various forms, for some fourteen years. Bayezid's claims were apparently supported by the main imperial military forces and high officials of the "new" capital at İstanbul. Cem's challenge depended on a number of different sources of resistance, and even included attempts to establish alliances with influences far from the Ottoman imperial homeland. Thus, Cem first tried, but failed, to defeat Bayezid with the support of Egyptian/Syrian Mamluk forces lent by Sultan Kā'it Bāy of Cairo. He then sought refuge with the Knights of Saint John on their island fortress at Rhodes. The knights decided not to join in the succession fray but turned Bayezid's brother over to the French kingdom. Several Christian states' use of the Ottoman pretender as their possible preferred ally over the next ten years forced Bayezid to keep close surveillance over his army to avoid possible betrayals. This limitation on the sultan's power in the early years of his reign (at least until Cem's death in 1495) held the Ottomans back from carrying out the major yearly military campaigns that had characterized most reigns up to and including that of Mehmed II.

Life's Work

Bayezid scored some early successes in maintaining and even expanding Ottoman control over key Balkan zones (capture of Herzegovina in 1483, seizure of the lower Danubian fortress of Kilia in 1484, and increased control over the Dniester River approaches to Crimea on the north coast of the Black Sea). The new sultan did not possess for some years, however, sufficient strength to fortify his southeastern provinces against the threat of Mamluk Egyptian/Syrian forays into agriculturally rich Cilicia. By 1491, an inconclusive peace was signed that would leave this southeastern zone in an indecisive position until Bayezid's son and successor Selim I marched into the area with force.

Bayezid's main attentions prior to the rise of Ṣafavīd Iranian threats to his eastern imperial flank would remain tied to Balkan Europe and the Krim Tatar zone of the north Black Sea coast, where Poland's kings aimed at making Moldavia (now part of Romania) a Slavic dependency. This was a claim that Bayezid would only reverse militarily in 1499. During the same period, he became seriously engaged in the Aegean Sea itself, where the Ottomans faced a formidable trade and military rival in the powerful city state of Venice.

Perhaps to detract attention from rising heterodox religious discontent and sedition in the eastern provinces, Bayezid pursued an openly aggressive policy toward his closest Christian rival, Venice. The break began in 1491, when the Venetian *balyos* (the diplomatic representative recognized by his father after the 1453 conquest) was expelled from İstanbul. Political tensions turned to material frustrations when, in 1496 (one year after the death of his rebellious brother Cem), Bayezid closed Ottoman ports to Venetian trade. For the next four years, clashes with the ships of Venice occurred throughout the eastern Mediterranean and the Aegean zones.

This protracted war of maritime encounters, which Pope Alexander VI would have liked to expand into a full-scale crusade, had an important effect on Bayezid's priorities as ruler. First, it made it necessary for the Ottomans to spend money on the development of seaports in western Turkey. Also, a new supreme naval commander, Kemal Reis (a former pirate captain whose ships had raided as far west as France and Spain), was named head of a largely rebuilt and heavily armed Ottoman navy.

The peace that was finally signed in 1502 restored most of Venice's trading privileges but limited its physical control of key ports considerably: Only Albania on the Adriatic and the Morea (southern Greece) could be called Venetian preserves in Ottoman territory by the first years of the sixteenth century. A second major repercussion of these years of Ottoman emphasis on naval development was a gradual assimilation of Mediterranean renegade captains into Turkish service. In addition to Kemal Reis, Bayezid encouraged a number of other important raiders (*gazis*) to pledge loyalty to his sultanate. Among these would be some of the great captains of the next generation, whose home ports were in North Africa. These would, by the end of Bayezid's son's reign, play a major role in attaching the provinces of Algiers, Tripolitania, and, eventually, Tunisia to the Ottoman realm.

Bayezid himself, however, did not live to see the rebirth of expansive Ottoman military power under his son Selim or, especially, Selim's successor Süleyman the Magnificent. Many historians note that, after the Venetian peace of 1502, Bayezid tended to withdraw more and more from direct management of imperial matters. This decision to retreat from direct responsibilities of rule offered the possibility for Bayezid to live a contemplative life. He was himself interested in music and poetry, and invited a number of recognized scholars of history, science, and religion to frequent his court in İstanbul. One of these, Kemal Pasha Zade, wrote a commissioned history of the Ottoman Empire under Bayezid's auspices. There were, however, negative factors that stemmed from Bayezid's decision to let others take responsibility for key affairs of state. On the one hand, apparently the influence of certain less tolerant religious leaders who were protégés of the court rose. This even went to the point of allowing zealots to denounce violently their rivals with the tacit and sometimes direct support of the sultan. On the other hand, increasing social and religious ferment in the Ottoman eastern Anatolian provinces, spurred on by unorthodox proponents of Shī‘a Islam under the banner of Ṣafavīd Shah Esmā‘īl I, had spread considerably by the early 1500's. The sultan's lack of a determined policy of reaction nearly assured that a party of political opposition to him would emerge.

Bayezid's approach to the problem of Shī‘a heterodoxy and its willingness to sponsor anti-Ottoman rebellions in far-flung provinces was to try to convince Esmā‘īl to respect the integrity of a single unified community of Islam. By 1508-1509, the futility of expecting Esmā‘īl to reason with the Ottoman sultan was apparent: Esmā‘īl invaded Iraq and added it to the Ṣafavīd domains. Concerned Turkish military leaders feared that Syria and perhaps Ottoman Cilicia would be next. When an Ottoman army led by Grand Vizier ‘Alī Pasha and Prince Ahmed only barely succeeded in expelling Esmā‘īl's supporters from the southeast province around Kayseri (August, 1511), a party of militant opposition to Bayezid's rule began to plan his overthrow.

Although, as Bayezid's eldest son, Ahmed should have been considered the legal successor, military professionals most anxious to see a strong force dispatched to the East preferred the candidacy of Selim. Bayezid's appointment (in 1507) of Ahmed to the same Amasya provincial governorate that he had held prior to defending his claim to the succession in 1481 seemed to be a sign that the sultan was unaware of such preferences. Thus, Selim and his supporters decided not to await Bayezid's demise before claiming the throne. They revolted against Bayezid and divided the army against itself. Several incidents of open clashes occurred before Bayezid was formally deposed

(April, 1512). Only a month later, while attempting to return to forced exile at his birthplace in Demotika, Bayezid died, presumably of natural causes.

Within a year after Bayezid's demise, his son Selim (the Grim) had begun to mount a major military reconquest of threatened Ottoman provinces in the East. In only two years, Esmā'īl would be defeated and a military route opened for Selim's conquest of the core countries of Arabistan: Syria and Egypt.

Summary

The reign of Bayezid II demonstrates that, despite the obvious imperial determination and military capacities of the Ottoman Empire, certain signs of internal dissension that would paralyze the political apparatuses of state in later centuries were already present in 1500. One of these is represented by the divisive influence of Cem's fourteen-year-long challenge to his brother's succession. Intrigues involving supporters of different scions of the Ottoman family as claimants to the throne had not been unknown before this date but had never affected so many different interest groups, both domestic and foreign.

Another negative characteristic of Bayezid's reign that would be repeated again and again in later centuries was his tendency to delegate active authority to govern. The sultan's retirement to the intellectually and aesthetically rarefied atmosphere of the imperial court left the field open for self-seeking politicians, military authorities, and religious zealots to play a larger role in high Ottoman affairs than had been possible under his predecessors. Although Selim's overthrow of his father in 1512 prepared the way for a reversal of these trends during the next two great reigns, the elements operating in Bayezid's period of rule would return to weaken many of the original bases of Ottoman imperial authority in the seventeenth century.

Bibliography

Creasy, Edward S. *History of the Ottoman Turks*. London: R. Bentley, 1878. This detailed historical work is based on the massive mid-nineteenth century German classic by Von Hammer-Purgstall. The author states that he not only abridged Von Hammer but also incorporated a wide range of other sources, including memoirs of Europeans who witnessed the events described. For Bayezid's time, however, there were very few primary sources to be consulted. Thus, the historical accuracy of many of Creasy's subjective impressions must be accepted with caution.

Fisher, Sidney N. *The Foreign Relations of Turkey, 1481-1512*. Urbana: University of Illinois Press, 1948. This work covers the precise reign dates of Bayezid. It is therefore one of the most complete and detailed studies of Bayezid, even though emphasis is on relations with foreign powers, both European and Muslim.

Inalcik, Halil. "The Rise of the Ottoman Empire." In *The Cambridge History of Islam*, edited by P. M. Holt, Ann K. S. Lambton, and Bernard Lewis, vol. 1. Cambridge, England: Cambridge University Press, 1970. The most concise survey of the entire early period of Ottoman expansion, with a specific section on Bayezid. The material on Bayezid is useful both for its cultural foci and for its discussion of social subgroupings, especially that of the Turcomans.

Itzkowitz, Norman. *Ottoman Empire and Islamic Tradition*. New York: Alfred A. Knopf, 1972. This book contains a short but complete subchapter on Bayezid, placed in a general section entitled "From Emirate to Empire." More important perhaps than this chronological coverage of each sultanic reign is the fact that the three other sections of the book deal with various Ottoman institutions such as bureaucracy and provincial structure that shed light on conditions, either practical or legal, that Bayezid faced.

Shaw, Stanford J. *History of the Ottoman Empire and Modern Turkey.* Vol. 1, *Empire of the Gazis: The Rise and Decline of the Ottoman Empire, 1280-1808*. New York: Cambridge University Press, 1976. Of several general works on Ottoman history, this volume contains perhaps the most information on Bayezid's reign. Provides useful information on key cultural questions, including undercurrents of religious discontent and some elements of courtly literature from the late fifteenth and early sixteenth centuries.

Byron D. Cannon

PIERRE BAYLE

Born: November 18, 1647; Carla-le-Comte, France
Died: December 28, 1706; Rotterdam, the Netherlands
Areas of Achievement: Philosophy and historiography
Contribution: Bayle was a great skeptical arguer, criticizing philosophical
  theories both old and new, and exposing the weaknesses of Catholic and
  Protestant theologies. His criticisms helped pave the way for modern tol-
  eration and provided the principal arguments for the Enlightenment.

Early Life

Pierre Bayle was born in the small town of Carla-le-Comte, near the
Spanish border south of Toulouse, where his father was a Calvinist minister.
He grew up during the increasing persecution of Protestants in France. He
was first sent to a Calvinist academy at Puylaurens. Next, he attended the
Jesuit college in Toulouse, because there was no advanced Protestant school
left in his area. His studies with the Jesuits led him to consider the controversial arguments used by Catholics to convert the Protestants. On the basis
of intellectual considerations, he soon became a Catholic, the worst thing a
son of an embattled Calvinist minister could do. He soon redeemed himself
by converting from Catholicism back to Protestantism, again on the basis of
intellectual arguments. This second conversion made Bayle a *relaps*, someone who has returned to heresy after having abjured it. As such, he was subject to banishment or imprisonment. For his protection, he was sent to the
University of Geneva to complete his studies in philosophy and theology.

To earn his living, Bayle returned to France in disguise and was a tutor in
Paris and Rouen. In 1675, he became professor of philosophy at the Calvinist academy at Sedan, where he was the protégé of the fanatically orthodox
Protestant theologian Pierre Jurieu, who was to become his most bitter enemy. Bayle and Jurieu taught at Sedan until it was closed by the French
government in 1681. They then went to the Netherlands as refugees and
were reunited as faculty members of the new academy in Rotterdam, the
École Illustre, and as leading figures in the French Reformed church in that
city.

Life's Work

Bayle's career as an author began shortly after his arrival in Rotterdam.
He published a work he had drafted in France, *Lettre sur la comète* (1682;
*Miscellaneous Reflections Occasion'd by the Comet Which Appear'd in De-
cember, 1680,* 1708), in which he began his critique of superstition, intolerance, bad philosophy, and bad history. This was followed by *Critique
générale de l'histoire du calvinisme de M. Maimbourg* (1682; general crit-

icism of Father Maimbourg's history of Calvinism), an examination of a very polemical history of Calvinism by a leading Jesuit. In 1684, Bayle edited *Recueil de quelques pièces curieuses concernant la philosophie de M. Descartes*, a collection of articles about Cartesianism, which was then under attack by the Jesuits. The collection contained articles by Nicolas de Malebranche, Bayle, and others. From 1684 to 1687, Bayle published a learned journal, *Nouvelles de la République des Lettres*, in which he commented on the theories then appearing of Gottfried Leibniz, Malebranche, Antoine Arnauld, Robert Boyle, and John Locke, among others.

Because of his acute judgment, which appeared in his early writings, Bayle became one of the central figures in the Republic of Letters and was in direct contact with many of its leading personalities. From 1684 to 1685, Bayle devoted himself exclusively to scholarly writing. His brothers and his father died in France as a result of the religious persecution against Protestants. He declined when the Jurieu family offered the opportunity of an advantageous marriage. He rejected a position as professor at the University of Franeker, preferring to remain in Rotterdam, contending against various kinds of opponents.

In 1686, Bayle published *Commentaire philosophique sur ces paroles de Jésus-Christ "Contrain-les d'entrer"* (*A Philosophical Commentary on These Words in the Gospel, Luke XIV, 23: "Compel Them to Come In, That My House May Be Full,"* 1708). This essay was directed against the Catholic persecution of the Protestants in France. In it, Bayle developed the most extensive argument of the time for complete toleration, going further than John Locke did in *A Third Letter for Toleration* (1692). Bayle advocated tolerating Muslims, Jews, Unitarians, and atheists, as well as Catholics (who were then persecuted in the Netherlands). Bayle's views used skeptical arguments as a basis for complete toleration of all views, claiming that an "erring conscience" had as many rights as a nonerring one, since it was impossible to tell who was right or wrong. Bayle's tolerance brought him into conflict with his erstwhile mentor, Jurieu, who became the theorist of intolerance and a dominant figure in the French Reformed church while in exile. Their differences became so great that Jurieu denounced his colleague as a menace to true religion and a secret atheist. During the late 1680's, Bayle began a furious pamphlet war against Jurieu and criticized the liberals who sought to develop a rational, scientifically acceptable version of Christianity. Bayle's many controversies led to his dismissal from the Rotterdam professorship in 1693. The rest of his life was devoted to skeptical, polemical scholarship.

Bayle's greatest work, *Dictionnaire historique et critique* (1697; *An Historical and Critical Dictionary,* 1710), began as an effort to correct all the errors he had found in previous dictionaries and encyclopedias and was a way of skeptically criticizing philosophical, scientific, and theological theories. The dictionary consists almost exclusively of articles about deceased people and defunct movements, with a few articles about places. Bayle decided to omit persons who had been adequately dealt with in the previous biographical dictionary of Louis Moreri from 1674. Thus, many famous people, such as Plato and William Shakespeare and René Descartes, are missing, while many obscure people are given articles of substantial length. The format of Bayle's dictionary, in folio volumes, was to set forth a biography of a personage on the top of the page, with long footnotes below, and with notes to the notes on the side. This gives the book a look somewhat like that of an edition of the Talmud. The core of the dictionary is in the notes and the notes to the notes, in which Bayle digressed to discuss and dissect old and new theories on a variety of subjects. He skeptically challenged Scholastic philosophy, Cartesianism, and the new philosophies of Leibniz, Malebranche, Ralph Cudworth, Baruch Spinoza, Locke, and Isaac Newton. He challenged Catholic and Protestant theologies and sought to show that they were unable to give a consistent or credible explanation of the problem of evil. Throughout *An Historical and Critical Dictionary,* Bayle claimed that his skepticism was a means of undermining or destroying reason in order to make room for faith. He cited Blaise Pascal to show this. Also throughout the work, however, Bayle questioned the moral or religious sincerity of the leading figures of the Old Testament, the Church Fathers, and the religious leaders of the Reformation. He reported all varieties of immoral sexual conduct, unethical practices, and hypocritical behavior of everyone from Noah and his children, to the heroes of Greek mythology, to kings and queens, to saints and church leaders.

An Historical and Critical Dictionary shocked the learned and religious worlds. The French Reformed church tried to ban it; it was attacked by many, with the result that it quickly became a best-seller. In the second edition (1702), Bayle had promised his church that he would explain what they found most outrageous: his article on King David, his defense of atheists, his Pyrrhonian skepticism, and his inclusion of so much obscene material. He wrote four lengthy clarifications of these matters, which only infuriated his opponents more. The clarification on skepticism became one of his most important statements on the relationship of skepticism and religion. The material in the second edition became basic to discussions of philosophy and theology in the eighteenth century. It was used extensively by George Berkeley, David Hume, Voltaire, and many others.

In the four years after the appearance of the second edition of the dictionary, Bayle wrote several works continuing his attacks on his many opponents, particularly his orthodox, liberal, and rational opponents. Critics insisted that he was trying to undermine all philosophy, science, and religion. He insisted that he was a true believer, trying to destroy reason to buttress faith.

Summary

Pierre Bayle was one of the most important skeptical arguers of the seventeenth century, who provided what was called "the arsenal of the Enlightenment." His many critical works, especially *An Historical and Critical Dictionary*, raised the central problems and questions of the time, challenging all the philosophical and theological solutions that had been offered previously. From the time that Bayle was alive and continuing after his death, there has been debate about his real intentions. Some see him as a chronic outsider, criticizing all views while apparently maintaining just a modicum of religious faith.

Regardless of his intent, Bayle influenced thinkers for the next hundred years. Leibniz wrote *Essais de théodicée sur la bonté de Dieu, la liberté de l'homme, et l'origine du mal* (1710; *Theodicy: Essays on the Goodness of God, the Freedom of Man, and the Origin of Evil*, 1952) to try and answer Bayle's skeptical attacks on religious solutions to the problem of evil. Berkeley and Hume took some of their basic argumentation from Bayle, and French Enlightenment figures from Voltaire onward built upon his criticisms. Immanuel Kant used him as a source for the antinomies of pure reason. Thomas Jefferson recommended Bayle's works as one of the initial purchases for the Library of Congress. Bayle continued to be influential until *An Historical and Critical Dictionary* was replaced by modern encyclopedias, and his skepticism was replaced by modern scientific positivistic views. In the late twentieth century, a strong revival of interest in his writing and impact among scholars occurred. He has since been recognized as one of the seminal figures in eighteenth century thought.

Bibliography

Bayle, Pierre. *Historical and Critical Dictionary, Selections.* Translated by Richard H. Popkin and Craig Brush. Indianapolis: Bobbs-Merrill, 1965. A collection of forty articles, exhibiting the range of Bayle's views.

Bracken, Harry M. "Bayle Not a Sceptic?" *Journal of the History of Ideas* 25 (1964): 169-180. An attempt to clarify the sense in which Bayle was a skeptic and a fideist, in answer to E. D. James's "Scepticism and Fideism in Bayle's *Dictionnaire*," *French Studies* 16 (1962): 307-324. This article challenges the views of Popkin and others regarding Bayle's religious views.

Brush, Craig. *Montaigne and Bayle: Variations on the Theme of Skepticism.* The Hague: Martinus Nijhoff, 1966. A comparison of the two thinkers, showing some profound differences as well as general points of agreement.

Kenshur, Oscar. "Pierre Bayle and the Structures of Doubt." *Eighteenth Century Studies* 21, no. 3 (1988): 297-315. An attempt to define and describe Bayle's skepticism, challenging Popkin's fideist reading.

Labrousse, Elisabeth. *Bayle*. Translated by Denys Potts. New York: Oxford University Press, 1983. An overall view of Bayle's place in intellectual history, and an interpretation of what he argued against and what he upheld, by a leading Bayle scholar.

Mason, H. T. *Pierre Bayle and Voltaire*. London: Oxford University Press, 1963. A comparison of the two, with an effort to assess what Voltaire borrowed from Bayle.

Popkin, Richard H. *The High Road to Pyrrhonism*. San Diego: Austin Hill Press, 1980. Contains several articles dealing with Bayle's skepticism and his influence. See also the author's article on Bayle in *The Encyclopedia of Philosophy* (1967), edited by Paul Edwards.

Rex, Walter. *Essays on Pierre Bayle and Religious Controversy*. The Hague: Martinus Nijhoff, 1965. A study of Bayle's views in the context of seventeenth century French Protestant theology.

Robinson, Howard. *Bayle the Skeptic*. New York: Columbia University Press, 1931. Presents Bayle as an irreligious skeptic, the precursor of Enlightenment atheism.

Sandberg, Karl C. *At the Crossroads of Faith and Reason: An Essay on Pierre Bayle*. Tucson: University of Arizona Press, 1966. An interpretation of Bayle as a sincere Calvinist.

Richard H. Popkin

THE BECQUEREL FAMILY

Antoine-César Becquerel

Born: March 8, 1788; Châtillon-Coligny
Died: January 18, 1878; Paris, France

Alexandre-Edmond Becquerel

Born: March 24, 1820; Paris, France
Died: May 11, 1891; Paris, France

Antoine-Henri Becquerel

Born: December 15, 1852; Paris, France
Died: August 25, 1908; Le Croisic, France
Areas of Achievement: Physics and chemistry
Contribution: The remarkable Becquerel family spans four generations of science, with several of its members making important discoveries in physics and chemistry, particularly in the realms of electrochemistry, electromagnetic radiation, and radioactive decay physics.

Early Lives

Little is known of Antoine-César Becquerel's early life. He is known to have served in the French army as an officer in the engineering corps until 1815. In 1837, he was appointed a professor at the Museum of National History in Paris, where he began work on numerous projects in physics and chemistry.

Alexandre-Edmond Becquerel was the second son of Antoine, the family's founder. He did not attend a university but instead became assistant to his father at the Museum of Natural History at the age of eighteen. He later collaborated with his distinguished father on several important treatises. On the basis of his work, he received the doctor's degree in 1840 from the University of Paris.

Antoine-Henri Becquerel spent his early years at the Lycée-Louis-le-Grand. Already showing his brilliance, in 1872 he entered l'École Polytechnique, transferring two years later to l'École des Ponts et Chaussées, where he would later work for ten years as chief engineer. From 1875 onward, he researched various aspects of optics and engineering, obtaining his doctorate in 1888. Appointed under his father at the museum, he became professor of physics there in 1892, gaining the chair both his father and grandfather had held. In 1895, he also earned the physics professorship at l'École Polytechnique, where he had started. In 1899, he was elected to the French Academy of Sciences, continuing in the family tradition.

Life's Work

Antoine spent his life at the Museum of Natural History in Paris. His works, in the early 1800's, were devoted to research on phosphorescence, fluorescence, thermoelectricity, the magnetic properties of materials, crystal optics, the theory of primary cells, and the electrical conductivity of matter. He is best known for his work in 1829, when he invented a primary cell with weak polarization.

After receiving his doctorate in 1840, Alexandre-Edmond became professor of physics at the Agronomy Institute of Versailles. While there, he became deeply involved in investigations of electricity and magnetism. His most significant discovery was the magnetic property of liquid oxygen. He was able to show that light, through the action of inducing chemical reactions, could cause the flow of an electric current. He invented an instrument that measured light intensity by determining the electric current intensity produced. As a by-product, he determined a means of measuring the heat radiated by objects hot enough to be emitting visible light by establishing the intensity of that light. He also originated the platinum-palladium thermocouple, which is used for high-temperature measurements.

Alexandre-Edmond's interests became centered on fluorescence and phosphorescence phenomena. He was the first to discriminate between these ideas and used them for the study of ultraviolet and infrared radiation from 1857 to 1878. The problems where certain chemical materials absorbed light of one wavelength and then reemitted light of another wavelength fascinated him, particularly the circumstances in which substances were seen to glow in the dark. In 1859, he invented the phosphoroscope for doing detailed studies of light-emission intensity. As a side interest, he made the first complete solar spectrum photograph. His 1872 studies of the phosphorescence spectra or uranium compounds are considered the beginning of the path that led his son, Henri, to discover radioactivity.

Henri was involved, for most of his researches, with the phenomena of light. He had coauthored a series of memoirs with his father, Alexandre-Edmond, on the temperature of Earth, but his real interest was in light interactions in materials. Henri was the first physicist to observe rotatory magnetic polarization in gases. Expanding the experiment, he discovered the magnetic rotation of the plane of polarized light by Earth's magnetic field. From 1886 to 1890, he performed experiments on the absorption of light by crystals, particularly investigating the anomalies of light passage along different axes within the crystal body. He then utilized that work to devise a new method of spectral analysis.

Fascinated by phosphorescence, he continued his father's research. By determined and careful investigations, he discovered the laws relating to the emission of radiation by materials being bombarded by light waves. He also showed how the emitted phosphorescence decreased with time, and why it did so. The work for which Henri is best known involved his discovery in 1896 that uranium compounds emitted some type of invisible but highly penetrating radiation, a type of light wave that would contaminate photographic plates and greatly influence the electrical conductivity in gases. He had been researching the idea that fluorescing materials might be emitting X rays (which had recently been discovered by Wilhelm Conrad Röntgen). With the aid of potassium uranyl sulfate, a fluorescent material, wrapped photographic negatives, and a fortuitous series of cloudy days, he discovered that the fogging of plates by the chemical did not depend on sunlight or phosphorescence but instead was a result of something's being emitted by the compound itself. Ignoring the sun and the fluorescence process, he studied the radiation and showed that it was quite like X rays, particularly in causing air to ionize. The radiation was emitted continuously in an unending, uninterrupted stream, heading in all directions. At his suggestion, Madame Marie Curie undertook the study of those radiations for a large number of minerals. For a brief period, the radiation was called "Becquerel rays," but in 1898, at Curie's suggestion, the phenomenon was renamed "radioactivity."

Henri's observations were announced at the French Academy of Sciences meeting on February 24, 1896, in his article entitled "Émission de radiations nouvelles par l'uranium métallique." He confirmed his studies with detailed work on the materials emitting the rays and on the properties of the rays themselves in "Sur diverses propriétés des rayons uraniques" (1896). By 1899, he had discovered that the radiation could be deflected by a magnetic field, so that at least some part of it had to be tiny charged particles: "Sur le rayonnement des corps radio-actifs" (1899). On the basis of further investigations, in 1900 he was able to announce that the part that was influenced by the field was negatively charged speeding electrons, identical to those identified in cathode-ray tubes by Sir Joseph John Thomson. After identifying the uranium atoms as the radioactive portion of the compound in 1901, he concluded that the electrons radiated had to be coming from within the uranium atoms themselves. This was, in the physics world, the first real indication that the atom was not a featureless sphere, that it had an internal structure. For all of his illustrious work, but particularly for the discovery of radioactivity, Henri Becquerel was awarded, along with Pierre and Marie Curie, the 1903 Nobel Prize in Physics.

Members of the family continued achievements into the twentieth century. Henri's son, Jean-Antoine-Édouard-Marie, also a member of the Paris Academy of Sciences, concentrated his work on the interactions of electromagnetic energy with solid materials. Notably, he studied the propagation of circularly polarized waves in various magnetic media. In addition, he did work on the anomalous dispersion of light by sodium vapors, the Zeeman effect in pleochroic crystals, and (with Heike Kamerlingh Onnes) the phenomena occurring in a substance placed in a magnetic field at the temperatures of liquid air and liquid hydrogen.

Summary

The Becquerels are outstanding examples of a family whose members distinguished themselves in science. Of its members, Alexandre-Edmond and Antoine-Henri played the grandest roles in the history of physics. Antoine-César, a pioneer in the development of electrochemistry, set a precedent by gaining the professorship of physics at the Paris Museum of Natural History—a position which was passed on through succeeding generations. Alexandre-Edmond's discoveries on light, particularly its transmission in materials and its interactions with magnetic fields in minerals, laid the foundation for modern optical mineralogy and crystallography, vastly important in the fields of geophysical exploration and ore identification. His works, along with his father's, on phosphorescence and fluorescence, paved the way for modern chemical studies on reaction rates, mechanisms, and complex formations. Henri, the best known of the family members, founded the field of radioactivity and furthered the use of light-magnetic-field interactions, particularly important in geology, optics, and electromagnetism. Moreover, his experiments helped to refute the belief, widely held in the late nineteenth century, that physics had produced all that it ever would. The idea of radioactivity, coupled with X rays, new elements, and quantum and relativity ideas, heralded the new age of modern physics.

Bibliography
Abro, A. d'. *The Rise of the New Physics: Its Mathematical and Physical Theories*. New York: Dover, 1951. This work covers all the major ideas and experiments that have led to modern quantum physics. Besides the topic of radioactivity, it deals with the people who worked with the Becquerels to extend the realms of physics. Contains chapters for readers with mathematical background, which can be skipped. In-depth and difficult.
Curie, Marie. *Radioactive Substances*. New York: Philosophical Library, 1961. This work deals with the researches of Marie Curie and her husband, Pierre Curie, based on the discoveries of Henri Becquerel on radioactivity. Details their experiments, their hardships, and the discoveries they made. Tedious in spots, but presents a true picture of science at work.
Holmyard, Eric. *Makers of Chemistry*. Oxford, England: Clarendon Press, 1931. A history of chemistry from its obscure beginnings to the modern science of the 1900's. Details the explosion of chemistry programs in the nineteenth and twentieth centuries. Extensive pictures help tell the story of who did what of importance.
Ihde, Aaron. *The Development of Modern Chemistry*. New York: Harper &

Row, 1964. This book covers the history of chemistry from ancient concepts of matter to present technology. Chapters on electrochemistry and radioactivity deal with the materials on which the Becquerels worked, including discoveries and interrelationships between physics and chemistry. Extensive references and pictures of the proponents of many theories.

Magie, William. *A Source Book in Physics*. New York: McGraw-Hill, 1935. This is a collection of the most important abstracts from physics in the last three centuries, from Galileo to Max Planck. Henri Becquerel's discovery of radioactivity from uranium is presented, along with numerous articles on his predecessors. Allows the reader to see the high points of physics.

Ronan, Colin A. *The Atlas of Scientific Discovery*. New York: Crescent Books, 1983. Surveys the march of science, tracing the development of new fields of study and the new techniques they demanded. Excellent pictures; accurate and easy to read.

Taton, René. *History of Science*. Vol. 4, *Science to the Twentieth Century*. New York: Basic Books, 1964. This work covers science from the Renaissance to the present, including astronomy, physics, chemistry, biology, and mathematics. All the major finds and their discoverers are included from Europe and North America. Numerous illustrations are provided, as are some asides on other areas of the world. Detailed reading; does not flow well.

Toulmin, Stephen, and June Goodfield. *The Architecture of Matter*. New York: Harper & Row, 1962. This reference work deals with the evolution of the scientific ideas of animate and inanimate matter in terms of chemistry and physics. Various theories of matter are presented to illustrate turning points and breakthroughs. Covers significant experiments and ideas through time. Good references, lively exposition.

Arthur L. Alt

LUDWIG VAN BEETHOVEN

Born: December 17, 1770 (baptized); Bonn
Died: March 26, 1827; Vienna, Austria
Area of Achievement: Music
Contribution: Beethoven contributed greatly to Western classical music. Clearly reflecting the transition from the classical tradition in music to the Romantic, he made numerous innovations in the piano sonata, the string quartet, and the symphony.

Early Life
Born in Bonn in 1770, Ludwig van Beethoven did not enjoy the happiest of childhoods. His father, a minor musician in the court of the archbishop-elector of Cologne, was generally more interested in drinking than in making music and was often a trial to his family. He knew well enough, however, that his son had a talent for music. Hoping that the boy might be a wunderkind, another Wolfgang Amadeus Mozart, he pushed him into a severe musical training that left little time for the pleasures of childhood. Beethoven's playmates were the piano, the organ, and the viola.

Not another Mozart, the young Beethoven nevertheless began to develop his musical abilities slowly but surely. By his thirteenth year, he was composing and was serving as an assistant to his teacher Christian Gottlob Neefe, the court organist, with the result that he began to gain notice from members of the aristocracy, people who, throughout the rest of his life, were to be patrons and friends. The family of Emanuel Joseph Breuning, for example, welcomed the boy, and he spent much time with them.

With the help of Neefe, the Breunings, and the archbishop-elector, Beethoven, at the age of seventeen, journeyed to Vienna, the preeminent musical city of Europe. It was for him a dream come true. There, he met Mozart, then at the peak of his career, and impressed him, moreover, with his own extemporaneous pieces on the piano. His stay in Vienna, however, was to be cut short. Upon hearing of his mother's illness, he hurried back to Bonn to find that she had died. He lost not only a mother but also, in his words, his "best and most faithful friend."

Shortly after his return to Bonn, Beethoven suffered another blow—the death of his younger sister. His father's drinking, moreover, had reached the point at which he could no longer support the family, and that task now fell to Beethoven. With the same indomitable spirit that marked his whole life, he accepted the challenge and cared for his two younger brothers. He also met the challenge of his musical talent and continued to increase his social and intellectual contacts among both young and old in Bonn.

When Joseph Haydn passed through Bonn in 1790, he encouraged Beethoven to come to Vienna to study with him. It took two years for Beethoven to complete the arrangements, but in 1792, he journeyed once again to Vienna, the city that was to be his permanent home. Although his relationship with Haydn lasted only two years, Beethoven began building a reputation that was to become only stronger as the years passed.

Life's Work

In Vienna, Beethoven studied counterpoint with Haydn, but the relationship between them was not a positive one. Beethoven thought that Haydn's teaching was perfunctory, and Haydn was displeased by his student's slow development—particularly in contrast to the genius of Mozart—and by his personal mannerisms and his audacious compositions. The result was that Beethoven found a new teacher of counterpoint. The young composer was, however, in the right place at the right time, because Vienna was a city rich in musical tradition and alive with the spirit of revolution.

Like so many artists and intellectuals, Beethoven was caught up in the fervor of the political changes sweeping America and Europe, and he no doubt saw a clear relationship between such changes and those occurring in the world of music. Although composers still found their main employment in the Church, the court, and the opera house, new possibilities of support were being introduced. Public concert halls, for example, offered sources of income, as did increased patronage from an aristocracy that was becoming more interested in the arts. Not content with the somewhat demeaning position to which artists and composers were relegated in relationships with their patrons, Beethoven, through his own strength of personality, worked to define a new kind of relationship that enabled him to be the careful creator and craftsman he was. Indeed, the Viennese aristocrats were eager not only to give Beethoven the support he demanded but also to gain his friendship.

While it is a general custom to approach the works of a composer, writer, or painter in terms of periods such as style and chronology, one must remember that the works themselves do not necessarily fall neatly into such divisions. As for Beethoven, most musicologists see his work falling into three distinct periods. The first period ends at 1802 or 1803 and includes the Op. 18 string quartets, the early piano sonatas, and the first two symphonies. The compositions of this period show the singular influences of Mozart and Haydn. The second period covers approximately the next ten years and may well be considered Beethoven's most productive, with 1814 being his peak year. This second period includes the third symphony (*Eroica*) through the eighth symphony, the opera *Fidelio*, the Op. 59 string quartets, some piano sonatas, and two piano concertos. The last period includes the last piano sonatas and quartets and the powerful ninth symphony (*Choral*).

While Beethoven was fulfilling his early promise as a composer, he discovered in his late twenties that his hearing was gradually getting weaker. With the devastating realization that he was going deaf, he contemplated suicide. "But how humbled I feel when someone near me hears the distant sound of a flute, and I hear *nothing*; when someone hears a shepherd singing, and I hear nothing!" he wrote to his brother. His faith in his art, however, was stronger than his desire for death, and, despite this cruel blow, he prepared to go on with his life and his music.

Stone-deaf at thirty-two, Beethoven became more depressed and eccentric in his daily living; in his music, however, he sought hope amid despair. His third symphony, the *Eroica*, was dedicated to Napoleon I and was meant to celebrate the heroic ideals of revolutionary leaders. The symphony itself was revolutionary, representing a distinct break with the classical past. Its length and complexity caused consternation among some critics, but through the years it has become one of the most widely performed of Beethoven's works.

Following the *Eroica* and the opera *Fidelio*, Beethoven concentrated primarily on the symphony, and between 1806 and 1808 he completed his fourth, fifth, and sixth symphonies. The fourth symphony is light and jovial and seems to be an effort on the composer's part to capture in music the joy that he was unable to realize in life. The powerful fifth symphony, on the other hand, is generally seen as symbolic of Beethoven's struggle against, and victory over, fate. The sixth symphony (*Pastoral*) expresses the romantic feelings and moods aroused by a walk through the Vienna woods.

Having accepted his silent world, one in which he could hear music only in his mind, Beethoven turned meditative in his later work. Two works dominate this third period—the mass in D (*Missa Solemnis*) and the *Choral*. The former, which Beethoven himself believed to be his greatest work, is a complex vocal and instrumental piece that owes much to George Frideric Handel. More a symphony than a mass, it is considered both a personal and a universal confession of faith. The *Choral*, whose oulines developed over eight years, was first performed on May 7, 1824, with Beethoven sharing in the conducting. The occasion was the composer's public farewell, and a tumultuous one it was as the audience applauded and waved handkerchiefs in appreciation not only for the *Choral* but also for a glorious career of musical creativity.

Summary

Each lover of classical music has his own favorite or favorites among the many great composers who have made the music of the Western world what it is. No one, however, can dismiss the tremendous contributions to that music made by Ludwig van Beethoven. A bridge between the classical tradition and the Romantic in music, he did much to transform a number of musical forms. His innovations included expanding the length of the symphony and of the piano concerto and increasing the number of movements in the string quartet from four to seven. His experiments in harmony and rhythm brought a new dimension to the symphony, as did his expansion of the orchestra itself. Introducing the trombone, the contrabassoon, and the piccolo, he sought to give the orchestra a broader range through which to reflect the breadth and depth of his compositions. In regard to his own instrument, the piano, he did much to bring it from its status as a relatively new invention (1710) to one in which it was seen to become the dominant and versatile instrument it is today.

Surely the greatest testament to Beethoven's power of creativity and to his overall contribution to the world of music is the universal and lasting popularity of so many of his works. His symphonies—particularly the third, fifth, sixth, and ninth—are performed regularly by virtually all orchestras. The same is true for the fourth and fifth piano concertos and the violin concerto in D. The opera *Fidelio* is also widely performed, as are the *Missa Solemnis* and the piano sonatas and string quartets.

Beethoven had his arrogance and his uncompromising character. He also had pain and tragedy in his life. Most of all, however, he had genius—and the strength of spirit to bring that genius to the highest level of accomplishment. Some twenty thousand admirers attended his funeral. They were saying goodbye to the man. The genius, however, lives on in the music.

Bibliography

Comini, Alessandra. *The Changing Image of Beethoven: A Study in Mythmaking.* New York: Rizzoli, 1987. Examines the image of Beethoven and the mythmaking process that began even during his lifetime. Attempts to analyze the interior image of Beethoven held by those who contributed to the mythmaking process. A solid study that places Beethoven very clearly in his time.

Landon, H. C. Robbins. *Beethoven: A Documentary Study.* New York: Macmillan, 1970. Provides a good picture of many members of the aristocracy and ruling class who were close to Beethoven. Includes excerpts from diaries and letters that provide an insight not only into Beethoven himself but also into those who knew him well.

Matthews, Denis. *Beethoven.* London: J. M. Dent & Sons, 1985. One of a series of books on great musicians. A revision of an earlier number and a reassessment of Beethoven. Covers his life in the first five chapters and his music in the next eight. Finally attempts to place Beethoven in the world of music.

Solomon, Maynard. *Beethoven.* New York: Schirmer Books, 1977. A standard biography that divides Beethoven's life into four basic phases—the Bonn years, the early Vienna years, the period of heightened creativity, and the declining years. Good introduction to Beethoven. A good essay on the music closes the book.

Thayer, Alexander Wheelock. *Thayer's Life of Beethoven.* Princeton, N.J.:

Princeton University Press, 1964, rev. ed. 1967. Revised and edited by Elliot Forbes. One of the basic studies of Beethoven that attempts to correct errors and to add new material. Good treatment of the facts of Beethoven's life, but no analytical interpretation of the music.

Valentin, Erich. *Beethoven and His World*. New York: Viking Press, 1958. Focuses more on Beethoven's life than on the music. Presents an excellent picture of Vienna in the early nineteenth century and of the politics of the period. Good introductory work.

Wilton Eckley

GIOVANNI BELLINI

Born: c. 1430; Venice
Died: 1516; Venice
Area of Achievement: Art
Contribution: As the leading painter of the Republic of Venice over more than two generations, Bellini achieved a synthesis of major currents in art deriving from Italian centers such as Tuscany and Padua as well as from Northern Europe. His conquest of the poetry of light and color was the foundation of the greatness of Venetian painting in the sixteenth century.

Early Life

The year of Giovanni Bellini's birth is not known, but the approximate date of 1430 has been suggested. Sketchy evidence indicates that he was the second of two sons born to Jacopo Bellini and his wife, Anna Rinversi. Giovanni's brother, Gentile, was probably born about two or three years earlier, and a sister, Nicolosia, two or three years later. The close ages of the children is significant for Venetian art, as the brothers were frequently to work in close association, and a major artistic influence upon Giovanni was his sister's husband, the painter Andrea Mantegna, whom she married in 1453.

There is a scarcity of information about Giovanni's early life, but a few biographical facts do offer some insight. For example, it is known that Giovanni's mother was a native of the region of Pesaro, south of Venice on the Adriatic coast; Giovanni may have found it convenient to reside there while creating one of his early masterpieces, *Coronation of the Virgin* (c. 1473). The family connection with Pesaro suggests Giovanni's receptiveness to the world outside the city-state of Venice. Similarly, Jacopo Bellini's important early contact with the vibrant art of Tuscany is shown by his apprenticeship to Gentile da Fabriano.

During the early Renaissance, it became increasingly possible for a talented individual to transcend the status of craftsman to become an artist, a person endowed with intellectual as well as manual skills. Jacopo is this sort of transitional figure in the art of early fifteenth century Italy, and his sons—more particularly Giovanni—were to enjoy an even higher social position than their father. To Jacopo, however, goes the credit both for the technical education of his sons and for their introduction to Renaissance ideals, including the enthusiasm for antiquity and the respect for learning embodied in the concept of Humanism.

At an unrecorded date Giovanni married a woman named Ginevra Bocheta, and they later had a son, Alvise. His departure from his parents' household around 1459 may not indicate his artistic independence but only his move to new quarters. Gentile was the first of the brothers to win large public commissions, and it was in this field that he specialized, producing throughout his career many monumental decorations for the Venetian fraternal groups called *scuole*—literally, but not actually, "schools." While it is acknowledged that Giovanni was a more adventurous and accomplished artist than Gentile, the brothers' achievement has often been regarded collectively because of their joint dominance of Venetian art during their lifetimes and because they seemed to have esteemed each other very highly.

Giovanni's likeness is known from an anonymous and mediocre woodcut in the 1568 edition of Giorgio Vasari's famous work on the lives of painters as well as from a drawing (now in the Condé Museum of Chantilly, France) by one of Giovanni's students. This profile portrait shows the middle-aged Bellini as a handsome man with a well-proportioned face and a prominent but straight nose. Adjusting for the slightly different treatment of the face in the later woodcut, one might accept the argument of a prominent scholar that Giovanni pictured himself in a late work, *Feast of the Gods* (c. 1514), as the mythological figure Silvanus.

Life's Work

Bellini's independent career can be regarded as beginning around 1460. It is often impossible to determine the contributions of assistants to the collective work of a studio, and in the case of the Bellini family this is especially true in the production of the 1450's. There is also little basis for distinguishing some of the work of this period by Giovanni from that of his brother-in-law Mantegna, who may have studied with Jacopo and worked in his studio on the same basis as his sons. Thus, Bellini's earliest work can be conceived only in the general terms of a range of stylistic qualities and types of objects. Aside from preparatory drawings, it consists of small paintings of religious character, some executed on vellum and others on wooden panels of modest dimensions. The paintings on vellum have a delicacy befitting both their size and their derivation from the traditions of manuscript illustration, but the panels show added concern with the treatment of the human figure as a sculptural volume and with the placement of the figure in a natural landscape.

In Giovanni's early panels, the influence of Mantegna is believed to be manifest. A native of the region of Padua, Mantegna was an extremely precocious artist whose style is characterized by somewhat schematized and muscular linear forms rendered with tone to achieve an incisive sculptural effect. Bellini's debt to Mantegna may be seen in his firm contours and crisp detail as well as in his pictorial construction, but Bellini's adaptations are more sensitively observant of nature, as in his *Agony in the Garden*, dating from the early 1460's. The same subject as treated by Mantegna is more tautly composed, favoring drama over poetry; Bellini's landscape is almost pastoral, while Mantegna's represents, in one scholar's words, an almost "lunar ideal of natural landscape."

From Giovanni's studio in the 1460's came a remarkable outpouring of paintings of Christ, of the Madonna and Child, and of various saints. These show a mastery of form and a depth of feeling that place Giovanni, still only in his thirties, at the forefront of Venetian art. The works are freshly approached on both the technical and the emotional levels and show that, even at a considerable distance from sources of innovation in Tuscany and central Italy, Bellini is receptive to the more advanced artistic tendencies of his time. His *Pietà with Virgin and Saint John*, in the Brera gallery in Milan, is representative of the artist's fully developed early manner in the way it combines assurance of form with a powerful yet restrained rendering of its subject, the sorrow at Christ's death. Notwithstanding its relatively early date in Bellini's career, it is one of the great achievements of European art.

The next phase in Bellini's career is notable for the increasing use of the medium of oil paint and a growing affinity for Flemish art, within which oil techniques had been ascendant since the 1420's. Neither the oil medium nor the influence of Northern art were entirely novel in Venice in the early 1470's, but both were given prominence in Venice by the brief presence there of the Sicilian-born artist Antonello da Messina around 1475. It is evident that Antonello learned much of his technique from someone with close ties to Jan van Eyck or one of his contemporaries, because his style was formed far less by Italian art than by the Northern tradition of rendering exact detail and effects of light. The influence of Antonello's Flemish orientation upon Bellini's work, and thus upon later Venetian painting, was lasting; the oil medium allowed for more fluid and colorful rendering of surfaces than did the traditional, fast-drying tempera paints, and provided Bellini and his successors with a material which was well suited to the Venetian artistic temperament, which was by nature more spontaneous and emotional than that of their central Italian counterparts.

During the 1470's, Bellini's appreciation of monumental form seems to have been enhanced by contact with the work of great Italian predecessors such as Donatello and Masaccio, though there is only indirect evidence of this. The influence of the frescoes of Piero della Francesca seems likely; Giovanni could have seen his work at Rimini, on the road between Venice and Pesaro. There is something of Piero's austere integration of form, light, and color in the large panel of Bellini's *Coronation of the Virgin*, part of the Pesaro altarpiece of the early 1470's. A small panel of the *Adoration of the Child*, part of the *predella*, or frame, of this altarpiece, shows Bellini's ability to create a convincing landscape environment for his solidly painted figures, but more particularly it reveals a poetic mastery of effects of light and atmosphere that was unmatched by his Italian contemporaries. Another panel (of disputed date, but perhaps painted as early as 1475), the *Saint Francis in Ecstasy* in the Frick Collection in New York, is considered one of Bellini's masterpieces. Conceived as an independent picture, this painting has a design that recalls the art of Mantegna, but its underlying character is more reflective. Bellini's art, increasingly receptive to the beauty of landscape, is in perfect harmony with the spirit of Francis of Assisi, of all the saints the one most devoted to nature.

In the following decade, Bellini continued with much the same range of subject matter as before, but he painted with increasing assurance. An *Enthroned Madonna and Child* of the late 1480's, also know as the San Giobbe altarpiece, is monumental both in size and in conception: It is more than fifteen feet high and eight feet wide and was originally installed in a Venetian church, where its pictorial space could be viewed as an extension of the actual interior space of the church. Another dimension of Bellini's work in this period was to meet the continuing needs of the *scuole* for large commemorative paintings, a task he often shared with his brother, but none of these has survived.

A continuous sequence of portraits by Bellini's hand—as distinct from works of his studio—cannot be established, but there are several portrait masterpieces that are unquestionably his own. His *Portrait of Doge Leonardo Loredan*, an exquisitely detailed rendering of Venice's leader, was probably painted following Loredan's election in October, 1501. In this work, Bellini gives a sense of the whole person in two senses: physically, by choosing a composition which shows more of the subject's attire, and psychologically, by means of rare human insight. Bellini's approach to portraiture soon became the norm with the new generation of painters, and his ability to keep abreast of the innovations of his younger contemporaries made him a sought-after artist into his final years.

Among Bellini's most important paintings is a work of his last years, the *Feast of the Gods*. Loosely based upon a subject taken from Ovid's *Fasti* (c. A.D. 8; feasts), the painting was commissioned by a knowledgeable patron, possibly Isabella d'Este of the Court of Ferrara. Isabella, a woman of decided tastes as well as strong intellect, had begun a project of decorating some study rooms in her private apartment with paintings of pagan subjects, and she may have engaged Bellini to paint a companion-piece to a work by Mantegna. *Feast of the Gods* is a painting that celebrates classical mythology while paying respects to the lively world of Italian Renaissance culture. One of Bellini's few paintings on classical subjects, its humor, lyricism, and mildly erotic content show that he could be moved by antique as well as Christian themes.

Summary

Giovanni Bellini's exceptionally long and productive career spanned more than six decades. The larger part of his work belongs to the 1400's, when Italian art evolved a unity of approach to pictorial organization and content within which local and individual styles are still strongly manifest. Bellini was Venice's foremost painter of this period, providing one of many regional inflections to the technical and expressive development of Italian art.

Like his great contemporaries, Bellini sought with success to enhance the sense of reality in his paintings through the study of space, volume, light, and color, but, among his varied achievements, art historians have credited him with a particularly astute understanding of atmosphere. Bellini learned to give his landscape-based compositions the reality of specific times of day and conditions of atmosphere, and he applied his discoveries to reinforcing the mood of his chosen subject.

Though Bellini developed his sense of light and color within the medium of tempera paint, his use of oil paint was particularly consequential for Venetian art, which increasingly exploited the brilliance and versatility of the oil medium. Bellini's mastery of oil was accomplished well before 1500, but his continuing conquest of its capabilities late in his career serves as a reminder that he not only survived into the new century but also was an active participant in it. Bellini remained extraordinarily vital in old age, perhaps spurred by friendly rivalry with a younger generation of painters that included Giorgione and Titian. It is likely that Giorgione was in some fashion Bellini's pupil, but the influence of pupil upon teacher is also suggested by scholars. Not long after Bellini's death, when the *Feast of the Gods* came into the hands of Alfonso d'Este in Mantua, the young Titian was engaged to revise it. Titian's kinship with Bellini—to an extent one of taste as well as of technical practice—is virtually the only explanation for the fact that Titian's alterations, though regrettable from the perspective of art history, are nevertheless quite successful in their own terms.

After a half-century of work, Bellini achieved a style as unified and expressive as that of his greatest contemporaries. The German artist Albrecht Dürer, visting Bellini in Venice in 1506, had found him *optimo pytor* (a great painter) and *pest in Gemoll* (the very best). After hundreds of years, Bellini's achievement still places him in the highest rank of European artists.

Bibliography

Freedberg, S. J. *Painting in Italy, 1500-1600*. Baltimore: Penguin Books, 1970. This discerning guide to Italian painting of the fourteenth through the seventeenth centuries deals in proportion with the Bellini family, but it has a particular virtue in giving a sense of the proportion of one artist's achievement to another, when many belong in the category "great." A minor irritant is that illustrations are separated from the text.

Hartt, Frederick. *History of Italian Renaissance Art: Painting, Sculpture, Architecture*. Englewood Cliffs, N. J.: Prentice-Hall, 1979. This standard survey of the field discusses the Bellini family very extensively. An excellent prelude to specialized reading, it retains its value for convenient reference to artists and works referred to in scholarly works. The illustrations are integrated with the text.

Hendy, Philip, and Ludwig Goldscheider. *Giovanni Bellini*. New York: Oxford University Press, 1945. This volume consists of more than one hundred illustrations of Bellini's works with an introductory essay by Hendy. The text is aimed at a general audience and contains comparative information useful to the student without an extensive background in Renaissance art. Color reproductions are given of five key works.

Meiss, Millard. *Giovanni Bellini's "St. Francis."* Princeton, N.J.: Princeton University Press, 1964. This short monograph on one of Bellini's most beautiful and celebrated paintings shows that scholarship in art history can be graceful as well as illuminating. The excellent illustrations (only the title painting is shown in color) include many works by Bellini and others that help place the St. Francis work in context.

Robertson, Giles. *Giovanni Bellini*. Oxford, England: Clarendon Press, 1968. Robertson's full-length study has the advantage of later scholarly research to differentiate it from Hendy and Goldscheider's monograph. The author negotiates a quantity of detailed information with surprising clarity. The absence of color plates may be accounted for by the extent of the black-and-white illustrations, of which there are 120.

Wind, Edgar. *Bellini's "Feast of the Gods": A Study in Venetian Humanism*. Cambridge, Mass.: Harvard University Press, 1948. Despite its many erudite references to issues in ancient literature and Renaissance Humanism—many of which appear only in Latin or Italian—this excellent small monograph is directed to nonspecialists as much as to scholars. Both the text and the plates give a broad sense of Bellini's later career and his cultural environment, and, though Wind's conclusions are questioned by later scholars, his observations are unfailingly interesting.

C. S. McConnell

CARL BENZ

Born: November 25, 1844; Karlsruhe, Germany
Died: April 4, 1929; Ladenburg, Germany
Areas of Achievement: Invention and technology
Contribution: As one of the earliest inventors of a practical automobile, Benz made contributions of great importance to the modern way of life. He developed several features essential to automobile design and function.

Early Life

When Carl Benz was only two years old, his father, a railroad engineer, died of pneumonia. His widowed mother was left with only a small income for the support of her family. Benz was able to contribute to the family finances by profiting from his interest in technical matters. While still a child, he repaired clocks and watches for the neighbors and had his own darkroom. He used the darkroom to develop pictures he took for the visitors to the area of the Black Forest around Karlsruhe, where he lived.

At secondary school he remained interested in technical subjects and became an assistant to the physics instructor. After attending Karlsruhe Polytechnic, he gained valuable experience by working for a manufacturer of engines. Even at this time, he had in mind the construction of a horseless carriage and spent evenings drawing plans for it. In 1871, he went to Mannheim to work for a firm that made wagons, pumps, and cranes. Soon thereafter, in 1872, he opened his own shop to produce engines. He was apparently confident of success, as he was married to Berta Ringer, whom he had met on a job in Pforzheim, just before starting out on his own.

Benz's confidence was not misplaced. His engines sold well, and he found investors who provided funds for him to establish the Mannheim Gas Engine Manufacturing Company. The new company employed forty people and was profitable. The venture lasted only a short time, however, as his shareholders were more interested in profits than in experimentation. They refused to allow him to use any of the profits for work on a horseless carriage, and he withdrew from the company, losing his investment after only three months of operations.

A man with Benz's experience, ability, and money-making record could not fail to attract sympathetic investors for long, and on October 1, 1883, Benz and Company was founded. Two Mannheim businessmen, Max Caspar Rose and Friedrich Wilhelm Esslinger, were the investors in the new company for the production of "internal combustion engines after the plans of Carl Benz." While his new partners were not enthusiastic about his experiments with horseless carriages, they were willing to tolerate them as long as he attended to the primary business of the company—the production of stationary gas engines. They were not to regret their indulgence.

Life's Work

It is difficult to maintain that Benz was the first to invent the automobile because of the difficulty in establishing the definition of an automobile. Self-propelled, steam-driven vehicles had been in operation since the early nineteenth century. An Austrian, Siegfried Marcus, designed handcarts propelled by internal-combustion engines in the 1860's, and French experimenters constructed similar vehicles. In these circumstances it cannot be maintained that Benz was the first to produce an automobile, but his vehicles were the earliest practical, marketable horseless carriages.

The plans that Benz had been developing for nearly two decades quickly bore fruit once he had the necessary resources at his disposal. Probably the most important feature of the motorized tricycle he produced in 1885 was the engine. This is not surprising given his years of experience in designing and building engines. It was a four-cycle, or Otto-cycle, engine that burned gasoline. The Otto-cycle engine had existed since the late 1870's, and its principle of operation had been established in the 1860's. It is called a four-cycle engine because the explosion of gasoline in the combustion chamber occurs only on every fourth stroke of the piston. During the first stroke, as the piston moves downward, atmospheric pressure forces the gaseous fuel into the piston cylinder through a valve. When the piston reaches the end of its downward movement, a spring closes the valve to prevent the gas from escaping as the piston makes its return, or second stroke. At the top of the second stroke the gas is compressed in the combustion chamber above the piston to about one-third of its normal volume. The gas is then ignited, and its expansion as it burns forces the piston down in its third, or power, stroke. When the power rises on its fourth stroke, it forces the burned gas out through an exhaust valve that is opened mechanically.

In order to convert the liquid gasoline to a gaseous state, a carburetor is necessary. The carburetor used by Benz was very simple. He routed the hot exhaust gases through a pipe that passed through a chamber containing liquid gasoline, thus warming it. Air admitted through holes in an outer container flowed over the evaporating gasoline, and the mixture of air and gasoline proceeded on to the combustion chamber. The mixture could be left rich in gasoline or leaned by the addition of air as required by means of a pipe with holes between the carburetor and combustion chamber. A sliding cover allowed more, or less, air to enter the holes.

The innovation that made the Benz engine particularly important was the ignition system. For the most part, previous engines had used a heated tube for ignition. This system left much to be desired. Benz used an electrical ignition system consisting of a four-volt battery connected to an induction coil wrapped around an iron core. In the circuit was a flat spring that was magnetically attracted to the iron core when current flowed through the coil. The attraction of the spring, known as a trembler, broke the circuit, allowing the spring to return to its original position and to reestablish the circuit. The result was a rapid vibration of the trembler and the production of a series of charges to the spark plug, which sparked and ignited the gas in the combustion chamber. The spark had to be produced at the correct time. To achieve the correct timing, a rotor made of insulating material with a metal chip in its circumference was introduced into the circuit. The rotor was connected mechanically to the piston-driven shaft in such a way that the metal chip closed the circuit to the spark plug when the piston was at the top of the compression stroke. A switch allowed the circuit to be opened to stop the engine. This ignition system was the basis for all others from that time to the present.

Other features of his motorized tricycle included elliptical rear springs, rack-and-pinion steering, and water cooling. Belts and chains transmitted power from the engine to the solid rear axle. Benz later claimed that he had driven the tricycle in the spring of 1885, and many consider this to have been the first automobile powered by an internal-combustion engine. In the autumn of 1885, he tested the vehicle before witnesses. The test was a short one. In fact, Benz never made it to the road outside his workshop yard: He ran into a brick wall, but he and his passenger—his wife—escaped injury. There were other tests as he developed his design, but his first public notice came on June 4, 1886, when the *Neue Badische Landeszeitung* printed a description of the vehicle, followed on July 3, 1886, by a favorable report of a test-drive.

Benz continued to improve his invention by adding a sun and planet gear which provided a second gear. He applied for a patent for this feature in April, 1887. Further improvements included a larger engine (three horsepower instead of one horsepower), better springs, and more effective brakes. By 1887, the vehicle had reached such a stage of development that it was possible to market it.

The first customer for a Benz automobile was a Frenchman named Émile Roger, who saw one demonstrated at the Paris Exhibition of 1887. In the following year, Benz won a gold medal at the Imperial Exhibition in Munich. The publicity from these exhibitions apparently stimulated a number of orders. In 1889, the Benz Company employed fifty workers. Business was so brisk that Benz was able to find new partners who financed a move to a larger factory where the company began producing vehicles with four wheels in 1890.

The addition of a fourth wheel was one of the few concessions Benz was to make to those who wanted him to maintain an up-to-date design. He appears to have regarded the design of 1890 as final and refused to make changes in it. Even when he consented to the addition of a hood to the front of the car, it was only an empty shell added for the sake of appearance. He insisted on keeping the engine at the rear. In 1905, he finally bowed to pressure from his colleagues and allowed sweeping design changes, but he and his wife continued to drive their older models.

Photographs of Benz posing as driver of his automobiles show a man of medium stature, dark hair, and constantly changing facial hair. He always wore a large mustache, but his goatees came and went presumably in accord with fashions of the day. Pictures of him in later life indicate that he became thinner and the hair and mustache turned white. The later photographs are of a man with a prominent, sharp nose and deep-set eyes.

Benz was not alone in the attempt to build a horseless carriage. His most significant German rival was Gottlieb Daimler. Many argue that Daimler should be regarded as the inventor of a practical, engine-driven vehicle with internal combustion. His engine was better in many respects and his patent of August, 1885, predates Benz's by five months. Benz's adherents concede these points but note that Daimler's work involved a motorcycle rather than a three- or four-wheeled vehicle. Competition between the two involved more than mere claims to priority. The two companies vied for sales, especially in France and Germany. It was for the sake of the French market that the Daimler product became known as the Mercedes. The French distributor suggested the name of his daughter, Mercedes, as sounding more French than Daimler and, therefore, more acceptable to the French buying public. Rivalry between Benz and Daimler was strictly on a commercial basis; they had never met when Daimler died in 1900.

During the economic depression that followed World War I in Germany, both the Daimler and Benz companies faltered. That led to their merger to form Mercedes-Benz in 1926. By that time Benz had little to do with the active management of the company that he had founded nearly forty years before.

Summary

The inventive genius of Carl Benz was considerable. Working independently, he managed to invent the necessary components for an automobile and combine them in a practical machine. The fact that Daimler and others produced better engines and made wider use of them in boats and for other applications does not detract from his accomplishments. Whether a motorized tricycle actually qualifies as the first automobile and whether it deserves such a title more than a motorcycle are less important concerns in assessing Benz's career than his status as a pioneer in the marketing of automobiles. His contributions were certainly recognized as significant during his lifetime. Early examples of his cars were in museums, and two days before his death a procession of several hundred automobiles drove from Heidelberg to his house in Ladenburg, where dignitaries delivered a number of speeches acclaiming him as the inventor of the automobile.

As shown by the earlier inventions of Siegfried Marcus, it is one thing to produce a self-propelled vehicle but quite another to turn it into something that people will buy in significant numbers. It was to take the mass production techniques of Henry Ford and others to make the automobile into more than a plaything of the rich, but Benz and his rivals brought the idea of automobile ownership and its practicality into the minds of the buying public.

Bibliography

Nevins, Allan. *Ford: The Times, the Man, and the Company.* New York: Charles Scribner's Sons, 1954. Although devoted to Henry Ford, the first volume of this work contains considerable discussion of the development of the early automobile in general and of the contributions of Benz in particular. It also contains a useful bibliography for use in further research on the early development of the automobile.

Nixon, St. John C. *The Invention of the Automobile.* London: Country Life, 1936. This book is the story of Benz and Daimler and the creation of their company. Most of it is devoted to Benz, and it gives him the lion's share of credit for the invention of the automobile. In fact, it proclaims him as its inventor. Contains helpful illustrations and photographs of several Daimler cars as well as a comparative chronology of Daimler's and Benz's lives.

Poole, Lynn, and Gray Poole. *Men Who Pioneered Inventions.* New York: Dodd, Mead, 1969. A book intended for juvenile readers. Gives considerable credit to Benz and boldly recognizes him as the inventor of the automobile.

Roberts, Peter. *Veteran and Vintage Cars.* London: Paul Hamlyn, 1963. One of the more readily available picture books dealing with early automobiles. Contains a descriptive text as well as color photographs and reproductions of advertisements. Covers the period to 1914 and has illustrations of the Benz products.

Singer, Charles, et al., eds. *A History of Technology.* Vol. 5, *The Late Nineteenth Century, c. 1850 to c. 1900.* New York: Oxford University Press, 1958. A useful work for more detailed explanations of the technical aspects of the work of Benz and the other early designers of internal-combustion engines. The authors do not enter into the discussion of priority in the invention of the automobile.

Philip Dwight Jones

HECTOR BERLIOZ

Born: December 11, 1803; La Côte-Saint-André, France
Died: March 8, 1869; Paris, France
Area of Achievement: Music
Contribution: Berlioz, one of the foremost exponents of Romanticism, extended the art of orchestration in compositions of striking originality. In his writings, which include a treatise on orchestration and a colorful memoir of his life, he made contributions both to musical craft and cultural history. During his lifetime Berlioz's music attained more popularity outside France than within it, where the eccentric notoriety of the man often overshadowed his genius.

Early Life

Louis-Hector Berlioz was born on the morning of December 11, 1803, in the town of La Côte-Saint-André, about fifty-five kilometers northwest of Grenoble, France. Hector was the first of six children born to Louis-Joseph and Marie Antoinette Berlioz; his family, which had prospered over generations from tanning and other enterprises, could be traced on his father's side to the beginning of the seventeenth century. Louis Berlioz was a kindly but serious man, who had received his medical degree in Paris only months after Hector's birth; though culturally and intellectually refined far beyond the custom of his provincial locale, he came to be loved by the peasants he served. Hector's mother figures in his life much less prominently than her husband. As a devout Roman Catholic, she provided him with a religious upbringing, but it seems not to have had a lasting impact.

After briefly attending school in La Côte, Berlioz's education was directed with great success by his father at home. His studies included mathematics, history, and French literature, but geography became his favorite topic. At an early age, he also came to love Vergil's *Aeneid* (c. 29-19 B.C.), learning to read the Roman author in the original Latin. At age twelve, on a family holiday in nearby Meylan, he experienced his first feelings of romantic love, a passion for a young woman of eighteen named Estelle Deboeuf. This brief, one-sided experience only slowly lost its hold upon his imagination.

Part of Berlioz's education at home consisted of lessons in practical music making; Hector had learned to play the flageolet, a form of recorder, after finding one in a bureau drawer at home; in his teens, he was given a flute, which he soon learned to play capably. Later, he learned the guitar, but there was no piano in his home, and he never learned the instrument aside from picking out harmonies on its keys. Hector was not a child prodigy, but his natural musical gifts soon led him to compose short instrumental and vocal works, which he would play with family and friends. At the age of fifteen, he was naïvely offering his pieces to a well-known publisher.

Louis Berlioz had determined that his son should follow a medical career and set about preparing Hector and a young friend for medical studies, which commenced in Paris in 1821. Hector's intellectual interest in his subjects was sincere, and he later praised some of the lecturers, but, when the course of study turned to the dissection of human cadavers, he recoiled violently from the work.

By 1824, Berlioz no longer pretended that he was studying medicine. Since the previous year, he had been a student in the classes of the composer Jean-François Le Sueur, who took a warm interest in him, and much of his time was devoted to attending opera performances, reading scores in the library of the music conservatory, and composing. This development was viewed with dismay by Berlioz's parents, who had hoped that a few disappointments with music would convince him to abandon his plans for a musical career. Despite occasional modest successes in the performance of his works, his failure to pass a music examination in 1826 caused his father to demand his return to La Côte. Louis persuaded his son to attempt once more to pass the examination; if he failed, he would choose a different profession.

By living extremely frugally and giving lessons in singing, flute, and guitar, Belioz was repaying a loan given by an acquaintance to finance a concert, when the thoughtless creditor requested the balance owing from Berlioz's father. Enraged by Hector's improvidence, Louis paid the debt but terminated Hector's allowance, and the twenty-three-year-old composer was thrown into virtual poverty, surviving only by taking a job in a theater chorus. Disciplining mind and body, however, he continued his studies. After a period of months, he passed the examination qualifying him to compete for the Prix de Rome, a lucrative award of the Academy of Fine Arts of the Institute of France. Soon after, his father restored his allowance, and Berlioz was able to continue his operagoing on a grand scale. His favorite composers at the time were Christoph Gluck and Gaspare Spontini, but he despised the popular Gioacchino Rossini.

Like many of his contemporaries who regarded themselves as Romantic artists, Berlioz embraced the experience and display of emotion. In 1827, a company of actors arrived from England to present a season of performances of plays by William Shakespeare. This was Berlioz's overwhelming introduction to Shakespeare on the stage, and it was also the beginning of his love for the actress Harriet Smithson, who played Ophelia on opening night. Berlioz's involved and somewhat ostentatious passion for Henriette (as she is called in his memoirs) was to play a large part in the inspiration for his *Symphonie fantastique* (1830) and its sequel, *Le Retour à la vie* (1831), or *Lélio*, as it was later known. Unsuccessful attempts to get Henriette's attention, including public concerts of his own work, were finally abandoned, but the beautiful and talented Henriette had already left her mark on Hector's imagination.

Berlioz continued his musical studies at the conservatoire and began, around 1829, to write articles on music for the Paris press. Literary work, which he generally undertook to relieve his strained finances, often seemed to Berlioz to be a curse, but he had a natural capacity for writing and his contributions to music criticism are substantial. His literary experience also led him to compose music to poems by Victor Hugo and others, and the first composition to which Berlioz gave an opus number, *Huit Scènes de Faust* (1828), was based upon Johann Wolfgang von Goethe's *Faust: Eine Tragödie* (1808). In 1830, *The Death of Sardanapalus* was the subject of a composition that won for him the Prix de Rome on his fourth attempt. The fictional but grotesque story of Sardanapalus had been broached only three years before by the painter Eugène Delacroix, partly relieving Berlioz of the reputation for excess that had dogged his previous competition efforts.

In the spring of 1830, Berlioz again fell in love, this time with a nineteen-year-old pianist, Marie Moke. They were soon engaged, despite the prospect of being separated by Berlioz's impending year-long stay in Rome, a condition of the Prix de Rome stipend. Sensing that his absence would be a kind of spiritual imprisonment, he tried to gain an exemption from the requirement, but the authorities would not agree to it. His fiancée's family was similarly unyielding, making the engagement conditional both upon his absence and upon the success of a pending performance of his *Symphonie fantastique*. After the work was successfully presented in December, Berlioz left for Rome, stopping to visit his family at La Côte early in the new year.

In residence at the French Academy in Rome for only a few weeks, growing fears about his engagement drove him to abandon the academy. Soon he learned in a letter from Marie's mother that his fiancée was to marry a prosperous man of fifty-eight. Berlioz, enraged, became intent upon murder and suicide, and got as far as Nice before thinking better of his plan. Berlioz was allowed to return to the academy, but he was often moody, bored, and distracted in Rome, which was to him little more than a museum. Preferring nature to city life, he toured the surrounding countryside on foot, gathering impressions of its landscape and inhabitants that later inspired the symphonic work *Harold in Italy* (1834), a musical essay evoking the atmosphere of Lord Byron's poem *Childe Harold's Pilgrimage* (1812-1818, 1819). After more than a year in Italy, Berlioz returned to Paris, arriving in the capital on November 6, 1832. On the eve of his thirtieth year, he had been well-seasoned by artistic struggles and by painful episodes in his personal life.

Life's Work

The professional difficulties of Berlioz's career were often concerned with finances or with the quality of performances that could be extracted from the French orchestras of the day. Sometimes these circumstances met to produce concerts that were financial as well as artistic failures, but more often Berlioz, an excellent conductor, fared well with Parisian audiences. A concert of December 9, 1832, designed to reintroduce himself to the public, featured the *Symphonie fantastique* and *Lélio*. Harriet Smithson, his unrequited love of four years past, was in the audience, doubtless uneasily aware that the two works had grown out of the composer's passion for her in 1827-1828. The following day they met for the first time, and after months of fervent but strained courtship they were married. In August, 1834, their only child, Louis, was born.

The two works of that fateful December concert were conceived as a spiritual autobiography in music. From the moment Berlioz discovered his tragic muse in Henriette's portrayals of Ophelia and Juliet, he had been immersed in a painful rapture which for a time had made creative activity almost impossible, and *Symphonie fantastique* was both a fulfillment and an exorcism of the composer's torment. It is a "program symphony," evoking "an episode in the life of an artist," and follows a novelistic scenario including a ball, a march to execution, and a witches' Sabbath. For all of its eccentricities and weaknesses, it is an influential landmark in music. *Lélio*, however, is generally regarded as a gratuitous, provocatively egotistic, and somewhat incoherent sequel. The true artistic sequel to the *Symphonie fantastique* is Berlioz's *Harold in Italy*, featuring a solo viola part which gives the symphony something of the nature of a concerto.

The German poet Heinrich Heine, who was a friend of the composer, described Berlioz as "an immense nightingale, or a lark the size of an eagle," whose music "causes me to dream of fabulous empires with fabulous sins." This characterization encompasses something of the spirit of the man as well as his appearance: The composer's artistic soul was both lyric and violent, as his appearance could seem either wistful or dramatic in turn. He was of medium height and angular, with a pronounced beaklike nose framed by intense, deep-set eyes and a great mass of hair.

The decade of 1835 through 1845 brought Berlioz fame both as composer and as conductor, but his successes were punctuated by the same kind of difficulties he had faced in previous years. He seems to have been a difficult man and was rarely at peace with the official cultural apparatus or with his colleagues. Financial problems continued and were intensified by the failure of Henriette's career following a leg injury (by 1842, Berlioz had separated from her, though his affection survived to her death in 1854). His journalistic work and his need continually to promote his own compositions strained his health, which was not robust. Nevertheless, these were the years in which he composed some of his greatest works, including the *Messe de morts*, or *Requiem* (1837), the opera *Benvenuto Cellini* (1834-1838), the symphony *Roméo et Juliette* (1839), and the dramatic cantata *La Damnation de Faust* (1846), derived in part from his early *Huit Scènes de Faust*.

The *Requiem*, commissioned by the government for a civic funeral, shows Berlioz in full command both of his musical materials and of his sense of public occasion. Berlioz specified for the work 190 instruments and 210 voices, not including timpani and brass choirs to be heard at a distance. Certain passages achieve a great acoustical and emotional effect, but other parts of the mass are models of delicacy. Berlioz's reputation for colossal effect is only partly justified, for he knew how to use large musical forces with restraint.

In 1842, Berlioz began a series of trips abroad which were to bring him many artistic triumphs and, not incidentally, a further source of income. He was in demand both as composer and conductor, and the accounts he gives in his memoirs of his travels in England, Germany, Austria, Hungary, and Russia show him directing his own works as well as those of Gluck, Ludwig van Beethoven, and others. His journeys also gave him an opportunity to meet many of the leading performers and composers of Europe, including Franz Liszt, Robert Schumann, and Richard Wagner, with whom he had a long-standing but ambivalent relationship.

In his forties, Berlioz's musical style began to show signs of retreat from the adventurous Romanticism of his youth. Official honors had already come his way: In 1839, he was made a member of the Legion of Honor and was given a modest salary as an official of the conservatory library. His treatise on orchestration and his *Voyage musical en Allemagne et en Italie* (a musical voyage in Germany and Italy) were published in 1844. Beyond these signs of increasing acceptance, however, the subtle moderation of his artistic outlook can be traced to other circumstances. He was drained by work undertaken for the sake of paying for two households—Henriette's and his own; his son, Louis, who had become a sailor, was often troublesome. More important, though, the melancholy streak in his character came to overrule his penchant for ostentation and experimentation. Berlioz turned more and more to the poetry of Vergil, which had stirred him as a child; a current of classicism emerged in his musical thought, expressing a conception of beauty that had perhaps lain dormant in him since youth. From this sensibility emerged much of Berlioz's late work: *L'Enfance du Christ*, first performed in December, 1854, belongs to this late phase of his career; *Les Troyens* (1856-1858), with a libretto by the composer, is its culmination.

Berlioz's musical work might well have ended with the staging of *Les Troyens*—he was suffering increasingly from an ill-defined internal malady—but a final commission, the two-act opera *Béatrice et Bénédict* occupied him during 1860-1862. Based upon Shakespeare's *Much Ado About Nothing* (1598-1599), it is a gracious comedy which Berlioz found to be a relaxation after the immense labors of *Les Troyens*.

Berlioz's last years brought him personal loss; in 1862, his second wife, Marie Recio, died suddenly. Her mother selflessly continued to look after the composer. In 1867, he was shattered by the news of his son's death in Havana from a fever. Their relationship had been a close one, marked on the father's side by patience and on the son's by intense devotion. In his grief and physical suffering, Berlioz told a close friend that he hardly knew how he managed to continue living. Yet in the winter of 1867-1868, he made a successful last tour to Russia on the invitation of the Grand Duchess Helena. To this evidence of his undiminished artistic renown, he is said to have exclaimed "Why am I so old and feeble?" In fact, he was to survive only one more year. In March, 1868, he suffered a serious fall while visiting the rocky coast near Nice; although by August he had recovered enough to attend a musical festival in Grenoble, he was unwell and began to experience loss of memory. Returning to Paris, he died on March 8, 1869.

Summary

Hector Berlioz was an artist whose career was formed to a great extent by the era into which he was born, the extraordinary period of upheaval when Napoleon I sought to subjugate Europe. The military conflicts of the period from 1805 to 1815 were followed in France by a reactionary politics which robbed the nation of economic and cultural vitality. Although Berlioz was, by most standards, not a political person, he was obliged to struggle against the cultural environment produced by politics. The soil on which his artistic genius had to take root was shallow and impoverished, and throughout his life—even discounting his contrary personality and his own exaggerations of his trials—he had to struggle against many odds, though they were perhaps more persistent than they were overwhelming.

The factor of temperament in Berlioz was undoubtedly strong. His precocious affinity for Vergil's poetry is shown in an anecdote from his memoirs, where he recalls bursting into tears while reciting to his father the episode of the death of Dido in the *Aeneid*. Sensitivity to landscape—a legacy both of his formative environment and early literary experiences—become bonded, in the encounter with Estelle, to an enduring conception of ideal love. Around all of these circumstances lingers an echo of classical myth with a primitive accent, which the young provincial carried with him to Paris. Berlioz's innate depth of sensibility was to be both a strength and a burden: It was a source of creative vitality which made him steadfast in the face of mediocre convention, but it also caused conflict in his professional relationships and probably narrowed his musical sympathies beyond necessity.

In his early years in Paris, Berlioz became a leading figure of the Romantic movement, acquiring a reputation as a somewhat rebellious genius. His unquestioned originality in certain spheres of musical composition was countered by a frequent lack of judgment in others. As an orchestrator he charted new territory, but his harmony and rhythm have often been criticized. Berlioz's sense of melody has also had many detractors, but in fact he was a fine and original melodist at times and was capable of great delicacy of feeling. His reputation as a seeker after effects is not unjustified, but many of the effects are astonishingly impressive—as in the offstage brass choirs of the *Requiem*, for example.

Berlioz's defiance of authority, his artistic daring, and the vigor of his journalistic rhetoric closely harmonize with the modern image of the Romantic artist, but the view of life he evoked in many of his major works exceeds the usual bounds of Romantic darkness. His capacity for despair, as man and artist, contrasts with more resilient figures such as Victor Hugo and Eugène Delacroix, who were his contemporaries. Though he gravitated toward classical ideals in his later music, clarity and harmony were never his secure possessions, either in art or in life.

Bibliography

Barzun, Jacques. *Berlioz and the Romantic Century.* 3d ed. 2 vols. New York: Columbia University Press, 1969. First published in 1950, Barzun's massive study was conceived in the spirit of the poet W. H. Auden's remark that "whoever wants to know about the nineteenth century must know about Berlioz." The author succeeds in being charming as well as thorough, and he provides an unmatched bibliography.

——————. *Berlioz and His Century: An Introduction to the Age of Romanticism.* Chicago: University of Chicago Press, 1982. This condensation of Barzun's two-volume work on Berlioz concentrates on the composer's life rather than his music. It has no sense of being a mere editing of the earlier books, but it is an introduction to Romanticism only in the most oblique way; as such, it will not mislead the reader, but it cannot be substituted for a true survey of the period of Berlioz's life.

Berlioz, Hector. *The Memoirs of Hector Berlioz, Member of the French Institute, Including His Travels in Italy, Germany, Russia, and England, 1803-1865.* Edited and translated by David Cairns. London: Gollancz, 1969. One of the great documents of nineteenth century European culture, but one that often has to be read skeptically. Apart from some portions of the book that provide details of Berlioz's concerts abroad, it is highly entertaining. Berlioz declined to write an autobiography in the manner of Jean-Jacques Rousseau, but there is a quantity of intense self-revelation nevertheless.

Elliot, J. H. *Berlioz.* London: J. M. Dent & Sons, 1938. A volume in the Master Musicians series, it efficiently fulfills all the standard requirements of biography, description, and analysis. Its perspective, however, though intelligently critical, appears inordinately fastidious. Excellent appendices—a calendar, list of works, and the like—redeem the author's somewhat limited enthusiasm for his subject.

Rushton, Julian. *The Musical Language of Berlioz.* Cambridge, England: Cambridge University Press, 1983. A work of critical scholarship rather than biography, this book may be consulted by the general reader for its introductory and concluding chapters and for its more recent bibliography.

Wotton, Tom S. *Berlioz.* New York: Johnson Reprint Corporation, 1969. Barzun honored Wotton as the foremost Berlioz scholar of his time, but the style and diction of the book are rather antiquated.

C. S. McConnell

CLAUDE BERNARD

Born: July 12, 1813; Saint-Julien, France
Died: February 10, 1878; Paris, France
Areas of Achievement: Physiology and medicine
Contribution: Bernard is called the "father of physiology," having developed the experimental methods and conceptual framework needed to change physiology from a primarily deductive science based on statistics to one which could discover empirical data using procedures borrowed from chemistry.

Early Life

Claude Bernard's parents were vineyard workers, and Bernard retained a lifelong attachment to the vineyards, returning there each fall to relax and help with the grape harvest and, later, to make his own wine. In the fields of his boyhood, he learned to observe nature and developed the manual dexterity and precision necessary for both wine making and scientific research. His father apparently died while Bernard was still a youth, though little is known concerning him. It is known, however, that Bernard adored his pious mother.

His early schooling was in the Jesuit school at Villefranche and later at the Collège de Thoissey, where he studied the humanities but little science or philosophy. When he finished this education, he became a pharmacy apprentice and during his evenings attended the theater and wrote a light comedy, *La Rose du Rhône*, and a five-act drama, *Arthur de Bretagne* (1887). His goal of becoming a playwright was shattered when the well-known literary critic Saint-Marc Girardin judged his drama as lacking merit and the author as without literary promise. The critic urged him to study medicine instead.

Bernard entered medical school in 1834 but divided his time between attending lectures and studying and giving lessons at a girls' school to help his mother pay the bills. His grades were only average, and when he took the internship examination in 1839, he ranked twenty-sixth out of twenty-nine. He began his internship, which was split between two hospitals. At one of these, the Hôtel Dieu, he became an unpaid assistant to a clinician and professor of physiology at the Collège de France, François Magendie. This experience had a life-changing effect on Bernard, for Magendie was an outspoken devotee of both experimentation and skepticism. Magendie recognized Bernard's talents in the laboratory and in 1841 hired him as an assistant on several projects. Bernard was granted his medical degree on December 7, 1843, on the basis of his thesis, *Du suc gastrique et de son rôle dans la nutrition* (1843; gastric juice and its role in metabolism). Earlier the same year, his first publication had appeared, *Recherches anatomiques et physiologiques sur la corde du tympan, pour servir à l'histoire de l'hémi-*

plegie faciale (1843; anatomical and physiological research on the chorda tympani).

In 1844, Bernard failed the examination for a teaching position with the faculty of medicine. Disheartened, he resigned his position with Magendie and considered becoming a country doctor in his home village. A colleague suggested that he find a wife with a good dowry instead, and in July, 1845, he married the daughter of a Parisian doctor. His marriage to Marie Françoise Martin was a matter of financial convenience, allowing him to continue his research, but it was also to be the source of much unhappiness in the years ahead. His wife obtained a legal separation from him in 1870, partly because of her opposition to his vivisectionist experiments. Both sons born to the marriage died in infancy, and the two daughters, like their mother, renounced him and apparently refused to be reconciled with him even on his deathbed.

Between 1843 and 1845, he made discoveries on the chemical and nerve control of the gastric juices and on the role of bile and began experiments with curare and on the innervation of the vocal cords and the functions of the cranial nerves. With the money from the dowry, he was able to continue this research as well as initiate others, and he published a number of papers on various subjects through the mid-1840's.

Life's Work

The year 1848 is generally taken to be the year from which Bernard's mature work dates. In December, 1847, he became an assistant to Magendie at the Collège de France, and the following year began teaching the course on experimental medicine during the winter terms. He also became a charter member and the first vice president of the Société de Biologie, which indicates his growing stature within the scientific community. In 1848, his research led him to two discoveries which were to provide not only new facts but also new ways of conceptualizing bodily functions. First, in his observations on the differences between the urine of carnivores and herbivores, he discovered the part played by the pancreas in the digestion of fats. He published the results of this discovery in *Du suc pancréatique, et de son rôle dans les phénomènes de la digestion* (1848; pancreatic juice and its role in the phenomena of digestion). Second, he discovered the glycogenous function of the liver. Formerly it was believed that the body could not produce sugars and was therefore dependent upon plants for their source. Bernard's discovery explained the constancy of sugar in the body and was instrumental in leading Bernard to a concept, which he first articulated in the late 1850's, of *milieu intérieur*, or internal environment.

Between the time that he first described this condition of a constant interior environment and his death, Bernard developed and extended the idea until it became the generalized and widely accepted biological notion of homeostasis. In his last comments about it, published in 1878, he explained that the organism does not exist in the *milieu extérieur* (the external environment of air or water) but rather in a liquid *milieu intérieur*, which is made of all the intracellular liquids of the organism. These liquids are the bases of all forms of cellular metabolism and the common factor of all simple chemical or physiological exchanges. The body's task is to maintain the stability of the *milieu intérieur*; hence, the task of the physiologist is to discover how this regulation occurs.

Bernard's work in the 1850's and 1860's was directed precisely to this task. In 1851, he discovered the control of local skin temperature by sympathetic nerves, and later he showed the importance of the nervous system in regulating the vascular system. In 1856, he demonstrated that curare blocks motor nerve endings, and the following year he reported that the toxic effect of carbon monoxide resulted from blocked respiration in the erythrocytes. He was finally able to isolate glycogen in a pure form in 1857.

He started teaching in the early 1850's, and in his lectures he argued against vitalism in favor of what he called experimental determinism. He contended that the laws governing the functioning of the organism were precise and rigorous, with the laws of physics and chemistry being fundamental for understanding living phenomena. By varying conditions, the experimental biologists could make the organism respond in a strictly determined manner.

In 1865, Bernard had more time to work on his philosophical ideas, for he became too ill to teach or to conduct research. He retired to the vineyards and wrote his most famous work, *Introduction à l'étude de la médecine expérimentale* (1865; *An Introduction to the Study of Experimental Medicine*, 1927), which for many years was his only work translated into English. In this work, he showed his indebtedness to his mentor, Magendie, and to Auguste Comte's positivism; both stressed the necessity of making observations and determining facts from the evidence. Bernard was unwilling to be shackled by their strict Baconianism, and, against current opinion, he argued that the forming of hypotheses was an essential and necessary part of the scientific process.

The following year, the minister of public education asked Bernard to prepare a report on the state of physiology in France to be published on the occasion of the World Exposition of 1867. Instead of the objective, factual, historical report that was commissioned, Bernard wrote an ideological tract that continued his philosophical thinking. In his *Rapport sur les progrès et la marche de la physiologie générale en France* (1867; report on the progress and course of general physiology in France), he described his vision of a new brand of physiology founded on the concept of the *milieu intérieur* and the elucidation of regulatory functions. This report demonstrated what Bernard hoped physiology would become—not what it was.

In later years, Bernard continued to pursue his interests in the phenomena characteristic of all living organisms. He had begun to explore this issue in his lessons at the Sorbonne in 1864, and, when offered the chair of comparative physiology at the Musée d'Histoire Naturelle in 1868, he insisted that the chair be renamed "general physiology." This willingness to treat general biological problems instead of strictly medical ones not only restructured the way in which questions about living material, life processes, and the properties of living beings were framed and studied but also freed physiology from its subservience to medicine and established it as an independent discipline.

In 1869, Bernard returned to his teaching duties at the Collège de France. He attracted a large and diverse audience, including, at times, Louis Pasteur, and entertained them with demonstrations to support both his physiological and philosophical views. Bernard's ideas were publicized through ten works, the best known being *Leçons sur les propriétés des tissus vivants* (1866; lessons on the properties of living tissues) and *Leçons sur les phénomènes de la vie communs aux animaux et aux végétaux* (1878-1879; lessons on the phenomena of life common to animals and plants).

Summary

The painting *Claude Bernard's Lesson in the Laboratory* by Léon Lhermitte delineates one of the most important aspects of Claude Bernard's work—his teaching and mentoring of younger scientists. In this picture, Bernard, with dark hair and eyes, is dressed in a white gardener's apron and wears a metal pince-nez around his neck. Near him are several of his disciples, including the electrophysiologist Arsène d'Arsonval; Bernard's most famous student, Paul Bert; and Louis Ranvier, the founder of histophysiology. Not all of Bernard's students agreed with him, but the discussions furthered the understanding of science in general and physiology in particular. As a teacher, Bernard ensured the continuation and independence of the new discipline of physiology.

During his lifetime, Bernard showed that general biological laws could be derived from specific experimental data; incorporated the latest techniques and findings of physics and chemistry into biology; developed the concepts of homeostasis, internal secretions, and organismic self-regulation; demonstrated the unity between physiology and medicine; and provided a philosophical basis for experimental biology. These contributions defined modern physiology, and current work in regulatory biology and much neurophysiology is the outgrowth of Bernard's scientific and philosophical initiatives.

In recognition of his work and status, he was given a chair in physiology at the University of Paris in 1854 and elected to the Academy of Medicine in 1861. In 1867, he was made a commander of the Legion of Honor and served as president of the Société de Biologie. In 1868, he was elected to the

Académie Française and served as its president in 1869. In 1870, he was appointed to the senate by Napoleon III and barely escaped from Paris before the Prussian army arrived.

After his illness-enforced retirement in 1865, Bernard never fully recovered his health, although he was able to do some teaching and research. His mind was ever active, and it is reported in many sources that as he grew older, he repeated more and more often, "My mind abounds with things I want to finish." He became seriously ill in early January, 1878, and died on February 10, 1878, probably of kidney disease. He was the first scientist upon whom France bestowed the honor of a public funeral.

Bibliography

Bernard, Claude. *An Introduction to the Study of Experimental Medicine.* Translated by Henry Copley Green. New York: Dover, 1957. This classic by Bernard has been widely read. Bernard's purpose in writing it was to describe the basic principles of scientific research, that is, to outline and explain his philosophy of science. For a philosophical treatise, this book is remarkably clear and easy to follow.

Hall, Thomas S. *Ideas of Life and Matter, 600 B.C. to A.D. 1900.* Vol 2. Chicago: University of Chicago Press, 1969. Hall succinctly describes Bernard's answer to four questions: How is the organism constituted? What part or parts of it appear to be alive? By what sign does one recognize "living"? and What does "life" mean?

Holmes, Frederic L. *Claude Bernard and Animal Chemistry: The Emergence of a Scientist.* Cambridge, Mass.: Harvard University Press, 1974. This work focuses on Bernard's early research period (1842-1848), during which he began to develop his views on experimentation, which in turn would lead him to one of his most famous discoveries—the role and function of the liver. Holmes also describes the scientific environment within which Bernard worked to provide a context for his thought and activities.

_____. "Claude Bernard, the *Milieu Intérieur,* and Regulatory Physiology." *History and Philosophy of the Life Sciences* 8 (1986): 3-25. Holmes explains the intellectual context in which Bernard developed the concept of *milieu intérieur* and shows how twentieth century physiologists have reinterpreted Bernard's original ideas to fit the concept of homeostasis. This article demonstrates the problems involved in understanding a scientist-philosopher in his own period instead of trying to make him say what is currently believed to be true.

Olmsted, J. M. D. *Claude Bernard, Physiologist.* New York: Harper & Row, 1938. This is probably the best-known biography of Bernard and is very good despite the pre-World War II date of publication.

Roll-Hansen, Nils. "Critical Teleology: Immanuel Kant and Claude Bernard on the Limitations of Experimental Biology." *Journal of the History of Biology* 9 (Spring, 1979): 55-91. Kant and Bernard proposed similar methodologies for biology. This article examines those methodologies, compares them, and shows how Kant's program had ethical and moral implications, while Bernard's approach was related to questions of science policy. The article describes the similarities and differences between Bernard and many of the natural historians and physicians of his period.

Sara Joan Miles

GIAN LORENZO BERNINI

Born: December 7, 1598; Naples
Died: November 28, 1680; Rome
Areas of Achievement: Art and architecture
Contribution: The sculpture and architecture of Bernini are considered to be among the most complete expressions of the thought and feeling of the Counter-Reformation. He is also one of the most representative practitioners of the High Baroque style.

Early Life

Although born in Naples, Gian Lorenzo Bernini was largely reared in Rome, where his father, Pietro, a minor Florentine sculptor, had obtained employment on the decorative program of Pope Paul V. The young Bernini was, by all accounts, a child prodigy who showed an early aptitude for his father's profession. At the age of eight, he is said to have carved a marble head that excited general admiration, and, by the time he was ten or eleven, he had attracted the personal attention of Pope Paul. The principal artistic influences on the young sculptor were, first, his father, who guided and encouraged the boy's early efforts with the utmost devotion, and, second, the Vatican itself, where he drew and studied the masterpieces of ancient sculpture and Renaissance painting.

Bernini's earliest surviving works are not precisely datable; early biographers and some modern scholars accept a date as early as 1610, while a majority place them around 1615. These juvenilia include a lifelike portrait of Bishop G. B. Santoni and a mythological group, *The Goat Amalthea with the Infant Jupiter and a Faun*, long regarded as an ancient Hellenistic piece because of its textural realism. Slightly later, and somewhat larger in scale, are marble figures of Saint Sebastian and Saint Laurence. The latter was Bernini's patron saint and is represented enduring martyrdom on a flaming grill. In order to achieve a convincing facial expression, the sculptor is said to have stuck his own foot into a fire while observing his face in a mirror. Although the story may be apocryphal, it does reflect Bernini's concern for psychological authenticity and his typically Baroque penchant for studying his own reactions.

More ambitious still were a series of life-size marble groups, produced between 1618 and 1625 for the great connoisseur and collector Cardinal Scipione Borghese. The first, *Aeneas, Anchises, and Ascanius Fleeing Troy*, focuses on the physical and psychological contrast between three stages of life: manhood, old age, and childhood. A similar contrast heightens the drama of *Pluto and Persephone*, which represents the god of the underworld abducting his screaming victim. The vigorous, determined figure of the abductor is juxtaposed to the soft, vulnerable girl in his arms. The imprints of his grasping fingers on her pliant flesh is often cited as an example of Bernini's vivid illusionism. *Apollo and Daphne* again makes the most of a violent and erotic myth in which the nymph turns into a laurel tree at the moment the god seizes her. The capture of seemingly instantaneous action and reaction and the transformation of skin into bark is a tour de force of the sculptor's art.

Work on the *Apollo and Daphne* was interrupted by a new commission from Scipione Borghese for a statue of David. David had been a favorite theme of the Italian sculptural tradition, but Bernini represents him in a new way: neither before nor after the encounter with Goliath but in the very act of hurling the stone. This pose implies the presence of the opponent in the spectator's space, so that the tension and energy of the figure seem to extend into his environment, a characteristic Baroque strategy. The *David*'s face is said to be a self-portrait, based on the image in a mirror held for the artist by his close friend, Cardinal Maffeo Barbarini. While the *David* was in progress, Barbarini was elected pope and, as a result, new vistas were opened to the twenty-four-year-old Bernini.

Life's Work

When Barbarini became Pope Urban VIII in 1623, Bernini's activities were redirected to the service of the Church. Initially, the pope encouraged the artist to study painting and architecture to supplement his mastery of sculpture. Architecture did indeed become an important aspect of Bernini's career, but although he is said to have produced more than 150 paintings, only a few are identified, including several self-portraits which show him as a handsome man with a long face and prominent, dark eyes.

The major artistic challenge facing the new papacy was the internal decoration of the recently completed St. Peter's, and this responsibility fell to Bernini. In 1629, at the age of thirty, he was officially named architect of St. Peter's, but by then he had already been at work for five years on the baldachin, the enormous bronze structure under the dome of the cathedral that marks the place where Saint Peter is believed to be buried. This monument, modeled on the canopy held over living popes, rises dynamically on its vine-covered corkscrew columns to a height of ninety-five feet.

Bernini also supervised the design of the four gigantic piers that surround the baldachin. Each pier contains a niche with a colossal statue of a saint, one of which, Saint Longinus, was executed by Bernini himself. Longinus' agitated robe demonstrates the sculptor's ability to make drapery, a requirement in ecclesiastical commissions, convey emotional excitement.

Another of Bernini's early projects for St. Peter's was the tomb of Urban VIII, which displays a rich contrast of colors and textures between a central core in gilt bronze and peripheral figures in white marble. The artist's taste for momentary action is reflected in the presence of a skeleton shown in the process of writing the epitaph. The effigy on Urban's tomb reflects Bernini's talent for portraiture. Several busts from this period, of the pope, of Borghese, and of the sculptor's mistress, Costanza Bonarelli, re-create not only the features but also the personalities of the sitters.

One of Bernini's rare failures was a scheme to add bell towers to the façade of St. Peter's. One tower was actually begun, but, because of unsound foundations, had to be demolished. This reversal coincided with the death, in 1644, of Pope Urban, and Bernini fell temporarily out of favor with the papal court. This misfortune, however, turned to his advantage by permitting him to accept private commissions, the most notable of which was the Cornaro Chapel in the Church of Santa Maria della Vittoria, executed between 1645 and 1652. The chapel is a total ensemble involving architecture, painting, and sculpture in several media, which culminates in a vision of the *Ecstasy of Saint Teresa*. Bernini regarded it as the most beautiful of all of his creations.

The artist regained papal approval with his spectacular design for the Four Rivers Fountain, constructed between 1648 and 1651, and, with the pontificate of Alexander VIII, he again enjoyed the close friendship and enthusiastic patronage of the pope. It was during this period that Bernini designed the piazza in front of St. Peter's, shaped by two colonnades which he likened to motherly arms reaching out to embrace the faithful. For the interior of the cathedral, he constructed a climactic spectacle in the apse, the *Cathedra Petri* (chair of Peter), a characteristically multimedia amalgam of sculpture and architecture. The Scala Regia (royal stairway), incorporating an equestrian statue of the Emperor Constantine, and the dramatic tomb of Alexander VII in St. Peter's are further legacies of the collaboration between the pope and the sculptor.

Late in his career, starting about 1658, Bernini undertook a number of architectural projects. His palace designs either were not built or were substantially remodeled; nevertheless, they exerted considerable influence. His three churches are all central plan structures and, predictably, function as showcases for the sculpture and painting within. Perhaps the most remarkable of the three is S. Andrea al Quirinale, built between 1658 and 1670.

Bernini left Rome only once. In 1665, at the insistence of Louis XIV, he traveled to Paris, where he spent five months engaged in various sculptural and architectural projects for the king. His bust of Louis XIV is a result of this trip, but for the most part his style was too dynamic and exuberant for the sober, classic taste of the French court.

Bernini's latest works, such as the *Angels* for the Ponte Sant'Angelo, *Beata Lodovica Albertoni*, and the portrait of Gabriele Fonseca, all dating from after the French expedition, reflect the intense spirituality of the aging artist. Bernini remained active and productive almost until his death, which occurred nine days before his eighty-second birthday.

Summary

Throughout his long career Gian Lorenzo Bernini demonstrated exceptional skills of hand, mind, and spirit. His almost legendary technical facility in the production of sculpture, seen particularly in his early works, was matched by an equally remarkable talent for conceiving and planning large-scale monuments and supervising their execution by others. These abilities are displayed in his many and varied ecclesiastical commissions. Bernini's particular contribution to Counter-Reformation religious art, however, consisted in his ability to make visionary experiences vividly real and to find visual and physical metaphors for spiritual states.

Another aspect of Bernini's genius was its seeming universality. An English visitor to seventeenth century Rome wrote in his diary that "Bernini . . . gave a public opera wherein he painted the scenes, cut the statues, invented the engines, composed the music, writ the comedy, and built the theatre." This ability to synthesize different art forms is characteristic of many of the artist's most impressive and distinctive monuments. Architecture, painting, sculpture, marble, bronze, stucco, and pigment are combined with the imagination of a stage director. Bernini's extraordinary versatility is seen also in the range of his production within his primary field of sculpture: mythological groups, devotional images, portrait busts, tombs, and fountains. In all of these types, he set the standard for Baroque sculpture.

Bernini was generally regarded by his contemporaries as the greatest artist of his day, and his style was widely emulated. His reputation declined rather drastically in the eighteenth and nineteenth centuries but soared again in the twentieth century. This revival was spearheaded by scholarly investigation, but his work is now widely appreciated by the art-loving public and by the tourist as well.

Bibliography

Baldinucci, Filippo. *The Life of Bernini.* Translated by Catherine Enggass with a foreword by Robert Enggass. University Park: Pennsylvania State University Press, 1966. The most important source on Bernini's life and career, published two years after his death, by a contemporary scholar and critic. Short and readable, with an informative foreword.

Bauer, George C., ed. *Bernini in Perspective.* Englewood Cliffs, N.J.: Prentice-Hall, 1976. A collection of writings about Bernini from the seventeenth to the twentieth century, with an introduction by the editor. Includes a biography by the artist's son. Contains black-and-white illustrations and a bibliography.

Hibbard, Howard. *Bernini.* Harmondsworth, England: Penguin Books, 1965. Scholarly but concise and highly readable text. Focuses on sculpture but touches on other areas as well. Includes black-and-white illustrations, a short bibliography, and notes. Paperback edition.

Lavin, Irving. *Bernini and the Unity of the Visual Arts.* 2 vols. New York: Oxford University Press, 1980. A study of the interaction of the arts in Bernini's oeuvre, dealing with several of his chapels and altars and, in greatest depth, with the Cornaro Chapel. Includes a catalog of relevant works, a bibliography, and extensive color and black-and-white illustrations.

Wallace, Robert. *The World of Bernini, 1598-1680.* Alexandria, Va.: Time-Life Books, 1970. A popular but reliable survey of the times, as well as of the life, of Bernini. Includes lavish illustrations, many in color.

Wittkower, Rudolf. *Gian Lorenzo Bernini, the Sculptor of the Roman Baroque.* London: Phaidon Press, 1955, rev. ed. 1981. The definitive work on Bernini's sculpture, with chapters on various genres. Contains a catalog, a bibliography, a chronological table, and extensive illustrations.

_____. "Gianlorenzo Bernini." In *Art and Architecture in Italy, 1600-1750.* Harmondsworth, England: Penguin Books, 1958, rev. ed. 1973. This chapter in a history of the period is an excellent short survey of all aspects of Bernini's career. Includes black-and-white illustrations, notes, and a bibliography. Paperback edition.

Jane Kristof

THE BERNOULLI FAMILY

Jakob I Bernoulli

Born: December 27, 1654; Basel, Swiss Confederation
Died: August 16, 1705; Basel, Swiss Confederation
Areas of Achievement: Mathematics, physics, and astronomy

Johann I Bernoulli

Born: August 6, 1667; Basel, Swiss Confederation
Died: January 1, 1748; Basel, Swiss Confederation
Area of Achievement: Mathematics

Daniel Bernoulli

Born: February 8, 1700; Groningen, the Netherlands
Died: March 17, 1782; Basel, Swiss Confederation
Areas of Achievement: Physics, mathematics, and medicine
Contribution: The Bernoulli family contributed to the flowering of mathematical analysis in the eighteenth century which applied advanced mathematical techniques to problems arising in physics, technology, medicine, and the emerging field of probability theory. Members of the family dominated Continental mathematics from the later seventeenth to the later eighteenth centuries.

Early Lives

Jakob I, Johann I, and Daniel Bernoulli are the most important members of the Bernoulli dynasty, but at least five others went on to achieve recognition from their contemporaries for their mathematical talents. There were so many Jakobs and Johanns that it has become standard to place Roman numerals after their names to help keep their identities clear. Johann I and Jakob I were brothers, and Daniel was the the son of Johann I.

The Bernoullis were descended from a line of merchants. Johann I and Jakob I's grandfather moved to Basel in 1622 and continued his profession as a druggist. His son, Nikolaus, became a minor local official. Jakob received his theological degree in 1676, while studying mathematics against his father's wishes. He traveled extensively: He spent two years in Geneva as a tutor, then went to France to learn René Descartes' approach to natural philosophy. He traveled to England in 1681, meeting Robert Hooke and Robert Boyle. He settled down somewhat in 1683, giving lectures, writing papers, and teaching himself more mathematics. He became a professor of mathematics at the University of Basel in 1687 and made himself master of the newly developed Leibnizian methods of infinitesimal mathematics.

Johann failed as an apprentice and received his father's permission to enter the University of Basel in 1683, where Jakob had just begun lecturing. He began to study medicine in 1685, receiving his doctorate in 1694 for a mathematical account of the motion of muscles. Before receiving an offer for a post in 1695, Johann studied mathematics with Jakob and both became quite expert at Leibnizian calculus. Johann left for the chair of mathematics at Groningen, the Netherlands. In 1700, Daniel Bernoulli was born to Johann. Daniel obtained his master's degree in 1716 and was taught mathematics by his father and his elder brother Nikolaus II. Attempts to place him as a commercial apprentice failed, and he studied medicine at several different universities, at last settling in Basel with a doctorate in 1721, his thesis concerning respiration. His first attempts to obtain a university post failed, but his *Exercitationes quaedam mathematicae* (1724; mathematical exercises) landed him a post at the St. Petersburg Academy.

Life's Work

Jakob became professor of mathematics at Basel in 1687, the same year that he published a significant article on geometry. He and Johann were both soon led into problems of infinitesimal geometry. The work of the brothers over the next several years was focused on the solution of puzzles that the leading mathematicians of Europe had proposed to demonstrate their own skill. Often a problem would be devised, solved by its formulator, and presented as a challenge to other mathematicians. One such problem was the shape of the curve that represented the motion of a body in constant descent in a gravitational field. Solutions would be offered, corrected by others, or counterproblems issued. This manner of solving problems greatly expanded the class of functions that could be analyzed using the tools of Leibnizian calculus. Jakob and Johann contributed to these sometimes-peevish arguments and mild polemics that nevertheless broadened the scope of calculus.

In 1695, Johann went to Groningen. He had no hope of getting the chair of mathematics at Basel, because his brother occupied it. The brothers were antagonistic toward each other. Jakob had taught Johann mathematics and apparently could never accept his younger brother as a professional equal. Both were sensitive, critical, and in need of recognition. Their intellectual gifts differed, as can best be seen by the famous problem of the brachistochrone posed by Johann in 1696. The brachistochrone is the curve a body makes as it moves along the path that takes the least time to travel between two points. Jakob solved the problem using a detailed but formally correct technique. Johann recognized that the problem could be rephrased in such a way that existing solutions could be adapted to the solution of this problem. Johann solved the problem in a more ingenious way, but Jakob recognized that his approach could be generalized. He laid the foundations of the field of the calculus of variations, which solves a wide variety of problems by using the methods of calculus to vary terms in an expression that takes a maximum or minimum. The brothers argued in print over each other's solutions to another variational problem from 1696 to 1701.

Jakob I spent the remaining years of his life working on more problems and compiling the results of his life's work. By the time of his death, he had accumulated a significant amount of original work on series (the finite sum of an infinite number of terms), gravitational theory, and engineering applications. Nikolaus I, Jakob's nephew, helped to have Jakob's most famous and original work, *Ars conjectandi* (1713; art of conjecture), published posthumously. Though incomplete, the work contains, among other things, Jakob's final statements on probability theory. His contributions to probability theory are recognized to have been decisive in the further development of the field.

Johann broadened the scope of the new calculus in the mid-1690's by calculating the details of the application of these methods to functions in which variables appear in the exponent. It was at this time that the brothers participated in their rancorous series of exchanges in print over the brachistochrone and other variational problems. Both brothers share the credit for the early development of the calculus of variations, for although Jakob first realized the generalizability of the technique, both followed up on this idea and applied it to other problems. After his brother's death, Johann published several works which presented formal solutions to variational problems that were reminiscent of Jakob's style.

Jakob's death in 1705 was the cause of Johann's return to Basel, where he took the vacant chair of mathematics. He became involved in the priority disputes between Sir Isaac Newton and Gottfried Leibniz over the invention of calculus and demonstrated the superiority of Leibniz's notation in the solution of particular problems. After 1705, Johann worked primarily on theoretical and applied mechanics. He published *Théorie de la manœuvre des vaisseaux* (1714; theory of the movement of ships), dealing with navigational problems and ship design. He also won three prizes offered by scientific academies by espousing the Cartesian vortex theory to explain the motion of planets. He criticized some aspects of Cartesianism, but some scholars claim that his undisputed status and support for Descartes' vortex theory delayed Continental acceptance of Newtonian physics, which banishes such vortices in favor of forces.

Daniel Bernoulli obtained a position in the St. Petersburg Academy in 1725 and remained there until 1733. In 1727, Leonhard Euler joined him. His most productive years were spent in St. Petersburg. He wrote an original treatise on probability, a work on oscillations, and a draft of his most famous work, *Hydrodynamica* (1738; *Hydrodynamics by Daniel Bernoulli*, 1968). He returned to Basel to lecture in medicine but continued to publish in the areas that interested him most—mathematics and mechanics. His father, Johann, tried to establish priority for the founding of the field of hydrodynamics by plagiarizing his son's original work and predating the publication. This is only the worst of many examples of the antagonism that Johann felt toward his son.

Daniel began lecturing on physiology, which was more to his liking than medicine, in 1743 and was offered the chair of physics in 1750. He lectured on physics until 1776, when he retired. His most important contributions center on his work in rational mechanics. He returned to probability theory in 1760 with his famous work on the effectiveness of the smallpox vaccine, arguing that the vaccine could extend the average lifespan by three years. He published a few more minor works on probability theory through 1776. Throughout his career, Daniel won ten prizes of the Paris Academy on topics involving astronomy, magnetism, navigation, and ship design.

Summary

The Bernoulli family was instrumental in developing many new fields of mathematics in the eighteenth century. They mastered the Leibnizian notation of calculus and successfully applied it to a range of problems. Their contributions to probability theory, the calculus of variation, differential and integral calculus, and the theories of series and of rational mechanics dominate even introductory textbooks in physics, mathematics, and engineering. The three Bernoullis who are the most famous of the eight who achieved contemporary recognition are Johann I, Jakob I, and Daniel.

Jakob was much more interested in mathematical formalism than his more intuitive younger brother Johann. Jakob's main contribution was in the ingenious solutions to individual problems. The cumulative weight of these mounting solutions reflected on the power and scope of the newly emerging analytical techniques. He also contributed in important ways to probability theory, algebra, the calculus of variations, and the theory of series. Johann can claim similar contributions, for the brothers often worked on similar problems and criticized each others' solutions in print. Johann also contributed to theoretical and applied mechanics. Daniel's contributions include founding the field of hydrodynamics and making essential contributions to rational mechanics, probability theory, and the mechanics of physiology.

Other Bernoullis of note include Nikolaus I (1687-1759), Nikolaus II (1695-1726), Johann II (1710-1790), Johann III (1744-1807), and Jakob II (1759-1789). All received recognition from their contemporaries but did not make as many or as important contributions as their more famous relatives.

Bibliography
Bell, Eric T. *Men of Mathematics.* New York: Simon & Schuster, 1937. Addressed to the general reader, this book uncovers the history that has

led up to the major ideas of modern mathematics.

Brett, William F., et al. *An Introduction to the History of Mathematics, Number Theory, and Operations Research.* New York: MSS Information, 1974. Written for undergraduates, this book shows the student that those who developed mathematics are creative and inquisitive, are human in every sense of the word, and sometimes find solutions that are useful but inaccurate.

Brown, Harcourt. "From London to Lapland: Maupertuis, Johann Bernoulli I, and *La Terre applatic*, 1728-1738." In *On Literature and History in the Age of Ideas: Essays on the French Enlightenment Presented to George R. Havens*, edited by Charles G. S. Williams. Columbus: Ohio State University Press, 1975. This article is based on the voluminous collection of letters of the Bernoullis at Basel. A significant number of excerpts from these letters (in French) are used to detail the controversy over the shape of the Earth.

Lick, Dale W. "The Remarkable Bernoulli Family." *The Mathematics Teacher* 62 (May, 1969): 401-409. Presents brief biographical information on eight of the most prominent members of the family. Interweaves historical and technical aspects but presents only a few simple equations. Includes a twenty-three-item bibliography.

Turnbull, H. W. *The Great Mathematicians.* 4th ed. New York: New York University Press, 1961. Aims at revealing something of the spirit of mathematics without burdening the reader with technical details. Uses a biographical approach to show how mathematicians think. Chapter 8 deals with the Bernoullis and Euler.

Roger Sensenbaugh

FRIEDRICH WILHELM BESSEL

Born: July 22, 1784; Minden, Westphalia
Died: March 17, 1846; Königsberg, Prussia
Areas of Achievement: Astronomy and mathematics
Contribution: Bessel greatly increased the accuracy of the measurements of stellar positions both by using more advanced instruments and by developing methods to account for instrument and observer error. The most famous discovery resulting from these observations was the first accurate determination of the distance to a star.

Early Life

Friedrich Wilhelm Bessel was born to a civil servant and a minister's daughter. One of nine children, he went to the local *Gymnasium* but left after only four years to become a merchant's apprentice. He showed no particular talent at school. At the age of fifteen, he began his unpaid seven-year apprenticeship to a merchant firm in Bremen. He excelled at his accounting job and received a small salary after one year. He spent his spare time teaching himself geography and languages because of his interest in foreign trade. He also learned about ships and practical navigation through self-study. Determining the position of a ship at sea—a long-standing problem in navigation—intrigued him. He therefore began to study astronomy and mathematics to understand the theory behind the existing methods.

Bessel began to make observations of stars on his own, which he was able to compare to observations reported in numerous professional journals of astronomy. One of his earliest tasks was to determine the orbit of Halley's Comet based on several observations of its position. He studied existing methods to determine the easiest way to do this, and he used observations made in 1607 to supplement his own. The precision of his observations and the scrupulous care given to minimizing or correcting for observational errors would characterize his professional work throughout his life. He made the observations, adjusted (or reduced) the 1607 data to make them directly comparable to his own, and submitted the results to Wilhelm Olbers in 1804. Olbers, a physician and highly esteemed amateur astronomer, was impressed with the agreement between Bessel's observations and Edmond Halley's calculation of the orbit. He urged Bessel to improve it further with more observations. Olbers was impressed enough to recommend Bessel in 1806 for a position as assistant at a private observatory near Bremen. Bessel made further observations of the comet and published the results in 1807 to wide acclaim.

Life's Work

In 1809, Bessel was appointed director of the new observatory at Königsberg, where he remained for the rest of his life. His early fame came from his reduction of the earlier observations of James Bradley. Bradley's measurement of the apparent position of stars had to be corrected for the motion of Earth, the bending of starlight as it passes through the air, and instrument errors. With sufficient care, any observation can be reduced to a universal coordinate system.

While waiting for the construction of the observatory, Bessel worked on reducing Bradley's observations of more than thirty-two hundred stars with the goal of producing a reference system for measuring the positions of other stars. Bessel received the Lalande Prize of the Institute of France for his production of tables of refraction based on these observations. In 1818, he completed the reduction and published the results in his work, *Fundamenta astronomiae* (1818; fundamental astronomy). This work provided the most accurate positions of a chosen set of stars. Accurate positions of a few stars are required to form the basis for extremely accurate measurements of positions for all other stars. This work has been said to mark the birth of modern astrometry. Bessel also provided accurate proper motions of many stars. (The so-called fixed stars actually move a very small amount over the centuries. When all perturbing effects are removed, the motion that is left to the star is called its proper motion.)

Bessel's next important contribution was to increase the accuracy of the measurement of stellar positions and motions. In 1820, he determined the position of the vernal equinox with great accuracy. The equinox is employed as the origin of the coordinate system used to record a star's position. He further improved accuracy in his work *Tabulae regiomontanae* (1830; *Refraction Tables*, 1855), in which he published the mean positions for thirty-eight stars for the period 1750-1850. In 1821, he noticed a systematic error in observation that was peculiar to each observer and called it the personal equation. This systematic error was reduced as each observer became more experienced, but it never disappeared. Bessel devised a method to remove the error.

Identifying and measuring the proper motion of stars was crucial in producing an important contribution to astronomy. The slight but periodic variation in proper motion of a few stars was not accountable by considering the motion of Earth or instrumental factors. In making the observations which later appeared in the *Refraction Tables*, Bessel suggested that the variations in proper motion of the stars Sirius and Procyon could be explained by the existence of an as-yet-unseen companion star. More than a century later, the companions to these stars were observed, as well as companions to many others.

Bessel also made important contributions to mathematics. Prior to Bessel, it was common for observers of the heavens to record their data and only later, if ever, reduce that data. Bradley, whose observations Bessel used extensively, carefully noted any possible perturbing effects in his observations. Nevertheless, reduction of the data for the positions of the stars was put aside in favor of recording lunar data. Bessel emphasized the need for the data reduction to be done immediately by the observer. Such reduction required extensive manipulation of complicated equations. In the process of developing ways to remove errors, Bessel noticed that he could use a class of functions which solved problems involving the perturbing influence of one planet on the orbit of another. He systematically investigated and described this class of functions in 1824. These functions, which bear Bessel's name, are not restricted to astronomy: They are used in the solution of a wide variety of problems in physics, mathematics, and engineering.

Another direct benefit of increased accuracy in stellar positions was Bessel's determination of the distance to a star, which is his most important contribution to astronomy. Although many astronomers had earlier claimed to have measured stellar distance using methods based on questionable assumptions, and although two of Bessel's contemporaries also correctly determined such distances, Bessel's comprehensive treatment of the data and his high accuracy of observations were convincing to his contemporaries.

As Earth moves in its annual orbit around the sun, the stars appear to move across the dome of the sky. By determining the location of a star at opposite ends of Earth's orbit and using some simple trigonometry, the distance to a star can be measured. Yet this so-called parallax (the apparent motion of an object caused by the motion of the observer) was small because the stars are very far away. The parallax had therefore never been measured. Indeed, some opponents of the heliocentric theory, according to which Earth revolves around the sun, used this failure to measure parallax as an argument against the theory. Astronomers had a rough figure for the radius of Earth's orbit and some idea of the extent of the solar system, but there did not seem to be a way to determine stellar distances that did not require the assumption that all stars had the same intrinsic brightness.

Earlier attempts at measuring parallax involved circumventing the problem of the immeasurably small parallax by looking at two stars that appeared to be very near to each other but were of different brightnesses. It was thought that the dimmer star would be farther away and that observing the relative change of position could lead to a determination of stellar distances. This method did not work, because not all stars are of the same intrinsic brightness. Most stars that appear near to each other are in fact binary stars and really are near each other.

Bessel used a different approach: He assumed that stars with large proper motions are closer than stars with small proper motions. He chose the star known as 61 Cygni, because it had the largest proper motion known. He used a new measuring device called the Fraunhofer heliometer (after Joseph von Fraunhofer, a nineteenth century optician), which was designed to measure the angular diameter of the sun and the planets. Its manner of comparing the images from two objects to determine angular diameter was more accurate than earlier instruments. Using nearby stars for comparison and observing for eighteen months, Bessel was able to measure a parallax of slightly under one-third of a second of arc, which is equal to the width of a dime viewed from twenty miles. From this amount of parallax, Bessel calculated that 61 Cygni was 10.9 light years or seventy trillion miles away. He completed his calculations and published the results in 1838.

The last six years of Bessel's life were marked by deteriorating health, but he managed to complete a number of works before his death from cancer in 1846.

Summary

Friedrich Wilhelm Bessel made important contributions to astronomy, mathematics, and geodesy. His work marks the turning point from a concern with planetary, solar, and lunar observations to investigations of the stars. His measurement of the distance to a star is noteworthy because it settled the centuries-old question of whether stars exhibited parallax. The care he took in his observations set much higher standards for the science of astronomy. Bessel's goal was to observe the stars accurately enough to predict their motion and to establish a reference system for their positions. As part of that plan, he developed methods for the careful determination of instrument and observer error, conducted years of observations himself, and developed the mathematical techniques to reduce the data. Bessel's lasting achievement was to raise the science of observing, reducing, and correcting astronomical data to an art.

Bibliography

Clerke, Agnes. *A Popular History of Astronomy During the Nineteenth Century*. New York: Macmillan, 1887. Although written during the period it was supposed to cover, this work has several redeeming qualities. Expressly written for a general audience, the book's language is clear and precise. A valuable record of what near-contemporaries thought of Bessel.

Herrmann, Dieter B. *The History of Astronomy from Herschel to Hertzsprung*. Translated by Kevin Krisciunos. Rev. ed. New York: Cambridge University Press, 1984. Traces the history of astronomy from 1780 to 1930. Written from the Marxist perspective.

Hoskin, Michael A. *Stellar Astronomy: Historical Studies*. Chalfont, England: Science History, 1982. A collection of material published in *Journal for the History of Astronomy*, with the addition of some new material. Attempts a synthesis of existing scholarship on the history of stellar (as opposed to planetary) astronomy as of the early 1980's.

Pannekoek, Anton. *A History of Astronomy*. New York: Interscience, 1961.

Traces the history of astronomy from antiquity to the present. Part 3, "Astronomy Surveying the Universe," contains information on Bessel and places him in the historical context of nineteenth century astronomy.

Williams, Henry Smith. *The Great Astronomers*. New York: Simon & Schuster, 1930. Reprint. New York: Newton, 1932. Book 5 deals with Bessel, among other subjects. Concerns parallax and Bessel's contributions to measuring the distance to 61 Cygni. Describes the work of Bessel's contemporaries who measured the parallax of other stars at about the same time.

Roger Sensenbaugh

FRIEDRICH VON BEUST

Born: January 13, 1809; Dresden, Saxony
Died: October 24, 1886; Altenberg Castle, Austro-Hungarian Empire
Areas of Achievement: Diplomacy, government, and politics
Contribution: Beust played a leading role from his position in the Saxon government in suppressing the Revolutions of 1848 in the German states and in formulating reactionary policies adopted by the governments of those states over the following two decades. First in the Saxon government, then in the Austrian, he was Otto von Bismarck's most formidable opponent during the Prussian chancellor's attempt to unify the small German states under the leadership of Prussia. Beust was also the architect of the political settlement in 1868 which created the Austro-Hungarian Empire.

Early Life

Friedrich Ferdinand von Beust was the scion of an aristocratic Saxon family whose members had served the Saxon monarchy for more than three centuries by the time he was born in Dresden on January 13, 1809. His father, an officer in the Saxon court, married the daughter of a Saxon government official just prior to the Napoleonic Wars, which formed the backdrop to Beust's early life.

When the Napoleonic Wars ended in 1815, the diplomats representing all the nations of Europe gathered in Vienna to establish a new political order in Europe, or, more accurately, to restore insofar as possible the old order that had been destroyed by the French Revolution and Napoleon I. Although there was widespread popular support in the German states for the creation of a nation which would include all German-speaking people, nationalist hopes were frustrated through the machinations of the Austrian representative at the Congress of Vienna, Metternich. The German universities remained hotbeds of support for the unification of the small German states under a liberal, constitutional government until 1819, when Metternich convinced the leaders of all the German states to suppress the *Burchenschaften*, the student fraternities in the universities which had been among the most enthusiastic and sometimes violent organizations calling for the unification of Germany. By the time Beust entered the University of Leipzig, the voices of liberalism and nationalism had been legally silenced on German campuses.

Beust's parents determined that he should pursue the traditional career of his family and sent him to the Universities of Leipzig and Göttingen to study law and government. Accordingly, he entered the University of Leipzig in 1826, when the repressive policies imposed on the German states by Metternich in 1819 were effectively stifling liberal and nationalist ideas. The professors who lectured in Beust's classes were largely champions of the status quo and critical of liberalism and nationalism. His own opposition to those two powerful forces of the nineteenth century formed during his university years and determined the course of his life.

After completing his studies, Beust entered the Saxon bureaucracy in 1830 and married a Bavarian heiress chosen for him by his parents. He served in various diplomatic capacities in Berlin, Paris, Munich, and London, where he gained a reputation as a capable spokesman for conservatism before assuming the post of Saxon foreign minister in 1849.

Life's Work

Beust immediately became the most influential member of the Saxon ministry and was primarily responsible for its reactionary policies in 1849. On Beust's advice, the Saxon king rejected the constitution proclaimed by the Frankfurt Parliament. The parliament, composed of elected representatives from all the German states, came into being as a result of the Revolutions of 1848, which convulsed most of Europe. In 1849, it attempted to promulgate a constitution which would have established a union of all the German states. The government of the new nation would have been a constitutional monarchy with a parliament elected by universal manhood suffrage. The rejection of the Frankfurt constitution in Saxony led to the outbreak of revolution in the capital city of Dresden. Beust's first act as foreign minister was to request military assistance from Prussia to suppress the revolutionaries, who included among their numbers Mikhail Bakunin and Richard Wagner. Both men gained considerable prominence in later years and were among Beust's most outspoken critics. The assistance was quickly forthcoming. Consequently, Beust fell into disrepute with German liberals and nationalists but became the hero of conservatives and reactionaries throughout the German states.

Upon the successful suppression of the revolt, Beust assumed the ministry of education and public worship in addition to his duties as foreign minister. For the next decade and a half, he was the dominant force in the Saxon government. He reorganized the police and used them to crush resistance to the monarchy, including especially student demonstrations at the university. The next year, he overthrew the liberal constitution adopted in Saxony in 1848 and restored the full powers and prerogatives of the monarchy. In 1851, he sided with Austria in that country's successful effort diplomatically to defeat an effort by Frederick William IV of Prussia to unify the small German states under Prussian leadership. In 1853, Beust assumed the Ministry of Internal Affairs and the post of Minister-President of Saxony in addition to his other duties, making him by far the most powerful individual in the country.

With the domestic situation well in hand, Beust devoted most of his attention to foreign affairs after 1853. He became the leader of the aristocratic faction in the German states which opposed a political or economic unification of Germany. He took the lead in proposing at the Bamberg Conference in 1854 that the small German states should form a closer union among themselves to make them better able to resist pressure from the two great monarchies, Austria and Prussia. Largely through Beust's efforts, the unification of Germany was delayed for yet another decade.

In 1864, Beust's policies led him into a direct conflict with the Chancellor of Prussia, Otto von Bismarck, who was intent on territorially aggrandizing the state of Prussia at the expense of the small German states. At Bismarck's urging, the Prussian press began vitriolic denunciations of Beust in that year, condemning him as a "particularist" (one who wished to preserve the independence of the small states within the Germanic Confederation). When Bismarck's policies of expansion led to war with Austria in 1866, Beust convinced the Saxon king to side with the Austrians. Beust tried to rescue a disastrous situation after the Austrian defeat at Hradec Kralové by traveling to France and seeking aid from Napoleon III, but his mission failed. He then resigned his post when Bismarck refused to negotiate with him at the ensuing peace conference. It appeared that Beust's public career was over, but events proved otherwise.

Unexpectedly, Austrian Emperor Franz Joseph asked Beust to assume the duties of Austrian foreign minister in December, 1866 (he became Minister-President of Austria the following year). The Hungarians had used the opportunity presented by Austria's defeat at the hands of Prussia to pursue their ancient dream of independence. Beust's primary responsibility when he assumed his new post was somehow to pacify the Hungarians and preserve the empire intact. The result of Beust's efforts was the creation of the so-called dual monarchy of Austria-Hungary which in effect granted the Hungarians control of their own domestic affairs but left their foreign policy in the hands of the Habsburg monarchy.

In 1868, Beust was appointed Chancellor of the Empire and awarded the title of count. He continued to direct the foreign policy of his adopted empire. Initially, he remained adamantly opposed to Bismarck's ambitions and consequently sought close relations with France. Even after the defeat of the French at the hands of Prussia in 1870-1871 and the proclamation by Bismarck of the German Empire, Beust was unwilling to accept the idea of a unified Germany. When it became obvious that there was nothing he could do to reverse the decision of the war, Beust reluctantly sought a détente with Bismarck, who accepted eagerly, since it meant Austrian recognition of the new German Empire. In July, 1871, Beust announced the agreement to his governments and consummated it with a personal meeting with Bismarck at Gastein the next month.

Later that year, Beust managed to dissuade Franz Joseph from instating a plan to grant greater local autonomy to the various ethnic groups within the empire. Very shortly thereafter, he was relieved of his post as chancellor without explanation. He requested and received appointment as Austrian ambassador to England, in which capacity he served for seven years. In 1878, he was transferred to Paris, where he retired from public life four years later. Beust died at his villa at Altenberg (near Vienna) on October 24, 1886.

Summary

Friedrich von Beust was a leading spokesman for those aristocratic elements in the Germanic Confederation that successfully prevented the democratic unification of the German states in 1848-1849. He was also instrumental in preventing a more authoritarian but still peaceful unification in 1851. Taken together, his successes prepared the way for the creation of the German Empire by force of arms completed under Bismarck's leadership and the distinctly Prussian and militarist nature of the new state which resulted. In addition, the delaying tactics adopted by Beust and those he represented against the installation of representative, constitutional government exacerbated the class conflicts that convulsed the German states throughout the latter half of the nineteenth century and contributed both to the coming of World War I and to the eventual triumph of National Socialism in the first half of the twentieth century.

The opposition of Beust and those he represented to pluralism in the Austrian Empire also had disastrous consequences long after Beust died. The struggle of the various ethnic groups within and without the empire for autonomy or self-determination led directly to the events at Sarajevo in June of 1914 that sparked the outbreak of World War I, with calamitous results for all nations involved. Beust alone did not bring about the apocalyptic events of the first half of the twentieth century. He was, however, a clever and effective champion of the policies that led directly to the catastrophic events that befell the generations of Germans that came after him.

An ancient proverb holds that the road to Hell is paved with good intentions. Beust's intentions from his own perspective were good. He intended to preserve intact the institutions of pre-1848 Europe and to crush the twin threats of liberalism and nationalism which would destroy those institutions. His very success paved the road to the modern hell of total war.

Bibliography

Beust, Friedrich von. *Memoirs of Friedrich Ferdinand, Count von Beust*. Translated by Henry de Worms. 2 vols. London: Remington, 1887. Beust's memoirs offer a wealth of information about the man and his policies but must be used with great caution because of Beust's tendencies toward self-glorification and magnification of his own importance in the unfolding of historical events.

Ellis, William Ashton. *1849*. London: Remington, 1892. This is the only book-length treatment of the Saxon revolution available in English. Ellis is very critical of Beust's role in the events of 1849, describing him as the chief culprit in the crushing of liberal democracy in Saxony.

Kann, Robert A. *The Multinational Empire: Nationalism and National Reform in the Habsburg Monarchy 1848-1918.* 2 vols. New York: Columbia University Press, 1950. Kann's book is the most complete account of Beust's career in the Austrian government. Kann treats Beust kindly and is especially complimentary concerning Beust's role in the formation of the dual monarchy.

May, Arthur J. *The Hapsburg Monarchy, 1867-1914.* Cambridge, Mass.: Harvard University Press, 1951. May offers a balanced account of Beust's career in the Austrian government. Beust emerges from May's pages as an egotistical but competent statesman.

Taylor, A. J. P. *The Habsburg Monarchy, 1809-1918: A History of the Austrian Empire and Austria-Hungary.* Rev. ed. London: Hamish Hamilton, 1948. An outstanding account of Beust's foreign and domestic policies during his career in the Austrian government, including especially his duel with Bismarck.

Paul Madden

OTTO VON BISMARCK

Born: April 1, 1815; Schönhausen, Prussia
Died: July 30, 1898; Friedrichsruh, Germany
Areas of Achievement: Government and politics
Contribution: Bismarck, known as the "blood and iron chancellor," occasioned the unification of the several German states into the German Empire of 1871-1918. Though his image is that of the aristocrat in a spiked helmet, he was above all a diplomat and a politician, skillfully manipulating the forces at work within Germany and among the European states to achieve his goals.

Early Life

Young Otto von Bismarck was influenced both by his father's and his mother's heritages. His father was a Prussian Junker, an aristocrat of proud lineage but modest financial means. The family estates were not particularly large or productive, but provided a setting of paternalistic rule over peasants long accustomed to serve. From his mother and her family, Bismarck learned the sophistication of the upper bourgeoisie, the cosmopolitanism of city life and foreign languages, and something of the ideals of the Enlightenment. Both sides of the family took pride in service to the Prussian state and its ruling dynasty, the Hohenzollern. The Junker aristocrats often served in the military, while the upper bourgeoisie chose the civil service.

Bismarck received a rigorous classical education and attended Göttingen and Berlin universities. He tried his hand at a career in the Prussian diplomatic and civil service. Though his excellent family connections and quick mind should have assured his success, his early career was a disaster. He was temperamentally unsuited to the discipline of a subordinate position, and he alienated his supervisors time after time. "I want to play the tune the way it sounds good to me," he commented, "or not at all. . . . My pride bids me command rather than obey." Like all young men of his class, Bismarck served a few months in the army and remained a reserve officer throughout his life, but he never considered a military career. At age twenty-four, he resigned from the Prussian bureaucracy and took charge of one of the family's estates. Then his life changed under the influence of pietist Lutheran families; he married Johanna von Puttkamer, a woman from one such family, in 1847, and settled down to the domesticity of country life.

The revolutions of 1848 roused him from the country and brought Bismarck into politics. He quickly made a name for himself as a champion of the Hohenzollern monarchy against the liberal and democratic revolutionaries, and, after the failure of the revolution, the grateful King Frederick William IV appointed him to a choice position in the diplomatic corps. He represented Prussia at the German Diet at Frankfurt am Main and then at the courts of Czar Alexander II of Russia and Emperor Napoleon III of France, making a name for himself as a shrewd negotiator and a vigorous advocate of Prussian interests.

Life's Work

Bismarck was recalled to Berlin by King William I of Prussia in 1862 to solve a political and constitutional crisis. The Prussian Diet was refusing to pass the royal budget, because it disagreed with military reforms instituted by the king and his government. To break the deadlock, Bismarck told parliament that "great questions will not be settled by speeches and majority decisions—that was the great mistake of 1848 and 1849—but by blood and iron," and he went ahead with the royal policies in spite of parliamentary opposition. In spite of his reputation as an old-fashioned Prussian monarchist, Bismarck was making an attempt to attract middle-class German nationalists to the support of the Prussian monarchy and its military establishment. When the newly reformed Prussian armies proved their effectiveness by defeating Denmark in 1864 and Austria in 1866 and by setting Prussia on the pathway toward a united Germany, Bismarck was a hero.

Now only France could block German unity. Through a masterful (if rather deceitful) set of diplomatic maneuvers, Bismarck forced the hand of Napoleon III, causing him to declare war on Prussia. Faced by the apparent aggression of a new Napoleon, the southern German states (except for Austria) joined with Prussian-dominated northern Germany. In the Franco-Prussian War which followed, France was defeated and the German Empire was proclaimed. Its capital was Berlin, and its reigning monarch was simultaneously the King of Prussia, William I; but the triumph was Bismarck's.

Even his old enemies among the German liberals were forced to recognize his genius. Yet, under the leadership of the Prussian-Jewish National Liberal politician Eduard Lasker, they pressured Bismarck to create a constitutional government for the newly formed empire. Bismarck's constitution was a masterful manipulation of the political power structure of the age. It contained a popularly elected parliament to represent the people (the *Reichstag*), an aristocratic upper house to represent the princely German states (the *Bundesrat*), and a chancellor as the chief executive—himself. Only the emperor could appoint or dismiss the chancellor, and as long as Bismarck held the ear of William I, his position was secure. As a further means of controlling power, Bismarck retained the positions of Prussian prime minister and Prussian foreign minister throughout most of the period.

Bismarck was a man of great physical stature, who enjoyed the outdoor life of the country squire, riding horses and hunting game. He indulged himself in eating, drinking, and smoking, and, though he fell ill from time to time, he revived again and again with great vigor. He was an eloquent speaker, though with an amazingly high-pitched voice, and he was a master of the German language. He loved the domestic haven of his family life, and he was capable of bitter hatred of his political opponents, at home and abroad. For a statesman famed for his cool exploitation of realistic politics, he showed surprisingly irrational passion when faced with determined opposition.

Bismarck continued to face both domestic and foreign challenges throughout his tenure as chancellor. He opposed the power of the Catholic Center Party in the so-called *Kulturkampf*, the German version of the struggle between the Catholic church and the modern state. He sought to limit the growth of the Social Democratic Party by a combination of social legislation and limits on the political freedoms of left-wing parties. He exploited the forces of anti-Semitism and economic nationalism to undermine the German liberal and progressive parties. He made many political enemies, but he was able to retain power by balancing forces against one another and shifting coalitions among political groups.

In foreign affairs, Bismarck used the talents he had once displayed in causing three wars to keep the peace once he had achieved his major goal of German unity. He caused great bitterness in France by taking Alsace-Lorraine in 1871. Yet he simultaneously wooed Austria and Russia, establishing a "Three Emperors' League" among the three conservative states to preserve the status quo. Bismarck organized the Congress of Berlin of 1878 to settle conflicts in the Balkans, and when it was successful he chose for himself the title of the "honest broker." As nationalism in Eastern Europe and colonial rivalries overseas continued to threaten the peace of the world, Bismarck skillfully sailed the German ship of state on the safest course he could.

In 1890, however, the seventy-five-year-old Bismarck clashed with his new sovereign, the thirty-one-year-old Emperor William II. When the young man wanted to do things his own way and forced Bismarck to resign, the British magazine *Punch* published one of the most famous cartoons in history, entitled "Dropping the Pilot." Bismarck retired to his estates, where he was the object of honors from the great and powerful and much adulation from the public. Yet he loved the reality of power, not mere applause, and he died a frustrated and embittered man in his eighty-third year.

Summary

Otto von Bismarck is known to history as the "blood and iron chancellor" and the practitioner of realpolitik. He was no sentimental humanitarian, and military power always figured strongly in his calculations. Yet he was not a single-minded dictator or heavy-handed militarist as he is sometimes portrayed.

Above all, Bismarck was a diplomat and a politician. He kept open several options as long as possible before choosing a final course of action. His shift from a parliamentary alliance with the liberals in the 1870's to an alliance with the Catholics and the conservatives in the 1880's was designed to achieve a single goal: the perpetuation of the power of the traditional elites of feudal and monarchical Germany and the emerging elites of business and industry. Prior to Bismarck, liberalism and nationalism seemed inevitably linked, and those movements were opposed by the aristocratic establishment; Bismarck broke that link and attached German nationalism to the Prussian conservatism that he valued.

For all of his skill, walking the tightropes of domestic and foreign policy as Prussian prime minister and German chancellor for twenty-eight years, he could not create a system that would endure. The forces of liberalism and socialism continued to grow, pushing Germany toward either democracy or revolution, and the Hohenzollern monarchs were swept away in 1918. The forces of radical nationalism and pan-German racism were not checked by the new republic, and Adolf Hitler's Nazism led Germany to disaster between 1933 and 1945. The German unity which Bismarck created lasted only twenty years after his death, and the map of the German-speaking states of Europe after 1945 bears little resemblance to that of Bismarckian Germany. Yet in a country that has seen so much political instability and military defeat in the twentieth century, the figure of Bismarck still looms large and continues to fascinate practitioners of statecraft and writers of history.

Bibliography

Crankshaw, Edward. *Bismarck*. New York: Viking Press, 1981. A standard volume for the general reader, colorfully written by an Englishman with a flair for political biography. Crankshaw is critical of Bismarck but does not see in him the roots of Nazism.

Gall, Lothar. *Bismarck: The White Revolutionary*. Translated by J. A. Underwood. 2 vols. London: Allen & Unwin, 1986. Though no biography of so controversial a figure as Bismarck will ever be accepted as definitive, this one by a West German historian comes close. Gall argues that Bismarck was a conservative who revolutionized German politics and European international affairs.

Hamerow, Theodore S., ed. *Otto von Bismarck: A Historical Assessment*. 2d ed. Lexington, Mass.: D.C. Heath, 1972. An anthology on Bismarck drawn from German, English, and American authors, introduced and edited by a knowledgeable American professor. Several of the pieces are unavailable in English except in this volume.

Kent, George O. *Bismarck and His Times*. Carbondale: Southern Illinois University Press, 1978. A brief and lucid account of Bismarck and his age, suitable for American college students and the general reader. Kent is familiar with the primary and secondary sources, and his excellent notes provide a springboard for further reading.

Pflanze, Otto. *Bismarck and the Development of Germany.* Princeton, N.J.: Princeton University Press, 1962. The first volume of a life's work on Bismarck by the acknowledged American scholarly master of the subject. It takes the story through German unification in 1871.

Stern, Fritz. *Gold and Iron: Bismarck, Bleichroeder, and the Building of the German Empire.* New York: Alfred A. Knopf, 1977. A study of Bismarck and his Jewish banker Gerson von Bleichroeder which sheds important light on both the personal and the economic aspects of the men and their time.

Taylor, A. J. P. *Bismarck: The Man and the Statesman.* New York: Alfred A. Knopf, 1955. A cleverly written portrait of Bismarck by an Oxford don famous for his acid commentaries on German history. He sees the chancellor as a man interested only in his personal power, who simply used the persons and institutions around him for his own aggrandizement.

Wehler, Hans-Ulrich. *The German Empire, 1871-1918.* Translated by Kim Traynor. Dover, N.H.: Berg, 1985. A leading West German historian, who emphasizes the social and economic aspects of the Bismarck era, summarizes his argument in this useful book. Wehler sees Bismarck as representing the traditional elites of Prussia, whose "fatal successes" contributed to the German disasters of the twentieth century.

Gordon R. Mork

GEORGES BIZET

Born: October 25, 1838; Paris, France
Died: June 3, 1875; Bougival, near Paris, France
Area of Achievement: Music
Contribution: Bizet is one of the foremost French composers of the nineteenth century and the author of one of the most popular operas of all time, *Carmen.*

Early Life
  Georges Bizet was an only child of musically inclined parents. His father, Adolphe Arnaud Bizet, was a teacher of voice and a composer. His mother, Aimée Marie Louise Léopoldine Joséphine Delsarte, was a gifted pianist. Bizet began informal music studies with his mother at age four. Groomed for a musical career, at age eight he began piano lessons with the celebrated teacher Antoine François Marmontel and was admitted to the Paris Conservatoire shortly before his tenth birthday. A brilliant student, Bizet excelled in his courses, winning the Premier Prix in *solfège* (sight-singing) and in Marmontel's piano class. His virtuosity was such that he could easily have launched a concert career in his late teens, had he wished to do so. The young Bizet, however, had his heart set on becoming a composer.
  His first attempts in composition date from 1850, when he was twelve years old. His early works consist of virtuosic piano pieces, choruses, and a one-act comic opera. Bizet's first major work, the Symphony in C, was composed when he was seventeen. Aside from an abundance of charming themes, this work displays a mastery of orchestration unusual in a composer at any age.
  In 1857, Bizet won the prestigious Prix de Rome for his cantata *Clovis et Clotilde.* That enabled him to travel to Rome, where he remained for three years, imbibing Italian culture and refining his skills as a composer. During this time, his attitude toward composition changed drastically. Always a composer of immense natural gifts, he decided to adopt a more rational approach to writing music. This, however, produced an identity crisis that resulted in a creeping paralysis of his creative powers and a series of projected and abandoned works.
  Bizet's problems in Rome were compounded when the Académie des Beaux-Arts, under whose aegis the Prix de Rome was offered, refused to accept his opera *Don Procopio* (1859) in place of the mass he had originally been obliged to write according to the stipulations of the prize. Bizet, for whom the Christian faith held little appeal, was reluctant to write religious music. An ode-symphony, *Vasco de Gama* (1860), was brought to completion and accepted by the Académie.

Life's Work

In 1860, Bizet returned to Paris, where he persisted in his desire to forge a career as a composer, even in the face of tempting offers to teach and make concert appearances. In 1861, he presented his third submission to the Académie in the form of the *Scherzo et marche funèbre* and an overture entitled *La Chasse d'Ossian*, both of which were well received. His final submission, in 1862, was a one-act comic opera, *La Guzla de l'émir*. Though the music for this opera has disappeared, much of it was incorporated into Bizet's first important stage work, *Les Pêcheurs de perles*. Premiered in 1863, it was received coolly by the critics, who criticized its apparent imitation of Richard Wagner and Giuseppe Verdi in orchestration, harmony, and dynamics.

By 1863, Bizet's Rome pension had run out, and he was compelled to earn a living making transcriptions and arrangements for the publishers Choudens and Heugel. The sixteen-hour days he often worked affected his health, which had never been good. Since childhood, he had suffered from a chronic ulceration of the throat which continued to bother him and which would eventually prove fatal. He was also afflicted with articular rheumatism. Nevertheless, he found the time to begin a new operatic endeavor, *Ivan IV*, which, though finished in 1865, was never produced. His next opera, composed in 1866, was *La Jolie Fille de Perth*, based on the 1828 novel *The Fair Maid of Perth* by Sir Walter Scott. It premiered in December of the following year and was reviewed enthusiastically by the press, the only one of his operas to be so received. During the period 1865-1868, Bizet wrote a considerable amount of piano music, most of which, though published, remains obscure. Full of effects in imitation of the orchestra, these pieces also reveal the composer's ongoing fascination with Lisztian virtuosity as well as with the works of Ludwig van Beethoven and Robert Schumann. He also composed a number of songs, the finest of which is "Adieux de l'hôtesse arabe" (1866).

In 1868, Bizet underwent another period of soul-searching as a composer, resulting again in a series of aborted projects. He also endured a severe bout of quinsy. Adding to his despair was the rejection of a new opera, *La Coupe du Roi de Thulé*, which he had submitted in a competition sponsored by the Paris Opéra. In the following year, at the age of thirty-one, Bizet married Geneviève Halévy, the daughter of his former composition teacher at the Paris Conservatoire. Their union was not a harmonious one, as she came from a family with a history of mental illness and was herself emotionally unstable. Their only child, Jacques, born in 1872, inherited this trait and committed suicide when he was fifty.

At the outbreak of the Franco-Prussian War, Bizet enlisted in the National Guard and remained with his wife in Paris. After the war, Bizet resumed work on two operas, *Clarissa Harlowe* and *Grisélidis*, neither of which reached completion. These were followed, however, by his opera *Djamileh*, a one-act work with a libretto by Louis Gallet, which was premiered in May, 1872. Bizet's highly original harmonies bewildered audiences and annoyed the critics. As a result, the opera was a complete failure. Among his most engaging works for orchestra is the incidental music to Alphonse Daudet's *L'Arléssienne*, a melodrama produced at the Théâtre du Vaudeville in October, 1872. Once again, the production was ill-fated, and Bizet's music was not well received. Nevertheless, the individual numbers, twenty-seven in all, are brilliant studies in orchestration. Four of them were arranged by Bizet for full orchestra (the original scoring having been for a small ensemble of twenty-six performers), and the resulting suite, premiered the following month, was greeted with approval by audiences and critics alike.

It was in the year 1872 as well that Bizet began work on his most important opera, one that would elevate him, though posthumously, to greatness. He was offered the services of Henri Meilhac and Ludovic Halévy as librettists and chose Prosper Mérimée's novel *Carmen* (1845; English translation, 1878) as his subject. Already by 1873 the first act was completed, and in the summer of 1874 the score was finished. Some aspects of the opera were controversial from the outset, especially its conclusion with a murder, which was unprecedented at the Opéra-Comique. Bizet's realistic portrayal of the seamier aspects of Merimée's *Carmen*, as well as his highly original and difficult music, caused considerable consternation among the proprietors of the theater. The opera's initial reception in the spring of 1875 seemed to confirm their worst fears. It was dismissed as obscene and Wagnerian, though it ran for forty-eight performances in its first year. It was successfully staged in Vienna in October, 1875, and this led directly to its worldwide popularity.

Bizet's brilliant musical characterization of the principal characters, José and Carmen, his exploitation of exotic musical material and colorful orchestration, and his depiction of violent human emotion imbue the opera with a sensual vitality and pathos that continue to enthrall modern audiences. It is worth noting, however, that Bizet never set foot in Spain. Nor did he utilize Spanish musical folklore extensively, though he did resort to quoting a few popular songs of the day.

Bizet, dejected at the poor reception of *Carmen* and suffering from a bout of quinsy, became seriously ill in May, 1875. His condition worsened when he contracted rheumatism and a high fever. That was followed by a heart attack on June 1, and he died in the early morning of his wedding anniversary. After a funeral ceremony attended by four thousand people, he was buried in Père Lachaise cemetery in Paris.

Summary
  Although he lived for the relatively short span of thirty-seven years,

Georges Bizet produced a sizable body of work. His output—encompassing some twenty-seven operas, ten orchestral works, more than fifteen choral works, and dozens of songs and pieces for piano—was prodigious but uneven. He showed scant interest in writing chamber music, solos for instruments other than piano, or concerti. The love for literature that he displayed early in life probably dictated his preference for writing music that had some dramatic or literary connection. Bizet is an example of a composer who has suffered from his own success. The enormous popularity of a few of his works, such as *Carmen* and *L'Arléssienne*, has tended to overshadow the rest of his oeuvre. Though not all of his music is of the same quality and many pieces were left unfinished, much beautiful music awaits discovery by anyone willing to probe beneath the surface of his accomplishments.

Posterity's judgment of Bizet has fluctuated between extremes of adulation and disdain. Only in the latter half of the twentieth century has a clearer image of his achievements begun to emerge. Though he was receptive to forward-looking trends in the music of his own time, his style was highly original and not easily imitated. As a result, his influence on succeeding generations is difficult to gauge and is not necessarily commensurate with his intrinsic stature as a composer. Yet he must be counted among the greatest musical geniuses of nineteenth century Europe.

Bibliography
Curtiss, Mina. *Bizet and His World*. New York: Alfred A. Knopf, 1958. A singular biography that sheds much light on Bizet's personal life. Progessing in chronological fashion, the discussion focuses on Bizet's relationship to such figures as Charles Gounod, Ludovic Halévy, and many others. Little emphasis is placed on analysis and critique of Bizet's music, and the text includes no musical examples. In addition to a selected bibliography and an index, the appendices include translations of Bizet's unpublished correspondence, a list of the contents of Bizet's music library, a catalog of his works, and accounts of their posthumous presentations.
Dean, Winton. *Bizet*. London: J. M. Dent & Sons, 1948. A standard biography by the preeminent Bizet scholar, writing in the English language. In addition to a carefully researched biographical discussion interspersed with musical examples, the author includes valuable appendices: a catalog of Bizet's works, a calendar of Bizet's life, and a list of individuals associated with Bizet and short biographies on them. Includes an extensive bibliography and an index.
_____. "Bizet's *Ivan IV*." In *Fanfare for Ernest Newman*, edited by Herbert Van Thal. London: A. Barker, 1955. Documents the history of Bizet's opera *Ivan IV*, which was never performed in his lifetime. Discusses the probable chronology of its composition and treats the problems involved in its posthumous productions. Presents an act-by-act critical

examination of the music and the drama and establishes Bizet's use of ideas from *Ivan IV* in his later operas, especially *Carmen*.

_____. *Carmen*. London: Folio Society, 1949. For devotees of the opera, an invaluable work that is divided into three parts. Part 1 presents an English translation (by Lady Mary Lloyd) of Mérimée's *Carmen*. Part 2 discusses the genesis of the libretto by Halévy and Meilhac. Part 3 treats the music of the opera and emphasizes the relationship of the music to the dramatic action.

Shanet, Howard. "Bizet's Suppressed Symphony." *The Musical Quarterly* 54 (October, 1958): 461-476. Seeks to explain the mystery of Bizet's Symphony in C, a masterpiece written when the composer was only seventeen years old but which waited eighty years for its first performance. Why did Bizet never have it performed, and why did his widow forbid its performance or publication? An engaging article that appeals to layperson and scholar alike.

Walter Aaron Clark

LOUIS BLANC

Born: October 29, 1811; Madrid, Spain
Died: December 6, 1882; Cannes, France
Areas of Achievement: Politics and philosophy
Contribution: The founder of humanitarian socialism, Blanc developed his dissatisfaction with the misery of the French people into an imperative to transform the basic governmental and economic system to end forever the capitalist exploitation of the working class.

Early Life

Louis Blanc was born in Madrid during the closing, turbulent days of the Napoleonic Empire. His father served King Joseph Bonaparte as an inspector general of Spanish finances. The French hold over Spain, however, was never secure. Joseph, already forced out of his capital several times by the successes of the British army under Sir Arthur Wellesley, finally left the country in 1813. The French bureaucrats, officials, and advisers departed with him. This exodus split the Blanc family. The father abandoned his wife after the birth of a second son, and Louis, the elder, was sent to live with his maternal grandmother in Corsica. Only after 1815, with the establishment of the Restoration Monarchy, did life become more settled. The father returned, managing to secure a royal pension, and Louis was reunited with his family. In 1821, he and his younger brother, Charles, were enrolled in the Royal College at Rodez, which they attended on scholarship. The school was run by the Catholic clergy, who instructed their pupils in the truth of Bourbon Legitimism and Scholastic theology. The Enlightenment and the Revolution were denigrated, if mentioned at all. Louis was a dedicated student. He won prizes in philosophy and rhetoric and excelled at biblical study, from which he derived a sense of obligation to work for the betterment of society. He completed his formal education in 1830 when he was nineteen years of age.

Blanc left Rodez to find work in Paris and arrived there in August, soon after the revolution which had replaced the Bourbon Dynasty with the Orleanist monarchy of Louis-Philippe. Trained as a gentleman, Blanc had difficulty finding work, especially with the new government, which looked with suspicion on all of those associated with the previous regime. To support himself, therefore, Blanc took a variety of part-time jobs such as tutoring, house cleaning, and clerking. He received some money from an uncle but spent much time visiting museums, palaces, and public monuments. In 1832, the prospect of more steady employment led him to leave the capital to accept a post as a tutor with a family in Arras.

While in Arras, he met Frédéric Degeorge, a newspaper editor and champion of democratic republicanism, who introduced him to political journalism and prompted his admiration of one of Arras' most famous native sons,

Robespierre. The association with Degeorge heightened Blanc's desire to return to Paris and to begin a real career as a writer. He returned in 1834, armed with a letter of introduction, and began work on *Bon Sense* (common sense), a paper founded two years earlier by a group of men who feared the growing power of Louis-Philippe. In 1836, Blanc became the journal's editor-in-chief. He was only twenty-four years of age.

Journalism had become his way to right wrongs and to pave the way for the establishment of a more just society. He wanted to inspire men of goodwill to cooperate in a common program to safeguard individual freedom and to exact reform through evolutionary, but decisive, change. He became involved in election politics and, in 1837, was instrumental in forming a committee to present qualified voters with a slate of progressive candidates in the forthcoming elections. This group failed to form an effective coalition out of the various opposition groups, however, and had little practical effect on the results. The government list was returned with a large majority. The failure did not shake Blanc's faith that government power could be made responsive to the general need. Therefore, he believed it should not be limited but used as the instrument of progress. Such active *étatism* put Blanc at odds with his newspaper's conservative ownership. He insisted, however, that a man should follow his convictions rather than his position and, in 1838, resigned. His entire editorial staff quit with him.

Blanc wanted to create a new kind of newspaper, one committed to the transformation of society, and one which would become a rallying point for all of those who were dedicated to democratic change and who believed in the need for the reorganization of work. This newspaper, *Revue de progrès politique, social et litéraire*, (review of political, social, and literary progress), began publication in January, 1839. In the following year, its pages contained a series of Blanc's articles which formed the key to his own thought and the basis upon which his subsequent political and intellectual career rested.

Life's Work

Blanc believed that society was divided into two classes, the bourgeois and the people, or the oppressors and the oppressed, and that only through political action could the oppressed achieve liberation and the ability to develop their true nature. Blanc asserted that exploitation was endemic to the system of his time where not only the rich exploit the poor but also the poor exploit one another and the father exploits his family. Daughters, to earn money for survival, are often driven to prostitution. Thus, capitalist society leads to the breakdown of the family, to the enslavement of women, to the increase of crime, and to moral decay. Only if the forces of the people succeed in capturing the state can the state be used to liberate man from the horrors of poverty.

This new government must be popularly elected and run by energetic deputies who will serve the interests of the mass of the voters, not the special interests of the capitalists whose oppression will end only after they are absorbed fraternally into a classless society. Blanc hoped that this process of fraternalization could be accomplished peacefully. He suggested that this could be done through the manipulation of the credit system, controlled by the state, which would force the capitalists to transfer money into state banks to be directed toward investments in public enterprises. Thus, the capitalists would be induced to participate in their own destruction. The economic sector would then be organized into ateliers, or social workshops, a production unit of men of the same craft or profession working together at the local level. The bosses would be elected by the workers and would oversee the distribution of earnings. Each man would produce according to his aptitude and strength and would be awarded wages according to his need. The production from the local ateliers would be adjusted to overall production through central organizations that would establish general principles and policies.

The heart of his concern for human welfare lay in his early religious training which taught him the value of charity. Blanc's God, however, was hardly Roman Catholic. Blanc believed in a pantheistic deity which existed in all beings and bound them together in a sacred spirit of fraternity. The perfect society was one with collective ownership of property and complete unity of objective. People would live communally with competition being replaced by cooperation. Blanc envisaged this transformation as being accomplished peacefully through proper education.

His Utopian vision, however, stood in stark contrast to the society in which he lived. The July Monarchy preserved the Napoleonic laws forbidding workers to engage in common action to establish wages and conditions of work. The government, dominated by a strict laissez-faire ideology, made no attempt to improve the standard of living of the working class; nor did many individual employers concern themselves with bettering the lot of their workers. Indeed, many capitalists believed that, since poverty was inevitable, it would not help to call attention to it. Strikes almost never succeeded because the authorities called out the soldiers and the police to suppress the malcontents and jail their leaders.

Thus, the Revolution of 1848, which overthrew the regime of Louis-Philippe, became an opportunity for deliverance. Blanc and other social reformers viewed the advent of the Second Republic as the beginning of the economic transformation of society. Blanc, however, had developed no clear idea of how to put his concepts into practice, nor did there exist any organized political party to support him. The moderate republicans viewed the Revolution as essentially political and were not interested in an economic agenda. Nevertheless, some deference had to be made to the demands of the workers, whose power had formed the backbone of the rebellion. Consequently, the provisional government recognized the socialist principle that the workers could demand government intervention in the industrial life of the nation, and it proclaimed the principle of the right to work. It also established a system of national workshops to guarantee each citizen a job.

Blanc was made president of a special commission to study the improvement of the status of workers. He intended to use his power to enact legislation in accord with his socialist principles. He wanted the people to produce according to their ability and to consume according to their need. Competition would be replaced with workers' associations. Workers would unite like brothers and receive comparable wages. He wanted the state to provide medical insurance and old-age pensions. His commission, he hoped, would assume an active role in the settling of wage disputes. Finally, he wanted to pave the way for the nationalization of the railroads, the factories, the insurance companies, and the banks. His success, however, was limited.

The Luxembourg Commission managed to push the government into passing a law that reduced the workday from eleven hours to ten hours in Paris, and from twelve hours to eleven hours in the provinces. It also had some success in wage disputes. Blanc's schemes, however, for the most part, received a cool reception by the provisional government, whose leadership viewed them as a threat to society. While these social reforms antagonized the middle class, they raised the hopes of the workers and added to the growing class tension. The national workshops scheme ended badly. Blanc had hoped for a plan to help workers become established in a particular profession, but the scheme had never been more than a program of unemployment relief—workers being thrown together without any distinction for their trade and receiving the wages of indigents. Blanc disavowed all connection with it.

The workshops had been established only as a temporary expedient to stall the dangerous masses, and, when the situation in Paris was deemed less volatile, the government began disbanding the groups. In June, a decree was issued that drafted all unwed workers into the army and sent all others connected with the program into the provinces, where they would become less threatening. This outrage sparked six days of street fighting, which left Paris in ruins and the army in control. Blanc's dream of a new France lay in the smoldering wreckage.

Blanc fled to England, where he remained until 1871. During the early days of the Third Republic, he served as a representative to the Chamber of Deputies from Marseilles, but his years of exile had put him out of touch with the new generation of leftist leaders. The Marxists scorned his nonrevolutionary approach. His last days were lonely. He had outlived most of his friends, his wife died in 1876, and his younger brother, Charles, died in January, 1882. Blanc himself was to die within the year. France gave him a state funeral, and the city of Paris named a street after him. One hundred and fifty thousand people were present for his interment at Père Lachaise cemetery. Suddenly in death, he received the recognition that he had once enjoyed in his days of power.

Summary

Like many of his countrymen, Louis Blanc tried to give definition to the revolutionary slogans of Liberty, Equality, and Fraternity. He began his attempt with two main assumptions, both of them drawn from Jean-Jacques Rousseau—that man is basically good, and that this goodness can emerge in a proper society. The conclusion was, therefore, inescapable: Injustice exists because of a bad environment, and the fault lies in institutions not in human nature. Upon such Cartesian assumptions, Blanc built his entire system. His basic dedication to social justice, however, flowed more naturally from a belief that human concern was a logical extension of the teachings of Christ.

Though his ideas formed the basis of modern French humanitarian socialism (as well as influencing the writings of Karl Marx), their application during his lifetime was nonexistent. The Luxembourg Commission was a practical failure. Nevertheless, it furnished an important precedent for state involvement in regulating conditions of work and in collective bargaining mediation. Blanc's system was hopelessly Utopian, but he had made it clear that political liberty is closely related to a society's standard of living and that without significant popular enjoyment of the nation's wealth real democracy is impossible.

Bibliography

Berenson, Edward. *Populist Religion and Left-Wing Politics in France, 1830-1852*. Princeton, N.J.: Princeton University Press, 1984. The first in-depth study of the coalition of democrats and republicans who tried to build social reform on political democracy. Focuses on the interaction of politics and ideology at the national and local levels. Particularly valuable discussion of the diversity of the Montagnard coalition of the Second Republic, of which Blanc was one of the main leaders.

Blanc, Louis. *The History of Ten Years, 1830-1840*. London: Chapman and Hall, 1845. A survey of the first crucial decade of the reign of Louis-Philippe, focusing largely on political events. Valuable for Blanc's partisan descriptions, complete with appropriate moralizing.

Duveau, Georges. *1848: The Making of a Revolution*. Translated by Anne Carter. New York: Pantheon Books, 1966. Disdains formal analysis in favor of a narrative re-creating events through vivid episodes and colorful portraits of the main participants. Contains a lengthy portrait of Blanc, as well as other leaders, in the book's concluding chapters. Blanc's role as head of the Luxembourg Commission is presented side by side with the deliberations of the Provisional Government. Limited almost exclusively to Paris.

Loubère, Leo A. *Louis Blanc, His Life and His Contribution to the Rise of French Jacobin-Socialism.* Evanston, Ill.: Northwestern University Press, 1961. A descriptive approach to the thought of Blanc, relating it to the circumstances of the times. Main thrust is on Blanc's intellectual development as fashioned by public experience. Shows how principal events were responsible for the change and growth of Blanc's socialist philosophy.

Price, Roger. *The French Second Republic: A Social History.* Ithaca, N.Y.: Cornell University Press, 1972. A graphic re-creation of the wretched working-class conditions and the structure of French society which led to the collapse of the July Monarchy.

Soltau, Roger Henry. *French Political Thought in the Nineteenth Century.* Reprint. New York: Russell & Russell, 1959. A competent survey of the leading political thinkers of the age. Blanc's social ideas are all the more extraordinary when placed in the context of his more conservative contemporaries.

Wm. Laird Kleine-Ahlbrandt

GEBHARD LEBERECHT VON BLÜCHER

Born: December 16, 1742: Rostock, Mecklenburg-Schwerin
Died: September 12, 1819; Krieblowitz, Silesia
Area of Achievement: The military
Contribution: Blücher served the cause of Prussia well throughout his life, especially during the French revolutionary and Napoleonic periods. Although he was not a great strategist, his considerable and undisputed ability as a leader of men and his strong support for military reforms following defeat at Jena in 1806 enabled Prussia to play a major role in the final victory over France, thereby contributing to Prussia's subsequent rise as a major power.

Early Life

Gebhard Leberecht von Blücher was born the son of a former cavalry officer who had served in the armies of the Duke of Mecklenburg-Schwerin and the *Landgraf* of Hesse-Cassell. The family was of old but poor East Elbian nobility and, at the time of Blücher's birth, was nearly penniless. The young Blücher entered Swedish military service at age fifteen. He had been sent to live with his married sister on the island of Rügen, then a part of Sweden. Early during the Seven Years' War, Blücher joined a Swedish regiment of hussars as a cadet. Cavalry service was a well-established tradition in the family. In 1760, Blücher was captured by the Prussians, and, when he was offered a commission in the Prussian army, he joined the regiment which had captured him, after obtaining a formal release from Swedish service. Such shifts of allegiance were neither uncommon nor dishonorable prior to the age of nationalism.

In 1773, when Blücher was passed over for promotion in favor of a person of higher nobility, he resigned his commission. He was in part passed over because of his so-called wild life, primarily gambling, drinking, and reckless displays of horsemanship. For Blücher, gambling was a substitute for the excitement of war, and he frequently compared the skills of gambling to the skills of war. For the next fifteen years, Blücher pursued the life of a noble landlord, first in Prussian Poland and then on his own estate in Pomerania. He married and became the father of five children by his first wife. After her death, he married a second time. At heart, however, he continued to long for the life of a soldier and repeatedly requested reinstatement.

Life's Work

Blücher's efforts to return to military life finally succeeded in 1787, when King Frederick William II commissioned him as a major in his old regiment. In 1790, Blücher was promoted to colonel of his regiment. He saw action after the Battle of Valmy (September, 1792) and distinguished himself repeatedly in the 1793 and 1794 campaigns against revolutionary France. In 1795, he was promoted to major general (one star), and in 1801, to lieutenant general (two stars). During the period of peace, Blücher, though primarily a soldier, served successfully as administrator of Münster, which had been annexed to Prussia in 1802. In this capacity, he worked together with Freiherr vom Stein, and the two developed respect for each other. Blücher was among those who advocated war against Napoleon I in 1805 and 1806, despite the fact that he recognized serious shortcomings in the Prussian army. "The army is good," he told a friend, "but the leaders are not well chosen. They include too many princes and old wigs who have outlived their usefulness." Blücher was also motivated by an ever-growing dislike for the French in general (he referred to them as "parlez-vous") and Napoleon in particular.

When Prussia finally joined the war, though belatedly, Blücher participated in the disastrous Battle of Auerstedt (October, 1806). During the inglorious retreat following the humiliating defeat at Jena and Auerstedt, Blücher distinguished himself as commander of the rear guard, covering the flight of the army. While the bulk of the Prussian forces was captured by the pursuing French, Blücher's troops finally retreated northward toward Lübeck, where he was forced to surrender, having run out of ammunition and provisions. Following the disastrous defeat of 1806 and the institution of military reforms, all Prussian officers who had been captured had to justify their action before a commission of inquiry. Blücher was the only one of the field commanders who had surrendered to pass that scrutiny. The commission concluded that "this surrender belongs to the very few which were justified."

Blücher was soon exchanged and appointed governor general of Pomerania, a position in which he again held civil as well as military duties. The king was forced to dismiss him, however, in 1811, under French pressure. Napoleon had become fearful of Blücher's proven ability and undisguised hatred for the French. As early as 1805, having come under the influence of the Prussian military reformers, Blücher advocated the establishment of a national army based on conscription according to the French revolutionary model, in place of the moribund army of unpatriotic mercenaries and impressed peasant boys. He also advocated more humane treatment of the soldiers, better pay, the establishment of self-contained divisions consisting of infantry, cavalry, and artillery, and other military reforms which the French had introduced early in the Revolution.

In 1809, Blücher and other progressive officers attempted to persuade Frederick William III to join Austria's anti-French uprising, but they were unable to convince the cautious and timid king to give the order. The king not only feared defeat but also was extremely distrustful of his subjects, and he did not like the idea of arming the masses. Blücher even considered leaving Prussian service and offering his sword to the Austrians. He spoke of forming a Prussian legion under Austrian command. As Napoleon's empire began to weaken, Blücher and General August Neithardt von Gneisenau, though not the Prussian military establishment, again advocated a popular uprising and guerrilla war, taking their inspiration from the successful Spanish uprising. In 1808, Blücher wrote to a friend, "I don't know why we cannot display as much respect for ourselves as the Spanish do."

In 1812, Blücher was forced into temporary hiding because Napoleon, preparing his Russian campaign, wanted to arrest him. During this period, Blücher suffered from a serious mental illness, which was a recurring problem, though it usually found expression only in depression and hypochondria. In 1813, Blücher was recalled to active duty, only one of two generals of the 142 in the Prussian army in 1806 who retained troop command. He commanded the joint Prussian-Russian "Army of Silesia" as a three-star general. In the summer of 1813, his army invaded Saxony and defeated the French in a series of engagements, including the Battle of Wahlstatt, and played a major role in the decisive allied victory in the Battle of the Nations (Leipzig), in October, 1813. For his part in this significant victory, he was promoted to field marshal. His impetuous and aggressive leadership earned for him the title "Marshal Forward" (*Vorwarts*), bestowed upon him by the Russians.

Blücher, in keeping with the new concepts of warfare, urged a continuous and unorthodox winter pursuit of Napoleon and with his forces crossed the Rhine River during New Year's night of 1814. The Austrians, on the other hand, wanted to negotiate with Napoleon, their emperor's son-in-law, and retain him on the throne of a reduced and chastened France as a counterweight to growing Russian power. Blücher, however, had no understanding of political considerations, seeing all matters solely from the military viewpoint. Though the allies still suffered some defeats, Blücher urged them to maintain the pressure until the final capture of Paris and Napoleon's abdication in March, 1814. Throughout this period, Gneisenau served as Blücher's capable chief of staff, complementing Blücher's daring and courage with competent staff work, the value of which Blücher fully and publicly recognized. Blücher, celebrated, decorated, and rewarded for his services, was always quick to praise others and give them credit. While accompanying the victorious monarchs during a visit to Britain, he received an honorary doctorate from the University of Oxford and later accepted a similar honor from the University of Berlin.

Ill health and his strong disagreement with the victorious coalition's lenient treatment of defeated France caused him to retire from military service. He was, however, immediately recalled as Prussia's field commander when Napoleon returned from Elba in 1815. Blücher joined forces with the British under the Duke of Wellington in the southern Netherlands (modern Belgium), moving his forces dangerously close to the French frontier. On

June 16, 1815, the Prussian forces, on Wellington's left flank at Ligny, were defeated by Napoleon's surprise attack, which was designed to separate the two allied forces. Napoleon then turned northward against Wellington, hoping to force him to retire to England. Blücher, though severely injured when he was pinned under his horse, which was killed during a French charge, managed to rally most of his disheveled army; instead of retreating along his line of communication toward Germany as conventional military doctrine would have dictated and as Napoleon expected him to do, Blücher retreated northward, slipped away from the pursuing Marshal Michel Ney, and joined Wellington at Waterloo on the evening of June 18. His timely arrival to assist the exhausted British turned a stalemate, or possibly a French victory, into a total French rout. For this victory, Blücher received a unique award, the "Blücher Star"—the Iron Cross superimposed on a golden star. Blücher had already received the Grand Cross of the Iron Cross in 1813 (awarded only seven times during the war). Following this final contribution to the allied cause, Blücher retired again and returned to his Silesian estates, where he devoted much time to his passion for gambling. He died in 1819 after a short illness, and his funeral became an occasion for great praise and more honors.

Summary

Gebhard Leberecht von Blücher was a man of limited formal education, a fact he clearly recognized and often lamented. Although he did not understand the essence of the French Revolution—the emphasis on democratic reforms—he recognized the benefits that a national, patriotic army offered. Though he is not considered to have been a military genius or even a capable strategist, he did join others in promoting reforms that led to the creation of the *Landwehr* (Prussian militia) and a national conscript army, so important in subsequent German history. Blücher is frequently described as being impatient with maps but able and willing to delegate authority, accept advice, and make quick and sound decisions under the pressure of battle. "Gneisenau stirs and I move forward," he said in reference to his chief of staff. Blücher was one of the few German officers of the old order to make the transition from the organizational and strategic concepts of classical (limited) warfare to the new concepts of revolutionary-national warfare. His most important contributions to victory over Napoleon were his insistence on aggressive action, close pursuit, and, above all, his folksy manner and sincere feeling for his troops. His soldiers in turn repaid him with steadfast loyalty, devotion, and obedience, even when his demands were excessive. He saw matters only from the military viewpoint and was greatly opposed to the lenient postwar diplomatic settlement.

Blücher was also firmly convinced that the army, as well as the Prussian nobility, should occupy privileged positions within the state, though he demonstrated none of the arrogance so common among his fellow aristocrats. At no time did he accept military subordination to civilian authority. His forthright, honest, and earthy character and his physical attractiveness made him a natural, charismatic leader and war hero, much admired by the German population; he is probably the most popular hero in German military history. Blücher, along with Gneisenau, is considered by Marxists to have been among the progressive Prussian officers of the War of Liberation. Karl Marx described him as "the model of a soldier."

Bibliography

Craig, Gordon A. *The Politics of the Prussian Army, 1640-1945.* Oxford, England: Clarendon Press, 1955. A general history, placing Prussian reforms into a broader context. Includes an index and a general bibliography.

Henderson, Ernest F. *Blücher and the Uprising of Prussia Against Napoleon, 1806-1815.* New York: Knickerbocker Press, 1911. A critical and balanced history of the period with primary emphasis on Blücher's contributions to the allied victory. Some original sources are listed in the text. Very little is included on his early life and career.

Paret, Peter. *Clausewitz and the State.* New York: Oxford University Press, 1976. Emphasizes military and civil reforms in Prussia with numerous references to Blücher. Includes a very comprehensive listing of primary sources and an extensive index.

―――――――. *Yorck and the Era of Prussian Reforms, 1807-1815.* Princeton, N.J.: Princeton University Press, 1966. After an introduction to warfare under the old order, this work concentrates on reforms and reorganization in state and army after Jena. Includes several appendices pertaining to the reform movement, an index, and an extensive bibliography.

Parkinson, Roger. *Clausewitz: A Biography.* London: Wayland, 1970. A balanced treatment of Clausewitz's life and work with detailed description of the battles and frequent references to Blücher as a military leader and a supporter of reforms. Includes a bibliography, an index, and illustrations.

Frederick Dumin

LUIGI BOCCHERINI

Born: February 19, 1743; Lucca
Died: May 28, 1805; Madrid, Spain
Area of Achievement: Music
Contribution: Boccherini was one of the most prolific composers of all time, creating almost five hundred instrumental compositions from trios to symphonies. With Joseph Haydn and Wolfgang Amadeus Mozart, he helped to establish the style and structure of the classic string quartet and concerto.

Early Life

Ridolfo Luigi Boccherini was born Februry 19, 1743, in Lucca, Tuscany, the third of five children of Leopoldo and Maria Santa Boccherini. Leopoldo Boccherini was one of the first musicians to play solos on the double bass. After having seen Luigi display a remarkably sensitive ear at an early age, Leopoldo hoped that his son would develop musical talent and began giving him cello lessons when he was five. After a few months, his father sent him to Abbate Domenico Francesco Vanucci, maestro di cappella at Lucca's cathedral. This composer, cellist, singer, and choirmaster taught the young Boccherini cello, harmony, and composition (as well as Latin and Italian) at the seminary of San Martino. When Boccherini was thirteen years of age, Vanucci realized that his pupil knew at least as much about music as he did.

After Boccherini gave his first public performance during the Festival of the Holy Cross in September, 1756, his father sent him to Rome. He auditioned for the celebrated cellist and composer Giovanni Battista Costanzi and was immediately accepted. Boccherini and his father were appointed cellist and double-bass player in the orchestra of the Imperial Theatre in Vienna in December, 1757. In 1760, Boccherini wrote six trios for two violins and cello obligato, his Op. 1, and its admirers in Vienna included Christoph Gluck. Other family members also found success in Vienna as one brother and two sisters danced in the ballet, and his other brother, Giovanni-Gastone, after failing as a dancer, a singer, and a violinist, became a librettist, eventually collaborating with Joseph Haydn.

Despite the advances he made in Vienna as cellist and composer, Boccherini wanted to spend the rest of his life in his native town and, in August, 1760, petitioned the Grand Council of Lucca for a position as cellist in the council's chapel, but received no reply. After a major success with a 1764 concert of his works in Vienna, he finally won his Lucca appointment, but the inexperienced Boccherini had expected too much and was disappointed in that the council did not pay for his compositions except for the expenses of getting the music copied. On December 9, 1764, attracted by the renown of Giovanni Battista Sammartini, he left for Milan.

In Milan, Boccherini wanted to exchange views with other talented composers and musicians. Such contacts led in 1765 to what historians of classical music consider to be the first formation of a string quartet for regular public performances. This quartet, which consisted of Boccherini (apparently the originator of the idea), Filippo Manfredi, Pietro Nardini, and Giovanni Giuseppe Cambini, played compositions by Haydn and Boccherini. In the spring of 1765, Boccherini returned to Lucca and to his official duties.

Later that year, Boccherini missed two performances, the first sign of an incurable condition which may have been tuberculosis and which grew steadily worse, forcing him eventually to abandon his ambitions as a virtuoso concert cellist. When his father died in 1766, the young composer became anxious over assuming sole responsiblity for his career. Needing an experienced adviser, he went to the violinist Manfredi, fourteen years his senior, who invited Boccherini to tour with him.

Life's Work

Early in 1767, they arrived in Paris, where Boccherini's music had already been published. Boccherini was soon befriended by the Baron de Bagge, an influential patron of the arts; the music publisher Vénier; and Madame Brillon de Jouy, a prominent harpsichordist, for whom he composed his Op. 5. Through the Baron de Bagge, he met the intellectual elite of France, becoming aware of the musical avant-garde.

In 1768, the Spanish ambassador to France invited Boccherini and Manfredi to Madrid, where they hoped for the patronage of the Prince of the Asturias, the heir to the Spanish throne, and were lured by the legend of the favorable treatment of artists in the court of Charles III and by the illusion of wealth possible in a country enamored of Italian music. The king and the prince, however, had little musical judgment and were guided entirely by the Italian violinist and composer Gaetano Brunetti. After receiving helpful advice about composition from Boccherini, Brunetti became jealous of this potential rival and decided to prejudice the court against him.

At the end of 1769, Boccherini received a major boost to his career when he met the Infante Don Luis, brother of the king, and composed six quartets (Op. 8) in his honor. Luis was much more sophisticated about music than were his brother and nephew and delighted in supporting musicians slighted at court. Impressed by Boccherini's talent and his personal charm, Luis appointed him cellist and composer of his chamber on November 8, 1770. Boccherini was to be paid thirty thousand reals annually, more than Luis' confessor and his personal physician, and the composer's art flourished for the next fifteen years.

Sometime after entering the service of Luis, Boccherini married Clementina Pelicho—sources do not provide a date—and their first child, a daughter, was born in 1776. When Luis also married and moved to Las Arenas,

Boccherini and his family followed. The composer settled down for the next nine years to work on chamber music almost exclusively, since only a small number of musicians were available in Las Arenas.

By 1783, the Boccherinis had three daughters and two sons, but Clementina died suddenly in 1785. After Luis died later that year, Charles III continued the composer's salary, appointing him cellist of the Chapel Royal. Boccherini never actually performed this duty because of his illness. The death of Don Luis left Boccherini free to dedicate his works to any patron, and Frederick William II, king of Prussia, appointed him composer of his chamber, although Boccherini continued to live in Madrid. Frederick William, also patron to Haydn and Mozart, was fond of the Italian's works since he himself was an amateur cellist. Among the many pieces Boccherini presented to the Prussian monarch was *La Tirana* (1792), his most famous quartet.

Boccherini's most important Madrid patrons during this time were the Countess-Duchess of Benavente-Osuna and her husband, the Marquess of Benavente. The Duchess of Osuna made him director of a sixteen-piece orchestra that performed in her palace. Because the Marquess was an ardent guitarist, Boccherini transcribed several of his piano pieces for his benefactor's instrument. At the request of the mother of the Marquess, he composed *La Clementina* (1786), his only opera, with a libretto by Ramón de la Cruz.

In 1787, Boccherini married Maria del Pilar Joaquina Porreti, daughter of his late friend the cellist Domingo Porreti. He then ceased composing and performing for the Duchess of Osuna and withdrew into isolation. He may have decided to devote himself entirely to composition since his productivity increased, despite ill health, during 1787-1796. Almost no documentation exists for the events of Boccherini's private life during this period. While some sources place him at the court of Frederick William, there is no substantial evidence that he ever left Madrid.

Boccherini's fortunes began to take a bad turn in 1798. After Frederick William died, his son halted the composer's pension. Boccherini then had to accede to the instructions of his Paris publisher, Ignaz Joseph Pleyel, also a composer. The correspondence between the two reveals many of Boccherini's problems with this demanding, perhaps jealous, publisher. When Pleyel advertised himself as the sole proprietor of Boccherini's works, the composer demanded to know if he was still alive. Pleyel's published Boccherini scores were full of errors, and many pieces languished in drawers until the publisher deemed the time right for his financial benefit.

Boccherini was nevertheless highly regarded in France, and in 1799 he dedicated six quintets, Op. 57, to that nation. As a result, he was invited to become one of the five directors of the Conservatoire in Paris, but he did not want to leave Spain, which he regarded as his native country. When Lucien Bonaparte arrived in Madrid as France's ambassador in 1800, he became

Boccherini's final patron. The composer was paid richly for organizing the music for the ambassador's parties in the palace of San Bernardino.

After Lucien Bonaparte left Madrid in 1801, Boccherini had nothing on which to live except what he earned from the sale of his works. The pension continued by Charles IV was meager. Despite increasingly bad health, he composed as much as before. Two of his daughters died during an 1802 epidemic, and his wife and another daughter died in 1804. Boccherini began a set of six quartets around this time but was too weak to continue after writing the first movement of the second. He died, apparently of pulmonary suffocation, on May 28, 1805. A century later, Lucca asked Madrid for the composer's ashes, and they were transferred to his birthplace in 1927 and interred in the Basilica of San Francesco.

Summary

Luigi Boccherini was considered second only to Haydn as a composer for cello and violin in the late eighteenth century, but, as tastes shifted from classical to Romantic music, he was considered, despite some proponents such as Frédéric Chopin and Aleksandr Borodin, to be passé. Boccherini's rococo style was thought too delicate and ornate, too superficial and monotonous. Because his music is charming, gentle, and even effeminate, he was called "Haydn's wife" by the violinist Giuseppe Puppo. Still, Mozart is thought to have been influenced by Boccherini, and Ludwig van Beethoven adapted many of his methods and idioms.

Boccherini was almost forgotten when what is still his best-known work, the minuet from the String Quartet in E Major, Op. 13, No. 5, was rediscovered in the 1870's as a jewel of the rococo art. In 1895, the Dresden cellist Friedrich Grützmacher published his free arrangement of the Cello Concerto in B Flat. Boccherini was known primarily for these two works, partly because most of his music was available only in flawed editions, until after World War II, when he began to be reevaluated. The Quintetto Boccherini, formed in Rome in 1949, helped renew interest in the composer, making tours throughout the world as well as making many recordings.

Boccherini has finally been recognized as a significant pioneer in the development of chamber music. He helped the technique of string instruments to progress from an almost primitive simplicity to a subtle sophistication. With Haydn and Mozart, he clarified and solidified the sonata form. He contributed to the maturity of the string quartet by writing as if for four blended soloists rather than for a small orchestra, and he virtually invented the quintet and sextet. He has most often been praised by critics for the balance, symmetry, and lyricism of his compositions. Of Boccherini, Sir William Henry Hadow, an English critic and composer, wrote, "So long as men take delight in pure melody, in transparent style, and in a fancy alert, sensitive and sincere, so long is his place in the history of music assured."

Bibliography

Cowling, Elizabeth. *The Cello*. New York: Charles Scribner's Sons, 1975. History of the instrument and its composers and players from the sixteenth century to 1960. Includes an excellent brief biography of Boccherini combined with analysis of his contribution to the literature of the cello.

Gérard, Yves, ed. *Thematic, Bibliographical, and Critical Catalogue of the Works of Luigi Boccherini*. Translated by Andreas Mayor. New York: Oxford University Press, 1969. Compiled to supplement Rothschild's biography. Corrects errors in earlier catalogs of Boccherini's compositions.

Griffiths, Paul. *The String Quartet*. New York: Thames and Hudson, 1983. Traces the development of the string quartet from 1759 to 1913. Evaluates Boccherini's contribution to this development and compares his chamber music to that of Haydn and Mozart.

Newman, William S. *The Sonata in the Classic Era*. Chapel Hill: University of North Carolina Press, 1963. History of the sonata from 1740 to 1820. Provides an overview of Boccherini's life combined with a brief but detailed analysis of his contribution to the sonata form.

Rothschild, Germaine de. *Luigi Boccherini: His Life and Work*. Translated by Andreas Mayor. New York: Oxford University Press, 1965. The only biography in English is very brief but contains all the relevant information known to exist. Emphasis is on Boccherini's life, with little analysis of his work. Includes a bibliography and an appendix with all extant Boccherini letters, all to his publishers.

Michael Adams

GERMAIN BOFFRAND

Born: May 7, 1667; Nantes, France
Died: March 18, 1754; Paris, France
Area of Achievement: Architecture
Contribution: Boffrand developed an approach to interior decoration resulting in rooms where sculpture, architecture, paintings, and furnishings all
interacted to convey a unified mood. His most successful rooms, still in
existence, are the salons of the Prince and Princess of Soubise at the Hôtel
de Soubise in Paris (1732-1739). Boffrand's lively, livable floor plans are
best exemplified in his design for the Hôtel Amêlot de Gournay, later
Montmorency, of 1712. His concern with the interrelationship of the room,
the plan, and the site resulted in works of visual, intellectual, and emotional harmony.

Early Life
Germain Boffrand's conception of architecture as environmental sculpture
is in part the result of his early training. His father was a provincial sculptor
who apprenticed his son in 1781 to François Girardon, the most honored
official sculptor during the second half of the seventeenth century in France.
Boffrand never denied his training in sculpture. Indeed, toward the end of
his career in 1745, he published a treatise on the casting of Girardon's
monumental bronze equestrian statue of Louis XIV.
Girardon had worked with Jules Hardouin-Mansart at Versailles, which
may have been the means by which Boffrand became an apprentice at the
royal office of architecture, Service des Bâtiments du Roi, under Hardouin-
Mansart in 1785. Boffrand was only nineteen when he began work on the
early drawings for the Place Vendôme. The experience Boffrand gained in
this project would be useful for him after 1732, when he joined the federal
department of bridges and roads, of which he eventually became the director.
Boffrand's connection with the theater during his youth perhaps had an
impact on his ability to produce an architecture that conveyed a particular
mood and idea. Boffrand's theatrical architectural space is not surprising for
an eighteenth century French architect trained in the royal office of architecture, since the major architectural patron of the seventeenth century in
France was Louis XIV. Louis' palace, Versailles, was the stage upon which
this king's play of absolute monarchy and controlled court life was enacted,
and Versailles was, in part, the travail of Hardouin-Mansart, Boffrand's
teacher.

Life's Work
Contemporary information about Boffrand's career comes from official
documents in the French archives of state; from his buildings; from accounts

of his works and character from French and other European architects, including the letters of Johann Balthasar Neumann, written on a study trip to Paris in 1724; and from Boffrand's own book *Livre d'architecture* (English translation, 195?) of 1745.

Between about 1702 and 1719, Boffrand worked under conditions that allowed him a certain amount of freedom of design. His patrons were non-French nobility, including the Duke of Lorraine and Maximilian II Emanuel, Elector of Bavaria. Being French gave Boffrand an elevated status distinct from that of the local architects. In addition, he maintained his contacts in Paris and erected speculative buildings in the districts of Saint Germain and Saint Honoré. These new areas of the city, developed on the left bank of the Seine River, became the most fashionable addresses in Paris.

Yet Boffrand's freedom probably was one of necessity, since there were few government commissions between the death of Louis XIV and the coming of age of Louis XV. While he was often experimental, he was also literate, exhibiting a knowledge of architectural theory written by his contemporaries as well as the books of earlier architects, particularly the late Renaissance Italian Andrea Palladio.

From 1702 to 1722, Boffrand worked for the Duke of Lorraine on many projects, including the palace Château Lunéville. Beginning at Lunéville as the representative of his architectural mentor Hardouin-Mansart, Boffrand eventually became first architect to the duke in 1711, three years after Hardouin-Mansart's death. Two aspects of Lunéville are experimental, while also revealing an interest in the literature of architecture—the chapel and the design of the *corps-logis*, or main body, of the palace. Like the chapel at Versailles, which Hardouin-Mansart initiated but which was completed by his brother-in-law, the chapel at Lunéville consisted of a tall, open nave ringed by aisles and galleries that stood on load-bearing, free-standing columns. Such a design takes its origin from the Greco-Gothic ideal described by the Abbé de Cordemoy in his *Nouveau Traité de toute l'architecture* (1706). R. D. Middleton singled out the chapel at Lunéville as the first work to put Cordemoy's ideas into practice. Using load-bearing columns at Lunéville, Boffrand focused the weight of the building on slender supports, allowing the walls and interior space to be more open, as was the case in Gothic interiors. Rather than use complex Gothic colonettes, Boffrand employed classical columns for support. The understanding of structural engineering revealed in the chapel at Lunéville is similar to the thinking followed by nineteenth and early twentieth century architects in creating the curtained, walled skyscraper.

Palladio's influence is obvious in the hunting lodge Boffrand built for the Elector of Bavaria in 1705. This structure, Bouchefort, was an octagon with four porticoes set in the center of a circular courtyard, which was the terminus of seven avenues leading into the forest of Soignies, near Brussels.

The plan of the central pavilion was inspired by Palladio's Villa Almerico, called Rotonda, which was a square with four identical porticoes.

Other innovative plans by Boffrand were the x-shaped Malgrange II, never built but perhaps related to the Althan Palace in Vienna of around 1693, by Johann Bernhard Fischer von Erlach, and the Hôtel Amêlot de Gournay, one of the speculative structures Boffrand erected in Paris in 1712. At Amêlot de Gournay, Boffrand took a rectangular lot and organized the structure around an enclosed oval courtyard, articulating the space with ovals and polygons into a convenient, rhythmically organic design.

Received directly into first-class membership in the Academy of Architects in 1709, Boffrand also rejoined the royal building service in that year. His primary contributions to the development of the Rococo-style interior began with a French royal commission in 1710—the salon of the Petit Luxembourg Palace. At Luxembourg, he used a continuous band of molding, the impost, in a new way. The impost, set below the ceiling, curved up over the doors, windows, and mirrors, visually uniting the room and giving no indication of the corners where one wall joined another. With this innovation, Boffrand eliminated the box-shaped room. At Malgrange I, he continued this process of unification in the oval salon of 1711, linking the walls and the ceiling as well through the use of decorative floral-relief sculpture. Although the design elements were complex, Boffrand maintained unity through the use of symmetry and repetition. Boffrand's masterpiece in Rococo design was the salon of the Princess of Soubise, where all the design elements work together, projecting a remarkable sense of light and harmony.

During the economic crisis of 1719-1720, known as the Mississippi Bubble, Boffrand lost his fortune. In addition, his affiliation with the court of Lorraine ended. Although he did continue some activities in the private realm, most of the second half of his career was devoted to public projects and consultancies. He served as architect and member of the board of the general hospital system in Paris from 1724, worked on the restoration at Nôtre Dame de Paris between 1725 and 1727, and joined the central administration of the French bridges and highway department in 1732. He consulted with Austrian architect Neumann over the design of the Würzburg Residenz in 1724. François Cuvilliés consulted with Boffrand in the 1730's and took the salon of the Princess of Soubise as his inspiration for the salon of the Amalienburg hunting lodge in Munich.

Summary

Germain Boffrand's *Livre d'architecture* encapsulates his career and sheds light on his interests as well as those of his contemporaries. Dedicated to the King of France, the chapters reveal Boffrand as an architect and an intellectual. The first chapter, a dissertation on good taste, is followed by a statement of principles of architecture extracted from Horace, an ancient Roman poet and critic. An essay on the shape and use of Doric, Ionic, and Corinthian forms and decorative systems is followed by comments on interior furnishings and plans, on elevations, and on his own buildings.

Defining good taste as the ability to distinguish between the good and the excellent, Boffrand praised the ancient Greeks, crediting them with developing enduring principles of architecture based on observation of nature and thoughtful reflection. The Greeks, he believed, began with utilitarian rustic huts, which they developed into convenient, efficient, well-proportioned structures. These principles were absorbed into Roman culture and were lost, according to Boffrand, with the fall of Rome.

Boffrand's ideas about classical architecture were not original, but his perceptions of Gothic architecture put him in the avant-garde of his time. In his *Livre d'architecture*, Boffrand suggested that the Goths took branches, vines, and leaves, and used them as the basis of their high, decorated vaults. He pictured Gothic vaults as a forest where the tree branches joined overhead. With this image, Boffrand likened the origin of Gothic architecture to that of the ancient Greeks as explained by the ancient Roman architect Vitruvius, since both began with the natural, rude hut. Boffrand's text may have been an influence upon Marc-Antoine Laugier, who proposed the primitive hut as the source of all good design.

Boffrand concluded his introductory chapter with remarks on his interests in building sites and the importance of expressing the spirit of the owner of a house in architectural terms. These concerns bring to mind Boffrand's readings of Palladio's four books on architecture and Boffrand's applications of these ideas in his buildings. Boffrand's thoughtful, humane understanding of how climate, setting, and ornamentation of a building could affect the mood and spirit of its inhabitants is his legacy to later generations of architects and builders.

Bibliography

Blomfield, Reginald. *A History of French Architecture: From the Death of Mazarin Until the Death of Louis XV, 1661-1774*. Reprint. New York: Hacker Art Books, 1973. This two-volume set is very accessible to English readers, but much of the information is out-of-date and inaccurate. It should be read in conjunction with Kalnein.

Blunt, Anthony, ed. *Baroque and Rococo Architecture and Decoration*. London: Elek, 1978. The chapter on France by Christopher Tadgell is concise and insightful. The other chapters set Boffrand in the context of German and Austrian Rococo architecture.

Garms, Jörg. "Projects for the Pont Neuf and Place Dauphine in the First Half of the Eighteenth Century." *Journal of the Society of Architectural Historians* 26 (1967): 102-113. This essay on two of the major city-planning projects in eighteenth century Paris reveals the context in which

Boffrand's design project for the Place Louis XV can be understood.

Kalnein, Wend Graf, and Michael Levey. *Art and Architecture of the Eighteenth-Century in France*. Harmondsworth, England: Penguin Books, 1972. This book is an up-to-date general work on eighteenth century French art. The treatment of Boffrand is evenhanded and quite complete, including illustrations of floor plans as well as photographs of buildings.

Kimball, Sidney Fiske. *The Creation of the Rococo*. New York: W. W. Norton, 1964. By focusing on establishing which French architect was the first to begin the development of the Rococo style, Kimball tends to diminish the importance of Boffrand's work. Yet there is much information on Rococo architects quoted verbatim from the French state archives that can only be found in France or in this book.

Middleton, R. D. "The Abbé De Cordemoy and the Graeco-Gothic Ideal: A Prelude to Romantic Classicism." *Journal of the Warburg and Courtauld Institutes* 25, nos. 1 and 2 (1962): 278-320. An exhaustive and excellent account of the interest in medieval architecture in France from the sixteenth to the eighteenth century. Useful for the presentation of the background of Boffrand's interest in Gothic architecture and for elucidating the relationship between his chapel at Lunéville and eighteenth century architectural theory.

Alice H. R. H. Beckwith

JAKOB BÖHME

Born: April 24, 1575; Alt-Seidenberg, near Görlitz, Silesia
Died: November 17, 1624; Görlitz, Silesia
Areas of Achievement: Philosophy and religion
Contribution: In a series of books Böhme developed a profound meta-physical system, rich in myth and symbol, which attempted to explain the nature of God, the origin of the universe and of man, and the Fall of Man and the way of regeneration. His complex and difficult thought influenced many German, French, and English philosophers and poets.

Early Life

Jakob Böhme was born on April 24, 1575, in the village of Alt-Seidenberg, near Görlitz, in what is modern East Germany. He was the fourth child of Jakob Böhme, a prosperous farmer, and his wife, Ursula. The family had been well established in the community for several generations, and Jakob's father was a Lutheran church elder and local magistrate. Information about Böhme's early life is scanty. He received an elementary education at the local school, and in 1589 he was apprenticed to a shoemaker, probably for a period of three years. He then traveled as a journeyman, and in 1594 or 1595 he settled in Görlitz. In 1599, he became a citizen of that town and probably at the same time became a master shoemaker. In May, 1599, he married Catharine Kuntzschmann, the daughter of a local butcher, who was to bear him four children.

The following year, 1600, was a highly significant one for Böhme. It marked the arrival in Görlitz of a new Lutheran pastor, Martin Moller. Moller was well read in the German medieval mystical tradition, and he espoused a Christianity of pure and inward spirituality. Böhme was attracted to Moller's teaching and joined his Conventicle of God's Real Servants. Moller's influence was a lasting one. In that same year came an experience which dramatically changed Böhme's life. As he happened to glance at a pewter dish which was reflecting bright sunlight, he experienced a moment of suddenly heightened awareness. This feeling stayed with him as he went outside to the fields; he felt that he could see into the innermost essence of nature, and he later said that the experience was like being resurrected from the dead. More experiences of illumination followed over the next ten years, and these clarified and amplified what he had seen and understood in his initial experience. These experiences were the foundation of his life's work. In 1612, he felt compelled to write, and the result was a long, rambling, but thrilling book, *Aurora: Oder, Die Morgenröthe im Aufgang* (1634; *The Aurora*, 1656). This work marked Böhme's first step on the road to becoming one of the most original and profound thinkers in the history of the Western religious tradition.

Life's Work

Böhme had originally written *The Aurora* for his own use only, but a nobleman, Carl von Ender, found the manuscript at Böhme's house, borrowed it, and had some copies made. Unfortunately for Böhme, news of his book came to the attention of the pastor of Görlitz, Gregorius Richter, a strict defender of religious orthodoxy, who had succeeded Moller in 1606. Richter was enraged at Böhme's bold assertions and assailed him from the pulpit in virulent terms, while Böhme himself sat quietly in the congregation. The next day the town council told Böhme to hand over the manuscript of *The Aurora* and not to write anymore. Böhme agreed to keep silent, and for seven years he kept his promise. He became prosperous, and as a member of his trade guild he was active in the day-to-day commercial life of the town. In 1613, he sold his business and entered the linen and wool trade, which involved him in yearly journeys to Prague and possibly to the Leipzig Fair.

During this period of silence he was making some learned and influential friends, including Tobias Kober, physician of Görlitz, and Balthasar Walther, who was director of the chemical laboratory in Dresden. From Kober Böhme learned about the work of Paracelsus, and Walther introduced him to the Jewish mystical tradition embodied in the Cabala. Both became major influences on his work, and Böhme also learned from his educated friends some Latin terms which he would later incorporate into his works. One of his friends, Abraham von Franckenberg, gives the following picture of Böhme's physical appearance: "His person was little and leane, with browes somewhat inbowed; high temples, somewhat hauk-nosed; his eyes were gray and somewhat heaven blew, and otherwise as the windows of Solomon's Temple: He had a thin beard, a small low voice. His speech was lovely."

In January, 1619, prompted by the urgings of his friends, Böhme decided that he could no longer keep silent. Taking up his pen once more, he produced a constant stream of lengthy books over a period of nearly six years until his death. The first of these was *Von den drei Principien göttlichen Wesens* (1619; *Concerning the Three Principles of the Divine Essence*, 1648), which was quickly followed by *Vom dreyfachen Leben des Menschen* (1620; *The High and Deep Searching Out of the Threefold Life of Man*, 1650) and *Viertzig Fragen von der Seele* (1620; *Forty Questions of the Soul*, 1647). In all of these works Böhme labored to give expression to his central insights: that all life, even that of God Himself, is composed of a dynamic interplay of opposing forces: fire and light, wrath and love. Only as a result of interaction with its opposite could anything in the universe gain self-knowledge; the clash of opposites is what drives the universe on, at every level. Within God, all opposing energies are held in a dynamic and joyful state of creative tension, a unified state which Böhme described as "eternal nature." Only in the human world ("temporal nature") does the equilibrium between the opposites of darkness and light become disturbed, and this brings with it the possibility of evil and suffering.

As Böhme's fame spread, he cultivated a large correspondence with noblemen, physicians, and others in positions of authority, who encouraged him to continue with his work. To keep up with the demand for Böhme's writings, his friend Carl von Ender employed several copyists, and because Böhme was still officially banned from writing, some of his manuscripts had to be smuggled out in grain sacks. Still they kept coming: In addition to a number of short, devotional treatises, he produced *Von der Gerburt und Bezeichnung aller Wesen* (1622; *Signatura Rerum: Or, The Signature of all Things*, 1651), a difficult but profound book full of alchemical terminology; *Von der Gnadenwahl* (1623; *Concerning the Election of Grace*, 1655), which he considered to be his greatest work; and *Erklärung über das erste Buch Mosis* (1623; *Mysterium Magnum*, 1654), a lengthy exegesis of the book of Genesis.

In 1624, Böhme once more encountered persecution. Some of his devotional works had been printed by his friends under the title of *Der Weg zu Christo* (1622; *The Way to Christ*, 1648). The book came to the notice of Gregorius Richter, and Richter again denounced Böhme from the pulpit. Incited by the preacher, a mob stoned Böhme's house. Richter then wrote a pamphlet against Böhme, accusing him of blasphemy, heresy, drunkenness, and of poisoning the whole city with his false doctrines. He requested that the Görlitz council imprison him. This time, however, Böhme replied to his accuser, refuting Richter point by point in writing. The town magistrates, under pressure from Richter, ordered Böhme to be banished, but the next day they rescinded their decision.

Later in the year, Böhme traveled to Dresden, where he had been called to appear before the Electoral Court. He was well received in the city by eminent men, and the several prominent Lutheran theologians who questioned him at length about his beliefs refused to condemn him. He returned to Görlitz, where he began work on *Von 177 theosophischen Fragen* (1624; *Theosophic Questions*, 1661). This work, in which Böhme's thought reached a new level of profundity, was left unfinished at his death on November 17, 1624.

Summary

Jakob Böhme's achievements were many. Drawing on his own experience of enlightened states of consciousness, he took many disparate strands of thought, including Lutheranism, the German mystical tradition, Renaissance Neoplatonism, the ideas of Paracelsus and the alchemical tradition, and the Cabala, and forged them into a new synthesis. His work constitutes a profound exploration of the nature of existence, both human and divine; it is at once a philosophical system, a mystical vision, and a mythological drama.

Perhaps its most significant aspect is Böhme's attempts to unify life without destroying its essential polarity—it is a metaphysics which includes a compelling explanation of the origin and nature of evil. His description of the process by which God comes to self-consciousness is powerful and original; his emphasis on intuitive rather than rational means of knowing is challenging, as is his insistence that man can know, on the level of direct experience, the totality of the universe. His theory of language, which centers on a universal, paradisal "language of nature" is worth more serious consideration than some have been prepared to give it.

Böhme has had an enormous influence on the history of ideas. G. W. F. Hegel called him the father of German philosophy, and the nineteenth century German philosopher Friedrich Schelling described him as "a miraculous phenomenon in the history of mankind." Arthur Schopenhauer and the twentieth century Russian philosopher Nicholas Berdyaev also felt his influence. In seventeenth century England, where Böhme's thought was very readily received, there was a sect known as the Behmenists, and there was even a proposal that Parliament should set up two colleges specifically for the study of Böhme. In the nineteenth century, the English Romantic poets William Blake and Samuel Taylor Coleridge were directly inspired by Böhme's work, and Coleridge's comment that Böhme was "a stupendous human being" is not an exaggeration: The self-taught shoemaker from Görlitz made a lasting contribution to the Western philosophical and religious tradition.

Bibliography

Boehme, Jacob. *The Way to Christ*. Translated with an introduction by Peter Erb. New York: Paulist Press, 1978. The most accurate and reliable translation of nine of Böhme's most accessible treatises, most of which are devotional in tone and do not explain in detail the theogony and cosmogony that is Böhme's main contribution to the history of ideas. An informative introduction places Böhme's work in the context of Lutheran theology, offers a comparison between Böhme and his contemporary, Johann Arndt, and provides a useful explanation of Böhme's sometimes confusing use of Latin terms.

Brinton, H. H. *The Mystic Will: Based on a Study of the Philosophy of Jacob Boehme*. New York: Macmillan, 1930. The most reliable and perceptive study in English of Böhme's thought. Not marred by the narrow Christian bias of Martensen and Stoudt. It is particularly useful for its analysis of how two of Böhme's most important ideas—the silent unmanifest Being (*Ungrund*) and the figure of Wisdom (or Sophia)—emerge and develop during the course of his work. Full of interesting observations, Brinton's book also includes a useful chapter on the reception of Böhme's works in seventeenth century England.

Hartmann, Franz. *Jacob Boehme: Life and Doctrines*. Reprint. Blauvelt,

N.Y.: Steinerbooks, 1977. An enthusiastic account of Böhme's life and work, some of which has been modified by modern research, but which remains useful in spite of its tendency toward hagiography. The main part of the book consists of short extracts from Böhme's works, organized thematically and punctuated by passages of theosophic commentary. The translations are extremely free.

Martensen, Hans L. *Jacob Boehme (1575-1624): Studies in His Life and Teachings.* Notes and appendices by Stephen Hobhouse. Rev. ed. London: Rockcliff, 1949. Originally published in 1882 in Danish, this is an honest attempt by a Danish bishop and theologian to grapple with the complexities of Böhme's thought. Martensen is basically sympathetic to Böhme, but he objects to some of Böhme's doctrines from the standpoint of a strongly biblical Protestant theology. Martensen is tolerably good when he sticks to exposition; his judgmental pronouncements have far less value.

Stoudt, John Joseph. *Sunrise to Eternity: A Study in Jacob Boehme's Life and Thought.* Preface by Paul Tillich. Philadelphia: University of Pennsylvania Press, 1957. The fullest account in English of Böhme's life. Carefully researched, accurate, and lively, it takes into account the findings of modern German scholarship—information which was not available to Hartmann or Martensen, above. The account of Böhme's thought is marred by Stoudt's insistence that it follows a certain pattern of development: Böhme is supposed to have rejected his early enthusiasm for alchemy and "pansophism" in favor of a Christ-centered Christianity, but such a pattern simply does not exist.

Bryan Aubrey

SIMÓN BOLÍVAR

Born: July 24, 1783; Caracas, Venezuela
Died: December 17, 1830; Villa of San Pedro Alejandrino, near Santa Marta, Colombia
Areas of Achievement: Government, politics, and the military
Contribution: The liberator of northern South America, Bolívar epitomized the struggle against Spanish colonial rule. His most lasting contributions include his aid in the liberation of Bolivia, Columbia, Ecuador, Peru, and Venezuela, and his farsighted proposals for hemispheric solidarity among Latin American nations.

Early Life

Simón José Antonio de la Santisima Trinidad Bolívar was born the son of wealthy Creole parents in 1783. Orphaned at the age of nine (his father had died when Simón was three), the young aristocrat, who was to inherit one of the largest fortunes in the West Indies, was cared for by his maternal uncle, who managed the extensive Bolívar urban properties, agricultural estates, cattle herds, and copper mines. Appropriate to his class, Bolívar had a number of private tutors, including an eccentric disciple of the French philosophe Jean-Jacques Rousseau, Simón Rodríguez. The tutor schooled the impressionable Bolívar in Enlightenment ideas that would later indelibly mark his political thinking.

When Bolívar was sixteen, he went to Spain, ostensibly to further his education, although his actions suggested that he was much more interested in ingratiating himself with the Spanish royal court. While at the court, he met, fell in love with, and married María Teresa Rodríguez, the daughter of a Caracas-born nobleman. During his three-year stay in Madrid, Bolívar came to see the Spanish monarchy as weak and corrupt; moreover, he felt slighted because of his Creole status. He returned home at the age of nineteen. His wife died six months after they returned to Caracas, and Bolívar, although he enjoyed female companionship, never remarried.

Bolívar returned to Europe. In Paris, he read the works of the Enlightenment feverishly and watched with disillusionment the increasingly dictatorial rule of Napoleon I. He also met one of the most prominent scientists of his day, Alexander von Humboldt, who had recently returned from an extended visit to the New World. Humboldt was convinced that independence was imminent for the Spanish colonies. While in Paris, the five-foot, six-inch, slender, dark-haired Bolívar also joined a freemasonry lodge. There he met radicals who espoused similar views. After Paris, Bolívar went to Italy, where he vowed to liberate his native land from Spanish rule. This second trip to Europe, which culminated in 1807, would play a pivotal role in shaping the transformation of this young aristocrat into a firebrand revolutionary.

Life's Work

After he returned from the Old World, Bolívar spent the better part of the next twenty years in various military campaigns until in 1825, after many defeats, hardships, and bouts of self-imposed exile, Bolívar and his patriot army drove the Spanish royal forces from the continent. In the early years of the conflict against Spain, he vied for leadership of the revolutionary movement with Francisco de Miranda, an expatriate Venezuelan who viewed with suspicion Bolívar's enormous ego and his insatiable lust for glory. After a bitter dispute between the two, Bolívar, believing that Miranda had absconded with the patriot treasury, turned Miranda over to Spanish authorities. Miranda was subsequently taken to Spain in chains and died in a Spanish prison several years later.

As a commander of the patriot forces, Bolívar demonstrated an uncanny ability to adapt his strategy to the particular circumstances. Faced with poorly trained and poorly equipped troops, Bolívar compensated by using the mountainous terrain of the Andes to his advantage, by delegating responsibility to exceptional field commanders, and by using his persuasive powers to attract new troops. Bolívar endured all the hardships and privations of the military campaigns alongside his soldiers. Moreover, the sheer force of his personality and his single-minded dedication to the goal of a liberated continent inspired his troops.

Despite his military prowess, Bolívar suffered a number of difficult defeats from 1810 to 1818. On two separate occasions during this early phase of the struggle, Royalist forces dealt the rebels serious setbacks and Bolívar was forced to flee South America. He used those occasions to raise funds, secure arms and soldiers, and make alliances with other states that might provide aid for the upcoming campaigns.

Bolívar also demonstrated the ability to unite conflicting ethnic groups and classes of Venezuelans and Colombians into an improvised army. He coopted as many different sectors of South American society as possible during the seemingly interminable war years. A perfect illustration of this penchant for compromise was his visit to Haiti during one of his exiles. There Bolívar extracted much-needed aid from Haitian president Alexandre Pétion. The Haitian president, the leader of a nation where a successful rebellion had liberated the slaves, insisted that Bolívar abolish slavery when he returned to Venezuela. Bolívar, who had set his own slaves free in 1811, agreed to do so, knowing that the Creole elite's economic viability was dependent on slave labor.

Another ethnic group which Bolívar courted were the *llaneros*. Led by their fierce regional chieftain (caudillo), José Antonio Páez, these mobile horsemen dominated the Orinoco River basin and initially supported the Royalist cause. Páez derived his power from control of local resources, especially nearby haciendas, which gave him access to men and provisions.

Caudillos such as Páez formed patron-client relationships with their followers, who pledged their loyalty to their commander in return for a share of the spoils. As the abolition of slavery infuriated the Creole elite, the inclusion of Páez and other caudillos in the patriot army also upset members of the upper class, since their property often was ravaged by overzealous guerrilla bands. Bolívar's charisma enabled him to hold this fragile coalition together. After victory was achieved, however, that consensus would be lost, the fissures and fault lines of class and ethnicity would reassert themselves, and the edifice of unity would come tumbling down.

Because of Bolívar's ability to bring together people of diverse ethnic and class interests into a formidable army, the tide of the war changed. Bolívar's army was helped in its efforts to end colonial rule by South America's other liberator, José de San Martín, who began his campaign in the viceroyalty of Rio de la Plata (modern Argentina) and defeated Royalist forces in what is modern Chile and Peru. The two liberators met at an epochal meeting in Guayaquil, Ecuador, in 1822 to plan the final campaign against the Spanish forces in Peru. By 1825, five new nations were created from the Spanish colonial viceroyalties of Peru and New Granada: Venezuela, Colombia, Ecuador, Peru, and Bolivia.

The liberation of the continent was only one of Bolívar's many objectives. A human dynamo who thrived on constant activity, Bolívar also wanted to ensure that the fledgling republics of South America made a successful transition from colonies to nations. A man of words as well as action, Bolívar wrote prolifically amid his grueling military campaigns on almost every conceivable topic of his day. His main political writings—*La Carta de Jamaica* (1815; *The Jamaica Letter*, c. 1888), *Discurso pronunciado por el general Bolívar al congreso general de Venezuela en el aeto de su instalacion* (1819; *Speech of His Excellency, General Bolívar at the Installation of the Congress of Venezuela*, 1819), and his constitution for the new nation of Bolivia (1825)—demonstrate the evolution of his political thinking (and its growing conservatism) over time.

Although Bolívar fervently believed in democracy, he understood that Latin Americans lacked the political experience to adopt the model of democracy found in the United States. The colonial legacy of three centuries of autocratic rule would not be eclipsed overnight, and a transitional period was needed, during which the people had to be educated for democracy. His primary model, roughly sketched in *The Jamaica Letter*, was along the lines of the British constitutional monarchy.

Bolívar's first well-developed theory of government was presented to the Colombian Congress of Angostura in 1819. There, his eclectic mixture of individual rights and centralized government was described in detail. Many of the basic rights and freedoms articulated in the French Declaration of the Rights of Man and Citizen and the United States Bill of Rights were contained in his Angostura Address. Faithful to his promise to Pétion of Haiti, he asked that the congress of Great Colombia abolish slavery. To diminish the popular voice, he limited suffrage and asked for indirect elections. Moreover, the heart of Bolívar's political system was a hereditary senate, selected by a military aristocracy, the Order of Liberators. A strong executive would oversee the government, but his power was checked by his ministers, the senate, and a lower house which oversaw financial matters. Bolívar was elected the new nation's first president in 1821.

Bolívar preferred ideas to administration, opting to delegate responsibility for the day to day management of government to his vice president. Bolívar grew increasingly skeptical that a workable democracy could be implemented. His last political treatise, the constitution he wrote for the new nation of Bolivia (named for Bolívar) demonstrates this skepticism. This document included a three-house congress and a president elected for a life term with the power to choose a successor. This latest political creation was nothing more than a poorly disguised monarchy. The constitution pleased no one. When Bolívar tried to convince Great Colombia—a nation which Bolívar had fashioned, composed of Venezuela, Colombia, and Ecuador—to adopt the new constitution, his plea fell on deaf ears. To enact the goals of his administration, Bolívar then did in practice what his constitution permitted on paper: He ruled as a dictator.

Not only did Bolívar meet resistance in implementing his political agenda but he also was frustrated with his farsighted proposals for hemispheric cooperation and solidarity. Convinced that the newly formed Latin American states individually were powerless to withstand outside attack by a European power, he advocated a defensive alliance of Hispanic American states, which would provide military cooperation to defend the hemisphere from invasion. Bolívar invited all the Hispanic American countries, as well as the United States, Great Britain, and other European nations, to send delegates to a congress in Panama in 1826. It was hoped that the Panama Congress would create a league of Hispanic American states, provide for military cooperation, negotiate an alliance with Great Britain, and settle disputes among the nations. Bolívar even articulated the hope for the creation of an international peace-keeping organization. Unfortunately, few nations sent official delegates and Bolívar's visionary internationalist ideas remained dreams for more than a century.

Bolívar's last years were difficult. The new nations he had helped create were racked with internal dissension and violence. After a serious dispute with his vice president Francisco Santander in 1827, a weary Bolívar, suffering from tuberculosis, ruled as a dictator. A year later, an attempt on his life was narrowly averted. Finally, Bolívar was driven from office, when it was discovered that his cabinet had concocted a plan to search for a European monarch to rule after he stepped down. Although he knew nothing of the scheme, he suffered the political consequences. Bolívar resigned from office in 1830, almost penniless. He died on the coast near Santa Marta, Colombia, in 1830. He had asked to be buried in his home city of Caracas, but Bolívar had so many political enemies that his family feared for the safety of his remains. In 1842, his body was finally taken home.

Summary

Not until the wounds of the independence period were healed by time were the accomplishments of Simón Bolívar put in their proper perspective. In retrospect, his successes and his visionary ideas more than compensated for his egocentrism and the defeats he suffered. As a committed revolutionary and a military general, he had few peers. By sheer force of his dynamic persona and his tireless efforts, he ended colonialism and ushered in a new era of nationhood for South America.

On the political front, his successes were tempered by the political realities of the times. Bolívar knew that the new nations were not ready for independence and a long period of political maturation was needed before democracy could be achieved. His dictatorial actions in his last few years betrayed his own republican ideals, but Bolívar, ever the pragmatist, was convinced that the end justified the means. What Bolívar could not foresee was how elusive democracy would be for South America.

Similarly, his ideas for hemispheric solidarity were not accepted. Not until the creation of the Organization of American States and the signing of the Rio Pact in 1947 would the first halting steps toward Pan Americanism be taken. Bolívar's fears of the growing power of the United States and its potentially damaging effects on Hispanic America proved prophetic. One hundred fifty years after his death, Bolívar is lionized throughout Latin America not only for what he accomplished but also for what he dreamed.

Bibliography

Bolívar, Simón. *Selected Writings*. Edited by Harold A. Bierck, Jr. Translated by Lewis Bertrand. Compiled by Vicente Lecuna. 2 vols. New York: Colonial Press, 1951. A brief, complimentary biographical essay by Bierck introduces this solid collection of Bolívar's most significant political writings.

Bushnell, David. *The Santander Regime in Gran Colombia*. Newark: University of Delaware Press, 1954. A thorough academic monograph on the Santander regime, which examines Bolívar's increasingly despotic measures in his last years.

Hispanic American Historical Review 63 (February, 1983). To celebrate the bicentennial of Bolívar's birth, editor John J. Johnson dedicated an entire issue of the preeminent journal in the field to a reappraisal of Bolívar. Four essays by independence period specialists reexamine and reassess both the man and his place in history. Includes John Lynch's "Bolívar and the Caudillos," Simon Collier's "Nationality, Nationalism, and Supranationalism in the Writings of Simón Bolívar," David Bushnell's "The Last Dictatorship: Betrayal or Consummation?" and Germán Carrera Damas' "Simón Bolívar, El Culto Heroico y la Nación."

Johnson, John J. *Simón Bolívar and Spanish American Independence, 1783-1830.* New York: Van Nostrand Reinhold, 1968. An excellent analytical overview of Bolívar's life and times. This book includes an abbreviated sample of some of the most important political writings by Bolívar.

Lynch, John. *The Spanish American Revolutions, 1808-1862.* New York: W. W. Norton, 1973. One of the best one-volume syntheses of the revolutionary era. Lynch's adroit analysis provides an overview of the internal and external factors that impinged on the struggle for independence. Includes a good examination of the personalities involved in the fighting.

Masur, Gerhard. *Simón Bolívar.* 2d ed. Albuquerque: University of New Mexico Press, 1969. One of the best biographies in English of Bolívar. Masur's even-handed narrative is generally sympathetic and conveys an appreciation for the difficulties that Bolívar faced in reconciling the divergent factions that threatened to divide the movement for independence.

Allen Wells

ALEKSANDR BORODIN

Born: November 12, 1833; St. Petersburg, Russia
Died: February 27, 1887; St. Petersburg, Russia
Area of Achievement: Music
Contribution: Borodin made a significant contribution to the repertory of
  Russian national music, with particular excellence in the domains of op-
  era, symphonic music, chamber music, and song.

Early Life

Aleksandr Porfiryevich Borodin was born out of wedlock to Prince Luka
Stepanovitch Gedianov and Avdotya Konstantinova Antinova. Following Aleksandr's birth, his father had him registered as the legal son of Porfiry Borodin,
one of his servants, in accordance with a custom of the time and arranged for
his mistress to marry Christian Ivanovitch Kleinecke, a retired army medical
practitioner. Aleksandr was educated by private tutors, with emphasis placed
on foreign languages (German, French, and English). Prior to his death, Luka
granted freedom to his son. Avdotya, after her husband's death, bore another
son, Dmitry, through another liaison, and bought a house near the Semyonov
Parade Ground, which is where Aleksandr spent his youth and adolescence.

Aleksandr composed a Polka in D Minor that he entitled "Hélène." Piano
study, attendance at symphonic concerts at the university during the winter and at Joseph Gungl's concerts at Pavlovsk in the summer, and self-
instruction on the cello moved the youth toward serious creativity; indeed, in
1847, he composed a Trio in G Major on a theme from Giacomo Meyer-
beer's *Robert le diable*, and a concert for flute and piano. There followed, in
quick succession, two piano compositions, a fantasy on a theme by Johann
Nepomuk Hummel, and a study, *Le Courant*. While developing his emerging
musical talent, Borodin evinced an equally strong interest in chemistry.

In the fall of 1850, Borodin was an external student at the Academy of
Physicians. By 1855, he completed his course of study with distinction.
Borodin moved up the ladder of academic success with alacrity. He gained
experience as a surgeon but came to realize that he was ill-suited for this
calling. On May 5, 1858, he was awarded the doctor of medicine degree.
After travels to Western Europe connected with his scientific career, he
corresponded in the fall of 1859 with Modest Mussorgsky, from whom he
acquired an appreciation for the music of Robert Schumann. Later that year,
his teacher Nikolai Zinin arranged for Borodin to work in Heidelberg so as to
gain the kind of experience that would enable him to assume a professorial
position in chemistry upon his return.

Life's Work

The Heidelberg period, which extended to 1862, proved to be a turning point in Borodin's life. It was here that he developed a friendship with the Russian chemist Dmitry Mendeleyev and attended lectures by such luminaries as Hermann Helmholtz and Gustav Robert Kirchhoff, the latter a pioneer with Robert Wilhelm Bunsen in the field of spectrum analysis. Travel to Freiburg (where he heard the famed organ there), Italy, and the Netherlands turned the once-sheltered Borodin into a cosmopolite.

In May, 1861, Borodin met his future wife, the twenty-nine-year-old Ekaterina Sergeyevna Protopopova. He traveled with her to Mannheim to hear such Wagnerian epics as *Tannhäuser* (1845) and *Lohengrin* (1848), and settled with her in Pisa. In terms of composition, he produced in this period a Sonata in C Minor for cello and piano (a three-movement work based on the fugue theme from Johann Sebastian Bach's Sonata in G Minor for violin), a Scherzo in E Major for piano duet, several incomplete chamber works, and, most significantly, a Sextet in D Minor for strings. This last composition was written, according to its creator, to please the Germans. Its two movements reflect Mendelssohnian traits, as, for example, in the lively sonata-allegro first movement with its "feminine" second subject and in the theme and variation second movement based on the song "How Did I Grieve Thee?" employed previously by the composer. Particularly interesting is the pizzicato variation, a technique that came to be identified with the Russian as it had been with Mendelssohn. The four-movement Quintet in F Minor for strings establishes Borodin as a master of the early Romantic style associated with the German school, notably in the use of classical forms, lyrical and evocative melodic lines, excellence in part-writing, and elfinlike scherzo movements. In addition, there is present a nostalgic yearning for the homeland, an awareness of the contributions of Mikhail Glinka in particular, and a Russian imprint on the Germanic fabric.

Borodin returned to St. Petersburg in September, 1862, and by December he was actively engaged in the world of academia. Apart from lecturing and translating scientific books, he gravitated again toward musical creativity, especially after meeting Mily Balakirev, mentor of the so-called Russian Five. After hearing the incipient works by this quintet of nationalists, the groundwork was laid for a shift from mainstream German Romanticism to Russian nationalism. Despite a fitful approach to large-scale composition, necessitated by his vocation, Borodin, under Balakirev's guidance, produced his First Symphony in 1867; it was premiered under Balakirev's direction on March 7, 1868, before the Russian Musical Society's directorate and, on January 16, 1869, it received its first public hearing. Encouraged by Balakirev, Borodin acquired the confidence to pursue his creative avocation on a surer footing. Although the opera-farce *Bogatiri* was a dismal failure at its premiere on November 18, 1867, the songs, which include "Pesnya tyomnovo lesa" (song of the dark forest) and "Falshivaya nota" (the false note) were more successful.

Borodin's personal life was solidified with his marriage to Ekaterina on April 17, 1863, in St. Petersburg. That fall, the couple moved to an apartment in a building owned by the Academy of Military Medicine, and, except for occasional travel, it was the composer's abode until his death. Throughout his life, the composer-scientist was found attractive by adoring young women; however, with the adoption of seven-year-old Liza Bolaneva, his marriage was established on solid footing.

In April, 1869, the critic Vladimir Stasov suggested that Borodin begin the opera that would be named *Prince Igor*, which was based on a twelfth century epic. By March, 1870, however, when his original interest in the project waned, he adopted some of the music he had already committed to paper for use in his Symphony No. 2 in B Minor. During the early 1870's, professional responsibilities created continuing impediments to uninterrupted musical achievement. In addition to lecturing on chemistry and supervising student work, Borodin became a leading advocate for medical courses for women. During 1874-1875, the "Polovtsian Dances" and other segments of *Prince Igor* were completed, and between 1874 and 1879 he finished the String Quartet in A Major. On March 10, 1877, Eduard Napravnik conducted the completed Second Symphony with limited success. After some revision, the work was accorded a more favorable response when it was conducted on March 4, 1879, by Nikolay Rimsky-Korsakov. The four-movement work is notable for its coloristic treatment of the orchestra, particularly for the passages for winds and harp, for its rhythmic drive and meter changes, and for its juxtaposition of long-breathed, folkloric melody and exciting, Tartarlike abandon.

Having achieved the succor that comes after so arduous an experience as seeing his Second Symphony through to a public performance, Borodin visited various German universities with a view toward gaining a better understanding of their laboratories. On one such trip, he called on Franz Liszt at Weimar (July, 1877) and met with the Hungarian master on five different occasions over a three-week period. A few more numbers were added to *Prince Igor*, but a streak of procrastination prevented the opera from moving forward to completion; it was left to Rimsky-Korsakov and Aleksandr Glazunov to orchestrate much of it after Borodin's death. Ironically, Borodin squandered much of the little time he had dallying with musical jokes, such as a polka contrived to be performed with "Chopsticks" as the accompaniment. While other composers contributed their talents to compositions on this motif, among them Rimsky-Korsakov and Anatoly Lyadov, and saw the entire set published in 1880 under the title *Paraphrases*, Balakirev rebuked the perpetrators of this farce for wasting time and effort on such trifles. Meanwhile, through Liszt's influence, Borodin's music obtained a hearing in Western Europe. The Symphony No. 1 was performed in Baden-Baden, Germany, on May 20, 1880, the year in which the composer wrote his symphonic poem, *In the Steppes of Central Asia* (dedicated to Liszt).

A setting of Alexander Pushkin's poem "Dlya beregov otchizni dalnoy" (for the shores of thy far native land) was prompted by the death from alcoholism of Mussorgsky on March 28, 1881. The String Quartet No. 2 in D Major, dedicated to Borodin's wife, suggests an evocation of the idyllic period in Heidelberg. It is best known today for its third movement, the *Nocturne*, in which the cello is given a soaring melodic line of incomparable beauty. Although Ekaterina's health was always precarious, it was Borodin who suffered an attack of cholera in June, 1885, leading, eventually, to the heart disease that took his life.

The European taste for Borodin's music spread to France and Belgium, and, in appreciation of her efforts on his behalf, the composer dedicated to the Belgian Countess of Mercy-Argenteau his six-movement *Petite Suite* for piano (1885). With César Cui, he enjoyed huge successes in Liège and Brussels. In 1886, despite the illnesses of his wife and mother-in-law, Borodin collaborated with Rimsky-Korsakov, Lyadov, and Glazunov on a string quartet in honor of the publisher, M. P. Balaiev. Two movements of his Third Symphony were completed, the second of which is a scherzo whose material is drawn from *Prince Igor.* Although interest in the opera was revived in 1887, only an overture and several additional numbers were actually completed. On the evening of February 27, 1887, at a lavish ball for the families and friends of the faculty of the Medical Academy, Borodin, attired in red shirt and high boots, and in apparent good spirits, succumbed suddenly to heart failure and died instantly. His beloved Ekaterina survived him by five months.

Summary

Of Aleksandr Borodin, Sir William Hadow said: "No musician has ever claimed immortality with so slender an offering. Yet, if there be, indeed, immortalities in music, his claim is incontestable." It is assuredly a phenomenal achievement when an individual rises to a position of eminence in fields as diverse as music and science, the one so intuitive and subjective but requiring the utmost discipline, the other so measured and objective. Borodin was somehow able to bring his analytical mind to bear on his creative impulses.

Borodin was a remarkable creative artist, a respected scientist, and a human being of the utmost sensibility and refinement. That he found the time and the inclination to cofound the School of Medicine for Women in St. Petersburg and to teach chemistry there from 1872 until his death, bespeaks of a man well ahead of his time. Borodin's compassion for humankind, his life of industry, and his zeal in the pursuit of excellence serve as reminders to a skeptical world that a job worth doing is a job worth doing well. When his music was adapted for use in the box-office triumph *Kismet,* which opened at New York's Ziegfeld Theatre on December 3, 1953, American audiences were introduced to Borodin's art in popularized format, and they were touched. Since that time, these treasures, in the original versions and touchups, have earned an honored place in the concert halls of the world. Borodin's is a music that contains a civility that transcends national boundaries.

Bibliography

Abraham, Gerald. *Borodin: The Composer and His Music.* London: William Reeves, 1927. A very thorough traversal of Borodin's life and works. Contains musical analyses.

_____. *On Russian Music.* Freeport, N.Y.: Books for Libraries Press, 1970. Two of the book's chapters deal expressly with Borodin and his music. One is devoted to "The History of Prince Igor," while the other deals with "Borodin's Songs."

Abraham, Gerald, and David Lloyd-Jones. "Alexander Porfir'yevich Borodin." In *The New Grove Dictionary of Music and Musicians,* edited by Stanley Sadie, vol. 3. London: Macmillan, 1980. An outstanding encyclopedia entry covering the salient biographical data and providing a clear-cut overview of Borodin's music according to genre. Contains a catalog of works and a fine bibliography.

Asafiev, B. V. *Russian Music from the Beginning of the Nineteenth Century.* Translated by Alfred J. Swan. Ann Arbor, Mich.: J. W. Edwards for the American Council of Learned Societies, 1953. This influential work treats Borodin's music in the context of broad categories of subject matter. The approach allows the reader to see the composer's contributions vis-à-vis those of his principal contemporaries and in the light of the aesthetic trends then prevalent in Russia.

Calvocoressi, Michel D., and Gerald Abraham. *Masters of Russian Music.* New York: Alfred A. Knopf, 1936. Presents a fine traversal of the major events in the composer's life and touches on the high points of representative compositions.

Dianin, Sergei. *Borodin.* Translated by Robert Lord. New York: Oxford University Press, 1963. This is a major life and works study of Borodin, with very important coverage of his ancestry, his childhood, and his adolescence. The music is discussed according to genre. Includes a chronological catalog of works and a genealogical table. A first-rate piece of scholarship.

Habets, Alfred. *Borodin and Liszt.* Translated by Rosa Newmarch. London: Digby, Long, 1895. Reprint. New York: AMS Press, 1977. Part 1 covers Borodin's life and works, touching on significant biographical details. A chapter entitled "The Scientist" presents insight into this major aspect of the artist's dual allegiances.

Lloyd-Jones, David. "Borodin in Heidelberg." *Musical Quarterly* 46 (1960): 500. A thorough account of Borodin's stay in Heidelberg. Emphasizes his development as a composer, offers succinct comments and insights into specific compositions, and places the musical contributions in the context of his personal life and his scientific career.

David Z. Kushner

FRANCESCO BORROMINI
Francesco Castelli

Born: September 25, 1599; Bissone, near Lake Lugano
Died: August 3, 1667; Rome
Area of Achievement: Architecture
Contribution: Borromini was one of the most innovative architects of the Baroque era, but his contemporaries were highly critical of his work and believed that it violated the principles of sound architectural design. For this reason, his immediate influence was slight, but he is now considered one of the giants of Baroque architecture.

Early Life

Francesco Borromini's father, Giovanni Domenico Castello-Brumino, and his mother, Anastasia di Leone Garovo Allio, were members of two of the many families of masons and stone cutters who lived near one another on the Swiss border near Lake Lugano. Their son Francesco Castelli, who was later to change his name to Borromini, was born in Bissone, in what is the modern Swiss Canton of Ticino, in 1599. His early life remains a mystery. When he was fifteen, or perhaps even at the age of nine, he went to Milan, where he received a thorough grounding in the mason's and stonecarver's crafts. There was a considerable amount of building going on in Milan in the early seventeenth century, and the work on the great cathedral was in its final phases, but it is not known what, if any, work Borromini may have designed or executed.

Many of Borromini's kinsmen had gone to Rome to work on papal building projects, and two of them had achieved considerable distinction. One was Domenico Fontana, the most important architect during the papacy of Pope Sixtus V, and the other was Borromini's uncle, Carlo Maderno, who completed the construction of St. Peter's during the reign of Paul V. Borromini idolized his uncle, and it was probably about 1619 that he was able to join him in Rome.

Maderno was then Rome's leading architect, and Borromini began working for him at once, carving some of the architectural decoration for the portico of St. Peter's. Within a few years, he had established himself as Maderno's principal architectural draftsman and most trusted assistant, and he continued to work very closely with him until Maderno died in 1629. In 1621, Borromini was paid for carving some of the capitals for the drum of the dome of Sant' Andrea della Valle in Rome, and two years later Maderno let him prepare the design for the lantern of the dome. The double capitals with heads of cherubs look forward to the bizzare decorations of his maturity. He was also responsible for the design of the decorative grille of the Cappella del S.S. Sacramento in St. Peter's.

By the mid-1620's, Borromini had begun working for Gian Lorenzo Bernini, who was designing the crossing and the apse of St. Peter's. Bernini was the great favorite of Pope Urban VIII, and during the late 1620's he began to take on more and more work in St. Peter's. Whatever hopes Borromini may have had of ever replacing his uncle as architect in charge of the church faded during those years. Shortly after Maderno's death, however, Bernini received the coveted appointment in February of 1629.

Life's Work

Bernini was virtually an artistic dictator; in the early 1630's, Borromini had no choice but to continue to work under him, at St. Peters' and also at the Palazzo Barberini, the pope's family palace, which Maderno had begun shortly before his death. It was not until the early 1630's that Borromini was able to break with Bernini and pursue an independent architectural career.

His first commission came in 1634. The Spanish Order of the Discalced Trinitarians asked him to erect their church and monastery of S. Carlo alle Quattro Fontane. Borromini built the dormitory, the refectory, and the cloisters first and, in 1638, began working on the church, which was completed in 1641 and consecrated in 1646. The façade, however, was not completed until 1665-1667. The church therefore marks the beginning as well as the end of Borromini's architectural career.

The plan of San Carlo is derived from a series of intricate geometric constructions in which two circles and an oval are inscribed within two equilateral triangles. The oval determines the shape of the dome and the apexes of the triangles give the location of the half-oval side chapels. What is so unusual about Borromini's plan is the fact that it contradicts what had been one of the most important principles of architectural practice from the Renaissance onward: the concept of planning in terms of basic arithmetical units, such as the diameter of a column. By developing his plan as a series of geometric relationships, he was returning to the method of planning that had been common during the medieval period but which had been largely abandoned during the Renaissance.

In 1637, the Oratorians of the Congregation of St. Philip Neri engaged Borromini to build an oratory for musical performances, a library and living quarters for the fathers next to their church of S. Maria in Vallicella. This was a major commission and the building went up rapidly. The oratory was vaulted in 1638 and inaugurated in August, 1640. The façade is an architectural creation of great distinction. It curves slowly inward and is crowned by a pediment that for the first time combines the triangular pediment with the curved one, thus uniting in a single architectural form two motifs which had always been considered as contrasting alternatives.

No work by Borromini, though, approaches the complexity of S. Ivo della Sapienza, the church of the Roman Archiginnasio, which was later the university. He had been appointed the architect of the Archiginnasio as early as 1632, but it was not until 1642 that he began work on the church. It was built at the end of a long, arcaded courtyard and while the lower part of the façade echoes the arcaded motif, the upper part is a remarkable construction which would seem to be composed of a curved drum, a low, stepped dome, and an enormous lantern topped by a spiral ramp. The strangeness of the lantern appears to be at odds with what seems to be the rather logical division of the dome into its two parts, the drum and the dome itself. Inside the church, however, this apparent clarity is seen to be deceptive, for the dome actually extends well into the drum. Once again, Borromini insisted on creating architectural forms which his contemporaries considered to be at odds with accepted architectural practice.

Like San Carlo, the plan of San Ivo is based on a geometrical construction. This time two equilateral triangles have been joined so that, if lines are drawn to connect their points of intersection, a regular hexagon is formed and this becomes the basis for the ground plan of the church. Hexagonal plans are virtually nonexistant in earlier Italian architecture, and Borromini's use of the figure may have been intended to represent the six-pointed Star of David, a symbol of wisdom.

While Borromini did not lack commissions, he never achieved the stature of Bernini, who for more than fifty years basked in the sun of papal patronage. Only Pope Innocent X, who was elected in 1644, favored him. Indeed, it was for Innocent that Borromini began to rebuild the family church of S. Agnese in 1653. After Innocent died in 1655, work ceased and the church was later completed by others. In 1646, Innocent had set Borromini to work on the remodeling of one of the oldest churches in Rome, the venerable church of S. Giovanni in Laterano, but the vault which he planned was never built.

During the last years of his life, Borromini was finally able to complete the façade of S. Carlo alle Quattro Fontane. There, where he began his career, he brought it to a climactic conclusion. The curved façade, one of the first fully curved Baroque façades on a church, is filled with contradictory elements which challenge traditional practices and concepts of design and which subsequent generations considered the antithesis of "proper" architecture. Today, however, its richness of decoration and mingling of architecture and sculpture have given it a secure place among the great monuments of Baroque architecture.

Borromini's disappointments and jealousy over Bernini's triumphs left him embittered and quarrelsome. He had few friends and lived as a recluse, devoting himself entirely to his work. As he grew older, his sense of persecution deepened, and eventually, in 1667, he tried to take his own life by falling on his sword. He lived for a few hours, taking the time to dictate to his confessor a strangely objective and dispassionate account of the reasons for his suicide.

Summary

Francesco Borromini, obsessed with the problems of his art, was a shy and misanthropic bachelor who lived in sparsely furnished rooms surrounded by his library of nearly one thousand books. In his will, he asked that he be buried in the tomb of his uncle, Carlo Maderno, one of the few people with whom he ever developed a warm relationship. His rivalry with Bernini was fueled by his conviction that Bernini was deficient in the technical knowledge that was Borromini's stock-in-trade. In the modern sense of the word, Borromini was a true professional, an expert within a limited range of concerns. Bernini, on the other hand, like his Renaissance predecessors, saw architecture as primarily a matter of design for which skill in drawing was sufficient training.

Borromini's buildings were seen by his contemporaries as new and in many ways unsettling solutions to architectural problems. His fascination with complex geometric plans, his unorthodox use of architectural motifs, his refusal to accept the traditional separation of architecture and sculpture, and his interest in architectural symbolism led his contemporaries to consider his buildings as creations of fantasy rather than reason.

From the Renaissance onward, architecture had been seen as the process by which man, guided by reason, could create structures that reflected the rational nature of the universe. With Borromini, this process comes to an end. His architecture is so complex, so full of contradictions that it seems to defy human reason. In reality, though, behind its apparent irrationality there lies a degree of order of such subtlety that human reason can no longer understand it. One is reminded that humankind must depend upon faith, not reason, to find answers about the nature of the universe. Borromini's expression of this view makes him one of the most eloquent architectural spokesmen of the religious ideals of the Counter-Reformation.

Bibliography

Blunt, Anthony. *Borromini.* Cambridge, Mass.: Harvard University Press, 1979. The best general book available in English on Borromini.

_____, ed. *Baroque and Rococo: Architecture and Decoration.* New York: Harper & Row, 1982. An excellent short chapter by Blunt on Borromini's architecture.

Connors, Joseph J. *Borromini and the Roman Oratory: Style and Society.* Cambridge, Mass.: MIT Press, 1980. A detailed discussion of the building history of the oratory of the Congregation of St. Philip Neri, one of Borromini's major architectural projects. Includes a catalog of drawings.

Hauptman, William. "Luceat Lux Vestra Coram Hominibus: A New Source for the Spire of Borromini's S. Ivo." *Journal of the Society of Architectural Historians* 33 (1974): 73-79. An investigation of the possible sources for the lantern of Borromini's church of S. Ivo della Sapienza and a detailed study of its iconographic meaning.

Portoghesi, Paolo. *The Rome of Borromini: Architecture as Language*. Translated by Barbara Luigia La Penta. New York: George Braziller, 1968. The author's detailed analyses of Borromini's buildings are often difficult to follow, but there are many illustrations that provide full coverage of all phases of Borromini's career.

Scott, John Beldon. "S. Ivo Alla Sapienza and Borromini's Symbolic Language." *Journal of the Society of Architectural Historians* 41 (1982): 294-317. A carefully documented study of the building history, ceremonial functions, and symbolic content of Borromini's church.

Wittkower, Rudolf. *Art and Architecture in Italy, 1600-1750*. 3d ed. Baltimore: Penguin Books, 1973. The basic study of Italian Baroque art. The chapter on Borromini is an excellent introduction to his work and art theory.

_____. "Francesco Borromini, His Character and Life." In *Studies in the Italian Baroque*. Boulder, Colo.: Westview Press, 1975. The English version of a lecture given in 1967 at an international congress honoring the tercentenary of Borromini's death. Wittkower's essay is an incisive study of Borromini's psychological makeup. Appendices.

Eric Van Schaack

HIERONYMUS BOSCH
Jeroen van Aeken

Born: c. 1450; 's-Hertogenbosch, North Brabant
Died: 1516; 's-Hertogenbosch, North Brabant
Area of Achievement: Art
Contribution: Bosch produced strikingly original paintings, whose brilliant style, flickering brushstroke, and fantastic, nightmarish visions influenced twentieth century Surrealists. Bosch's message, however, is rooted in the preoccupations of the early sixteenth century. His obsessions—sin, death, and damnation—reflect orthodox Christian concerns.

Early Life
Hieronymus Bosch is the most fascinating early Netherlandish painter, in part because he is the most puzzling. Little is known about his life. Like most northern Renaissance artists, he left no self-portraits, letters, diaries, or theoretical writings. Contemporary sources mention several works by him, but none of these survives. Conversely, the paintings that are attributed to him are all undocumented. Hundreds of works bear his name, but few of these signatures are authentic.

The two principal archival sources for Bosch are the city records of his hometown, s'-Hertogenbosch, and the account books of one of the town's confraternities, the Brotherhood of the Blessed Virgin. These documents reveal that Bosch's family had settled in 's-Hertogenbosch by the year 1426 and that Bosch entered the family business: His grandfather, three uncles, his father, and his brother were all painters, and Bosch was probably trained by a family member, most likely his father. Since Bosch's name does appear with regularity in the 's-Hertogenbosch archives, he must have lived there throughout his life. His family name was van Aeken (possibly a reference to the city of Aechen), but by 1504 he adopted Bosch as his surname, to refer to the town where he lived and worked.

Bosch, like his grandfather, uncles, and father, was a member of the Brotherhood of the Blessed Virgin, a large and wealthy confraternity devoted to the worship of the Virgin Mary. Much of Bosch's activity for the brotherhood was created for their new chapel in the cathedral of 's-Hertogenbosch. He painted a panel of living and dead members, offered advice on gilding and polychroming a sculpted altarpiece, and designed a crucifix, a chandelier, and a stained-glass window. None of this work survives.

Sometime between the years 1479 and 1481, Bosch was married to a wealthy woman, Aleyt Goyaerts van den Meervenne, the daughter of pharmacists. It has often been noted that alchemical equipment appears to underlie many of the forms in Bosch's most important work. Bosch could have become acquainted with such apparatuses through his in-laws.

There was no active court life in 's-Hertogenbosch, but documents show that the nobility elsewhere were patrons of Bosch. In 1504, Philip the Handsome, Duke of Burgundy, commissioned an altarpiece of *The Last Judgment*, now lost, and Henry III of Nassau owned *The Garden of Earthly Delights* by 1517. Margaret of Austria's inventory of 1516 includes paintings by Bosch, and in the middle of the sixteenth century Philip II, King of Spain, favored his works.

Life's Work

Bosch's art stands outside the mainstream of early Netherlandish painting. While Bosch's holy figures are plain and at times awkward, most Netherlandish artists, such as Jan van Eyck, Rogier van der Weyden, and Hans Memling, idealize and dignify the Holy Family and saints. While Bosch tended to paint thinly and rapidly, most Netherlandish painters used a painstaking technique of multilayered glazes and meticulous brushwork. Whereas Bosch shows little interest in the individual, portraiture is a hallmark of the early Netherlandish school. In addition, Bosch depicts themes that are new to large-scale painting, such as the *Haywain* and *The Ship of Fools*, and interprets traditional themes, such as *Hell* or *Christ Carrying the Cross*, in a strikingly original way. More fundamentally, evil and corruption dominate Bosch's world. Hermit saints, such as Saint Anthony, strive to resist temptation through the contemplative life, but, as Max J. Friedländer observes, with Bosch, "innocence was pale." God is small and passive, mankind weak and sinful, and the Devil powerfully seductive. The disturbing quality of Bosch's works is far from the grace, beauty, and serenity that typify early Netherlandish painting.

Bosch's obsession with sin, death, and corruption expresses an undercurrent that is easily detected in northern Europe. Some in the North accepted new ideas, such as the humanistic belief in the dignity of man; however, for others, the time around 1500 produced only fear, conflict, and uncertainty. Millennial fears were widespread; the *Malleus malificarum*, a handbook on witchcraft, was a best-seller. The disturbing quality sensed in Bosch's paintings can also be found, for example, in the contemporary work of German artists such as Matthias Grünewald, Hans Baldung Grien, and Hans Burgkmair and in sculptures of Death, alone or with a lover.

Dating early Netherlandish paintings is notoriously hazardous. None of Bosch's works can be dated with certainty. Scholars generally agree that the early works, generally dated before 1485, such as the *Adoration* in Philadelphia, are characterized by an uncertain sense of foreshortening and perspective, timid brushwork, and simple, traditional compositions. As Bosch matured, his brushwork became freer, more painterly; his perspective and foreshortening improved; and his paintings achieved a power, an immediacy not seen earlier. The *Landloper* in Rotterdam, the *Adoration Triptych* in

Madrid, and *The Crowning with Thorns* in London are generally viewed as late works, dating after 1500.

Scholars have suggested varying theories to explain Bosch's art. Some explanations, such as one that holds that Bosch was a member of a heretical sect, must be rejected as totally lacking in evidence. Others are more convincing. Astrology, alchemy, and Netherlandish folklore have been shown to be among the sources to which Bosch turned for his imagery. The widespread use of Nertherlandish proverbs in Bosch's oeuvre has also been noted.

Bosch uses a pictorial language that is largely lost to modern viewers. For example, his *Saint John the Baptist* shows an upright bear beneath a tree, a well-known symbol of the desert, used, for example, by Andrea Pisano on the Campanile and by the Limburg brothers (Pol, Hermann, and Jehanequin) in the *Belles Heures*. The saint's pose seems at first glance inappropriate; he seems to lounge on the ground. Yet his recumbent position, head in hand, refers to his dreamlike state, favorable for visions.

Modern scholarship has tried to place Bosch's art in its historical context. His images of Saint Anthony should, in part, be seen against the large numbers of victims suffering from Saint Anthony's Fire, a disease that produced hallucinations. Walter S. Gibson suggests that Bosch's works may have appealed to members of the societies of rhetoric and to the rich intellectual community of 's-Hertogenbosch.

Most scholars agree that Bosch held traditional, orthodox Christian views. For example, some of his works, such as the Philadelphia *Adoration* and the Madrid *Adoration Triptych*, show Eucharistic symbolism. In the interior of the latter work, Bosch uses Old Testament prototypes and alludes to the Virgin as altar; on the exterior, he depicts *The Mass of Saint Gregory*. Many of his works moralize against sin, specifically lust (*The Ship of Fools* and *The Garden of Earthly Delights*) or avarice (*The Death of the Miser* and *Haywain*. Others point the way to a devout life. The numerous images of *Christ Carrying the Cross* suggest that one should imitate Christ, as the writings of Thomas à Kempis had advised. Bosch recommends the contemplative life through his depictions of hermit saints such as Saint Anthony.

Bosch's work remains, to a great extent, a puzzle. The meaning of two wings in Rotterdam, for example, remains a mystery. No literary or visual precedents are known. There is also considerable disagreement as to the interpretation of individual motifs. For example, the letter "M" that appears on the knives in Bosch's *The Garden of Earthly Delights* had been explained alternately as referring to the painters Jan Mandyn or Jan Mostaert; to Malignus, the Antichrist; to the word "mundus," meaning "the world"; to the male sex organ; and to a cutler of 's-Hertogenbosch.

The Garden of Earthly Delights, Bosch's most famous work, reveals the artist's variety of sources, fertile imagination, brilliant style, and moralizing message. The title dates from a later time; the contemporary title is unknown. The interior left wing shows Adam and Eve in the Garden of Eden. Bosch makes their identity clear by their nudity, the apple orchard behind, the serpent coiled around the palm tree in the left middle ground, and the animal-filled garden. The moment depicted is rare in large-scale painting: the introduction of Adam to Eve. Adam's position, seated on the ground, seems inappropriate, but it refers to an earlier incident, his creation from the earth. Adam gazes eagerly at Eve, who modestly casts down her eyes. The rabbit to her right refers to her fertility.

This is clearly not the typical Garden of Eden. Creepy, slimy animals crawl out of the pool in the foreground. Animals fight, kill, and devour one another. Monstrous animals and bizarre rock formations further indicate that this is a corrupt earth. The central panel shows hordes of naked young men and women frolicking in an outdoor setting. Both blacks and whites are included to suggest all of mankind. Bosch indicates their lust in several ways; directly, by depicting embracing couples; metaphorically, through oversize strawberries and fish; and by association, through references to fruits, animals, gardens, dancing, and bathing.

Bosch condemns these amorous activities. Genesis I:28 had advised: "Be fruitful and multiply and replenish the earth and subdue it and have dominion over the fish of the sea and over the fowl of the air and over every living thing that moveth upon the earth." Clearly, mankind has disobeyed God. No children are shown, and the oversize fish and birds overwhelm the people. The mouse about to enter the bubble that holds an embracing couple suggests that their act is unclean. The owl, which was thought to be evil in contemporary Dutch folklore because he attacked day birds, is embraced by a lustful youth. The hollowness and fragility of earthly things are indicated by the numerous egg shapes, glass tubes, shells, and bubbles, as well as by such motifs as the figures standing on their heads, precariously balanced on a narrow ledge encircling a cracked globe that bobs in the water.

The right interior wing depicts Hell, a nightmarish vision with fire and ice, monstrous devils, and countless tormented souls. A literary source for this wing is known. The anonymous *Vision of Tundale*, which was published in 's-Hertogenbosch in 1484, describes a monster who ingests and excretes damned sinners. Bosch also illustrates traditional punishments for specific vices. The glutton vomits; the avaricious excrete coins; the proud woman admires her reflection in the polished rear end of a demon.

Another traditional motif is the world upside down: The rabbit, dressed in a hunting jacket, blows a hunter's bugle as he carries, hanging by the feet from a pole, his booty: a man. Bosch reflects a popular Dutch saying with the woman whose arm is burned by a candle (the modern equivalent is "burning the candle at both ends"). The man who coasts on an oversized skate into a hole in the ice suggests the saying "to skate on thin ice."

Summary

Although much of the content is traditional, Hieronymus Bosch's work stands apart, to some extent because of his wide variety of sources. Yet, more important, Bosch was able through his technical skill to translate his strikingly imaginative visions into visual form. His ability, for example, to express textures convincingly, whether ice or fire, metallic sheen or watery bubble, the strings of a lute or the smoke of Hell, made his visions believable. Bosch convinces one of the impossible. One accepts as reality, for example, the Tree-Man with barren trunks for legs, a broken egg-shell body, and a face that wistfully directs its gaze at the viewer. Irrational visions haunt and frighten because they seem so real. Bosch's message is moral: Beware the consequences of sin. His worldview is pessimistic: Mankind goes straight from a corrupt Eden to a world full of sinners, to a nightmarish Hell. No alternative is offered; the power of his art is overwhelming.

Bosch had a tremendous impact on his age. Hundreds of works dating from 1500 to 1530 show the imprint of his style. His nightmarish visions continue to haunt later generations. The Surrealists were his children; indeed, even as late as the 1980's a play based on *The Garden of Earthly Delights* was performed in New York.

Bibliography

Bosch, Hieronymus. *The Complete Paintings of Bosch*. Edited by Gregory Martin and Mia Cinotti. New York: Harry N. Abrams, 1971. A comprehensive catalog of the contemporary documents that mention Bosch. This thorough catalogue raisonné includes more than seventy paintings attributed to Bosch. Martin's introduction emphasizes Bosch's pessimism. Numerous color photographs, some detailed, as well as black-and-white reproductions of all cataloged works.

De Tolnay, Charles. *Hieronymus Bosch*. New York: William Morrow, 1966. An expanded edition of De Tolnay's 1937 monograph. Bosch's paintings are divided into three chronological periods. His work is interpreted in the light of the dream theories of Sigmund Freud and Carl Jung. Abundantly illustrated with high-quality details of Bosch's works. Somewhat dated.

Friedländer, Max J. *Early Netherlandish Painting*. Vol. 5, *Geertgen tot Sint Jans and Jerome Bosch*. Edited by G. Lemmens. Translated by Heinz Norden. Leiden, the Netherlands: Sijthoff, 1969. The English translation of the 1927 edition. This is the fundamental discussion of Bosch's style and character. Includes a section on Bosch's drawings and engravings. Contains high-quality photographs of many works by Bosch and his school. Extremely well written.

Gibson, Walter S. *Hieronymus Bosch*. London: Thames and Hudson, 1973. A thoughtful, balanced survey of Bosch's life and art.

_____. *Hieronymus Bosch: An Annotated Bibliography*. Boston:

G. K. Hall, 1983. This comprehensive annotated bibliography includes more than one thousand items, many little known and inaccessible. A concise introduction places the literature on Bosch in its historical context and evaluates the varying interpretations of Bosch's art and the sources for his unusual style. Extremely useful.

Snyder, James. *Northern Renaissance Art*. Englewood Cliffs, N.J.: Prentice-Hall, 1985. Includes one chapter on Bosch. Less cautious than Gibson. Good introductory text, meant for college undergraduates.

Diane Wolfthal

JACQUES-BÉNIGNE BOSSUET

Born: September 27, 1627; Dijon, France
Died: April 12, 1704; Paris, France
Areas of Achievement: Religion, literature, and historiography
Contribution: Bossuet was one of the most eloquent orators in seventeenth century France. In his sermons and funeral orations, he expressed profound psychological insights in a very refined and effective style. His major contributions were to rhetoric and sacred oratory.

Early Life

Jacques-Bénigne Bossuet was born in the Burgundian city of Dijon, where his father, Bénigne, was a lawyer. From 1636 to 1642, he attended a Jesuit school in Dijon, where he studied rhetoric, Greek, and Latin. During his lifetime, Bossuet read an enormous amount of works written in both Latin and Greek. His lengthy study with the Jesuits would help him years later to understand the many influences of the classical tradition on the development of Christian theology. In October of 1642, he began his preparation for the priesthood and his formal study of theology at the College of Navarre in Paris. Bossuet's major professor was the learned theologian Nicolas Cornet, who convinced Bossuet that a solid understanding of the early church fathers and Saint Thomas Aquinas was essential for the proper exposition of biblical texts. In 1652, Bossuet was ordained a priest and also received his doctorate in theology. Later in 1652, he moved to the French city of Metz, where he soon established a reputation as a very eloquent preacher. His fame would spread throughout France by the end of the 1650's. Even before he reached the age of thirty, Bossuet had enriched the cultural and spiritual life of France through his sermons.

Life's Work

Although Bossuet had a long and distinguished career as a bishop, as the private tutor for King Louis XIV's eldest son, as a respected member of the French Academy, and as a writer on such varied subjects as the history of Christianity, biblical exposition, and political theory, his fame rests largely on several well-crafted sermons and funeral orations that he delivered between the 1650's and the 1680's. Although his contemporaries greatly admired his very learned historical work *Discours sur l'histoire universelle* (1681; *A Discourse on the History of the Whole World*, 1686), this book and other of his extensive writings on the differences between Roman Catholicism and Protestantism are considered irrelevant by many contemporary theologians. Bossuet's eloquent sermons and funeral orations, however, included such universal themes as fear, despair, hope, the search for moral values, social injustice, and death that these speeches still continue to move even those readers who may not share Bossuet's religious beliefs.

Divine Providence constituted the unifying theme in Bossuet's works. Readers since his day have revered *Sermon sur la providence* (1662; *Sermon on Providence*, 1801), *Sermon sur la mort* (1662; *Sermon on Death*, 1801), and *Oraison funèbre d'Henriette Anne d'Angleterre* (1670; *Funeral Oration for Henrietta of England*, 1801). These masterpieces of French prose illustrate Bossuet's creativity in expanding the meaning of divine Providence in order to enrich his listeners' understanding of widely different human emotions.

On March 10, 1662, Bossuet preached his *Sermon on Providence* at the Louvre, then the French royal court. Twelve days later, he delivered *Sermon on Death*. These were part of a series of fourteen Lenten sermons that he gave at the royal court in 1662. Based on the sermon titles, listeners may well have thought that these two sermons would differ significantly in perspective and in subject matter. Yet these two sermons both illustrate the Christian belief that divine justice eventually rewards the just and punishes evildoers.

Bossuet argues quite sensibly that worldly success and pleasure are ephemeral. He uses a curious but effective comparison in order to convey this truth to his listeners. He reminds them that "pure wine" pleases the palate, whereas watered-down or "mixed wine" merely satisfies the thirst. Bossuet affirms that the pleasures of "pure wine" represent the eternal joys of the beatific vision, whereas the satisfaction from "mixed wine" symbolizes the happiness and disappointments of daily life. Bossuet begins *Sermon on Providence* by citing Saint Luke's contrast between the cruel rich man whose soul will never leave Hell and the virtuous but poor Lazarus, who is spending eternity in Paradise. Bossuet ends this sermon with an equally powerful biblical image. He tells his listeners that if they imitate Lazarus, who was never discouraged by injustice in this life, they too "will rest in the bosom of Abraham and possess with him eternal riches."

Despite its title, Bossuet's *Sermon on Death* presents a highly optimistic view of the human condition by stressing the essential grandeur and excellence of each person. This sermon develops extensively the opposition between appearance and reality. Bossuet makes a curious reference to chemical compounds in order to explain the meaning of death for Christians: "The nature of a compound is never more distinctly observed than in the dissolution of its parts." He justifies the relevance of this comment by stating that each man and woman is composed of a soul and a body that separate upon death. The body will return to dust, whereas the soul will return to Heaven. Physical death is thus both an end and a beginning. Each person possesses a dual nature: The body is mortal and the soul is immortal. In *Sermon on Death*, Bossuet explains that an acceptance of this dual nature consoles humans in their period of grieving and enables them to endure suffering in this life because of the belief that pure happiness awaits them in Paradise. In this well-structured sermon, Bossuet describes eternal life as a reality that no one should wish to deny.

Bossuet's contemporaries greatly admired the formal beauty in his sermons and funeral orations. After his ordination in 1652, Bossuet served fifty-two years as a priest and thirty-three years as a bishop. Since he was such an influential clergyman, he was often asked to deliver funeral orations for famous French persons, including Queen Maria Theresa (Louis XIV's first wife) and Michel Le Tellier (Chancellor of France). Although these two dignitaries were both exemplary Christians, their deaths were not personal tragedies for Bossuet himself.

In 1670, however, Bossuet had to deliver the funeral oration for Princess Henrietta Anne of England, the twenty-six-year-old wife of Louis XIV's only brother. This was an essentially painful responsibility for Bossuet. For more than a year, he had served as Henrietta's spiritual director, and he had come to admire her kindness, her virtue, and her courage. On June 29, 1670, she became suddenly ill and died the next morning. Bossuet himself gave her Extreme Unction, and he was at her side when she died. Such a tragic loss inspired Bossuet to compose his most moving and personal funeral oration. Near the beginning of this oration, Bossuet describes the true paradox of death. He tells his listeners: "Madame (Henrietta) is no longer in the tomb; death, which seemed to destroy everything, has established everything." He stresses that only Henrietta's body has died and that death has freed her soul for eternity. He explains that Henrietta had grown spiritually largely as a result of the real tragedies in her short life. The execution of her father, Charles I, in 1649 and her exile from England gave her the opportunity to reflect on eternal spiritual values that social upheavals cannot destroy. Had she enjoyed an uneventful childhood and adolescence at the English royal court, Bossuet preaches, she might have become a vain and superficial princess. Divine Providence, however, transformed her into a sincere Christian whose brief but exemplary life should inspire in others a profound love for God. Henrietta realized that "the favors of this world" are nothing in comparison to those favors that will be experienced in Heaven.

During his distinguished ecclesiastical career, Bossuet tried consistently to balance his intellectual pursuits with his responsibilities as a priest and as a bishop. He feared that worldly success would detract from his spiritual growth. In 1681, he accepted the position of bishop in the relatively small French city of Meaux. Although he continued to write and preach during the last two decades of his life, Bossuet spent most of this time tending to the spiritual affairs of his diocese. He died in Paris on April 12, 1704, at the age of seventy-six.

Summary

Jacques-Bénigne Bossuet's contemporaries recognized and appreciated his unique contributions to the moral, political, and religious life in the France of King Louis XIV. In his sermons and funeral orations, Bossuet developed persuasive intellectual arguments to support the religious value system on which French society was then based. He convinced his listeners that it was perfectly sensible for them to accept orthodox Christian dogma. It is difficult to overestimate Bossuet's influence on generations of French preachers who strove to imitate the eloquence and psychological depth in his sermons. His insightful remarks on divine Providence helped listeners to endure with optimism the travails and suffering of daily life. Bossuet's affirmation of universal dignity and his commitment to tolerance improved the quality of religious life in France. Although he participated actively in discussions with Protestant clergymen, Bossuet always respected the beliefs of those with whom he disagreed. Bossuet's compatriots also admired his writings on political theory. In *A Discourse on the History of the Whole World*, he argued that the French monarchy, although imperfect, was a very useful form of government, because it preserved stability in society and also prevented the country from falling into the political chaos that France had experienced during its civil wars of the sixteenth and seventeenth centuries.

Since the seventeenth century, Bossuet has been admired as a brilliant orator who combined eloquence with profound erudition. Although he wrote in a consistently formal style and never modified his acceptance of orthodox Catholic theology, he always adapted his arguments to the specific public he was addressing. Critics still admire both his skills as an orator and his keen insights into the complex motivation for human behavior. His elegant and well-structured speeches were never flowery or overly sentimental. Bossuet expressed himself with restrained passion.

Bossuet attained a stylistic perfection that no other French preacher has equaled. His speeches have often been favorably compared to the tragedies of Jean Racine and to Madame de La Fayette's psychological novel *La Princesse de Clèves* (1678; *The Princess of Clèves*, 1679). Such comparisons are both appropriate and thought-provoking. Like Racine and La Fayette, Bossuet was a profound writer whose aesthetically pleasing and yet understated works have created an enriched understanding of the human condition.

Bibliography

France, Peter. "Bossuet: The Word and the World." In *Rhetoric and Truth in France: Descartes to Diderot*. Oxford, England: Clarendon Press, 1972. This chapter examines the importance of rhetorical theory and practice in Bossuet's sermons and funeral orations. It demonstrates Bossuet's creative uses of imagery and argumentative techniques and analyzes the emotional effect of Bossuet's speeches both on contemporary listeners and on modern readers.

Judge, H. G. "Louis XIV and the Church." In *Louis XIV and the Craft of Kingship*, edited by John C. Rule. Columbus: Ohio State University Press, 1969. This is a very informative study of the indirect influence of Bossuet and other French preachers on political decisions made by Louis XIV. It demonstrates that French clergymen, including Bossuet, generally supported Louis XIV's claim that the Catholic church in France possessed much independence within the Church.

Perry, Elisabeth. *From Theology to History: French Religious Controversy and the Revocation of the Edict of Nantes*. The Hague: Martinus Nijhoff, 1973. An excellent study of religious controversies between French Catholic and Protestant theologians in the 1670's and 1680's. It describes very well Bossuet's active participation as an apologist for Catholic dogma.

Roberts, William. "Bossuet's *Henriette-Marie*: Indebted to Saint-Amant?" *Papers on French Seventeenth-Century Literature* 17 (1982): 537-551. Roberts notes that the French poet Saint-Amant had written in 1649 three poems on the execution of King Charles I of England. Roberts argues persuasively that these poems may well have influenced the funeral oration that Bossuet delivered in 1669 for Henrietta Maria.

Stanton, Domna. "The Predicatory Mouth: Problematics of Communication in Bossuet's *Oeuvres oratoires*." *Papers on French Seventeenth-Century Literature* 16, no. 1 (1982): 103-121. This essay proposes a fascinating Freudian interpretation of selected sermons by Bossuet. It shows that Bossuet was keenly aware of the many difficulties involved in communicating ideas clearly to listeners and readers.

Terstegge, Georgiana. *Providence as "Idée-Maîtresse" in the Works of Bossuet*. Washington, D.C.: Catholic University of America Press, 1948. This is the major English-language book on Bossuet. It argues persuasively that divine Providence is the unifying theme in Bossuet's works and examines numerous thematic and stylistic uses of Providence by Bossuet. Contains an excellent bibliography of secondary sources on Bossuet's writings.

Edmund J. Campion

SANDRO BOTTICELLI
Alessandro di Mariano Filipepi

Born: c. 1444; Florence
Died: May, 1510; Florence
Area of Achievement: Art
Contribution: Botticelli has been celebrated for the linear flow of his paintings and for the graceful and thoughtful cast of so much of his work. One of the greatest colorists of Renaissance painting, Botticelli created idealized figures that suggest great spirituality and somewhat less interest in humanity than was depicted in the works of many of his contemporaries.

Early Life

Sandro Botticelli was born Alessandro di Mariano Filipepi. Not much is known about his childhood or family life, except that, like many Florentine painters, he came from the artisan class. He grew up in an international city, already renowned for its art and commerce, for its wool and silk products, and for its bankers and princes—the Medicis, who determined much of the city's politics and art and who would become his patrons. Around 1460, Botticelli was apprenticed to Fra Filippo Lippi, one of the greatest Florentine painters of the early Renaissance. Known especially for his coloring and draftsmanship, he was to exert a lifelong influence on Botticelli's work. Lippi conveyed enormous human interest in his religious paintings, a characteristic Botticelli emulated while expressing a much more exquisite sensitivity to the devotional aspects of his subjects.

Botticelli's earliest commissioned paintings date from about 1470. The figure of *Fortitude*, now in the Uffizi in Florence, reveals many of his mature qualities and interests, as well as details he learned to apply in Lippi's workshop. *Fortitude* is portrayed as a full-figured woman with a characteristically swelling midsection and delicately featured face. The small head, angled toward her left shoulder, and her eyes, following the line of her left arm, suggest a contemplative, even melancholy, figure, whose thoughts are drawn together as tightly as her tiny closed mouth. The only expansive part of her face is her forehead, which is high and wide, and decorated with a pearl-studded crown (a touch borrowed from Lippi). This is a monumental work, which suggests both great volume and extraordinary finesse.

A companion piece from this period, *Judith and Her Maid*, depicts the characters walking through a beautiful landscape, returning to the Israelite camp after Judith has severed the head of Holofernes with a sword. Sword in one hand, and olive branch in the other, the picture of Judith with her head inclined toward her right shoulder resembles the figure of *Fortitude*. Although the sword is bloody, her expression is contemplative and in marked contrast to the maid, whose head juts forward under the strain of carrying

Holofernes' head. Judith, in the foreground of the painting, seems to inhabit a space of her own, a spirituality to which the maid and the background landscape must be subordinated. Judith's face resembles Lippi's Madonnas, and the utterly composed quality of her expression is starkly contrasted with the battling troops, just visible on a plain below the path of Judith's progress. In this painting, Botticelli first seems to grasp the division between the realms of the mystical and the natural that is characteristic of his later work.

Life's Work

Botticelli is renowned for painting several versions of *Adoration of the Magi*, which can be studied as evidence of his artistic development. There is, for example, a painting (1482) in the National Gallery of Art, Washington, D.C., that is remarkable for its vivid color and for its striking portrayal of individual figures—all of them arranged in highly distinctive reverential positions. At the apex of the painting are the Madonna and Child, framed by a monumental yet open-ended and airy architectural structure; its triangular roof (through which the blue sky can be seen) is paralleled by the human triangle of the Magi presenting their gifts to the Christ Child. This is a beautiful painting which reads like a moment of suspended time. It also has a subtlety and suggestiveness to it that is less apparent in a version at the Uffizi (c. 1475), in which the portraits of figures at the Adoration are more individualized and realistic but also somehow less important, because they contribute less to the meaning of the whole composition. In a recent restoration of this picture, however, it was discovered that the painting had been cropped, so that earlier comments by art historians on the painting's restrictiveness have had to be revised. As in the earlier painting of Judith, the restored Uffizi *Adoration* shows Botticelli employing an open landscape in the background to give perspective to the spiritualized content of his enclosed space.

The power of spirit over space is evident in Botticelli's painting *Saint Augustine in His Cell* (c. 1495). Augustine is presented as a massive, robed figure, holding a book in his powerful left hand while his right hand, with open tensile fingers, is stretched diagonally across his upper body. That he is in the grip of intense thought is also indicated by the lines of concentration on his forehead and his strongly focused eyes. While he is surrounded by the implements of the scholar and the churchman, his gaze is clearly heavenward, for he transcends all earthly instruments, which are merely the means to a spiritual end.

In such paintings, Botticelli retains enough objects and pays enough attention to the human body to create a sense of realism, but in comparison with his contemporaries it is evident that he is more concerned with the spiritual presence of his subjects. Thus, they are less individualized in terms of their clothing or bodily structure. For all of his massiveness, Augustine has none of the muscularity associated with Renaissance painting. Similarly, the details of a scholar's study are kept to a minimum and the sense of a domestic scene is not emphasized, especially when compared with the paintings of Saint Jerome by Domenico Ghirlandajo, Jan van Eyck, and Petrus Christus, which served as models for Botticelli's Augustine.

As significant as his religious painting is Botticelli's treatment of classical subjects. Two of his most famous paintings, *Primavera* (c. 1478) and *The Birth of Venus* (c. 1480's), reflect his concern for line and form rather than for story or for close copying of his Greek models. The central figures of *Primavera* has been taken to be Venus, surrounded by the dancing Graces of spring. The figure's expression suggests much of the same pensiveness of his Madonnas, as does her oval-shaped, tilted head and rounded body. Although an allegorical scene is being illustrated, which includes Flora (the figure of spring), Mercury, Zephyr, and Cupid in order to suggest the arousal of passion in the new season, most commentators have been struck by the elegant choreography of the setting, in which the Graces appear to be dancing while lightly touching one another and entwining their hands. There is a dreaminess, a magical lightness to this locale that evokes the feeling of spring.

For sheer elegance, Botticelli never surpassed *The Birth of Venus*. She stands in the nude on a seashell, blown to shore by the entwined allegorical figures of the winds at her left. Like so many of his female figures, Venus has soft lines—narrow, rounded shoulders and breasts and an upper body that swells out gracefully to wide hips and a rounded stomach. It is the continuity and fullness of his figures that constitutes beauty, not muscle tone or bone. Venus' attendant, at her left, moves toward her with billowing clothes, while the serene goddess stands perfectly poised with knees slightly bent, her hair flowing in the wind. Botticelli had classical sources for this rendering of Venus, but as in *Primavera*, the overwhelming impression of the painting is of the arrival of beauty and perfection, of an aesthetic ideal that is meant to be treasured in and for itself and not particularly for what it represents in myth.

Summary

Ethereal feminine beauty is so much a part of Sandro Botticelli's classical and religious paintings that it has been speculated that he was deeply influenced by the Neoplatonists, who equated the concept of Beauty with Truth. Botticelli's Venus and his Madonnas could have the same expression, these critics argue, because their perfection was emblematic of the divine. Clearly the unity of his paintings and the way they minimize narrative in favor of tableaux suggests a Platonic bias. The softness of his colors, the vagueness of his landscapes, and his lack of interest in the structure of the human form are reflective of a sensibility that yearns toward some deep, inner mystical sense of the origins of things.

Although Botticelli was viewed as a technically resourceful painter in his time, he was eventually eclipsed by Leonardo da Vinci, whose range of human gestures, dynamic compositions, and use of light and shade made Botticelli seem old-fashioned. Not until the late nineteenth century, when he was taken up by the English Pre-Raphaelites, was Botticelli reinstated. To them, he represented the simplicity and sincerity of early Italian art. Similarly, the English art critic John Ruskin used Botticelli as an example of an artist who presented nature and human figures as expressions of a divinely created world. Art historians still marvel at the refinement, purity, and poignancy of Botticelli's painting. His figures have an otherworldly aura that is attributed to the artist's own faith. His paintings are not so much illustrations of his subjects as they are the subjects themselves—as though the apprehension of eternal beauty and perfection were itself a matter composed of his rhythmical lines, soothing colors, and elongated shapes.

Bibliography
Baldini, Umberto. *Primavera: The Restoration of Botticelli's Masterpiece.* New York: Harry N. Abrams, 1986. Although this book concentrates on one painting (it includes several essays by different art critics), it also provides important criticism of Botticelli's other works and a helpful description of his period in history. A useful bibliography, an index, and handsome color plates make this an indispensable volume on the artist.
Ettlinger, Leopold D., and Helen S. Ettlinger. *Botticelli.* New York: Oxford University Press, 1977. An excellent introduction to Botticelli's oeuvre, including 138 illustrations, eighteen in color. An annotated bibliography and an index make this a particularly useful resource.
Hatfield, Rab. *Botticelli's Uffizi "Adoration": A Study in Pictorial Content.* Princeton, N.J.: Princeton University Press, 1976. As the subtitle indicates, this is a specialized study, aimed at developing a vocabulary to describe the pictorial content of Botticelli's paintings. All plates are in black and white. Essentially a book for advanced scholars, this might prove useful to students concentrating on one aspect of the artist's career.
Lightbrown, Ronald. *Sandro Botticelli.* 2 vols. Berkeley: University of California Press, 1978. This is a superb study, with individual chapters on the artist's early life, his early works, his relationship with the Medicis, his period in Rome, his religious and secular paintings, and his drawings. An appendix of documents, notes, an annotated bibliography, and an index make this an essential and accessible scholarly work.
_____. *Sandro Botticelli.* Vol. 2, *Complete Catalogue.* Berkeley: University of California Press, 1978. This is an enormous work of scholarship, identifying paintings attributed to the young Botticelli, autograph paintings, workshop paintings, drawings, works wrongly attributed to Bot-

ticelli, and lost works. This book will help to correct errors made in earlier volumes of art criticism and history. Each catalog entry includes a description of the work, its condition, location, history, and background. Also notes whether the work exists in other versions.

Venturi, Lionello. *Botticelli.* 2d ed. London: Phaidon Press, 1971. A competent introduction to Botticelli's life and work, with helpful references to his place in the history of art criticism. Forty-eight large color plates make this an especially good volume for studying the paintings.

Carl Rollyson

LOUIS-ANTOINE DE BOUGAINVILLE

Born: November 12, 1729; Paris, France
Died: August 31, 1811; Paris, France
Areas of Achievement: Exploration and the military
Contribution: Bougainville is best known as the leader of the first French expedition to sail around the world. He fought the British during the French and Indian Wars and later during the American Revolutionary War.

Early Life

Louis-Antoine de Bougainville was the youngest of four children. He was born in Paris on November 12, 1729. His father was a notary in the Paris Courts of Justice. Although his mother died while Louis-Antoine was an infant, he seems to have had a happy childhood.

His biographers have generally been kind to Bougainville. He was physically short, inclined to be plump or, by some accounts, even fat. His portrait shows him as a splendid French gentleman with a filled-out face, rosy cheeks, and a reddish, somewhat bulbous nose. He is described as tactful, compassionate, and good-humored. He seems to have been an adventurer, a gambler, and somewhat of a ladies' man. Loyal to his friends, king, and country, he was concerned for the welfare of his companions and those under his command. The translations of his writings indicate that he was a better-than-average journalist.

At his father's urging, he studied law and mathematics at the University of Paris. In 1755, he published a treatise on integral calculus which brought him academic recognition, the most notable being his election to membership in the British Royal Society of London. It is not known whether he ever practiced law, but he did have influential friends in law, politics, and government who helped him gain important positions. Bougainville spent several months as secretary to the French ambassador in London, where he enjoyed an active social life, perfected his English, and made the acquaintance of (and often befriended) many prominent Englishmen. He read the accounts of English naval explorers, particularly the account of Admiral George Anson's voyage around the world.

Life's Work

Bougainville lived at a trying time for his country. Yet if France had been on the rise, he might not have had his moment in the sun. In 1756, at the beginning of the Seven Years' War, General Louis de Montcalm was appointed military commander of the French forces in what was then France's colony in North America, a large tract of land consisting of Canada, the Great Lakes, and the Mississippi basin, including Louisiana. Bougainville was Montcalm's aide-de-camp and friend from 1756 until 1760, when Montcalm was killed in the Battle of Quebec. As Montcalm's aide, he learned to deal with the native Indians. He did this so successfully that he was adopted by an Iroquois tribe. He visited most of the French forts of this territory and took part in many of the skirmishes and battles. He was wounded in the Battle of Ticonderoga.

Since he spoke English and had diplomatic experience, he frequently would be sent to negotiate the terms of surrender in these battles. As the years passed, he watched France's power fade and the friction between the French military and colonial government increase. At this juncture, General Montcalm sent Bougainville to France with two objectives: to defend Montcalm from the accusations of Governor Philippe de Rigaud de Vaudreuil, and to encourage the French government to support the war effort in North America or risk losing Canada to the English. He accomplished the former aim but succeeded only in getting lip support for Montcalm. Returning empty-handed to Canada, he took part in the losing defense of Quebec against General James Wolfe. After the death of Montcalm, he rose to second in command of the remaining French forces and eventually played a part in negotiating France's surrender of Canada to the English, then commanded by General Jeffrey Amherst.

The Pacific was the next stage in the European rivalry between France and England. On his return to France, Bougainville convinced King Louis XV that despite France's defeat in the Seven Years' War, it still might be possible to block the English from the Pacific. Bougainville was given permission to try but no money to establish a French settlement in the Malouine (Falkland) Islands. He raised his own funds and, with a small group of French Canadians, in 1764 landed on and took possession of the Malouine Islands for France. The English, who had claimed but not settled these islands, demanded that France withdraw its colony. The French, thoroughly drained by the Seven Years' War, were powerless to resist. Instead, they negotiated an agreement with Spain to turn the settlement over to Spain rather than give it to the English. As part of this political maneuvering, Bougainville was given the job of handing over another French colony to another foreign power. In return, he was given two ships and orders to sail around the world—and in the process explore the South Pacific for France. It was this voyage that brought renown to Bougainville as the first Frenchman to circumnavigate the globe.

Bougainville was not alone in the exploration of the South Pacific. The English in the same year sent an expedition under Samuel Wallis and Phillip Carteret. They became separated during bad weather while passing through the Straits of Magellan and each continued alone, unaware of the other's progress. Bougainville followed closely behind. Bougainville finally caught up with and passed Carteret off the west coast of Africa, returning to home port first. Several colorful and complimentary accounts, including his own, have been made of Bougainville's voyage. He unsuccessfully searched for the then-legendary southern continent. Several new islands and channels were discovered. One of the islands today bears his name. He visited Tahiti and his description of it and its people captivated the French imagination. His supply ship carried Jeanne Baret, the first woman to sail around the world. She was apparently the mistress of the expedition's naturalist, Philibert Commerson, who had successfully disguised her as his valet. She was not discovered until they had reached Tahiti. Bougainville brought a Tahitian back with him to Paris. This "noble savage" was the talk of Paris. Commerson, a botanist, found a brightly flowered vine in Brazil which he named bougainvillea. While Bougainville's voyage added little to what was known of the Pacific, it was of importance to the French. It gave them a small victory after a series of dismal failures in the international power struggles of the eighteenth century.

Shortly after Bougainville had completed his account of the journey, he was again pressed into military service for France. In 1778, the French, at the urging of Benjamin Franklin, signed a treaty with the fledgling United States of America to take their part against the English. Bougainville was given the command of a French battleship and went to war against the British again. This French adventure was, on the whole, less than successful. The one success was the naval battle in Chesapeake Bay, which led to the surrender of Major General Charles Cornwallis to George Washington. Thus, the French were instrumental in depriving their enemy of a large colony in North America in revenge for their loss of Canada twenty years earlier.

Bougainville married at the age of fifty and had four sons by this marriage. One of them, Hyacinthe, followed in his father's footsteps, joining the navy, and making several voyages of exploration, including a trip to Tahiti. Bougainville, a supporter of the royalty during the French Revolution, barely escaped the guillotine. He spent the last eighteen years of his life in good health, honored by Napoleon I and the people of France. He was preceded in death by his second son and by his wife. Bougainville died on August 31, 1811, in his home in Paris.

Summary

Louis-Antoine de Bougainville can be described as a model eighteenth century aristocrat. He was intelligent, well educated, adventurous, socially outgoing, and, in the latter part of his life, financially comfortable. He dedicated most of his life to public service, first as a junior army officer and later as naval commander. In his public life, he was a patriot, loyal to his country, king, and commanding officers, and in return he received their loyalty.

He is most renowned for being the first Frenchman to command a vessel that circumnavigated the earth. This voyage was noteworthy for a reason that was given little or no public acclaim but in retrospect was more important than any real or imagined victory over the English. Bougainville made accurate notations of the longitude of the places he visited. He used a method suggested by Galileo and Jean Cassini's tables of the eclipses of the moons of Jupiter to determine the time it was in Paris compared to the time it was where they were. Unfortunately, this method of establishing the longitude of a place did not become widely used, partly because of the difficulty of the astronomical observations needed. Once this practice, pioneered by Bougainville, became commonplace, navigators were able to determine their destination accurately, as well as where they were in relation to their destination. Thus, the guesswork was taken out of overseas transportation and trade became more practical.

Bibliography

Allen, Oliver E., et al. *The Pacific Navigators*. Alexandria, Va.: Time-Life Books, 1980. The third chapter of this book relates biographical material on Bougainville, centering on his part in the exploration of the South Pacific. Contains his portrait and a map which traces his voyage across the Pacific. Also includes references to the solution to the longitude problem. Illustrations.

Bougainville, Louis-Antoine de. *Adventure in the Wilderness: The American Journals of Louis-Antoine de Bougainville, 1756-1760*. Edited and translated by Edward P. Hamilton. Norman: University of Oklahoma Press, 1964. A very readable translation of Bougainville's American journal. Also contains a short but valuable introduction that describes Bougainville and sets the historic and geographic stage for his journal. Contains several portraits, two of Bougainville, and several sketch maps, including a very useful place-name map of New France and the British Colonies.

Brown, Lloyd A. *Map Making: The Art That Became a Science*. Boston: Little, Brown, 1960. The chapter "The Science of Longitude" describes the method used by Bougainville to establish the longitudes of the places he visited.

Dunsmore, John. *French Explorers in the Pacific*. Vol. 1, *Eighteenth Century*. New York: Oxford University Press, 1965. Relates the stories of seven French navigators of the eighteenth century, the first of whom was Bougainville. The bulk of this chapter deals with Bougainville's voyage across the South Pacific from the Straits of Magellan, past Tahiti, and around the Solomon Islands. Briefly describes the remainder of the trip through the Dutch East Indies, across the Indian Ocean to the Île de France (Mauritius), around the southern tip of Africa, and back to France.

Hammond, L. Davis, ed. *News from New Cythera: A Report of Bougain-*

ville's Voyage. Minneapolis: University of Minnesota Press, 1970. This short but valuable book contains a long introduction to the translation of a newsletter written by Bougainville, in which he describes his encounter with the Island of Tahiti. In the introduction Hammond cites the historic significance of this voyage and gives a short biography of Bougainville.

Ross, Michael. *Bougainville*. London: Gordon & Cremonesi, 1978. A short but difficult biography. Contains many references to French history and historical personages.

Theodore P. Aufdemberge

TYCHO BRAHE

Born: December 15, 1546; Knudstrup Castle, Scania, Denmark
Died: October 24, 1601; Prague, Bohemia
Area of Achievement: Astronomy
Contribution: Brahe realized early that the existing means for observing and measuring celestial bodies and their motions were inaccurate. His great achievements are to have significantly improved existing instruments, to have invented some new instruments, and to have made amazingly accurate observations.

Early Life

Tyge Brahe Ottosøn was the eldest of ten children born to Otto Brahe. The Brahes were an old and noble family with both Danish and Swedish branches. Tyge's father was privy councillor to the King of Denmark at the time of Tyge's birth and ended as governor of Helsingborg Castle in Scania—then part of Denmark. Tycho was not reared with his parents and younger siblings. His father's brother Jørgen, who was childless, stole him while he was still a baby. Initial turmoil in the family was stilled when Otto's second son was born. It was therefore in the home of his uncle that Tyge was reared, showing so much early scholarly promise that, in addition to the requisite training for a young nobleman in horseback riding and swordsmanship, he was allowed to learn Latin in the hope that he would become a statesman and counselor to the king.

At thirteen, he entered the University of Copenhagen, head held high above a piped collar and small rapiers by his side. Thirteen was not an unusual age for university entry at the time. He studied, as did most of his colleagues, philosophy, rhetoric, and law. The curriculum was in Latin. His academic career was planned for him: After finishing his studies in Denmark, he would go to one of the more famous German universities and study law, still in preparation for a career in government. The problem was that young Tyge (he took the name Tycho upon graduation) was not interested in law. An event that took place on August 21, 1560, when he was nearly fourteen, came to fascinate him so deeply that it, in effect, determined his choice of career. He heard that an eclipse of the sun had been predicted for that day. The fact that the prediction proved to be correct and that the sun was indeed eclipsed seemed to him divine.

It was not considered good form for a man of Brahe's social station to become a mere scientist, and his fascination with astronomy was greeted with far less than enthusiasm by his uncle and father. His astronomical studies were performed in secrecy and at night. When he went to Germany, a tutor accompanied him to ensure that he did not stray from his legal studies. The two arrived in Leipzig in 1562, when Brahe was not quite sixteen.

Anders Sørensen Vedel, the tutor, kept a rapt eye on his charge, and Brahe studied law by day and reserved his nights for gazing at the stars. He also managed to study mathematics, which would be necessary for him in his further astronomical studies, and he met two of the more famous astronomers of his day, who happened to reside in Leipzig—Bartholomaeus Scultetus and Valentin Thau. The instruments he used for his observations were quite crude: a globe, a compass, and a radius.

Life's Work

The tutor eventually became aware of his charge's illicit nightly activities, and the two of them were called home to be under Jørgen Brahe's intense scrutiny. Yet Jørgen died not long afterward, leaving the nineteen-year-old Brahe a wealthy and independent man. Brahe could embark on his life's work. For a while, out of a sense of duty, he performed his responsibilities as a nobleman and oversaw the Tostrup estate in Scania which was part of his inheritance. In 1566, however, he decided to make his scientific studies the center of his life and activities. To the accompaniment of his family's scorn, Brahe moved to Wittenberg and worked with Kaspar Peucer, a then-famous astronomer, until an outbreak of the plague forced his return to Denmark. Later, he went to Augsburg because of its famous instrument makers; he wanted new, more precise, better designed instruments made for his observations. He had a new globe, sextant, and radius made. His fame in the scientific community began to grow.

Brahe concentrated his early studies on the apparent movements of the planets and the fixed stars. His father's death and an appointment as cantor of the Roskilde Cathedral devoured much of his time, but he steadfastly continued his work. His growing fame changed the attitudes of his family and peers toward his work: His uncle Steen Brahe had a lab outfitted for him. His first major breakthrough was the observation of a new star, first seen on November 11, 1572. The star, which he appropriately called Stella Nova in a book entitled *De nova et nullius aevi memoria prius visa stella* (1573; about the new star), appeared in the Cassiopeia constellation. Large and bright, the new star remained visible until 1574. The accuracy of the observations, down to the minute details, caused a sensation in the scientific community, and Brahe was established as a great scholar.

Brahe, by now a grown man, cut quite a striking figure. Bejeweled and flamboyantly dressed, he was stocky, with reddish-yellow hair combed forward to hide incipient baldness, and he sported a pointed beard and a flowing mustache. When he was a young man in Germany, Brahe had been in a duel, and his opponent sliced off a large piece of his nose, for which Brahe had a substitute made of gold and silver and painted to look natural. He always carried a box with glue and salve.

Brahe's plan was to settle abroad and continue his studies, but the king changed his plans by donating to him the small island of Hveen, in the channel between Denmark and Sweden. The position of the island was perfect for his purposes, and Brahe accepted the generous offer. On Hveen, he built his famous observatory: the architecturally beautiful Uraniborg (after the muse of astronomy Urania), which contained a chemistry lab, his famous mural quadrant, and observatories in the attic. He also built the smaller, but equally famous, Stellaburg, which, except for a cupola, was built underground. This building contained many observational instruments, including his renowned revolving quadrant. It also had portraits, in the round, of the greats of astronomy: Timocharis, Hipparchus, Ptolemy, Nicolaus Copernicus, and himself.

On the official front, Brahe became royal mathematician and lecturer at the University of Copenhagen. Little is known about his private life. He married a bondwoman, Kirstine, by whom he had eight children, five girls and three boys. Brahe did not reveal this part of his life in his own writings, and his contemporaries restricted themselves to expressing disapproval of this alliance. In his observatories, he continued his work, making surprisingly accurate observations of celestial bodies. He always had a number of students living with him, who helped him in his observations.

By 1582, Brahe had reached a point at which he could propose his own astronomical system. He rejected both the static Ptolemaic system with the sun and planets moving around Earth in individual orbits and the Copernican system, which has Earth and the other planets moving around the sun. Brahe's system is an amalgam. For reasons involving both the laws of physics and the Bible, he could not accept a system that makes Earth simply one of the planets that revolve around the sun. In Brahe's system, Earth is static and the moon and the sun revolve around it, with the other planets revolving around the sun. It remained for Brahe's student Johannes Kepler to reinstate the correct Copernican system reinforced by Brahe's minutely correct measurements and observations.

On Hveen, Brahe had his own printing press and published, besides his own works, calendars and horoscopes for the king and other high dignitaries. Like many of his contemporaries, Brahe did not distinguish sharply between astronomy and astrology, but he apparently did not think highly of horoscopes and only made them under duress. Many kings and dignitaries from around Europe visited the island to see the famous observatories.

At Hveen, Brahe did the bulk of his scientific work. He made accurate observations of the sun, moon, and planets. Many scholars find that his greatest achievement, besides his introduction of the use of transversals on the graduated arcs of astronomical instruments and his improvements of existing instruments (such as the equatorial armillae, which are spheres used to establish differences in longitude and latitude), was his catalog of fixed stars, which stood until such improved instruments as telescopes and clocks of precision came into use.

Unfortunately, Brahe did not adhere to his scientific studies. As he grew older, his idiosyncrasies became more obvious and he became involved in some petty suits that alienated the king, who had been one of his staunchest supporters. Brahe's intransigence finally caused the king to confiscate land that had been bequeathed to him, leaving Brahe without an adequate source of income.

Finally, in July, 1597, Brahe left native shores and moved to Rostock, Germany. He sent a submissive letter to King Christian IV, in which he asked the king to take him back into his good graces. The letter elicited a direct and angry response from the king, who said that until Brahe came to his senses, admitted his faults, and promised to do as he was told, he should not return.

Brahe, determined not to give in, decided to find a new mentor. He approached Emperor Rudolph II in Prague. Rudolph had a reputation as a patron of the sciences and indeed took Brahe and his collaborator Kepler under his wing. The two famous astronomers had, at times, a stormy relationship, and, after several years, Kepler had a nervous breakdown and left Prague. Brahe died on October 24, 1601, in Prague.

Summary

Tycho Brahe was a transitional figure in the history of astronomy. His theoretical work was flawed and actually a step back from the work of Copernicus. His great achievements were in the areas of practical and spherical astronomy. He devised new and more sophisticated instruments for observations and recorded an astounding body of observations that represented a quantum leap forward in knowledge about the movements and relative positions of celestial bodies.

Brahe's observatories on the island of Hveen represented the state of the art in sixteenth century astronomical observations. Here he gazed at the stars, recorded his observations, made his mathematical computations, and had his most famous instruments built and installed: three equatorial armillae; a mural quadrant, which he used to determine time; and sextants with transversals on the graduated arc and improved sights that allowed for pointing the instrument with great precision to measure distances and angles.

Brahe's legacy, which has made him, in one biographer's somewhat hyperbolic phrase, "a king among astronomers," is his large body of accurate observations and measurements performed by means of instruments and methods devised by him.

Bibliography

Dreyer, J. L. E. "The Place of Tycho Brahe in the History of Astronomy." *Scientia* 25 (March, 1919): 177-185. A concise outline of Brahe's scientific achievements, including descriptions of his most important instruments. Places Brahe in the history of astronomy, trying to assess his importance relative to other greats such as Ptolemy, Copernicus, and Kepler.

_____. *Tycho Brahe: A Picture of Scientific Life and Work in the Sixteenth Century.* Reprint. New York: Dover, 1963. The most detailed work on Brahe in terms of his work and studies. Early in the book, Dreyer sets the general scientific and astronomical stage Brahe was to enter. While somewhat technical, the book gives a thorough and minute description of Brahe's instruments and observations.

Gade, John Allyne. *The Life and Times of Tycho Brahe.* Princeton, N.J.: Princeton University Press, 1947. Gade gives the social and political backdrop to Brahe's life and work. His emphasis is not so much on technical descriptions as on Brahe the man and the community member. Gade writes amusingly of Brahe's childhood and youth and gives a fairly complex psychological profile of the adult scientist and nobleman. The most personal portrait of Brahe extant.

Gray, R. A. "Life and Work of Tycho Brahe." *Royal Astronomical Society of Canada Journal* 17 (1923). Starts with a careful statement of the Ptolemaic and other theories current before the advent of Brahe. Lists among Brahe's achievements his statement that comets are not, as previously believed, within Earth's atmosphere. Also mentions Brahe's improvements on existing instruments.

Parsonby, Arthur, and Dorothea Parsonby. *Rebels and Reformers: Biographies for Young People.* London: Allen & Unwin, 1917. Takes the reader into Brahe's physical world at Hveen, describing the buildings and instruments in great but nontechnical detail. Mentions Brahe's difficult personality. Outlines his major scientific contributions, listing as the most important his catalog of fixed stars. Very didactic.

Per Schelde

JOHANNES BRAHMS

Born: May 7, 1833; Hamburg
Died: April 3, 1897; Vienna, Austro-Hungarian Empire
Area of Achievement: Music
Contribution: One of the greatest composers of his century, Brahms left an enduring corpus of works. He demonstrated that the forms and genres of Viennese classicism continued to have artistic validity in the late nineteenth century and that they were not incompatible with the ethos of Romanticism.

Early Life

Johannes Brahms was the son of Johann Jakob Brahms, a double bassist in the municipal orchestra of Hamburg, and Johanna Henrika Christiane Nissen, a small, crippled woman who was seventeen years her husband's senior. Though romantic biographers often exaggerated the humble origins of their subjects, accounts of Brahms's childhood in a Dickensian tenement in Hamburg are largely accurate, and it appears true that Brahms was required at an early age to play the piano in dockside taverns and dance halls in order to augment the family income. Certainly Brahms's childhood was not altogether wretched: It seems clear that his parents offered considerable affection (Brahms worshiped his mother throughout her life) and did what could be done, given their straitened circumstances, to develop their son's gifts.

Brahms's remarkable musical talent was discovered at an early age by his father. He was given competent instruction at the piano by Otto F. W. Cossel and distinguished, if conservative, instruction in composition by Eduard Marxsen. Though Brahms was not a prodigy on the order of Wolfgang Amadeus Mozart or Felix Mendelssohn, his talent developed rapidly. In the 1848-1849 season, he gave two public piano recitals, performing works as formidable as Ludwig van Beethoven's *Waldstein* Sonata, Op. 53. He was also composing prolifically, though the works from this period are no longer extant; Brahms, ever self-critical, later destroyed these "youthful indiscretions" by the trunkful.

In 1853, Brahms seized an opportunity to participate in a concert tour with the flamboyant Hungarian violinist Eduard Reményi. The tour proved to be a turning point in Brahms's life. Through Reményi's offices, Brahms was introduced first to Franz Liszt in Weimar and then to Robert and Clara Schumann in Düsseldorf. The initial meeting with the Schumanns—he the leading spirit in the German Romantic musical movement and she the greatest female pianist of the century—took place on September 30, 1853. The three immediately experienced a remarkable personal and musical communion, and Brahms became virtually a member of the Schumann household. At this time, Brahms was twenty years old, small, slightly built, blond, unbearded, and androgynously fair of face (not the bearded, well-fleshed, cigar-smoking doyen of later photographs), and he seems to have exercised a complex fascination on both the Schumanns. So impressed by Brahms's playing and compositions was Robert Schumann that he was moved to issue a review in the prestigious *New Journal for Music* declaring Brahms to be a "young eagle" who had sprung forth "fully armed." Schumann had, in effect, anointed Brahms as his musical heir; the younger man's public career had begun.

Life's Work

The first works which Brahms allowed posterity to see date from the period of the first meeting with the Schumanns. It is easy to see why Robert Schumann admired the three piano sonatas (Opp. 1, 2, and 5) which Brahms presented to him. Though the shadow of Beethoven looms over these works, they display an emerging individuality, a formal mastery, and a seriousness of purpose which justify Schumann's description of Brahms as already "fully armed." The Sonata in F Minor, Op. 5 is particularly impressive: It is a big-boned work in five movements whose carefully organized ideas are alternately fiery and lyrical. Brahms's unique, thick-textured, robust, and occasionally awkward keyboard idiom, doubtless deriving from his own idiosyncratic piano technique, is already fully present.

The years from 1854 to 1856 were years of personal turmoil for Brahms. Early in 1854, Robert Schumann suffered a nervous collapse which required his institutionalization and which led ultimately to his death in 1856. Brahms devoted much of his energy during this time of trial to the emotional support of Clara. There is no doubt that Brahms believed himself to be in love with Clara at this time. The degree of intimacy to which Brahms and Clara progressed is not known. Shortly after Robert's death, the two evidently agreed to maintain their friendship on a purely platonic basis.

The years of Schumann's illness had not been productive ones for Brahms. Shortly before Schumann's collapse, Brahms had completed his first major chamber work: the Piano Trio in B Major, Op. 8. It was an auspicious beginning. The next large works date from the end of the decade. In 1857, Brahms accepted a post as pianist and choral conductor at the small court of Detmold. There he had an opportunity to work with the court's forty-piece orchestra. In 1859, Brahms completed his first work employing full orchestra, the Concerto No. 1 in D Minor, Op. 15. The work had a complicated genesis: Brahms had first intended to write a symphony, and the work lacks the surface brilliance of most Romantic concertos. Though it was not well received at first, it is a great, if somewhat austere, work. The piano part is in some respects ungracefully written, and the work was long considered unplayable.

Though Brahms was by no means a reactionary, he found himself increasingly allied in the 1850's and 1860's with musical conservatives such as the Schumanns and violinist Joseph Joachim in opposition to radical Romantics such as Franz Liszt and Richard Wagner. Brahms himself had little interest in critical polemics of any sort, but in 1860 he allowed his name to be placed on a manifesto decrying the so-called music of the future of Liszt and his cohorts. Ultimately, Brahms was made to suffer for this gesture: He became the *bête noire* of radical critics and was the victim of critical vituperation for the remainder of his life. To these thrusts, Brahms appeared stoically indifferent; on later occasions, he expressed admiration for the works of Wagner, the leader of the opposing camp.

In 1863, Brahms accepted a post as director of the Vienna *Singakademie* (choral society) and for the remainder of his life resided chiefly in Vienna. The city of the Habsburgs, with its *Gemütlichkeit* and its memories of Franz Schubert, Mozart, and Beethoven, thus became the backdrop for Brahms's supreme achievements as a composer. The move was probably a healthy one for Brahms: The sunniness of the Viennese doubtless helped to mitigate Brahms's North German dourness and enabled the composer to show on occasion a more genial and charming face. As Brahms aged, he seemed in some respects to personify the aging of the century itself; his works increasingly assumed that cast which generations of critics have called "autumnal." Brahms's late works are indeed the Indian summer of Romanticism, warmed by a low sun whose rays shine obliquely.

Brahms's great work of the 1860's, and the work which firmly established his international reputation, was the *German Requiem*, Op. 45, for chorus, soloists, and orchestra. Despite its title, this is not a liturgical mass. Brahms assembled his own text from the German Bible, and as Karl Geiringer has observed, Brahms's requiem is not so much a prayer for the dead as an attempt to comfort and reassure the living who mourn. The occasion which gave rise to this work was the death of Brahms's mother in 1865; the great seven-movement edifice which he constructed in her memory was completed in 1868. Brahms's compositional technique was by this time completely assured in both choral and orchestral idioms, and the *German Requiem* shows Brahms working at a sustained level of inspiration throughout.

Among numerous other works which Brahms composed in his fourth decade, mention should be made of the Piano Quintet in F Minor, Op. 34 (1864), the Horn Trio in E-flat Major, Op. 40 (1865), and the orchestral *Variations on a Theme by Haydn*, Op. 56a (1873). The quintet for piano and strings began life as a duet for two pianos but is heard to greatest effect as a quintet. The trio Op. 40 was written for the unusual combination of violin, French horn, and piano; in its euphony and elegiac quality, it is purest Brahms. The Haydn variations show Brahms in his highest spirits; although the theme was not original with Haydn, a measure of his good humor pervades the work.

As Brahms entered his forties, he had not yet completed a symphony. It is part of the lore of the composer that he shrank from comparison with Beethoven in this genre. It is ironic, then, that his Symphony No. 1 in C Minor, Op. 68 (1876) was promptly dubbed "Beethoven's Tenth," and it is revealing that Brahms was not displeased by the nickname. The work borrows the key of Beethoven's Fifth Symphony and appropriates some of the emotional world of the Ninth as well, but these borrowings are not the result of a nullity on the part of Brahms; rather, they reveal the composer emboldened by the sureness of his own voice. Brahms was to write three more symphonies in 1877, 1883, and 1885; each is the product of consummate craftsmanship, and each has become a repertory staple.

Brahms's productivity did not diminish in his later years. Among the notable works of his last two decades are the Violin Concerto in D, Op. 77 (1878), the Piano Concerto No. 2 in B-flat, Op. 83 (perhaps his greatest utterance in concerto form), the second and third piano trios (1882 and 1886), the *Four Serious Songs*, Op. 121 (1896), and the miniatures for piano entitled variously *Intermezzo*, *Capriccio*, and *Ballade*, Opp. 116-119 (1892). These works for piano are an anthology of gems and have a valedictory quality; in some cases, they are an exquisite sort of sublimated café music.

The event which hastened Brahms's end shortly before his sixty-fourth birthday was the death of his great friend and artistic companion Clara Schumann in 1896. Shortly thereafter, Brahms was found to be suffering from cancer of the liver, to which he succumbed in April of 1897.

Summary

It was fashionable in progressive circles at the turn of the century to disparage Johannes Brahms. Hugo Wolf railed against Brahms's vacuousness and "hypocrisy"; George Bernard Shaw declared his style to be "euphuistic," and quipped that "his *Requiem* is patiently borne only by the corpse." These views seem today to be quaint at best and monuments to critical vanity at worst. A remarkable percentage of Brahms's works have remained in the active repertory, and they seem to appeal equally to the learned and the casual listener. Though the formulation may be simplistic, it can be said that Brahms—like Beethoven—speaks both to the intellect and to the heart. As a builder, Brahms was masterful both in design and in execution, and admirers of craftsmanship will not fail to respond to this. Brahms kindly supplied enough recondite features in his works to subsidize a large corps of scholars. At the same time. Brahms had the courage to speak directly and ingenuously to his listeners on an emotional level. This combination of sophistication and directness is the stamp of a great artist.

Bibliography

Gál, Hans. *Johannes Brahms: His Work and Personality*. Translated by Joseph Stein. Reprint. Westport, Conn.: Greenwood Press, 1977. Gál, a composer as well as a musicologist, was coeditor of the collected works of Brahms; his study is informed by an exhaustive knowledge of Brahms's works.

Geiringer, Karl. *Brahms: His Life and Work.* 2d rev. ed. London: Allen & Unwin, 1948. Geiringer's work remains the standard study in English of Brahms's life and creative achievement. The book is divided into two parts: a chronological account of Brahms's life and a critique of his works organized by genre. Offers an appendix containing an interesting sampling of Brahms's correspondence.

Latham, Peter. *Brahms.* London: J. M. Dent, 1948, rev. ed. 1966. A valuable shorter appraisal of Brahms in a two-part life-and-works format. Contains vivid, epigrammatic descriptions of major works.

Newman, William S. *The Sonata Since Beethoven.* Chapel Hill: University of North Carolina Press, 1969. Newman's study of the sonata principle contains a section of generous dimensions discussing Brahms's affinity for the sonata form, in general, and his sonatas for violin, piano, and clarinet, in particular.

Ostwald, Peter. *Schumann: The Inner Voices of a Musical Genius.* Boston: Northeastern University Press, 1985. Contains a well-documented and thoughtful account of the relationship between Brahms and Schumann. Essential for the student who would understand the Johannes Brahms-Robert Schumann-Clara Schumann triangle. Ostwald, a practicing psychiatrist, bases much of his presentation on previously inaccessible documents.

Schauffler, Robert H. *The Unknown Brahms: His Life, Character, and Works.* New York: Dodd, Mead, 1933. An anecdotal account of Brahms's personal life, Schauffler's work is based in large part on interviews with actual acquaintances of Brahms, and herein lies its chief value. In his attempt to unravel the enigma of Brahms's sexuality, Schauffler provides an early specimen of the so-called psychobiography. Schauffler's discussion of the works is old-fashioned and florid but not altogether exiguous.

Schönberg, Arnold. "Brahms the Progressive." In *Style and Idea.* New York: Philosophical Library, 1950. An essay by the influential atonal composer demonstrating the progressive aspects (rhythmic complexity and subtlety of motivic manipulation) of Brahms's art. A useful counterpoint to the prevailing view of Brahms as an autumnal composer.

Steven W. Shrader

LOUIS BRAILLE

Born: January 4, 1809; Coupvray, near Paris, France
Died: January 6, 1852; Paris, France
Areas of Achievement: Invention, technology, and social reform
Contribution: Braille was responsible for the invention of what has become a
worldwide system for teaching the blind to read and write.

Early Life

Louis Braille was born in 1809 in Coupvray, France. His mother, Constance Braille, was the daughter of a farming family in the countryside near Coupvray. His father, who also bore the name Louis, was a harness-maker. While playing in his father's workshop, the three-year-old Louis suffered an accident which would lead, first to sympathetic ophthalmia, and then to total blindness. Because there were no special educational facilities for the blind in the provincial areas of France at that time, the child spent the next seven years of his life in a state of relative solitude. Then, in 1819, when Braille was ten years old, he received a scholarship that enabled him to go to the Royal Institute for the Blind in Paris. It was there that, at the age of fifteen, Braille helped develop a new system of tactile coded impressions that could be used by the blind both to read and to write. This work represented a vast improvement over earlier methods. Although some time passed before this invention gained widespread acceptance, Braille was such a model student at the institute that, once he earned his completion certificate, when he was seventeen, he was appointed as a teacher in the Institute for the Blind.

Life's Work

As his career as a teacher progressed, Braille played a role in several of the changes that affected not only the organization but also the philosophy of education for the blind in France and other countries. Before 1784, when Valentin Haüy founded what would eventually become the National Institute for the Blind in Paris, few, if any, institutional provisions had existed for special assistance to the blind either in France or elsewhere in Europe or in the United States. This is not to say that the blind had not been the focus of considerable popular attention during prior generations. Indeed, Haüy and others associated with the new institute tried immediately to address some of the most important public-image questions that both he and, ultimately, Braille would face throughout their careers as educators of the blind.

One of these was the task of counteracting traditional prejudices, ranging from innocent pity or emotional compassion to open fear, visibly present among the majority of the population in their attitudes toward the blind. In Haüy's generation, the methods used to achieve this end were not always effective. In some cases, for example, arguments were introduced that underlined special characteristics of the blind. When these had to do with presumed extraordinary talents possessed by the blind by dint of one missing sense (heightened capacities of sense perception through touch or hearing), educators of the blind could emphasize certain positive points. To a certain extent, this was being done at the institute when Braille began there as a student: Many blind children were given training in music, so they could "prove" to society that they had talents worthy of recognition and praise.

On the other hand, there was another stream of literature, supported in part by Haüy, that suggested that the blind possessed a distinct inner nature that touched the realm of the mysterious. Anyone with a tendency to react negatively to obvious differences between the blind and persons with normal vision might also have been tempted to interpret suggestions of this special characteristic more in negative than in positive terms.

Even before Braille came to the Institute for the Blind in Paris, a debate had already challenged the Société Philanthropique (the founding inspiration behind the institute) for offering only charitable assistance to the blind children who came under its care. Some argued that more practical attention needed to be given to preparing blind children for life as participating members of society. In Haüy's generation, such pressures tended to focus on a list of so-called suitable occupations for which the blind could be trained. Most of these were simple manual trades that could be learned through the sense of touch.

In practical terms, the members of the institute knew that, in order for the transmission of intellectual knowledge to occur, some technical method needed to be found to enable the blind both to read the same texts that were available to the literate majority population and to write without assistance. The most obvious method—one that was already in use by the time Braille became a student at the institute—was to print texts with raised letters. Although the blind could thus follow any printed text by tactile progression, there were two disadvantages in this early system. First, the method was rather slow, since the full form of each letter was fairly complicated and difficult to feel. Second, because of the relative complexity of the forms of the letters, the likelihood of errors in reading, particularly if one tried to move rapidly, was fairly high.

On the other hand, those who insisted that fuller integration into so-called normal society would be a desirable by-product of educating the blind to read had also to keep other, less practical, considerations in mind. Prejudices against presumed special inner moral and psychological characteristics of the blind might rise if a communications system were devised for or by them that was not as immediately accessible to the "normal" majority as simple raised letters were. Haüy himself discovered, well before Braille made his contribution, that controversy would rise over any form of innovation that went further than the simple method of raised letters: Representation of sounds by raised symbols rather than letters (the Haüy method), for example, never became an established technique for teaching the blind to read.

There are several reasons why the work of Braille—which was technologically rather commonplace—needs to be placed in the wider context of the time and society in which he lived. Braille's system of printing writing by means of a "code" of dots rather than actual letters was obviously meant to simplify the reading process for the blind. Because knowledge of what eventually came to be known as Braille involved mastery of a "secret" code, however, some of Braille's contemporaries believed that the new system ran counter to the normal integrationist objectives that education for the blind was meant to serve. As a consequence, Braille techniques did not spread as rapidly or as widely as the modern observer, more accustomed to practical criteria for judging the effectiveness of technological innovations, might imagine.

Despite its rather slow start (Braille was not used, even in the institute where Braille taught, until 1829), progress toward the official adoption of the six-dot reading code was made gradually. By the mid- to late 1830's, Braille's insistence on the fact of increased teaching efficiency through the use of his system gained important recognition. A special school was founded on the outskirts of Paris (at Maisons Alfort), in which Braille was used exclusively. Later, as the success of the Maisons Alfort program became obvious, the school moved to the center of Paris, on the rue Bagnolet.

By the late 1840's, the use of Braille was enhanced considerably by two new developments. First, in 1847 the first Braille printing press was invented and used in France, soon to be exported for use throughout Europe and the United States. Second, the French government decided to establish a series of branch schools for the blind that would use the same Braille methods as the Paris Institute to provide elementary levels of instruction through reading, as well as manual trade training at the departmental level. From the mid-nineteenth century onward, the most qualified graduates of these provincial elementary schools would qualify to continue their education in full academic subjects at the National Institute for the Blind in Paris.

Braille himself did not live to see the full effects of the application of his reading code for the blind. Because of health complications caused by tuberculosis, he was forced to retire from teaching at the institute in 1837. At the time of his death in 1852, Braille lived in seclusion and was a nearly forgotten man. His reputation as an important contributor to modern education came only in stages. In 1887, the town of Coupvray, Braille's birthplace and the site of his grave, erected a monument to his memory in the center of the town square. In 1952, one century after his death, and at a time when the techniques he had pioneered were in use throughout the world, Braille's remains were transferred from Coupvray to a place of national prestige in the Panthéon in Paris.

Summary

The life of Louis Braille is more representative in many respects of the history of an issue than the history of an individual personality. Before Braille's time, both in France and elsewhere in Europe or the United States, institutions that cared for the blind functioned more as asylums than as places where useful trades could be taught. Intellectual stimuli, and even basic educational instruction, remained even more remote than possibilities for simple vocational training. Until an effective menas of communication had been found, learning was restricted to areas concentrating on the senses of touch and/or hearing.

The importance of the contribution of Braille, therefore, should be considered not only in practical terms (development of a simplified system of representing the letters of the alphabet by means of a code of raised dots) but also for its effect on attitudes toward the types of schooling that have since become possible for the blind. Even though the use of Braille to teach reading was initially limited to special schools for the blind, an important difference was in the making: Those who had formerly had no access to normal texts, be they in literature or the sciences, were now able to prepare themselves for interaction with society. Eventually, as Braille became more common and less expensive as a system of printing, this movement in the direction of fuller social and intellectual integration of the blind went further. By the early stages of the twentieth century, the blind were able to attend regular schools and follow the same academic curricula as their fellow classmates, using the same books, printed in Braille for their special use.

Bibliography

Davidson, Margaret. *Louis Braille*. New York: Scholastic Book Services, 1971. A work of historical fiction, designed mainly for young readers, recounting the life of Braille. In addition to Braille himself, the author portrays the people who influenced him, both as a youth in Coupvray and later, during his adult years.

Hampshire, Barry. *Working with Braille*. Lausanne, Switzerland: UNESCO, 1981. This book updates the 1954 United Nations Educational, Scientific, and Cultural Organization (UNESCO) analysis of methods of adapting Braille for international use. It is particularly important for its discussion of the impact of technological changes that have facilitated rapid communication beyond the imagination of original inventors of the Braille system.

Kugelmass, J. Alvin. *Louis Braille: Windows for the Blind*. New York: Julian Messner, 1951. Although this biography was designed for a popular reading audience, it is the result of fairly extensive research into relevant resources in French and other languages. These lend an impression of historical accuracy, as well as some sense of the technical details of

Braille's system, to what is otherwise a simple account of Braille's life.
Mackenzie, Sir Clutha. *World Braille Usage*. Paris: UNESCO, 1953. Provides a historical review of the processes that were followed over a century's time to alter the original system of Braille in order to meet the needs
of blind readers and writers of Asian and African languages. It includes a
brief review of Braille's life and work as well as a history of the World
Braille Council.
Paulson, William R. *Enlightenment, Romanticism, and the Blind in France*.
Princeton, N.J.: Princeton University Press, 1987. A scholarly historical
study of changing cultural values that affected French attitudes toward the
blind from the mid-eighteenth through to the mid-nineteenth centuries. It
is in Paulson's book that the question of prejudices, particularly toward
the presumed mystical inner nature of the blind, is developed most fully.

Byron D. Cannon

DONATO BRAMANTE
Donato di Pascuccio d'Antonio

Born: 1444; Monte Asdruvaldo, near Urbino, Papal States
Died: April 11, 1514; Rome
Area of Achievement: Architecture
Contribution: One of the greatest architects of the Italian Renaissance, Bramante stands out for the pure classicism of his buildings. His influence extended throughout Europe. Except for the long nave, St. Peter's in Rome is basically his design.

Early Life

Donato di Pascuccio d'Antonio took his father's nickname "il Bramante" ("the dreamer") as his cognomen. At first a painter, he may have studied at Mantua with Andrea Mantegna and with Piero della Francesca at Urbino. Their influence is visible in Bramante's interest in the science of perspective. At Mantua, he may have met the architect Leon Battista Alberti, designing there his noted church of S. Andrea.

In the 1470's, Bramante primarily designed architectural decorations for interiors and façades. In the new ducal palace at Urbino in about 1476, he helped decorate the *Studiolo* of the Duke of Urbino. In this small office, the walls are covered with pictures formed by inlaid wood of different tones so as to create an atmosphere both of intimacy and of illusionary space. Bramante also made illustrations of illusionistic perspective in the duke's chapel and library.

At Urbino, Bramante had access to the graceful architectural plans of Luciano Laurana, patronized by the Duke of Urbino along with Piero della Francesca. Alberti may have contributed to the design of the new palace, influencing Bramante, who would soon become an architect. Alberti's classically inspired treatise on architecture, as well as those of Filarete and Francesco di Giorgio, were certainly available as manuals for Bramante. In the Palazzo del Podestà in Bergamo in 1477, Bramante created the illusion of "opening" a wall by painting on it a loggia or corridor, with philosophers seated between the columns.

From about 1479 to 1499, Bramante was in Milan. His first project there was to construct the three-aisled, barrel-vaulted, domed church of S. Maria presso (near) S. Satiro, a diminutive ninth century Carolingian church. About this same time (1481) can be dated the large print prepared by Prevedari. It contains fanciful classical architectural themes and is signed by Bramante.

Commissioned by Cardinal Ascanio Sforza, Bramante's plan for the cathedral of Pavia in 1488 foreshadowed in boldness his future conception for St. Peter's. A high dome was to rest on eight massive piers, creating a large central space. The choir was to be cruciform, its three arms ending in apses, the whole arranged in a harmonious hierarchy of proportions. In 1492, Bramante left the project, which was completed after his death and much altered by later architects.

Bramante designed the loggia (or *ponticella*) of Ludovico Sforza and decorated some rooms in Castello Sforzesco, of which all that remains is his painting of mythical Argus. The Brera Pinacoteca contains paintings certainly by Bramante: *Christ at the Pillar* and eight frescoes of artists and warriors which, with his *Heraclitus* and *Democritus*, once decorated a room in Milan's Palazzo Panigarola. In these, Bramante painted shadows which reflected the actual light source and give the figures an impression of three-dimensionality.

Leonardo da Vinci came to Milan in 1482, and his writings manifest a respect for Bramante. The latter may have learned to appreciate the "central space" concept from Leonardo's sketches of Greek-cross type churches. Both worked for the monks of S. Maria delle Grazie, where Leonardo painted the *Last Supper* and where, from 1492 to 1497, Bramante constructed a choir and transepts. The crossing of nave and transepts here is a spacious open square surmounted by a dome-on-pendentives spanning sixty-five feet. Outside, this interior dome appears as a sixteen-windowed cylinder or drum with sloping roof and a lantern. The crossing was planned as a crypt area for the ducal Sforza family of Milan, Bramante's employers.

During these same years, Bramante designed, for Cardinal Sforza, Duke Ludovico's brother, several cloisters for the Abbey of S. Ambrogio (1492-1497), some additions to the ducal palace at Vigevano, where he resided while in Milan at least until 1495, and a west façade for the abbey church at Abbiategrasso (1497). He also designed a partial city plan, whose main feature was a large square like that of S. Marco in Venice, but here serving as a court area between palace and cathedral. The work was interrupted by the French invasion of Milan in 1499, which relieved Bramante of several unfinished projects.

Life's Work

Also in 1499, Bramante arrived in a Rome electric with building activity in preparation for the coming jubilee year. The popes had even authorized the use of the Colosseum and other ancient monuments as stone quarries. Bramante received immediate employment to design a cloister for S. Maria della Pace, a two-storeyed arcade or loggia that on the ground level appears as a wall in which round arches have been cut. Its Ionic pilasters continue above, supporting a horizontal architrave. Between these, slender columns ride directly above the centers of the arches below, creating twice as many openings above as below.

Bramante's famous *Tempietto* absorbed him in 1501-1502. As a sort of monumental reliquary built upon the spot where Saint Peter was reputedly crucified, it had the round design and central plan customary for churches commemorating martyrdom. It is a two-storeyed drum of only fifteen feet in diameter, with a dome and a lantern. Around it is a Doric colonnade supporting a classical triglyph-metope architrave. Above, the drum is pierced by alternating windows and shell-topped niches. It achieves perfectly the avowed Renaissance aim to imitate the dignity of classical antiquity.

Appalled by the wholesale destruction of ancient Rome in the interests of Holy Year, Bramante campaigned for preservation of the past, or at least of an exact plan of imperial Rome. His first years there saw him devoted to drawings and three-dimensional projections of ancient monuments (his own new technique). His study of antiquity taught him much about Roman building secrets, most notably that of inserting brick ribs into walls before filling them with concrete. The new St. Peter's, built on a scale many times greater than normal, would depend on this knowledge.

Bramante's career in Rome (1500-1514) is closely tied to the regime of Pope Julius II (1503-1513). The architect rearranged the streets of Rome for this pope, receiving the nickname "Ruinante" because of his destruction of old streets and of so much of old St. Peter's. Julius invited the congenial, well-read architect to accompany him on military campaigns so that they could enjoy evenings of Dante together. In 1504, Bramante designed the courtyard of St. Damasus with three levels of columned arcades, to ensure papal privacy.

In 1505, he won the competition to design and supervise the construction of the new St. Peter's, to be the crowning glory of Christendom. Fundraising for the project would destroy Christian unity. The fourth century Constantinian edifice was falling apart, and under Pope Nicholas V (1447-1455) a major restoration was begun. Julius decided on a complete reconstruction, the domed choir of which would contain his own massive tomb carved by Michelangelo with forty figures (the *Moses* is the masterpiece of a much-reduced monument in the church of St. Peter in Chains).

Bramante's concept was a Greek-cross design with a gigantic central hemispheric dome flanked by four equal naves ending in apses. Each corner would have a chapel surmounted by smaller cupolas, and, farther out, four towers would give the building the form of a perfect square with the four apsidal projections. This original design can be seen in the Uffizi Gallery, Florence, and in Caradosso's official souvenir medal. Though finally altered into a Latin cross, the present basilica retains Bramante's spirit and his entirely new massive scale. At his death, only the central piers for supporting the dome were in place. Significant but largely unnoticed is Bramante's bedrock substructure for this colossal edifice. Remarkable, too, is his sculptural modeling of walls. This awareness of the "plastic potentiality" of a wall, also used by Filippo Brunelleschi, was late Roman in origin and important in subsequent Baroque development.

Nicholas V also began the refurbishment of the papal residence into the imposing Vatican palace. Bramante's last important design (1514) was the Palazzo Caprini, planned as his own private residence. It is better known as the House of Raphael, since it was bought in 1517 by the painter.

Summary

Otto H. Förster, a scholar of Donato Bramante, has urged the theory that Bramante in 1510, and not Raphael, was the author of a treatise on the architecture of imperial Rome addressed to Julius II. It is full of confidence that the dome of St. Peter's could rival that of the Pantheon, the scale of which Raphael and others found impossible to contemplate. In it the author is critical of the Palazzo della Cancellaria, a building often attributed incorrectly to Bramante. It is, in fact, difficult to verify Bramante's part in many structures because of the damage and reconstructions of the centuries.

Despite his reputation for magnanimity, Bramante did not get on well with Michelangelo, who in a letter of 1542 voiced the suspicion that the older artist had enviously persuaded Julius to pull him away from the precious sculptural project for the great tomb in order to paint in the Sistine. Still, in a letter of 1555 the sculptor remarked, "Bramante was as gifted an architect as anyone from antiquity until now. . . . His plan for St. Peter's was clear and pure, full of light. . . . Whoever departs from Bramante's plan departs from the truth." Thus, one may assert Bramante's influence over Michelangelo the architect. Sebastiano Serlio imitated Bramante's use of columns; Andrea Palladio's S. Giorgio Maggiore in Venice manifests Bramantean influence.

In 1517, Bramante was satirized as arriving at the Gates of Heaven and immediately proposing improvements. He would replace the difficult road to paradise by a spiral ramp so that Heaven could be attained on horseback; "and I would tear down this Paradise and build a new one with finer accommodations for the blessed. If you agree, I'll stay; if not, I'll head for Inferno." Thus were perceived the confident assertiveness and integrity of Bramante at about the time of his death in 1514.

Bibliography

Baroni, Constantino, ed. *Bramante*. Bergamo: Istituto Italiano d'Arti Grafiche, 1944. In Italian, a fifty-page biography. Useful for its 134 excellent black-and-white photographs.

Burckhardt, Jacob. *The Architecture of the Italian Renaissance*. Translated by James Palmes. Chicago: University of Chicago Press, 1985. Offers a useful organization into genres but the book's style is difficult. Excellent illustrations and bibliography.

Durant, Will. *The Renaissance*. New York: Simon & Schuster, 1953. Views Bramante in the context of Renaissance Italy. A very readable appreciation.

Förster, Otto H. *Bramante*. Vienna: A. Schroll, 1956. The best book on Bramante, in German. Useful for its numerous illustrations.

Pevsner, Nikolaus. *An Outline of European Architecture*. Baltimore: Penguin Books, 1963. A good survey of major architectural achievements and theory. Bramante is seen in a wider European perspective.

Rossiter, Stuart, ed. *Rome and Environs*. Chicago: Rand McNally, 1971. Thorough descriptions of art and architecture in Rome for the scholarly traveler. Bramante's buildings receive generous and detailed coverage. Identifies all buildings in which Bramante may have had some role.

Daniel C. Scavone

ANTON BRUCKNER

Born: September 4, 1824; Ansfelden, Austro-Hungarian Empire
Died: October 11, 1896; Vienna, Austro-Hungarian Empire
Area of Achievement: Music
Contribution: Rising from modest rural origins, Bruckner first established himself as one of the leading organists of his time, then persevered in his creative work to produce a great series of choral and symphonic works. Musically eloquent and possessing a unique sense of spiritual aspiration, the finest of Bruckner's large-scale compositions belong to the essential repertoire of nineteenth century music.

Early Life

Anton Bruckner was born to Anton and Theresa Bruckner on September 4, 1824, in the village of Ansfelden, in the Austro-Hungarian Empire. His family was for generations engaged in modest occupations such as broom-making and innkeeping, but both Bruckner's father and his grandfather had become schoolteachers, a position of modest status but substantial responsibilities. One of the tasks of a schoolteacher in those days was to oversee the basic musical education of his students. Thus, it was Bruckner's father who first instructed him in singing and in the playing of various instruments. Though young Anton seems to have played a child's violin as early as age four, he showed no special talent until the age of ten, when his godfather and cousin, Johann Weiss, took him into his own home in the nearby town of Hörsching to instruct him in the playing of the organ. One likely cause for Anton's move may have been the crowded Bruckner household; he was the first of eleven children, though only five survived to maturity.

Under his cousin's guidance, Anton studied the rudiments of music theory and continued his organ studies. In 1836, he composed his first organ work, a prelude which suggests that Bruckner knew some of the music of Franz Joseph Haydn and Wolfgang Amadeus Mozart, the foremost Austrian composers of the late eighteenth century. Later, Bruckner was to be influenced by the music of Johann Sebastian Bach and the Counter-Reformation master Giovanni Palestrina, but his months of study in his cousin's home were cut short when Anton was needed at home to deputize for his ailing father in the schoolroom. In 1837, the elder Bruckner died, leaving Anton nominally the head of the family.

With surprising resourcefulness, Anton's mother immediately arranged for him to become a student and choirboy at the Augustinian monastery of St. Florian, which boasted a splendid Baroque church containing one of the finest organs of the time. The young student flourished in the environment of the monastery and was able to continue his musical studies with the church organist. His progress as an instrumentalist was rapid, and although little is known of his intellectual growth it is likely that Bruckner was a diligent student, for in October, 1840, he left St. Florian to enter the preparatory course for public school teachers in Linz and was graduated from it the following year without having to repeat the course, as was usually necessary. In Linz, Bruckner was exposed to an increasing range of musical influences. It was there that he heard for the first time a symphony by Ludwig van Beethoven, but he did not record the impression it made upon him.

Upon completing the preparatory course for teachers, Bruckner was assigned as an assistant teacher to the small town of Windhaag, where he endured appalling conditions of employment. Living in the teacher's house, he had to eat his meals with the servant girl. In addition to classroom duties, he was required to ring the church bells at 4:00 A.M., help the village priest dress for services, and work in the fields during the harvest. After fifteen months in Windhaag, an understanding school inspector transferred Bruckner to nearby Kronstorf. At this time, his only stated ambition was to become a schoolteacher, despite evidence that he was capable of either a religious or a musical vocation. Bruckner's need for financial security and his sense of responsibility toward his needy family were undoubtedly factors in his reluctance to declare an interest in a career as a performing musician; even his appointment as assistant organist at St. Florian in 1849 did not quell his insecurity about abandoning a steady, if ill-paying, job as public school teacher. After assuming the permanent post of organist at St. Florian in 1851, Bruckner was still reluctant to entrust his future to music, and he continued to enroll in preparatory courses in order to be qualified for high school teaching. He even applied, unsuccessfully, for a routine clerical position in 1853.

Despite his insecurity about finances, Bruckner's growth as a musician was steady. In 1856, while living in Linz, where he had recently been appointed cathedral organist, Bruckner began studying with the noted Viennese musician Simon Sechter. This elderly organist and conservatory professor was the author of a treatise on musical composition which codified rigorous rules of harmony and counterpoint based upon the musical practices of past centuries.

In accepting private students, Sechter requested that they set aside creative work in composition during their period of study with him, and Bruckner largely complied with this condition for the six years of Sechter's rigid but benevolent instruction. Bruckner's sacrifice was perhaps less significant than it was for other musicians, since he continued improvising at the organ, in itself a creative experience akin to composition. Music historians have regretted that Bruckner seems always to have been indifferent to writing down even the outlines of his acclaimed organ improvisations, and Bruckner himself once remarked upon this fact by saying "One does not write as one plays."

Life's Work

After completing his study with Sechter—which was carried on by mail and in occasional vists to Vienna—Bruckner's creative output increased remarkably, but at age thirty-nine he continued to seek instruction from established musicians. His next teacher was an opera conductor, Otto Kitzler, who introduced Bruckner to the work of Richard Wagner, the German composer of monumental "music-dramas" such as *Tristan und Isolde* (1859) and *Der Ring des Nibelungen* (1874). The influence of Wagner's music and personality upon Bruckner is as unquestionable as it difficult to assess. Wagner's music released powerful forces in Bruckner's creative personality, but it is clear that the younger composer did not comprehend the literary and ideological content of Wagner's work, even after making Wagner's acquaintance in 1865. Wagner was a sophisticated, cosmopolitan personality, while Bruckner was a man with country schooling and manners; it is a testimony to the unique genius of each that they were able to appreciate each other. Bruckner's formal, even obsequious manner may well have been a source of concealed amusement to the self-possessed Wagner.

Bruckner's career as a composer had blossomed in the early 1860's with the composition of a Mass in D Minor and two symphonies. The second of these symphonies, long forgotten by the composer, was later acknowledged by him as "only an attempt," and numbered as "Symphony 0." The composition of Bruckner's great chain of nine symphonies began in 1865 with the Symphony No. 1 in C Minor. Two more masses followed in the years 1866-1868 before the completion of the Symphony No. 2 in C Minor in 1872. This work begins the first of two great creative waves in Bruckner's mature career, encompassing work on the second, third, fourth, and fifth symphonies between 1871 and 1876. By all standards, this first period of mastery occurred very late in the composer's life; at the time of the completion of Symphony No. 4 in E-flat Major, he had just passed his fiftieth birthday, and although he was enjoying professional success as an organist, choral composer, and, to a lesser extent, choral director, his life was a lonely one. In 1867, he had suffered a nervous breakdown and spent three months recovering at a hydropathic establishment in Bad Kreuzen, where he was assailed by thoughts of suicide and a mania for numbers. It is reported that he would count the stars or the leaves on a tree and was possessed by the idea that he had to bail out the Danube River. Though simple overwork contributed to Bruckner's depression, his inherently solitary and often-melancholy disposition magnified his sense of his life's disappointments. On the personal side, his utter inability to find a partner in marriage weighed unusually heavily upon him. Bruckner was a very religious man, even by the standards of his time, and he would not countenance a sexual relationship outside marriage. Since his romantic interests were rather ineffectually aimed at young women aged sixteen to nineteen, Bruckner's search for a mate seemed almost designed to fail.

Later, Bruckner was unable to take professional disappointments in stride. While the opposition to his music by powerful critics such as Eduard Hanslick was often malicious, the occasional incomprehension of his scores by conductors and orchestral players was essentially a transitory problem, and much of his music was well received. The episode of mental collapse he experienced in 1867-1868 was fortunately not to be repeated, but Bruckner continued to be plagued by doubts about his work, which he sought to resolve by repeated and often ill-advised revision of his scores. The creative period of the early 1870's was followed by a period of revision in 1876 through 1879. He regained his confidence and composed a series of masterpieces in the years 1879 through 1887, including his *Te Deum* (1883-1884) and the magisterial Symphony No. 8 (1884-1886), but another period of revisions ensued in 1887, lasting until 1891.

The most frequently reproduced photographs of Bruckner show him in later life as a dignified and remote man, posing rather formally in his studio—often seated next to the great Bösendorfer grand piano that was left to him by a friend of earlier years. With close-cropped hair and baggy trousers (said to aid an organist's foot-pedalling), Bruckner had nothing of the appearance of a typical artist of his era. He seemed to his friends almost completely unaware of the effect of his awkward appearance and manners, and he was once admonished to take care in dressing so as not to disadvantage himself in his professional life.

Bruckner's formative years occurred during the reign of the Austrian Emperor Franz Josef, a period of unrelieved political conservatism and social rigidity; reflecting this background, Bruckner approached most relationships in an archaic and servile manner that irritated many of his acquaintances. Nevertheless, as a professor of music theory at the University of Vienna and as a private teacher, he gained the love and respect of his students not only by his competence but also by his humanity, which must have been all but invisible to the public.

The growing recognition given Bruckner's music in the 1880's was a partial consolation for the relative neglect he had suffered, which can be measured by reference to the fact that his main rival in the field of symphonic composition, Johannes Brahms, received enormous sums for the publication of his four symphonies, while few of Bruckner's works were published in his lifetime, and then only with subsidies from friends and admirers. The burden of Bruckner's many professional responsibilities seems to have had little effect on his ability to complete massive compositions. By 1890, however, in declining health, he gave up the last of his teaching positions to devote his full efforts to the completion of his Ninth Symphony. This work was intended to bear the dedication, *Dem lieben Gott . . .* , "To the dear Lord, if he will accept it," revealing a faith that is perhaps as naïve as it is profound. The first three movements of the Ninth Symphony were composed during the period 1891 through 1894, and the fourth was begun in late 1894. By that time, Bruckner had accepted the emperor's offer of accommodation in an annex of the Belvedere Palace, where he labored on the finale of the symphony until days before his death on October 11, 1896. Although speculative completions of the finale have been recorded, the symphony has been performed for generations as a complex but unified work of three movements, concluding with an adagio that embodies, in its final passages, a profound and valedictory innocence.

Summary

Anton Bruckner's great works were composed after a long musical apprenticeship, and they display a technical and expressive consistency which makes possible a degree of generalization about them. A Bruckner symphony tends to be expansive, developing on a scale where the formal logic of late eighteenth and early nineteenth century music is of limited use as an organizing principle. The grandeur of Bruckner's musical thought was often expressed in compositions of demanding length which some listeners perceive as formless. In reality, Bruckner's music is highly organized, but it is unusually complex and polymorphous, and seldom adheres to familiar forms. Many of Bruckner's obvious structural ideas, such as periodicity within movements, dramatic contrast of blocks of thematic material, and complete rests within movements (which the composer compared, perhaps only half seriously, to pausing to take a deep breath before saying something important), were novel in their time and were often remarked upon disparagingly.

Bruckner's harmony became increasingly daring in his mature compositions, but in this he was not out of step with contemporary trends. His harmonic practice has been often attributed to the influence of Wagner's music, but it might also be regarded as Bruckner's inevitable victory over the rigidity of Sechter's rules. Similarly, Bruckner was able to turn a conventional mastery of contrapuntal technique into a creative resource, achieving remarkable powers of thematic metamorphosis and large-scale integration. In all areas of endeavor, Bruckner blended orthodoxy with inspired inventiveness. Many of his contemporaries, acknowledging his idiosyncrasies but not his inspiration, thought him to be a naïve musician, but the more discerning of his colleagues, such as Gustav Mahler, knew the stature of the man from their earliest experience of his music. The public was soon to follow in its appreciation of Bruckner's singular genius. He is recognized as the composer of a magisterial body of music that stands somewhat outside its time, looking as much to the past as to the future, but which forms part of the great continuity of European music.

Bibliography

Barford, Philip. *Bruckner Symphonies*. London: British Broadcasting Corporation, 1978. One of the BBC Music Guides, this slim volume discusses the symphonies in terms understandable to the layperson and with a minimum of musical examples. A brief concluding section, "Understanding Bruckner: A Personal View," is excellent.

Doernberg, Erwin. *The Life and Symphonies of Anton Bruckner*. London: Barrie & Rockliff, 1960. This solid study, divided into independent sections dealing first with the composer's life and then with his symphonies, frees Bruckner from many of the character stereotypes that for so long created an almost unbridgeable gap between perceptions of the man and his music. Excerpts from Bruckner's letters are provided in sufficient quantity for the reader to imagine something of his personal trials and his musical triumphs.

Schönzeler, Hans-Hubert. *Bruckner*. London: Calder and Boyars, 1970. The author is a musicologist as well as a conductor who has been an advocate of Bruckner's music, and his account of the composer is notably sympathetic to Bruckner's cause. The book stands apart from others in its quanity of useful illustrations. There is no bibliography, but a chronological list of works is provided.

Simpson, Robert. *The Essence of Bruckner*. 2d ed. London: Victor Gollancz, 1977. This book is the product of twenty-five years of reflection upon Bruckner's symphonies by a noted British composer. Each work is examined in detail, satisfying the most exacting analytical standard. A concluding chapter, "Reflections," is essential for the nonspecialist reader.

Watson, Derek. *Bruckner*. London: J. M. Dent & Sons, 1975. The growth of interest in Bruckner's music in the English-speaking world brought about the publication of this new account of the composer in the Master Musicians series. Readable. The many appendices are very useful.

Wolff, Werner. *Anton Bruckner: Rustic Genius*. New York: Cooper Square Publishers, 1973. The author, whose father was the founder of the Berlin Philharmonic Orchestra, met Bruckner in the early 1890's, when the composer was invited to dinner. As conductor, author, and lecturer, Wolff later championed Bruckner's cause. The bibliography dates from the original edition (1942) and consists almost exclusively of German-language entries.

C. S. McConnell

PIETER BRUEGEL, THE ELDER

Born: c. 1525; near Brée, Brabant
Died: September 5, 1569; Brussels
Area of Achievement: Art
Contribution: In an era when portraiture dominated, Bruegel teamed his subjects with their larger environment, greatly elevating landscape art. Bruegel's miniaturist style also chronicled the many facets of everyday sixteenth century Flemish life.

Early Life

Pieter Bruegel, called the Elder, hailed from the Brabant region, the Flemish countryside which straddles the southern part of the Netherlands and northern Belgium. Little can be ascertained about his early life, or when and where it exactly began. Although 1525 is often cited as the year of Bruegel's birth, scholars have hypothesized various dates ranging from 1520 to 1530. When the artist arrived in Antwerp to commence his career, he was listed as Peeter Brueghels. Since country-born Flemings often lacked surnames, one near-contemporary, the early seventeenth century biographer Carel van Mander, states that the artist adopted "Bruegel" or "Brueghels" from his place of birth. Other scholars speculate that it was a family name, although such a nomenclature often was preceded by "van." The artist's origin also remains unclear. Three Flemish towns bore some form of the name Bruegel, and at least the same number of families shared the appellation. Since two of the towns are close together, near the city of Brée in modern Belgium, this area frequently has been cited as Bruegel's birthplace.

Excepting the folktales which come from each of the artist's alleged hometowns, his biography begins in 1545, when he first apprenticed with Pieter Coecke van Aelst, a successful painter, architect, and ornamental/tapestry designer. Bruegel's master maintained operations in both Brussels and Antwerp, and subscribed to the Italian Renaissance style then dominating art. It remains difficult to trace Bruegel's creative evolution during his apprenticeship because guild rules dictated that students could not sign or sell any of their work; they were totally under the direction of the masters. Yet some very tangible benefits resulted from Bruegel's association with Coecke. The master's wife, Mayken Verhulst, was a talented miniaturist who may have imparted some of her skills to Bruegel. The apprentice also married the Coeckes' daughter, Mayken, some years later, in 1563. After the death of both Bruegels, Mayken Verhulst instructed the couple's young, artistic sons, Pieter and Jan.

Life's Work

Coecke's sudden demise in December, 1550, led his apprentice to Hieronymus Cock, a copper-plate engraver who became less known for his personal artistry than for a rare ability to capitalize on the spirit of the day. Antwerp at mid-century was Europe's most active commercial center, attracting traders from all over the Continent and spawning a cosmopolitan, consumer-oriented existence. Art proved to be a major beneficiary of the economic climate. Realizing the public's increasing desire for affordable creations, Cock opened the Four Winds publishing house. The owner/ entrepreneur successfully marketed prints of popular artists, such as Hieronymus Bosch, and used a broader approach to fulfill the demand for art: Cock engaged young, local talents to execute new works.

Bruegel thus arrived at Four Winds. Within several months, he became a master in the Antwerp chapter of the Guild of St. Luke, a brotherhood including painters, graphic artists, ornamental and interior designers, glassworkers, and others. Most craftspersons of the era proved to be extremely versatile. Bruegel himself was to draw and paint in oils; he also skillfully engraved at least one of his own works, though print-related processes usually were reserved for other craftspersons.

One advantage of Bruegel's association with the publisher Cock was that his employer dispatched him to Italy in 1552, possibly in search of new subject matter or because the trip might yield popular Italian-style art. During the journey, Bruegel witnessed the burning of the Calabrian seaport, Reggio, by Süleyman's Turks. The scene is later documented in *Sea Battle in the Straits of Messina*, Bruegel's only real historic painting.

Besides the exposure to Italy—which inspired several seascapes—the artist gained much from his trip across the Alps. Mountain vistas often appear in his work, with results that never could have been attained had he not ventured forth from the Flemish flatlands. It also is said that Bruegel acquired a new perspective: His paintings frequently seem to be executed from a higher ground, looking down. This approach, perhaps a manifestation of his Alpine travels, was rather uncommon during the mid-1500's.

Returning to Antwerp in 1553, Bruegel continued his employment with Four Winds, creating drawings largely for public consumption. Some of his earlier works, such as the *Seven Deadly Sins* series (1556-1557), show elements of fantasy. Scholars thus debate whether Bruegel was creatively motivated by Bosch (1450-1516) or whether he imitated the established artist to satisfy public demand. Many factors may explain Bruegel's attraction to fantasy: a possible escape from politics, particularly Catholic Spain's harsh rule over the Reformist-leaning Low Countries; the superstition and magical beliefs which sometimes dominated daily life; or the artist's inclination toward social commentary and satire. Yet, as one expert notes, Bruegel rendered *The Temptation of Saint Anthony* without signing it. A previous Bosch engraving bore the same title and a similar style. Commercial factors therefore could have prevailed in some of Bruegel's earlier drawings.

Although association with the publishing firm perhaps muted the artist's powers of self-expression (at least through 1557), the connection served him well in other ways. Four Winds, complete with coffeehouse, became an intellectual center and mecca for art dealers. The atmosphere netted Bruegel excellent contacts, including a string of patrons who supported his best-known work—the oil paintings created from 1557 until the end of his life.

The biographer van Mander describes Bruegel's steadfast friendship with one patron, Hans Franckert: With this Franckert, Bruegel often went out into the country to see the peasants at their fairs and weddings.

> Disguised as peasants they brought gifts like the other guests, claiming relationship or kinship with the bride or groom. Here Bruegel delighted in observing the droll behavior of the peasants, how they ate, danced, drank, capered or made love.

Perhaps the artist derives his greatest twentieth century renown from these rustic scenes. Combining peasant life with miniaturist technique, he produced his acclaimed *The Blue Cloak* in 1559. The painting illustrates anywhere from seventy-five to one hundred sayings common during the sixteenth century. Some, such as a variation on the "he speaks from both sides of his mouth" theme, continue to be used. *The Battle Between Carnival and Lent* (1559) and *Children's Games* (1560) give further substance to this Bruegelian genre. The two paintings reveal literally hundreds of adults and youths, respectively, amusing themselves. Given the abundant activity and immense cast of characters illustrated, it is interesting to note that each of the three works only measures about four feet by five feet.

Later paintings concentrate more on smaller-scale activities. *Peasant Wedding* (1568) and *Peasant Dance* (1568) are well-known examples of Bruegel's ability to make the everyday, bucolic life-style of sixteenth century Flanders accessible to modern viewers. *Parable of the Blind* (1568) and *The Cripples* (1568) hold additional virtues. With its theme of "the blind leading the blind," the former painting depicts six men, each suffering from a different form of eye disease. Similarly, *The Cripples* shows various implements used by the era's handicapped. These subjects also sport foxtails, a sign of the Beggars, a political order seeking independence from Spain.

Indeed, scholars debate the level of sociopolitical commentary found in Bruegel's work. Some say that he moved from Antwerp to Brussels in 1563 partly to escape the volatile atmosphere pervading the port city. The primary reason for the relocation, however, remains simple: marriage. According to van Mander, Bruegel was permitted to marry Mayken Coecke only on the condition that he move to Brussels. The artist had previously been living with a servant girl, and apparently his new family wanted him to forget the relationship.

Subsequent to his marriage and move, Bruegel became a more prolific painter, perhaps because of his distance from the commercial lure of Four

Winds. His work included landscapes populated by lively peasants, as well as biblical scenes. Some of the religious themes, however, may have masked political intentions. Soldiers garbed in sixteenth century regalia, marching through Alpine paths and snowy fields far from the Holy Land, dominate *The Road to Calvary* (1564) and *The Massacre of the Innocents* (1566). Artists of the era sometimes placed historical figures in contemporary surroundings, but Bruegel's inspiration remains subject to speculation. With orders from King Philip II of Spain, the Duke of Alba raised twenty thousand soldiers to invade the Low Countries during the mid-1560's, just as Bruegel executed his somber themes.

Arguments about Bruegel's politics notwithstanding, the last years of his short life proved to be the most successful. A wealthy patron, Niclaes Jonghelinck, offered the artist his first commission: a series of six "seasons" paintings to be used for the decoration of a mansion. Out of this endeavor came *Hunters in the Snow* (1565), perhaps Bruegel's finest work. Public recognition soon followed. Shortly after 1569 commenced, the Brussels City Council advanced the artist money for a series of paintings commemorating the opening of a new canal. The paintings remained unfinished: Bruegel died on September 5, 1569.

Summary

Pieter Bruegel, the Elder, left behind approximately 150 drawings, fifty oil paintings, various prints, and a legacy: his two sons, Pieter, the Younger (1564-1638), and Jan (1568-1625). His namesake largely became known as an imitator of his father's work; Jan, however, helped to usher in a new creative era with his elaborate, Baroque nature subjects. Nicknamed "Velvet" Brueghel (both sons reinstated the "h" in their family nomenclature), he also developed a lifelong friendship and collaborated with one of the era's most outstanding painters, Peter Paul Rubens. The Bruegel art dynasty, in fact, survived for about two hundred years.

The reputation of Pieter, the Elder, outlived him, too, but not by more than a few decades. Changing trends—some spawned by the heated political events occuring during the mid-1500's—rendered his work unfashionable. Interest in Bruegel only resurfaced at the dawn of the twentieth century, with the very first exhibit of the artist's work in 1902. Perhaps nostalgia for a diminishing peasant life-style fostered this revival. Surely one of Bruegel's major contributions was in replacing elite faces with those of the rural lower classes. Yet, while Bruegel painted people, he refused to confine himself to the then-dominant portraiture. His crowded street scenes do not so much depict individuals as a social landscape. Bruegel also forced his vibrant peasants to share attention with the wheat-covered fields and steep Alpine paths which offered the essence of human activity.

Bibliography
Delevoy, Robert L. *Bruegel*. Translated by Stuart Gilbert. Lausanne, Switzerland: Editions D'Art Albert Skira, 1959. Using an advanced approach, this book explores Bruegel's artistic techniques as well as the content of his work. A biographical chapter debates various theories about the artist's life. Also included are an extensive bibliography, a list of major Bruegel exhibitions, translated documents, and color plates.

Denis, Valentin, ed. *All the Paintings of Pieter Bruegel*. Translated by Paul Colacicchi. New York: Hawthorn Books, 1961. A catalog of Bruegel's works containing 160 plates, this volume cites lost paintings and those which may not have been created by the artist. An introductory chapter presents Bruegel as one who withstood prevalent artistic influences and only gradually introduced his concepts into the mainstream. Also featured are selected criticism, biographical notes (timeline), and a brief bibliography.

Foote, Timothy. *The World of Bruegel c.1525-1569*. New York: Time-Life Books, 1968. Portrays the artist as an innovator who, nevertheless, reflected—rather than attempted to comment on—social conditions. Also explores Bruegel's predecessors, peers, and successors; contemporary artistic trends; and the politics and religious attitudes of the sixteenth century. Contains a bibliography, a listing of other European masters, and both color and black-and-white plates.

Glück, Gustav. *Peter Brueghel, the Elder*. New York: George Braziller, 1936. Depicts Bruegel as having been a nonjudgmental, realistic painter of a chaotic world. Emphasizes the master's artistic progression and increasing ability to convey nature accurately. Glück also argues that Bruegel defined later genres of Dutch painting. This oversize book features forty-nine superb color plates and a bibliography.

Klein, H. Arthur, and Mina C. Klein. *Peter Bruegel, the Elder: Artist of Abundance*. New York: Macmillan, 1968. Bruegel appears as a social critic in this general biography. Details of the artist's environment and contemporary life-style are explored. Heavily illustrated in black and white, the book uses both Bruegel's works and those of his peers. Also contains a short color section and list of American museums housing Bruegel paintings.

Lynn C. Kronzek

FILIPPO BRUNELLESCHI

Born: 1377; Florence
Died: April 15, 1446; Florence
Areas of Achievement: Architecture, art, and engineering
Contribution: Brunelleschi's architectural accomplishments, as well as his
dedication to the principles of perspective, established a vigorous new
classical Renaissance style that influenced building design for centuries.

Early Life

Filippo Brunelleschi was born in Florence in 1377, the second of three
sons of Ser Brunellesco di Lippi and Giuliana degli Spini, the daughter of an
established Florentine banking family. His father was a notary and middle-
level public official frequently employed in various capacities by the republican government. Young Filippo thus grew up in a household heavily involved in the complex politics of Tuscany's leading city. His elder brother,
Tommaso, became a goldsmith and died in 1431, while his younger brother,
Giovanni, entered the priesthood and died in 1422.

As a child, Brunelleschi received the traditional education of boys of his
class. Although his father may have wished him to follow him in a notary
career, young Filippo early exhibited a penchant for art and mechanics. The
elder Brunelleschi consequently apprenticed his second son to the Silk Guild
for training as a goldsmith. His training there included a study of literature
and the abacus as well as rigorous mathematical instruction. In 1398, Brunelleschi applied for registration as a goldsmith with the Silk Guild and was
admitted as a full master six years later.

Even before this last event, the young artist had established a reputation
for himself as one of the most promising figures in the Florentine artistic
community. In the early 1400's, he made several silver figures for the altar
of the cathedral in Pistoia. Two busts of prophets and two full-length figures
of saints survive from this endeavor.

One of the turning points in Brunelleschi's early career concerned his
participation in the 1401 competition sponsored by the Signory and Guild of
Merchants for the commission to do a series of relief sculptures for the north
doors of the Florence cathedral baptistery. Brunelleschi was one of the two
finalists, but in 1402, the judges selected a panel submitted by his fellow
goldsmith Lorenzo Ghiberti as the winner. Brunelleschi's competition panels
on the theme of the sacrifice of Isaac have been preserved in the National
Museum of Florence. Brunelleschi's defeat in the competition had important
consequences for his future. Virtually the rest of Ghiberti's long career was
consumed by the task of the north doors and a subsequent set for the eastern
entry. Brunelleschi found himself free for other endeavors, and he increasingly became more interested in architecture in preference to sculpture.

Life's Work

Although he was active in many artistic and engineering projects, Brunelleschi's main contribution during the last four decades of his life was in the field of architectural inventiveness. He most probably left Florence shortly after his 1402 defeat and spent several years in Rome with his fellow Florentine, the sculptor Donatello. In Rome he studied ancient buildings in minute detail, making careful drawings of classic arches, vaulting, and other architectural features.

The Florence to which he returned in the early 1400's provided a fertile field of opportunities for the energetic and talented young Brunelleschi. The city's wealthy elite had an increasing thirst to commission city palaces, country villas, and burial chapels. Even more important, the civic Humanists dominating the Florentine government were eager to employ painters, sculptors, and architects to make Florence the premier city in Italy. The most imporant project to the city fathers was the completion of the great cathedral of Santa Maria del Fiore, an undertaking that gave Brunelleschi his most challenging and famous commission.

Begun in 1296 and designed in the traditional Tuscan Gothic style, the cathedral essentially stood finished by the late fourteenth century except for the dilemma of constructing a dome to cover the 140-foot octagonal space created by the crossing at the east end. No previous architect had found a solution to the technical problems and expense entailed by this problem. It remained for Brunelleschi, who had been involved with various facets of the cathedral's construction as early as 1404, to provide the answer.

In 1418, the cathedral's officials announced a competition for a workable design for the dome. Based on his studies of ancient Roman and Byzantine vaulting, Brunelleschi proposed an innovative solution that entailed constructing the cupola without the traditional costly wooden centering or exterior scaffolding. After two years of feasibility studies, the commission finally jointly awarded the prize to Brunelleschi and his rival Ghiberti, but the latter soon largely retired from the project.

Brunelleschi personally invented much of the machinery necessary to erect his revolutionary dome. His eventual plan utilized a skeleton of twenty-four ribs (eight of them visible from the exterior) that enabled the cupola to be self-supporting as it rose from its base 180 feet from the ground. The ribs soared some one hundred feet and converged in an oculus meant to be topped by a lantern tower. To keep the weight of the structure to a minimum, Brunelleschi designed the first double shell in architectural history and placed the brickwork in herringbone patterns on the framework of the stone beams. When completed in 1436, his masterpiece was by no means a mere copy of classical patterns, but a unique and daring creation notable for its visual impressiveness from the outside, unlike such Roman structures as the Pantheon. It became the single most identifiable architectural landmark in the city. In 1436, Brunelleschi won yet another competition, this one for the design of the lantern that anchored the top of his cupola. This lantern was not completed until 1461, fifteen years after his death. He also designed the lateral tribunes that graced the structure.

Despite its overwhelming importance, Brunelleschi's work on the Florentine cathedral was not representative of the main thrust of his architectural style. Much more typical were his plans for the Ospedale degli Innocenti (foundling hospital), a building commissioned by the Silk Guild in 1419. His most important contribution to the project was a graceful portico of rounded arches that extended across the façade. The entire exterior reflected Brunelleschi's dedication to proper geometrical proportions, symmetry, and classical detail.

Classical elements also dominate the two basilican churches which Brunelleschi designed in his native city, San Lorenzo and Santo Spirito. Although neither was completed before his death and each was somewhat modified from his original plans, both reflected his dedication to mathematical proportion and logical design to provide visual and intellectual harmony. Their interiors of Roman rounded arches and pillars became hallmarks of the Renaissance style.

One of the Florentine master's greatest undertakings in church architecture was the Pazzi Chapel, a chapter house for the monks of the cloister of Santa Croce. Although his commission came in 1429, actual work did not begin until 1442 and continued into the 1460's. In this chapel, Brunelleschi again produced an edifice noted for harmonious proportions and clarity of expression, breaking with Gothic mystery and grandeur in favor of restraint and geometrical harmony. The interior, dominated by a dome-covered central space, became a highly influential model for future architects. Brunelleschi employed darkly colored pilasters against lightly colored walls to create a harmonious and peaceful atmosphere notable for its simplicity and classical beauty.

Churches were by no means Brunelleschi's sole architectural preoccupation. Despite the proliferation of palace-building in Florence during this time, only one such structure—the Palazzo di Parte Guelfa—was definitely designed by him. His model for a palace for Cosimo de' Medici was rejected as too ostentatious and imposing. Florence and other cities throughout Tuscany frequently employed him as a consultant to design fortifications and bridges and to supervise other public works projects. In 1430, for example, he became involved in an unsuccessful scheme to divert the Arno River in order to turn the city of Lucca into an island.

Brunelleschi did not completely abandon sculpture after his loss in the competition of 1401. His polychrome wood statue of the Virgin for the Church of Santo Spirito perished in a 1471 fire, but several other works have been attributed to him, including the terra-cotta evangelists in the Pazzi Chapel.

A lifelong bachelor, in 1417, Brunelleschi adopted five-year-old Andrea di Lazzaro Cavalcanti, more commonly known as Il Buggiano, as his heir. This foster son became his apprentice in 1419 and eventually collaborated with his mentor on many projects. Brunelleschi continued working actively on his numerous projects until his death on April 15, 1446. In 1447, city officials authorized the interment of his remains in the same cathedral which had played such an important part in his long and productive career.

Summary

At the time of his death, only a few of Filippo Brunelleschi's designs had been completed. Most, such as the great basilicas of San Lorenzo and Santo Spirito and the lantern for his great dome, were finished only many years after his death. Nevertheless, during his active career of nearly half a century, Brunelleschi established himself as the premier architect in Florence and the first architect of the new Renaissance style. Unlike his younger contemporary Leon Battista Alberti, he never produced a book about his architectural theory, but his landmark buildings served as textbooks by themselves for numerous future architects such as Michelangelo.

With his profound respect for classical values, Brunelleschi personified the self-confident optimism of the early Renaissance Humanists. Much like Leonardo da Vinci later in the century, he was interested in a wide variety of subjects, including hydraulics, watchmaking, and practical mechanics. Sometime between 1410 and 1415, he drew two panels, now lost, which effectively rediscovered the principles of linear perspective. This had a profound impact upon painters of the era, such as Brunelleschi's young acquaintance Masaccio. Linear perspective helped revolutionize the style of fifteenth century Italian painting.

It is through his architectural accomplishments, though, that Brunelleschi made his major contribution. He was undoubtedly the pivotal figure in assuring Florentine supremacy in the field throughout the fifteenth century. Works such as his great cathedral dome and the Pazzi Chapel revived admiration for classical styles without resorting to slavish imitation of Greco-Roman forms. Brunelleschi thus created a vibrant, self-confident classical Renaissance style that profoundly influenced architecture for centuries.

Bibliography

Battisti, Eugenio. *Filippo Brunelleschi: The Complete Work.* New York: Rizzoli, 1981. A translation and revision from an earlier Italian version, this scholarly study thoroughly examines Brunelleschi's life and career, including such aspects as his military engineering, theatrical machinery, and verse. Contains a detailed documentary chronology of his life and times and a chronological bibliography from 1568 to 1980.
Fanelli, Giovanni. *Brunelleschi.* Florence, Italy: Scala Books, 1980. Briefly

discusses Brunelleschi's career and major buildings and is chiefly useful for its lavish and detailed color illustrations of his major works. It particularly focuses upon his great dome.

Hyman, Isabelle, ed. *Brunelleschi in Perspective*. Englewood Cliffs, N.J.: Prentice-Hall, 1974. A useful monograph divided into two sections. The first is a collection of fifteenth and sixteenth century documents and writings about Brunelleschi; the second consists of twelve articles written by nineteenth and twentieth century authors. Contains a useful chronology of his life.

Manetti, Antonio di Tuccio. *The Life of Brunelleschi*. Edited by Howard Saalman. Translated by Catherine Enggass. University Park: Pennsylvania State University Press, 1970. Manetti was the probable author of the *Vita di Filippo Brunelleschi* that appeared in the 1480's. As a young man, Manetti had known and idolized Brunelleschi, and this work is a laudatory treatment that despite its inaccuracies and biases remains the best early source of information about the great architect. This particular edition, with texts in both English and Italian, contains an introduction discussing the problems of authorship, chronology, and reliability.

Murray, Peter. *The Architecture of the Italian Renaissance*. London: B. T. Batsford, 1963. A standard survey that contains a useful chapter on Brunelleschi, showing his influence on architects of the fifteenth and sixteenth centuries. Contains a critical bibliographical essay on early treatises and more recent works.

Prager, Frank D., and Gustina Scaglia. *Brunelleschi: Studies of His Technology and Inventions*. Cambridge, Mass.: MIT Press, 1970. A brief monograph which discusses Brunelleschi's machines, innovative construction methods, and masonry work. Contains useful illustrations of his machines and problems concerning the construction of his dome.

Tom L. Auffenberg

LEONARDO BRUNI

Born: c. 1370; Arezzo, Republic of Florence
Died: March 9, 1444; Florence
Areas of Achievement: Historiography, literature, and politics
Contribution: Bruni was a leading Italian Renaissance figure, a Humanist scholar whose work was important in the development of historiography.

Early Life

Leonardo Bruni was the son of Cecco Bruni, a small grain dealer in Arezzo. As a result of civil war, Bruni and his father were imprisoned in 1384, with the young Bruni held apart from his father in a castle room on the wall of which was a portrait of Petrarch. Bruni would later write that his daily viewing of the painting of this famous Italian poet and Humanist inspired him with an eagerness for Humanist studies. The years following the war and his imprisonment were difficult for Bruni. His father died in 1386, his mother in 1388; family resources declined sharply.

In spite of the family hardship, Bruni moved the forty miles to Florence, perhaps to live with relatives, and began his studies. From 1393 to 1397, he studied law in Florence and came to the attention of the medieval scholar Lino Coluccio Salutati. In 1396, another scholar, Manuel Chrysoloras, moved to Florence and did much to broaden Bruni's career and education. In 1397, Bruni shifted to the study of Greek, in which Chrysoloras educated and then inspired him to complete a series of translations of several classical literary items from ancient times, many of which had been overlooked for centuries. These included works by Xenophon, Saint Basil, Procopius, Polybius, Demosthenes, Plutarch, Thucydides, and Aristotle. Before he was thirty-five, Bruni's achievement in this work led to his stature among contemporaries as the leading authority on the subject of ancient literature.

Life's Work

As a result of his recognition as a literary figure and because of his proficiency in Latin and Greek, Bruni received an appointment in 1405 as a secretary to Pope Innocent VII. Except for a brief period in 1410 and 1411, he would spend ten years with the papal court in Rome. In 1411, when he was forty-one years of age, he married. While little is known about his wife or her family, it is known that she brought to the marriage a dowry that reflects a family of wealth and status. Bruni also became a close acquaintance of Baldassarre Cossa, who became Pope John XXIII during the Schism of the Papacy until the famous deposition in 1415 at the Council of Constance. As a result of the loss of power by his patron, Bruni returned to Florence, where he settled into an active life in historical study and writing, Florentine politics, and personal investments.

It was as a historian that Leonardo Bruni became a great Renaissance scholar. Through translations, dialogues, biographies, commentaries, and his monumental *Historiae Florentini populi* (1610; history of the Florentine people), Bruni changed historical writing and thought so significantly that he was referred to as the "father of history" for at least two centuries after his death. Numerous Italian historians were influenced by his methods and style, and his impact extended into other disciplines. Although there is no complete chronology of Bruni's historical works, the list is impressive. It begins with his *Laudatio Florentinae urbis* (in praise of the city of Florence) and the *Dialoghi ad Petrum Paulum historum* (dialogues dedicated to Pier Paolo Vergerio), both produced between 1401 and 1405.

Laudatio Florentinae urbis is an attempt to present a thorough view of the Florence city-state in its geographic and historical perspectives, a total view of the city. The work is based, in part, upon the model of Aristides' eulogy of Athens in ancient Greece. Bruni sought to explain how Florentine institutions and politics evolved from the Italian past, in itself a new historical method. It was also in this work that Bruni's civic Humanism emerged. He expressed the view that the health of the state must ever be based upon the educated and ethical sense of the citizenry, factors which, in his view, had contributed much to the glory and fame of Florence. *Dialoghi ad Petrum Paulum historum* was a combination of two dialogues that served as reproductions of conversations between scholars from two Florentine generations. Here Florence is presented as the preserver of the best features of republican Rome and classical Greece. Together the two works are credited with marking the beginning of a new Humanism, a new civic sentiment, and a new view of the past.

Bruni's greatest work was his *Historiae Florentini populi*, the first and, as some would argue, the greatest achievement of Renaissance historical writing. Bruni intended this work to be a complete history of Florence to 1404 in order to explain the greatness of this Italian city-state. He concluded that the civic virtue of its citizens and the republican form of its government were key explanations for its greatness. In his view, Florence was the shining example of what men living in political freedom could accomplish. The setting for much of his history was the conflict between Florence and Milan. Although some scholars have criticized Bruni's continued use of the rhetorical methods of Greek and Roman historians and his heavy emphasis upon the symbols of the classical age, the work served as a model for historians for many years. Bruni's research was in response to clearly articulated questions and in pursuit of relevant causal relationships. He became more than a chronicler and instructed those who followed him that history must be true, utilitarian, documented, instructive, readable, thematic, respectful of the past, viewed in epochs or eras, and focused upon those matters which human beings can control, specifically politics. Finally, *Historiae Florentini populi* is important for the significant narrative techniques it introduced.

There are other writings for which Bruni received recognition. These include his *De militia* (1421; on knighthood), in which he advanced the establishment of the idea of a citizen-army for Florence; his 1427 funeral oration for a Florentine general, Nanni degli Strozzi, who had fought successfully against Milan, thus serving to promote the interests of freedom and humanity; his *De studiis et litteris* (1421-1424; *Concerning the Study of Literature*, 1897), one of the first treatises to advance a program of education based upon the humanities that offers a demonstrated concern for women as well as men. In his later years, he published his memoirs, *Rerum suo tempore gestarum commentarius* (1440-1441; commentary on the history of his own times), a perspective on contemporary history that substantially departed from the work of previous chroniclers.

The success of his literary career led Bruni into a prominent political role in Florence by the middle of the 1420's. He became a member of a number of prominent trade and professional guilds, served as an ambassador to Pope Martin V in 1426, and in 1427 became the Chancellor of Florence. In the latter position, he would play a major role in the political and military affairs of the state, an influence he would continue until his death in 1444. Tax records indicate that by 1427 he was one of the wealthiest persons in Florence, possessing a series of farms, houses, and investments. In 1431, his son Donato married into a prominent family and would himself occupy a visible place in the affairs of Florence for many years. Clearly Bruni spent a considerable amount of time promoting his personal political power and personal wealth.

The important role of Bruni in the affairs of Florence is borne out by the elaborate public funeral given upon his death in 1444. This proved to be an event of major importance, attended by figures of prominence from a wide area. His funeral oration was given by a leading statesman, and one of the most gifted sculptors of Florence prepared a marble tomb for him. Niccolò Machiavelli, the famous author and statesman of the Italian Renaissance, was buried beside Bruni upon his death in 1527.

Summary

Leonardo Bruni was one of the outstanding figures of the Italian Renaissance. In the first half of the fifteenth century, he was the leading figure in the development of Humanism, history, and political thought. His translations of ancient Greek texts from Aristotle and Plato made a major contribution to European scholars for centuries. He was clearly the greatest authority on ancient literature for his time. His own biographies, dialogues, histories, and commentaries created a virtual revolution in historical writing and thought. He divided the past in new ways, placed a new emphasis upon sources, developed new narrative forms, and established Humanism as a political necessity in the struggles among the Italian city-states. He is the most important example of civic Humanism in the early Renaissance.

Bibliography

Baron, Hans. *The Crisis of the Early Italian Renaissance: Civic Humanism and Republican Liberty in an Age of Classicism and Tyranny.* 2 vols. Princeton, N.J.: Princeton University Press, 1955. An outstanding study of the Italian Renaissance with Bruni as the central figure. Contains one volume of text and one volume of notes. Includes detailed analyses of Bruni's major works. Baron is the leading scholar of Bruni.

_____. *From Petrarch to Leonardo Bruni: Studies in Humanistic and Political Literature.* Chicago: University of Chicago Press, 1968. An extension of the above work. Baron subjects Petrarch's and Bruni's writings to critical analysis based upon additional sources made available and upon the large amount of interest and reinterpretation of Humanism and the Renaissance in the 1960's. A superb analysis of the evolution of Humanism from its Renaissance origins to the middle of the twentieth century.

Bondanella, Peter, and Julia Conaway Bondanella, eds. *Dictionary of Italian Literature.* Westport, Conn.: Greenwood Press, 1979. A brief but excellent summary of the major contributions of Bruni. Primary emphasis is upon his writings, with clear understanding of the influence of his *Laudatio Florentinae urbis* and *Dialoghi ad Petrum Paulum historum.*

Cochrane, Eric. *Historians and Historiography in the Italian Renaissance.* Chicago: University of Chicago Press, 1981. A superb study of the emergence, growth, and decline of Renaissance historiography. Places Bruni in historical perspective. References are made to several hundred historical writings of the period. An outstanding work on an important period in the development of historical writing.

Martines, Lauro. *The Social World of the Florentine Humanists, 1390-1460.* Princeton, N.J.: Princeton University Press, 1963. An excellent social study of the early Renaissance. This is an analysis of the social position of the Humanist scholars in Florence primarily in the first half of the fifteenth century. Provides insight into the political and financial position of Bruni. An unusual examination of the social lives of a number of prominent scholars.

Wilcox, Donald J. *The Development of Florentine Humanist Historiography in the Fifteenth Century.* Cambridge, Mass.: Harvard University Press, 1969. A study of the influence of Leonardo Bruni upon the writing of history in the fifteenth century. Much of the emphasis and analysis is based upon *Historiae Florentini populi.* The method and manner in which later historians were shaped by and reacted to this work is given attention. The role of moral commitment in Bruni's writing is clearly identified.

Frank Nickell

GIORDANO BRUNO

Born: 1548; Nola, near Naples
Died: February 17, 1600; Rome
Areas of Achievement: Philosophy and astronomy
Contribution: With his daring and speculative theories in astronomy and philosophy, Bruno anticipated many of the achievements of modern science, but his stubborn personality and arcane interests brought him into inevitable conflict with the authorities of his time.

Early Life

Giordano Bruno was born in 1548 in Nola. He was the son of Juano Bruno, a professional soldier, and his wife, Fraulissa Savolino. As a child, Bruno was named Filippo; he took the name Giordano when he entered the Dominican Order. He was sometimes known as "the Nolan," after the town of his birth, and he often referred to himself in this fashion in his works.

From contemporary records and his own writings, Bruno seems to have been a particularly intelligent and impressionable child. He left several accounts of odd, almost visionary experiences in his youth, including an extended, quasi-mystical dialogue with the mountain Vesuvius which first revealed to him the deceptiveness of appearances and the relativity of all material things. These were to become two dominant themes in his philosophy.

As a youth, Bruno was sent to Naples, where he attended the Studium Generale, concentrating in the humanities, logic, and dialectic. It is clear that Bruno had a thorough grounding in Aristotle and his philosophy and also was well acquainted with the works of Plato and the writings of the Neoplatonists, who were then creating considerable intellectual activity and controversy, especially in Italy.

In 1565, when Bruno was seventeen, he entered the Dominican Order, moving within the walls of the monastery of San Domenico in Naples. There he took the name Giordano. Bruno's decision to enter the Dominican Order is puzzling, for in retrospect it clearly stands as the major mistake in his often-turbulent life. Although he was well suited for the intellectual studies of the Dominicans, he was quite unfit for the accompanying intellectual discipline and submission required for the monastic and clerical life. His thoughts were too wide-ranging and innovative to be restrained within traditional confines, a situation which eventually placed him in mortal conflict with the Church.

Bruno spent eleven years in the monastery of San Domenico. He studied Saint Thomas Aquinas, Aristotle, and other traditional figures, but at the same time was reading in the mystical doctrines of the Neoplatonists, the new works of Desiderius Erasmus, and other reformers and seems to have become suspiciously well acquainted with the works of heretics such as

Arius. These unorthodox diversions brought him into conflict with the Dominican authorities, and reports were made that Bruno was defending the Arian heresy. Arius had taught that God the Father and God the Son were not the same in essence. When the Dominicans learned that Bruno was suspected of defending Arianism, charges were prepared against him. Learning of this, he fled the monastery in 1576. He was aged twenty-eight, and he would spend the rest of his life in exile or in prison.

Life's Work

When Bruno fled the monastery, he embarked upon twenty-one years of wandering throughout Europe. Many of his stops lasted merely a matter of months, and the most productive, for only three years. Controversy and conflict dogged him on his travels—much of it a result of not only his daring and speculative thought but also his unrestrained attacks on those who opposed him in any degree and his innate lack of common sense or practical judgment. Employment was difficult and income was insufficient and insecure. Yet, during this period, Bruno wrote and published an enormous body of work whose content far outpaced even the most advanced thinkers of his time.

Bruno's first extended sojourn was in Geneva. There, safe from the power of the Church, he soon plunged into local intellectual conflicts. In 1579, he published a scathing attack on Antoine de la Faye, a noted professor of philosophy at the University of Geneva. Bruno's assault was more than an academic exercise, for he seemed to undermine de la Faye's theories, which were the basis for the quasi-theological government of Geneva. Bruno, the renegade Dominican on the run, had put himself in disfavor with the Calvinists of Switzerland. He was arrested, then released; he soon left Geneva, moving first to Lyons, then to Toulouse, France. In 1581, Bruno went to Paris, where he found his first real success. He lectured on his own techniques of memory, and the results were so impressive that King Henry III summoned Bruno to court to explain his methods. As a result, the king appointed Bruno to the Collège de France. Bruno held the post for two years, lecturing on philosophy and natural science and publishing a number of books, many of them on his art of memory.

Still, he managed to alienate many fellow professors and intellectuals in Paris. Some were outraged by his arrogant and self-proclaimed superiority, while the more conventional were troubled by his unorthodox views and desertion of his monastic vows. In 1583, Bruno left for London, with a letter of recommendation to the French ambassador Michel de Castelnau.

The London period, from 1583 through 1585, was the most productive of Bruno's career. Perhaps he was stimulated by the intellectual climate of England, for not only did he deliver a series of lectures at Oxford, explaining the Copernican theory, but also he had among his acquaintances men such as Sir Philip Sidney, Sir Walter Raleigh, and Sir Fulke Greville, noted figures of the English Renaissance. In 1584, Bruno produced a series of six dialogues expounding his philosophy; three of these dealt with cosmological issues, and three with moral topics.

In *Cena de le Ceneri* (1584; the Ash Wednesday supper), Bruno laid the foundation for his scientific theories. He began with the view of Nicolaus Copernicus that the sun, rather than the earth, was the center of the solar system. Bruno recognized that the sun was itself a star, and he concluded that other stars must have their attendant planets circling them. He came to the conclusion that the universe was infinite, and that it therefore contained an infinite number of worlds, each world capable of having intelligent life upon it. Such a theory ran counter to the traditions of both the Catholic church and the newer Protestant faiths.

Bruno continued the development of his theories in *De l'infinito universo e mondi* (1584; *On the Infinite Universe and Worlds*, 1950). He systematically criticized the prevailing Aristotelian cosmology, and in its place put forth a precursor of the modern theory of relativity later developed by Albert Einstein. Bruno maintained that sensory knowledge could never be absolute, but only relative, and it is this relativity that misleads humans in their attempts to understand the universe. Human perceptions are incapable of truly and completely comprehending the universe, and that universe itself can be accurately comprehended only as a total unity, rather than in isolated parts. Therefore, neither senses nor imagination can be fully trusted, but only reason, which allows humans to penetrate to the divine essence of creation.

Bruno also developed a theory that the universe was composed of "minima," extremely small particles much like the atoms proposed by the ancient Roman philosopher Lucretius. Like Lucretius, Bruno thought that certain motions and events were inevitable and that the universe develops inexorably out of inherent necessity. In order to resolve the conflict between this deterministic view and free will, Bruno postulated that the universe itself was divine; he projected a universal pantheism in which the Creator manifests Himself through and within creation.

Finally, Bruno resolved the difficulty of the relationship of human beings to God, of the finite to the infinite, or ignorance to knowledge. These were long-standing puzzles to theologians and philosophers, for it seemed impossible that the limited mind of man could comprehend or understand the perfect and infinite attributes of divinity. Bruno believed that there was an identity of opposites at work in which the essential elements of creation and divinity are found in all parts of the universe. Opposition is only relative and illusory; on the most fundamental level, everything is the same, and everything is therefore divine.

In 1585, Castelnau was recalled to Paris, and Bruno, left without a patron, was forced to leave England. For the next six years, he wandered through

Europe, accepting and losing posts at a number of universities in Germany and the Holy Roman Empire. He continued to write and publish prolifically, including his special area of memory, and, in the fall of 1591, he received an invitation from a Venetian nobleman, Zuane Mocenigo, to come to Venice and teach him the art of memory.

Bruno accepted, believing that he would be safe in Venice, which was at that time a fairly liberal and independent state which carefully guarded its freedom from the Papacy. There was a dispute between Bruno and his patron, however—apparently the nobleman believed that he was being cheated and that Bruno planned to flee to Germany—and on May 23, 1592, Bruno was arrested by the Venetian Inquisition. He was questioned through September, but no decision was made.

On February 27, 1593, Bruno was delivered into the hands of the Roman Inquisition, and for the next seven years he was held in prison, repeatedly questioned and examined, and urged to recant his heresies and confess his sins. Bruno tried to play a crafty game, willing to admit minor infractions, but pretending not to comprehend how his cosmological and philosophical writings could run counter to the teachings of the Church. Finally, in February, 1600, the Inquisition found him guilty and delivered him to the secular authorities for punishment. When Bruno heard the decision, he replied, "Perhaps you who pronounce my sentence are in greater fear than I who receive it." On Saturday, February 17, 1600, Bruno was burned in the Square of Flowers in Rome.

Summary

Giordano Bruno was a philosopher of great insight and imagination, yet a thinker who could link science to magic and yoke philosophical understanding to mnemonic tricks. He was poised amid the thought and traditions of the Church, the mystical teachings of the Neoplatonists, and the rapid advances of the sciences, especially astronomy. From the combination of these three traditions, he forged a new and highly individual vision of the cosmos and mankind's place in it.

Bruno's influence was recognized by both scientists and Humanists in the years following his death. Scientists, even to modern times, admire the startling insights which he drew concerning the infinite number of worlds in an infinite universe. Bruno's early recognition of the concept of relativity and the place which it must play in humanity's conception and understanding of the universe is also a prime legacy which Bruno left to science.

Humanists of the period were profoundly influenced by his insistence on the need for tolerance in matters of religion and belief. Perhaps because Bruno himself was so often a victim of the intolerance of the age, he was especially eloquent in his plea for patience and understanding.

Finally, Bruno combined the sense of infinite expansion and relativity of all things with a new approach to human knowledge and culture. He refused to divide the world into the sacred and the profane, the Christian and the heathen, the orthodox and the heretic. Instead, he saw human life and culture as a single strand and the universe as a divine manifestation which carried with it all knowledge and truth. To Giordano Bruno, the cosmos was God's creation and therefore all good, and man's role was not to judge but to understand.

Bibliography

Boulting, William. *Giordano Bruno, His Life, Thought, and Martyrdom*. New York: E. P. Dutton, 1916. As indicated by its title, this biography is a highly favorable account of Bruno's life and thought. On the whole, it presents his philosophical and scientific views in a fair and unbiased light.

De Santillana, Giorgia. *The Age of Adventure: The Renaissance Philosophers*. Boston: Houghton Mifflin, 1957. An introductory survey of Bruno and his work, with particular attention paid to his influence upon later scientists and writers.

Feingold, Mordechai. "The Occult Tradition in the English Universities of the Renaissance: A Reassessment." In *Occult and Scientific Mentalities in the Renaissance*, edited by Brian Vickers. Cambridge, England: Cambridge University Press, 1984. An enlightening study of Bruno's 1584 visit to Oxford and the state of learning at that time, with special emphasis on which areas of knowledge were believed to be beyond the boundary of conventions.

Kristeller, Paul Oskar. *Renaissance Thought and Its Sources*. New York: Columbia University Press, 1979. Does not have an extended treatment of Bruno as an individual, but is an excellent source for understanding the intellectual climate of his times and how it developed.

Singer, Dorothea. *Giordano Bruno: His Life and Thought*. New York: Henry Schuman, 1950. A sympathetic but generally unbiased biography of Bruno, with emphasis upon his thought and theory. The volume contains several helpful appendices and an excellent annotated translation of the dialogue *On the Infinite Universe and Worlds*.

Yates, Frances. *Giordano Bruno and the Hermetic Tradition*. Chicago: University of Chicago Press, 1964. By one of the most distinguished scholars of Renaissance thought, Yates's account of Bruno's place is invaluable. Particularly good in situating him within the confines of a broad philosophical stream.

_____. *Lull and Bruno*. Boston: Routledge & Kegan Paul, 1982. The section "Essays on Giordano Bruno in England" is particularly valuable for its studies of Bruno's lectures on Copernicus at Oxford and his views of religion and the established church.

Michael Witkoski

MARTIN BUCER

Born: November 11, 1491; Schlettstadt, Alsace
Died: February 28, 1551; Cambridge, England
Areas of Achievement: Church reform and religion
Contribution: During the Reformation, Bucer served as mediator between Huldrych Zwingli and Martin Luther and attempted to reconcile the Roman Catholic church and the Protestants. He made lasting contributions to the liturgy of Protestant sects, particularly in England.

Early Life

Born on November 11, 1491, to Nicholas Butzer, a shoemaker, and his wife, an occasional midwife, Martin Bucer lived in Schlettstadt, in the Alsace region, until he was ten years old. By the time he had moved to Strasbourg and was put under the care of his grandfather, also a shoemaker, Bucer had already acquired the religious and scholarly zeal that characterized his entire life. At fifteen, however, he had to decide whether to follow family tradition and become an apprentice shoemaker or to continue his education by the only means available to poor young men, service in the Church. Although he did not really want to become a monk, he joined the Dominican Order and spent the next ten years in the monastery at Schlettstadt. There he was subjected to medieval Scholasticism, embodied in the works of Thomas Aquinas, and deprived of the new learning of the Humanists, notably the reformer Desiderius Erasmus.

The turning point in Bucer's life occurred ten years later, when he was transferred to the Dominican monastery at Heidelberg, a university town. There he was caught in the conflict between the medieval Scholasticism advocated by the Dominicans and the Humanism taught by the university professors. Bucer, a voracious reader, soon became a devoted follower of Erasmus, and his liberal leanings were strengthened by his meeting with Martin Luther, who came to Heidelberg in April of 1518 to defend his views. When he received his bachelor of theology degree and was made master of students in 1519, Bucer also received permission to read the Bible; he subsequently wrote biblical commentaries and grounded his own religious beliefs in Scriptures, not in the writings of the Church Fathers.

After joining the local literary society and meeting other religious insurgents, Bucer, whose models were Luther and Erasmus, became convinced that his views were incompatible with his life as a Dominican and attempted to win his release from his monastic vows. That first step in his break from the Catholic church occurred in 1521; after brief stints as a court chaplain to Count Frederick of the Palatinate and as a parish priest, he married Elizabeth Silbereisen. While his marriage did not result in his immediate excommunication, Bucer's fervid defense of Luther's teachings, particularly the primacy of the Bible and the emphasis on faith rather than good works, eventually and inevitably brought him to the attention of his church superiors. Bucer was regarded as a threat because he used his preaching ability and debating skill to challenge conservative theologians who were reluctant to engage him in religious disputations. When, in 1523, he refused to go to Speier to meet with his bishop, Bucer was excommunicated. He was left virtually homeless when he lost his religious and political supporters and the Council of Wissembourg requested that he leave the city in May of 1523.

Life's Work

When he arrived, uninvited, in Strasbourg in 1523, Bucer found a city congenial to his Reformation views and strategically located between the warring strongholds of the Swiss Reformer Huldrych Zwingli and Martin Luther. In the eight years between his first sermon and his appointment in 1531 as official head of the Strasbourg clergy, Bucer brought his adopted city to prominence as a theological center. Under his unofficial leadership, ties were established between the church and the state; a public school system, with a religious emphasis, was inaugurated; and religious tolerance of a sort was established, though that tolerance was repeatedly tested by the Separatists and Anabaptists.

For the most part, Bucer's biblical commentaries were written during this period—a commentary on Romans, written in 1536, was the exception. Rather than using the traditional grammatical approach, he relied on close readings of the passages, which were placed in their historical context and compared to similar passages from elsewhere in the Bible. This comparative approach was especially helpful in his commentaries on the Gospels, but some critics believe that his best exegesis is contained in his work on the Psalms. (Unfortunately, this work was published under a pseudonym, Aretius Felinus, in order to gain for it an objective reading in Catholic France, but the stratagem left him open to charges of duplicity and earned for him the ire of both Luther and Erasmus.)

Shortly after Bucer arrived in Strasbourg, the Supper Controversy, the conflict over the meaning of the Eucharistic phrase "This is my body," between Zwingli and Luther threatened Reformation unity. Zwingli's followers—and Bucer must be included among them—maintained that the bread and wine were merely symbols of Christ's body and blood, not His actual body and blood, as Luther's followers, and the Roman Catholic church, believed. Although he sided with Zwingli, Bucer attempted to reconcile the two factions, who became engaged in pamphlet wars, by glossing over the real doctrinal differences and by attempting, through ambiguous language, to effect an apparent compromise where none was, in fact, possible. Bucer's conciliatory efforts were, unfortunately, hampered by his own writings, which revealed his own theological beliefs and which were attacked by Lutherans,

Zwinglians, and Catholics: The middle ground was treacherous territory.

From 1524 until 1548, when he was exiled to England, there was hardly a religious conference in Germany or Switzerland that Bucer did not attend in his role of theological conciliator. The first significant conference, the Marburg Colloquy of 1529, established a tenuous peace between Luther and Zwingli on all religious doctrine except for the Supper Controversy, but the real differences between the two opponents kept surfacing. Working with Wolfgang Capito, another Strasbourg Reformer, Bucer drafted in 1530 at the Diet of Augsburg the Tetrapolitana, or Confession of the Four Cities—Strasbourg, Zurich (Zwingli's stronghold), Basel, and Bern—but the ambiguous language concerning the Eucharist resulted in its rejection by Luther and Zwingli, both of whom wanted changes of a more specific kind. After Zwingli died in 1531, Bucer renewed his efforts at establishing concord, and the resulting Wittenberg Concord of 1536 did effect a consensus, if not a lasting peace, primarily because of Bucer's gift of obscuring meaning through ambiguous wording. While Philipp Melanchthon secured Luther's approval of the compromise, Bucer's efforts with the Zwinglians, already suspicious because of Luther's endorsement, effectively brought the moderate Zwinglians into the Lutheran fold while permanently alienating the ultra-Zwinglians.

The Protestant cause, already adversely affected by the Luther/Zwingli hostilities, suffered another setback when Philip of Hesse, a supporter of the Reformers, sought their religious sanction for his bigamy. Appealing to Scripture, the authority for the Reformers, Philip approached Bucer through an intermediary. Although he had not sanctioned Henry VIII's earlier divorce from Catherine of Aragon and although his initial response to Philip's request was negative, Bucer weighed the religious and political factors and reluctantly acquiesced to Philip. In fact, Bucer wrote a defense of bigamy, but his ultimate response was typically equivocal: He sanctioned Philip's secret bigamy. Unfortunately, Bucer's attempts to keep the marriage a secret were thwarted by Philip, who made it public and who also sought approval from the Catholic church.

Although the Reformation was an accomplished fact, the Catholic church was intent on returning the Reformers to the fold, and Bucer himself participated in several councils whose ostensible purpose was to unite all Christians. In 1540, the year of Philip's bigamous marriage, the Colloquy of Worms was convened, but no real progress was made, despite Bucer's efforts, which included secret meetings with liberal Catholic reformers. The following year, Bucer attended the Diet of Regensburg, which was called by Emperor Charles V, who had two aims: religious unity and military assistance against an impending Turkish invasion of the Holy Roman Empire. The authorship of the Regensburg Book, which served as the basis for the ensuing discussions, was unknown; the material, however, was drawn from the secret meetings conducted at the earlier Colloquy of Worms. At these secret meetings, Bucer had made compromises which, when they were made public, brought criticism from the Protestants, especially the Lutherans. When both sides rejected the Regensburg Book, Bucer apparently despaired of effecting a Protestant/Catholic reconciliation, and he became very anti-Catholic. Subsequent meetings, which were also futile, were held, but they were conducted, as Bucer suspected, more for political than for religious reasons. Charles V, who had been conducting secret negotiations with the pope, the French, and the Turks, finally attacked the Protestant German princes in 1546 and quickly defeated them. After the defeat of the Smalkald League, Charles V instituted the Augsburg Interim, which reflected not only his ideas but also some of the articles of the Regensburg Interim, which had been drafted in part by Bucer. Despite the similarities between the two documents, Bucer adamantly opposed the Augsburg Interim because it was the product of force, not negotiation, and because he had become more intolerant of the Catholics. Bucer resisted Charles V until 1549, when he was officially requested to leave Strasbourg.

Although he had various options, Bucer chose to accept Archbishop Thomas Cranmer's invitation to aid the Reformation effort in England. After all, his Cologne Ordinances had been included in the First Book of Common Prayer, and he had many friends and supporters in that country. Soon after his arrival at Cambridge, where he taught, he was again embroiled in the Supper controversy, this time, however, with Catholic opposition.

In his service to Edward VI, he refuted the Catholic elevation of good works over faith, resisted the radical views of the Scottish Reformers, wrote *De regno Christi* (1557), a design for converting England into the Kingdom of Christ, and aided in the development of the English Books of Prayer. For his efforts he received the doctor of theology degree from Cambridge before he died on February 28, 1551. Even in death he was involved in controversy: English Catholics under Mary tried and condemned him posthumously for heresy, then exhumed and burned his body in 1555; Elizabeth, the Protestant queen, atoned for the Catholic desecration in 1560.

Summary

Unlike his more famous Reformation contemporaries—Luther, Zwingli, and Calvin—Martin Bucer was a mediator occupying the middle ground in most of the religious controversy of the sixteenth century. Rather than establishing his own sect, he sought to reconcile the intransigent extremes within the Reformation movement. His ecumenical efforts with such divergent groups as the Anabaptists and Catholics led him to make concessions, although for the goal of church unity, that undermined his credibility with his colleagues. Though he never abandoned the essential tenets of his faith, he did appear occasionally too willing to compromise, even to surrender, on the details that preoccupied other Reformers. Though he was inevitably unsuccessful in mediating what were irreconcilable differences, he did succeed in negotiating the reform of several German cities which were attempting to resolve questions about the disposition of church property and the use of images in worship services. Under his leadership, Strasbourg became an influential Reformation city which attracted young Reformers, most notably Calvin, who incorporated some of Bucer's ideas in his *Institutes of the Christian Religion* (1536).

Because he occupied the middle ground on theological disputes, Bucer is not a theologian whose influence is readily traced. His theology, because of his wide reading, was eclectic and drawn from many sources, some of them—Anabaptist and Catholic—inherently contradictory. Bucer's contribution was in his synthesis of theology, not in his creation of it. Centuries later, his ecumenical approach to theology seems more appropriate to the times than the dogmatic intransigence of his more famous contemporaries.

Bibliography

Eells, Hastings. *Martin Bucer*. New Haven, Conn.: Yale University Press, 1931. The definitive biography of Bucer, this lengthy book contains valuable information about the historical context, theological differences between the Reformers, and the personalities of the major figures. The book is well organized, well indexed, and very readable. Though his sympathies are clearly with Bucer, Eells is fairly objective in his discussion of Luther, Zwingli, and the Roman Catholic church.

Höpf, Constantin. *Martin Bucer and the English Reformation*. Oxford: Basil Blackwell, 1946. A thorough review of Bucer's influence on the English Reformation. Höpf, who includes copious illustrations, original correspondence, and a comprehensive bibliography, extends Bucer's influence beyond his *Censura* (wr. 1550) of the First Edwardian Prayer Book and details how Bucer's psalms were printed in the English primers. Bucer, for Höpf, was more influential in England than either Zwingli or Luther.

Pauck, Wilhelm, ed. *Melanchthon and Bucer*. Philadelphia: Westminster Press, 1969. Pauck includes his translation of Bucer's *De regno Christi*, which he introduces by discussing Bucer's substantial contribution to the Reformation and explaining how Bucer's Strasbourg experiences affected his recommendations for England in *De regno Christi*. Of particular interest are Pauck's comments about the relationship of church and state.

Stephens, W. P. *The Holy Spirit in the Theology of Martin Bucer*. Cambridge, England: Cambridge University Press, 1970. A close examination of the Holy Spirit in Bucer's theology. Stephens provides an introduction establishing Bucer's theology in the context of his times and summarizes the various influences that affected the development of his religious thought. There is also an excellent bibliography.

Wendel, François. *Calvin: The Origins and Development of His Religious Thought*. Translated by Philip Mairet. New York: Harper & Row, 1963. Although the book concerns the many sources of Calvin's theology, Wendel establishes Bucer as being particularly influential. Bucer's influence is especially prominent in the predestination material found in Calvin's *Institutes of the Christian Religion*, and Calvin's theology is regarded as being aligned with the theology of the Tetrapolitan Confession of 1530.

Thomas L. Erskine

COMTE DE BUFFON
Georges-Louis Leclerc

Born: September 7, 1707; Montbard, France
Died: April 16, 1788; Paris, France
Areas of Achievement: Biology and natural history
Contribution: Buffon wrote one of the earliest multivolume natural histories that saw nature as a complete entity. He also worked toward a concept of evolution and geological change that would contribute to later investigators in the field.

Early Life

Georges-Louis Leclerc was born in the region of Dijon, France, from an upper-middle-class family, where his father was the lord of Buffon and Montbard. He was the eldest of five children and he grew up in a house in Dijon, where his family held an important position in society. Between 1717 and 1723, he attended a nearby Jesuit college, where he showed some promise in mathematics. He then began legal training for three years, a future career suited to his position in society. His career path was interrupted in 1727, when he became close friends with a Swiss mathematics professor and went to Angers to pursue his interest in medicine and botany. His activities during the next four years remains obscure, although there are unsubstantiated reports that he fought a duel and traveled extensively.

Buffon returned to Paris in 1732 and began to make rapid advancement in both political and scientific circles. His mother had died a year earlier and left him a sizable inheritance. Even though his financial future was secured, he devoted a considerable amount of time building on his inheritance and soon became a wealthy man. For the next few years, he directed his attention to areas of mathematics and physics. He wrote a paper on timber strength for the navy and contributed a study on probability theory. In 1734, he was elected as an associate to the French Royal Academy of Sciences and for the following six years Buffon would follow his interests wherever they led him through a number of different scientific areas. Buffon worked in botany, mathematics, and chemistry, as well as performing microscopic research on animal reproduction. In 1739, he was appointed Curator of the Royal Gardens of the King of France. This was a major turning point in Buffon's life, because from this point onward he would concentrate more of his attention on biological and botanical areas. Also by this time, he completed his study of the physics of Isaac Newton (1642-1727), including a translation of Newton's *The Method of Fluxions and Infinite Series* in 1740. Throughout his career, Buffon would view nature from a mechanical point of view.

Life's Work

Buffon returned to Montbard in 1740 to administer and enlarge his family estates. For the next forty-eight years, he divided his time between his financial concerns and his scientific interests. He spent summers on his estate and returned to his botanical responsibilities in the fall in Paris. During his tenure, he expanded the Royal Gardens extensively and saw them become an important center of scientific research. During this period of his life, he gradually began to publish his forty-four volume *Histoire naturelle, générale et particulière* (1749-1789; *Natural History, General and Particular,* 1781-1812). He became a leading scientist of his time and was a member of the many influential scientific societies of Europe. Louis XV made him Comte de Buffon and ordered a statue made in his likeness. Although scientific and financial matters seemed to fill his life, he was married to a pretty, twenty-year-old woman in 1752. Their marriage lasted until her death in 1769, when he was left with a five-year-old son.

Buffon's life's work is contained in his monumental forty-four-volume natural history. He began work in 1740 on this unprecedented attempt to write a comprehensive history of all the natural sciences. He developed a network of correspondents throughout the world, who sent him summaries of scientific research. In Paris, he organized a team of collaborators, who helped him sort and digest the vast amount of information at hand. The first three volumes of *Natural History, General and Particular* were published in 1749, and these include titles on the theory of the earth's history and the history of man. These volumes were published by the royal press and hence were not examined by the censors. As a result, their publication brought a storm of protest from the Catholic clergy, who were incensed over Buffon's rejection of the Genesis view of creation. Yet he could not be considered an atheist; like many other thinkers of the Enlightenment, he remained a Christian despite his rejection of tradition. Indeed, Buffon wrote a retraction, but he then continued to publish volumes in his natural history without swerving from his commitment to scientific investigation.

Periodically throughout his life, volumes of his work would be published. Buffon worked on a series of volumes on quadrupeds between 1753 and 1767. These were followed by volumes on birds between 1770 and 1783. A final series on minerals appeared between 1783 and 1788. In addition, there were a number of volumes called supplements, which were published between 1774 and 1789. Among this last group is one of his most famous works on the geological periods of the earth, *Époques de la nature* (1778; *The Epochs of Nature*). Taken as a whole, these forty-four volumes make three major contributions to biological sciences: the rejection of a rigid system of identification and classification of biological forms; the opening of a continuing debate on the nature, formation, and diversification of biological species; and the entrance of the concept of evolution into the vocabulary of science through research on anatomy, fossil records, and vastly extending geological time.

Buffon began the first volume of his natural history based on the belief in the continuity and unity of nature. He declared in that volume that nature knows only individuals and cannot be placed into logical categories such as classes and genera. This assertion flies in the face of biological classification, which had reached a degree of success and scientific acceptance with the work of Linnaeus (1707-1778). Linnaeus saw the biological world as discontinuous, each species of organism separately created and placed in the world. For Buffon, each organism was not made according to some ideal design but functioned in the world in a practical manner. Thus, in 1749 Buffon would claim that the classification of organisms was impossible, because it did not take into account the entire organism, only some structural parts. Yet he did not believe that organisms could evolve over time and pass on these traits to future generations. In time, as his knowledge of organisms grew, he would accept classifications of birds and other mammals, but always with the mental reservation that the system was artificial and arbitrary. Having lived a long and active intellectual life, Buffon would often reconsider his earlier conclusions. As a consequence, later commentaries would often disagree as to his precise thoughts on a specific subject.

One major problem in any classification system is that of how to split organisms into various categories: in other words, to identify each separate species or genus as distinct from another one. Linnaeus believed that each species of organism was separately created by God and continued through direct descent to his time. Buffon's concept of species, when he came to accept this concept, is closer to modern notions than to those of his own time. He argued on the basis of reproduction that those similar individuals that could constantly reproduce over time were a species. He also differed from Linnaeus in another aspect: Buffon thought that physical characteristics were less important than those of habit, temperament, and instinct. Buffon's ideas on species are closer to later biological descriptions of subspecies and varieties.

Buffon was also probably the first person to open discussion on a large number of questions surrounding evolution. While his answers to these questions were to result in a rejection of the concept of evolution, they nevertheless became part of the scientific literature. In his work on *Epochs of Nature*, Buffon attempted to establish a chronology that was vastly different from the accepted one. Biblical interpretation placed the age of the earth at somewhere between 4000 and 6000 B.C.; Buffon's experiments on cooling of the earth gave him a figure of seventy-five thousand years. In fact, in his notes he had worked out a figure of three million years, but he thought that he would be misunderstood by his readers. He also proposed a theory of how minerals were transformed by physical and chemical agents and suggested that coal was the product of organic matter. He raised questions regarding sedimentary rocks and fossils within these strata, and this led to questions with regard to the extinction of species. Through his investigations in these areas, Buffon opened the doors for future research that would produce major discoveries in the natural sciences.

Summary

Comte de Buffon was a man of the Enlightenment, who believed that rational thought and observation would provide answers to the mysteries of the natural world. He largely rejected the myths of the past and wanted to provide his carefully considered evaluation of the problems of nature. Because he believed that an organism should be treated as a whole, he suggested the possibility of comparative anatomy; the study of behavior followed, since an organism also responded to its environment.

Through his efforts, the attempt to measure the chronology of the earth became a scientific enterprise on the part of geologists. Buffon had studied the human species by the same methods he applied to other organisms. In one of his volumes, he described the first men as living on the earth while it was still hot; thus, they were black and capable of living in tropical temperatures. It was through the use of human intelligence that mankind invented fire and tools which enabled them to adapt to all climates. Buffon saw his work as organizing and analyzing facts and following them to a rational and ordered conclusion; this is an intellectual and scientific framework that future investigators would use to advance their own discoveries.

Bibliography

Eisley, Loren. *Darwin's Century*. Garden City, N.Y.: Doubleday, 1958. The section on Buffon is brief and scattered in several parts of the text. Buffon is included in this work to provide the background for Charles Darwin's theory of evolution. This work is recommended as a general text on eighteenth century natural science, since the author's writing is highly accessible to the lay reader.

Lovejoy, A. O. "Buffon and the Problem of Species." In *Forerunners of Darwin, 1745-1859*, edited by Bentley Glass, O. Temkin, and W. L. Strauss, Jr. Baltimore: Johns Hopkins University Press, 1959. This article describes in some detail the major problems associated with classification of species and how Buffon's ideas on species fit with those of his predecessors and that of Linnaeus.

Mayr, Ernst. *The Growth of Biological Thought: Diversity, Evolution, and Inheritance*. Cambridge, Mass.: Harvard University Press, 1982. Mayr is a leading authority on Darwin and on the history of biological evolution. Each major section contains information on Buffon and his contributions to biology. The material is sometimes difficult, but the treatment is definitive.

Nordenskiöld, Eric. *The History of Biology*. New York: Tudor, 1928. Chapter 8 of this volume summarizes Buffon's major contributions. Even though the work is dated, the presentation of the materials is competent and provides useful information.

Wilkie, J. B. "The Idea of Evolution in the Writings of Buffon." *Annals of Science* 12, nos. 1-3: 4. This three-part article examines in some detail the questions of how Buffon may have considered the idea of evolution. Even though Buffon would have rejected the modern concept of evolution, there are concepts of transformation of species in Buffon that link him to later developments in evolutionary theory.

Victor W. Chen

JACOB BURCKHARDT

Born: May 25, 1818; Basel, Switzerland
Died: August 8, 1897; Basel, Switzerland
Area of Achievement: Historiography
Contribution: Burckhardt, a uniquely gifted historian and literary artist, was a pioneer in the development of modern *Kulturgeschichte*, the study of nonpolitical aspects of civilization. His lasting contribution was in Renaissance historiography, where his work became a model for the treatment of culture in the study of civilization.

Early Life
Part of an influential, aristocratic Swiss family, Jacob Burckhardt recalled his early childhood in Basel as being very happy. For three centuries, Jacob's ancestors utilized their financial abilities to amass a considerable fortune in the silk industry and international trade, which they parlayed into political power. The Burckhardts held one of the two burgomaster positions in the city for nearly two centuries, while other members of the family served the community as professors and clergymen. Jacob's own father, one of the less affluent Burckhardts, studied theology in Heidelberg and was pastor of the Basel ministry at the time of his son's birth. In 1838, the senior Burckhardt became the administrative head of the Reformed church in the Basel canton. Jacob recalled his father as being pleasant, a good scholar, and a capable artist. It was his father's artistic ability that first stimulated the youth's enduring love for art.

The joys of early childhood turned to sorrow with the unexpected death of his mother in 1830. This experience made a lasting impression on twelve-year-old Jacob, as he became painfully aware of the transitoriness of all living things. Throughout his adult life, Jacob experienced difficulty in establishing lasting relationships, and it may well have been memories of his mother's death that influenced his decision to remain a bachelor.

Burckhardt's patrician heritage instilled in him an aristocratic prejudice, a sensitivity to beauty and form, a deep, abiding respect for the dignity of mankind, and a Protestant morality, all of which would be reflected in his life as a teacher and scholar. As he matured into adulthood, however, his personal appearance seemed to belie his conservative nature. As a young man, he was notable for his uniquely stylish clothes, distinct coiffure, finger rings, and excessive taste for red wine and cigars. In later years, he dropped the foppish airs but retained his taste for wine and cigars.

The public school in Basel provided Burckhardt with an excellent primary education in the classics but left him undecided as to a vocation. After a brief stay in French-speaking Neuchâtel, where he wrote an essay on Gothic architecture, he entered the University of Basel in 1837 to study theology.

Eighteen months later, he experienced a prolonged religious crisis that resulted in his abandoning his orthodox religious beliefs and rejecting the ministry. Because of the support and encouragement of his father, Burckhardt attended the University of Berlin from 1839 to 1843 to pursue his historical interests. While there, Burckhardt was praised by the renowned classical scholars August Boeckh and Johann Gustav Droysen for his extensive knowledge of antiquity, but Burckhardt ultimately took his degree in 1843 under the eminent scientific historian Leopold von Ranke. Burckhardt greatly admired Ranke and his seminars, but the two never established a close relationship. Although master and student have been used to illustrate two diametrically different approaches to historiography, it should be noted that Ranke had praise for his student, and in 1872 Burckhardt was offered the chair of history at the University of Berlin as Ranke's successor—an offer that he refused because of his abhorrence of German politics.

Burckhardt's closest association in Berlin was with the pioneer art historian Franz Kugler, who encouraged Burckhardt to combine his love for history with his love for art and directed the attention of the fledgling student to Italy and the Renaissance.

Life's Work

In 1843, the University of Basel awarded Burckhardt a Ph.D. in absentia and the following year invited him to become a lecturer on history and art—a position he held with distinction for nearly fifty years. Because the university did not have an official vacancy until 1858, Burckhardt had to supplement his lecturing income with a variety of other jobs. For two years, he was the editor of the conservative *Basler Zeitung*, and he taught at the local grammar school for most of his career. In 1846, Burckhardt was given permission by the author to revise Kugler's text on art history, which brought in some revenue, and he was offered a lucrative position at the Academy of Art in Berlin. Burckhardt had no desire to return to Berlin but did so out of friendship to Kugler. For the next twelve years, Burckhardt taught at Basel, Berlin, and Zurich, with lengthy visits to Italy in 1847, 1848, and 1853. Despite his excessive work load and extensive travels, he was able to publish two important works during this period. His first major work, *Die Zeit Konstantins des Grossen* (1853; *The Age of Constantine the Great*, 1949), attested his love for ancient civilization. Although the study showed the important role Christianity played in the cultural life of the Middle Ages, Burckhardt's sympathies lay clearly with the decaying ancient world. His second publication, *Der Cicerone* (1855; *The Cicerone*, 1873), was a detailed study of Italian art, and it became the most popular travel guide to Italy in Europe. In 1855, Burckhardt accepted a teaching position at the new polytechnical institute in Zurich, not only to increase his earnings but also to gain access to the rich collection of Renaissance materials housed there. Three years later, there was a vacancy at the University of Basel, and Burckhardt readily accepted that university's only chair of history.

Family influence, formal education, work experience, and foreign travel provided Burckhardt with the inspiration for his life's work. After observing at first hand the political turmoil in Germany, the quiet, freedom-loving Swiss was repulsed by those scholars who saw history as past politics or a chronology of state development. It was the nonpolitical past, more specifically, the moral and mental past, that fascinated Burckhardt. His objective was to undertake a meticulous study of thought and conduct, religion and art, scholarship and speculation in an attempt to penetrate the *Kultur* of the people and discover what he called "the spirit of the age." Thus, in 1842 he announced that it was to *Kulturgeschichte* that he intended to devote his life, and the fulfillment of this self-established goal is represented par excellence in *Die Kultur der Renaissance in Italien* (1860; *The Civilization of the Renaissance in Italy*, 1878).

Burkhardt divided this book into six sections, each of which discussed a specific aspect of Italian *Kultur*. The section on the state as a work of art provided the political framework, as it emphasized the conflict between emperors and popes, but it was not political history in the traditional sense. His intent was to demonstrate how the state became free of outside control and, in the process, produced what Burckhardt called the modern "state-spirit." This phenomenon had its counterpart in the evolution of modern individualism, which was explained in the second section of the book. The development of the individual was characterized primarily by the rebirth of secularism and the perception of the Italian Humanists as independent entities, free of any corporate structure, such as the Church. While rebirth was the general theme of the entire work, it was of specific concern in the third section on the revival of antiquity. Here, Burckhardt argued that while the rebirth of Humanism complemented the newly emerging spirit of secular individualism, it was the result of what was happening in Italy and not the cause. Individualism and secularity would have evolved without the rebirth of antiquity. The last three sections of the work provided evidence of how the new secular individualism operated in society and how it influenced the culture and moral life of the age.

Summary

After more than a century, Jacob Burckhardt's history of the Italian Renaissance remains one of the most controversial works ever published. With justification, critics have stated that the work is too static and that it exaggerates the creativeness of Italy. It is too sharply delimited in time and space, as it neglects the other European countries and fails to consider the creative forces at work in the late Middle Ages. Burckhardt overemphasizes individualism, immorality, and irreligion in Italy and exaggerates the rediscovery of the classical world. Furthermore, Burckhardt's work is limited to a study of the upper class, is devoid of any economic analysis, and is based on the debatable assumption that there was a common spirit of the age that characterized all Italy for two hundred years.

Yet even the most ardent critics regard the book as a penetrating analysis of history and civilization. Burckhardt's work was unique in that he was one of the first to interpret the psychology of an epoch with power and insight. His methodology was highly original, as he employed a topical approach that permitted him to study what he termed "cross sections in history" from a variety of directions. His work treated civilization as a unit in a series of parallel discussions, each approaching the central problem from a different point of view. Critics of Burckhardt should also remember that he approached history as an artist, not as a philosopher, and with regard to written history he always considered himself an "arch dilettante," whose vocation was teaching.

Though Burckhardt lived another forty years after completing his history of the Renaissance, he never again published. With his health waning, Burckhardt requested to be relieved of his position in art history in 1885, and in 1893, suffering from acute asthmatic troubles, he surrendered his chair of history. Four years later, he died in his small two-room apartment over the local bakery in Basel. Although Burckhardt never published again, three of his major historical works were published posthumously: *Griechische Kulturgeschichte* (1898-1902; *History of Greek Culture*, abridged 1963), *Weltgeschichtliche Betrachtungen* (1905; *Force and Freedom: Reflections on History*, 1943), and *Historische Fragmente* (1929; translated in *Gesamtausgabe: Judgments on History and Historians*, 1958).

Bibliography
Burckhardt, Jacob. *The Civilization of the Renaissance in Italy.* Translated by S. G. C. Middlemore with an introduction by Benjamin Nelson and Charles Trinkaus. Vol. 1. New York: Harper & Row, 1958. The introduction contains an excellent summary and response to the critics of Burckhardt. Discusses what Burckhardt intended to do with his work as opposed to what others would have liked him to have done.

_____. *Letters.* Selected, edited, and translated by Alexander Dru. New York: Pantheon Books, 1955. With none of Burckhardt's biographies having been translated, this introduction contains the best biographical information available in English. Also included is a bibliography of all the principal editions of Burckhardt's letters.

Ferguson, Wallace K. *The Renaissance in Historical Thought.* Boston: Houghton Mifflin, 1948. The most scholarly coverage of Burckhardt in English. Contains little on his early life but gives detailed information on his place in Renaissance historiography. Good synopsis of his major works.

Gooch, G. P. *History and Historians in the Nineteenth Century.* New York: Longmans, Green, 1913. Rev. ed. Boston: Beacon Press, 1959. The best work on nineteenth century historiography. Attempts to establish Burckhardt's place among nineteenth century scholars. Apologetic in nature, containing little criticism of Burckhardt.

Thompson, James Westfall. *A History of Historical Writing.* Vol. 2. New York: Macmillan, 1942. Reprint. Gloucester, Mass.: Peter Smith, 1967. A good first source of Burckhardt. Brief, chronological, and factual, with little attempt at analysis. Must be supplemented by one of the other sources, as Thompson's omissions can be misleading.

Weintraub, Karl Joachim. "Jacob Burckhardt: The Historian Among the Philologists." *The American Scholar* 57 (Spring, 1988): 273-282. A concise, readable discussion of Burckhardt's posthumously published history of Greek culture. Taking as his point of departure the harshly critical response to this work among scholars of Burckhardt's time, Weintraub illumines Burckhardt's conception of cultural history.

——————. *Visions of Culture.* Chicago: University of Chicago Press, 1966. Second only to Ferguson in scholarly analysis of Burckhardt's history of the Renaissance. Surpasses Ferguson in biographical information and concentrates on Burckhardt's contribution to *Kulturgeschichte.*

Wayne M. Bledsoe

PEDRO CALDERÓN DE LA BARCA

Born: January 17, 1600; Madrid, Spain
Died: May 25, 1681; Madrid, Spain
Areas of Achievement: Theater and drama
Contribution: Calderón continued the Golden Age of drama after the death of Lope de Vega Carpio, bringing to Spain some of the greatest dramatic literature and *autos sacramentales* in the seventeenth century.

Early Life

The bright Spanish cultural renaissance had its center in the *fin de siècle* spirit, and Pedro Calderón de la Barca was born into it, in 1600, in Madrid. His parents were very much part of the establishment; his father, strong-willed and demanding, was secretary to the Council of the Royal Treasury. It was his mother's wish before her death in 1610 that Pedro enter the priesthood; his father, on his deathbed when Calderón was fifteen, turned her request into an order, a dying command that was to plague Calderón throughout his career, until he finally took holy orders at the age of fifty-one. Without his parents to guide him, Calderón was forced to examine his life alone, with the guilt of disobedience mixed with a sense of not knowing who he was. No early portrait of Calderón exists, but a graphological analysis of his handwriting done by one scholar reveals a shy, nervous, and sensitive young man, not so much challenging his faith or loyalty to the Catholic church as questioning his own place in it. This combination of an inquiring mind together with a mandate by his dead parents confused Calderón during his youth and possibly led him to explore answers to his dilemma in the dramatic mode, dramatizing over and over the conflict between predestination and free will.

Calderón's schooling, however, was not neglected. From 1614 to 1620, his academic virtuosity reflected his internal confusion and indecision. At the Imperial Jesuit College, he received an excellent education in the classics, religion, and (later, at the University of Alcala) rhetoric and logic. In Salamanca he studied law. It was, however, a minor poetry contest in 1620, part of a celebration in honor of Saint Isadore, patron saint of Madrid, that was to turn Calderón's life away from the traditional pursuits of priesthood or law to writing. Lope de Vega, the acknowledged master dramatist of the Spanish Golden Age, was a judge and saw fit to praise Calderón's entry. Inspired, Calderón began to write plays at a rate that rivaled Lope de Vega's (who is said to have written fifteen hundred plays in his lifetime). His first play (discounting youthful efforts), *Amor, honor y poder* (love, honor, and power), was performed in Madrid at the court of Philip IV in 1623 and was immediately followed by *La selva confusa* (the entangled forest) and *Judas Macabeo* (Judas Macabee), both in 1623. Calderón's military service in

Italy and Flanders interrupted his dramatic writing for a short time. Returning from Spain's triumph at Breda, Calderón wrote *El sitio de Breda* (the siege of Breda), performed in 1625 and, judging from accurate geographical details in the play, conjectured to be based on his own experiences in battle.

The court life of the Spanish Golden Age could only emerge from more than one hundred years of relatively peaceful royal succession since Ferdinand and Isabella, who united Spain and defeated the Moors in a decisive battle at Granada in 1492. When Lope de Vega died in 1635, Calderón was his successor at the court of Philip IV, during the construction of the king's great court theater, El Coliseo del Buen Retiro.

Life's Work

"The sober celebration of order triumphant"—this phrase, from James E. Maraniss' study, *On Calderón* (1978), summarizes Calderón's life's work, manifested in his dramatic approach to his secular plays (1630 to 1651) as well as his religious attitudes expressed in the *auto sacramentale* form he favored after 1651. Throughout his career, which lasted more than fifty years, Calderón viewed the function of the stage as the reestablishment of order in the face of the constant threat of political, moral, and spiritual rebellion. By 1635, at the beginning of Calderón's succession as director at the court of Philip IV, he had written thirty plays, of which three—*La dama duende* (wr. 1629, pr. 1636; *The Phantom Lady*, 1664), *El príncipe constante* (1629; *The Constant Prince*, 1853), and *La vida es sueño* (1635; *Life Is a Dream*, 1830)—have joined the permanent repertory of classical world drama, performed, adapted, and modernized in many countries. The latter play, considered his masterpiece, embodies the themes and the style of virtually all the secular plays: A hero, wrongly deprived of his royal honor, examines his own consciousness to recover his station and his free will. The gongoristic style of bombast and exaggeration, together with the insertion of poetic monologues, denotes the dramatic style of the period, of which Calderón and Lope de Vega, along with Tirso de Molina, were masters.

Calderón's appointment coincided with the construction and occupation of the royal palace, Buen Retiro, begun in 1629 and opened in 1634, featuring the Coliseo del Buen Retiro, a special theater space expressly designed for the performance of his plays. It was this permanent home and captive audience of sympathetic courtiers, together with encouragement of his early work, that allowed the prolific Calderón to continue his career as playwright well into mid-life. The theatrical companies of that day, licensed by the king, gave private performances to the royal court, usually before their public debut; consequently, Calderón's position at court gave him easy access to the commercial theater outside the royal palace. One memorable evening performance of *El mayor encanto, amor* (1635; *Love, the Greatest Enchant-*

ment, 1870) took place on an island in the garden lake, with the audience attending from gondolas; a sudden storm toppled several vessels and blew out the candles, causing the six-hour play to be postponed.

The many performances at court in the years between 1635 and 1650, described by one biographer as "counted among the rare blissful hours in theatrical history," perfected Calderón's dramaturgical skills and gave the theater world such masterpieces as *El alcalde de Zalamea* (1643; *The Mayor of Zalamea*, 1853), *El mágico prodigioso* (1637; *The Wonder-Working Magician*, 1959), *El médico de su honra* (1637; *The Surgeon of His Honor*, 1853), and *A secreto agravio, secreta venganza* (1637; *Secret Vengeance for Secret Insult*, 1961); these plays were collected from time to time during this period and published in several volumes under Calderón's supervision.

A series of personal blows, including the death of his brothers and mistress in 1650, forced him to retreat into a monastic life. Calderón's retreat into priesthood did not end his perpetual examination of the idea of free choice as moral basis. The *autos sacramentales* of his later period reflect once again the metaphysical struggle between earthly desires and the willful renunciation (a word used often by Calderón's biographers) of those desires by the Christian soul. The *autos sacramentales* were allegorical pieces in which abstractions such as Everyman, Error, and the World were personified in Manichaean battles with temptations to sin and moral compromise. By far the most frequent figure was the World, whose tribulations on the stage actually continued for Calderón his never-ending struggle to reconcile his ethical standards with his own human weaknesses, as he saw them. His most popular *auto sacramentale*, *El gran teatro del mundo* (wr. 1635, pr. 1649; *Great Theater of the World*, 1856), was written before his investiture and contains all the elements of the genre: A Director in gaudy symbolic costume of stars and rays calls together the World, the Law of Grace, and various actors in the Play of Life to "celebrate/ My power infinitely great." As the play-within-a-play moves to its patrological conclusion, the Poor Man retreats to a subservient position and the Rich Man justifies his place in the importance of historical events, thus reinforcing the conservative view. Despite modern reservations about the outcome, the play is studied as a model of the type.

During his most fruitful years at court, Calderón kept careful accounts of his work, publishing them in several volumes under the editorship of his brother and other friends, rejecting publicly the imitations and acknowledging the authentic works as his own. Near the end of his life, after publishing five volumes of his work, he provided an official list of his secular and religious pieces. Thus, despite the paucity of biographical documentation of Calderón's life—caused in large part by his habit of keeping secret his social and private activities—his canon is definitive and relatively uncontested, and includes some 180 plays.

Summary

Spanish literature, with the exception of a few masterpieces, is not nearly as widely known in Western culture at large as are French and English literature. Spain, while flourishing in its own cultural climate, did not export her ideas and creative artists. Spain's participation in the Thirty Years' War promoted more crossbreeding of cultures, but it remained for the scholars of the nineteenth and twentieth centuries to renew the world's interest in Miguel de Cervantes, Lope de Vega, Tirso de Molina, and the other giants of Spanish literature.

Although his works were performed in some European countries during the eighteenth century, Pedro Calderón de la Barca's contributions to world literature have been only lately appreciated. His defense of royalist principles, in a time when the rising middle class was questioning monarchies elsewhere, makes even more remarkable his popularity and the currency of his ideas in today's humanistic studies. Further, the dramatization of the philosophical question of free will versus predestination had found no greater craftsman since the Greek tragedians. Finally, the *autos sacramentales* provide a religious continuity from the medieval pageant plays of all European countries to the modern work of T. S. Eliot and Christopher Fry. Calderón should not be considered a minor local phenomenon isolated by the Pyrenees from the mainstream of Western ideas, but rather a gifted, prolific, and articulate spokesperson for the universal themes of the late European Renaissance: man's relation to his God, his country, and his fellowman, and the nature of his being.

Bibliography

Aycock, Wendell M., and Sydney P. Cravens, eds. *Calderón de la Barca at the Tercentenary: Comparative Views*. Lubbock: Texas Tech Press, 1982. An important collection of papers on the three-hundredth anniversary of Calderón's death. The essayists concentrate on comparing some of Calderón's contributions with other artistic impulses, such as German Idealist philosophy, Euripides, Mexican cleric characters, and William Shakespeare.

Cascardi, Anthony J. *The Limits of Illusion: A Critical Study of Calderón*. Cambridge, England: Cambridge University Press, 1984. Valuable for the breadth and variety of its inquiry. Concentrates on Calderón's unique notion of a universal dramatic theme—illusion. Index.

Edwards, Gwynne. *The Prison and the Labyrinth*. Cardiff: University of Wales Press, 1978. This imagery study of Calderón's tragedies illuminates the texts by characterizing his moral dilemma as physical enclosures from which his true psychological and spiritual self cannot escape without free will. "Disposition and environment may incline" man's will in one direction or another, says Edwards, but "they cannot force." Contains a bibliography and an index.

Gerstinger, Heinz. *Pedro Calderón de la Barca*. Translated by Diana Stone Peters. New York: Frederick Ungar, 1973. Begins by describing Spain's Golden Age and its theater, then proceeds through Calderón's dramaturgy, worldview, religious attitudes, modern interpretations, and permanent legacy to dramatic literature. The second section treats nine plays individually, adding a valuable bibliography and handy index. Contains a chronology with English play titles.

Hesse, Everett W. *Calderón de la Barca*. Boston: Twayne, 1967. Treats the Spanish theater of the Golden Age, the political and social arena, the structure of Calderón's work, the works in which he excelled, and Calderón's critical reception. Particularly valuable is Hesse's discussion of such subgenres as cloak-and-sword plays, honor tragedies, and mythological plays. Selected bibliography and index.

Honig, Edwin. *Calderón and the Seizures of Honor*. Cambridge, Mass.: Harvard University Press, 1972. These essays were generated from Honig's translations of Calderón's plays in 1961 and 1970 and constitute the clearest, most easily accessible glosses on the plays available to the average reader. An appendix offers passages in the Spanish original.

Maraniss, James E. *On Calderón*. Columbia: University of Missouri Press, 1978. Stressing Calderón's sense of "order triumphant," Maraniss moves through the canon examining the structural integrity of each play, the symmetry and careful alternation of the plots, and the repeatedly demonstrated dramatic restatement of acknowledged social principles.

Mujica, Barbara Louise. *Calderón's Characters: An Existential Point of View*. Barcelona, Spain: Puvill, 1980. A strong essay that examines the characters of Calderón's plays with an eye toward their existential choices and the sense of free will in the face of despair. Mujica claims that "the type of character—free and *en situation*—which is the hallmark of existentialist fiction is also the hallmark of seventeenth-century Spanish theater, in particular, Calderón's."

Wardropper, Bruce W., ed. *Critical Essays on the Theatre of Calderón*. New York: New York University Press, 1965. Essays on Calderón's themes, characters, structure, political viewpoint, and theoretical perspectives. The opening article, by A. A. Parker, is a good summary of the justifications for ranking Calderón among the great writers of a great literary age.

Thomas J. Taylor

JOHN CALVIN

Born: July 10, 1509; Noyon, Picardy
Died: May 27, 1564; Geneva
Areas of Achievement: Theology and religion
Contribution: Calvin was one of the most important theologians of the Protestant Reformation of the sixteenth century. The Reformed church that he established in Geneva became a model for Calvinist churches throughout Europe. Calvinism itself became the most dynamic Protestant religion of the seventeenth century.

Early Life

John Calvin was born in Noyon, Picardy, on July 10, 1509, the second son of Gérard Cauvin and Jeanne le Franc Cauvin. His father was the secretary to the Bishop of Noyon and fiscal procurator for the province, and his mother was the daughter of a well-to-do innkeeper. The young Calvin was tutored for a career in the Church, and in 1523 he entered the Collège de la Marche at the University of Paris. It was there that he Latinized his name to Calvinus for scholarly purposes. Next, he attended the Collège de Montaigne, an institution of great importance in the Christian humanistic tradition of the day. After having received his master of arts degree, he studied law at the University of Orléans. He returned to Paris in 1531, where he furthered his studies with some of the greatest Humanists of the period.

Sixteenth century Europe was in ecclesiastical ferment. The Roman Catholic church had long been under attack because of its weaknesses and abuses. Religious reformers had, for more than a century, called for a thorough cleansing of the Church. In 1517, Martin Luther had initiated the action which ultimately became the Protestant Reformation. Given this environment, Calvin was soon affected by these ideas of protest and of reform. During this period of transition, Calvin published his first book, a study of Seneca's *De Clementia* (c. A.D. 55-56; *On Clemency*), which revealed him to be a forceful and precise writer.

Soon after the publication of this work, Calvin was converted to Protestantism. Fearing for his safety, he fled Paris and went first to Angoulême and later to Basel. He devoted himself to a study of theology, concentrating on the Bible, as Luther had done. In 1536, he published the results of his study in the first edition of his most important work, *Christianae religionis institutio* (*Institutes of the Christian Religion*, 1561). This work was to be refined, expanded (quadrupled in size from this edition to the final, 1559 edition), and developed over the course of his life. It quickly won for him a reputation as a Protestant authority. Indeed, most scholars agree that it is the single most important work produced during the Reformation.

The *Institutes of The Christian Religion* provided the foundation for a different form of Protestantism. Calvin's training as a lawyer helped him to produce a work which was well organized, clear, and logical. There were two primary themes within the work: the absolute majesty of God and the absolute depravity of man. On the one hand, God is omnipotent and omniscient, and therefore He knows all that was, is, and will be. Man, because of his corrupt nature, cannot determine his salvation; only God can do so. Indeed, because of God's omniscience, He has predetermined who is to be saved and who is to be damned.

The doctrine of predestination, while it did not originate with Calvin, made good works useless. While this may seem fatalistic, to Calvin it was not. A member of the elect would most assuredly perform good works as a sign that God was working through him. Hence, one of the elect would work hard and strive for earthly success in order to prove himself as having received God's grace. Calvin also stated that Christ is present in spirit when believers gather prayerfully; priests are not necessary, for they have no special powers. He also rejected all sacraments except for baptism and the Eucharist.

Life's Work

Shortly before the *Institutes of the Christian Religion* was published, Calvin left Basel for Ferrara, Italy. There, he visited the Duchess of Ferrara, a sympathizer who had protected a number of reformers. Calvin made a strong appeal to her for further financial support of the Reformation. This was the first of many of his efforts to acquire aristocratic support, which was essential in an age when aristocrats still controlled much power and wealth. Calvin returned to Basel, traveled to France, and, in 1536, stopped in Geneva, a city-state which had just become Protestant.

At this time, everyone in a given place had to be of the same religion. Geneva had revolted against its bishop, but the city had not determined which Protestant ritual it would follow. Calvin, thus, stepped into a religious vacuum. He held public lectures on the Bible, and he printed a tract to prepare the Genevese for his concept of the Reformed faith. His dour version of Christianity, however, was met with antipathy by many less austere Genevese. In 1538, Calvin and his associate, Guillaume Farel, were ordered to leave Geneva.

Calvin went to Strasbourg for the next three years. There he developed a liturgy in French, created an organization for running a parish, and attended many religious debates on the Holy Roman Empire. He debated with Lutheran theologians, especially Philipp Melanchthon, and with Catholic theologians as well. During the debates, he became convinced that Roman Catholics could never be negotiated with and that there would never be a reunion with the Roman church. He also became convinced that Lutheranism had not resulted in enough reforms within its church. In 1540, he married

Idelette de Bure. They had one child, who died in infancy. Idelette died in 1549, and Calvin never remarried. A naturally reticent man, Calvin rarely permitted outsiders a glimpse of his personal life.

In 1541, Calvin was asked by the Genevese council to return. He was promised total cooperation in building the religious state that he wanted. His first activity was to propose a series of ecclesiastical ordinances, which were ratified on January 2, 1541. The ordinances were to become the cornerstone of Reformed church (Calvinist/Presbyterian) polity throughout Europe. The ministry was divided into four categories: doctors, pastors, lay elders, and deacons. The doctors were to study the Bible and to develop theology; Calvin was the only doctor at that time. Pastors were to proclaim the word of God; elders were to oversee the carrying out of the Reformed church's dicta, that is, they were to be moral policemen; deacons were to help those who could not help themselves, that is, to perform benevolent works. The Company of Pastors was the official governing body of the Reformed church. Under the leadership of Calvin, the Company of Pastors determined religious assignments, worked with Protestants in other countries, and determined theology. The Company of Pastors also worked with the elders to control Geneva.

There were occasional sharp conflicts with the city council, but Calvin won absolute control of the city by 1555. All Genevese were forced to accept the moral laws of the Reformed faith or to suffer the consequences. From 1555 until his death in 1564, fifty-eight people were executed and 786 were banished in order to preserve the morals of the community. The most celebrated case was that of Michael Servetus, a somewhat eccentric Spanish theologian, who wished to debate Calvin on the doctrine of the Trinity. Calvin warned him not to come to Geneva. Servetus ignored the warning, came to Geneva in 1553, was arrested and convicted of heresy, and was burned. Calvin was not a believer in religious toleration.

With Geneva under his absolute control, Calvin devoted more time to the spread of his Reformed church to other areas. He created in 1559 a religious academy, which ultimately became the University of Geneva. Protestants from all over Europe were encouraged to come to Geneva to study. As his native land was his particular area of interest, hundreds of refugees were trained in the new theology and then were assisted in their return to France. Calvin also established an underground network throughout France to bind these French Reformed, or Huguenot, parishes together. Representative assemblies of pastors and elders were also encouraged. Drawing upon his earlier experiences in France and elsewhere, Calvin appealed to sympathetic French nobles for protection for the Huguenots. His most notable convert was the King of Navarre, although this ultimately resulted in the French Wars of Religion.

The last years of Calvin's life were spent in dominating Genevese theological issues, in working with Calvinists everywhere, and in developing the *Institutes of the Christian Religion* further. In the 1560's, he had serious health problems, and he permitted his heir apparent, Theodore Beza, to take over most of the responsibilities of managing the affairs of the Reformed church. On May 27, 1564, Calvin died. Throughout his life he had devoutly believed that he had been called by God to reform His church; this he had done. His powerful intellect and his unswerving devotion to his theology do much to explain Calvin's enormous impact on Western theology and on Western religion.

Summary

John Calvin's intellectual talents, quick mind, forceful writing style, and precise teaching skills enabled him to become one of the most important figures in Western religious history. While in Geneva, he created a religious dictatorship which became a model for Reformed church/Calvinist churches throughout Europe. His *Institutes of the Christian Religion* became one of the most important documents in Western theology. Even during his lifetime, his significance was well recognized, and Geneva itself was called a Protestant Rome.

Calvinism, as this second-generation Protestantism came to be called, quickly became the most dynamic theology in a Europe wracked by religious debate. Although Calvinism was austere in the extreme, its success may be explained. First, the Roman Catholic church was so corrupt and so filled with abuses that a thorough purging was viewed as absolutely necessary by most religious reformers of the day. To many, Luther had simply not gone far enough; Calvin, on the other hand, created an absolutely cleansed church. Second, Calvin's rules for a godly life were clear and succinct in comparison with those of the Roman church, and this clarity was appealing to those who hoped for salvation. Third, Calvin's tenet of predestination, while on the surface appearing to be fatalistic, came to be a rationale for the behavior of the middle class. While Calvin had stated that no one could know whether one was a member of the elect, it was believed that God's grace could be measured by one's success. Although this conclusion is much debated by historians, it is nevertheless true that the Calvinist areas of Europe were to be the most economically successful over the next several centuries.

Following Calvin's death, Calvinism became the dominant Protestant theology in the religious wars that occurred over the next century. Calvinist leaders played major roles in a number of European wars. Calvinism became the dominant religion of the Low Countries, southwestern France, Scotland, central Germany, and southeastern England. In each of these areas, strong economic growth took place, an educated middle class emerged, and demands for political power developed. Indeed, the period from 1550 to 1700 and afterward cannot be understood without an awareness of the impact of the theology of John Calvin.

Bibliography

Bouwsma, William J. *John Calvin: A Sixteenth-Century Portrait*. New York: Oxford University Press, 1988. This work by a distinguished historian has been acclaimed as the best modern biography of Calvin. At the same time, as the subtitle indicates, Bouwsma uses Calvin's experience "to illuminate the momentous cultural crisis central to his century." Includes sixty pages of notes, a bibliography, and an index.

Calvin, John. *Institutes of the Christian Religion*. Edited by John T. McNeill. 2 vols. Philadelphia: Westminster Press, 1960. These volumes are an annotated edition of Calvin's work and include a lengthy introduction and an extensive bibliography.

Haller, William. *The Rise of Puritanism*. New York: Columbia University Press, 1938. While his prose is at times turgid, Haller offers insight into the spread of Calvinism into England. His study is useful for understanding why Calvinism spread so rapidly.

Kingdon, Robert M. *Geneva and the Coming of the Wars of Religion in France, 1555-1563*. Geneva: Librairie E. Droz, 1956. Important for understanding Calvin's methods of exporting his theology to other areas of Europe.

McNeill, John T. *The History and Character of Calvinism*. New York: Oxford University Press, 1954. A carefully balanced source that offers an excellent interpretive discussion of the theory and practice of Calvinism. Includes a lengthy biography of Calvin, followed by a series of chapters on the spread of Calvinism throughout Europe and to the United States.

O'Connell, Marvin R. *The Counter Reformation, 1559-1610*. New York: Harper & Row, 1974. Places Calvin and the spread of Calvinism in perspective. Includes an excellent bibliography.

Parker, Thomas H. L. *John Calvin: A Biography*. Philadelphia: Westminster Press, 1975. Parker's work is a concise, single volume on the life of John Calvin. Particularly useful for a study of the impact of university life on Calvin and upon Calvin's scholarship. Well written and easily understood. Useful bibliography.

Wendel, François. *Calvin: The Origins and Development of His Religious Thought*. New York: Harper & Row, 1963. First published in French in 1950, Wendel's work is essential for an understanding of the evolution of Calvin's theology.

William S. Brockington, Jr.

JEAN-JACQUES-RÉGIS DE CAMBACÉRÈS

Born: October 18, 1753; Montpellier, France
Died: March 8, 1824; Paris, France
Areas of Achievement: Law and government
Contribution: Cambacérès served France as a skilled jurist, an able legislator, and a prudent administrator during the revolutionary period. As second consul to Napoleon I, he effected a new civil code, controlled the media, and served as a moderating influence on the emperor. Without personal political ambitions, he dedicated himself to maintaining Napoleon's power and to serving his country.

Early Life

Jean-Jacques-Régis de Cambacérès was born in Montpellier, France, on October 18, 1753, one of eleven children of Jean-Antoine and Marie-Rose (née Vassal) Cambacérès. The Cambacérès family was a distinguished one, long active in politics. Cambacérès' father served as Mayor of Montpellier, and Cambacérès was destined for a career in law. He attended the Collège d'Aix, rather than the one at Montpellier, which was judged not good enough for the young Cambacérès. A bright and diligent scholar, he excelled and developed a reputation for exactitude and a painstaking devotion to detail— these traits were to stand him in good stead later when he was helping to draft the civil code for France.

By 1569, he was practicing law in Montpellier, where he later (in 1774) became councillor of the local fiscal court (*Cour des comptes et des aides*). In 1771, he renounced his estate, a political move in keeping with the tenor of the times; Cambacérès was adept at gauging political barometers. His father had suffered some financial reverses, and Cambacérès had attempted to restore the family's financial position. He was ultimately to become a very rich man through his services to Napoleon. Because of his growing legal reputation, he was elected in 1789 president of the criminal tribunal at Hérault, and when the states-general were convened that year he was chosen as the nobility's second representative for the Montpellier district. When Montpellier was judged to be entitled to only one representative from the nobility, he returned from Paris. That political setback did not daunt Cambacérès, who in 1790 helped found the Société des Amis de la Constitution et de l'Égalité at Montpellier.

Because of his political activity and legal reputation, he was elected in 1792 to the National Convention. A political moderate, he attempted to steer a middle course and avoid the impending excesses of the leftists, but the trial of King Louis XVI eventually forced him to take a stand, qualified as it was. After losing the fight to have the convention judged not competent to try the king, he did find the king guilty, but he recommended that the king's execution be effected only if France were invaded.

Cambacérès' "moderation" was politically dangerous, and he attempted to divert suspicion by absorbing himself in legislative and judicial matters. He submitted in 1793 a plan, containing 695 articles, for a civil code, but though the code reflected the politics of the times, it was not revolutionary enough for the convention; a shorter version, with only 297 articles, was rejected as well. When the convention became more moderate, after Robespierre's downfall in 1794, Cambacérès emerged as one of its leaders, serving as president of the convention and later as president of the Committee for Public Safety. In that role, he helped conclude the peace treaties of 1795 with Prussia and Spain. He also called for a general amnesty and attempted to prevent vindictive behavior and new persecutions. When the convention was dissolved, he became a member of the Council of Five Hundred, but the Directory which came to power regarded his moderation with suspicion. His third draft of the civil code was also rejected, and he retired from his position as president of the Council and returned to practicing law.

Life's Work

Cambacérès returned to the government, serving as minister of justice, in June, 1799, just prior to the *coup d'état* of the Eighteenth Brumaire, which overthrew the Directory and established the consulate. Although he took no active part in the revolution, Cambacérès played a typically discreet role in assisting Napoleon and Emmanuel Sieyès with the coup. In recognition of his help and of his acknowledged legal prowess, Napoleon, who was named first consul in December, 1799, named Cambacérès second consul. (Charles François Lebrun, a sixty-year-old Norman with financial experience and more conservative views than Cambacérès, was named third consul.)

Although as second consul he was theoretically second in command to Napoleon, Cambacérès had no political ambitions of his own and directed his considerable abilities and energies to furthering Napoleon's interests. Cambacérès succeeded, through negotiating with selected ministers and reducing the size of the legislative body and the Tribunate, in reducing the number of influential opponents of Napoleon and engineered the assemblies' 1802 election of Napoleon as consul for life. Cambacérès' strategy effectively brought an end to representative government in France, and Napoleon was free to enact the long-desired civil code and to become emperor only two years later. Napoleon's ascension resulted in a promotion for the loyal Cambacérès, who became arch-chancellor of the empire, presiding in the emperor's frequent absence over the senate.

Although Napoleon held all the real power, Cambacérès was the emperor's trusted adviser and confidant, a bureaucrat who worked diligently to help Napoleon retain control of France. As his voluminous papers indicate, Cambacérès was in constant communication with Napoleon, even when the emperor was on one of his numerous military campaigns. One of Cambacérès' primary functions was to serve as an unofficial minister of propaganda for Napoleon, who recognized the value of the press. Cambacérès not only reviewed political articles and decided the fates of individual generals but also inserted articles in selected journals. He also was involved in ordering that books be written on selected topics, and in 1806 he printed the fictitious *Ms. trouvé dans le cabinet du roi de Prusse à Berlin*, a book about the partition of Poland. Though he was primarily concerned with domestic affairs, he did oversee the publication and distribution of maps of battles and campaigns. Even the discussions of the Council of State were edited by Cambacérès before they were subsequently printed in the *Moniteur*, the government's journal. This control was extended in 1811, when a special decree gave Cambacérès control over the telegraph linking Paris to major European cities—he effectively determined what messages would be transmitted.

In addition to managing the news, Cambacérès was active in the elaborate patronage system Napoleon and he devised in order to create a new supportive nobility to replace the old nobility. Since titles were not attached to land or to family but were granted by the state for service, people were encouraged to serve the state and to remain loyal to the new empire.

Cambacérès served not only as Napoleon's second in command but also as his personal legal adviser, though Napoleon's personal affairs certainly impinged upon his public political life. When the emperor wanted his marriage to Joséphine nullified, Cambacérès handled the intricate and delicate negotiations.

During his Napoleonic years, Cambacérès exercised considerable power over the media, the government, and the legal system, which he helped create. He also served as a moderating influence on Napoleon. Yet his most important attempted interventions—to save the life of the Duc d'Enghien and to forestall the military campaigns of 1812-1813—were futile.

When Napoleon abdicated and the Bourbons were restored to power in 1814, Cambacérès survived and even endorsed the return of the monarchy, the current stabilizing force in France. When Napoleon returned to power the following year, Cambacérès was persuaded to resume his pre-Restoration duties, this time to direct the Ministry of Justice and preside over the Chamber of Peers, though he had undoubtedly had reservations about the likelihood of Napoleon's continued success. The Hundred Days did, indeed, end with Napoleon's defeat at Waterloo; upon Louis XVIII's final restoration to power, however, Cambacérès was not as fortunate as he had been before. He was exiled and moved to Belgium. Although he was permitted in 1818 to return to France and to regain his civil and political rights, he did not again hold public office. Six years later he died in Paris.

Summary

As the titular head of the French government during Napoleon's frequent, extensive absences, Jean-Jacques-Régis de Cambacérès theoretically had a considerable amount of power. In fact, some historians have maintained that he governed France while Napoleon was away. As his own voluminous correspondence to the emperor indicates, Cambacérès was essentially an adviser and the administrator of Napoleon's policies, though he certainly had a hand in drafting key legislation and in coordinating and supervising the various codes that were implemented during Napoleon's reign.

Because Napoleon would not or could not delegate authority, the power to decide significant events was his alone; yet that centralized authority caused delays in dealing with governmental affairs and produced administrators unwilling to take the initiative and assume responsibility. Napoleon's grand schemes, including the reform of the codes, required implementation by an administrator who could handle detail, however trivial. Cambacérès, the legal technician, was the consummate lawyer, equally at home in administrative, legal, and financial matters. He also discharged some military tasks for Napoleon. Though he did not serve on the commission Napoleon appointed in 1800 to prepare a new draft of the civil code, Cambacérès' previous three drafts and his ideas found their way into the civil code adopted in 1804.

Cambacérès was a political survivor, an administrator, and a legislator who steered a middle course between extremes in the hope of serving in a stable, efficient French government. His moderation, his vacillation, and his desire to please all parties have made him as suspect to contemporary historians as he was to his political colleagues on the far Left. During his political career he was a Republican, an anti-Terrorist, a regicide, a Jacobin, an enthusiast, and a sometime supporter of Napoleon and the Bourbons—in short, whatever was expedient and consonant with his advocacy of a stable government.

Given his aversion to political chaos and corruption, which were rampant from 1795 to 1799, his support of Napoleon seems almost inevitable. He seems to have been attracted by Napoleon's authoritarianism and expediency and his desire to effect needed change. Although Cambacérès may have been more inclined to authoritarianism than Napoleon, his actions were as moderate as his views, and while he counseled Napoleon, he seems not to have urged his views with any vigor. Richard Boulind, who has studied Cambacérès' ties to Napoleon, sees Cambacérès' homosexuality as the key to their productive working relationship. In a classic case of alter egos, Cambacérès, possessed with "feminine" tact, reflectiveness, and precaution, balances and is attracted to the "masculine" Napoleon, who is assertive and decisive. Regardless of how this working relationship is seen, there is no question about Cambacérès' having been the ideal statesman to complement Napoleon and his dreams for France.

Bibliography

Bergeron, Louis. *France Under Napoleon*. Princeton, N.J.: Princeton University Press, 1981. Part of Bergeron's book concerns the patronage system instituted under Napoleon's rule. Bergeron explains the system, examines Cambacérès' role, and shows how the system benefitted both the recipients and Napoleon. Details of Cambacérès' social and financial ascent are provided.

Boulind, Richard. *Cambacérès and the Bonapartes*. New York: H. P. Kraus, 1976. Boulind includes the unpublished papers of Cambacérès, both letters to Napoleon and papers on the personal and dynastic interests of Napoleon. His introductions to both parts provide the most extensive discussion in English of Cambacérès. Boulind provides a brief biography and a psychological reading of the relationship between Cambacérès and Napoleon.

Cronin, Vincent. *Napoleon Bonaparte: An Intimate Biography*. New York: William Morrow, 1972. As the title suggests, Cronin's book mingles history with anecdotes and personal details. He is helpful in providing a comparison and contrast between Napoleon and Cambacérès and in detailing the degree to which Cambacérès advanced Napoleon's cause.

Holtman, Robert B. *Napoleon's Propaganda*. Baton Rouge: Louisiana State University Press, 1950. Holtman examines the means by which Napoleon and Cambacérès managed the news during Napoleon's rule. According to Holtman, Cambacérès was the primary agent of control—news releases, the telegraph, fabricated books, and the like.

Marquart, Robert. "The Fortunes of Cambacérès." *Revue de l'Institut Napoléon* 127 (1973): 43-52. Marquart provides a thorough discussion of Cambacérès' acquisition of an immense fortune through prudent management and imperial generosity. Marquart's findings attest the social and financial rise of a class that replaced the old nobility.

Thompson, J. M. *Napoleon Bonaparte: His Rise and Fall*. New York: Oxford University Press, 1952. Thompson's book is particularly helpful in its discussion of Cambacérès' role in obtaining Napoleon's canonical divorce from Joséphine. Thompson details Cambacérès' painstaking preparation of the case and sees the divorce as evidence of the deterioration of Napoleon's character under stress.

Thomas L. Erskine

LUÍS DE CAMÕES

Born: c. 1524; probably Lisbon, Portugal
Died: June 10, 1580; Lisbon, Portugal
Area of Achievement: Literature
Contribution: Camões is the author of *Os Lusíadas* (1572; *The Lusiads*, 1655), the national epic of Portugal. Celebrating the voyage of Vasco da Gama, the poem recites the heroic history of the Portuguese nation.

Early Life

Luís de Camões (sometimes written Camoëns) was born in 1524, the year Vasco da Gama died. He was probably born in Lisbon, although by 1527 his family was living with Luís' grandparents in Coimbra; most likely they fled from Lisbon to escape the plague, which reached the capital in that year.

Luís' father was Simão Vas de Camões, a gentleman of no great power or wealth. Little is known of Anna de Macedo or Sá, Luís' mother, beyond her name. When his father returned to Lisbon to take a position in the king's warehouse, Luís remained in Coimbra with his mother in the home of her family, who were influential people there.

As Luís grew into manhood, Coimbra was undergoing its own development into the educational center of Portugal. Under the guidance of John III, a great university was permanently established. In or near 1539, Luis entered the university and must have read Vergil, Ovid, Lucan, and Cicero in the original Latin. He learned to speak Spanish fluently and was also exposed to Italian, Greek, geography, history, music, and many other subjects. During this period, he developed many friendships with young aristocrats, from whom he learned courtly tastes and manners. He also suffered his first taste of love, leading to some of his earliest, most tragic lyrics. After the conclusion of his studies, he left Coimbra for Lisbon, never to return.

Life's Work

When Camões traveled to Lisbon to make his fortune, in or near 1543, he began a life of adventure and accomplishment as exciting as any legendary hero's. He started quietly enough: Camões took a position as a tutor to the young son of a count. During these years, he learned all he could of his country's history and culture. Camões was considered charming and attractive. Surviving portraits from this time show a handsome man with reddish-gold hair and blue eyes. In 1544, in church, he saw a young girl, Catarina de Ataíde, and fell immediately and passionately in love with her. For the rest of his life, Camões would consider Catarina the great spiritual love of his life; many of his most beautiful lyrics are dedicated to her.

While still in Lisbon, Camões also wrote three well-received comedies: *Auto del-Rei Seleuco*, performed in 1542, *Enfatriões*, performed in 1540, and *Filodemo*, performed in 1555. As he became more widely known as a writer, Camões was drawn deeper into the inner circles of the court, where he found many who admired his talents and charms, and many who despised his smugness and sharp tongue. Never one to feign modesty, he dedicated impassioned poetry to a series of lovers, in spite of his devotion to Catarina. Finally, his brashness led to his disgrace at court, though the actual sins committed are uncertain. Because of the scandal, he enlisted, under duress, in the army in 1547, served two years in northern Africa, and lost the use of his right eye in a battle at Ceuta in Morocco.

Camões returned to Lisbon no wiser than he had left; his wild living soon earned for him the nickname *Trincafortes*, or Swashbuckler. His absence had done nothing to restore his favor with the court, but he found himself equally capable of carousing with a lower class of companion. For the next two years, the poet earned a meager living as a ghostwriter of poetry and did all he could to enhance his reputation as a scalawag. On June 16, 1552, the intoxicated poet was involved in a street fight with a member of the royal staff, whom he stabbed. Camões was promptly arrested and sent to prison, where he languished for eight months.

When the stabbed official recovered, Camões' friends obtained the poet's release, but under two conditions: He was to pay a large fine and to leave immediately on an expedition to India. On March 26, 1553, he set sail on the São Bento, playing out the dangerous existence of the warrior-adventurer described in his epic. The voyage to India took six months, and the seafaring life was not an easy one. Boredom, hunger, scurvy, cold, seasickness, and storms—Camões and his companions had suffered it all before the ship rounded the Cape of Good Hope.

In September, 1553, the ship reached the Indian city of Goa, the Portuguese seat of power and wealth. During his residence there, Camões observed the local people and their exotic costumes, manners, and traditions, and began writing *The Lusiads*. He took part in several expeditions up the Malabar Coast, along the shores of the Red Sea, and through the Persian Gulf.

Camões continued to write poetry and satire, and to work on his epic; his play *Filodemo* was performed for the governor. The success of his play nearly brought him advancement and a return home, but it was not to be. A satire mocking local officials was wrongfully attributed to him, and the officials concerned goaded him into an intemperate display of public indignation. To restore order, he was sent to a new position as trustee for the dead and absent in Macao, China.

In Macao, Camões was happy for a time. He enjoyed the company of a woman he loved, and he continued to write new poems and to polish his epic. The silks, jades, porcelains, and teas of China provided him with new material, and he spent much time alone dreaming and writing. After three years in Macao, he was accused, apparently falsely, of misappropriating funds. Camões was forced to sail again for Goa to stand trial.

On the voyage to Goa, fate intervened. A typhoon struck the ship off southern Indochina, and the ship was wrecked. Camões grabbed the box containing his manuscripts before he was swept off the ship; when he recovered his wits, he was floating on a scrap of wood, and the manuscripts were still in his hand. He struggled to shore and was taken to a fishing village on the Mekong River. In 1561, he somehow was able to return to Goa. Yet his troubles did not end there. He learned that Catarina, his great inspiration, had died, and a few days later he was again cast into prison to face the misappropriation charges. No evidence was produced against him, and he was released. Camões remained in India for several more years, living again a life of poverty.

In the spring of 1567, he arranged passage to Mozambique, and in 1569, after an absence of seventeen years, he set sail for home, arriving in Lisbon in 1570 with the completed manuscript of *The Lusiads* his only possession. He dedicated his time to finding a publisher for his greatest work. Finally, in 1572, the poem was published, and he was granted a small royal pension. Of the next several years of the poet's life little is known, but he appears to have written almost nothing after his return to Lisbon. In 1580, he died of the plague, and his body was placed in an unmarked mass grave.

Summary

Had he written only the three comedies and his large variety of *Rimas* (1595; *The Lyrides*, 1803, 1884), Luís de Camões might be acknowledged as one of the finest European poets of the sixteenth century. With *The Lusiads*, however, Camões was able to capture the passion and nobility of a nation, and it is as the creator of the national epic of Portugal that he will always be remembered.

The Lusiads tells the dramatic story of Vasco da Gama's discovery of a sea route to India, but in the process, da Gama as narrator relates virtually the entire history of "the sons of Lusus," or the Portuguese. *The Lusiads* relies heavily on Camões' classical learning, especially his reading of Vergil (for its structure and tone) and Ludovico Ariosto (for its ottava rima). Yet Camões brought much that was new to the epic. Of the epics written before his, none is grounded so heavily in actual events; Camões demonstrated how actual historical figures could be given the stature of mythical heroes. Unlike Homer or Dante or others, Camões described countries, peoples, and storms at sea that he had witnessed at first hand.

The Lusiads was immensely popular when it was published and has never been out of print since. Schoolchildren throughout the Portuguese-speaking world still memorize its opening stanzas, and the poem has been translated into English many times. English poets such as John Milton, Lord Byron,

William Wordsworth, and Elizabeth Barrett Browning have treasured and praised *The Lusiads*, which has been called "the first epic poem which in its grandeur and universality speaks for the modern world."

Bibliography

Bell, Aubrey F. G. *Luis de Camões.* London: Oxford University Press, 1923. This is a brief treatment that includes a biography of the poet, a description of his moral character as revealed by the poetry, an analysis of *The Lusiads*, and a chapter entitled "Camões as Lyric and Dramatic Poet." A difficult book, its approach assumes that the reader is familiar with previous biographies and with the major Romance languages.

Bowra, C. M. "Camões and the Epic of Portugal." In *From Virgil to Milton.* New York: St. Martin's Press, 1945. An explication of *The Lusiads* as an epic poem, a poem of the ideal in manhood, demonstrating Camões' indebtedness to classical tradition and especially to Homer, Vergil, and Ariosto. The discussion of how the poet reconciles his use of pagan divinities with his Christian message is particularly illuminating.

Burton, Richard Francis. *Camoens: His Life and His Lusiads.* 2 vols. London: Bernard Quaritch, 1881. This is a commentary on *The Lusiads* in five sections: biography; bibliography emphasizing English translations; history and chronology of Portugal through the death of the poet; geographical study of the world as it was understood by da Gama and Camões; and annotations of specific passages in the poem. Appendix includes a table of important episodes in the poem and a glossary.

Freitas, William. *Camoens and His Epic: A Historic, Geographic, and Cultural Survey.* Stanford, Calif.: Institute of Hispanic American and Luso-Brazilian Studies, Stanford University, 1963. A historic and geographical study using *The Lusiads* as a source for information on Portugal's clashes with other nations. The final chapter traces the poem's roots of nationalism through the next four centuries of Portuguese history. Includes a bibliography of biographical, critical, and historical works in several languages as well as twenty illustrations, including portraits and maps.

Hart, Henry H. *Luis de Camoëns and the Epic of the Lusiads.* Norman: University of Oklahoma Press, 1962. A comprehensive, readable biography, filled with colorful detail of the scenery, culture, and history through which the poet walked. Appendices provide several examples of Camões' poems and a listing of books on the Orient which he may have read. Includes a generous bibliography and eight illustrations.

O'Halloran, Colin M. *History and Heroes in the "Lusiads": A Commemorative Essay on Camoëns.* Lisbon: Commissão Executiva do IV Centenário da Publicação de "Os Lusíadas," 1974. A short book examining the use Camões made of the history of Portugal in the creation of the heroes and kings in his poem. Discusses the poem as a record of and tribute to

Portugal's national drive to conquer new lands and convert the people there. It is interesting and accessible, but all quotes from the poem are in Portuguese.

Cynthia A. Bily

CANALETTO
Giovanni Antonio Canal

Born: October 18, 1697; Venice
Died: April 20, 1768; Venice
Area of Achievement: Art
Contribution: Among the most popular of the Old Masters, Canaletto preserved in his canvases the world of eighteenth century Venice. His realistic portrayal of the commonplace and his brilliant clarity influenced numerous artists in Italy and England.

Early Life

The son of Bernardo and Artemisia Barbieri Canal, Giovanni Antonio Canal, named Canaletto—little Canal—to distinguish him from his father, was born in Venice on October 18, 1697. After nearly a century of artistic decline, Venice was experiencing a renaissance during Canaletto's youth. Luca Carlevaris, the city's most successful topographical painter of the early 1700's, was creating a local market for the kind of work Canaletto would produce. He may have been Canaletto's teacher; it is clear that Carlevaris was an important influence.

A scene-painter came to Venice in 1712 and introduced the idea of moving the vanishing point from the center of a backdrop to the side or even offstage. Canaletto, who was helping his father and his brother Cristoforo design sets for theatrical and operatic productions, frequently employed this device. In 1716, another topographical artist, Marco Ricci, settled in Venice and would affect Canaletto's early handling of light, shadow, and background. Ricci was among those who combined actual scenes with imaginary, romanticized landscapes to create the capriccio, a form Canaletto adopted in the 1740's.

In 1719, Canaletto accompanied his father and brother to Rome, where they prepared the scenes for two of Alessandro Scarlatti's operas, both of which were performed during the 1720 Carnival. Probably these were the last theatrical pieces Canaletto produced. While he was still in Rome, he almost certainly saw the work of the Dutch painter Gaspar van Wittel, who had moved to Italy in 1699 and had helped popularize urban views. Canaletto may even have studied briefly under van Wittel, and at this time he may have executed twenty-one Roman scenes that have been attributed to him.

Life's Work

By 1722, Canaletto was back in Venice, though the first work that is indisputably his dates from three years later. In 1725 and 1726, he executed four paintings for Stefano Conti, three of them offering views of the Grand

Canal. These canvases are large: a yard tall and more than four feet wide; Canaletto did his best work on a large scale. Although he is famous for his luminous shadows, light backgrounds, and clear blue skies, his early works, including those for Conti, are painted on a dark, reddish-brown ground like that used by Ricci. Dark clouds hang in the sky, and figures are small.

In other respects these paintings exhibit characteristics of Canaletto's later work. He painted slowly, in part because he insisted on using only the best ingredients for his colors. For example, he is the only artist of the period known to have used the then newly discovered Prussian blue; after more than two and a half centuries, his paintings have therefore retained their brightness. Also typical are the high viewpoint and the realism: One sees the peeling stucco and worn bricks of a Venice past its prime.

For these four works, Canaletto received ninety sequins, a fairly high price for the time. Some two years later, in July, 1730, the future British consul Joseph Smith, Canaletto's greatest patron, wrote in a letter: "[Canaletto is] so much follow'd and all are so ready to pay him his own price for his work (and which he vallues himself as much as anybody)." According to one account, Carlevaris died of apoplexy brought on by the great success of his rival Canaletto.

As the French scholar Charles de Brosses was to complain in the late 1730's, the English on the grand tour were especially fond of Canaletto, and in the late 1720's he began catering to this audience by painting festivals and ceremonies. In such pictures, he drew on his experiences in the theater to convey a sense of drama and action, and he demonstrated great skill with both figures and architectural detail. This ability is evident in six large paintings of the Piazza San Marco, the first of many commissions Canaletto received from Smith. In these pictures one also finds another of Canaletto's traits: a willingness to sacrifice topographical accuracy for artistic needs.

The Stonemason's Yard (c. 1728) is the masterpiece and culmination of Canaletto's early phase, with its realistic portrait of Venetian squalor, its dramatic depiction of people working, and its mixture of sunlight and shade (chiaroscuro). Heightening the sense of everyday life are elements such as a half-naked baby squalling on the ground in front of its mother on the far left and a woman getting water from a well on the right.

By 1729, Canaletto was turning away from chiaroscuro in favor of luminosity, even in shadows. The painting of the reception of Count Bolagno is bathed in light. The background is white rather than reddish-brown; the colors are clear and bright, especially the gold and silver of the barges. The contrast of light and dark derives from the costumes of the figures, and the threatening clouds of the earlier works have vanished from a blue sky.

Between approximately 1727 and 1732, Canaletto prepared a series of fourteen paintings for Smith; these appeared in a book of engravings which includes twelve views of the Grand Canal with *A Regatta on the Grand*

Canal (c. 1732) and *The Bucentoro at the Molo on Ascension Day* (c. 1732). Smaller than most of his earlier works, the twelve views of the Grand Canal seem wooden, lacking the sweep and drama of the other two paintings in the volume, which are painted on a larger scale and were probably added as an afterthought. The frontispiece to this volume contains the only definite portrait of Canaletto. His keen eyes—at the age of sixty-six he boasted of painting without glasses—gaze from an oval frame. Beneath long wavy hair, a high forehead, and a full nose, a faint smile suggests his contentment with being the city's most popular painter.

Smith apparently had the Venetian tourists in mind when he issued the volume, intending to suggest the type of work they could secure from Canaletto. In this regard the pictures succeeded. Indicative of the artist's popularity are purchases by the fourth Earl of Carlisle and the Duke of Bedford. When the Swedish Count Carl Gustaf Tessin wrote on July 16, 1736, about the leading Venetian painters, he placed Canaletto first and commented on the high prices he commanded. Demand for Canaletto's work increased to such an extent that he began to portray character types rather than individuals, to rely on assistants such as his nephew, Bernardo Bellotto, for much of the painting, and to use dots and dashes to suggest light.

The War of the Austrian Succession, which erupted in 1741 and reached Italy the next year, sharply reduced the number of visitors from northern Europe to Venice; even an expanded second edition of engravings failed to revive business for Canaletto. He now turned to other forms and subjects, devoting himself to drawings and engravings. He may have paid a second visit to Rome about 1740, for shortly afterward he executed a number of pictures on Roman themes. These may, however, have been based on illustrations rather than observation. He definitely toured the Brenta Canal as far as Padua, an excursion that led to many of his best drawings, with fine lines that resemble engraving. The careful attention to detail and drama that recalls his paintings of the 1720's characterizes these efforts, many of which he later translated into oils.

Never reluctant to alter a view for aesthetic ends, Canaletto began to execute capriccios; among these is *The Ponti della Pescaria and Buildings on the Quay* (1742-1744), one of thirteen "overdoors" Smith commissioned, in which the artist moved statues from the library to the bridge. Even more fanciful is a view of the Rialto with the bridge Andrea Palladio had designed for the site; that structure had never been built. Canaletto did not altogether abandon topographical scenes, though. *Entrance to the Grand Canal: Looking East* (1744) is in many ways the finest of his renditions of this view, bathed in the Venetian sunlight as only Canaletto could render it and rich in painstaking detail, showing none of the haste that mars some of the other works of this phase in his career.

Perhaps he lavished time on this piece because orders from patrons other than Smith were limited. When he was told about the possibility of commemorating the nearly completed Westminster Bridge in London, Canaletto resolved to visit England to secure the commission. Two of his most important customers, the Dukes of Richmond and Bedford, were involved in the construction, and if the English could not come to Venice, Canaletto would go to the English.

In addition to painting Westminster Bridge, Canaletto secured a number of commissions from the British aristocracy. For his patron, the Duke of Richmond, he executed two of his most famous views in 1747, *Whitehall and the Privy Gardens* and *The Thames and the City of London from Richmond House*. New admirers also appeared, among whom where Sir Hugh Smithson, first Duke of Northumberland, Lord Brooke, and the Earl of Warwick, for whom Canaletto painted five views of Warwick Castle. From the Dean of Westminster came a request to commemorate the procession of the Knights of the Bath from Westminster Abbey to the House of Lords.

Still, Canaletto's popularity had declined. Antiquarian George Vertue even reported the rumor that the painter claiming to be Canaletto was an impostor. Actually, the English were witnessing the change in Canaletto's style, particularly in his treatment of figures, that had begun a decade earlier.

Later commentators have also criticized Canaletto's English works, but at their best, such as his *Old Walton Bridge* (1754), they rival his best paintings. They also provide a record of a mid-Georgian London that has largely vanished and create a panoramic cityscape freed from smoke and suffused with Italian sunlight. Even if more than half of *The Thames and the City of London from Richmond House* consists of sky, the figures are wooden and small, and the vessels on the river are Italian barges rather than English craft, the picture ably re-creates the sense of eighteenth century England, the crowded spires of Sir Christopher Wren's churches punctuating the horizon, with the great dome of St. Paul's serving as the focal center. With his views of Whitehall and Charing Cross, Canaletto captured what Samuel Johnson called in another context "the full tide of human existence" that London exhibited, conveying the city's mood as well as its topography.

In 1755, Canaletto returned to Italy, where his last years were difficult. Occasionally he received commissions, but at his death on April 20, 1768, he had twenty-eight unsold paintings. In 1760, John Crewe came upon the painter sketching in St. Mark's Place, probably hoping to attract passersby. If that was his motive, he apparently succeeded in this instance, for in 1836 Lord Crewe sold a Canaletto painting of the Piazza; most likely it was the one acquired in 1760.

The Venetian Academy, founded in 1750, finally admitted Canaletto in 1763. For his reception piece he presented the Academy with *Portico of a Palace* (1765), a complex study in perspective, rather than a more typical cityscape because such work still lacked prestige. Had Canaletto painted historical scenes or portraits, he would probably have gained admission to the Academy much sooner. The last recorded work by Canaletto, executed in 1766, shows that he could still draw firmly and well. The scene is full of life, architectural features and figures receiving equally detailed attention. Although he depicts an interior, a rare setting for him, he fills the church with the light that is his trademark.

Summary

French novelist Théophile Gautier called Venice the city of Canaletto, not because Canaletto was born, lived, worked, and died there but because he, more than any other artist, commemorated and celebrated it in his art. An excellent technician—even in his oils he developed the ability to record his impressions without revision—he lovingly rendered every brick and ornament. Although he frequently repeated scenes in his eight hundred paintings and four hundred drawings, each version exhibits subtle differences because he shifted a building's proportions, added or removed figures, and changed the lighting. Always present is a sense of drama, for he saw Venice—and London—as the backdrop for human action.

Despite the decline in his popularity after 1740, he influenced a number of artists. Among the Italians are his nephew, Bellotto, Migliara Borasto, and Giambattista Cimaroli of Brescia. In England, where his impact was greater, Thomas Girtin, John Constable, and J. M. W. Turner learned from his work. In *Ducal Palace and Bridge of Sighs, Canaletto Painting* (1833), Turner pays tribute to the master in his first oil of Venice.

Although English art critic John Ruskin expressed the dominant Romantic dissatisfaction with Canaletto's neoclassicism, Édouard Manet admired his drawings, and James McNeill Whistler liked his paintings. The late twentieth century shares this enthusiasm, recognizing that Canaletto did not only paint "things which fall immediately under his eye," as Owen McSwiney claimed. Instead, he mixed sun and shade, palaces and laundry hanging out to dry, columns, bridges, and canals, and beggars and patricians, to create a personal view of his world. If the result is rarely profound, it is almost always pleasing in its ability to convey a mood as well as a sense of place.

Bibliography
Constable, W. G. *Canaletto: Giovanni Antonio Canal, 1697-1768*. Rev. ed. Oxford, England: Clarendon Press, 1976. The definitive study of Canaletto's life and work, it provides a catalogue raisonné of Canaletto's output and reproduces the majority of his paintings, drawings, and engravings. Includes Owen McSwiney's letters to Lord March about the artist, a detailed account of Canaletto's estate at his death, and a selective bibliography.
Levey, Michael. *Canaletto Paintings in the Royal Collection*. London: Phai-

don Press, 1964. The British Royal Family owns the most extensive collection of Canaletto's works. This catalog reproduces the holdings in black-and-white full-page illustrations and offers a short biography of the artist.

_____. *Painting in Eighteenth-Century Venice*. London: Phaidon Press, 1959. Rev. ed. Ithaca, N.Y.: Cornell University Press, 1980. Provides a well-illustrated overview of eighteenth century Venetian art. Arrangement is by type of work: historical painting, landscapes, views, genre, and portraits. Good section on Canaletto.

Links, J. G. *Canaletto*. Ithaca, N.Y.: Cornell University Press, 1982. A comprehensive study of the artist, with illustrations conveniently located in the text. Drawing on recent research, Links clarifies some puzzles about Canaletto, such as his relationship with Joseph Smith and his activities in England.

Moschini, Vittorio. *Canaletto*. Milan: Aldo Martello, 1954. A lavishly illustrated text that reproduces many important paintings in full color. The detailed chronology is especially useful. Contains a bibliography of works dealing with the artist from 1733 to 1753.

Joseph Rosenblum

ANTONIO CANOVA

Born: November 1, 1757; Possagno, near Venice
Died: October 13, 1822; Venice
Area of Achievement: Art
Contribution: Canova fixed the ideal style in neoclassical sculpture for generations. His works were considered the standard of international artistic excellence in his day and his name and opinion held great authority.

Early Life

Antonio Canova was born on November 1, 1757, in Possagno, to Angela and Pietro Canova. In 1761, at age twenty-six, Pietro, a stonemason, died. In 1762, Angela remarried and moved to a village west of Possagno, leaving young Antonio in the care of Pasino Canova, his paternal grandfather, who was also a stonemason. In 1768, Antonio was apprenticed to Giuseppe Bernardi, known as Torretti, in nearby Pagnano. He received his first formal lessons in this active studio which manufactured garden sculpture. There, Canova would have absorbed proficiency in handling stone, in efficient delegation to specialized assistants of the various mechanical steps in the production process, and in the administration of the technical and financial aspects of a studio.

In autumn of 1768, Torretti took the young Canova to his other studio in Venice. For the first time Canova was able to study Greco-Roman sculpture in private Venetian collections. He also studied the collections of plaster casts in the palace of Filippo Farsetti and frequented the academy. In 1770, Senator Giovanni Falier, who had shown an interest in Canova's work, commissioned two baskets of fruit in stone and two life-size figures.

Encouraged, Canova left Torretti's studio and in 1775 established his own studio in the cloister of Santo Stefano in Venice. At this time he won second place in a competition organized by the Venice Academy. Having achieved a reputation for portraiture, he carved the naturalistic life-size marble *Daedalus and Icarus* (1779), his first truly original work, for the procurator Pietro Vittor Pisani. Exhibited at the annual Venetian art fair of the Ascension, it was a great public and financial success. With this money Canova left for Rome October 9, 1779.

On November 4, 1779, via Bologna and Florence, Canova arrived in Rome. He was received by the Venetian ambassador Girolamo Zulian, who provided him with a studio in the embassy palace. There he was able to study private and public collections and the sculpture of Roman churches. The young Canova also benefitted from his acquaintance with the most advanced artists and critics of the age.

Life's Work

In the winter of 1780, Canova visited Naples, where he saw great collections of antiquities. Back in Rome, he exhibited a plaster cast of his *Daedalus and Icarus* to the influential artist and archaeologist Gavin Hamilton, who recognized his talent. Hamilton advised Canova on the direction his style should take and was instrumental in turning him from the Baroque to the revolutionary neoclassical style first propagated by the German archaeologist and historian Johann Joachim Winckelmann. The young sculptor became determined to study antique style thoroughly.

Winckelmann's aesthetic revolution carried an enormous moral charge. He condemned the excesses of the Baroque as not only offensive to sensibility but also injurious to rationality, man's highest faculty. He favored the pure Greek art with its noble simplicity and calm grandeur over the corrupt Roman art.

In 1781, Ambassador Zulian commissioned the marble *Theseus and the Minotaur*. This gave Canova the chance of proving himself in the new style. He accepted the advice of men he had grown to respect, restrained his natural inclination toward liveliness, and altered his style in accordance with the new doctrine of tranquil grandeur.

In 1783, the Venetian Giovanni Volpato, to whose daughter Canova had been briefly engaged, attained for Canova the commission for the monumental *Tomb of Pope Clement XIV* (1783-1787). Here he purifies the Baroque elements represented by such funerary monuments as Gianlorenzo Bernini's *Tomb of Pope Urban VIII* by replacing Bernini's lavish allegorical approach with figures in noble, body-clinging draperies, their restraint and pose reinforcing the clean severity of the entire composition. The figures do not interact but appear to be juxtaposed, an arrangement which heightens the quiet solemnity. At the unveiling of this piece in 1787, Canova's international reputation was established. The immediate, enormous success made him the most celebrated sculptor of his time.

Canova's work on the tomb of Clement XIV was so intense that, as a result of his constant running of the drill which had to be pressed against the stone with his chest, he suffered severe deformation of the ribs. This injury was connected to the cause of his death. Canova's output would vary between two stylistic extremes: powerful, life-size monuments and intimate figures of an erotic nature. Works such as the tender *Cupid and Psyche* (1787-1793) were calculated to give greatest satisfaction when contemplated in a private manner.

Canova's sculpture combined the purity of white marble and the simplicity of antique forms with the softness of execution. His mature works were so successful because the references to the ancients were always clear. Their sensuality was often heightened by the working of the marble and by the definite sense of line and silhouette. Except for a few works, Canova's productions are of a translucent delicacy.

Canova's human figures display his knowledge of formalized anatomy. He did not try to portray the body realistically. Part of the appeal of such pieces as *Hebe* (1796) is the intricate, undulating lines which abstract the forms, aided by the unnatural whiteness of the marble, and thus negate realism. Canova's movement toward abstraction was evident by the ease with which his works translated into outline engraving without losing total effect.

With the rise of Napoleon I, circumstances in France changed for sculpture. Neoclassicism, because it assumed a political position of patriotism and social progress, was the ideal style for propagandizing the very meaning of the Empire. Canova's popularity generated commissions from Napoleon and his family. In most of these pieces he sought to depict the dynasty as successors to their imagined imperial Roman ancestors.

The period from 1800 to 1814 was extremely productive for Canova. Two of his greatest masterpieces, *Pauline Borghese as Venus Victorious* (1804-1808) and the *Tomb of Archduchess Maria Christina* (1805-1809), were produced during this period. The tomb deliberately detaches itself from the church, focuses the viewer's attention exclusively on itself, and remains stoically silent about the possible meaning or resolution of death. It is strangely lacking in both instruction and celebration. The participants do not face the observers; they simply participate in the endless procession to the grave. The portrait of Pauline Borghese is an ideal image where the elements of classicism, technical virtuosity, and a submerged sensuality are joined in a subtly evocative whole. This cool yet voluptuous figure shows the wide range of sexuality which Canova's outline style can express. With these two works, Canova reached the peak of his career; unlike most artists he managed to stay there for the rest of his life.

In his later life, Canova traveled extensively between Venice, Rome, Vienna, Paris, and London. His reputation for neutrality, for his dedication to basic ethical causes as well as his reputation as an artist, made Canova the ideal papal agent at the Congress of Paris in 1815. The Papal States won back most of their vast artistic treasures through Canova's shrewd diplomatic tactics. From Paris he traveled to London, where he saw the Elgin marbles. There he quickly realized that most of the works on which he had based his style had been Roman copies, and he identified the copies as affected, exaggerated, and conventional. His advanced age, however, prevented any further change in his artistic direction.

Very little is known about Canova's intimate life. Although he experienced enduring hurt over his father's early death and his mother's abandonment, there appeared to be a detachment from conventional personal affections or passions. Yet throughout his life Canova was a modest, kind, and generous man, especially to young and struggling artists and to his half brother, who seemed not to deserve his generosity. In 1820, the first sharp symptoms of his fatal illness appeared and undermined his strength as he continued to work. Scarcely able to eat, suffering from severe abdominal pain, he died on October 13, 1822. He was buried in the new Tempio, the church which he built for Possagno, his native town.

Summary

Antonio Canova's achievement was to remain the ideal exemplar for academic sculptors throughout most of the nineteenth century. He worked in enough genres to provide a variety of imitable forms. His superficially simple antique style was pure and graceful without overemphatic voluptuousness. It was repeated all over Europe and America but with an intensification of hardness and dryness which became too evident in the studio repetitions and other copies of his art.

Canova was the one man who actually made sculpture in accordance with Winckelmann's theories. The lack of high-quality sculpture in the classical manner after Canova's death resulted from following those theories which deadened more talents than they inspired since imitation soon became mechanical. Eventually it was the entire neoclassical style within which Canova worked, with all of its moral and political overtones, that was completely rejected.

Because of the highly polished purity of Canova's marble forms and their intentional connections with the masterpieces of antiquity, he has received negative criticism from modern critics who favored the sketch over the finished work and who condemned imitation as the enemy of spontaneity. Late nineteenth century criticism condemned his sensuality and his idealization of nature. The twentieth century turned against him for precisely opposite reasons: He was considered too blandly realistic and too lacking in sensual fervor.

During Canova's lifetime and well after his death, however, his excellence was not questioned. The success of his style entailed its spread in the form of originals, copies by assistants, and engravings which he himself commissioned.

The greatest following of Canova's style was in France. His own style was partly formed from French ideas as a result of his friendship with the antiquarian Quatremère de Quincy. Their exchange of letters over many years enlightened Canova with a program of classical aesthetics. The Frenchman made subject suggestions and gave encouragement and approval. Canova even tried tinting some of his statues according to ancient practice as suggested by Quatremère's researches.

Canova was highly influential among such contemporary French artists as the sculptors Antoine Chaudet and Joseph Chinard and the painters Anne-Louis Girodet, François Gérard, Pierre Guérin, and J. A. D. Ingres. These painters were inspired by his delicately linear representations of the nude. Many of Girodet's works adapt Canova's figures to paint. Ingres' *Bather of Valpinçon* (1808) was influenced by Canova's *Venus Italica* (1804-1812).

Canova's popularity in England is evidenced by the large number of his works in English collections. The sculptor and draftsman John Flaxman, who obtained at least one commission from Canova, was strongly influenced by his style.

Canova's significance, in part a result of his diplomatic activities, passed beyond the boundaries of the art world and made him a figure accessible to a broad public. With the exception of Peter Paul Rubens, no other artist had ever been able to ingratiate himself and his art to so many European courts during his lifetime.

Bibliography

Boime, Albert. *Art in an Age of Revolution, 1750-1800.* Vol 1, *A Social History of Modern Art.* Chicago: University of Chicago Press, 1987. A brief treatment of Canova's career and the significant political implications of his art in the light of events at the end of the eighteenth century.

Clark, Anthony M. *The Age of Canova.* Providence: Rhode Island School of Design, 1957. An appreciative evaluation of Canova's work in this brief catalog for the exposition of his work held in the Museum of Rhode Island School of Design, fall, 1957.

Honour, Hugh. *Canova's Theseus and the Minotaur.* Reprint. London: Phaidon Press, 1969. An excellent, in-depth, and scholarly essay explaining the complete evolution of this, the first neoclassical piece of sculpture by the artist. Bibliography, detailed notes, black-and-white reproductions.

Honour, Hugh, et al. *The Age of Neoclassicism.* London: Arts Council of Great Britain, 1972. A comprehensive catalog for the fourteenth exhibition of the Council of Europe housed in the Royal Academy and Victoria and Albert Museum, fall, 1972. Includes eleven essays on seminal aspects of neoclassical culture, ideas, and specific art forms; bibliographical outline for each artist; historical sketch of each artwork; plates.

Licht, Fred. *Canova.* Photographs by David Finn. New York: Abbeville Press, 1983. This elaborate and handsome volume, the only major recent work in English, presents Canova's sculpture by means of photographic and textual interpretation. More than three hundred color and black-and-white photographs sensitively convey both the grandeur and delicacy of Canova's sculpture. Contains detailed analyses on individual works. Epilogue, notes, chronology, and an excellent bibliography.

Praz, Mario. *On Neoclassicism.* Translated by Angus Davidson. London: Thames and Hudson, 1969. Chapter 6 is an analytical review of the predominantly adverse criticism accompanied by reassessment of Canova's art within the larger context of the aesthetics of neoclassicism.

John A. Calabrese

THE CARRACCI FAMILY

Ludovico Carracci

Born: April 21 (baptized), 1555; Bologna, Papal States
Died: November 13, 1619; Bologna, Papal States

Agostino Carracci

Born: August 16, 1557; Bologna, Papal States
Died: February 23, 1602; Parma

Annibale Carracci

Born: November 3, 1560; Bologna, Papal States
Died: July 15, 1609; Rome
Area of Achievement: Art
Contribution: From the mid-1580's onward, the paintings and frescoes of the Carracci family of Bologna made their city one of the major centers of reaction against the so-called mannerist style, an elegant and often over-refined style that had dominated Italian art for sixty or seventy years. When Annibale went to Rome in the early 1590's, his work laid the foundation for the magnificent pictorial accomplishments of the Baroque period.

Early Lives

The Carracci family came to Bologna from Cremona, and Ludovico's father was a butcher named Vincenzo. Agostino and Annibale were his second cousins, the sons of Antonio Carracci, who was a well-known tailor. Ludovico began his artistic studies with Prospero Fontana. According to the Carracci's seventeenth century biographer, Carlo Cesare Malvasia, his work was so laborious that Fontana nicknamed him "the ox" and advised him not to continue with his studies. Ludovico then went to Florence. For a time he worked with Domenico Passignano and later traveled through northern Italy, where he saw at first hand the works that were to be so important in his artistic development, which were by Correggio and Parmigianino, the great sixteenth century masters of Parma and of the region known as Emilia, and by Titian and Paolo Veronese in Venice. By 1578, he was back in Bologna and was a member of the local painters' guild.

Agostino initially received some training as a goldsmith and also studied with Fontana. His real master, though, was Domenico Tibaldi, from whom he learned the art of engraving. His engravings, after works by Michelangelo and Baldassare Peruzzi, brought him some success, and he later went to

Venice, where he produced engraved copies of works by Veronese and Tintoretto.

Annibale's training was much less formal, and it is possible that his cousin Ludovico was his only teacher in painting and that he learned engraving from his brother Agostino. In the spring of 1580, Annibale went to Parma in order to see and to paint copies of the works that had made such a deep impression on Ludovico a few years earlier. By late 1580 or early 1581, he was in Venice with Agostino; by about 1582, the brothers had returned to Bologna.

Life's Work

In the early 1580's, all three of the Carracci were involved in the development of a unique combination of artistic workshop and art academy, which they called the "Academy of the Eager Ones" or the "Academy of the Progressives." Considerable emphasis was put on drawing from life, but there were also lessons in anatomy and perspective as well as in architecture. What the Carracci developed at their "academy" was a program of practical and theoretical instruction aimed at reforming the art of painting, which, as they saw it, had deteriorated into a vapid and boringly repetitive set of formulas, devoid of life and energy.

In the early 1580's, the Carracci began to emerge as individual artists, but they also often worked together. By 1584, they had completed their first major joint commission, which was the series of frescoes illustrating the *History of Jason* in the Palazzo Fava, Bologna (modern Società Majestic Baglioni). Unfortunately, the frescoes are not in good condition, but their strong illusionism and richness of color can still be appreciated, and there is a remarkable lack of artifice in the easy and naturalistic poses of the figures. This was the first major public manifestation of their doctrine of artistic reform. The fresco cycle in the former Palazzo Magnani was also a joint production, and, when asked to tell which parts each of them had painted, they are said to have replied: "It's by the Carracci. All of us made it."

For the next ten years, the Carracci were actively engaged in creating altarpieces for Bolognese churches, many of which can now be seen in the Pinacoteca Nazionale, Bologna. While Agostino devoted much of his time to engraving and to teaching, he was also a painter of note, and *The Last Communion of Saint Jerome* (1591-1593) is his masterpiece of the period, admired by artists as diverse as Nicolas Poussin and Peter Paul Rubens. Ludovico's painting of the *Madonna of the Bargellini Family* (1588) is one of his strongest early paintings, and critics have recognized the qualities of his work. Yet it is clear that by the end of the 1580's, Annibale had emerged as the most important artist of the three, a painter of great power whose richness of color is matched by his masterful drawing. His *Madonna with Saint John Evangelist and Saint Catherine* (1593) reveals his brilliant synthesis of the formal order of the High Renaissance with the colorism of Venice and Parma. Annibale also had a lighter side. He was one of the first artists to produce caricatures in the modern sense of the art of caricature, and in his early twenties he painted a number of genre paintings. *The Bean Eater* (c. 1585) in the Colonna Gallery, Rome, is one of the best—a small-scale scene of everyday life rendered with an astonishing boldness and naturalism.

In the mid-1590's, the Carracci were invited to go to Rome to work for Cardinal Odoardo Farnese, the brother of the Duke of Parma and Piacenza. Annibale accepted the cardinal's invitation, and Agostino later joined him; Ludovico chose to remain in Bologna, where he continued to direct the Carracci's academy, and, in order to ensure that the academy would continue, he tried to have it officially incorporated into the professional association of Bolognese artists. Ludovico's own late work is uneven, and it is unfortunate that the fresco cycle that he and his pupils executed in San Michele in Bosco (about 1605) is lost and is known only from engravings. Two of the finest works from Ludovico's later period are the enormous paintings *Funeral of the Virgin* (1606-1607) and *Apostles at the Tomb of the Virgin* (c. 1612). He died in Bologna in 1619.

After Annibale's arrival in Rome in 1595, he developed into an artist of great historical importance. In the Palazzo Farnese, he was first asked to decorate the ceiling and upper walls of a room, now known as Camerino Farnese (Farnese's little room), with scenes illustrating the adventures of Hercules and Ulysses. In 1597, he began work on a fresco cycle in one of the principal rooms of the palace, the so-called Farnese Gallery.

The Farnese Gallery is Annibale's masterpiece, and subsequent generations considered it worthy of comparison with Raphael's frescoes in the Vatican Palace and Michelangelo's Sistine Chapel ceiling. A fictive architecture provides the framework for what appears to be framed easel pictures moved up the ceiling. There are bronze medallions, simulated marble statues, and naturalistic figures of youths sitting on pedestals—all painted with such convincing illusionism that distinctions between the real and the painted worlds seem to vanish. The theme is the power of love, and incidents illustrating the loves of the gods and goddesses of antiquity fill the ceiling and the upper walls. Many of the frescoes' stories are drawn from *Metamorphoses* (c. A.D. 8) by the Roman poet Ovid; yet behind this joyous and lighthearted exuberance, Annibale's contemporaries discerned a serious moral allegory.

In the execution of the Farnese Gallery, Annibale had been helped by Agostino, but about 1600 Agostino left Rome and went to Parma, where he remained until his death in 1602. His principal work there was a fresco cycle for the Palazzo del Giardino, but it was not finished when he died and was completed much later by other artists. Annibale continued to work on the Gallery, whose lower walls were probably not finished until about 1604.

Among his surviving easel paintings from the Roman period are some religious works of great power, such as the *Mourning of Christ*. His late landscapes were also of great importance for the subsequent history of painting. The finest of these landscapes are the ones that he and his pupils painted for the chapel in the Aldobrandini Palace (modern Galleria Doria-Pamphili, Rome).

In the early part of 1605, Annibale suffered a breakdown, at least partially caused by his bitterness over the small sum of money he was paid for the Farnese Gallery. For the next four years, he was unable to work, and in the summer of 1609 he died in Rome. He was buried in the Pantheon, an unusual honor and one which had also been accorded to Raphael.

Summary

The three Carracci had a major role in the reformation of the mannerist style, and, while they often worked together, they were distinct and highly individual artists. Ludovico was a gifted teacher, and several of the younger men who were trained by him in the Carracci's academy after Annibale left for Rome went on to become important artists. Two of these students, Guido Reni and Domenichino, later became major figures of the Baroque era; yet there were many others of lesser distinction but considerable talent whose work provided the basis for the flourishing seventeenth century schools of painting in Bologna and Emilia.

Agostino was more interested in art theory than were the other Carracci, and, according to one of his biographers, he was a student of mathematics and philosophy. He also composed verses and was a musician. To some extent, his posthumous fame has been dependent upon his reputation as a theorist and an intellectual, but his qualities as an artist should not be discounted. He was a fine engraver, and his engravings after Venetian masters such as Veronese helped to spread the fame of their art. Yet he was also an excellent painter, although not as productive as his brother or his cousin.

Annibale's work gave new life to the tradition of monumental art in the grand manner. In Rome, under the influence of the work of Michelangelo, Raphael, and the sculpture of antiquity, his art matured and his combination of idealism and illusionism provided the greatest inspiration for the younger generation of painters. The Farnese Gallery was the first great fresco cycle of the Baroque era and set a precedent for the fresco cycles of the next two centuries.

Bibliography

Bellori, Giovanni Pietro. *The Lives of Annibale and Agostino Carracci.* Translated by Catherine Enggass. University Park: Pennsylvania State University Press, 1967. Giovanni Pietro Bellori's book was first published in Rome in 1672. This translation of the portion devoted to the Carracci is the only contemporary biography available in English. Most of the work is devoted to a description of the Farnese Gallery and an explanation of its symbolic meaning.

Boschloo, Anton Willem Adriaan. *Annibale Carracci in Bologna: Visible Reality in Art After the Council of Trent.* Translated by R. R. Symonds. 2 vols. The Hague: Government Printing Office, 1974. A detailed study of Annibale's work in Bologna and its relationship to the art of his contemporaries and predecessors.

Dempsey, Charles. *Annibale Carracci and the Beginnings of the Baroque Style.* Locust Valley, N.Y.: J. J. Augustin, 1977. An extensive review of the critical evaluations of Annibale's work and a discussion of the Carracci Academy and its role in the reform of painting.

Freedberg, Sydney J. *Circa 1600: A Revolution of Style in Italian Painting.* Cambridge, Mass.: Harvard University Press, 1983. Three lectures given at Cornell University in 1980 and dealing with Annibale and Ludovico Carracci and Caravaggio. Excellent exposition of the nature of the artistic accomplishments of the Carracci. The final lecture dealing with Ludovico is particularly illuminating.

Martin, John Rupert. *The Farnese Gallery.* Princeton, N.J.: Princeton University Press, 1965. The basic study of Annibale's work in the Palazzo Farnese. Richly illustrated and fully documented.

Posner, Donald. *Annibale Carracci: A Study in the Reform of Italian Painting Around 1590.* 2 vols. New York: Phaidon Press, 1971. The standard monograph on Annibale. Contains excellent plates and detailed catalog entries of extant works.

Wittkower, Rudolf. *Art and Architecture in Italy, 1600-1750.* 3d ed. Baltimore: Penguin Books, 1973. Still the basic study of the period. The chapter on the Carracci is an admirable summary, and there are excellent bibliographies for all the major artists of the period.

Eric Van Schaack

CATHERINE DE MÉDICIS

Born: April 13, 1519; Florence
Died: January 5, 1589; Blois, France
Areas of Achievement: Government and politics
Contribution: Catherine de Médicis contributed to maintaining a strong centralized monarchy in spite of challenges from noble and religious factions. Her attempts to balance Roman Catholic and Calvinist interests in France also encouraged at least a minimum of toleration in the seventeenth century.

Early Life

Catherine de Médicis' father, Lorenzo de' Medici, was *capo dello stato* in Florence, *gonfalonier* of the Church, and, after a victorious expedition, Duke of Urbino. His uncle, Pope Leo X, hoping to restore the Medicis to their earlier status, arranged a marriage between Lorenzo and Madeleine de la Tour d'Auvergne, a distant relation of Francis I, King of France. The young couple were married at Amboise in 1518, and within a year their daughter was born. Two weeks later, Madeleine was dead of puerperal fever, and five days later Lorenzo also died.

The baby Catherine was the last legitimate heir of the family. Immediately, she became a tool in the hands of her guardian, Pope Leo X, and of his half brother Giulio, later Pope Clement VII, to recoup the Medici fortune. Catherine's childhood was spent in Rome and Florence, where she was at times ignored and at other times the center of attention. In 1527, during a Florentine revolution, she was the hostage of anti-Medici forces and handled her desperate situation with great diplomacy. At the age of ten, she returned to Rome, where Pope Clement VII negotiated a marriage between Catherine and Henry, the second son of Francis I.

On October 26, 1533, Catherine and Henry, both fourteen years of age, were married at Avignon. Small and thin, with strong rather than beautiful features and the bulging eyes of the Medicis, Catherine was vivacious, self-assured, witty, bright, and eager to learn. As a new wife, she traveled everywhere with the French court and joined a group of young women, protégées of her father-in-law, to study Latin, Greek, French, mathematics, science, astronomy, and astrology. She hunted, danced, and rode using a sidesaddle she invented. Still a child when she married Henry, she had to call upon all of her habits of diplomacy to handle two major crises. The first was her husband's attachment to his mistress Diane de Poitiers. Catherine handled this problem by being a patient and loving wife and by making an ally of her rival. The second difficulty was more critical and became especially important in 1536, when Henry's older brother died and Henry became the heir to the French throne. That difficulty was her inability to bear children and the possibility that Henry would obtain a divorce to marry a fertile bride and leave Catherine without resources. Catherine's charm and vivacity saved her from this fate, and, after ten years of marriage, she presented Henry with an heir.

During the next thirteen years, Catherine bore ten children, including four sons, and settled into a mutually respectful relationship with Henry and Diane de Poitiers. When Francis died in 1547, Henry arranged a coronation ceremony for Catherine, an unusual innovation for sixteenth century French kings. In 1551, when Henry went to war in Burgundy, he left Catherine as his regent, and, although Diane was his chief adviser, he also consulted with his wife. In 1559, Catherine was one of the architects of the Treaty of Cateau-Cambrésis, which temporarily calmed the Franco-Spanish rivalry. The new amity was sealed with the marriage of Philip II of Spain and Catherine's daughter Elizabeth. A tournament was held to celebrate this alliance, and, during one event, a splinter from a broken lance pierced the French king's eye and he died.

Life's Work

Although she did not know it at the time, Catherine's life's work began with the death of her husband. Francis became king at the age of fifteen. A year earlier, he had married Mary Stuart, Queen of Scotland and niece of the Guises, a prominent French noble family. Mary's relatives assumed responsibility for advising the young king. If Francis had lived, Catherine would not have become an important political figure in France. When Francis died, Charles IX, aged ten, assumed the throne. After observing the arrogant despotism of the Guises, Catherine determined to become regent to her son.

During her years as regent, Catherine responded to two major crises in the face of four significant enemies. One struggle was to preserve royal authority against two noble families—the Guises and the Bourbons—who were determined to dominate the king and the royal family. The Bourbons were the hereditary kings of Navarre and the next in line to inherit the throne after Catherine's sons. The other major crisis for Catherine was the religious conflict between Roman Catholics and Protestant Calvinists, called Huguenots, in France. To complicate her task, the Guises became associated with the Roman Catholic position and often looked to the Spanish for assistance, while the Bourbons, at least the Queen of Navarre and her brother-in-law the fiery Prince of Condé, openly adhered to the Protestant faith. Even before Francis II's death, the Prince of Condé had mobilized Huguenot support against the Guises in a conspiracy aimed at kidnapping the king and executing his Guise advisers. His efforts failed, but the lines of conflict were drawn. Catherine also faced a powerful Spanish king, Philip II, who would act in his own dynastic interest even though he was Catherine's son-in-law. Finally, she had to deal with an inadequate treasury and the imminent bankruptcy of the Crown. As a woman and a foreigner, Catherine's task was doubly difficult.

The queen mother's response to the religious difficulties was to organize a national religious council to mediate between French Protestants and Catholics. The Colloquy of Poissy, which met in 1561, succeeded in getting the French religious parties to talk together, but it also polarized them. The Guises and other staunch Roman Catholics united and sought help from the Spanish king to challenge royal efforts at mediation. Religious passions intensified. In January, 1562, when Catherine issued the Edict of Toleration granting government protection to the Huguenots, the Catholics left the royal court, and the first of the French Religious Wars began.

During the next ten years, France was torn by three major civil wars motivated by religious and noble rivalry. Catherine tried desperately to maintain a balance among all of these forces, but she failed. The third and most savage of the first set of religious wars ended in August, 1570, with the Peace of Saint-Germain and a backlash against the Guises and their Spanish allies. A new party, the Politique Party, grew out of this disgust with foreign influence. Composed of Roman Catholic and Huguenot moderates who believed that the integrity of the state was more important than religion, this party reflected Catherine's own position.

Catherine's diplomatic expertise became especially important in 1572, in negotiating defense treaties with the English and the Ottoman Turks against Philip II and in gaining the throne of Poland for her third son, Henry. As Henry departed for Poland, Europe was rocked by news of the Saint Bartholomew's Eve Massacre. The occasion was the wedding of Catherine's daughter Marguerite to Henry, King of Navarre, heir to the French throne after Catherine's sons. All the important nobles of France were gathered in the capital, including the Huguenot leaders. Whether Catherine and Charles IX intended to kill all the Protestants in Paris on August 23, 1572, or whether Catherine only meant to kill one or two of the Protestant leaders, the result was a massacre of Protestants by Catholics in the capital city and in other cities throughout the nation. War broke out again and, in spite of their losses, the Huguenots managed to retain several key fortresses. When Charles IX died in 1574, and Henry III returned from Poland, the new king was also unable to seize the Protestant strongholds and to subdue the opposition. In 1576, peace was negotiated on the basis of the status quo. Henry III, Catherine's favorite son, was an adult when he came to the throne, and Catherine no longer played an important policy-making role. Since the king was unmarried and preoccupied with war, his mother continued to direct the ambassadors and to send and receive letters from agents and diplomats throughout Europe.

In June of 1584, Catherine's youngest son died of influenza. Thus, the Protestant Henry of Navarre would inherit the throne if Henry III were to die. War raged, and, fearing the Spanish king would send in troops, Henry III was forced to put himself at the head of the Catholic League in order to control its excesses. The Estates General refused to grant the government more money to fight the wars they did not want. On December 23, 1588, Henry III summoned the Cardinal of Guise to the royal chamber, where armed guards killed him. Shortly thereafter, Henry had the Duke of Guise assassinated as well. Catherine was in the castle at Blois that evening on her deathbed, when Henry carried the news of the Guises' deaths to her. She was not pleased; by destroying one faction, Henry had put himself in the hands of the other; he no longer had a weapon against the Bourbon and Protestant nobles. The collapse of Spain would give Geneva and the Calvinists the victory.

Catherine died less than two weeks later on January 5, 1589, and her son was assassinated before the end of the year. Henry IV, the Protestant King of Navarre, officially inherited the throne, but the war continued until 1595, when he had reconquered the north and converted to Catholicism. Henry was able, however, to protect his Huguenot friends and relatives by issuing the Edict of Nantes that granted the Huguenots several armed cities and freedom to worship.

Summary

Catherine de Médicis set out to destroy the resistance to royal power, to secure for her sons the French throne, to build a government with a centralized power in the hands of the French monarchy, and to limit the authority of the nobles. She succeeded in gaining those ends even as she failed to achieve them peacefully and permanently. Accused by contemporaries and historians of being a Machiavellian, Catherine must at least plead guilty to being a realist in her exercise of power. She changed sides, made secret agreements, and even sent ambassadors to the infidel Turk to negotiate a treaty against the Spanish in 1570. She met with all parties and used every means available to achieve her ends. She condoned war and murder in the interest of her duty as the regent of France.

It may have been her failure to balance the dynastic and religious conflicts that brought on the civil wars, but it was her success at identifying the factions in the conflict and her attempts to balance them that allowed Henry IV to obtain his throne intact with Huguenots alive to tolerate. The religious civil wars were horrible, but some of the changes as a result of the wars moved France closer to the centralized, bureaucratic state that was more nearly modern than was the sixteenth century dynastic structure. The wars served to redistribute the land from the hands of a few large noble families to those of a number of smaller families who were loyal to the monarchy. The most significant result of the civil wars, however, was the creation of the Politique Party, a party that recognized the need for a strong monarchy regardless of religious affiliation and regardless of noble demands for power. Catherine's contribution to French government in the sixteenth century was the principle of centralized power in the hands of the monarchy.

Bibliography

Héritier, Jean. *Catherine de Medici*. Translated by Charlotte Haldane. New York: St. Martin's Press, 1963. Long biography of Catherine as a great national and moderate leader who preserved for Henry IV a kingdom which was battered but intact.

Neale, J. E. *The Age of Catherine de Medici*. New York: Harper & Row, 1943. Short and colorful presentation of Catherine's rule as foolish, misguided, and middle-class.

Roeder, Ralph. *Catherine de Medici and the Lost Revolution*. New York: Viking Press, 1937. Presents the problem of sixteenth century France as the inability of Catherine to balance the dynastic and religious conflicts of the age.

Sichel, Edith. *Catherine de' Medici and the French Reformation*. London: Constable, 1905. Presents Catherine as the evil nemesis of the political problems of France, never quite in control of her plans. Sichel also relates the art and literature of the period of the French Reformation to Catherine's reign.

Strage, Mark. *Women of Power: The Life and Times of Catherine de' Medici*. New York: Harcourt Brace Jovanovich, 1976. A conventional rehash of the story focusing on Catherine's relationship with Diane de Poitiers and Margaret of Valois.

Sutherland, N. M. "Catherine de Medici: The Legend of the Wicked Italian Queen." *Sixteenth Century Journal* 9 (1978): 45-56. An analysis of the attitudes of historians about Catherine de Médicis and her role in history from her contemporaries to the present day.

Van Dyke, Paul. *Catherine de Médicis*. 2 vols. New York: Charles Scribner's Sons, 1923. General study of Catherine within the context of her time. Catherine is held responsible for not solving the religious and political problems but not through inherent malice.

Loretta Turner Johnson

CATHERINE THE GREAT

Born: May 2, 1729; Stettin, Pomerania, Prussia
Died: November 17, 1796; St. Petersburg, Russia
Area of Achievement: Monarchy
Contribution: One of the early enlightened monarchs, Catherine attempted to create a uniform Russian government with a modern Westernized code of laws that represented all levels of Russian society with the exception of the serfs. In the forty-four years of her reign, she sculpted Russia into one of the great world powers of the time and laid the foundation for what would become modern Russia.

Early Life

Catherine the Great was born Sophie Friederike Auguste von Anhalt-Zerbst in Stettin, a seaport in Pomerania. Her parents, Prince Christian August and Princess Johanna Elizabeth of Holstein-Gottorp, were minor members of the German aristocracy. As a result of her strained relationship with her mother, Sophie developed into an independent young woman. Russian monarchs held the prerogative of choosing their successors, and her cousin Duke Karl Peter Ulrich of Holstein-Gottorp had been summoned to Russia by the childless Empress Elizabeth as the heir to the throne. It only remained to find him a wife, and, after several months of searching, Elizabeth decided on Sophie, and both she and her mother were invited to Russia in January, 1744.

Elizabeth was pleased with her choice, and Peter fell in love with the princess. On June 28, 1744, Sophie converted to Russian Orthodoxy, was given the name Catherine, and on the following day the couple were publicly engaged. From the time he arrived in Russia, Peter, whose health was never good, had a series of illnesses which left him permanently scarred and most probably sterile. Their marriage, which occurred on August 21, 1745, was not consummated immediately and probably not at all.

Married to a man who displayed a mania for Prussian militarism and who preferred to play with toy soldiers and conduct military parades than be with her, Catherine was left to develop her own interests. She began to read, a pastime almost unheard of in the Russian court, and mastered the technique of riding astride, an activity in which she took great pleasure, often going for long rides. Neither interest could overcome the lack of an heir, which, as the empress pointed out to her on more than one occasion, was Catherine's only reason for being. Starved for affection and more than a little aware that her position depended on producing a child, she took a lover, Sergei Saltykov. Twice she became pregnant and miscarried, but on September 20, 1754, Catherine delivered a male child, Paul Petrovich, who was probably the son of Saltykov.

The empress took control of the child from the moment he was delivered, and Catherine was once again left alone. Totally barred from any involvement in the political life of the court, she consoled herself with reading the works of such writers as Voltaire, Cornelius Tacitus, and Montesquieu. Saltykov was replaced by Count Stanislas August Ponistowski, and, in 1761, she met and fell in love with Count Grigory Orlov. During this time her husband's behavior became more and more eccentric. Russia was at war with Prussia, yet Peter made no secret of his pro-Prussian sentiments, even going so far as to supply Frederick II with information concerning Russian troop movements.

Elizabeth died in December, 1761, leaving Catherine's husband, Peter III, as the new emperor. Catherine was six months pregnant with Orlov's child at the time, a son who was born in April, 1762, but no one really noticed. Peter III immediately ended the war with Prussia and then allied himself with Prussia to make war on Denmark, declaring himself more than willing to serve Frederick II. Added to this insult to Russian patriotism, Peter outraged the Church by reviling Russian Orthodox ritual and by ordering the secularizing of church estates and the serfs bound to those estates. Most important to his final overthrow, he offended the elite Guards, dressing them in uniforms that were completely Prussian in appearance and constantly taunting the men.

In June, 1762, Catherine, with the support of the powerful Orlov family and the Guards, acted. In a bloodless coup, she seized the crown in St. Petersburg and published a manifesto claiming the throne. Dressed in a Guard's uniform and astride her stallion Brilliant, she led her troops against her deposed husband in his stronghold at Peterhoff. He offered his abdication, and, with its acceptance, Catherine became Empress of Russia.

Life's Work

Catherine began her reign by declaring that she had acted only because it was the will of the people. Aware that she had come to the throne by the might of the powerful Orlov family and with the backing of the Guards, she realized the need not to antagonize the nobility or the Church. As a result, her manifesto justifying her seizure of the throne explained her actions as needed to establish the correct form of government, an autocracy acting in accord with Russian Orthodoxy, national custom, and the sentiment of the Russian people. While her words were a welcome relief from the brief reign of Peter III, her actions were not unilaterally accepted—after all she was a German by birth and had no blood claim to the throne, even if she was ultimately claiming it for her son. To complicate matters, Peter III died, in all probability murdered at the behest of the Orlovs, and in 1764 Ivan VI, himself deposed by Elizabeth, was killed in his prison cell during an abortive rescue attempt. Catherine was forced to deal with a throne which many thought she had murdered the legitimate claimants to gain.

At the time she took the throne, she still retained much of her early beauty. She had a clear, very white complexion, which was set off by her brown hair and dark eyebrows. Her eyes were hazel, and in a certain light they appeared bright blue. She had a long neck and a proud carriage, and in her youth she was noted for her shapely figure. As she aged, she grew increasingly heavy: When she collapsed immediately before her death, it took several men to carry her to her bed.

Despite her rather tenuous hold on the throne, the new empress rapidly took charge. She ended the hated war against Denmark and quickly went to work trying to reform Russia into what Peter the Great had envisioned for it. An advocate of economic growth and expansion and an opponent of trade restrictions, she abolished most state monopolies and authorized grain exports. Under her reign, Russia had some of the most liberal tariff policies in Europe. Determined to improve agriculture, in 1765 she established the Free Economic Society for the Encouragement of Agriculture and Husbandry.

Faced with the chaos of the Russian legal system, Catherine was determined to create an effective centralized government. She set to work codifying the laws of Russia, and in 1766 she published a work in which she drew freely from writers such as Montesquieu, Cesare Bonesana Beccaria, and Denis Diderot. It confirmed the need for an autocratic ruler as the best form of government to fill the needs of Russia; yet it developed the idea that the government was responsible to the needs of the people. All subjects, except the serfs, were entitled to equal treatment under the law, and all had the right to petition the sovereign. The standard use of torture in conjunction with legal proceedings and the common use of capital punishment were shunned, the only exception being in the case of national security.

Not content with this venture alone, she set to work on a series of legal codes to cover nearly all aspects of the Russian social order. In 1782, she published a work which gave minute instructions for the administration of the urban population. This was followed in the same year by two charters which delineated the rights and obligations of the various levels of society. Despite these laws, she did not deal with the one level of society that by the end of the century made up 90 percent of the population—the peasantry. Russian serfs were bound to the nobles, who had complete control over them. The wealth of a noble was based on how many serfs, or souls, he owned, not on how much land he controlled. Catherine maintained her position by the support of the nobility. To create any law that interfered with the nobles' rights over their serfs would alienate the nobility and without any question would lead to her being deposed in favor of her son. For this reason, while she remained acutely aware of the serfs' plight, she did nothing to change their status as property and refused them the basic right to petition the monarch, a right held by all other levels of society.

Two major problems that plagued her reign were wars and the frequent threat of impostors making claims on her throne. In 1768, the Ottoman Empire declared war on Russia over the question of Russian troops in Poland, and the war continued until the Ottomans surrendered in 1774. Russian territory was greatly increased in the settlement, but in 1787 the Ottoman Empire again declared war on Russia, a conflict which lasted until 1791. In 1782-1783, the Crimea was under siege but was subdued and incorporated into Russia in 1784. In 1788, while Russia was at war with the Turks, war with Sweden erupted and lasted until 1790. In 1793, Catherine annexed part of Poland, and in 1794 a full-scale rebellion erupted in that country but was finally crushed by Russian troops, leaving the area firmly in Russian control.

From the beginning of her reign, rumors abounded that Peter III was not dead, and at intervals impostors came forward to claim the Crown. Some of these amassed considerable followings, especially in the case of the Pugachov Revolt of 1773-1774, but all were quickly eliminated. Most of the impostors spent the rest of their lives in banishment in Siberia. Catherine was always aware of the fragility of her hold on the throne, and in later years she reacted in fear to the news of the French Revolution, taking stern measures to ensure that no such ideas developed in Russia. In 1793, she broke all relations with France, including the importation of any French goods, and, despite her earlier support of publishers, in 1796 she imposed rigid book censorship and limited the number of presses to those completely under government control. Any hint of republican thinking was quickly investigated, and anyone even remotely suspect was quickly banished.

At the height of this fear of French republicanism, and having outlived nearly all of her friends and advisers, she suffered a stroke in November, 1796, and died at the Winter Palace in St. Petersburg. Her relationship with her son had always been strained, and there were rumors that she intended to remove him as her heir in favor of his son Alexander. If she left a testament to this effect it was never found, although forgeries of such a document continued to appear. The new emperor, Paul I, had his murdered father's body exhumed, and, after crowning the remains with his own hands, he had the bodies of both of his parents buried together at the Peter and Paul Cathedral in St. Petersburg.

Summary

Under Catherine the Great, Russia was changed from a chaotic, badly managed nation to one of the major forces in Europe. Laws were codified and a powerful centralized government was formed. As a result of numerous wars, the lands of the nation were greatly increased. There was also a great increase in national wealth.

Despite her failure to deal with the question of the serfs, Catherine can be viewed as one of the first enlightened monarchs, attempting to create a moral society and eliminating corruption in government. She introduced smallpox inoculation to Russia in 1768, and in 1786 she published a statute setting up general education in the twenty-six provincial capitals. In a highly illiterate nation, this was a radical step forward. She encouraged advancement in agriculture and made every effort to improve the life of the Russian people.

Bibliography
Alexander, John T. *Catherine the Great: Life and Legend.* New York: Oxford University Press, 1989. This work gives a largely unbiased portrait of a complex and powerful woman. Alexander considers all aspects of Catherine's life and manages to deal honestly with the reality of her legendary love life. Excellent bibliography.
Bergamini, John D. *The Tragic Dynasty: A History of the Romanovs.* New York: G. P. Putnam's Sons, 1969. A generally detailed look at the life of Catherine although greater emphasis is given to her sexual appetites and her relationship with her two famous lovers than to the political aspects of her reign.
Cowles, Virginia. *The Romanovs.* New York: Harper & Row, 1971. Cowles deals with Catherine's love of opulence and the scandals of her life, emphasizing her love of grandeur and her numerous lovers.
Grey, Ian. *The Romanovs: The Rise and Fall of a Dynasty.* New York: Doubleday, 1970. Catherine is depicted as a ruthless sovereign who plotted her way to the throne even before the death of Empress Elizabeth.
MacKenzie, David, and Michael W. Curran. *A History of Russia and the Soviet Union.* Chicago: Dorsey Press, 1978. A text covering the history of Russia. Contains several detailed chapters on Catherine which show her life in a historical perspective. Excellent bibliography of historical texts on the period.

C. D. Akerley

COUNT CAVOUR

Born: August 10, 1810; Turin, French Empire
Died: June 6, 1861; Turin, Italy
Areas of Achievement: Politics and government
Contribution: As prime minister between 1852 and 1861, Cavour gave Piedmont the economic and diplomatic leadership of Italy and played a key
role in the country's political unification. He is generally regarded as the
founder of modern Italy.

Early Life
Count Camillo Benso di Cavour was born in Turin on August 10, 1810.
His mother, née Adèle de Sellon, came from a line of wealthy Huguenots who
had been expelled from France by Louis XIV and had settled in Geneva. His
father, the Marquis Michele Benso di Cavour, was the head of an ancient
noble family, a businessman and administrator who rose to high office in the
reactionary regime of Restoration Piedmont. Cavour soon rejected this world.
As a second son, he was expected to make his living in the army, but, while
attending Turin's Royal Military Academy, he was frequently punished for
rebelling against military routines. He was graduated in 1826 and served
in the army for five years, while formulating increasingly liberal political views. After the Revolution of 1830, in which Charles X of France was
overthrown, Cavour was put under surveillance by Piedmontese authorities
as a dangerous radical. In November, 1831, he resigned his commission.
Cavour was eager for a political career, but his ambitions remained blocked
by Piedmont's autocratic government for the next sixteen years. Instead, he
engaged in various economic activities, supervising family estates, investing
in new factories, banks, and railway companies, and speculating profitably in
government securities and foreign exchange. He also devoted himself to the
study of political and economic developments in Great Britain and France,
visiting both countries periodically and acquiring a deep admiration for the
ideas of Jeremy Bentham and the practices of François Guizot and Sir Robert
Peel.
By the mid-1830's, he had become an advocate of the *juste milieu*, or
middle way, which he thought would obviate the dangers posed by the extremes of reaction and revolution. Specifically, he recommended a parliamentary government controlled by an educated, wealthy elite which would
promote social progress by means of gradual, rational reform. Thus, after
briefly espousing radical opinions in his youth, Cavour adopted a liberal-
conservative stance which he maintained for the rest of his life.

Life's Work
Cavour's political opportunity finally arrived as a result of King Charles

Albert's reluctant reforms during the revolutionary atmosphere of the late 1840's. In 1847, Cavour was one of the founders and the editor of a moderate liberal newspaper, *Il Risorgimento*. In 1848, he served on the commission which established a restricted parliamentary franchise similar to his own ideal and, in June, was elected to the Chamber of Deputies.

Initially, Cavour's chances of rapid political advancement must have appeared slim, for he had neither parliamentary allies nor a commanding personal presence. He was short and stocky, with a round face, thinning, reddish hair, a scanty beard, and spectacles, and was more familiar with the French language than Italian, which he spoke imperfectly and unattractively. Yet he proved an engaging character, self-confident, down-to-earth, humorous, and conscientious, with the somewhat racy image of an incorrigible gambler, a lifelong bachelor, and a womanizer. More important, he was a highly skilled politician, well versed in parliamentary practice, and an extremely penetrating, logical speaker. He quickly won the allegiance of conservatives by backing Massimo d'Azeglio's center-right government and of leftists by supporting the Siccardi laws against ecclesiastical privileges. It thus came as no surprise when he was appointed minister of marine, commerce, and agriculture in October, 1850, added the Finance Ministry six months later, and became the dominant figure in the government. He was able to seize complete power in 1852, when Azeglio resigned in protest at the senate's rejection of a civil-marriage bill. Cavour was a rationalist who generally sympathized with attempts to reduce the Church's authority, but on this occasion he agreed to King Victor Emmanuel II's demand that the bill be abandoned and was appointed prime minister on November 4.

In the early years of his premiership, Cavour concentrated on domestic affairs, attempting to convert backward Piedmont into the most progressive and powerful country in Italy. Accordingly, he resisted royal attempts to subvert parliament's constitutional supremacy, resumed the attack on the Church by dissolving half of the monasteries in 1855, and increased military expenditure. In addition, he terminated Piedmont's dependence on costly loans from the Rothschilds' Paris bank and promoted economic growth by expanding bank credit, financing the development of mines, railways, and utilities, and maintaining tariff agreements that he had negotiated earlier as finance minister. As a result, Piedmont became the only liberal, reforming state in the peninsula and the acknowledged leader of the Italian national cause.

Cavour's important contribution to that cause was a tribute to his remarkable flexibility and opportunism. At heart a Piedmontese nationalist, he was concerned to further the interests of his native state. To do so, he invariably opposed revolutionary efforts by republicans such as Giuseppe Garibaldi and Giuseppe Mazzini but otherwise was prepared to modify tactics and objectives in the light of experience and circumstances. In the 1840's, he expected the Italians themselves to expel Austria and create a Turin-based, northern kingdom to the exclusion of the central and southern parts of Italy. Austria's easy victories over Piedmont in 1849, however, convinced him that little could be achieved without foreign aid and he carefully avoided hostilities until the Crimean War. Before its outbreak, Cavour was reluctant to meet British and French requests for help and only did so in 1855 in order to foil Victor Emmanuel's plan to replace him with a more warlike minister. Nevertheless, participation in the war proved a boon.

On the one hand, the army's creditable performance increased Piedmont's prestige in Italy. On the other, at the Congress of Paris in 1856 Cavour raised the Italian question in an international forum for the first time and learned that Napoleon III was sympathetic to the idea of a moderately powerful, independent kingdom in northern Italy. Subsequently, he maintained contact with the emperor and, in 1858, negotiated the secret Pact of Plombières, committing France to send military assistance in return for territorial concessions if Cavour engineered a crisis in which Austria appeared the aggressor. He was able to do so in April, 1859, largely because of Austria's foolish ultimatum demanding unilateral demobilization by Piedmont. During the resultant war, however, stiff Austrian resistance led Napoleon to withdraw after two narrow victories and negotiate the Armistice of Villafranca with Emperor Francis Joseph. Cavour, who was not invited to the talks, was bitterly disappointed at the peace terms, which obliged Austria to cede only Lombardy and ordered the restoration to the central Italian duchies of absolutist rulers who had been ousted during the war and replaced by Piedmontese sympathizers. On learning that Victor Emmanuel had accepted the terms, he angrily resigned on July 11, 1859.

In the last two years of his life, a series of unexpected developments enabled Cavour to achieve goals he had previously dismissed as impracticable. While he was out of office, the faltering alliance with the French was replaced by British support. Foreign Minister Lord John Russell criticized the Villafranca agreement as unworkable, insisting that Italians be allowed to determine their own future, and pressured Victor Emmanuel into reinstating Cavour in January, 1860. On his return, he was thus fully confident that Piedmont's control would soon be extended into central Italy. In March, after he had guaranteed Napoleon's acquiescence by ceding Nice and Savoy to France, plebiscites were held in Modena, Parma, Romagna, and Tuscany, whose subjects voted overwhelmingly for annexation. At this juncture, Cavour looked for a lengthy period of peace in which the new territories could be consolidated, but his hopes were rudely shattered by Garibaldi's startling conquest of Sicily and Naples between May and September, 1860. Desperate to prevent Italian leadership's falling into popular, democratic hands, he first convinced Napoleon that his purpose was to protect the pope from advancing revolutionaries and then boldly sent the army south. Having taken Umbria and the Marche, the central and eastern parts of the Papal States, it entered Naples, where Garibaldi relinquished authority to Victor Emmanuel in late October. Subsequently, the people of Naples, the Marche, and Umbria voted for annexation by Piedmont. In January, 1861, elections were held for a national parliament which, on March 17, gave the Italian crown to Victor Emmanuel. Tragically, Cavour was unable to enjoy the fruits of his triumph, for soon afterward he contracted a fever, probably malaria, and died on June 6, 1861.

Summary

Count Cavour's achievements fully justify his reputation as one of the most successful statesmen in modern European history. In a mere eight years, he made Piedmont the leading Italian state and, with a rare combination of diplomatic skill, opportunism, and military daring, unified most of the peninsula. When he died, the only remaining independent territories were Venetia and Rome, which were added in 1866 and 1870, respectively. Yet Cavour's legacy was by no means untarnished. Essentially, the process of unification entailed the imposition on all Italy of Piedmont's political system, which gave power to the largely anticlerical upper middle class. In conjunction with Cavour's seizure of papal territory, the extension of the political system contributed to the rift that was to divide church and state for the remainder of the century. It also aroused intense hostility among the thousands who had fought or voted for annexation expecting democracy, and aggravated the serious class and regional conflicts that racked Italian society. Equally detrimental were Cavour's methods of controlling parliament, such as tampering with elections, invalidating unfavorable returns, and disarming opposition by giving office to its moderate elements. The latter practice underlay the *connubio* (marriage), which united Cavour's moderate conservative deputies and Urbano Rattazzi's center-left group from 1852 to 1857, when leftist electoral losses facilitated a return to the Right.

Such expedients enabled Cavour to establish a virtual dictatorship, unfettered by king, cabinet, or parliament. Whether he viewed them as temporary, emergency measures is unclear because he died so soon after the prolonged national crisis ended. After 1861, the imitation of these measures by less talented politicians produced many of the features which characterized later Italian politics, including a tendency to tolerate autocratic power, the absence of cabinet responsibility, and reliance on fluctuating centrist coalitions which survived only by avoiding controversial issues. Thus, Cavour can be viewed as the founder not only of the Italian state but also of traditions responsible for its chronic political weakness.

Bibliography

Coppa, Frank J. *Camillo di Cavour*. Boston: Twayne, 1973. A brief, well-written biography by an American Catholic scholar, focusing on aspects of Cavour's career not normally stressed. Particularly useful for church-state relations and diplomacy prior to Plombières. Contains a detailed bibliography with some omissions.

Hearder, Harry. *Cavour.* 2d ed. London: Historical Association, 1985. An updated version of a 1972 pamphlet. Provides an excellent introduction, with sections on Cavour's life, opinions, and achievements and a well-balanced assessment of his contribution to Italian history. Contains a useful, short bibliography.

Mack Smith, Denis. *Cavour.* New York: Alfred A. Knopf, 1985. A fully documented, lucid biography, containing much fresh information and new insights. Good on all aspects of Cavour's life but particularly economic policies and the development of his character. Contains a useful bibliographical note. Essential reading.

_____. *Cavour and Garibaldi, 1860: A Study in Political Conflict.* Cambridge, England: Cambridge University Press, 1954, reprint 1985. A seminal work based on newly released archival material. Brilliantly clarifies the complex events of 1860, demonstrating the conflicts between Italian leaders and undermining traditional myths about Cavour. The 1985 reissue includes the author's reflections on the controversy generated by the original edition.

Whyte, A. J. *The Early Life and Letters of Cavour, 1810-1848.* London: Oxford University Press, 1925. A scholarly account of Cavour's life before his entry into parliament, making extensive use of his correspondence. Offers useful insights into his character and his preparations for a political career.

_____. *The Political Life and Letters of Cavour, 1848-1861.* London: Oxford University Press, 1930. The sequel to the above entry, with similar qualities. Deals with Cavour's political career, emphasizing his diplomatic activities.

Ian Duffy

BENVENUTO CELLINI

Born: November 3, 1500; Florence
Died: February 13, 1571; Florence
Areas of Achievement: Art and literature
Contribution: Cellini is acknowledged as perhaps the finest goldsmith in
Renaissance Italy. His sculpture, represented by his bronze *Perseus*, was
also superb. He is, however, best known for his lively and spirited auto-
biography, which transmits his spirit and that of his age.

Early Life

Benvenuto Cellini was born in Florence at the beginning of the Cinque-
cento. He was the son of Giovanni Cellini, an architect and engineer, who
was also a passionate amateur musician, and of Elisabetta Granacci, the
daughter of a neighbor. Cellini describes his parents' marriage as a love
match: Elisabetta married without a dowry. Benvenuto was born to them
after some twenty years of marriage, during which time they had one daughter. Cellini's father dearly wished him to become a musician, a flutist, while
Benvenuto himself wished to study art. This struggle, a friendly one, continued between the two for many years. When Benvenuto reached the age of
fifteen, he apprenticed himself, against his father's will, as a goldsmith in
the studio of Andrea di Sandro Marcone. He was not paid wages and so was
not compelled to do much of the menial labor that fell to paid apprentices.
He used his extra time to study drawing, a study he continued all of his life
and one of the things that made him much more than a mere craftsman.

About a year into this apprenticeship, he became involved in a duel in
support of his younger brother; the duel rapidly developed into a brawl. In
this year, 1516, Benvenuto was banished from Florence for six months. He
went to Siena and worked for a goldsmith there, until he was recalled to
Florence by the Cardinal de'Medici at the elder Cellini's request (the Celli-
nis were Medici adherents through all the changes in Florentine government;
Benvenuto continued this tradition, although his vigorous sense of *amour
propre* meant that his relations with the great were always rather testy).
Benvenuto was then sent by his father to study music in Bologna, but the
youth also worked with a goldsmith there. He returned to Florence after
several months and eventually made peace with his father on the art or music
question.

Leaving for Rome at about age sixteen, Benvenuto ended up in Pisa for a
year. While in Pisa, he worked as a goldsmith and studied the local antiquities. Returning to Florence, he studied the work of Michelangelo, whom
he regarded as the greatest modern sculptor. Finally, in 1519, he did travel to
Rome but returned, after two years, to Florence, from where in 1523 he had
to flee under sentence of death for fighting.

Benvenuto fled to Rome and soon began to receive important commissions from the Bishop of Salamanca, Sigismondo Chigi, from his wife, Porzia, and from Pope Clement VII. At this time, he was artistically mature; he began to work for himself and not for other goldsmiths and established a shop of his own in Rome. What would be the pattern of his life had taken shape: a peripatetic habit, often set in motion of necessity, because of his terrible temper and tendency to violence; many important commissions; a great reputation for his work coupled with frequent disputes with his patrons; and much trouble with the law.

Life's Work

In Rome, Cellini's fine work in drawing, jewelry, and larger pieces such as serving plates and candelabras very soon caught the notice of rich and influential patrons. He was a musician, briefly, in Clement's orchestra; he did many drawings in the style of Michelangelo and Raphael; he made jewelry, and set and estimated the value of jewels; he made cast and carved plate and ornamental silver; and he designed and struck medals and coinage. He was also drawn to military life during this period and participated in the defense of Rome in 1527, during the invasion of Italy by the Holy Roman Empire. He claimed to have shot the Constable of Bourbon and the Prince of Orange during the defense, and there is some evidence that his claims could be true. At this time, his sculptor's knowledge of structure and spatiality, translated into engineering, was useful in ordering the pope's artillery. Later he would design fortifications in Florence. (It was common for sculptors in this period to be called on to use their engineering skills to design weapons, fortifications, and buildings for their cities of residence.)

While in Rome, Cellini was often distracted from his art by his music and also by romantic dalliance. His ambition to excel in all branches of goldsmithing, coinage, and sculpture also served to distract him from the relatively single-minded pursuit of one medium which was the norm, then and now, for craftsmen. Most artists specialized in certain aspects of their art. Cellini was an endlessly ambitious and curious student of many arts and always was a leader in technical innovations in sculpture and goldsmithing.

After the invasion of Rome, Cellini left for Florence, intending to raise a company and become a captain under the famous condottiere Orazio Baglioni. On hearing this, Cellini's father sent him to Mantua so that he would not be called on to fulfill his obligation to Baglioni. Cellini went to Mantua, executed some small works for the duke there, quarreled with him, and returned to Florence, where he discovered that his father and sister Cosa had died of the plague. His brother and another sister remaining, he stayed in Florence until Clement declared war on the city and requested Cellini's presence in Rome.

In danger of being arrested as a traitor or spy because of these communications from Clement, Cellini traveled to Rome in 1529. He received at this time the commission from Clement for the famous morse (a clasp or button for a cope), now lost. Its design is recorded in three eighteenth century drawings in the British Museum: God the Father, in half relief is over a large diamond in the center of the morse, and the diamond is supported by three children. At this time also, Cellini began to make the steel dies for the pope's coinage and was appointed *maestro della stampe* at the papal mint.

After Clement's death in 1534, Cellini seized the opportunity of the resultant civic disorder to kill a rival goldsmith, Pompeo; he was absolved of this murder by the new pope Paul III, partly because of the support of influential friends such as Cardinal Francesco Cornaro and Cardinal Ippolito de'Medici, and partly because the new pope wished to retain him as master of the mint.

In 1536, Holy Roman Emperor Charles V arrived in Rome for his triumphal entry as conqueror of the city. Cellini had been commissioned by Paul to make the gifts for the emperor and empress: a crucifix in gold and a jeweled golden case for a richly illuminated Book of Hours. The works were not finished at the time of the arrival of the emperor (April 6, 1536), and the pope told Cellini to offer himself along with the gifts in order to see the work to its conclusion. By the time this was done, an enemy of Cellini (of which he always seemed to have a good supply) had slandered him to the pope, who became angry at Cellini, underpaid him for his work, and refused to send him with the book to the emperor, who had requested his presence.

At this point, Cellini decided to travel to France (he left April 1, 1537). He met at this time Ippolito I, Cardinal d'Este of Ferrara, who commissioned a basin and a jug from him; this friendship later proved to be his entrée with the King of France, Francis I. Becoming ill, Cellini returned to Rome. He was soon recalled to France by Francis through the Cardinal d'Este but, before he could leave, he was arrested by the pope and imprisoned in the Castle Sant'Angelo for allegedly stealing the papal jewels, entrusted to him at the time of the invasion of Rome in 1527. Pier' Luigi, the pope's natural son, was apparently behind this plot; Cellini writes that Pier' Luigi wanted to obtain Cellini's property. Francis requested Cellini of the pope but was refused.

During Cellini's long prison stay, which severely impaired his health, he survived poisoning attempts and political maneuvering; he was finally extracted from the papal clutches in 1539 by means of the deft diplomacy of the Cardinal d'Este, at the behest of Francis. Cellini brought out of prison a long poem he had composed there, which he reproduced in his autobiography, *La vita di Benvenuto Cellini* (*The Life of Benvenuto Cellini*, 1771), which was not published until 1728. The Cardinal d'Este brought Cellini back to France, where he arrived in 1540. Soon after his arrival, Cellini became dissatisfied with his treatment by the cardinal and tried to leave France on a pilgrimage to the Holy Sepulchre. This near loss made the cardinal more attentive and drew the attention of the king, who gave Cellini a large salary and a small castle in Paris in which to work. In 1542, Cellini was granted letters of naturalization by the king, and in 1543 he completed for the king the great saltcellar.

This saltcellar, one of Cellini's most famous works, has two figures in gold: a male representing the sea who holds a small ship (which holds the salt) and a facing female figure representing the land. Her hand rests on a small temple (which holds the pepper). The legs of the figures are inter-twined as they halfway recline on an oval base. The piece is beautifully ornamented and enameled, and can be seen in any illustrated collection of Cellini's works. Cellini created many other works for Francis. Among these was a silver candlestick: a life-size figure of Jupiter, mounted on rollers, holding a (functioning) torch in one hand. Several pieces he did in France do survive: the *Nymph of Fontainebleau* (1545) and an accompanying satyr are among them. He began to make models for a monumental figure of Mars and accompanying smaller allegorical figures for a fountain at Fontainebleau, but this work never reached completion. Cellini had incurred the ire of the king's mistress, Madame d'Étampes; he apparently did not realize the extent of her power, especially in the realm of art commissions. She resented Cellini's obliviousness to her power and bitterly opposed his projects; her op-position was sufficient to prevent any new projects of his from coming to fruition.

Frustrated in his work, in 1545 Cellini asked leave to travel to Florence. The king denied him permission while the Cardinal d'Este told him he could leave; he left on what was meant to be a brief trip, but he never returned. In his autobiography, he often regrets his departure from France. In Florence, he visited Cosimo I de'Medici and described for him all that he had done for Francis. Cosimo asked Cellini to make, for the piazza of Florence, a statue of Perseus, symbolizing Cosimo's own victory over the Gorgon of republi-canism. The *Perseus* would be in grand company—Michelangelo's *David* (1501-1504) and Donatello's *Judith and Holofernes* (1456-1457) already stood in the piazza. This was Cellini's chance to make his name as a sculptor in his home city, a city renowned for sculpture. He regarded the commission as an honor but received only about a third of the money he requested for the piece. The piece was finally finished and revealed fully to the public on April 27, 1554. It was greeted with great public acclaim; art criticism was a democratic activity in the Florence of those days. Cosimo, standing half-hidden at a window of the palace, heard the praise of the crowds. He appar-ently wanted to know the sentiments of the crowd before he expressed his own. The acclaim of the public allowed him to be equally pleased with the piece.

During his stay in Florence, Cellini had begun to work in marble. He restored an antique Ganymede for Cosimo and did a life-size Christ in white marble on a cross in black marble; this was to be for his own tomb (the piece is now in the Escorial). At this time, he induced Cosimo to have a competition among the Florentine sculptors for a beautiful block of marble, meant for a statue of Neptune, that had been quarried for Bandinelli (a hated rival of Cellini who had since died). Cellini did not get this commission, he thought, because of the opposition of Cosimo's wife, who thought him too haughty. At the end of his autobiography, he portrays himself as involved in rather acrimonious negotiations with Cosimo for making the *Neptune* from a different block of marble. This task was never accomplished.

Soon afterward, Cellini left Cosimo's service and established his own shop again, doing goldsmith's work for many clients. His life is poorly documented after this time, because it is not included in his autobiography and because he had fewer dealings with influential people. The writing of his autobiography is his most important work of this period, during which he also wrote his treatises on sculpture and on goldsmithing, *Trattati dell' orefi- ceria e della scultura* (1568; *The Treatises of Benvenuto Cellini on Gold- smithing and Sculpture*, 1898), which he published himself much later.

In 1557, in Florence, Cellini was condemned to four years in prison for sodomy, though this sentence was reduced to four years of confinement in his own house. During this time, he dictated his autobiography to a fourteen-year-old boy, while working at projects in his studio. In 1559, a version of his autobiography was completed, and Cellini gave it to the famed Benedetto Varchi, a Florentine writer and scholar, for criticism. Varchi liked the collo- quial style and told Cellini to retain it. Cellini continued work on his autobi- ography until 1562. He died in Florence in 1571.

Summary

Benvenuto Cellini's life represents what is meant by the phrase Renais- sance man. He was an immensely able, curious, and active practitioner of many civilized arts: drawing, music, sculpture, goldsmithing, swordplay, military strategy and architecture, conversation, and literature. His appear- ance was apparently pleasing, though no contemporary likenesses exist. He was social, well connected, and confident, and felt himself the equal of any by virtue of his skill. His directness and enthusiasm in *The Life of Benvenuto Cellini* seem to represent the spirit of his age.

As an artist, Cellini was both an excellent craftsman and a technically innovative and formally inventive sculptor. He could combine the Renais- sance virtues of beautiful form and new technologies into works that can stand with the best of his day. It is unfortunate that, because of his tempera- ment, the circumstances of his life, and the occasional uncooperativeness of patrons, his skill was not generally allowed the scope it needed. It is also unfortunate that, because many of his works were executed in precious met- als, few of them survive, many having been melted down.

His greatest work, however, is not so much a work of art, perhaps, as of personality. His autobiography provides a most vivid picture of life in the Renaissance; it is undoubtedly tainted by exaggeration and boasting, but even these characteristics reveal aspects of an age of great energy. Cellini was an extremely subtle observer; through his description, figures that would otherwise be little more than names are revealed in detail. His own personality is revealed without caution and a thoroughly charming self-portrait of a fascinating man appears.

Bibliography

Avery, C. "Benvenuto Cellini's Bust of Bindo Altoviti." *The Connoisseur* 198 (May, 1978): 62-72. An unusual look at one of Cellini's portrait bronzes. Not very penetrating, but it does give some account of a mode of work in which the sculptor excelled and for which he is little remembered.

Cellini, Benvenuto. *The Life of Benvenuto Cellini*. Translated with an introduction by John Addington Symonds. Garden City, N.Y.: Doubleday, 1961. This is the standard English translation of Cellini's autobiography. It is faulted on several counts, largely for its tendency to clean up and standardize Cellini's vigorous and colloquial Italian, yet it is coherent and very readable. Includes footnotes that put into context the many characters in Cellini's story.

_____. *The Treatises of Benvenuto Cellini on Goldsmithing and Sculpture*. Translated by C. R. Ashby. London: E. Arnold, 1898. This work by Cellini describes his beliefs about the trades to which he devoted his life.

Pope-Hennessy, John. *Cellini*. New York: Abbeville Press, 1985. This magnificent work contains full photodocumentation of Cellini's surviving works and drawings, and the casts of some that have been lost. Pope-Hennessy has written an absorbing and readable essay on Cellini's life and works for the book. Contains much information not in Cellini's autobiography. His descriptions of Cellini as an accountant, record-keeper, and litigant are especially fascinating, revealing Cellini's nonswashbuckling side. The book is probably the best source on Cellini next to the autobiography and makes good use of many contemporary sources. Includes a good index, notes, and a bibliography.

Vasari, Giorgio. *Lives of the Painters, Sculptors, and Architects*. Translated with an introduction by William Gaunt. London: Dent, 1963. This four-volume work is a trove of biographical information on Renaissance artists, compiled and written by a fellow artist and contemporary. Although there is no separate entry on Cellini, he is mentioned in many of the other artists' biographies. Includes an index.

Ann Klefstad

MIGUEL DE CERVANTES

Born: September 29, 1547; Alcalá de Henares, Spain
Died: April 23, 1616; Madrid, Spain
Area of Achievement: Literature
Contribution: Poet, playwright, and novelist, Cervantes is Spain's greatest
  writer, chiefly because of *Don Quixote de la Mancha*, the first real Euro-
  pean novel and one of the supreme works of world literature.

Early Life

In 1547, the year that Miguel de Cervantes Saavedra was born, Henry VIII
of England and François I of France died, leaving Charles I of Spain (and V
of the Holy Roman Empire) undisputedly the dominant ruler in Europe and
the Spanish dominions the most powerful empire on earth. The sixteenth
century is known in Spanish history as the *siglo del oro* (the golden century), partly because of Cervantes, who is the greatest of all Spanish writers.
His parents were impoverished members of the gentry, and Miguel, the
fourth of their seven children, was born in Alcalá de Henares, some twenty
miles from Madrid. His father, Rodrigo, was an apothecary surgeon, who
was usually in debt and was even sent to debtors' prison. In 1551, he moved
the family to Valladolid, and in 1553 to Córdoba, once the greatest city of
Moorish Spain. There Miguel probably studied under Father Alonso de Vi-
eras and later at the Jesuit College of Santa Catarina, where he is likely to
have seen his first plays. For six years after 1558, the family's whereabouts
cannot be determined, but in 1564, they appeared in Seville, the major city
of Andalusia. There Miguel attended the new Jesuit college and saw the
great actor Lope de Rueda and his company perform. The residence in Seville was brief, however, for in 1566, the family moved to Madrid, the new
seat of the royal court under Philip II. There, Cervantes became a student in
the city school. When Queen Elizabeth de Valois died, Cervantes' teacher
composed a commemorative book in 1569 that included four poems by
young Cervantes on the death of the queen.

That same year, however, a warrant was issued for Cervantes' arrest for
wounding a man in a duel, apparently in the royal court, because the penalty
was for Cervantes to have his right hand amputated and to be exiled for ten
years. Not waiting for the sentence to be carried out, Cervantes escaped to
Rome, then proceeded to Naples, where he enlisted in the Spanish army,
where his brother Rodrigo joined him. In 1571, the brothers were among the
troops aboard the immense fleet of two hundred galleys and one hundred
additional ships that engaged the equally formidable Turkish armada at Lepanto in the Gulf of Corinth. On the eve of the battle, Cervantes was ill with
malaria and was ordered to stay below, but he insisted that he be posted
"where the danger is greatest and there I shall remain and fight to the

death." During the Battle of Lepanto, the greatest naval combat in history to that date, Cervantes held his post on the deck of the *Marquesa*, and at the end of the day, when the Spanish were victorious, he was found there covered with blood, his sword in his right hand, his left hand shattered, and his chest bleeding from two severe wounds. The victorious admiral, Don Juan of Austria, must have been aware of Cervantes' valor, for that day he ordered an increase in his pay. It was three weeks before Cervantes had his wounds properly treated at the hospital in Messina. It is not clear whether his left hand was amputated or was crippled and useless for the rest of his life. Nevertheless, Cervantes considered that day in battle as one of the greatest of his life and said that he would rather have been in the battle than have missed it and the wounds he suffered. After six months' hospitalization, Cervantes recovered, rejoined the fleet, and was present when Don Juan captured the Turkish flagship on which the galley slaves rebelled and killed their captain, the grandson of the pirate Barbarossa. He was also present when Don Juan captured Tunis without a battle in 1573. Garrisoned in Naples for a year, he fell in love with a woman who became the model for Silena in his first novel, *La Galatea* (1585; *Galatea: A Pastoral Romance*, 1833).

On a voyage home in 1575, his ship was attacked by Algerian galleys, and after a sharp fight the ship was captured and the survivors, including Miguel and Rodrigo de Cervantes, were taken as slaves to Algiers. Cervantes later described the event in a verse epistle to the king's secretary, Matteo Vásquez. Because Cervantes was bearing letters of praise from Don Juan of Austria and the Duke of Sessa, his ransom was made impossibly high. During five years of brutal captivity, though usually loaded down with chains, Cervantes masterminded four escape attempts. Each was thwarted, yet, despite the strong danger of being mutilated, impaled, hooked, or burned alive, as some of his confederates had been, he kept trying. Each time he was caught, he claimed sole responsibility for the plot. Each time, he was chained and imprisoned more severely, yet his courage, resourcefulness, and lust for freedom were irrepressible. At one time he may have planned to organize a massive slave insurrection. According to one account of Algerian captivity, the pasha lived in perpetual fear of "the scheming of Miguel de Cervantes." Apparently only greed for his ransom kept his master from putting him to a horrible death. Such ransom as was provided was inadequate for both Cervantes brothers, so Miguel relinquished his share so that Rodrigo could go free. Not until three years later was Miguel finally ransomed, in October, 1580. His captivity provides the basis for the captive's tale in part 1 of *El ingenioso hidalgo don Quixote de la Mancha* (1605, 1615; *The History of the Valorous and Wittie Knight-Errant, Don Quixote of the Mancha*, 1612-1620; better known as *Don Quixote de la Mancha*).

Life's Work

Back in Spain, after twelve years' absence, Cervantes sought preferment and was sent on a confidential mission to Spanish territory in North Africa. Thereafter, he spent seven months in Lisbon seeking employment and even requesting a post in the New World. When his money ran out, he began to devote himself to literature, turning to the theater, for which he wrote, in his own words, "twenty or thirty plays," of which all but two have been lost. One of the survivors is *El trato de Argel* (1585; *The Commerce of Algiers: A Comedy*, 1870), about Christian lovers imprisoned in Algiers. Artistically, it is not impressive, but it is valuable as a realistic picture of Algerian life and the lot of prisoners, one of whom, a soldier named Saavedra who assists his fellow captives, is a self-portrait. The other play, *El cerco de Numancia* (wr. 1885, pb. 1784; *Numantia: A Tragedy*, 1870), dramatizes the tragic siege of a city in Spain by Scipio the Younger. Rather than yield to the Romans, every citizen chooses death. The play became symbolic of Spanish courage and was performed during Napoleon I's siege of Saragossa in 1809, to strengthen the resistance of the defenders.

During his years with the theater, Cervantes had an affair with Ana de Villafranca, who in 1584 bore him an illegitimate daughter, Isabel. Shortly thereafter, Cervantes was married to Catalina de Salazar y Palacios. Though she was eighteen years younger than he, though his business often kept them apart for the next thirteen years, and though they had no children, the marriage endured for the rest of his life.

The next year, Cervantes published his first novel, *Galatea*, in the then-popular genre of pastoral romance. His income from literature was not enough to support his family, however, for with his father's death in 1585, Cervantes had to care for his wife, mother, two sisters, daughter, and a niece. Accordingly, he took a position to procure grain in Andalusia for the Spanish Armada. Outraged at his confiscating some wheat from powerful churchmen, the Vicar General of Seville had Cervantes excommunicated, but Cervantes managed to get the ban removed. Further commissions sent him through many Andalusian towns and cities in search of grain and olive oil. Having difficulty collecting his salary, Cervantes applied for one of four positions vacant in America, but the Council of the Indies rejected him. Instead, he returned to work as a royal commissioner, traveling extensively through Andalusia and between Seville and Madrid. His intimate knowledge for nearly thirteen years of roads, inns, folklore, and travelers and their speech provided him with a rich background for his exemplary novels and for *Don Quixote de la Mancha*. Finally in 1594, Philip II abolished the royal commissions, and Cervantes, then forty-six years old, had to look for new employment.

His first job was to collect back taxes in the provinces of Málaga and Grenada. In 1595, he won first prize (three silver spoons) in a poetry competition at Saragossa, and the next year he wrote a celebrated sonnet satirizing the English sack of Cadiz. In 1597, he was still collecting taxes, and when an accountant made an error that showed Cervantes' accounts to be short, he was imprisoned for seven months in Seville. There he may have begun *Don Quixote de la Mancha*. In 1598, Philip II decreed that the theaters be permanently closed, thus interrupting Cervantes' career as a playwright. When the king died later that year, Cervantes wrote a poem in his honor and then wrote and read in the cathedral of Seville a far better sonnet satirizing the monarch's exceedingly grand catafalque. In the final years of the century, Cervantes probably wrote some of his exemplary novels and continued work on *Don Quixote de la Mancha*. He associated with most of the leading writers of the day, such as Lope de Vega, Francisco de Quevedo, and Luis de Góngora. When the new king, Philip III, moved the court to Valladolid, all the writers followed him there, including Cervantes in 1604.

At the beginning of 1605, part 1 of *Don Quixote de la Mancha* was published. Probably parts of it had already circulated in manuscript, for there is evidence that it was already known in literary circles. The first edition quickly sold out, and Cervantes soon found himself internationally famous, though still in financial difficulties, for he had sold the work outright and got no royalties. His new fame did not prevent him and most of his household, though innocent, from being imprisoned briefly in the summer of 1605 after testifying about a fatal duel fought in front of their home.

There is no record of Cervantes for the next three years, but in 1608, he appeared in Madrid, which was to be his main residence for the rest of his life. These final years were those of his most intense literary activity, for he was working on part 2 of *Don Quixote de la Mancha* as well as on more plays, a long poem, and a series entitled *Novelas ejemplares* (1613; *Exemplary Novels*, 1846). These are actually long short stories or short novellas, intended to instruct as well as to entertain. Cervantes prided himself on being the first person to write novels in the Castilian tongue. In the prologue, he presents a vivid description of himself as a man of average height with stooping shoulders and a somewhat heavy build, with an aquiline countenance, chestnut hair, a smooth brow, a hooked nose, a once golden beard turned silver, a large mustache, and a small mouth with only half a dozen teeth remaining. One of the works he mentions in the prologue is *Viage del Parnaso* (1614; *The Voyage to Parnassus*, 1870), a narrative poem that in eight chapters tells of a journey to Mount Parnassus, home of the Muses, where a battle is fought between good and bad poets. The poem is of considerable autobiographical importance, for in it Cervantes discusses the other poets of his day, his relationship with them, and his evaluation of his own work. In 1615, he published *Ocho comedias y ocho entremeses* (English translation, 1807), none of which had yet been performed. His full-length plays have not made a lasting mark, but the interludes made him the greatest

Spanish creator of one-act comedies.

Meanwhile *Don Quixote de la Mancha* went through innumerable editions in Spain and abroad. In 1614, a spurious sequel attributed to Alonso Fernández de Avellaneda appeared—a meretricious work lacking any literary distinction and full of obscenities and vulgar details, together with insulting comments on Cervantes' poverty, advanced age, and crippled hand. Incensed, Cervantes turned back to his own work in progress and completed part 2 of *Don Quixote de la Mancha*, which was published in the fall of 1615, about half a year before the author's death. In the remaining months of his life he completed *Los trabajos de Persiles y Sigismunda* (1617; *The Travels of Persiles and Sigismunda: A Northern History*, 1619), the dedication and prologue to which he wrote after he had received extreme unction, only four days before he died of dropsy on April 23, 1616, the same day and year that William Shakespeare died. A few years before his death, Cervantes had joined the Tertiary Order of the Franciscans, and they buried him in an unknown grave.

Cervantes' poems, plays, and exemplary novels are minor works, but *Don Quixote de la Mancha* is generally regarded as one of the world's supreme works of literature, ranking with the masterpieces of Homer, Dante, and Shakespeare. Cervantes conceived of it as a satire upon books of chivalry. Having read chivalric romances until his wits are scrambled, Alonso Quejana decides to become a knight errant, renames himself Don Quixote de la Mancha, dons a suit of battered armor, proclaims his skinny nag to be the war horse Rosinante, and, accompanied by a peasant, Sancho Panza, as his squire, goes forth to set the world right. At first, he is a figure of satire, as he confuses illusion with reality, mistakes windmills for giants, inns for castles, and flocks of sheep for armies, wears a barber's basin for a helmet, and generally causes chaos and confusion by meddling in matters which do not need mending. Gradually, he evolves into a heroic figure, even a Christlike one. An aged man, lean as a rake, with no help but his lance, sword, and the often-reluctant help of the commonsensical Sancho, he tries single-handedly to right wrongs, help the oppressed, succor widows and orphans, and bring about justice, only to be mocked, reviled, ridiculed, beaten, and almost crucified for his efforts. In a famous essay, the Russian novelist Ivan Turgenev contrasts Don Quixote with Shakespeare's Hamlet, finding the latter to be obsessed with himself, whereas Don Quixote is quite selfless in his desire to help others. The novel develops and deepens from comedy into tragicomedy. The nineteenth century French critic Charles Sainte-Beuve called it the "Bible of humanity." Far from being opposed to chivalry, Cervantes was chivalric to a fault, and in his life he showed many of the traits of Don Quixote himself. It is Quixote's gallantry, his idealism, and his panache that has made him, rather than the historic El Cid, the symbolic national hero of Spain.

Summary

In the *Exemplary Novels* and in *Don Quixote de la Mancha*, Miguel de Cervantes wrote a model of clear Castilian prose and portrayed a realistic panorama of Spain, particularly of the lives of ordinary people, even while he created a hero whose idealism makes him confuse reality with his illusions. It is that idealism and those illusions that have made Don Quixote a legend. Edmond Rostand's Cyrano de Bergerac takes him as a model. From the beginning, *Don Quixote de la Mancha* was immensely popular and profoundly influential. In England, it inspired Francis Beaumont's play *The Knight of the Burning Pestle* (1613), the picaresque novels of Henry Fielding and Tobias Smollett in the eighteenth century, and such novels as *The Spiritual Quixote* (1773) and *The Female Quixote: Or, The Adventures of Arabella* (1752), and Charles Dickens' *The Pickwick Papers* (1836-1837). Don Quixote and Sancho Panza are surely in the background of Tom Sawyer and Huckleberry Finn. W. Somerset Maugham has Don Quixote reappear as a character in his novel *Catalina* (1948), and Graham Greene's *Monsignor Quixote* (1982) has a twentieth century priest who claims to be a descendant of the don go on a similar pilgrimage around Spain. Innumerable artists have illustrated *Don Quixote de la Mancha* or done paintings inspired by it, including Francisco Goya, Honoré Daumier, Gustave Doré, and Pablo Picasso. There are dozens of operas, operettas, ballets, and songs based upon *Don Quixote de la Mancha* as well. There are several film and television versions of *Don Quixote de la Mancha*, as well as a popular musical. Don Quixote is one of the best-known and best-loved literary characters in the world, and the term "quixotic" has come to mean gallantly chivalrous, romantically idealistic, and courageously visionary.

Bibliography

Bell, Aubrey F. G. *Cervantes*. Norman: University of Oklahoma Press, 1947. Studies Cervantes' work in the context of the Renaissance and of his life and times; argues that *Don Quixote de la Mancha* must be read in relationship to all Cervantes' writings.

Byron, William. *Cervantes: A Biography*. Garden City, N.Y.: Doubleday, 1978. The most complete life and times, providing graphic detail on Cervantes' activities, the Battle of Lepanto, his captivity, the theater, and the like. Analyzes the writings both for their intrinsic artistry and as part of the literary scene of the golden age.

Cervantes, Miguel de. *The Ingenious Gentleman, Don Quixote de la Mancha*. Translated by Samuel Putnam. New York: Viking Press, 1949. The best modern translation.

Duran, Manuel. *Cervantes*. Boston: Twayne, 1974. Number 329 in the Twayne World Authors series, Duran's study examines the universality of Cervantes' work, the clarity of his style, his relationship with his public, the humor and realism of his fiction, his compassion for the humble, and his democratic spirit.

Flores, Angel, and M. J. Benardete, eds. *Cervantes Across the Centuries.* New York: Gordian Press, 1969. A collection of critical essays dealing with the genesis, composition, style, realism, and social and historical background of *Don Quixote de la Mancha.*

Fuentes, Carlos. Introduction to *The Adventures of Don Quixote de la Mancha.* New York: Farrar, Straus & Giroux, 1986. This introduction by Mexico's leading novelist discusses the influence of Desiderius Erasmus on Cervantes and the duality of realism and imagination in *Don Quixote de la Mancha* and argues that this work can be considered the beginning of a modern way of looking at the world.

Nabokov, Vladimir. *Lectures on Don Quixote.* San Diego, Calif.: Harcourt Brace Jovanovich, 1983. Six lectures, originally given at Harvard in 1951 and 1952, plus two essays on narrative and commentary, dealing with the structure, main characters, victories and defeats, and cruelty of *Don Quixote de la Mancha.*

Predmore, Richard L. *Cervantes.* New York: Dodd, Mead, 1973. A clear and concise biography by a leading Cervantes scholar, lavishly illustrated with 170 pictures from Cervantes' time and by later artists.

Riley, Edward C. *Cervantes' Theory of the Novel.* New York: Oxford University Press, 1962. Gathers Cervantes' scattered ideas on literature into coherent theories for the art of poetry, drama, and the novel. Argues that Cervantes created the modern European novel and speculated more about the problems of literature than any writer before the eighteenth century.

Russell, P. E. *Cervantes.* New York: Oxford University Press, 1985. A slim volume (117 pages) in the Past Masters series. Deals with Cervantes as poet and dramatist, examines his parodies of chivalric romance, analyzes Don Quixote as a Romantic hero, investigates his madness, and gives a close reading of both parts of the novel.

Robert E. Morsberger

PAUL CÉZANNE

Born: January 19, 1839; Aix-en-Provence, France
Died: October 22, 1906; Aix-en-Provence, France
Area of Achievement: Art
Contribution: Cézanne's innovative and brilliant style challenged the conventions of nineteenth century art and had a major influence on twentieth century cubists and abstract artists.

Early Life

Paul Cézanne was born at Aix-en-Provence, a town in the south of France, not far from Marseilles and the Mediterranean. His father's family came from the Italian Alpine village Cesana (hence the surname) in the seventeenth century and had a history of minor business activities. Louis-Auguste, Paul's father, started out as a hat maker, at which he was a success, and eventually became a banker in Aix. He lived with Anne-Élisabeth-Honorine Aubert for several years before marrying her in 1844, and Paul was one of their children born before they were married. The family was financially secure, and Paul was educated locally. Interested in art, he took some instruction at the local École des Beaux Arts. One of his closest friends then, and in later life, was Émile Zola, who was to become one of France's greatest men of letters.

Cézanne's enthusiasm for art was tolerated by his father, but he was expected to make a career in the law. He was a good student and entered the University of Aix-en-Provence to study law, but after passing his first-year exams, he asked his father if he might join his friend Zola, who had gone to Paris to make his way as a journalist. Cézanne wanted to study at the prestigious Académie des Beaux-Arts in Paris. His father allowed him to quit school in late 1859, but he kept him in Aix until April, 1861, when he took him to Paris to study as an artist. Cézanne was refused entrance to the school and joined the Académie Suisse, a studio in which young artists banded together to work with live models. He was virtually untrained and his work showed little promise. Often difficult and inclined to be morose and withdrawn, he was often unhappy with himself and his work. His father supported him, but not generously. In September he gave up, returned to Aix, and joined the family bank.

Life's Work

Cézanne's self-portraits reveal a thick-set, hard-mouthed peasant glaring out of the canvas, and if there is one thing that marks him as a man and as an artist it is his weighty, determined stubbornness which the paintings suggest. Once back in Aix, he began to draw again and to take some classes locally. In 1862, his father gave in once again and allowed him to return to Paris, and he began to associate with a group of young artists whose work had been rejected by the conservative power structure of artists, critics, and teachers who controlled the Académie des Beaux-Arts and the annual Salon, an exhibition of supposedly the best art being produced in France. Camille Pissarro became his closest friend, but he also came to know Édouard Manet, Auguste Renoir, and Claude Monet, all, in one way or another, out of step with established standards of taste in the art world.

This group of painters would ultimately be called the "Impressionists," a name which was originally imposed on them with contempt because of their insistence on a new, looser, lighter style of painting in which they attempted to catch the transitory nature of visual experience. There was considerable difference in their individual contributions to the movement, and it can be argued that Manet, whose work was sometimes accepted by the Salon, was on the fringe of the group. The artist most clearly not quite an Impressionist was Cézanne. After attempting to get his work accepted by the Salon and being pointedly rejected, he joined the Impressionists in exhibitions outside official circles, and he continued to exhibit with them for several years, and, like them, he was to be ridiculed and neglected.

In the late 1860's, he established a relationship with the model Marie-Hortense Fiquet, who was often a subject of his paintings; they had a child, Paul, in 1872. Like his father, Cézanne did not wed his mistress for several years. He sold practically nothing, was still dependent upon his father, and often disappeared for months at a time. In 1877, he exhibited for the last time with the Impressionists and was so derided for his work that he simply gave up public exhibitions.

His early work was often awkward, his colors muddy, his themes uninviting. Rape, murder, or other emotionally excessive subjects seemed to mirror personal problems with which he was attempting to deal in his art. There is much piling on of paint with the palette knife, and a sense of great power not quite successfully expressed. In the 1870's, he was closest to being something of an Impressionist. He spent a considerable amount of time with Pissarro, who was something of a teacher-father to him, and began to paint less morbid subjects, his colors becoming brighter, and his draftsmanship more sophisticated. He was still tonally serious, and he never quite gave way to the looser, feathery style of the Impressionists. Where the Impressionists attempted to record the evanescence of experience, its constant change, he chose to seek its basic structures, painting the planes, the conjunctions, the solidity of objects. By 1880, he had finally developed a style all his own, entirely different from that of any other painter, incorporating the "open air" freshness of Impressionism to the austere monumentality of painters such as Nicolas Poussin and Gustave Courbet. In a sense, he invented himself.

Cézanne went his own way, almost forgotten, spending most of his time around Aix, painting landscapes, still lifes, and portraits very slowly, painstakingly, in planes of color placed sometimes at seemingly perverse angles, eschewing line for mass, teasing volume, depth, relationships out of small dabs of color, knowing that colors laid flatly side by side suggest depth or protrusion to the human eye. At close range it resembles a jigsaw puzzle.

Cézanne seemed to reject the idea that a painting was supposed to be an accurate rendering of reality. His paintings start with reality, but ultimately are independent of it: They are aesthetic experiences with their own internal logic. He often subverted the commonly held idea that paintings represent one point of view. He deliberately tipped one end of a table, while the other end was left perfectly flat. He represented his subjects from more than one point of view in ways which are often subtle shifts of perspective. What looks simply like bad draftsmanship was, in fact, deliberate distortion, which creates rhythms, associations, patterns transcending normal representational painting.

This experimental urge is absorbed in a tender solemnity of tone which suggests that the paintings, however simple in subject, have a haunting metaphysical weight, often reminiscent of the same deep stillness in the work of Jean-Baptiste-Siméon Chardin. The subject, ultimately, is less important than the experience of its aesthetic presence. He painted more than sixty studies of Mont Sainte-Victoire, a rather unimposing mountain which can be seen on the horizon just across the road from his last studio on the Chemin des Lauves on the outskirts of Aix. The paintings are all quite magnificent, all disturbingly alike factually and aesthetically different, often quite clearly presaging the cubist attempt to turn reality into design.

In the late 1890's, he began to receive some public recognition, and a group of young artists became aware of the fact that he was not only a formidable painter, but also that he had broken new ground in how one might think about art.

Cézanne worked doggedly, never entirely satisfied, avoided by most because of his notorious irascibility, completely committed to his work. He was beginning to get the attention he had deserved, but seemed not to need it. Watercolors became more important than ever to him, proving his long-held theory that there was no such thing as line and modeling; there were only contrasts. His oils are gloriously rich in his later years, and his work kept exploring the old themes, a few apples, a jug, the old hill, bits and pieces that can still be seen on the tables in the studio as he left it. He suffered from diabetes, but continued to work. He caught a cold while painting on October 15, 1906, but he was painting the next morning. He died a week later.

Summary

It is generally accepted that Paul Cézanne is one of the greatest artists in the history of painting. His own work as a colorist and as an exponent of an entirely original style in both the oil and the watercolor might be sufficient proof of this judgment, but he was much more than simply a superlative practitioner. For all of his rough provincialism, he was a theorist who not only put his theories into practice but also showed the way for the entirely new art of the twentieth century. It is difficult to think how that art might have gone had Cézanne not provided it with three singularly important clues.

His own work—beginning so unpromisingly, slowly accumulating form and individuality, absorbing the influences of the past and that of his contemporaries, especially the struggling Impressionists, blossoming into one of the most singularly distinctive styles in the history of painting—proved that there was always room for making art new if ambition, will, and talent could hold out against indifference, neglect, and derision.

His decision not to become a follower of Impressionism, to be a second-class artist, but to use it to go forward into his own realm of expression allowed him to discover one of the most important secrets behind one of the major movements of twentieth century painting: that just as light is always on the move across the landscape, so is the eye. Therefore, the point of view need not be fixed in a painting but can express that movement in the single canvas. This insight was the key needed to trigger the cubist movement in modern art.

Perhaps even more important, he proved that art need not necessarily be an accurate representation of what the eye sees. Styles had changed through the centuries, as had theories about how the artist was to represent reality. Cézanne argued for the proposition (and put it into action in his art) that the work of art might start in nature but need not simply reflect it. It could transcend reality; it could be abstract.

He had said it best: "The eye is not enough, reflection is needed." And he had illustrated it best in paintings which at one and the same time could convey the aesthetic illusion of depth and the sense of flat design consistent with the nature of the medium. His one-man show of 1895, organized by his old friend Pissarro, started him on his way to the reputation he deserved. In 1907, a memorial showing of fifty-six paintings was displayed in Paris at the Salon which so long before had turned him away. From that moment onward, he was to be seen as the most influential painter of the century.

Bibliography

Callen, Anthea. *Techniques of the Impressionists*. London: New Burlington Books, 1987. So much of understanding Cézanne is dependent upon a recognition of the central concern of the artist and his Impressionist friends for technique. This book analyzes individual paintings by artists prior to the Impressionist period and during the period of Impressionist activity. Two Cézanne paintings are carefully discussed.

Cézanne, Paul. *Paul Cézanne*. Edited by Ellen H. Johnson. New York: Funk & Wagnalls, 1978. Book 18 of the Great Artists series. Contains a short, informed article by Johnson, which is mindful of the general audience. Large reproductions of several paintings, accompanied by short, but sensible notes.

Harris, Nathaniel. *The Art of Cézanne*. New York: Excalibur Books, 1982. A short, inexpensive, but generously illustrated discussion of the artist's life and his painting.

Lewis, Wyndham. *Wyndham Lewis on Art: Collected Writings, 1914-1956*. New York: Funk & Wagnalls, 1969. Lewis was a great admirer of Cézanne, whom he speaks about with the cogency of a practitioner of the same trade.

Rewald, John. *Paul Cézanne: A Biography*. New York: Schocken Books, 1968. Based on the correspondence of the painter and his friends, this biography has a homey intimacy and easy charm.

_____. *Paul Cézanne: The Watercolours, a Catalogue Raisonné*. New York: Graphic Society Books, 1984. The watercolors have often been ignored, but they are not only first-class art in their own right but also provide another way of understanding the artist's obsession with technique and that peculiar way in which he achieves dimensional effects by juxtaposing slabs of pure color.

Charles Pullen

CHANG CHIH-TUNG

Born: September 2, 1837; Nan-p'i, Chihli, China
Died: October 4, 1909; Peking, Chihli, China
Areas of Achievement: Government and education
Contribution: Chang Chih-tung was a leading scholar-official in China during the last half-century of the Ch'ing Dynasty. His educational, military, and economic reforms contributed greatly to the survival of China's last imperial dynasty.

Early Life

Chang Chih-tung came from a gentry family of modest means. His father, Chang Ying, provided him with a rigorous classical education, and Chih-tung responded with diligence and precocity. At age thirteen, he passed the prefectural exam, becoming a *sheng-yüan*. At fifteen, Chih-tung, in competition with almost ten thousand scholars, led the list of about one hundred who received the *chü-jen* degree in Chihli Province.

He delayed taking the metropolitan exam, deterred in part by his father's death in 1855. In 1863, however, he passed the Peking exam, becoming a *chin-shih* degree-holder and member of China's upper gentry. His palace examination, though somewhat controversial, apparently pleased Tz'u-hsi, the empress dowager, who appointed him to the Hanlin Academy in Peking.

From 1867 to 1881, Chang Chih-tung alternated between provincial posts in education in Hupeh and Szechwan, and positions at the Hanlin Academy. At the capital, he associated with a group of conservative Confucian scholars who called themselves the Ch'ing-liu, or purists. The Ch'ing-liu demanded that China adopt a militant stand against foreign encroachment and characterized the policies of moderating as constituting cowardly appeasement. Chang was no better than any of the purists, however, in his constant efforts to please Tz'u-hsi. He condoned her decision, in 1875, to defy Confucian tradition by breaking the normal line of succession and securing the throne for her nephew, Emperor Kuang-hsü. When a censor, Wu K'o-tu, committed suicide in 1879 to protest Tz'u-hsi's policies, Chang wrote a lengthy memorial criticizing Wu and justifying the empress dowager's actions.

Chang's memorials were usually less sycophantic and usually concerned foreign policy. He and the purists called for military action against Russia over the I-li and against France over the status of Annam. In the first instance, their bellicose posturing appeared to be effective, and Russia agreed to replace the earlier Treaty of Livadia (October, 1789) with the less favorable Treaty of St. Petersburg (February, 1881). Unfortunately, the purists, encouraged by their apparent success in I-li, prodded the throne into applying the same kind of threatening approach to France, which precipitated the Sino-French War (1883-1885). The fighting resulted in France's destruction of the Chinese fleet and shipyards at Foochow, and China reluctantly agreed to the unfavorable terms of the Li-Fournier Agreement (May, 1884).

Most of the purists were discredited for having pushed China into a losing war, and Chang might have suffered a similar fate. Fortunately for him, he had already embarked upon a more substantive career than that of warmonger. The bitter experience of witnessing China's ignominy during the Sino-French fiasco had radically altered Chang's perspectives on the West and on change, and he had become an energetic reformer.

Life's Work

Earlier, while still basking in the success at I-li, Chang received several rapid promotions and became Governor of Shansi Province in 1881. As governor, Chang initiated numerous industrial and educational projects to help reduce the deplorable economic conditions in Shansi. In 1884, during the Sino-French hostilities, the throne appointed Chang Viceroy of Liangkwang (Kwangtung and Kwangsi). At the conclusion of the war, the throne not only criticized Chang for his earlier bellicosity but also praised him for having undertaken several positive measures, including the defense of Kwangtung. Chang began to adopt the ideas of Feng Kuei-fen, who in the early 1860's had popularized the concept of *tzu-ch'iang*, or self-strengthening.

To Chang, strengthening China required the adoption of Western technology. He was, however, deeply concerned with the relationship between modernization and Westernization—the dilemma facing all Chinese reformers. His interest was not to alter China in a radical way but rather to save it by entertaining certain modifications. Thus, he insisted upon preserving Confucianism as the central core of Chinese culture. To this end, Chang promoted the slogan *Chung-hsueh wei t'i, Hsi-hsueh wei yung*, or "Chinese studies as the foundation, Western studies for their practicality." This signified that modernization should not entail Westernization, because Chinese values were superior to those of the West.

Among Chang's many proposals was the construction of a railway line between Peking and Hankow. The throne appointed Chang Viceroy of Hunan-Hupeh in 1889, with instructions to oversee this project. Having earlier constructed a foundry in Kwangtung, Chang also undertook to establish the Han-Yeh-P'ing Iron and Steel works in Han-yang. Though small and wiry, Chang was apparently tireless in his efforts to seek funds for these and other projects. His zeal, however, did not mean that he understood either the mechanics or the financial underpinnings of successful industrialization. When it became evident that he could not obtain the necessary capital for either of these projects, he turned them over to private corporations.

During the Sino-Japanese War of 1894-1895, when the Viceroy of the Anhwei-Kiangsu-Kiangsi area, Liu K'un-i, was commanding troops, Chang took over at Nanking on an interim basis. In his efforts to prepare China for continued war, Chang undertook the creation of a self-strengthening army, with German advisers and foreign weapons. Chang turned over this modern force to Liu upon the latter's return to Nanking, but he re-created essentially the same type of units on his resumption of the viceroyalty post at Han-yang.

During 1895-1898, Chang associated with many young zealous reformers, who ultimately became involved in the famous Hundred Days Reform during the summer of 1898. Prior to this abortive movement, Chang published his famous *Ch'üan Hsüeh P'ien* (exhortation to study). The reformers, reading their own convictions into this work, construed it as a rallying platform. For his part, Chang, who had originally financed and sponsored many of the reformers, became alarmed by their misrepresentation of his ideas. He also disliked their leader, K'ang Yü-wei for his constant representation of Confucius as a radical reformer. As the reformers moved toward constitutional monarchy, Chang, who distrusted participatory democracy, began to distance himself from them. When Tz'u-hsi's coup ended the Hundred Days Reform, Chang was one of the first to call for the severe punishment of the reform leaders. He even refused to join Liu K'un-i in memorializing the throne against the threatened deposition of the young emperor. Chang emerged from this movement the object of suspicion and hatred, both by court conservatives and young reformers. Whatever remaining ties existed between Chang and the new reformers ended in 1900, when Chang arrested and executed twenty conspirators who had been plotting the overthrow of Tz'u-hsi.

During the Boxer Rebellion (1899-1900), Chang joined a few other provincial leaders in guaranteeing the safety and property of foreigners in southern China. While he complied with orders from the court to send troops to the north, he kept his strongest units at home and sent untrained recruits to the capital. At the conclusion of the Boxer Rebellion, he and other moderate provincial officials requested that foreign powers not hold Tz'u-hsi accountable for Boxer outrages. Chang thus consolidated his position at the court and also endeared himself to many foreigners in China. He eventually made use of his ties to British representatives, asking them repeatedly to intercede on his behalf at the imperial court.

With the deaths of Li Hung-chang and Liu K'un-i, in 1901 and 1902, respectively, Chang became China's senior statesman. Among many reform activities, he spearheaded a commission to study the future of the civil service examination system. Calling at first for their gradual abolition, Chang suddenly suggested an immediate end to the exams and the creation of a national Confucian school system. Tz'u-hsi complied with alacrity and on September 2, 1905, abolished the examination system, ending what was probably the most salient feature of China's Confucian imperial system.

In the summer of 1907, Chang came to the capital as a grand secretary, but the court also made him a grand councillor and directed him to head the Ministry of Education. By this time, however, he was beset both by infirmity and considerable doubts about the Ch'ing Dynasty's ability to survive. The death of Tz'u-hsi in November, 1908, did little to improve his outlook. Chang had come to accept the idea of a constitutional monarchy but was frustrated by what he construed as moral decay in China. On October 4, 1909, the same day he submitted a memorial eulogizing Tz'u-hsi, he died, surrounded by friends and family.

Summary

An educational innovator who founded dozens of academies and modern schools and an initiator of numerous industrial and communications ventures, Chang Chih-tung unquestionably helped to arrest the continued decline of the Ch'ing Dynasty. Yet he embodied both the best and worst features of China's traditional elite class. Honest to a fault, Chang died a relatively poor man. Yet his loyalty to a dynasty led him to tolerate the venality and corruption of Tz'u-hsi, the empress dowager. He understood that China was weak and needed reform, but he also remained firmly convinced that China's traditional value system should remain virtually intact. In essence, he failed to grasp the relationship between technological modernity and the sociocultural foundations that were necessary for such modernization. His formulas for self-strengthening proved to be bankrupt rationalizations that failed to acknowledge inherent weaknesses in China's cultural tradition itself. His occasional opportunism was a reflection of the corrupt state of the Ch'ing Dynasty, and, in the end, most of his projects served only to retard the process of dynastic deterioration. Chang could neither save the dynasty nor conserve the Confucian tradition that he cherished. He died a famous and respected man but ultimately was a failed leader of a country that had become weaker during his own lifetime. Although he did not bear the principal responsibility for this decline, the empress dowager, the Ch'ing Dynasty, and, in large measure, the unaltered Confucian tradition that he supported, all contributed to China's decay.

Bibliography
Ayers, William. *Chang Chih-tung and Educational Reform in China*. Cambridge, Mass.: Harvard University Press, 1971. Although concentrating on Chang's role as an educational reformer, this well-documented work can serve as a biography of his life as well.
Bays, Daniel H. *China Enters the Twentieth Century: Chang Chih-tung and the Issues of a New Age, 1895-1909*. Ann Arbor: University of Michigan Press, 1978. A thorough and analytical account of Chang's career during the last fifteen years of his life.
Cohen, Paul A., and John E. Schrecker, eds. *Reform in Nineteenth Century China*. Cambridge, Mass.: Harvard University Press, 1976. Numerous articles discuss Chang's association with the Ch'ing-Liu reformers and his

other activities. Most of the articles provide an excellent background for a study of Chang.

Eastman, Lloyd E. *Throne and Mandarins: China's Search for a Policy During the Sino-French Controversy, 1880-1885.* Cambridge, Mass.: Harvard University Press, 1967. An excellent review of this period, with much discussion of Chang and the purists.

Hummel, Arthur W., ed. *Eminent Chinese of the Ch'ing Period (1644-1912).* 2 vols. Washington, D.C.: Government Printing Office, 1943-1944. Volume 1 contains a fairly detailed biography of Chang which is still accurate and useful.

Levenson, Joseph R. *Confucian China and Its Modern Fate.* 3 vols. Berkeley: University of California Press, 1958-1965. In volume 1, the author discusses the conflict between continuity and change during the Ch'ing Dynasty. Referring frequently to Chang, the author gives a superb analysis of the dilemma facing Confucian reformers.

Powell, Ralph L. *The Rise of Chinese Military Power, 1895-1912.* Princeton, N.J.: Princeton University Press, 1955. Offers substantial coverage of Chang's military reforms and his efforts involving the self-strengthening army.

Wright, Mary C. *The Last Stand of Chinese Conservatism: The T'ung-Chih Restoration, 1862-1874.* Stanford, Calif.: Stanford University Press, 1957. Although concentrating on the period prior to Chang's prominence, this classic is essential to understanding the struggle between conservatism and modernization in the late Ch'ing Dynasty. The author frequently refers to Chang's ideas and actions.

Hilel B. Salomon

JEAN SIMÉON CHARDIN

Born: November 2, 1699; Paris, France
Died: December 6, 1779; Paris, France
Area of Achievement: Art
Contribution: Perhaps the greatest French painter of the eighteenth century, Chardin drew his inspiration from the Dutch masters and the simple world of the Paris bourgeoisie that he knew so well. Yet he was not merely a genre painter, because many of the techniques that he employed both in his oils and in his pastels would be adopted and developed by generations of painters yet unborn.

Early Life

Jean Siméon Chardin was born on November 2, 1699, in Paris, the eldest surviving son of Jean and Jeanne Françoise David Chardin. He was baptized at the church of Saint Sulpice the following day, and he lived his entire life in the neighborhood of Saint-Germain-des-Prés. His father was a master cabinetmaker whose specialty was billiard tables, and one of his patrons was the King of France. Anxious to provide each of his children with a proper livelihood, the elder Chardin tried to persuade his namesake to train to take his place, but Jean would have none of it. His first love was art.

With reluctance Jean's father agreed to his son's choice of a career, but he did not understand the importance of the course of study pursued by aspiring artists. Without being consulted, young Jean was sent in 1718 to study with Pierre-Jacques Cazes, who was a professor at the Royal Academy but in all respects an inferior teacher. Cazes was so poor that he could not afford to hire models; instead, his students were forced to copy his sketches. Luckily, two years later Chardin was able to leave the studio of Cazes to become the assistant of Noël-Nicolas Coypel, from whom he learned to paint directly from nature. There was always a refreshing spontaneity in Chardin's art, a quality not often found in the work of many of his contemporaries, who usually painted from sketches.

In 1723, Chardin fell in love with Marguerite Saintard, a young woman whose family included prosperous lawyers and minor government officials; against all odds, she accepted his proposal of marriage. The contract was drawn up that same year, and the elder Chardin, conscious that his family would soon improve its social status, once again took charge of his son's life. Without his knowledge or permission, the aspiring young painter's name was submitted for membership in the Academy of St. Luke in 1724. More a guild than an assembly of artists, this once-proud organization was the refuge of men whose talents placed them in the second rank. While his father's action was the result of ignorance of the hierarchy of the arts, Chardin was faced with the difficult task of bringing his talents to the attention of those who could advance his career.

Each summer, during the morning hours of Corpus Christi Day, young artists who were not members of the Royal Academy were allowed to exhibit their works in the Place Dauphine. On June 20, 1728, Chardin showed a number of his paintings, all of them in the lowest category sanctioned by the academy. Since he had little formal education or training, he might not aspire to paint historical or religious subjects, but he could perfect his mastery of the still life. His bid for recognition was successful; on September 25, 1728, he was admitted to membership in the Royal Academy as a painter skilled in animals and fruits. The following year, he resigned from the Academy of St. Luke.

Life's Work

Despite his admission to the lowest level of membership, Chardin was a loyal member of the Royal Academy until his death. Although he failed in his attempt to gain an assistant professorship, he considered the academy to be extremely valuable as a teaching institution for the training of young artists. He regularly attended its meetings and exhibited at its salons. By the time of his marriage in February, 1731, to Marguerite Saintard, Chardin was already popular with critics and the public alike for his still lifes, which sold for modest prices but were always in demand. Some even called him the French Rembrandt. Yet it was his technique that set him apart from his contemporaries and earned for him his special niche in the history of art.

From the study of the works of the Dutch and Flemish masters, which were available in numerous engravings, Chardin developed the same fascination for the effects of light on objects in nature that made the work of the Dutch painter Jan Vermeer so exciting. Some even mistook Chardin's works for those of a Flemish painter. As he began to paint genre canvases, he often borrowed themes and compositions familiar in the works of the northern painters, but he achieved a freshness and originality which gave his work a special character. Always true to nature, Chardin nevertheless painted objects and figures according to his special vision. He rearranged his subjects to suit his exploration of the mysteries of light. Chardin placed his paints on canvas in a manner unlike any other artist of his day. Often he applied them rather thickly and blended his colors into one another with a subtlety that made it difficult to discern the subject of a painting when viewed at close range. When regarded at a distance, however, the various elements of his composition were easily recognizable.

Chardin's father died in the summer of 1731, and on November 18 of that year his son, Pierre-Jean, was born. Two years later, on August 3, a daughter, Marguerite-Agnes, was baptized. As his family grew, so did Chardin's reputation. The French ambassador to Spain commissioned two paintings, and in June, 1734, sixteen of his works were exhibited at the Exposition of

Young Artists. His personal life, like one of his canvases, was a mixture of light and shadow. In April, 1735, at the age of thirty-eight, Marguerite Saintard Chardin died after a long illness. It is interesting to note that no painting bears the date 1735, a year of grief for Chardin, who always sought to reassure his public of the basic goodness of human existence through his art. By 1737, when he exhibited eight paintings at the Salon of the Royal Academy, he had lost his daughter also. Some of his personal loss must have been assuaged by his professional success; his works were now appearing in engravings, and the circle of his admirers was growing ever wider.

He had no rival in the area of still life, but in the realm of genre painting there were several artists whose works were widely respected. To compete with them for the public's attention, Chardin had to develop a new approach to this category of art. Working with a rather narrow palette of soft and muted tones, he created works in which the composition was the central theme and the actual subject matter often of a secondary importance. These were works which appealed to artists, to connoisseurs such as the King of Prussia, the Queen of Sweden, and Louis XV of France, who obtained two Chardin canvases in 1740 for his collection. Because he devoted so much effort to perfecting a composition, Chardin often copied his earlier paintings at the request of patrons. That was a lucrative and steady source of income for a man who only worked on one painting at a time. Since he was dealing with a familiar composition, he could work faster than normal.

Within the structure of the Royal Academy, Chardin's activities increased as his reputation grew. He was appointed in 1739 to a committee responsible for keeping accounts and assessing taxes. His expertise in finance eventually led to his appointment as the first treasurer of the Royal Academy in 1755. He was promoted in 1743 to the post of adviser to the Royal Academy of Painting and Sculpture. Five years later, Chardin served on a committee to examine the pictures at the Academy Salon. His diligent service, broken only by a six-month illness in 1742, earned for him the recommendation of an annual grant, in 1752, and living quarters in the Louvre, in 1757. Just as his professional life reached this zenith, his private life was filled with trouble and tragedy.

A modest inheritance passed to Chardin at his mother's death in 1743, which enabled him to marry, on November 26, 1744, Françoise Marguerite Pouget, a wealthy widow. The following October, their daughter, Angélique-Françoise, was born, and the Chardins settled down to a comfortable life. Chardin also took pride in the progress of his son Pierre-Jean, who showed a remarkable talent for painting. Pierre-Jean received all the advantages and opportunities which had been denied his father. In April, 1754, while studying to be a painter of historical subjects, the highest level of achievement in the Royal Academy, he was allowed to compete for the academy's Grand Prize, which he won in August. Three more years of work with the best teachers earned for Pierre-Jean Chardin the chance to study at the French Academy in Rome. He left Paris in December, 1757, and died in Venice ten years later under mysterious circumstances. During that stormy decade, he wasted his opportunities, caused a scandal among the members of the French community in Rome with his outrageous behavior, was captured briefly by pirates in 1762, and publicly accused his father of cheating him out of his inheritance.

From scenes of domestic life, Chardin turned to portraits, but they were not well received by the critics; at the end of his career, he therefore returned to the still life. In 1755, he had taken charge of hanging the pictures at the annual Academy Salon for a friend who was ill; the task was awarded to Chardin permanently in 1761. It was a duty he enjoyed, and one that gave him great power over his fellow artists. A painter's reputation could be enhanced or damaged by the placement of his works at the salon. Chardin became well known for his fairness and tact. As the years passed, Chardin continued to paint and to attend faithfully to his duties at the academy, but increasingly the critics relegated him to the past, a pleasant old anachronism. They were wrong. At the very end of his life, Chardin discovered another area of artistic endeavor, the pastel. When his first pastel portraits appeared in the Salon of 1771, they caused a sensation. Suffering from gallstones and plagued with failing eyesight, he continued to work until his death from edema on December 6, 1779.

Summary

The art of Jean Siméon Chardin moved through four phases: from his mastery of the still life as a young man, to the charming pictures of domestic harmony and the artistically correct portraits of his mature years, and finally to the sensitive pastels at the end of his life. Yet the subjects which consumed six decades of creativity are unimportant when compared to the techniques which Chardin developed. Often he regretted the fact that he had not received the training provided by the Royal Academy; yet that omission allowed him to explore the full measure of his media and to maintain his creativity in the face of the potentially stifling rules and regulations of the academy.

Chardin was inspired by the art of the Netherlands, by the subject matter, by the palette, and by the techniques of the Dutch and Flemish masters. He was particularly fascinated by the effects of light on nature. The object, whether animate or inanimate, was of little importance to Chardin; it was the light and the shadow that motivated him. In nearly every canvas he painted, Chardin dealt with his fascination with light and the problems it might cause the artist. He painted objects as they appeared to him, not as they necessarily were. Chardin sought to portray the essence of his subjects, not their reality. In this respect, he was the precursor of Impressionism. Many of his contemporaries did not understand or appreciate his art; it remained for their children's children to rediscover Chardin's fresh and original approach to the painter's craft.

Genre painting, the celebration of the simple life, had long enjoyed a popularity among all classes, but especially the bourgeoisie. Too often, however, scenes of domestic life possessed a cloying charm. Chardin gave genre painting dignity. He seemed to prefer the most commonplace subjects, but he gave them a timelessness by carefully divorcing them from contemporary events or definite fashions. The men, women, and children who people his canvases are more symbols than personalities. They are suspended in time and space, captives of the same light that held Chardin spellbound. He was not a revolutionary; his celebration of bourgeois life was not political in its intent. He simply painted what was readily at hand. His muted colors and delicate contrasts were the palette of one who adored the subtle loveliness that lay all around him, but particularly in simple things. For more than fifty years, Chardin was a member of the Royal Academy, for nineteen its treasurer; in the last analysis, however, he was the servant of beauty.

Bibliography

Conisbee, Philip. *Chardin*. Lewisburg, Pa.: Bucknell University Press, 1986. Perhaps the most complete treatment of Chardin and his contribution to the art of painting in eighteenth century France. The quality of the plates is quite good, and in a number of cases the reader is able to examine specific details of some of Chardin's more important works.

De la Mare, Walter. *Chardin (1699-1779)*. New York: Pitman, 1950. While only ten of Chardin's most famous domestic scenes are featured in this slender volume, it is nevertheless of interest because of the excellent essay and notes by de la Mare. The whole work is not merely informative; it is beautifully written as well. One of the best introductions to Chardin and his work.

Furst, Herbert E. A. *Chardin*. London: Methuen, 1911. While the style of this work is old-fashioned and the prose at times a bit fulsome, this volume is an excellent treatment of the life and work of Chardin. The author obviously has a great admiration for Chardin, not only as an artist but also as a man; it is this quality of sensitivity that makes this book worthwhile.

Kalnein, Wend Graf, and Michael Levey. *Art and Architecture of the Eighteenth Century in France*. Harmondsworth, England: Penguin Books, 1972. Very useful as an introduction to the main events in the painter's life as well as to the elements of his style. More important, Chardin is placed in the context of his time, and his contemporaries in all the arts are given the same thorough and scholarly treatment.

Roberts, Warren. *Morality and Social Class in Eighteenth-Century French Literature and Painting*. Toronto: University of Toronto Press, 1974.

Chardin and his works are examined in the light of the society that produced them. Roberts views Chardin's representations of bourgeois domestic life as the antithesis of the bedroom art that was so popular among some members of the French aristocracy. Chardin is viewed not as a political revolutionary but as the perfect representative of his class.

Rosenberg, Pierre. *Chardin, 1699-1779*. Translated by Emilie P. Kadish and Ursula Korneitchouk. Cleveland: Cleveland Museum of Art, 1979. Although this work is essentially a catalog of a remarkable exhibit of Chardin's works, it contains a tremendous amount of biographical and historical data useful to the student of the period. Each of the artist's works is described. Contains notes and a bibliography for each work. The final bibliography is also extremely valuable.

Schwarz, Michael. *The Age of the Rococo*. Translated by Gerald Onn. New York: Praeger, 1971. This remarkably well-translated version of an earier German work is extremely valuable, because it examines the various types of painting which flourished in the eighteenth century, not only in France but also throughout Western Europe. The treatment of Chardin and his work is balanced.

Wildenstein, Georges. *Chardin*. Translated by Stuart Gilbert. Rev. ed. Greenwich, Conn.: New York Graphic Society, 1969. The essay that begins this revised edition of Wildenstein's 1933 work is an excellent introduction to the life and work of Chardin. Also useful is the chronology that precedes the superb collection of plates, both in color and in black and white, and the catalog of Chardin's work, which is divided according to subject.

Clifton W. Potter, Jr.

CHARLES III

Born: January 20, 1716; Madrid, Spain
Died: December 14, 1788; Madrid, Spain
Areas of Achievement: Government and politics
Contribution: Charles III's Bourbon Reforms rejuvenated the economic and political administration of Spain and its colonies. While upholding the doctrine of political absolutism, these reforms promoted Enlightenment ideals of humanitarianism, rationalism, and secularism in Spanish government and culture. As a consequence, Charles became the most successful of Europe's "enlightened despots."

Early Life
Charles was born in Madrid, Spain, on January 20, 1716, the first son of Phillip V of Spain and Elizabeth Farnese of Parma. He was born into Spain's Bourbon dynasty, which was founded in 1700 by his father, who was the grandson of Louis XIV, the great French Bourbon king. Phillip's accession to the throne was secured and legitimated by the War of the Spanish Succession (1700-1713). Charles's mother was very ambitious for her son, but her hopes for his accession to the Spanish throne seemed blocked by the aspirations of her older stepchildren, Louis and Ferdinand VI. As it happened, however, Louis died at a relatively young age, and Phillip and Ferdinand were both afflicted by melancholia, which eventually led to Charles's emergence as King of Spain.

Charles's preparation for the Spanish monarchy began early. In October, 1731, he became Duke of Parma and Piacenza, and in 1734 he became Charles IV, King of the Two Sicilies. In 1736, he married Maria Amalia of Saxony, niece of the Holy Roman Emperor. As monarch of the kingdom of the Two Sicilies, Charles imposed political absolutism on a very violent and contentious society, and he relied heavily on astute advisers to train him in the art of statecraft. His reign was characterized by a remarkable public building program, Enlightenment values, and subordination of the church to the state.

Life's Work
In August, 1759, Ferdinand VI of Spain died, and Charles resigned as King of the Two Sicilies in favor of his third son, Ferdinand, and left for Spain to become Charles III. He was well received by the Spanish people, but this festive mood was dimmed by the death of Maria Amalia. Charles never remarried. At this moment in life, he appeared homely and small in stature, colorless in personality, yet a man of considerable intelligence and devotion to duty and family. He reflected a curious blend of devout Roman Catholic faith and Enlightenment rationalism. He read extensively in history

and economics, and he exhibited a deep passion for hunting and other sports.

Charles was appalled by Spain's political, economic, and cultural back-wardness, and he resolved to restore his country to its former glory. He quickly initiated a road-construction program to promote better communication within the country and a stronger national economy. He also built irrigation canals in order to put more land under cultivation and he erected numerous public buildings in Spain's urban centers.

Even so, Charles's popularity never extended to his government, which was dominated by Italian ministers. This was an unfortunate mistake on Charles's part, because he himself had not been in Spain since 1731 and was largely uninformed about the country and its people. His inattention to this matter resulted in a number of unwise decrees that led to the Madrid Riot of March 23, 1766. This upheaval compelled the king to replace his foreign advisers with talented and reform-minded Spaniards such as Conde de Aranda, Conde de Floridablanca, Conde de Campomanes, and Gaspar Melchor de Jovellanos. As a group, they reinforced Charles's notions of political absolutism, colonial and economic reform, and subordination of church and nobility to the state.

Charles's early efforts to restore Spanish pride and power were not completely successful. In 1761, he joined the Family Compact with France in order to prevent England's victory over France and its hegemony in the New World and Europe. In 1762, Charles formally entered the Seven Years' War (1754-1763) and experienced disastrous reverses in the Caribbean and the Philippines. During the Paris peace negotiations of 1762-1763, France ceded the western half of Louisiana to Spain, but Charles had to relinquish the Floridas to England in order to regain Havana. He also managed to regain Manila.

In spite of this debacle, Charles reaffirmed his commitment to the Family Compact over the next two decades. By 1770, he was forced to concede British dominion over the Falkland Islands. During the American Revolution, he joined France in supporting the rebels in order to weaken and embarrass England. In 1779, Charles offered to mediate the dispute, but England's refusal led him to declare war and intervene militarily on the rebel side. The French-Spanish intervention proved decisive. Although a massive Spanish assault on Gibraltar was repulsed, Spain won a series of victories in North America and kept constant pressure on British military forces. In 1782, Spain captured Minorca. In 1783, Charles allowed the Family Compact to lapse, and in the Peace of Paris, in 1783, he received the Floridas and Minorca and secured a British pledge to leave Honduras.

One primary goal behind Charles's diplomatic and military policies was to protect New Spain's (Mexico's) silver district in the north-central plateau. In order to secure the objective, Charles's advisers proposed that a series of buffer zones be established between the silver district and Spain's enemies, namely the Americans, British, and Russians. Consequently, Texas, New Mexico, and Louisiana would contain the British and Americans east of the Mississippi River and behind the Great Lakes, and, in 1769, California was occupied to serve as a buffer against the Russians heading southward from Alaska.

Charles also instituted a series of political, economic, and military reforms that are collectively known as the Bourbon Reforms. In 1767, Spain retrenched to fortifications of the northern frontier of New Spain to more defensible locations. This realignment of presidios would save the king some eighty thousand pesos annually.

Charles revived the captain-generalcy as an administrative unit and applied it to Cuba (including the Floridas and Louisiana), Guatemala, Chile, and Venezuela; he also established the Viceroyalty of La Plata (Buenos Aires) in 1776. Most important of these administrative reforms was the introduction of the intendant system, which streamlined imperial administration, made it more efficient, and eliminated graft and corruption. The intendants assumed responsibility for finances, justice, war, and administration and proved to be very successful in meeting their objectives.

In economic reforms, Charles sought to open trade within the empire while denying it as much as possible to foreigners. He broke the Cadiz monopoly on colonial trade and allowed other Spanish ports to participate in it. Restrictions on internal trade were relaxed, as were trading relations between the colonies and the mother country. Charles abandoned the obsolete flota system of colonial trade in favor of individual registered ships sailing from colonial ports to Spain. By freeing the internal economic system of the empire, Charles succeeded in increasing intercolonial trade and promoted a rising middle class in the colonies and Spain. In general, however, these reforms did not take hold in Spain because of internal opposition, war, lack of an industrial base, and competition from other European economic powers.

The Bourbon Reforms were directed at internal Spanish problems, many of which related to the Church. Just as in the Two Sicilies, Charles had become concerned by the concentration of economic and political power in the Church, and he and his officials resolved to make it subordinate to the will of the monarchy. Charles systematically struck at the Church. For example, he decreed that no papal bull would be published without the prior consent of the government. He curbed the activities of the Holy Council of the Inquisition, and he expelled the Society of Jesus (Jesuits) from Spain and her colonies in March/April, 1767. Charles's motivations in the latter action have never been clearly presented. He apparently resented the society's popularity among the Spanish people, and he resented its refusal to subordinate itself to the king. Moreover, he suspected that the Jesuits had been behind the Madrid riots of 1766.

Summary

On December 14, 1788, following two days of high fever, Charles III died in Madrid. In the mourning that followed, it could be said that Spain was in a far better position after his reign than it had been before. Spain seemed well on its way toward political and economic recovery. The monarchy was stronger than ever before, and the privileges and power of the clergy had been contained. Prosperity was general throughout the land, and education flourished. Madrid had become a cleaner and more livable city, and the nation's road system had tied the country closer together than ever before. Moreover, Spain's cultural life had been deeply influenced by the Enlightenment. Yet this reform program did not long survive Charles because his successors were not equal to the standards he had set for the monarchy and nation. Consequently, Spain continued its slide into the nineteenth century.

Bibliography

Durant, Will, and Ariel Durant. *Rousseau and Revolution.* New York: Simon & Schuster, 1967. Although occupying a small portion of the volume, there is a fine and illuminating account of Charles's life and career. It reveals his character, personality, and cultural contributions to the Spanish Enlightenment.

Gibson, Charles. *Spain in America.* New York: Harper & Row, 1966. Part of the New American Nation series. A fine overview of Spanish imperial policy with a good but brief section on Charles and the Bourbon Reforms. Oriented toward the nonspecialist.

Herr, Richard. *The Eighteenth Century Revolution in Spain.* Princeton, N.J.: Princeton University Press, 1958. An excellent look at Spain's intellectual revolution that occurred under the Bourbons, especially Charles's reign. Determines that the origins of Spanish liberalism date from the Bourbon rule and emphasizes the role of France in Spain's intellectual upheaval.

Maria Aguilar, Julian. *La España possible en tiempos de Carlos III.* Madrid: Sociedad de Estudios y Publicaciones, 1963. Written for the specialist and in Spanish. An intellectual history of eighteenth century Spain.

Petrie, Sir Charles. *King Charles III of Spain: An Enlightened Despot.* New York: John Day, 1971. The most recent and best biography of Charles; a very positive view of his life and career with extensive information on his early years.

Stephen P. Sayles

CHARLES V

Born: February 24, 1500; Ghent, Burgundy
Died: September 21, 1558; Yuste, Spain
Areas of Achievement: Politics and religion
Contribution: Charles V initiated 150 years of Habsburg dynastic hegemony in Europe, stopped the Turkish advance in Europe, promoted reform, and expanded Spanish colonization in America.

Early Life

Charles V was born in Ghent, the ancient capital of Flanders and the heart of the Duchy of Burgundy. In 1477, Burgundy escheated to the Holy Roman Emperor, Maximilian I of the house of Habsburg. Maximilian's rivalry with the French over the Burgundian lands led to an alliance with Spain that resulted in the marriage of his son, Philip, to Joan, daughter of Ferdinand II and Isabella. Charles, as the eldest son of the couple, became Duke of Burgundy in 1506, King of Spain in 1516, and Holy Roman Emperor in 1519.

When Charles entered Spain in 1517, he could not speak the native language and was surrounded by a Flemish court that sought to monopolize high offices in the Spanish church and state. Physically, Charles appeared rather awkward, a lanky teenager with the jutting Habsburg jaw. After two years of ineffective kingship in Spain, Charles was elected Holy Roman Emperor to the dismay of many Spaniards, who believed that Charles would relegate their country to a peripheral province to be drained of wealth for imperial ambitions. Thus, almost immediately after Charles left Spain for his coronation, the Castilian cities initiated the Comunero Revolt (1520-1521) to force Charles's return and a reform of political administration.

The imperial election brought Charles problems outside Spain as well. Since the Investiture Conflict of the twelfth century, the powerful German princes, especially the seven imperial electors, had limited the emperor's power through the Germanic Diet, the major representative and administrative institution of the Holy Roman Empire. In addition, Germany's political weakness meant that its church was more directly under the control of the Papacy and, therefore, paid a disproportionate amount to the papal treasury. The desire of some of the princes to end papal taxation, obtain vast church lands, and maintain a decentralized political administration quickly merged with Martin Luther's call for a doctrinal reform of the Church following his attack on the sale of indulgences in Germany in 1517.

Charles held a diet of the Holy Roman Empire at Worms in 1521 to determine the fate of Martin Luther and his princely supporters. After listening to Luther speak, the emperor had the diet condemn the reformer with an imperial ban, though by that point most Protestant princes had left the meeting and, therefore, considered the ban unbinding upon them. Charles could not take action against the Protestants because of the Comunero Revolt and a simultaneous French attack in Italy that aimed to regain Naples from Spain.

Life's Work

In 1522, Charles returned to Spain and began his life's work, the forging of Habsburg hegemony in Europe based upon Spanish wealth and power. At Worms, he had received reports from Hernán Cortés about his conquest of Mexico. From that point, Charles's new empire in the Americas contributed its silver to the protection of his European inheritance. Cortés would be followed by Francisco Pizarro, conqueror of the Incas, and a host of lesser-known conquistadores. Charles reformed his court and from then on Spaniards predominated in high offices throughout his empire. His residence in Spain led Charles to appoint his brother Ferdinand as regent in Germany. Charles's decision to make Spain the center of his empire contributed to a resounding victory in Italy over the French king, Francis I, at the Battle of Pavia in 1525.

Charles could not enjoy his victory long, as a new and more dangerous enemy appeared to threaten his empire, Süleyman the Magnificent, Sultan of the Ottoman Empire. The Ottoman Turks mounted the greatest Muslim attack on Christendom since the eighth century. In 1529, Süleyman led a huge army into Austria (personal lands of the Habsburgs) and laid siege to Vienna; only inclement weather prevented the fall of the great city. Sensing an advantage, Francis renewed his attacks, forcing Charles to fight in Italy and Burgundy as well as southern Germany. The French and Turkish cooperation led to their formal alliance in 1535.

The Franco-Turkish War forced Charles to adopt a more conciliatory policy in regard to the religious conflict in Germany. (He was influenced as well by his own reform inclinations, which were similar to those of Desiderius Erasmus, the famous Humanist and counselor to the emperor.) Charles sanctioned a series of diets in Germany to reach a settlement on the religious conflict in order to meet the Turkish threat. The Diets of Speyer (1526) and Augsburg (1530) failed to achieve agreement, but they recognized the legal existence of the Lutheran religion pending the convocation of a general church council that Charles pledged to convene. In return, the German princes, Protestant and Catholic, rallied to Charles's war against the French and the Turks. As a result, the Turkish advance into Central Europe was finally halted during a decisive campaign in 1532.

Pope Clement VII sided with France during the war in order to avoid the emperor's pressure for a general council that might reduce the pope's authority. This proved disastrous as a combined German-Spanish army marched on Rome and sacked it in 1527. Clement agreed to call a general council, though it failed to materialize because of the renewal of war between Charles and Francis over Milan in 1535.

As the Franco-Turkish Alliance became operative during the war, Charles decided to deliver another blow against the Turks. In 1535, he organized a massive armada and captured Tunis, the base of Turkish power in the western Mediterranean. Following his victory, Charles triumphantly marched through Italy and appeared at the papal court, where he spoke in Spanish condemning the French for their alliance with the Turks and preventing the convocation of a general council. Charles finally secured a favorable peace with the Franco-Turkish Alliance in 1544 and gained the support of Francis for a general council. Charles then turned his attention toward resolving the religious conflict in Germany.

Pope Paul III recognized the urgent need to reform the Church but wanted to avoid any diminution of papal authority and any doctrinal compromise with Protestantism that might result from a general council. He sanctioned the Jesuit Order (founded by Saint Ignatius of Loyola), whose schools cleansed humanistic studies of paganism and used them to reinforce Catholic doctrine and improve the quality of the clergy. Having earned the reputation of a reformer, Paul agreed to call a general council in the city of Trent on terms that ensured papal domination of the council.

Charles tried to create a sympathetic atmosphere for a religious compromise at the pending council by convening the German Diet in Regensburg in 1541. Papal and Lutheran representatives agreed on several points, including a compromise position on faith and justification (double justification) but failed to settle issues surrounding the role of the Sacraments. In the end, even the agreement on double justification met with condemnation by the pope and Luther.

Charles abandoned his policy of peaceful negotiation in 1545 for three reasons: The Lutherans refused to participate in the Council of Trent because they correctly believed that it would be dominated by the pope; the French and Turks were no longer threatening; and Charles feared that the spread of Lutheranism among imperial electors would lead to the election of a Protestant emperor. Charles believed that with a victory over the League of Schmalkald, the alliance of Protestant princes, he could force the Lutheran princes to cooperate with the Council of Trent and reunite the Church.

The Schmalkaldic War, 1546-1547, ended with a dramatic victory for Charles at the Battle of Mühlberg. Yet the fruits of victory were spoiled at the Council of Trent, where the pope, fearing an overpowerful emperor, rejected Charles's demands to move slowly, saving doctrinal issues for later discussion with Lutheran representatives. Instead, Paul enumerated and condemned Protestant doctrines and clarified traditional Catholic orthodoxy. The initial decrees of Trent meant that Charles would have to pacify the religious conflict in Germany himself.

The result was the Augsburg Interim of 1548, which provided for clerical marriage, communion in two kinds, and the half-Protestant doctrine of double justification. Otherwise, the interim reimposed the rites of the old religion. The interim applied only to German Protestants and was almost universally hated: The pope believed that it was a usurpation of his authority; the Lutherans viewed it as the reimposition of a foreign (Roman) church; and it failed to bring about the religious reunification of Germany sought by moderates. The breach was irreconcilable.

Even princes who were neutral during the Schmalkaldic War grew impatient with Charles's German policies. Political concerns loomed as large as religious ones. Charles had humiliated great princes with arrest and imprisonment. Following the war, his attempts to create an Imperial League and to make the imperial office hereditary threatened the princes' traditional predominance in the Holy Roman Empire. In order to regain their religious and political liberties, Protestant princes struck an alliance with the young French king Henry II in 1552. In return for helping to secure Protestant liberty, France gained the strategic fortress cities of Metz, Toul, and Verdun in the Rhineland; thus, the gates into Germany were opened to French influence. In order to defend his lands from French attack, Charles quickly made peace with the Protestant princes. The final religious settlement for Germany was the Peace of Augsburg of 1555, which stated that each prince in the Holy Roman Empire would determine whether his state would be Catholic or Lutheran. The settlement also ended Charles's attempts to create strong monarchical power in the Holy Roman Empire.

Charles did not sign the Peace of Augsburg, as he began divesting his authority in Germany to Ferdinand. He divided his lands between Ferdinand and his son Philip: Ferdinand was given Germany and the imperial title, while Philip received Spain, Naples, the American Colonies, Burgundy, and Milan. Following the territorial division, Charles abdicated the Spanish throne in 1556 and retired into a Spanish monastery, San Jeronimo de Yuste, where he studied religious works and contemplated his failure to maintain the religious unity of Christendom. He died two years later.

Summary

At Yuste, Charles V considered his reign a failure. Yet his moderate policy toward the Protestants prior to 1545 was essential for the defeat of the Turks and the reform of the Catholic church. He led Spain into its Golden Age (1500-1650), when it became, for the first time in its history, the dominating political and cultural power in Europe. Philip II became the sword of the Counter-Reformation, while Spanish spirituality, exemplified by the Jesuits, was its soul. The Council of Trent represented a crucial turning point for Catholicism, as internal reform was essential for the reversal of Protestant gains in France, Poland, Hungary, and southern Germany.

If Charles was depressed for having lost part of Europe to Protestantism, he could take comfort in his opening of two new continents to Western influence. The colonial enterprise represented more a drain than a boon to Spain's resources prior to the 1530's. Given Charles's European commitments, he might have stalled the conquests rather than encouraged them. Mexico, Central America, and most of South America were all conquered during Charles's reign. He began the institutionalization of the colonial empire by creating the Council of the Indies and formulating the New Laws of 1541, which aimed to make the assimilation of Native Americans more humane.

Charles was both the end of one chapter in European history and the beginning of another. He was the last Holy Roman Emperor to dominate Europe and the last monarch to adhere to medieval ideals of chivalry. On the other hand, the division of his empire and development of Spain encouraged the emergence of the European state system and began the process of global Westernization that has continued into the twentieth century.

Bibliography
Brandi, Karl. *The Emperor Charles V: The Growth and Destiny of a Man and a World Empire.* Translated by C. V. Wedgwood. London: Jonathan Cape, 1939. This is a standard biography though somewhat slanted toward Charles's German concerns. Contains a detailed account of Charles as a classic Renaissance monarch who ruled each realm through traditional institutions but integrated them through dynastic policy. The thesis that Charles desired a world empire has long been contested.
Fernández-Santamaría, J. A. *The State, War, and Peace: Spanish Political Thought in the Renaissance, 1516-1559.* Cambridge, England: Cambridge University Press, 1977. An excellent analysis of the impact Charles V's imperial policies had on the evolution of Spanish political thought. Argues that Charles's elevation of Spain led to a modern theory of state and empire. Also provides a detailed analysis of debates arising from American conquests over the legitimacy and extent of Spanish authority in the New World.
Fischer-Galati, Stephen A. *Ottoman Imperialism and German Protestantism, 1521-1555.* Cambridge, Mass.: Harvard University Press, 1959. A survey of Charles's relations with the Turks and how they influenced his policies toward the Lutheran princes. Argues that early Protestant success was dependent on Turkish advances. Temporary guarantees of security granted in 1526 and 1532 could not be revoked because of the continued pressure of the Franco-Turkish alliance.
Koenigsberger, Helmut B. "The Empire of Charles V in Europe." In *The New Cambridge Modern History,* vol. 2, *The Reformation, 1520-1559.* Edited by G. R. Elton. Cambridge, England: Cambridge University Press, 1968. A good, short survey of political administration in Charles's hetero-

genous empire. This is the best place to begin a study of how Charles governed his empire: the type of institutions he had to work through in each area and the amount of revenue they contributed. This is also a good insight into Charles as the model Renaissance monarch, neither an absolutist nor a feudal monarch.

Lynch, John. *Spain Under the Hapsburgs*. Vol. 1, *Empire and Absolutism*. New York: Oxford University Press, 1964. A topical survey of Spain during the reigns of Charles and Philip. Particularly good on economic and social developments that contributed to the decline of Spain in the seventeenth century. Also demonstrates the impact of the American Colonies on the Spanish economy and Habsburg military campaigns. Good synthesis of a vast amount of secondary scholarship.

Wallenstein, Immanuel. *The Modern World-System: Capitalist Agriculture and the Origins of the European World-Economy in the Sixteenth Century*. New York: Academic Press, 1974. This book argues that Charles's empire and the impact of American silver contributed to the shift of Europe's economic axis from the Mediterranean to a Northwestern European core, which fostered the development of capitalist nation-states and an international division of labor based upon peripheral reaction to core demands. An intriguing argument but difficult reading for the novice in history and economics.

Daniel A. Crews

CHARLES XII

Born: June 17, 1682; Stockholm, Sweden
Died: December 11, 1718; Fredriksten, Norway
Areas of Achievement: The military, government, and politics
Contribution: As one of the greatest kings of the Vasa Dynasty, Charles XII
defended Sweden and won many victories for his country during the Great
Northern War against Russia, Poland, and Denmark. He brought Swedish
power to a high point and also initiated its decline.

Early Life

The future Charles XII was born on June 17, 1682, in Stockholm, to
loving parents, the reigning Vasa King of Sweden, Charles XI, and his wife,
Ulrika Eleonora, a former Danish princess. As a child, he was frail but
physically active. He survived a case of smallpox and throughout his life
loved riding and hunting. Charles also appreciated and enjoyed his formal
education. While he was uncomfortable and awkward speaking Swedish, he
was learned in Latin, German, and French. He liked reading biography and
military history and studying religion and mathematics (which he often applied to problems of ballistics and fortifications). His heroes were Alexander
the Great and Julius Caesar. As a young man, he was often wild, extravagant, irreverent, and drunken, but as king he became pious and abstemious,
drinking nothing alcoholic, with the exception of beer. Yet he was always
strong-willed and stubborn.

Charles was the first King of Sweden born to absolutism, and from the
beginning of his reign he expanded upon it. Charles XI died in 1697, and a
regency was established for his fifteen-year-old son and successor, but it
lasted only a few months. In 1697, at age sixteen, Charles XII crowned
himself king in Stockholm rather than in Uppsala, as dictated by tradition,
and he omitted the traditional oath. His first official acts were to build and
restore several palaces for a lavish court life and to enlarge and modernize
(for example, introducing flintlocks and bayonets) the Swedish military
establishment.

Life's Work

Unquestionably, the most important event of Charles's reign was the Great
Northern War (1700-1721). Yet he had little directly to do with its coming
about and was one of its casualties before it was over. The war was largely
caused by the dynamic and ambitious czar of Russia, Peter the Great, who
was ten years Charles's senior. Mistaking the new Swedish king's youth and
inexperience for ineptitude, Peter gathered to his emerging Russian Empire
two of Sweden's other historic rivals, Poland and Denmark, in an initial
alliance and seized an apparent moment of vulnerability to go to war with
Sweden.

In the opening weeks of the war, Charles moved swiftly and decisively, catching the enemy alliance almost completely off guard and proving himself to be a military genius. He soon came to be called the "Lion of the North." In 1700, with the aid of England and the Netherlands, he defeated Denmark and quickly turned to Poland. The price for Anglo-Dutch support had been a pledge of Swedish neutrality during the War of the Spanish Succession (1700-1714), in which England and the Netherlands engaged Sweden's tacit ally, the France of Louis XIV. In Poland, Charles quickly defeated the Polish-Lithuanian-Saxon armies and established a position of dominance, and the defeat of the Russians at Narva at the end of 1700 caused Peter to initiate a reorganization of his forces. In 1703, however, Russian victories along the Baltic Sea led to the founding of Peter's new capital, St. Petersburg. In 1704, Charles deposed the Saxon King of Poland, Augustus II, and replaced him with Stanisław Leszczyński, forcing Poland into a temporary alliance with Sweden and clearing the Russians from Polish territory. The mastery of Poland at this time marks an important high-water mark of Swedish power in the seventeenth and eighteenth centuries. Charles secured his rear in 1707 by signing a treaty with Prussia and a convention with the Holy Roman Empire to protect his earlier invasion of Saxony.

After concluding a secret alliance with the Cossack leader Ivan Stepanovich Mazepa in 1708, Charles launched an invasion of the Ukraine. Yet Peter's military reforms bore their first fruits with the great Russian victory over the Swedes and Cossacks at Poltava in 1709. The Swedish army was destroyed, Charles and Mazepa were forced to flee to the Ottoman Empire, and Augustus was reinstated as King of Poland. The Russo-Danish-Polish-Saxon alliance was reconstructed, and in 1710 Charles in turn concluded an alliance with Turkey. The Russians were then decisively defeated in a battle at the Pruth River in which Peter the Great was captured in 1711. Consequently, the peace which followed was dictated by the Turks, and Charles returned to the Ottoman Empire. Russia mainly lost territory in the Azov region on the Black Sea, which it had secured from Turkey in 1700.

Sultan Ahmed III and Charles had a falling-out in 1713, all Russo-Turkish hostilities ceased, and Charles was forced to return to Europe in 1714 to defend Swedish-occupied Stralsund. In 1715, the Netherlands, Britain, Prussia, Bremen, Verden, Holstein, and Hannover declared war on Sweden, and Stralsund fell to the Danes and Prussians. Charles invaded Norway in 1716, and in 1717 Peter finally failed in his attempts to secure an alliance with Louis XIV. Charles was killed in the trenches at the Siege of Fredriksten in 1718.

While as a warrior-king on campaign Charles lived a spartan, sober, and even pious existence, the Great Northern War nevertheless took a formidable toll on Sweden and its Baltic empire. With the king's continued absence from Stockholm, the absolutism of the monarchy began to erode. Because he remained unmarried and had no direct heir to the throne, while he was away at the war his weaker sister, Ulrika Eleonora, became the de facto head of state. The resurging power of the Swedish parliamentary forces, especially of its upper house, and the increasing demands of the prolonged war began to force change on the monarchy. In 1711-1714, while Charles was in Turkey, administrative and economic reforms were enacted in Sweden, allowing for new taxes to pay for the war in return for economic and political concessions on the part of the monarchy. Perhaps Charles believed that he could reestablish the absolute authority of the monarchy upon his return to Stockholm, but he never did return. Upon Charles's death in battle, he was succeeded to the throne by Ulrika Eleonora. She gradually lost more power to the nobility and clergy under a new constitution.

After 1715, Russian successes in Finland and the Baltic area, which eventually came to threaten Stockholm itself, and the general political and economic exhaustion resulting from a war of more than two decades finally forced Sweden to agree to an end to the hostilities. Under the Treaty of Nystadt in 1721, peace was formally declared, and Sweden lost some parts of its Baltic empire (for example, the province of Ingria, surrounding St. Petersburg, to Peter the Great's newly declared Russian Empire). The Peace of Nystadt was by no means a victors' peace. Instead, it led to better relations in the changing spectrum of Baltic and other powers in Northern Europe, culminating in Sweden's participation in the allied coalition against Napoleonic France less than a century later.

Summary

Charles XII was a single-minded and ambitious absolutist ruler and a formidable soldier who neglected the real needs of his kingdom and its empire for foreign adventure and personal glory. Of the twenty-one years of his reign, he spent all but three away from Stockholm fighting the Great Northern War. Through his military triumphs he revitalized, for a time, the power and status of the Swedish Empire, recalling the days of the greatest Vasa King of Sweden, Gustavus II Adolphus, and the Thirty Years' War and thus causing many historians to consider Charles second only in importance to Gustavus among the ruling members of the Vasa Dynasty.

Yet the Great Northern War and Peter the Great also were Charles's and the Swedish Empire's undoing. The Russian victory and the Treaty of Nystadt marked Sweden's fall and its replacement as a great power by the new Russian Empire of Peter the Great. With it, the tacit French-Turkish-Swedish anti-Habsburg coalition came apart too, and Poland was reduced to little more than a Russian puppet-state on the road to partition. Last, the reign of Charles signaled the beginning of Sweden's transition from an absolute to a constitutional monarchy under the later Vasa and Bernadotte Dynasties.

Bibliography

Bain, R. Nisbet. *Charles XII and the Collapse of the Swedish Empire, 1682-1719.* New York: G. P. Putnam's Sons, 1895. A standard biography of Charles, presenting a detailed account of his life and times. Dwells on his military prowess and sees his ambition as his undoing and that of the Swedish Empire.

Bengtsson, Frans G. *The Life of Charles XII, King of Sweden, 1697-1718.* London: Macmillan, 1960. A more modern, but nevertheless standard, biography. Portrays Charles in a more positive light than does Bain, but on the whole Bain's life of Charles reveals more to the reader.

Buzzi, Giancarlo. *The Life and Times of Peter the Great.* Translated by Ben Johnson. London: Hamlyn, 1968. This popular account of Charles's principal rival includes several sections on Charles and the Great Northern War. Profusely illustrated.

Hallendorff, Carl, and Adolf Schück. *History of Sweden.* Stockholm: C. E. Fritze, 1938. This standard Swedish history of Sweden has a good chapter on Charles and puts him into perspective with the rise and fall of the Swedish Empire under the Vasa Dynasty.

Hatton, R. M. *Charles XII of Sweden.* New York: Weybright and Talley, 1968. The best biography of Charles in English. A well-researched, well-documented, well-written, and balanced study of the man, his country, and his times.

Lisk, Jill. *The Struggle for Supremacy in the Baltic, 1600-1725.* New York: Funk & Wagnalls, 1968. Follows the rise of Swedish and then Russian power in the Baltic arena in the seventeenth century through the Great Northern War and the death of Peter the Great. Includes two important chapters on Charles and the Great Northern War.

Massie, Robert K. *Peter the Great: His Life and World.* New York: Ballantine Books, 1980. A Pulitzer Prize-winning biography of Peter the Great. Thorough and well written, with chapter 24 and more on Charles. Charles is treated fairly and not really overshadowed by Peter when they are both center stage.

Warner, Oliver. *The Sea and the Sword: The Baltic, 1630-1945.* New York: William Morrow, 1965. Essentially a general modern naval history of the Baltic basin. Includes a good and rather extensive chapter on Charles, Peter, and the war.

Dennis Reinhartz

CHARLES XIV JOHN
Jean-Baptiste-Jules Bernadotte

Born: January 26, 1763; Pau, France
Died: March 8, 1844; Stockholm, Sweden
Areas of Achievement: Politics and the military
Contribution: Charles XIV lived virtually two distinct lives. He was first a soldier in the French army with strong republican convictions, and then the conservative King of Sweden.

Early Life

On January 26, 1763, Jean-Baptiste-Jules Bernadotte was born at Pau in the southern province of Gascony. The son of Henri, an attorney, and Jeanne, he was reared in a typical provincial bourgeois manner. He abandoned his law education after the death of his father in 1780 and joined the army. An intelligent young man, with a better education than the French army was accustomed to, he rose through the ranks. On the eve of the French Revolution, he held the rank of sergeant major, the highest noncommissioned position in the army. When the Revolution opened the ranks of the officer corps to men of ability, Bernadotte was among the first to benefit. He was commissioned a second lieutenant in November, 1791.

Soon after France went to war with Russia and Austria in April, 1792, he was promoted to captain. He first saw combat at the head of a company in 1793. Promotions came quickly for able officers in those crucial years of the French Republic, and Bernadotte was catapulted in one year, 1794, from captain to general of division. Campaigning in Belgium and on the Rhine, he earned the reputation of a competent and careful division commander. He took an active part in the campaigns of 1795 and 1796. Then in February, 1797, Bernadotte was sent to Italy with reinforcements for Napoleon I. This was the first time that he served under the future Emperor of the French. As was the case with the other generals of division in the army of Italy, Bernadotte was senior in time served but with the same rank as Napoleon and resented the fact that he had to serve under an officer who had never commanded a division in combat until he was given the army of Italy in 1796. Bernadotte was also six years older than the twenty-seven-year-old aristocrat from Corsica and had much more combat experience. Yet Napoleon had already won stunning victories over the Austrians at Castiglione, Arcola, and Rivoli before Bernadotte had arrived and had established somewhat of a reputation. The newcomer from the Rhine had no choice but to take orders. He played a waiting game.

Life's Work

Bernadotte had spent all of his adult life as a soldier until 1798. In that year, he was appointed by the government of the Directory to be ambassador to Austria. His stay in Vienna was brief, as a lack of social graces combined with strong republican beliefs caused him to be quite unacceptable in the heart of aristocratic Europe. Returning to Paris after only a few months in Vienna, he met and quickly married Désirée Clary. In 1795, Napoleon had unsuccessfully sought her hand in marriage after his brother Joseph had married Désirée's sister Julie. As a result of his marriage, Bernadotte became a part of the extended Bonaparte family. Despite this relationship, he was seldom on good terms with the man who would rule France for fifteen years. When Napoleon went to Egypt in 1798, Bernadotte remained in Paris, and in July of the following year he was appointed minister of war by the Directory. It was his strong republican views that won for him this position, but he did not work well with the directors, and within a few months he was relieved of the office. When Napoleon returned to France and took part in the *coup d'état* of Brumaire, Bernadotte refused to have any part in the overthrow of the government. He sat on the sidelines while Napoleon made himself master of France with the title of first consul.

To ingratiate the staunch republican, Napoleon named Bernadotte councillor of state in January, 1800. Despite the fact that he remained a republican, he accepted the prestigious position and gave tacit support to the new regime. He was also given a command in the army, and between 1800 and 1804 he served in the west of France and in northern Europe. It seems to have been during the first decade of the nineteenth century that Bernadotte was transformed from a republican into a monarchist. Napoleon showered him with wealth, titles, honors, and decorations, which he could never have gained under a republic. Yet if the emperor was able to buy his loyalty and support, he was not able to purchase his affection. Bernadotte never came to like Napoleon.

In 1805, when war again broke out with Austria and Russia, Bernadotte commanded the I Corps of the Grand Army. At the Battle of Austerlitz, he held the left flank and supported Marshal Nicolas Jean de Dieu Soult's decisive attack against the center of the Russian line. His corps fought well, and he contributed to this, perhaps Napoleon's finest, victory. The following year, Bernadotte was made Prince of Ponte-Corvo. By the end of the summer of 1806, France was again at war with a Continental power. This time it was Prussia and the campaign was in southeast Germany. Unlike at Austerlitz, however, Bernadotte and his I Corps sat idly in between the Battles of Jean and Auerstadt on October 16. He was strongly criticized by Napoleon and the army for not marching to the aid of Marshal Louis N. Davout, who fought and defeated a Prussian army at Auerstadt that was more than twice the size of his III Corps. Although the emperor threatened to court-martial Bernadotte for his lack of initiative, no action was taken against him, and the I Corps, rested and unscarred, led the pursuit of the devastated Prussian army. Bernadotte received the surrender of the city of Lübeck and then marched east to support the main army. He was not at the Battle of the Eylau in February, 1807, but he was wounded in action at Spanden in June of the same year, shortly before the campaign came to a victorious conclusion with the defeat of the Russian army at Friedland. Upon his recovery from his wound, he was named Governor of Hamburg, Bremen, and Lübeck.

During the two years he spent in northern Germany he had various dealings with Serden, which had held territory on the south Baltic coast. The renewal of hostilities with Austria in the spring of 1809 brought Bernadotte back into Central Europe at the head of the IX Corps. Following the victory at Eckmuhl and a setback at Aspern-Essling, Napoleon engaged the Austrian army at Wagram on July 5. Bernadotte's Saxon Corps held the left center of the French line. When the Austrians attacked the French left, the Saxons broke and fled to the rear. Despite Bernadotte's efforts, it was necessary to fill the gap created by redeploying Marshal André Masséna's IV Corps. Napoleon was furious with Bernadotte. He accused him of losing the battle, which the French eventually won, and of cowardliness in the face of the enemy. Bernadotte was ordered to leave the army in disgrace and to retire to Paris.

The year 1810 was a pivotal one for Bernadotte. In 1809, the Swedish king, Gustavus IV Adolphus, was forced into exile, and his uncle was put on the throne with the title of Charles XIII. With the death of Charles XIII's adopted son, the Swedish Parliament elected Bernadotte crown prince. Having formally changed his name—he was now Charles John—and his religion, he left France with Napoleon's blessing, landing in Sweden on October 20, 1810. As crown prince, Charles John did not become involved with domestic affairs, but he did play an active role in foreign policy. He realized that Sweden's interests lay in cooperation with Russia and England, not France. Therefore, in 1813 he encouraged the Swedes to declare war on France in order to acquire Norway, owned by Denmark, as compensation for the loss of Finland, which had been taken by the Russians in 1809. Charles John led a Swedish army of twenty thousand men into Germany to fight against France. He defeated Marshal Nicolas Charles Oudinot at Gross-Beeren on August 23, 1813, and arrived at Leipzig on the last day of the three-day battle to witness the defeat of Napoleon. He played a minor role in the campaign of 1814 that forced the French emperor to abdicate in April of that year. He seems to have grasped at the hope of becoming King of France but was never seriously considered by the French. Most Frenchmen, and in particular those in the army, considered him to be a traitor.

Returning to Sweden, Charles John played no part in the campaign of the Hundred Days when Napoleon returned in 1815. Yet Sweden did receive Norway as a reward for having joined the grand alliance against France in 1813. When Charles XIII died in 1818, the once-strong republican was crowned Charles XIV, King of Sweden. His twenty-six-year reign was not particularly eventful. He had been put on the throne by the grace of Parliament, and he did not overstep the limitations placed on the Crown. He became progressively more conservative, and in the later years of his reign clashed with the reform-minded Parliament. Charles John died at Stockholm on March 8, 1844, and was succeeded by his son Oscar I.

Summary

As Charles XIV John, King of Sweden, the man born Jean-Baptiste-Jules Bernadotte found an improbable fulfillment of his ambitions. If his story sounds like something out of the pages of Alexandre Dumas, the reality was considerably less romantic. The reign of Charles XIV John came at a time in Sweden's history when power was decisively shifting from the throne to Parliament; this period was the foundation of modern Swedish democracy. Still, if Charles's role was sharply circumscribed, his years on the throne were peaceful and prosperous ones for Sweden, and history has labeled him as a good king.

Bibliography

Barton, Dunbar Plunket. *Bernadotte: The First Phase, 1763-1799*; *Bernadotte and Napoleon, 1799-1810*; *Bernadotte, Prince and King, 1810-1844*. London: John Murray, 1914, 1921, 1925. Taken together, these three volumes still represent the definitive work on Charles John. They provide a detailed account of his long and active life with numerous quotations from his correspondence. See also the abridged one-volume edition of Barton's work entitled *The Amazing Career of Bernadotte* (1929), which is much more widely available then the multivolume study.

Dewes, Simon. *Sergent Belle-Jombs: The Life of Marshal Bernadotte*. London: Rich & Cowan, 1943. This readable account, favorable toward its central figure, concentrates on Charles John's military career during the Napoleonic years. Dewes is primarily concerned with military affairs and tends to minimize the political and administrative aspects of Bernadotte's life.

Heathcote, T. A. "'Serjent Belle-Jambe': Bernadotte." In *Napoleon's Marshals*, edited by David G. Chandler. New York: Macmillan, 1987. A very good twenty-two-page chapter in an excellent study of the marshals of the Napoleonic Empire. The emphasis is on Charles John's early years and his career in the French army. There is virtually nothing on him as King of Sweden.

Scott, Franklin D. *Bernadotte and the Fall of Napoleon*. Cambridge, Mass.: Harvard University Press, 1935. This is a scholarly study of Charles John's role in the removal of Napoleon from the throne of France in 1814. Although it covers only a brief period of the life of Charles John, it provides a good understanding of the man and his ambitions and motivations. Wencker-Wildbery, Friedrich. *Bernadotte: A Biography.* London: Jarrolds, 1936. Written in a popular style with many undocumented quotes, this is a very readable account of the life of Charles John. It also contains a number of good pictures of him and his family into the twentieth century. Although it is reasonably accurate, it is not a scholarly work.

John G. Gallaher

CHARLES THE BOLD

Born: November 10, 1433; Dijon, Burgundy
Died: January 5, 1477; near Nancy, Lorraine
Areas of Achievement: Government and politics
Contribution: Charles the Bold attempted to build the Duchy of Burgundy into a unified kingdom. He was considered a serious threat to the stability and centralization of the French state.

Early Life

Charles was born on November 10, 1433, at Dijon, the son of the immensely popular Duke of Burgundy, Philip the Good, and his third wife, Isabella of Portugal. Perhaps because Charles was the only son of three to survive, Isabella zealously protected the infant. She tended to his needs personally, refusing to relinquish him to wet nurses, as was the normal custom of the age. As a youth Charles received the education properly fitting for a future military leader and political ruler. Charles became a skilled horseman, having received his first lessons at the age of two on a specially constructed wooden horse. Charles avidly pursued knowledge of military affairs as well during his early years.

The future duke was familiar with Latin, although he was by no means a Humanist. He read Sallust, Julius Caesar, and the deeds of Alexander the Great, although he was more interested in their martial activities than their literary style. Charles had an aptitude for languages and could conduct himself in Italian and Flemish as well as in his native French. He had limited knowledge of English as well. In appearance, he was tall, fleshy, and well proportioned. His hair, eyes, and coloring were dark, favoring his mother over his father.

Charles was most revealing in his character traits. Like his mother, he was always suspicious, was slow to embrace friends, and seldom had confidantes. He possessed an enormous ego and reveled in excessive flattery. Above all, as his name, Charles the Bold, indicates, he was an impulsive and rash man, who followed courses unrelentingly without accepting or listening to prudent advice.

Life's Work

Charles became the Duke of Burgundy upon the death of his father in June, 1467. He inherited a large network of territories that consisted of Franche-Comté, Nevers, Bar, Luxembourg, the Netherlands, Artois, and Picardy. His domain lacked cultural, linguistic, and geographic unity. Charles governed his regional conglomeration through a complex feudal system of political, ecclesiastical, and military appointees. Much depended on personal loyalty to the duke on the part of his underlords and his subjects.

Charles was a product of his age and his culture. He believed in the feudal concepts of chivalry. Chivalric virtues emphasized military prowess, personal loyalty to one's overlord, courtesy to one's peers, generosity, and intellectual gentility. Charles and his court at Dijon reflected a chivalric society. Burgundian dukes patronized the outstanding artists of the fifteenth century, including Claus Sluter, Jan van Eyck, and Rogier van der Weyden. Their generosity as patrons was well-known. Tapestries depicting heroic feats of Alexander the Great, Caesar, and Charlemagne lined the walls of Dijon. Charles continued this benevolent tradition by supporting the historians Georges Chastellain, Olivier de La Marche, and Philippe de Commynes.

Unfortunately, early in his reign he learned that reality was less pleasant than the courtly activities at Dijon. Urban centers, in particular, had little time for chivalry. Their citizens preferred practicality, and they resented excessive taxation and deprivation of privileges. With an eye toward independence, the cities Ghent and Liège rebelled in 1468. Charles responded quickly and forcefully with an army that brought both cities to heel. Because he suspected that the citizens of Liège had conspired against him with the French King Louis XI, Charles planned ruthless punishment for the city. Louis, in the meantime, had come to Peronne, which was within the duke's lands, in October, 1468. The king hoped to negotiate with Charles. The French monarch found himself a virtual prisoner at the castle of Peronne after Charles had received what he regarded as evidence of the king's treacherous complicity with Liège. Louis was forced to watch the systematic pillage, carnage, and burning at Liège at the hands of the fully enraged duke. Louis witnessed Charles's impetuosity, a lesson he learned to put to good use in his future dealings with the duke.

Events at Peronne and Liège merely provided the necessary impetus for descent into formalized warfare between the ambitious Duke of Burgundy and his natural rival, the equally acquisitive Louis, correctly labeled the "universal spider." In order to outwit the monarch, his legal overlord, Charles activated his political design. In 1468, Charles was married to Margaret of York, the sister of Edward IV, the King of England. Through his marriage, Charles hoped to keep the English alienated from any potential alliance with the French. With the English federation under his control, the duke actively pursued his grander plan. Charles embarked upon his dream of creating an independent Burgundian kingdom as a buffer state between France and Germany. This conceptualized kingdom would extend from the North Sea to Switzerland.

Alsace and Lorraine, the heart of the old Carolingian Lotharingia, were to become the nucleus of the future Burgundian realm. In 1469, under the conditions of the Treaty of Omer, Charles happily received the mortgage of Upper Alsace from the impoverished and improvident Duke Sigismund of Austria-Tirol. The fifty thousand Rhenish florins loaned to Sigismund permitted Charles to take a firmer step toward further aggrandizement.

At his next juncture, he negotiated with Frederick III, the Holy Roman Emperor. These transactions were seriously conducted from 1469 to 1471. His goal was to secure the emperor's promise that Charles would receive the imperial coronation upon the abdication or the death of the old emperor. Part of the diplomatic arrangements ensured the hand of Mary of Burgundy, Charles's only child, to Frederick's son, Maximilian. A planned meeting between the emperor and the duke in November, 1473, at Trier was intended to seal the negotiations as far as Charles was concerned. Charles may have expected the coronation on November 18, 1473. The emperor delayed and then slipped away from Trier, almost secretly, on November 24, without crowning Charles and without finalizing the marital arrangements between Mary of Burgundy and Maximilian.

Charles was disappointed, and gravely so, but did not sulk for long. He proceeded to expand his territory in Alsace and then to secure Lorraine by force toward the end of 1475. His aggressive movements alarmed the Swiss, who were neighbors of Alsace and Lorraine. The "spider" king, Louis, managed to spin a web of intrigue around the oblivious Charles. Louis fed the fears of the Swiss and, simultaneously, managed to ally them with Sigismund of Austria-Tirol in 1474, after the transactions with the emperor and Charles had failed and before Charles's final aggression against Lorraine. Then Louis added René II of Lorraine to the federation. René was a willing cohort since his territory had been snatched by the duke in 1475. Open warfare erupted between the German and Swiss league on one side and Charles the Bold on the other. Charles was soundly defeated at Grandson, Morat, and, finally, Nancy. The Battle of Nancy, fought in freezing cold on January 5, 1477, claimed Charles's life.

Charles's page later reported that the duke's horse had come to the edge of a ditch, stumbled, and unseated his rider. The duke died during the carnage of battle. His body was found several days later. It was an ironic and cruel trick of fate that the last of the proud and glorious house of Burgundy should come to an ignoble end, lying nude, stripped of clothing, weapons, and jewels, mutilated, and partly eaten by animals in a land that he coveted.

Summary

The political situation in Europe during the last half of the fifteenth century was in a process of rapid change. The balance of power between the monarchs and their magnates teetered in a precarious manner. Both sides battled furiously for control within and outside geographical boundaries. Louis and Charles the Bold were locked in such a conflict. Charles, in some ways, was a Janus-like figure. He idealized the chivalric virtues of military prowess and personal obligations. Yet he combined these with the Renaissance characteristics of fame and glory. He looked back to the Carolingian middle kingdom of Lotharingia with nostalgia as he tried to remold it into a new state. Yet he hoped that this new kingdom would balance the power between Germany and France. At the beginning of his reign, it seemed quite possible to political observers (including Louis) that Charles might very well succeed.

He reached his peak with the submission of Ghent and Liège. The acquisition of Alsace and Lorraine represented an anticlimax since rapid defeats in Switzerland and Lorraine caused the death of the duke and the collapse of the Burgundian state in 1477. Charles was to blame, in part. He often acted rashly and consistently refused to follow the advice of his seasoned advisers, a fact that writers such as Niccolò Machiavelli and even Desiderius Erasmus would find troubling.

Fortune turned against him as well. He had no sons. The male line, consequently, ended with Charles. His daughter, Mary, was married to Maximilian I, the German emperor's son, in 1477. While this seemed a prudent move at the time, Mary died five years later, and the entire Burgundian inheritance disappeared into the domain of either Germany or France.

Two significant historical developments resulted from Charles's career and his ambitions, neither of which was intentional. First, Charles provided the setting for the last stage of the Franco-Burgundian struggle with the monarch winning over the magnate. Centralization of France was completed with the fall of Burgundy. Second, a more remote event was the eventual independence of the Low Countries from German and French competition. The seeds of discontent were orignally sown during Charles's era but did not fully blossom until the seventeenth century, when the Netherlands attained the formal status of independence.

Bibliography
Calmette, Joseph. *The Golden Age of Burgundy: The Magnificent Dukes and Their Courts*. Translated by Doreen Weightman. New York: W. W. Norton, 1963. Places Charles in the environment of the age of Burgundian power. Calmette is the only historian to treat the Burgundian court within the context of its intellectual and artistic milieu.
Kirk, John Foster. *History of Charles the Bold, Duke of Burgundy*. 3 vols. Philadelphia: J. B. Lippincott, 1864-1868. A detailed and straightforward account of the life of Charles. Generous quotes from letters, reports, and treaties. Strictly conforms to the nineteenth century historiographical emphasis upon factual information. Would be most useful as a source for an in-depth study of the duke, even though its interpretation is dated.
Putnam, Ruth. *Charles the Bold, Last Duke of Burgundy, 1433-1477*. New York: G. P. Putnam's Sons, 1908. Standard biography that is part of a larger series dealing with heroic individuals. A lively account of the duke's life and an equally vivid portrayal of the mores of the fifteenth

century. The author stresses the role of the individual as hero in history.

Vaughan, Richard. *Charles the Bold: The Last Valois Duke of Burgundy.* New York: Longman, 1973. An excellent interpretation of Charles and his complicated relationship with his lands. The author penetrates the political motives of Charles, Louis, and other major figures. Ample quotes from diaries, dispatches, histories, and letters. Contains a full and detailed bibliography.

_____. "Chasing a Sphinx: Charles the Bold's Burgundy." *History Today* 37 (May, 1987): 24-29. A good, brief overview that points out the lack of cultural and linguistic unity that prevented Charles from making Burgundy a modern state.

Barbara M. Fahy

CHATEAUBRIAND

Born: September 4, 1768; Saint-Malo, France
Died: July 4, 1848; Paris, France
Area of Achievement: Literature
Contribution: The father of French Romanticism, Chateaubriand popularized the melancholy hero and deeply influenced many other nineteenth and twentieth century writers.

Early Life

The youngest of ten children, François-August-René de Chateaubriand was born at Saint-Malo, France, on September 4, 1768. His father, René-Auguste de Chateaubriand, had become rich as a shipowner and merchant sailor; with his wealth, he had purchased the château of Combourg. There the young Chateaubriand spent a lonely childhood, wandering the woods with his sister Lucile, four years his senior, who early recognized and fostered her brother's genius. Already as an adolescent he revealed himself as a dreamer. He later recalled that when he spoke with Lucile about the world, "it was the world that we carried within us," that of the imagination.

His father initially intended for Chateaubriand to pursue a naval career. To this end the youth attended the College of Dol, near Combourg, and then the Jesuit college of Rennes. Having rejected the sea, Chateaubriand next went to the College of Dinan to study for the priesthood but soon abandoned this field as well. An older brother, Jean-Baptiste, who was living in Paris and moving in court circles, then secured for him a military commission; Chateaubriand was to remark that both he and Napoleon I began their careers as sublieutenants. He was also to observe that he spent fifteen years as a soldier before devoting fifteen to writing and another fifteen to politics.

Actually, his military career was considerably briefer. When his father died in September, 1786, Chateaubriand left the army, returned to Combourg, and, in 1789, joined his brother at the French capital. An unintentional witness to the fall of the Bastille and the increasingly violent French Revolution that ensued, in July, 1791, Chateaubriand sailed to America to find true liberty, fraternity, and equality.

On the banks of the Ohio, he chanced upon a newspaper report of the flight of Louis XVI. He hastened back to France to fight for the monarchy. Lacking funds sufficient to join the émigré army, he married the rich and acerbic Céleste Buisson de la Vigne. Wounded and left for dead at the siege of Thionville, he managed to escape to England, where he made a living as a tutor and translator.

Life's Work

In the evenings, he also began to produce original works. Among the earliest of these is his "Lettre sur l'art du dessin dans les paysages" (1795; letter on the art of landscape painting), a significant contribution to the Romantic movement. From the Renaissance through the eighteenth century, artistic theory emphasized the importance of learning technique through imitation of past masterpieces. Chateaubriand recognized the importance of technical skill, but he argued that the painter must first immerse himself in nature and respond to it emotionally, then attempt to recapture these feelings in his work. The artist should faithfully record what he has observed— Chateaubriand had studied botany before going to America so that he would recognize and understand what he was seeing—but landscape painting should seek not photographic realism but rather the ideal. One sees here a number of concepts that recur in writings on Romantic literary theory.

Just as Chateaubriand's observations on landscape painting challenged the neoclassical aesthetic, so this *Essai sur les révolutions* (1797; *An Historical, Political, Moral Essay on Revolutions*, 1815) rejected the political attitude of the Enlightenment. Intended as the first volume of a detailed study of revolutions, it devotes relatively little attention to the one then engulfing Europe. Yet it does comment on events in France, denying the idea of progress and perfectibility, seeing the French Revolution as only one of an ongoing series of upheavals that left people no freer or happier than they were before.

The next year he apparently began to change his mind about religion, though he would never allow his devotion to Catholicism to interfere with his pleasures. He began work on *Le Génie du Christianisme* (1799, 1800, 1802; *The Genius of Christianity*, 1802), a spirited defense of traditional belief. Again he was rejecting the views of the eighteenth century philosophers, and, by couching his arguments in aesthetic and emotional terms, he was allying himself once more with the Romantics.

Some portions of this work were published in England, but Chateaubriand was still revising the manuscript when he returned to France in May, 1800. Seeking literary fame and needing money, he detached from *The Genius of Christianity* a novella intended to illustrate how religion improves literature; this piece he published separately in 1801. *Atala* (English translation, 1802), the first work by a European to use the American wilderness and the Indian as central features, told of the love of Atala for the Indian Chactas. Unwilling to betray the vow of chastity made to her dying mother, and unable to overcome her passion for her lover, Atala poisons herself. Here, as in *René* (1802; English translation, 1813), Chateaubriand portrayed the melancholy Byronic hero well before George Gordon, Lord Byron, himself, did so. The dreamlike landscapes that mirror the inhabitants' moods and at the same time seem to control their actions, the emphasis on emotion, the descriptions that fuse the senses (as when each blade of grass emits a different note) are devices that would influence succeeding generations of writers.

The popularity of *Atala* was matched, if not surpassed, by that of its parent work when it appeared in France the next year. The timing of its publication could not have been more fortunate for the author: On April 8, 1802, Napoleon concluded the Concordat, restoring Catholicism as the official religion of France; *The Genius of Christianity* appeared six days later.

Encouraged by the book's success and by recommendations from Chateaubriand's current mistress, Pauline de Beaumont, Napoleon appointed the author to the post of secretary to the French embassy in Rome (1803). Chateaubriand soon sought, and obtained, another assignment, that of chargé d'affaires to the puppet state of Valais. Yet before he could settle his affairs in Paris, he learned of Napoleon's kidnapping and execution of the Bourbon Duke of Enghien, an act meant to warn the Royalists against any attempted coup. Chateaubriand resigned his office and broke with the French ruler.

Using Royalist funds, he bought the newspaper *Mercure de France* and, on July 4, 1807, published a harsh attack on the dictator. Napoleon retaliated by forcing him to sell the paper, though at a profit sufficient to allow Chateaubriand to acquire a country house outside Paris, where he completed *Les Martyres* (1809; *The Martyrs*, 1812), another tale of doomed love. The heroine, Cymodocéa, is modeled on Natalie de Noailles, who had succeeded Pauline de Beaumont as Chateaubriand's mistress. Throughout his life, he would attract France's most beautiful and clever women, earning for himself the title "the enchanter." Short, stocky, broad-shouldered, and pale, he had a leonine head that compensated for any physical flaw, flashing gray eyes, and wild brown hair that gave him an aura of romance.

Set in the reign of Diocletian, *The Martyrs* presents a thinly veiled attack on Napoleon by comparing the French emperor to the Roman. Having arrested the pope and, therefore, having been excommunicated, Napoleon chose to ignore the criticism and sought to renew his friendship with the leading French Catholic author of the day. He arranged Chateaubriand's appointment to the prestigious Académie Française, but the writer's acceptance speech, so harsh that Napoleon censored it, showed that reconciliation was impossible.

In 1814, Chateaubriand wrote an even sterner indictment of the French ruler. "What have you done, not with a hundred thousand, but with five million Frenchmen . . . our relatives, our friends, our brothers?" he asked in *De Buonaparte et des Bourbons* (1814; *On Buonaparte and the Bourbons*, 1814). Again Chateaubriand's timing was perfect: The piece appeared on the day the allied troops entered Paris, and the newly crowned Louis XVIII claimed that the publication was worth 100,000 soldiers.

Yet Chateaubriand's relationship with the Bourbons was uneasy. On June 4, 1814, Louis issued a charter that reaffirmed individual rights and sought to establish a constitutional monarchy along English lines, with ministerial responsibility to the legislative majority rather than to the king.

Within two years, though, Chateaubriand was disillusioned. In his memoirs he was to write, "Descending from Bonaparte and the Empire to those who followed them, is like falling from . . . the summit of a mountain into an abyss." While supporting the freedoms won since 1789, Chateaubriand claimed that the king's ministers did not share the views of the majority of Frenchmen and were thus betraying the Charter of 1814.

On February 13, 1820, the Duc de Berry, son of the future Charles X, was assassinated at the opera. In his newspaper *Le Conservateur*, Chateaubriand wrote, "The hand that struck the blow does not bear the greatest guilt; they that have murdered the Duc de Berry are those that have been introducing democratic laws into the Monarchy for the last four years." The government of Elie Decazes fell, and its successor named Chateaubriand minister of state and envoy to Berlin. He did not remain in Prussia long before returning to Paris to devote himself to Juliette Récamier, Claire de Duras, and Delphine de Custine. In January, 1822, he again went abroad, this time as ambassador to the Court of St. James, where his chef, Montmireil, immortalized his name among many who never would read *René* or *Atala* by naming a thickly cut beefsteak for the diplomat. Chateaubriand left London in September to represent France at the Congress of Verona, and on December 28, 1822, he was named minister of foreign affairs. He was to claim that in this office he succeeded in doing what Napoleon had not—conquering Spain. A popular revolution had dethroned Ferdinand VII, and Chateaubriand persuaded France to intervene and restore the king to his throne.

In June, 1824, Chateaubriand was himself deposed, losing his ministerial position, though in 1827 he returned to a government post as ambassador to Rome. When Charles X named the conservative Jules de Polignac as chief minister, Chateaubriand resigned. As Chateaubriand feared, Polignac proved to be the downfall of the Bourbon monarchy; in 1830, the Orléans Louis-Philippe assumed the throne after a short revolution. Despite his treatment by the Bourbons, Chateaubriand refused to take the oath of allegiance to the new king, preferring to renounce his titles of peer and minister of state together with the salary they carried.

By then, he no longer needed this stipend, for he had been paid 550,000 francs for the rights to the collected works, and he received another 156,000 francs and a life pension for his memoirs, which appeared posthumously. Chateaubriand's last years were dedicated to the completion of this autobiography and to Juliette Récamier, who was with him when he died in Paris on July 4, 1848. At his request, he was buried in a simple tomb on the rock of Grand Bé off the coast of Saint-Malo.

Summary

In 1831, when the Gothic church of Saint-Germain l'Auxerrois faced demolition, Chateaubriand played an important role in its preservation, though he remarked that too many such buildings were appearing in the literature of the day. That writers were filling their pages with descriptions of Gothic cathedrals was, however, in large part attributable to Chateaubriand himself. Théophile Gautier claimed that *The Genius of Christianity* restored the popularity of Gothic architecture, just as *Les Natchez* (1826; *The Natchez*, 1827) unlocked the natural sublime and *René* invented the modern melancholy hero. Chateaubriand was an idol to a generation of French Romantics—the young Alphonse de Lamartine waited outside Chateaubriand's house for two days to catch a glimpse of the man—and later authors such as Gustave Flaubert and Charles Baudelaire were equally influenced by his works.

The first writer to appreciate the literary potential of the American frontier, Chateaubriand placed within that setting the brooding hero that Byron would popularize a decade later. The poet of sadness, night, suffering, and ennui, he gave the world the character who searches for a self he will never find. He also taught the French how to read their own classics. He was among the first to recognize the tragic sense that underlies much of Molière's comedy and the sadness and dreamlike qualities of Jean de La Fontaine, Blaise Pascal, and Jean Racine.

Honoré de Balzac wanted to be a literary Napoleon; Chateaubriand hoped to be a political Napoleon as well. He lacked the talent and temperament necessary to rival his fellow sublieutenant in the field or in the cabinet, but in the study he reigned supreme. As Bonaparte remarked, "Chateaubriand has received the sacred fire from Nature; his works bear witness to it. His style is not that of Racine but that of the prophet."

Bibliography

Evans, Joan. *Chateaubriand: A Biography.* New York: Macmillan, 1939. Relies primarily on Chateaubriand's autobiography but corrects and supplements this work with other accounts. Readable, with many fine vignettes but little analysis.

Hilt, Douglas. "Chateaubriand and Napolean." *History Today* 23 (December, 1973): 831-837. Traces Chateaubriand's political career under Napoleon and the author's subsequent portrayal of Napoleon in his memoirs.

Maurois, André. *Chateaubriand: Poet, Statesman, Lover.* Translated by Vera Fraser. New York: Harper & Row, 1938. Drawing heavily on Chateaubriand's own writing, Maurois artfully weaves his subject's own words into a readable narrative.

Painter, George D. *Chateaubriand: A Biography.* London: Chatto & Windus, 1977-   . A projected three-volume work, when complete it will be the definitive biography. Painter offers an extensively detailed account; the first volume traces the life from 1768 to 1793.

Porter, Charles Allan. *Chateaubriand: Composition, Imagination, and Poetry.* Saratoga, Calif.: Anma Libri, 1978. A stylistic analysis of Chateaubriand's major works. Like many of Chateaubriand's contemporaries, Porter sees discontinuities of time and space in the prose. Porter finds in these disjunctions a modern attempt to engage the reader in the creative process.

Sieburg, Friedrich. *Chateaubriand.* Translated by Violet M. MacDonald. Winchester, Mass.: Allen & Unwin, 1961. Concentrates on biography rather than literary analysis. Argues that "Chateaubriand's ambition and his desire for action were . . . forever undermining the foundations of his existence" and that his life is a tissue of contradictions.

Joseph Rosenblum

ANTON CHEKHOV

Born: January 29, 1860; Taganrog, in the Crimea, Russia
Died: July 15, 1904; Badenweiler, Germany
Areas of Achievement: Literature, theater, and drama
Contribution: Although Chekhov had a significant impact on the creation of modern drama with his four major plays, his most important influence has been on the development of the modern short story. With his numerous lyrical stories, Chekhov liberated the short story in particular from its adherence to the parable form and fiction in general from the tedium of the realistic novel.

Early Life

Anton Chekhov was born on January 29, 1860, in a small port town on the Sea of Azov in the Crimea. His grandfather was a former slave who bought his own freedom. In what is perhaps the best-known remark Chekhov ever made about his life, he said he felt the necessity to "squeeze the slave" out of himself. Chekhov's father, Pavel Egorovich, owned a small general store in which Chekhov worked as a child. When Chekhov was sixteen, however, his father had to declare bankruptcy and escape his creditors by going to Moscow. Chekhov's mother, along with the two youngest children, followed soon after. Chekhov stayed behind as a tutor to the son of one of his mother's former boarders.

After living in poverty and fending for himself for three years, Chekhov was graduated from high school in Taganrog and went to Moscow to enter medical school at Moscow University. Because his father had a low-paying job outside town and was only home on Sundays and holidays, Chekhov had to assume the role of head of his family's household and find work. Having shown an early interest in writing while he was a child in Taganrog, he sought to supplement his family's meager income by contributing anecdotes and stories to humorous magazines, especially at the urging of his elder brother Aleksander, who was already earning a small income by publishing in such magazines. At first Chekhov had little success with his writing efforts, but in March, 1880, his first story was published in the humor journal *Strekoza* (dragonfly). Chekhov later called this the beginning of his literary career.

Life's Work

In 1882, Chekhov became a regular contributor of jokes and anecdotes to a weekly St. Petersburg magazine, *Oskolki* (fragments), edited by Nikolai A. Leikin. He submitted a large number of short pieces to the journal, many under various pseudonyms. By 1884, he had published more than two hundred short pieces, but when his first collection, *Skazki Melpomeny* (1884;

Tales of Melpomene, 1816-1823), was published, he included only twenty of them. Also in 1884, Chekhov finished his degree and began practicing medicine. By the following year, when he went to St. Petersburg, he found, much to his surprise (because he did not consider his work significant), that he was quite well known as a writer there.

Chekhov's increasing desire to write more serious fiction, however, made him chafe against the restrictions of the humor magazines, as well as against Leiken's insistence that he stick to jokes. Thus, when Aleksey S. Suvorin, the owner of the influential newspaper *Novoye vremya* (new times), asked Chekhov to contribute more substantial stories to his newspaper, Chekhov was pleased to comply. During 1886 and 1887, Chekhov wrote a large number of stories and short pieces for Suvorin, including some of his best-known stories. His second collection, *Pystrye rasskazy* (motley stories), was published in 1886, and a third, *V sumerkakh* (in the twilight), was published in 1887.

Still, Chekhov was not personally satisfied with his work, believing it to be ephemeral. Moreover, in 1886, he began to suspect that he had tuberculosis, although he refused to have another doctor give him an examination. In this spirit of anxiety about his health and dissatisfaction with his work, Chekhov left on a trip to his hometown in the Crimea to visit friends and relatives. This trip seemed to rejuvenate him, for several important stories of the provincial life of the people he encountered resulted from it. Perhaps the most important result of the journey, however, was his lyrical story "Step'" ("The Steppe," 1915), which was published in a highly reputable literary monthly in 1888. Following the story's publication, Chekhov was given the Pushkin Prize for literature by the Academy of Sciences. Even Chekhov himself could no longer doubt that his work had more than ephemeral value.

Also in 1888, Chekhov turned to writing plays, beginning with *Leshy* (1889; *The Wood Demon*, 1925), which was so poorly received that he quit writing serious drama until 1895. This failure, along with a general sense of malaise, what Chekhov called a stagnation in his soul, was the cause of his decision to take a most treacherous journey to the penal colony on Sakhalin Island in the Northern Pacific to learn about the living conditions of the prison inmates. Taking extraordinary means to study the geography and history of the island, he embarked on April 21, 1890, and arrived on July 11. Chekhov spent three months on the island and did enough research on the inmates, he said, for "three dissertations." Although *Ostrov Sakhalin* (1893; the Island of Sakhalin) was the formal result of the trip, more lasting fictional results are such stories as "V sylke" (1892; "In Exile," 1912) and "V ovrage" (1900; in the ravine).

On his return to Moscow, Chekhov once again had the urge to travel, this time to Europe. He found Vienna, Venice, Rome, and Florence overwhelming in the beauty of their art and landscapes. On his return, Chekhov purchased a country estate about fifty miles outside Moscow in Melikhovo, where he became a country gentleman and landowner and wrote many of his most famous stories, such as "Chorny monakh" (1892; "The Black Monk," 1903), "Palata No. 6" (1892; ward no. six), "Student" (1894; the student), "Muzhiki" (1897; peasants), and "Dom s mezoninom" (1896; the house with an attic).

In 1895, Chekhov began writing plays again, working on *Chayka* (*The Seagull*, 1909), which was first staged at St. Petersburg in October, 1896, but, partly because of the nature of the production, was an abysmal failure. Once again, Chekhov swore never to write plays. Shortly thereafter, his health worsened and he began to hemorrhage from the lungs. After entering a clinic, he was officially diagnosed as having tuberculosis and was advised to spend the winter months in a warm climate; he soon left for Nice, France. While Chekhov was in France, the Moscow Art Theater asked for permission to stage *The Seagull*. Although Chekhov first refused, he later agreed and went to Moscow to meet the cast. Among them was Olga Knipper, whom Chekhov would marry a few years later.

Chekhov's ill health again forced him to leave Moscow, this time for Yalta, where he had a house built. On December 17, 1898, *The Seagull* opened and was a tremendous success. Thus encouraged, Chekhov rewrote his first failure, *The Wood Demon*, and renamed it *Dyadya Vanya* (*Uncle Vanya*, 1914), which the Moscow Art Theater staged in 1899. The following year, when the troupe began a tour of the Crimea with both *The Seagull* and *Uncle Vanya* among their repertoire, Chekhov was at last able to see his two plays on the stage. He was also able to spend more time with Olga Knipper. Soon after, Chekhov finished his third play, *Tri sestry* (1901; *Three Sisters*, 1920). He and Olga Knipper were married on May 25, 1901.

In 1902, Chekhov's health took another turn for the worse; it is a tribute to his determination and genius that during this year he worked on his final play, *Vishnyovy sad* (*The Cherry Orchard*, 1908), and completed it in October. It was scheduled to premier on January 29, 1904, on his forty-fourth birthday; it was also presented in celebration of his twenty-five years as a writer. When Chekhov arrived at the theater after the third act, much to his embarrassment, he was honored with speeches and applause.

Chekhov went back to Yalta for the rest of the winter; on his return trip to Moscow in the spring, his health became worse. On June 4, he and his wife went to Berlin to see a specialist; from there, they went to Badenweiler, a spa in Germany. Chekhov died early in the morning on July 15, 1904. His body was shipped back in a refrigerator car to Moscow, where he was buried by his father.

Summary

Anton Chekhov was one of the most influential literary artists at the close of the nineteenth century to usher in the era of modernism in narrative fiction, particularly in short fiction. When his stories were first made widely available in English in the famous Constance Garnett translations between 1916 and 1923, they were termed sketches or slices of life, lacking in all the elements that constituted the short-story form. Critics soon began to realize, however, that Chekhov's freedom from the prevailing conventions of social realism and formalized plot indicated the beginnings of a modern kind of narrative, which combined the specific detail of realism with the poetic lyricism of Romanticism.

Chekhov's most significant contributions to the short-story form, contributions which have influenced modern writers such as Ernest Hemingway and Raymond Carver, include the following: the presentation of character as a lyrical or psychological mood rather than as a two-dimensional symbol or as a realistic personality; the conception of a story as a lyrical sketch rather than as a highly plotted tale; and the assumption of reality as basically impressionistic and as a function of narrative perspective or point of view. The final result of these innovations has been the modernist and postmodernist view of reality as a fictional construct.

With Chekhov, the short story took on a new respectability and began to be understood as the most appropriate narrative form to reflect the modern temperament. Today, most critics agree that there can be no understanding of the short story as a genre without an understanding of Chekhov's contribution to the form.

Bibliography

Clyman, Toby, ed. *A Chekhov Companion*. Westport, Conn.: Greenwood Press, 1985. A collection of critical essays, especially commissioned for this volume, on all aspects of Chekhov's life, art, and career. Some of the most important critics of Chekhov's work are represented here in essays on his major themes, his dramatic technique, his narrative technique, and his influence on modern drama and on the modern short story.

Hahn, Beverly. *Chekhov: A Study of Major Stories and Plays*. New York: Cambridge University Press, 1977. Hahn focuses on *The Cherry Orchard* as the principal Chekhov play with which to introduce his dramatic technique, although she does discuss the earlier plays as well. This study is particularly notable for its study of Chekhov's relationship with Tolstoy and of his depiction of women in his plays.

Hingley, Ronald. *Chekhov: A Biographical and Critical Study*. London: Unwin Books, 1950, rev. ed. 1966. Hingley provides a general introduction to the life and work of Chekhov, focusing on both Chekhov's language and his relationship to the social issues significant in Russia during that time.

_____. *A New Life of Anton Chekhov*. New York: Alfred A. Knopf,

1976. A more detailed and more thoroughly biographical study than Hingley's earlier work, this biography makes use of many documentary materials not previously available, particularly eight volumes of Chekhov's letters. It also focuses more on the mysterious subject of Chekhov's relationships with women than do previous studies.

Kirk, Irina. *Anton Chekhov*. Boston: Twayne, 1981. A general introduction to the life and art of Chekhov, focusing primarily on Chekhov's stories as being the embodiment of the search for a philosophy of life and the search for love and home. Although most of the book focuses on discussions of the stories, one final chapter analyzes the plays.

Pitcher, Harvey. *The Chekhov Play: A New Interpretation*. London: Chatto & Windus, 1973. A detailed discussion of the four Chekhov plays in the light of several premises Pitcher establishes about their basic nature: for example, that they focus primarily on the emotional side of life, that they follow a certain structural formula, that they follow the ensemble approach of the Moscow Art Theater, and that the language of the characters is dominated by a feeling of informality.

Pritchett, V. S. *Chekhov: A Spirit Set Free*. New York: Random House, 1988. This study by a master of the short story is neither straight biography nor literary criticism but rather a leisurely mixture of the two, with an emphasis on the latter. Pritchett discusses many of Chekhov's stories in detail and attempts to distill the essential qualities of his art.

Winner, Thomas. *Chekhov and His Prose*. New York: Holt, Rinehart and Winston, 1966. A chronological study of Chekhov's development as a story writer, from his beginnings as a writer of humorist anecdotes, to his experimentation with his impressionistic style, through his final concern with the Russian social scene.

Charles E. May

CHENG CH'ENG-KUNG

Born: August 28, 1624; Hirado, near Nagasaki, Japan
Died: June 23, 1662; Taiwan
Areas of Achievement: Government, politics, and the military
Contribution: Cheng was a Chinese sea lord who fought for the failing Ming
   Dynasty against the conquering Manchus. He incorporated Taiwan into
   the Chinese cultural and political systems.

Early Life

Cheng Ch'eng-kung was born in the declining years of the Ming Dynasty
(1368-1644). The Ming were steadily losing ground against the expanding
Manchus, who would soon rule China as the Ch'ing Dynasty (1644-1912).
Cheng Ch'eng-kung's father, Cheng Chih-lung, was born in 1601 in the
coastal province of Fukien. Like many Fukienese, he took to the sea. He
lived in the Portuguese colony of Macao, where he was baptized and known
to the Europeans as Nicholas Iquan. Asian waters were dangerous, and there
was a thin line between commerce and piracy. Cheng Chih-lung controlled a
pirate fleet of Chinese and Japanese adventurers and built a trading empire.

Cheng Ch'eng-kung was born August 28, 1624, in Hirado, Japan, where
his father had a Japanese wife of the Tagawa family. He lived with his
mother until he was seven, learning Japanese culture to such an extent that
the Japanese would later adopt him as a cultural hero, describing him as "a
Japanese with a Chinese father." Meanwhile, his father was becoming an
important political figure at the Ming court. Initially attacked as a pirate, he
was so powerful that the court had no option but to grant him office. He
agreed to defend the southern coast against other pirates.

Now more secure, Cheng Chih-lung brought the seven-year-old Cheng
Ch'eng-kung to live with him in China. The boy studied the classical writings that were the focus of Confucian education. Cheng Ch'eng-kung was a
talented, diligent student, who took his first degree at fifteen, entering the
Imperial Academy in 1644. Had he lived at another time, he might have
become a major Confucian scholar or holder of high office within the civil
bureaucracy, the ultimate goal of Confucian studies. The Ming Dynasty was
collapsing, however, before the Manchus, who were expanding southward
from their ancestral home in Manchuria.

The Manchus were a vigorous, seminomadic warrior race, who had learned
Confucian ways from long ties to China. Even many Chinese saw their rule
as preferable to that of the Ming, which had grown corrupt and oppressive.
The Ming lost their capital, Peking (and their last formally recognized emperor), to the Manchus in April, 1644. The successor to the throne founded a
second capital at Nanking, which fell in June, 1645; a third successor
founded another capital at Foochow, Fukien.

Life's Work

Fukien was virtually controlled by Cheng Chih-lung, a fact which made his eldest son and heir, the young Cheng Ch'eng-kung, even more important. Cheng Ch'eng-kung was presented to the emperor, who made him a member of the imperial clan. He was known at court as Kuo Hsing-yeh, or "lord of the imperial surname," from which Europeans would derive his Latinized name, Koxinga. Cheng Ch'eng-kung's father was ordered to guard the main pass into Fukien against the Manchus. Cheng Ch'eng-kung himself was drawn into the military defense of the failing regime and given the court rank of earl and the military title of field marshal in 1645.

His father foresaw the fate of the Ming, which had little legitimacy after losing two capitals and two emperors. The Manchus, presenting themselves as reformers rather than conquerors, offered office and rewards to any Chinese who joined them; Cheng Chih-lung came to terms and abandoned the pass. The conflict between family ties and loyalty to the state has always been a major one for all Chinese, and Cheng Ch'eng-kung must have been torn between his father and the Ming court. The traditional version of his life has it that he remonstrated with his father, calling him a traitor. Certainly the young man came to a decision which marked a turning point in his life: He decided to stay with the Ming. With the critical pass unguarded, Foochow fell to the Manchus, and the third refugee emperor killed himself in 1646. Cheng Ch'eng-kung left Fukien with a small band of followers (legend says ninety men) and sailed for the southern province of Kwangtung, centered upon the great international port Canton.

Within a year, Cheng Ch'eng-kung commanded a major fleet, whose forces, when operating on land, were a formidable army. Considering that he was only twenty-two years old, this was a remarkable achievement. Part of the explanation lies in his personal abilities and magnetism. As a successful scholar and court figure, he was much admired, but he was also a man of action. He was physically impressive and inspired awe in even prejudiced Europeans who would meet him later. Many of his father's forces also saw the elder Cheng's defection as immoral and rallied to Cheng Ch'eng-kung.

Cheng understood well the importance of traditional models to the historically minded Chinese and always presented himself within the established tradition of loyalty in the face of adversity. This adversity heightened when his mother, who had come to China sometime earlier, died at the fall of Amoy in Fukien. With his new fleet and army, Cheng now operated against the Manchus in Fukien, retaking lost territory. There was now yet another refugee Ming court, in Kwangtung, and he pledged loyalty to this fourth refugee emperor.

In Cheng's later life, there is often confusion between his commitment to the Ming and his commitment to self-interest. One event that highlights this ambiguity is Cheng's murder of his cousin, Cheng Lien, while retaking

Amoy. Later, he also executed an uncle. Removing these potential competitors gave him control of the Cheng family's land and sea empire, including southern Fukien and islands off Kwangtung.

With this base, Cheng began to operate in the key Yangtze River valley of central China, even trying, but failing, to retake Nanking in September, 1659. After mopping up other Ming loyalist forces, the Manchus turned their entire attention to Cheng and began to take his mainland bases. He decided that it was necessary to relocate to continue the fight. He turned to the island of Taiwan, across a narrow strait from Fukien. Taiwan had been largely ignored by the Chinese. Its small population was split about equally between aboriginal tribal peoples of Malayan descent and Chinese immigrants from Fukien, attracted to the island's rich agricultural lands. The Portuguese had first seen the island's importance as a base for trade and had given it its European name, Formosa. The Dutch saw it as an important adjunct to their base at Batavia in the Indonesian islands and seized it in 1624.

The Dutch had occupied the island easily, suppressing several local uprisings, thus growing contemptuous of Chinese warriors. The Dutch had only lightly defended the island when Cheng's fleet, about one thousand ships, appeared out of the morning mists on April 3, 1661. Several hundred Dutch infantrymen marched out to meet the battle-hardened veterans of the Manchu wars. Cheng's men "discharged so great a storm of arrows that they darkened the sky," in the words of a Dutch observer. The Dutch stubbornly defended their fortifications, which fell months later. The siege was savage, and many Dutch civilians died, including missionaries, women, and children. This siege made Cheng, or as he was now known, Koxinga, an exemplar of the ruthless Asian warlord to the Europeans in the tradition of Attila and Genghis Khan.

The Cheng family's control of Taiwan was a positive one, as Cheng and his descendants encouraged Chinese immigration and founded a Chinese educational and administrative system. Cheng did not live to see these successes; he died, probably of malaria, in June, 1662, at the age of thirty-seven. When the Manchus finally took the island from his heirs in 1683, it was indisputably Chinese and became a Chinese province. In 1949, Taiwan became the bastion of another refugee regime, the Nationalist Chinese, who had been defeated by Mao Tse-tung's Communist forces. Under their administration, Taiwan grew to become the second strongest economy in Asia after Japan.

Summary

Cheng Ch'eng-kung was at the center of the events of the seventeenth century, which saw a major realignment in power relations in East Asia, affecting China and the Western powers. These were violent times, and Cheng Ch'eng-kung had the necessary qualities to thrive in them: ruthlessness, martial talents, and immense self-confidence. As he told the Dutch negotiators when they surrendered to him in Taiwan: "If I wish to set my forces to work then I am able to move Heaven and Earth; wherever I go, I am destined to win." Although he was one of the few Chinese to be known by a Latinized name, showing his stature in Europe, his reputation was to be a dreadful one until the more accurate historical portrayals of the twentieth century. To the Japanese, he became a model Samurai adventuring in romantic China. To the Chinese, however, he was always to exemplify loyalty and perseverance in the face of certain defeat. Eventually, he was made a protective deity of popular religion in Taiwan, which he first incorporated into China.

Bibliography

Coyett, Fredric. *Neglected Formosa*. Translated by Inez de Beauclair. San Francisco: Chinese Materials Center, 1975. These are the memoirs of the last Dutch governor of Taiwan. They are a key source for the battle of Taiwan and were the primary influence upon European attitudes toward Cheng.

Croizier, Ralph C. *Koxinga and Chinese Nationalism: History, Myth, and the Hero*. Cambridge, Mass.: Harvard University Press, 1977. Considered the standard analysis of Cheng's life and its meaning for later Chinese, both Communist and anti-Communist, as well as for the Japanese and for Europeans. An analytical bibliography of sources in Chinese, Japanese, and English is included. Well written and balanced in its interpretations.

Davidson, James W. *The Island of Formosa, Past and Present*. London: Macmillan, 1903. This work is not only a very readable history of Taiwan but also the first positive Western account of Cheng.

Hummel, Arthur W., ed. *Eminent Chinese of the Ch'ing Period (1644-1912)*. Washington, D.C.: Government Printing Office, 1943-1944. The standard reference for the lives of Cheng Ch'eng-kung and for his father, Cheng Chih-lung.

Hung, Chien-chao. *Taiwan Under the Cheng Family: Sinicization After Dutch Rule*. Ann Arbor, Mich.: University Microfilms International, 1985. A detailed analysis of the Cheng family's administration of Taiwan. Hung argues that, without the Cheng occupation, Taiwan would not have become an integral part of China, and thus world history would be quite different.

Jeffrey G. Barlow

CH'IEN-LUNG
Hung-li

Born: September 25, 1711; Peking, China
Died: February 7, 1799; Peking, China
Area of Achievement: Government
Contribution: Ch'ien-lung presided over an empire unprecedented in size and power. Under his rule, China reached its apex, enjoying a long span of peace, order, and prosperity.

Early Life

The Manchus, a vassal tribe of China situated on its northeast border, rose against China as early as 1616, seizing control of all Manchuria by 1621. Between 1610 and 1640, there was much unrest in China itself, with various factions competing for power (that is the gentry, the literati, the eunuchs, and the military). Some rebellious generals defected to the Manchus, and, in April, 1644, the beleaguered Ming Dynasty emperor killed himself. The new emperor failed to gain sufficient support for defense of China, and in June, 1644, Manchu troops captured Peking. It took them another forty-plus years to bring the entire country under their rule, but by the 1680's the Ch'ing Dynasty was in complete control of all China.

The Ch'ing Dynasty (1644-1912) was in its ninety-second year when Ch'ien-lung took the throne. Grandson of K'ang-hsi, considered the greatest of the Ch'ing rulers, Ch'ien-lung modeled himself upon this vigorous ruler, successfully blending Chinese and Manchu traditions. As a youth, Ch'ien-lung studied Confucian ethics and Manchu military arts, his teachers being a mixture of Chinese and Manchu scholars. The required curriculum included the classics, history, literature, philosophy, and ritual performances.

Under the Ch'ing Dynasty, all important decisions came from the emperor. This centralization of power placed a great burden on the emperors to keep abreast of events in their vast empire. Succeeding his father, Yung-cheng, a harsh but able ruler, Ch'ien-lung depended upon a smooth-running administrative machine to help him in decision making.

The chief government organ in Ch'ing times was a grand (later, privy) council, whose members met with the emperor daily to advise him on overall policies; the grand secretariat handled routine business. Below these organs were the six ministries, each having a Manchu and a Chinese minister, along with two Manchu and two Chinese deputy ministers. At all levels of government, Chinese officials were present in large numbers. This was a major factor in the success and long rule of the Ch'ing Dynasty. Conscientious and responsible, Ch'ien-lung was assisted by competent statesmen in the first half of his reign. He made several inspection tours of the country, acquainting himself with many areas while satisfying his taste for grandeur.

Life's Work

Militarily, Ch'ien-lung's armies pacified Chinese Turkestan (Sinkiang) between 1745 and 1749. Burma was subjugated between 1766 and 1770. Outer Mongolia, long considered a security threat, was also subdued so that, by 1759, the Ch'ing Empire extended from Outer Mongolia in the north to Kwangtung in the south to Central Asia in the west. Taiwan, too, acknowledged Ch'ing overlordship, and neighboring counties sent tribute missions regularly to Peking, recognizing their dependence on China's goodwill.

Economically, Ch'ing China outstripped any previous dynasty with growth in three particular areas: commerce, agriculture, and manufacturing. Internal trade provided much revenue, with foreign trade gaining fast by the late eighteenth century. China traded worldwide, and the maritime provinces benefited in particular. Western traders were tightly controlled during the Ch'ing Dynasty—until the nineteenth century. Even before Ch'ien-lung's reign, they were confined to southern China, and, by government decree in 1757, all foreign trade was conducted in the port of Canton. Here, all foreigners were treated alike, as inferiors, bearing tribute to China.

The British were the greatest seapower and trading nation of the world by the eighteenth century, and they continually pressured China for more trade rights. Yet the Chinese had little knowledge of England's power or of international law as it was developing in Western Europe. Ch'ien-lung exemplified this ignorance in his decree (1793) addressed to King George III, in which he informs the king that "as to your entreaty to send one of your nationals to be accredited to my Celestial Court and to be in control of your country's trade with China, this request is contrary to all usage of my dynasty and cannot possibly be entertained." He goes on to state that "we possess all things . . . and have no use for your country's manufactures."

As in previous dynasties, China was a Confucian state, following strict Confucian principles. Among these was stratification of peoples by class and by nation. Within China, there was a huge gap between superiors and inferiors (upper and lower classes). In foreign relations, this same stratification showed itself in the Chinese term for foreigners: "barbarians." Some forty years after Ch'ien-lung's death, England and other European nations would no longer tolerate what they saw as Chinese arrogance and would open Chinese ports all along the coast by military force.

Agriculture provided the greatest share of Ch'ing revenue, reaching highest development during Ch'ien-lung's reign. Traditionally, Chinese farming was a precarious occupation. It was labor-intensive (dependent on human manpower), applied to small plots of land. Recurring problems were those of absentee landlords and high taxation. Yet conditions improved considerably by the eighteenth century. New crops were introduced (such as sweet potatoes, sorghum, and maize) that could be grown even on poor land. Diet improved and, with the widespread practice of irrigation and the use of better fertilizers, many peasants were prospering. Until the last twenty years of Ch'ien-lung's rule, peasants were only moderately taxed. Manufacturing reached a peak, also, in the eighteenth century with the textile industry, the largest, most productive of them all. The cotton-goods industry, tea plantations, and porcelain factories filled orders for the court and for wealthy families as well as for exports worldwide. The decorative arts were especially prized in foreign markets, testified to by a European craze for chinoiserie.

As a patron of the arts, Ch'ien-lung collected paintings and porcelains, and himself produced many poems and much calligraphy (not held in high repute). He sponsored a mammoth work entitled *Ssu-ku ch'üan-shu* (1782-1787; complete library of the four treasuries), containing more than thirty-six thousand volumes, with four main categories of literature: classics, history, philosophy, and belles lettres. Scholarship flourished with contributions on statecraft and philosophy. The function and evaluation of literature were debated, and original writings came under careful scrutiny, their historicity being challenged. Ch'ing writers produced many works—poetry, essays, short stories, and novels. There is a dark side to Ch'ien-lung's interest in and sponsorship of learning. Imperial control was strong, and so-called heretical, subversive authors were punished. Unacceptable books were burned; records list 13,862 works being destroyed between 1774 and 1782.

The last twenty or so years of Ch'ien-lung's reign were years of dynastic decline. Ironically, part of this was the result of agricultural growth and overall peace and prosperity: China underwent a population explosion. From 1741 to 1796, the population nearly doubled. Production failed to keep pace, and new strains developed on the economy, state, and society. Distant wars in Central Asia, Nepal, Burma, and Western Szechwan, as well as the upkeep of a luxurious court, further drained the state's resources. Administrative laxity and corruption made the government less effective and increasingly costly. As a taste for wealth spread through the upper classes, myriad new taxes burdened the lower classes, the peasants in particular.

In his later years, Ch'ien-lung became increasingly autocratic. During the mid-1770's, he bestowed his favor on a young general of the imperial body guard, Ho-shen, who exerted an all-powerful influence in government. Ho-shen appointed relatives and henchmen to high positions and amassed for himself a large fortune. Organized resistance to government inefficiency and corruption flourished in secret societies, among them the White Lotus Sect, which led an open rebellion in 1793. Another, more extensive revolt erupted in 1796, taking nine years to suppress. Ch'ien-lung abdicated in 1796, while continuing to rule behind the scenes. Upon his death in 1799, his protégé Ho-shen was arrested by the new emperor, Chia-ch'ing, and was allowed to commit suicide that same year. Yet the dynastic decline was well in motion, and Chia-ch'ing was unable to restore the former glory.

Summary

There is much to admire in Ch'ien-lung's long reign. Certainly, in the first forty years, he strove to be an enlightened ruler, well grounded in the arts of emperorship. Ch'ing China prospered, not unfit to be mentioned with the Han and T'ang Dynasties as a golden era. Highly centralized, the Ch'ing Dynasty of the eighteenth century thrived through a combination of military, economic, political, and social adaptations, and, under a benevolent despot such as Ch'ien-lung had been in his early years, China reached its apex of power and prestige.

In his old age, Ch'ien-lung failed to keep the reins of government firmly in hand, and he must bear the blame for much of China's subsequent weakness as it faced the onslaught of a new enemy, the encroaching Western nations. A major cause of the Ch'ing decline by the late eighteenth century was the lack of competent officials at all levels of government. Many were ignorant of the country outside the state and provincial capitals; many were underpaid and, therefore, were caught up in the struggle for wealth to achieve security for themselves and their families. Worse, Ch'ien-lung, like his predecessors and successors, failed to reform an antiquated civil service examination system. The examination system stressed Confucian values, rewarding humanistic achievements rather than science, technology, and industry. Its narrow scope and impractical nature did not help develop administrative ability. Free expression was stifled while orthodox thought was encouraged. Not until the late nineteenth century was the system challenged, and only in 1901 was reform actually implemented. By then it was too late, and the dynasty fell in 1912.

Bibliography

Eberhard, Wolfram. *A History of China*. Translated by E. W. Dickes. Berkeley: University of California Press, 1950. A survey of Chinese history from prehistorical times to the mid-1970's, with a special focus on social and cultural developments. Includes twenty pages on the Ch'ing Dynasty, an excellent chart and statistics on population growth, brief notes and references in an appendix, and an index.

Fairbank, John K., Edwin O. Reischauer, and Albert M. Craig. *East Asia: Tradition and Transformation*. Boston: Houghton Mifflin, 1973. Chapter 9, "Traditional China at Its Height Under the Ch'ing," is very helpful. Covers the rise of the dynasty, its administrative structures, military expansion, culture, and population growth. Includes fine pictures, maps, and a detailed index.

Gernet, Jacques. *A History of Chinese Civilization*. New York: Cambridge University Press, 1982. There are three chapters on the Ch'ing Dynasty. Chapter 23, "The Enlightened Despots," is most valuable. Includes maps and charts, a chronological table, and a helpful index and bibliography.

Hsü, Immanuel C. Y. *The Rise of Modern China*. New York: Oxford University Press, 1970. Chapters 2 and 3 are on the Ch'ing Empire with five pages on Ch'ien-lung's reign. Special concern is taken with political, intellectual, social, and economic history. Includes helpful tables and charts of statistics, and extensive bibliographies after each chapter.

Latourette, Kenneth S. *China*. Englewood Cliffs, N.J.: Prentice-Hall, 1964. Includes one brief chapter on the Ch'ing Dynasty but covers the great emperors up to 1800 with particular emphasis on military campaigns, economics, and foreign relations. Contains a bibliography after each chapter, an appendix of proper names and Chinese words used in the text, and an index.

Rodzinski, Witold. *The Walled Kingdom: A History of China from Antiquity to the Present*. New York: Free Press, 1984. Contains brief but concise chapters covering all the dynasties and into the post-Mao era. Chapter 7, "China Under Manchu Rule," is most pertinent. Covers foundation, culture, and decline of the dynasty, and is critical of the Manchu emperors. Includes excellent maps, a page of suggested readings, and an index.

Schirokauer, Conrad. *Modern China and Japan*. New York: Harcourt Brace Jovanovich, 1982. Chapter 1, "China Under the Manchus," is brief but thorough. Covers geography, the reign of Ch'ien-lung, politics, economics, and the arts. Includes a fine map and illustrations, brief notes after each chapter, an annotated bibliography at the end of the book, and an index.

S. Carol Berg

FRÉDÉRIC CHOPIN

Born: March 1, 1810; Żelazowa Wola, Poland
Died: October 17, 1849; Paris, France
Area of Achievement: Music
Contribution: Chopin achieved eminence in two usually distinct areas of music: as a performer and as a composer. He became the foremost pianist of his time, despite the fact that his delicate style and unwillingness to perform in public placed him outside contemporary fashion and practice. His eminence as a composer is equally startling, for unlike every other composer of comparable stature, Chopin devoted himself almost exclusively to keyboard music. Against what some have perceived as the narrowness of his interests, one may posit the brilliance and diversity of his compositions.

Early Life

Frédéric Chopin was born in the Polish village of Żelazowa Wola, located thirty-four miles from the then-provincial city of Warsaw. His mother, Justyna, was the well-educated daughter of an impoverished, upper-class family. His father, Nicholas, a Frenchman by birth, was employed as a tutor by another and more well-to-do branch of that same family, the Skarbeks. Shortly after Frédéric's birth, the family moved to Warsaw, where Nicholas eventually secured a position as a teacher of French at the Lyceum. Impressed by the playing of his mother and older sister, Ludwika, Chopin began to play the piano at the age of four or five. At six he was already composing and taking lessons from Wojciech Zwyny. His first published work, the Polonaise in G Minor, appeared when he was only seven, and he made his first public appearance the following year (1818) at a charity concert. Soon afterward, he played before Poland's Grand Duke Konstantine and in 1825 was selected to demonstrate the aeolomelodicon before Czar Alexander I. While still a student at the Lyceum (1823-1826), Chopin began taking lessons from Josef Elsner, director of the Warsaw Conservatory. Elsner proved an especially fortunate choice; himself inclined toward the Romanticism that Chopin would perfect, he was willing to bend his own strict academic standards to accommodate his student's evident genius. While under Elsner's tutelage, Chopin composed his first major work, a set of variations on Wolfgang Amadeus Mozart's "La ci darem" from *Don Giovanni* (1787), which evidenced a surprising originality and maturity. The trip he made to Berlin in 1828 seems to have whetted his appetite for travel and, more important, for a wider musical world than Warsaw could then provide, and so, after having their request for a travel scholarship rejected by the government, his parents financed his 1829 trip to Vienna themselves. There with the help of a letter of introduction from Elsner, Chopin secured a publisher for his Mozart variations and, as part of his agreement with the publisher, Tobias Haslinger, gave a free concert in order to advertise his work. In fact, Chopin gave two concerts while in Vienna, both of which were successful. His audience was surprised by the lightness of his touch and delighted by his technical skills and use of Polish materials. Upon his return to Warsaw, he fell in love with Konstantia Gladkowska and continued to be well received by Polish audiences. Chopin grew restive, however, and on November 2, 1830, he again journeyed to Vienna, this time accompanied by his close friend, Tytus Wojciechkowski. News of the Polish revolt against the Russians reached them later that month. Wojciechkowski immediately returned to Poland. Chopin, at the urging of his family, remained in Vienna, where he expected to repeat his earlier success. In this he was mistaken. The few concerts he gave attracted little attention and even less cash. After eight months he left Vienna for Paris, learning en route that the revolt had failed and Warsaw had fallen.

Life's Work

Until his death nineteen years later, Paris was to be Chopin's home. The city was then the center of European culture, and thanks to a Viennese friend, Chopin quickly gained entrance to its cultural life. Just as important, Paris was also home to a large number of Polish émigrés, including Adam Mickiewicz, an exile, a poet, and a patriot. Unlike Mickiewicz, Chopin could return to Poland but chose not to do so. Although sensitive to the plight of his countrymen and even supportive of many of them, Chopin was not an activist; nor are his works nationalist in the same sense or to the same degree that Mickiewicz's poems and plays clearly are. Himself half French, Chopin quickly adapted to his new home, largely because it received him so warmly. His first concert on February 26, 1832, attended by Franz Liszt and Felix Mendelssohn, was a decided success, and in the autumn of that year he was invited to play for the Rothschilds. Having gained entry into the highest level of Parisian society, Chopin quickly became the most fashionable and highest paid piano teacher in the city. Financially secure, he could afford to give up the public concert hall performances he disliked so much and which were so ill-suited to both the character of his music and the delicacy of his playing. His immense and financially rewarding success in the salons of Paris, however, extracted its own price. By the 1830's, an important shift had occurred in the world of music. Aristocratic patrons of the arts, especially music, had begun to play a less significant role, while the mass audience was beginning to exert a far greater influence than ever before. Liszt's style of music and playing was well suited to this new audience; Chopin's was not. The aristocratic salons of Paris therefore played a most important role in nurturing Chopin's genius, but not without limiting or at least misunderstanding it as well, for what the Rothschilds and others prized was not Chopin's compositions but his playing, his imitations, and his improvisations in particular.

Three years after his introduction into this world, there began a sequence of events that was to have a profound effect on Chopin's life and art. Chopin met and fell in love with Maria Wodzinska in 1835, but when he proposed marriage, the family, having heard the rumors of the composer's poor health, refused to give their consent. Disappointed, Chopin paid a short visit to England and within the year had begun his famous liaison with Amandine-Aurore-Lucile Dupin, or George Sand, as she is better known. It was Sand who made the first overtures (in 1836), and these Chopin refused, disturbed by her evident masculinity. Yet in 1837 he became as passionately drawn to her as she was to him. Over the next nine years, he would transform that passion into some of his greatest music. (Over the same period, Sand's passion would undergo a quite different change in the direction of maternal devotion.) At Sand's suggestion, they spent the winter of 1838-1839 on the Island of Majorca. Poor food and even worse weather, coupled with the islanders' fear of contagion caused by Chopin's tubercular condition as well as their distaste for this evidently immoral bohemian household, made composing difficult and the worsening of Chopin's health inevitable. They returned to the mainland in February, but the seriousness of Chopin's condition (he had begun to hemorrhage) forced them to delay their arrival at Sand's country home in Nohant until June. Located 180 miles south of the French capital, Nohant was well suited to Chopin's needs. Sensitive to noise and other distractions, and physically weak, Chopin always found it difficult to write while in Paris, and so the summers he spent at Nohant (1839, 1841-1849) proved to be especially rewarding. Even as his art advanced, the relationship with Sand deteriorated into recriminations and finally separation, first as her passion cooled and then as the result of plots hatched by her two grown children.

Chopin's physical decline, which had begun on Majorca and which had worsened upon his learning of his father's death (May 3, 1844), advanced more precipitously following his estrangement from Sand. On February 16, 1848, he gave his first public concert in ten years; it was also the last one he would ever give in Paris. A second concert had been planned but had to be canceled when revolution broke out in the city's streets. The revolution of 1848 put an end not only to the French monarchy but to Chopin's patronage as well. Out of necessity, he accepted an invitation from Jane Stirling, a wealthy former pupil, to visit Great Britain. After spending much of the year traveling and performing in London and Scotland, Chopin returned to Paris in late 1848, too weak either to write or to teach. Generously supported by the Stirlings and comforted by his sister, he continued to decline. His death occurred on October 17, 1849, but preparations were so elaborate that the funeral had to be delayed nearly two weeks. Some three thousand mourners were in attendance as the funeral march from his Sonata in B Minor and (at Chopin's own request) Mozart's *Requiem* were played. Chopin was buried in Paris, and his heart was interred in Warsaw.

Summary

For Frédéric Chopin, playing and composing were integrally related. A brilliant if unusual performer, he preferred to be judged chiefly as a composer, and it was to this end that he increasingly devoted himself from the late 1830's onward. Chopin gave no public concerts from 1838 until 1848; in fact, he gave only thirty public performances during his entire career. Yet as Derek Melville has noted, "Curiously enough, the less he played in public, the more legendary he became." Unfortunately, the acclaim he received as early as 1837 as Europe's greatest pianist overshadowed his work as a composer. Even after his death, Chopin's compositions have rarely been given the credit they are due. That he wrote almost exclusively for the piano has been misunderstood as a major limitation, one that has barred him from the ranks of greatness. While his contribution to harmonic development has been acknowledged, critics have tended to slight his overall achievement.

The narrow range of that achievement is not a sign of weakness, however, but of a strength comparable to what his near contemporary, the novelist Jane Austen, managed to achieve on her "inch of ivory." To defend Chopin's breadth is impossible, and to defend his sense of musical structure along conventional lines is fruitless. This is not to say that he was, as often accused, inattentive to form or unable "to develop his materials on a large scale." Chopin's great strength lies not in his adherence to the conventions but in his innovations, including his use of a "departure and return pattern" in many of his works and his experimentation with organic form in a number of his later ones. When he felt the need, he was more than willing to learn and to adopt traditional techniques, such as counterpoint, which he began to study in earnest only in the 1840's. The very real narrowness of range of Chopin's oeuvre needs, therefore, to be reevaluated. As a performer, Chopin was physically too frail to compete with his contemporaries in terms of virtuosity and dramatic effects, and as a result both as performer and as composer he chose, or was perhaps forced, to explore and exploit the subtleties of his playing, his music, and his medium, the piano, in compositions and performances far better suited to the intimacy of the salon than to the impersonal space of the concert hall. Moreover, although he wrote almost exclusively for the piano, he did so with incredible variety: waltzes, nocturnes, preludes, études, scherzos, polonaises, and mazurkas, with the emphasis clearly on the solo piano (139 of his 167 compositions). In his desire to make the piano imitate the human voice, Chopin utterly transformed keyboard music and keyboard technique. One needs to realize that in Chopin's age, the piano was essentially a new instrument. The introduction of leather-bound hammers, for example, made possible the production of much softer tones than in previous times. Although it was John Field and J. N. Hummel who first began to compose music adapted to this new instrument and sound, it was Chopin who came to exploit the piano so masterfully.

Legend often portrays Chopin as at best a melancholy Romantic and at worst a pampered high society narcissist. Fact portrays a quite different figure, fashionable in his dress and fastidious in his conduct, sickly and shy, less proud than committed to his art, and not so much a recluse as an introvert. The facts are perhaps too few to draw as complete a portrait as one might like. For this reason one many turn to the music to distinguish more definitely the character of the man from the qualities of his music: passionate yet introspective; emotional but never sentimental; delicate and refined; expressive yet restrained; as much concerned with perfection as with originality. In many respects, he is the very embodiment of Romanticism, yet he is a strange avatar of the Romantic movement, for his music was clearly influenced by the classical style of Johann Sebastian Bach and Mozart at least as much as it was by the Italian opera of his own age. Chopin's influence on others has, however, been far greater than anyone's on him: on the keyboard music of Liszt, Arnold Schönberg, and others, and on the use of national—especially folk—materials by Antonín Dvořák, Manuel de Falla, Pyotr Ilich Tchaikovsky, and others. Chopin stands as the first and perhaps the most important of the modern composers who have become aware that the breadth, grandeur, and order that were both possible and inevitable in the classical period may no longer be advisable even if they are technically still possible. Narrowness, or specialization, Chopin proved, has its own possibilities and its own frontiers.

Bibliography

Abraham, Gerald. *Chopin's Musical Style*. London: Oxford University Press, 1939. A brief but important study of the "unfolding and maturing of Chopin's musical style," intended chiefly, but by no means exclusively, for performers and students of harmony. Abraham distinguishes three significant periods of development (1822-1831, 1831-1840, and 1841-1849) but fails to discuss the problems of chronology within each period. Nor does he consider the origins of Chopin's style. Nevertheless, long considered the standard work on the subject.

Chopin, Fryderyk. *Chopin's Letters*. Edited by Henryk Opienski. Translated by E. L. Voynich. New York: Alfred A. Knopf, 1931. Although it has been largely superseded by later editions, Opienski's work is noteworthy both for its relative extensiveness (given the time it was published) and for the excellence of Voynich's translations from the original Polish and French. The dating of many items is, however, incorrect.

_____. *Selected Correspondence of Fryderyk Chopin*. Edited and translated by Arthur Hedley. New York: McGraw-Hill, 1963. This volume is abridged from Chopin's correspondence, collected and edited by Bronislaw Edward Sydow. Although less exhaustive than Sydow's volume of nearly eight hundred items, Hedley's book does add appreciably to the slimmer Opienski work. Yet Hedley not only omits pieces included in Sydow but also abridges a number of items. Even so, this is an indispensable volume; the eleven-page appendix concerning the history and inauthenticity of the erotic "Chopin-Potocka Letters" is especially interesting.

Hedley, Arthur. *Chopin*. London: J. M. Dent & Sons, 1947. Especially noteworthy because Hedley's *Chopin* does not merely summarize previous scholarship. Recognizing the inadequacy of the standard English-language study, Frederick Niecks' *Fredrick Chopin* (1888), Hedley has examined materials at first hand and many for the first time. He devotes somewhat more than half of his authoritative study to Chopin's biography and the remainder to discussions of Chopin as performer, as teacher, and as composer and of Chopin's works according to type.

Huneker, James. *Chopin: The Man and His Music*. New York: Charles Scribner's Sons, 1900. Trained as a pianist, Huneker was the foremost American music critic at the time he wrote this study. Enthusiastic and knowledgeable, he devotes the first third of this book to biographical analysis, the import of which is clearly evident in his chapter titles "The Artist" and "Poet and Psychologist." The remaining chapters deal with each of the various kinds of musical compositions Chopin wrote.

Melville, Derek. *Chopin*. Hamden, Conn.: Linnet Books, 1977. Part of the Concertgoer's Companion series, Melville's book includes a surprising amount of material in its very few (108) pages. Besides going unnecessarily far in his efforts to undermine the credibility of George Sand's remarks about Chopin, Melville's writing is balanced and especially well informed. His lengthy annotated bibliography of works in English about Chopin and his music (pp. 62-78) is particularly useful.

Robert A. Morace

CHRISTINA

Born: December 8, 1626; Stockholm, Sweden
Died: April 19, 1689; Rome
Areas of Achievement: Monarchy and patronage of the arts
Contribution: Under Christina's short rule, Sweden benefited politically and socially through the Treaty of Westphalia, which brought an end to the devastating Thirty Years' War, and culturally by the importation of many works of art and manuscripts from cultural centers of Europe. During her residence in Rome, Christina was an enthusiastic patron of the arts, founding the learned society Accademia Reale in 1674, a precursor to the Accademia dell'Arcadia of eighteenth century Italy.

Early Life

Christina, Queen of Sweden from 1644 until her abdication in 1654, was born on Decmeber 8, 1626, daughter to the beloved King Gustavus II Adolphus of Sweden and his mentally unstable wife, Maria Eleonora, daughter of the Elector of Brandenburg. Gustavus was not only a war hero of epic proportions but also the famed Protestant king and commander of the Swedish troops in the Thirty Years' War as well as the last male member of the Protestant branch of the royal Wasa family. Christina was the only one of the couple's children to survive beyond her first year and was convinced that she was hated by her mother because of her sex—both mother and father had hoped for a male heir to the throne. Yet Gustavus accorded all the ceremony and honor to his daughter that a prince would have received, and he made her his heiress before the Riksdag in 1630. When Gustavus was killed at the Battle of Lützen in 1632, his five-year-old princess became queen, although she did not begin ruling until she reached eighteen years of age.

The young Christina showed an intellectual bent unusual for females of her time; she spent long hours studying and, apparently, preferred this activity to all others. The young queen displayed the same talent for languages that her father had possessed; she learned German, French, and Latin rapidly, reading Livy, Terence, Cicero, and Sallust. Soon she developed a liking for Cornelius Tacitus, who was one of her father's favorite writers and not an easy one to comprehend.

Christina's appearance also set her apart from other women. Her gait was mannish; she spoke in a deep, booming voice; and she showed a lack of interest in fine clothing and adornment. This latter trait developed in later years into a penchant for wearing (often shabby or dirty) men's clothes with little or no jewelry. She was decidedly homely, though portraits reveal large, beautiful eyes. In addition, her exceptional skill in horseback riding surpassed that of most men of her court.

Major figures in the young queen's life included the Chancellor Axel

Oxenstierna, her tutor in statesmanship, who essentially ruled in her minority; Bishop John Matthiae, her religious instructor, who was primarily responsible for teaching her tolerance of other religions; and Countess Catherine Palatine, her paternal aunt, who came closest to providing the young girl with a normal mother figure until Christina's mother sent her away. Maria Eleonora seems to have been too warped by grief to be able to nurture her child properly; in addition, the queen mother kept dwarves and buffoons at court, characters that frightened Christina, who was also misshapen. Oxenstierna and other advisers to the late king removed Maria Eleonora to Uppsala, fearing that her instability and prolonged, ostentatious grief would prove harmful to her daughter. Christina's childhood was therefore essentially lonely and devoid of a proper family environment.

An early romantic interest blossomed for Christina in her early teens, and she and her cousin Charles Gustavus (later Charles X of Sweden) became secretly engaged. By the time she reached the throne, however, her feelings for him had cooled, possibly as a result of her passionate if unanswered affection for the courtier Magnus De la Gardie; they never married. During this time, she also made the acquaintance of Countess Ebba Sparre, her best female friend (Christina had otherwise little interest in women), who may have been Christina's lover.

Life's Work

Christina's adult life lends itself to a discussion of two distinct time periods: her Swedish reign and her postabdication travels and eventual permanent residence in Rome. She came to power in Sweden during a particularly difficult time. The Thirty Years' War had been raging for twenty-six years, a situation that had taxed the Swedish population in terms of both men and money. In addition, the politics at the court itself featured a strengthened nobility worried about possible land confiscations to improve the royal finances. Christina proved herself to be an astute politician and strategist but a profligate spender with little comprehension of economic affairs. She improved Sweden's diplomatic relations with France, to some degree through her personal friendship with the French minister (later ambassador) Pierre-Hector Chanut, and brought her country to temporary, welcome peace by the Treaty of Westphalia. She strengthened the power of the Crown vis-à-vis the nobility by means of clever strategies, aligning herself with the estates of the bourgeoisie and the peasantry. Yet the royal finances continued to deteriorate.

For all of her enjoyment of diplomatic intrigues and political power (things she did not cease to seek even after her abdication), her spiritual life was apparently lacking. She had been reared in the Lutheran faith but had been repelled by its austerity and sternness; her religious instructor, Matthiae, had taught her religious tolerance. The war booty from the Continent, which boasted sumptuous Italian paintings, vibrant tapestries, and volumes of hitherto (in Sweden) unknown literature, introduced her to the cultural wealth, lacking in her native land, that the more southerly countries of Europe had to offer. Although Christina called, among others, foreign artists, musicians, doctors, and philosophers (including René Descartes) to her court to try to fill the cultural void, she soon realized that she could not remain in spartan Sweden. She chose to abdicate, a decision to which her unrequited love for De la Gardie may have contributed. She prepared for this step with great care, ensuring that her own candidate for the succession, her cousin and former fiancé Charles Gustavus, was officially accepted by the Riksdag as the heir to her throne. During this time, she became attracted to the Catholic religion, a faith with greater appeal to her aesthetic sense than Protestantism (it is recorded that she actually subscribed to her own private religion), and received instruction in secret from Italian Jesuit priests, for Catholicism was still illegal in Sweden at the time. Although the Riksdag refused initially to accept her bid for abdication, she persisted, citing as grounds her intention never to marry, her "weaker" sex, and her wish to retreat into private life. She also probably allowed an inkling of her Catholic interest to be perceived. It would have been a terrible embarrassment to Sweden if the daughter of its Protestant hero had converted to the opposing religion. To retain her on the throne would have been unthinkable. Her decision was accepted, and she abdicated on June 6, 1654.

After her abdication, Christina left in disguise for the Spanish Netherlands; the sponsor of her conversion to Catholicism was Philip IV of Spain. After a stay in Brussels, she continued to Innsbruck, where she made her formal profession of the Catholic faith on November 3, 1655; Pope Alexander VII received her in Rome with lavish ceremonies on December 23 of the same year. There she met Cardinal Decio Azzolino, who later became her closest friend and, some believe, her paramour; he supported her with advice and friendship for the remainder of her life, dying two months after she did as her sole heir.

Christina was not content to live quietly in Rome, practicing her new faith. Her interest in politics kept her in touch with the most powerful figures of Europe; on a more prosaic level, she needed money to maintain her extravagant life-style. Although she thought that she had provided for steady financial support by securing for herself the income from Sweden's Baltic possessions and other lands, political unrest and poor or dishonest administration of these areas made her financial situation shaky at best. For these reasons, she went to France in 1656 and entered into secret negotiations with Cardinal Jules Mazarin to place her on the throne of Naples, a political dream that was foiled, partially through the treachery of a member of her entourage, Gian Rinaldo Monaldeschi. She had him murdered at Fontainebleau on November 10, 1657, an act which later prevented her from ascending the Polish throne (to which she actually had some claim) and which gave her a reputation for bloodthirstiness. In 1660 and 1667, Christina made trips to Sweden, primarily to protect her financial interests. Finally, in 1668, she returned to Rome, where she remained until her death.

In her adopted home, the now-round, stout queen, eccentric as ever, continued her involvement in politics and culture; she supported certain papal candidates during conclaves and founded learned societies, in particular the Accademia Reale. She invited singers and other musicians to her rented palace, the Palazzo Riario, and bought works of art which were displayed there. Christina worked on her autobiography (of which there are several drafts extant) and began writing aphorisms, which are often rather unoriginal but occasionally revelatory of her feelings toward Azzolino. She died in the aftermath of a stroke on April 19, 1689.

Summary

Christina has never quite died in terms of controversy over her reputation. She has been by turns slandered and revered, seen as a murderess of her lovers and as a saint who sacrificed her crown for religion. Clearly the fact that she was female and that she never married contributes to the fascination surrounding her. She was an anachronism in some ways; a woman with a strong personality and a sharp intellect would fit into the modern world much more smoothly than into the Baroque Age. It was perhaps partly her own inability to feel comfortable in her time that made her restlessly give up one crown, go on to seek two or three others, and change religions and homelands. Her attractive personality reaches across time to pull modern readers and historians into her sphere, as the physically plain queen was able to attract young courtiers, cardinals, and even noblewomen to her. Christina remains enigmatic, and perhaps this is why much of what has been written about her has focused on the questions of whether she had sexual relations with Sparre, Azzolino, Monaldeschi, or other members of her court, or on questions of her alleged hermaphroditism or lesbianism.

Yet Christina made a lasting contribution to Swedish and Italian cultural life. She commanded that libraries from the Continent be bought and shipped to Sweden, modeled the Swedish court on that of Louis XIV, and surrounded herself with many talented minds. In Rome, she continued to support the arts to the extent that her reduced means allowed, making her home a meeting place for culture and scholarship.

Bibliography

Goldsmith, Margaret. *Christina of Sweden: A Psychological Biography.* Garden City, N.Y.: Doubleday, Doran, 1933. A straightforward biography that is, despite the title, not of a particularly psychological orientation. The thesis and conclusion, that Christina left no mark on history, leads one to wonder why the author decided to write about this important figure. The bibliography is useful.

Gribble, Francis. *The Court of Christina of Sweden and the Later Adventures of the Queen in Exile*. New York: Mitchell Kennerley, 1913. Despite the title, this work is actually also a biography of Christina with a good discussion of her aphorisms presented in the last two chapters. The author sees, perhaps correctly, the relationship with Azzolino as the most important aspect of her life. Contains illustrations and an excellent annotated index.

Mackenzie, Faith Compton. *The Sibyl of the North: The Tale of Christina, Queen of Sweden*. London: Cassell, 1931. A nonscholarly biography, written in a chatty style, with a tendency to romanticize. Too much attention is paid to Christina's alleged love affairs. Contains a short bibliography, an annotated index, and four illustrations.

Masson, Georgina. *Queen Christina*. New York: Farrar, Straus & Giroux, 1968. An excellent, informative introduction that proceeds chronologically from a brief overview of Gustavus' career to the funding of a monument to Christina by Clement XI in 1701. Gives succinct and helpful explanations of the often-confusing historical events of the seventeenth century. Includes a well-organized bibliography, an annotated index, and interesting illustrations.

Taylor, Ida A. *Christina of Sweden*. London: Hutchinson, 1909. An old-fashioned biography that, though engaging and basically accurate, suffers from its Victorian cast. Includes an annotated index and illustrations of major figures.

Woodhead, Henry. *Memoirs of Christina, Queen of Sweden*. London: Hurst and Blackett, 1863. This standard, two-volume treatment is indispensable for the serious student. It is well documented and gives a full picture of the political and historical climate surrounding Christina. The author takes the view that, despite her personal flaws, Christina made a considerable contribution to society. A selection of her aphorisms is given in English translation at the end.

Kathy Saranpa Anstine

CLAUDE LORRAIN

Born: 1600; Chamagne, Lorraine, France
Died: November 23, 1682; Rome
Area of Achievement: Art
Contribution: Claude established landscape in Roman and French painting as a subtle and varied means of artistic expression on an equal level with the older genres of religious and historical painting. He is one of the greatest masters of all time in the ideal landscape.

Early Life

Claude Gellée, known to the French as le Lorrain, was born in the village of Chamagne in the Duchy of Lorraine, the third of five sons. In 1612, his parents died and he went to Freiburg im Breisgau to live with an elder brother, Jean, a wood-carver. In 1613, he accompanied a relative to Rome and remained there to become a pastry cook. In this capacity, he obtained employment in the house of Agostino Tassi, the landscape painter. Gradually he learned the rudiments of painting from Tassi, who became his principal master at this time. Claude may have been one of the apprentices employed by the Cavalier d'Arpino and Tassi on the decoration of the Villa Lante, Bagnaia, which was completed by 1616.

At some time between 1616 and 1622, Claude went to Naples to work under the Flemish artist known in Italy as Goffredo Wals. This visit had a lasting effect on Claude. He was haunted by the beauty of the Gulf of Naples and reproduced to the end of his life the coast from Pozzuoli to Sorrento. In April, 1625, Claude departed from Rome for Nancy, the capital of Lorraine. There he worked as assistant to the Lorrainese court painter Claude Deruet painting architectural backgrounds to his vault frescoes for the Carmelite church. By the beginning of 1627, Claude returned to Rome. He remained in Rome until his death, with only one recorded absence, in 1660.

In 1627, Claude painted for both Italians and foreigners and was commissioned by Cardinal Guido Bentivoglio to make two landscapes, but no certain works by him survive from before 1630. During the early 1630's, he was active chiefly as a fresco decorator in the Palazzi Crescenzi and Muti. Although the fine quality of the Muti frescoes was a major factor in establishing his artistic reputation, he never again worked in the fresco medium.

Life's Work

Still comparatively unknown in 1633, by 1638 Claude was the leading landscape painter in Italy, with commissions to his credit from the pope, several cardinals, the King of Spain, and the French ambassador. From that time, patrons were never lacking, and his paintings, which fetched high prices, were in demand by both Italian and foreign collectors. At this time,

Claude's style began to attract the attention of imitators and forgers. In 1634, the artist Sébastien Bourdon thought it profitable to copy Claude's style and pass off one of his own paintings as a work of Claude. As a measure of his artistic reputation, in 1635 Claude began to record his compositions in the *Liber veritatis* (book of truth). Though incomplete at first, the *Liber veritatis*, from 1640 onward, formed a virtually complete inventory of Claude's production.

In addition to the influence of his early master Tassi, the roots of Claude's landscape style can be traced to the Dutchman Paul Brill and the German Adam Elsheimer. In Rome, Brill and Tassi had developed the late mannerist landscape tradition. This style, with its artificial nature, consists of the division of the picture into areas of dark greenish-brown foreground, light green middle distance, and blue hills on the far distant horizon. Each area of the composition is set out in coulisses, side pieces at either side of a stage arranged to give room for exits and entrances, starting from a dark tree in the foreground to create a sense of infinite distance. This artificiality of design is combined with stylized treatment of the trees, painted in a set formula of feathery fronds in silhouette. In paintings of the early 1630's, such as *The Mill* (1631), Claude followed Brill closely. The influence of Elsheimer is more evident in Claude's etchings of this period.

As a result of these influences, Claude developed a style that is neither as heroic nor as classical as that of his great contemporary Nicolas Poussin, but rather is capable of expressing both a more poetic mood and a livelier sense of the beauty and variety of nature. The most significant element of this style is his varied treatment of atmosphere and light: the calm glow of evening, the brilliance of noon, the cool light of early morning. Claude studied these carefully on his frequent sketching excursions into the Roman countryside using pen, wash, and even oils. He represented these lights with a subtlety unparalleled in his time and not excelled before Impressionism. Whereas Elsheimer explored the strong dramatic effects of moonlight or dark twilight, Claude aimed at serenity, minimizing value contrasts in order to preserve the calm unity of the whole.

The light of Claude's paintings usually emanates from an area of the sky immediately above the horizon, so that the viewer may gaze directly or almost directly into it. It spreads forward and outward through the composition, permeating the whole landscape with its radiance and joining background and foreground in one continuous spatial unity. By the late 1630's, Claude had carried these effects almost to the point of exaggeration. Shadowy masses of trees in the foreground are contrasted with a misty sunlit vista. In several of the seaport scenes, a corridor of light emanates from the sun, just visible above the horizon. The *Harbor Scene* (1634) is one of the earliest examples of this phenomenon in the history of painting.

Claude was intrigued by the pastoral life described in the poems of Vergil as well as by the mythic age when Aeneas founded Rome. Some works even depict themes from this early phase of the *Aeneid*. His knowledge of Vergil came through translations and conversations with learned friends, since he was not a Latin scholar. The pastoral illustrations from the *Vatican Virgil*, which was studied by his friends, along with actual Roman frescoes of country landscapes and architectural scenes, also influenced his development. Claude's painting at times included ruins, and it was an essential part of his intention to create a feeling of nostalgia for the past.

Claude did not develop a composition logically from the particular theme of a painting. His concern, which went beyond the theme of any given work, was the beauty of the Roman landscape which, in its pictorial possibilities, had gone unnoticed. The scenes he painted were given significance by his understanding of the particular light which bathes them. In short, the content of Claude's paintings is actually a poetic rendition of the subtle, changing light and atmosphere of the countryside.

Between 1640 and 1660, Claude refined his complete mastery over every type of landscape painting. His style became calmer and the lighting more diffused as in *The Marriage of Isaac and Rebecca* (1648). An idyllic pastoral mood permeates many of these mature landscapes. He turned to both sacred and classical literature for subject matter and included a conventional type of Arcadian shepherd for the pastoral scenes. He selected and combined all the familiar pictorial elements—tall trees against the sky, villages, distant hills, winding streams, fragments of classical architecture, large bodies of water—in such a way as to convey a sense of repose and enchantment.

In Claude's late phase, 1660-1682, the earlier process of idealization, of setting the imaginary world of the painting at a distance from the real world, was taken much further. The human figure, never very important, was reduced to insignificance, totally dominated by the scenery. His last paintings, such as *Ascanius and the Stag* (1682), represent a dreamland in which the forms are so shadowy that they hardly interrupt the continuity of the air in which light has a mysterious magical property.

Claude was a respected member of the colony of foreign artists in Rome. He remained on good terms with Poussin until his death in 1665. Claude never married but had a daughter, Agnese, born in 1653, who lived with him until his death. Though he amassed a small fortune, he lived frugally and quietly and had no ambitions beyond the pursuit of his art. He was seriously ill in 1663, suffered from gout in his later years, and died on November 23, 1682. He was buried in the French Church of Trinità dei Monti, above Piazza di Spagna in Rome. Biographies of him were first published by his friend Joachim von Sandrart in 1675 and by Filippo Baldinucci in 1728.

Summary

Claude Lorrain brought to its limit the study of light and atmosphere as a means of creating imaginative, pictorial unity. The experience of drawing had major significance for his paintings. He made many finished preparatory sketches and etchings for paintings which often reveal the evolution of his design. Claude's drawings illustrate the wide range and intensity of his observations. There is an endless variety to his sketches made from nature, and they are often bolder than his paintings. Most of the nature drawings, which include rapid pen sketches, black chalk, washes, and oils, were done before 1645. The majority of these embody some unexpected effect of light: changing light in a valley, a path through a sunlit wood, a tree seen *contre-jour*—pointed toward or nearly toward the chief source of light. In order to render precisely, for example, the complexity of light effects with reflections in a valley, he, at times, permitted the solidity of the hills to disappear. No artist before Claude had attempted such a subject. Claude was able to capture the infinity of nature within the narrowly defined boundaries of classical composition, that is, art derived from the study of antique exemplars. His methods showed that French classicism, best exemplified in the disciplined, rational approach of Poussin, could be softened to reveal the poetic side of nature.

Poussin constructs hollow, boxlike space filled with solid objects which recede in clearly defined steps. Claude creates looser space almost always leading the eye to infinity on the horizon. Atmosphere fills and unifies this space. Recession occurs by the subtle gradation of color, usually in trees which have no sharp outline. Poussin rarely represents water, but when he does it is the static surface of a river which clearly reflects the surrounding scene. Claude chooses to render the constant motion of the sea. The eye is led over the continuous surface of the sea to the horizon by no means other than color, tone changes, and minute variations in the surface of wave patterns which reflect light. Poussin's buildings are simple solid blocks; Claude's porticoes, façades, and towers are seen against the sun and lose their substance in the atmosphere. Poussin's trees are marble, Claude's reflect light.

Claude Lorrain is rightly regarded as one of the greatest landscape painters in history. It is his stress on the subjective side of nature, the attempt to capture a mood, that made his work so popular with the early Romantics, most notably Joseph Mallord William Turner. From his own time to the present, Claude has enjoyed a great reputation, especially in England, and his popularity has remained undimmed.

Bibliography

Kitson, Michael. *Claude Lorrain: Liber Veritatis*. London: British Museum Publications, 1978. An excellent catalog of the 1977 British Museum exhibit of the complete drawings from the artist's record of his own work, originally in bound sketchbook format. Includes text, notes, black-and-white plates, an index of patrons, and an appendix.

Manwaring, Elizabeth Wheeler. *Italian Landscape in Eighteenth Century England.* Reprint. New York: Russell & Russell, 1965. Chiefly a study of how the Italian landscapes of Claude Lorrain and Salvator Rosa became the major shapers of English taste for the conceptions about landscape beauty through their literary and poetic appeal.

Röthlisberger, Marcel. *Claude Lorrain: The Drawings.* 2 vols. Berkeley: University of California Press, 1968. A standard catalog of the artist's nearly twelve hundred known drawings. Volume 1 contains precise information to correspond with each black-and-white plate in volume 2. Information on types of drawing, style, and technique.

_____. *Claude Lorrain: The Paintings.* 2 vols. New Haven, Conn.: Yale University Press, 1961. A standard catalog of Claude's existing output as a painter, nearly 250 oils. The introduction to volume 1 includes a basic summary of artistic influences and stylistic development, and comments about frescoes and imitators. Each black-and-white plate of volume 2 has a corresponding text in volume 1.

Russell, H. Diane. *Claude Lorrain, 1600-1682.* Washington, D.C.: National Gallery of Art, 1982. This comprehensive volume is excellent in every respect. Illustrations of paintings and drawings are in color, two-tone, and black-and-white. Contains historical commentaries, an intricate chronology, a glossary, a fine bibliography, and appendices.

John A. Calabrese

CARL VON CLAUSEWITZ

Born: June 1, 1780; Burg, near Magdeburg, Prussia
Died: November 16, 1831; Breslau, Silesia
Areas of Achievement: The military and philosophy
Contribution: Clausewitz played an important role in Prussian military and political history during the Napoleonic Wars. He is best known, however, as the leading philosopher of war. His most famous work, *On War*, has been characterized as "not simply the greatest, but the only great book about war."

Early Life

Carl von Clausewitz was born into a Prussian family that, despite its pretensions to nobility, was in fact of middle-class origins. The elder Clausewitz had obtained a commission in the army of Frederick the Great but was forcibly retired during Frederick's purge of nonnoble officers after the Seven Years' War. Clausewitz seems, however, to have believed in the family's claim to noble status; on the basis of his own achievements, Clausewitz had his claim confirmed by the King of Prussia in 1827.

The ambiguity of Clausewitz's social position may be a key to understanding his life and personality, although it does not appear to have blocked his advancement. He tended, as his correspondence and comments by contemporaries reveal, to feel and to be treated like an outsider. Sensitive, shy, and bookish by nature, he could also be passionate in his politics, his love for his wife, and his longing for military glory. Slim and rather handsome, he frequently displayed coolness and physical courage in battle. His keen analytical intelligence was accompanied by a certain intellectual arrogance. These qualities may account for the fact that, although he rose to high rank in the Prussian service, he served always as a staff officer rather than as a commander.

Clausewitz entered the Prussian army as a cadet at the age of twelve; he first saw combat, against revolutionary France, at thirteen. After 1795, he spent five years in the rather dreary garrison town of Neuruppin. There, he applied himself energetically to his own education, a project in which he was so successful that he was able to gain admission to the new War College in Berlin in 1801. With this appointment, his rise to prominence had begun.

Life's Work

The director of the War College was Gerhard Johann von Scharnhorst, who was to become Clausewitz's mentor and a key figure in the Prussian state during the upheavals of the Napoleonic Wars. Many of Clausewitz's basic historical, political, and military views derived from the influence of Scharnhorst and other Prussian military reformers.

Clausewitz was graduated first in his class in 1803 and was rewarded with the position of military adjutant to the young Prince August. The same year, he met and fell in love with his future wife, the Countess Marie von Brühl. Yet the ambiguity of his social background and his poverty posed problems. Marie's family would resist this poor match for seven years, until Clausewitz's rapid promotion undermined their objections to a marriage.

Prussia had remained at peace with France since 1795 but, alarmed at the devastating French victories over Austria and Russia in 1805, mobilized for war in 1806. Clausewitz and most other Prussian officers anticipated the struggle with confidence, but the timing was poor and the nation was ill-prepared. The Prussian forces were shattered in humiliating defeats at Jena and Auerstedt. Both Clausewitz and Prince August were captured. The experience was both shocking and enlightening for Clausewitz. When he returned from internment in 1808, he joined Scharnhorst and the other members of the reform movement in helping to restructure both Prussian society and the army, in preparation for what Clausewitz believed to be an inevitable new struggle with the hated French. His enthusiasm was not, however, shared by the king, who was more concerned with maintaining his position in the much-reduced Prussian state. Clausewitz's disillusionment reached a peak when Prussia, allied with France, provided an army corps to Napoleon I to assist in the 1812 invasion of Russia. Along with about thirty other officers, Clausewitz resigned from Prussian service and accepted a commission in the Russian army. He fought at the bloody Battle of Borodino and witnessed the disastrous French retreat from Moscow. He then played a role, the importance of which is disputed, in negotiating the defection of the Prussian corps from the French army.

None of this won for him any affection in the court at Berlin, where he was referred to on at least one occasion as "Louse-witz." The eventual entry of Prussia into the anti-Napoleon coalition nevertheless led, after some delay, to his reinstatement in the Prussian army. Clausewitz participated in many key events of the "War of Liberation," but bad luck and the lingering resentment of the king prevented him from obtaining any significant command.

In 1818, Clausewitz was promoted to general and became administrative head of the War College. This position offered him little scope to test his educational theories or to influence national policy. Perhaps because of the conservative reaction in Prussia after 1819, as a result of which many of the liberal reforms of the war years were weakened or rescinded, Clausewitz spent his abundant leisure time quietly, writing studies of Napoleonic campaigns and preparing the theoretical work that eventually became his magnum opus, *Vom Kriege* (1832-1834; *On War*, 1873).

Clausewitz saw war as essentially a creative activity: Victory goes not to the general who has learned the rules but to the general who makes them.

Therefore, military theory must not attempt to prescribe a general's actions but should aim instead at educating his judgment so that, on the battlefield, he will be able to weigh all the factors that apply in his own unique situation. Clausewitz was scornful of military dilettantes such as Adam Heinrich Dietrich von Bülow, who tried to reduce the art of war to a mathematical equation. The strategist, like the artist, will make use of science, but the end result in both cases will be something quite different from the predictable, repeatable results of an experiment in physics. This outlook surely stemmed from Clausewitz's own experience of the overthrow of traditional armies by the radically new forces of the French Revolution.

Clausewitz's approach contrasts with that of his initially more influential contemporary, the Swiss theorist Antoine-Henri de Jomini. Where Jomini saw fixed values, Clausewitz looked for variable quantities. Where Jomini worried about physical forces, Clausewitz discussed the effects of morale and psychological factors. Where Jomini prescribed unilateral action, Clausewitz showed that war is the continuous interaction of opposites. Where Jomini sought to achieve certainty on the battlefield, Clausewitz stressed uncertainty, chance, suffering, confusion, exhaustion, and fear, factors that added to what he called the "friction" of war.

The most famous and often-quoted line from *On War*, possibly the only line ever read by most quoters of Clausewitz, is that "War is the continuation of politics by other means." His point was that war is not in any way a sphere separate from politics and that military operations must always serve a rational political end. The crux of the problem is that neither soldiers nor statesmen are infallible, even within their own areas of competence, and Clausewitz's dictum will work only if the generals and the politicians understand one another's limitations.

Clausewitz returned to active field duty in 1830, when revolutions in Paris and Poland seemed to presage a new general European war. Before leaving, he sealed his manuscripts with the warning, "Should the work be interrupted by my death, then what is found can only be called a mass of conceptions not brought into form . . . open to endless misconceptions." Although war was averted, Clausewitz remained in the east, organizing a sanitary cordon to stop the spread of a cholera epidemic from Poland. He returned home to Breslau in 1831, seemingly healthy, but contracted the deadly disease and died the same day. He was fifty-one years old. Despite his note of warning, his fiercely loyal wife continued his work. It was she who edited and published *On War*, the first volumes of which appeared in 1832.

Summary

Although Carl von Clausewitz wrote a considerable amount of history, particularly campaign studies, he is read almost exclusively for the military philosophy contained in *On War*. This book was received with the respect its famous author deserved but remained in obscurity until cited by Helmuth Karl Bernhard von Moltke as the key to his victories over Austria in 1866 and France in 1870-1871. It then became a virtual military cult object. *On War* has gradually assumed a status as the preeminent philosophical examination of war and military theory.

Unfortunately, many later interpreters have twisted Clausewitz's argument—and even altered the text—concerning the relationship of war and political policy, with the intent of winning greater independence for military leaders. Colmar von der Goltz, writing in 1883, reconciled these two seemingly irreconcilable ideas by saying that "war serves the ends of politics best by a complete defeat of the enemy," even though this formulation directly contradicted the lessons of Prussia's greatest military-political successes, that is, the victorious wars against Austria and France.

Although Clausewitz is often supposed to have been the "apostle of total war," in fact, this is merely the unfortunate by-product of his quasi-Hegelian analytical method, which led him to begin with a discussion of war as an "absolute," an ideal. Clausewitz was writing in the years before nuclear weapons, but his abstract discussion of absolute war seems now to be prophetic of today's balance of terror. There is even a group of modern strategic theorists who have been called the "neo-Clausewitzians," including such prominent nuclear strategists as Henry Kissinger and Herman Kahn. Clausewitz, however, recognized that war could be either total or limited and that in reality no war would be a perfect example of either.

That *On War* or its misinterpretation actually led to the debacle of World War I, as some have charged, is dubious. Few generals of this war ever read this notoriously difficult book. Furthermore, as Clausewitz himself recognized, war changes over time; societies fight the wars for which they are physically, socially, and psychologically equipped. The nature of war in any given environment is determined by Clausewitz's trinity of government policy, the capabilities of the army, and the attitudes of the population.

If Clausewitz's work is understood as descriptive in nature, it can be a useful tool for military analysis. If, instead, the reader tries to use it prescriptively, as Clausewitz feared might happen, he will constantly be misled by his own cultural preconceptions and by the tendency to see war in its ideal, absolute form, rather than in the disorderly form in which it actually exists. To see in Clausewitz's rather matter-of-fact description of war as "a continuation of policy" a justification for resorting to arms is to miss the point of his argument; no leader who truly grasps Clausewitz's description of the role of chance in war is likely to take the gamble lightly.

Bibliography
Aron, Raymond. *Clausewitz: Philosopher of War.* Translated by Christine Booker and Norman Stone. Englewood Cliffs, N.J.: Prentice-Hall, 1985.

Although not a good translation from the French, this book contains a useful biography of Clausewitz, a subtle analysis of his ideas, and an account of the scholarly controversies which they have spawned.

Clausewitz, Carl von. *On War*. Edited and translated by Michael Howard and Peter Paret. Princeton, N.J.: Princeton University Press, 1976. The best of three English translations of Clausewitz's major theoretical work. The volume also contains essays on Clausewitz by each of the editors as well as a guide to reading by Bernard Brodie, a prominent American strategic analyst.

Gallie, W. B. *Philosophers of Peace and War: Kant, Clausewitz, Marx, Engels, and Tolstoy*. Cambridge, England: Cambridge University Press, 1978. Treats Clausewitz's theories in their philosophical and military contexts.

Handel, Michael I., ed. *Clausewitz and Modern Strategy*. London: Frank Cass, 1986. A collection of essays discussing Clausewitz, his theories, and his influence on the military strategies followed by various nations, including Germany, France, and Italy.

Paret, Peter. "Clausewitz." In *Makers of Modern Strategy: From Machiavelli to the Nuclear Age*, edited by Peter Paret and Gordon A. Craig. Princeton, N.J.: Princeton University Press, 1986. A short essay on Clausewitz in an excellent anthology of essays on other strategic thinkers.

_____. *Clausewitz and the State: The Man, His Theories, and His Times*. Princeton, N.J.: Princeton University Press, 1976. The most sophisticated biography of Clausewitz.

Christopher Bassford

FERDINAND JULIUS COHN

Born: January 24, 1828; Breslau, Lower Silesia
Died: June 25, 1898; Breslau, Lower Silesia
Areas of Achievement: Botany and biology
Contribution: Cohn is considered one of the founders of modern bacteriology. As a botanist, he contributed to understanding the evolutionary position of many microscopic plantlike organisms by elucidating their life
histories.

Early Life
The eldest of three sons of a poor Jewish merchant, Issak Cohn, Ferdinand
Julius Cohn was born in the Breslau ghetto. He was a precocious child who,
it is said, was able to read at the age of two and enter school at the age of
four. At the age of seven he began higher school at the *Gymnasium* of
St. Maria Magdelina, and he began attending the University of Breslau at the
age of fourteen. Influenced at the university by professors Heinrich Goeppert
and Christian Nees von Esenbeck, he became interested in botany. Because
of the rules against Jews receiving advanced degrees at Breslau, he could not
be granted one there. Thus, in 1846, he moved to the more liberal University of Berlin, from which, a year later, he obtained a doctorate in botany. At Berlin, he was influenced by several professors, especially Christian Ehrenberg in microscopy and Johannes Müller in physiology. He was in
Berlin during the uprisings of 1848, with which he sympathized but in which
he did not actively participate. Returning the next year to Breslau at the age
of twenty-one, he became a privatdocent at the university, working under
Professor Jan Evangelista Purkinje in his Institute of Physiology. There he
began his work on the microscopic aspects of living organisms, at that time a
new area of biological investigation, particularly because of the newly proposed cell theory of Theodor Schwann and Matthias Schleiden. In 1859, he
became an extraordinary professor at the university, and in 1867, he married
Pauline Reichenbach. The remainder of his professional career was spent at
the University of Breslau, where he became an ordinary professor in 1872.

Life's Work
Cohn's interests were in microscopic organisms, both plant and animal,
which he used to try to understand their relationships with higher groups of
organisms and to understand their development and physiology. At first, he
studied various microscopic algae, and, especially using the unicellular *Pro-
tococcus pluvialis*, he concluded that these organisms had a regular life cycle
and various developmental phases including sexuality, and that the cellular
substance was similar in all cells, both plant and animal. The latter conclusion led him to call the cell substance protoplasm, the name Hugo von Mohl

had used for that in plant cells, rather than the term sarcode, which had been used by Felix Dujardin for animal cell substance. Cohn is best known for his studies of bacteria. He believed that these organisms were more plantlike than animal-like. He showed that they had stable characteristics of form which varied within certain limits, allowing them to be given firm generic names and, at least, provisional specific names. His hesitation about specific names was based on his knowledge that sometimes those of the same form had different fermentative properties. He recognized six genera of bacteria based on their shapes: micrococcus (ball-shaped); bacterium (short rods); bacillus (straight threadlike); vibrio (wavy-shaped); and spirochete (long, flexible spirals). The genera were placed into four larger groups: spaerobacteria for the round ones; microbacteria for the rod-shaped ones; desmobacteria for the longer rod- and thread-shaped ones; and spirobacteria for the wavy or spiral-shaped ones. Because of his clear presentation of the information about the characteristics of bacteria, their cultivation, and their physiology, Cohn helped found the modern science of bacteriology.

Cohn was involved in some of the most important aspects of the developing field of microbiology. He undertook to understand why some bacteria in hay infusions were able to withstand high temperatures. He was able to show that certain bacilli were able to form heat-resistant endospores. This discovery came at a time to help Louis Pasteur, and later John Tyndall, substantiate the attack on the idea of spontaneous generation of microorganisms. Because he was the major Germanic worker with bacteria, and because he had been trying to prove the importance of bacteria in causing diseases, the then-young Robert Koch wrote to Cohn asking if he could come and demonstrate his evidence for the bacterial cause of anthrax. Koch visited Breslau for three days and convinced Cohn and others at Breslau that he had definite proof that *Bacillus anthracis* was the sole cause of the disease. Cohn was very impressed with Koch's ability, supported his research program, and published his paper on anthrax in 1876, in the journal *Beitrage zur Biologie der Pflanzen* (contributions to the biology of plants), which Cohn had established in 1872 and used to publish many of his own findings.

Work in botany and the popularization of biology also occupied Cohn's time. From 1856 to 1886, he served as secretary of the botanical section of the Schlesiche Gesellschaft für Vaterländische Cultur (Silesian society for the culture of the fatherland), in which capacity he organized and edited a multivolume work on the cryptogamic flora of Silesia. Cohn wrote a popular work on bacteria, *Über Bacterien, die kleinsten lebenden Wesen* (1872; *Bacteria, the Smallest of Living Organisms*, 1881), and one on plants, *Die Pflanze* (1882; the plant). In this way, and by articles and lectures, he helped to interest the general public and students in biological subjects. In 1866, he was able to establish an Institute of Plant Physiology at the University of Breslau, the first of its kind in the world, thus fulfilling a long-held dream.

He made studies of tissues in plants that were involved with rapid movements which he believed to be similar to animal muscle tissue.

Summary

Ferdinand Julius Cohn is historically important as a major figure in the foundation of modern microbiology, and as a sponsor of Robert Koch in his important studies of disease-causing bacteria. Cohn placed microscopic organisms, particularly algae, fungi, and bacteria, which he considered to be plants, into a Darwinian evolutionary framework. By elucidating their life cycles, and when possible their sexuality, he furthered biological understanding. He recognized the importance of protoplasm as the universal living substance of cells. An important educator, he popularized botany and bacteriology by his writings and lectures.

Bibliography

Brock, Thomas D., ed. *Milestones in Microbiology.* Englewood Cliffs, N.J.: Prentice-Hall, 1961. Two of Cohn's important papers—with some deletions—in English translation are given: "Studies on the Biology of the Bacilli," concerned with the survival of spores of some bacteria after boiling, and "Studies on Bacteria," describing some of the problems in classifying bacteria and considering them best related to the fungi. Comments accompany the papers indicating their historical importance.

Bulloch, William. *The History of Bacteriology.* New York: Oxford University Press, 1938. Reprint. Mineola, N.Y.: Dover, 1979. Cohn's work is considered in the context of the history of bacteriology. His studies on the survival of bacteria after sterilization of their media are considered, as are his ideas about bacterial classification.

Cohn, Ferdinand. *Bacteria, the Smallest of Living Organisms.* Translated by Charles S. Dolley, with an introduction by Morris C. Leikind. Rochester, N.Y.: F. D. Phinney, 1881. Reprint. Baltimore: Johns Hopkins University Press, 1939. Originally published in German by Cohn in 1872, and in a small English edition by the translator in Rochester, New York, in 1881, this introduction to bacteriology was written for the general reader. It gives a brief history of the knowledge of bacteria and presents a summary of what Cohn and others knew and thought about bacteria. The reprint in the Johns Hopkins University Press book contains a short biography and the original complete bibliography of Cohn's writings.

Geison, Gerald L. "Ferdinand Julius Cohn." In *Dictionary of Scientific Biography,* edited by Charles Coulston Gillispie, vol. 3. New York: Charles Scribner's Sons, 1971. This scholarly biography of Cohn is the only substantial one in English. In addition to providing basic biographical information, it stresses Cohn's importance in the development of microbiology and botany. Provides a detailed bibliography.

Lechevalier, Hubert A., and Morris Solotorovsky. *Three Centuries of Microbiology.* New York: McGraw-Hill, 1965. Reprint. Mineola, N.Y.: Dover, 1974. Cohn's place in the development of bacteriology is considered briefly. The authors stress Cohn's studies of spontaneous generation of microorganisms in relation to Pasteur's work and the relationship between his work and Koch's bacterial studies.

Talbott, John H. *A Biographical History of Medicine: Excerpts and Essays on the Men and Their Work.* New York: Grune & Stratton, 1970. A brief biographical sketch of Cohn, with a composite drawing, stresses his contributions to botany. It includes a long quotation from the English translation of his book, *Bacteria, the Smallest of Living Organisms*, which emphasizes the importance of bacteria as disease organisms and as possible extraterrestrial initiators of life on Earth.

Emanuel D. Rudolph

JEAN-BAPTISTE COLBERT

Born: August 29, 1619; Reims, France
Died: September 6, 1683; Paris, France
Areas of Achievement: Government, politics, and patronage of the arts
Contribution: Colbert contributed to the reform of the administrative, economic, legal, and cultural foundations of the French monarchy. As the third in a succession of great French ministers of the seventeenth century, he exercised primary responsibility for implementing the system of absolute monarchy that governed France until 1789.

Early Life

Jean-Baptiste Colbert was born in the city of Reims in the Champagne region of France. Little is known of Colbert's childhood or education beyond the facts that he sprang from a family of wholesale cloth merchants turned financiers and that he attended the Jesuit college in Reims. Changes in trading routes and European economic patterns had dramatically reduced Reims's commercial significance by the 1620's, and the once prosperous Colbert family moved to Paris in 1629, seeking wider opportunities as bankers and financiers. Apparently, young Colbert remained behind in Reims to complete his education and in 1634 took up a position at a banking house in Lyons. Shortly afterward, however, he moved to Paris and took employment as an assistant to a notary. Sometime before 1640, he obtained a position as a royal war commissioner, a minor venal office his father probably purchased for him.

Colbert took his first real steps up the political and social ladders in the early 1640's. First, family connections allowed him to attach himself to the entourage of Michel Le Tellier, France's war minister. Then, with deliberate calculation he married Marie Charon, the daughter of a wealthy financier, who brought a very large dowry (100,000 livres) to the marriage. Sometime after Le Tellier acquired the post of secretary of state for war in 1643, Colbert became an assistant to the secretary and then his personal emissary to Jules Mazarin. From that point until early 1651, when he entered Mazarin's service, Colbert's loyalty to Le Tellier's cause and his aptitude for political and financial dealings proved themselves time and again. Indeed, despite his initial dislike for Colbert, it was those very qualities of loyalty, service, and efficiency that prompted Mazarin to request Le Tellier to release Colbert to enter his own service.

From 1651 until Mazarin's death in 1661, Colbert served Mazarin faithfully. During the turbulent years of civil war (the Fronde, 1648-1653) and Mazarin's two political exiles (1651-1653), Colbert acted as the minister's personal financial agent in Paris and as his representative at court. So great was his skill for these tasks that he managed to amass a fortune in Mazarin's name. Following the end of the Fronde and Mazarin's return to Paris, Colbert once again proved himself the loyal servant of his patron's interests, advising the minister on political matters and continuing to enlarge Mazarin's fortune (and his own) through the traffic in venal offices, manipulation of the monarchy's debts, and financial speculations. On his deathbed, Mazarin commended Colbert to Louis XIV's service.

Life's Work

Following Mazarin's death, Louis XIV's dramatic announcement of the plan to act as his own first minister meant that Colbert would never rise to the heights of political power or personal wealth Cardinal de Richelieu and Mazarin had attained. Nevertheless, as a member of the king's financial council (from 1661), as controller general of finance (from 1665), as secretary of state for the navy (from 1668), and as secretary of state for the king's household (from 1669), Colbert made his mark on the first half of Louis' reign in ways so profound as to set the political form of Louis' absolutism as the European model for centralized monarchy.

Colbert's rise in the power structure of Louis' government resulted from his zeal in pursuing reforms aimed at eradicating the very same ministerial abuses of power and finance he himself had helped Mazarin practice during the 1650's. With Mazarin's death, the greatest threat to Louis XIV's power and to his resolution to act as his own first minister came from Nicolas Fouquet, the king's powerful superintendent of finance. Fouquet was, in fact, the most logical successor to Mazarin's ministry. Clearly the richest man in France, Fouquet's willingness to finance the monarchy through loans and pledges based on his personal fortune had allowed Louis to pursue war against Spain to a successful conclusion in 1659. In short, Fouquet had personally acted as one of the monarchy's chief bankers throughout the 1650's. Such openhandedness in financing the monarchy was only possible because Fouquet had used his position in the government to enrich himself beyond all measure.

Within months after Mazarin's death, Louis and Colbert had spun an elaborate trap for Fouquet, which culminated in a dramatic arrest on charges of treason and financial peculation. Fouquet not only held a stranglehold on Louis' finances, but he also maintained private fortresses, troops, and a personal navy stronger than the king's. Additionally, Fouquet enjoyed tremendous popular support. Colbert, formerly on close terms with Fouquet, undertook personal charge of the prosecution and succeeded in gaining a conviction on the charges of financial misconduct. Many condemned Colbert as a hypocrite, claiming that Fouquet's crimes in the 1650's had been no worse than Mazarin's (or Colbert's own). At a personal level Fouquet was treated unfairly, but this case actually concerned crimes of the past less than it did the future direction of the monarchy. Through the Fouquet prosecution,

Louis signaled his absolute determination to subordinate the machineries of royal finance, administration, and justice to his personal will. Henceforth, the king would tolerate no overly ambitious or powerful subjects. Breaking Fouquet was an object lesson to anyone who might try to emulate the models of either the Cardinal de Richelieu or Mazarin.

Colbert himself belonged to that group of financiers and political actors who had risen to power under Richelieu and Mazarin. His own part in the Fouquet prosecution signaled his acceptance of Louis' lesson—the rules of high politics had changed. From his first efforts to assist the king in laying his trap for Fouquet through his death in 1683, Colbert never forgot that lesson. Beginning with the dismantling and royal seizure of Fouquet's financial empire, then moving on to the establishment of special chambers of justice to investigate, punish, and fine wrongdoers among the entire class of royal financiers, Colbert launched a financial reform that reversed Louis' kingdom from its position as the greatest debtor state in Europe to a status as the richest and most rationally administered.

Colbert proved tireless in his efforts to reform and regularize royal taxation, government contracting, financial administration, and economic regulation. He also showed himself equally willing to employ the monarchy's resources to build new manufacturing, to establish colonies and trading companies, and to reform the legal system. Altogether, this complex of reforms and royal initiatives constituted a whole that historians have labeled "Colbertisme" in its particular application to France and mercantilism in its more general application as the model for the economic and political thinking that dominated Europe in the eighteenth century.

The specifics involved in Colbert's mercantilism defy easy summary, but the main theoretical lines can be delineated. The state was to foster and support new manufacturing, both through direct subsidies and the establishment of prohibitive import duties. Regulating everything concerning the quality, type, and quantities of goods, France would become an economically independent state enjoying a surplus in the value of trade export over the value of imports. Colonies would provide raw materials and markets for finished goods. Trade with other European states was to be limited to exports paid in cash. Other trading nations such as the Dutch and the English constituted France's natural enemies, and France's greatness depended on undercutting or destroying these enemies' ability to compete economically. Finally, the success of the entire system must depend on a debt-free, centrally organized economy.

In practice, this theoretical framework called for a massive overhaul of the French economy and political administration. The task was obviously beyond the reach of Colbert's lifetime, and his success must be measured in terms of progress rather than actual accomplishments. France was an overwhelmingly agricultural nation, but Colbert did lay the basis for a new system of state-controlled manufacturing establishments, especially in the luxury trades. Moreover, despite hindrances to trade, the government regulations gained for French goods an unparalleled reputation for quality and value. His efforts to build a new navy and the merchant ships necessary for colonization and the protection of trade made considerable gains—enough so, in fact, that the French navy seriously challenged English/Dutch supremacy for a time. Most important, his efforts at reforming the tax collection system (not the actual tax burdens on the population), the management of debt, and the administration of the kingdom's finances yielded dramatic results in reestablishing the state's solvency.

Within the new political order Louis XIV's personal reign created, Colbert was only one of several powerful ministers who acted strictly in the king's name while serving at his pleasure. Such a system was bound to create disagreements and conflicts among these ministers, and Colbert was involved in his share. The most important of these long-running political enmities put him in conflict with Le Tellier, his former patron, and Le Tellier's son the Marquis de Louvois. Le Tellier and Louvois, as successive secretaries of state for war, pushed relentlessly for turning the royal treasury to the purposes of strengthening the French army. They also urged a militarist foreign policy on Louis as the best approach to building the monarchy. Colbert opposed both of these policies, urging economic warfare instead.

Initially successful in winning the king's ear, Colbert progressively lost ground to the Le Tellier/Louvois faction as the reign unfolded. Louis did indeed pursue an increasingly militaristic policy, and as he did Louvois' influence waxed, while Colbert's waned. Nor was this basic policy issue the only one on which Colbert suffered reverses. Although he was the superintendent of the king's buildings, he strongly opposed the lavish building program Louis launched in renovating the palace at Versailles. Colbert wanted Louis to make Paris itself his capital and the Louvre his principal residence. He did succeed in making dramatic improvements in the sanitation, police, and public works of Paris, but here, too, his basic policy was at odds with the king's wishes. Despite Colbert's efforts to make Paris the modern Rome, his death really marked the eclipse of the city of Paris as the focal point of French absolutism. Similarly, as a proponent of religious toleration, Colbert failed to sway the king from his policy of increasing persecution of French Protestants. Although he did not live to see the results, the revocation of the Edict of Nantes was to prove his views correct.

In another realm, Colbert fared better. As superintendent of the king's buildings, Colbert assumed responsibility for establishing Louis as the greatest patron of the arts, letters, and science that Europe had ever seen. Starting in 1662 with a European-wide system of French royal patronage for artists and intellectuals, Colbert went on to found the Academy of Inscriptions (1663), the Académie Royale des Sciences (1666), the Académie de France de Rome (1667), the Academy of Architecture (1671), and the first of the formal royal academies in the provinces. Colbert also reorganized and re-charted the two existing royal academies, the Académie Française and the Academy of Painting and Sculpture, making them true state-supported institutions. The system of royal academies Colbert created not only served to glorify Louis' reign but also served the important political purpose of bringing France's most noted artists, intellectuals, and scientists under royal control. Colbert's academies survived until the Revolution and as reconstituted under Napoleon still form the basis for the Institut de France. To the extent that French arts, literature, and science have dominated various cultural periods in the three centuries since Colbert's death, these academies may be claimed as his most enduring legacy to the world.

Summary

Jean-Baptiste Colbert's life remains particularly difficult to summarize. He was an intensely private man noted for his formidable and chilling personality. Moreover, the circumstances under which he served Louis XIV made it difficult for him to give free rein to his ambitions and personality. Historians long debated whether he may have been the actual architect behind the major policies of Louis' reign; while that interpretation has been rejected, the fact remains that he exercised primary responsibility for implementing the reforms and administrative machinery of Louis' reign. In that sense, he was the primary "contractor" building the edifice of absolutism that Richelieu, Mazarin, and Louis had designed.

A complex figure, Colbert defies easy categorization in the modern terms of government service. His career spanned a crucial transitional period in the development of political forms, and perhaps his greatest virtue lay in his ability to adjust to and then support inevitable changes. He died a bitter and cynical man. His influence clearly on the wane, he was acutely conscious of his failure to sway the king from policies he considered destructive to the monarchy's future. Although he was little mourned at his death, his legacies to France proved themselves of incalculable value.

Bibliography
Cole, Charles Woolsey. *Colbert and a Century of French Mercantilism.*
    2 vols. New York: Columbia University Press, 1939. This classic treat-
    ment of Colbert's economic ideas and his financial reforms furnishes the
    best starting point for understanding both Colbert's impact on France and
    the difficulties inherent in any attempt to synthesize any simple interpreta-
    tions. Strongly based in traditional scholarship, Cole's work provides a
    valuable compendium of historical scholarship.
Dent, Julian. *Crisis in Finance: Crown, Financiers, and Society in
    Seventeenth-Century France.* New York: St. Martin's Press, 1973. A solid

exposition of the financial workings of the seventeenth century French monarchy, starkly exposing the weaknesses of the financial administration Colbert set out to reform. Detailed and scholarly, this work offers a strong portrait of the world of the financiers, dealing with both their political and social worlds.

Maland, David. *Culture and Society in Seventeenth-Century France*. New York: Charles Scribner's Sons, 1970. The best survey in English treating French high culture, political involvements with patronage, and the institutional development of the academies. Treats personalities and conflicts as well as the more traditional historical facts.

Ranum, Orest. *Artisans of Glory: Writers and Historical Thought in Seventeenth-Century France*. Chapel Hill: University of North Carolina Press, 1980. Treating only one aspect of artistic and literary life (historical writing), Ranum traces the political influence in reshaping the boundaries of an intellectual discipline. Despite the seemingly narrow focus, this work offers many general insights into the world of patronage and letters Colbert sought to control. More important, Ranum's work suggests why such control was important to Colbert and the monarchy.

_____. *Paris in the Age of Absolutism*. New York: John Wiley & Sons, 1968. Ranum traces the cultural, social, and political histories of Paris from the reign of Henry IV through Colbert's death. Invaluable as a guide to understanding the aims and purposes of Colbert's cultural ideas and Louis' policies.

Root, Hilton L. *Peasants and King in Burgundy: Agrarian Foundations of French Absolutism*. Berkeley: University of California Press, 1987. While focused primarily on developments in eighteenth century France, this work actually demonstrates the profound effects of Colbert's financial and administrative reforms. Tracing the development of village corporatism in Burgundy, this work shows many connections between Colbert and struggles over political reform in the next century.

Trout, Andrew. *Jean-Baptiste Colbert*. Boston: Twayne, 1978. One of the few book-length studies of Colbert in English. An indispensable guide, but it suffers from serious limitations. Primarily intended as a summary and overview, it lacks the depth and coherence necessary to arrive at a clear picture.

Wolf, John B. *Louis XIV*. New York: W. W. Norton, 1968. As a scholarly biography of Louis XIV, this work contains invaluable material concerning Colbert's relations with the king. Particularly strong in explaining the political significance of Louis' decision to rule in his own right. Wolf offers a succinct, yet important, explanation of the new ministerial system developed in the 1660's.

David S. Lux

CHRISTOPHER COLUMBUS

Born: Between August 25 and October 31, 1451; Genoa
Died: May 20, 1506; Valladolid, Spain
Areas of Achievement: Navigation and exploration
Contribution: Columbus' discovery of America was the first recorded transatlantic voyage. It led directly to Europe's colonial settlement and exploitation of the New World, and it altered the course of history.

Early Life

Christopher Columbus' father, Domenico, was a wool weaver and gatekeeper in Genoa. In 1470, he moved his family to nearby Savona, where he worked as an innkeeper. Christopher Columbus (in Spanish, Cristóbal Colón) was the eldest of five children, of whom Bartolomé and Diego played a large part in his life. Christopher had little formal education, having become an apprentice at sea at about age ten, not entirely surprising in the great port city of Genoa. His knowledge of mathematics, astronomy, and Latin came with experience.

Columbus' early days at sea brought him as far as Tunis and Chios, a Greek island that was then a Genoese possession. He next traveled to Ireland, Iceland, and Madeira, where, in 1478, he married Felipa Perestrello e Moniz of a noble Portuguese family with a hereditary title to govern Porto Santo, one of the Madeira islands. They had a son, Diego, and Columbus resided in Porto Santo for perhaps three years and worked as a seaman or merchant.

In the early 1480's, having sailed in either capacity to São Jorge da Mina on Africa's Gold Coast, then the southernmost point in the known world, Columbus gained experience of the south Atlantic. By 1484, his hair prematurely white, he had conceived the plan for a great *empresa de las Indias* (enterprise of the Indies). In that year, the Portuguese king John II rejected Columbus' idea of reaching Cathay, the islands of Japan, and India by sailing westward. Portugal was deeply committed to its search for an African route to India.

The concept of sailing westward was not new; indeed, it did not even originate with Columbus. A mathematician from Florence, Paolo Toscanelli dal Pozzo, had articulated this idea in a letter with a map sent to Prince Henry the Navigator in 1474. It was, moreover, widely accepted that the world was round. Columbus had researched his plan well. Perhaps he had seen Toscanelli's letter in the archives. Certainly he had read Marco Polo and Ptolemy. These books and Pierre d'Ailly's *Imago Mundi* (c. 1483; shape of the world), which Columbus had studied—he made hundreds of marginal notes in his copy—were authoritative at that time, though filled with errors tending to understate the size of the earth. The miscalculation of the journey's length by about two-thirds nearly destroyed Columbus' project.

By 1486, Portugal's repeated failure to cut through the Congo or to attain the southern tip of Africa allowed Columbus' plan a second hearing. In 1488, however, Bartolomeu Dias rounded the Cape of Good Hope, and Columbus was again disappointed in Portugal. Henry VII of England entertained the offer of Columbus' agent, brother Bartolomé. Yet it was Ferdinand II and Isabella of Spain who, after shunting his proposals into committee for four years, finally, in the flush of victory over Muslim Granada early in 1492, awarded him his chance. The Franciscan friar and astronomer Antonio de Merchena helped him gain an interview with Isabella in about 1490, and court treasurer Luis de Santangel finally gained for Columbus Isabella's support by pledges of Jewish investment in the project.

During his pursuit of the Spanish royal court, Columbus had acquired in Córdoba a mistress, Beatriz Enríquez de Harana. She bore him a son, Fernando, who wrote an affectionate and thorough biography which is a chief source for modern knowledge about Columbus.

Life's Work

Fernando relates the exorbitant terms by which the Spanish monarchs agreed to grant Columbus 10 percent of all the gold or other goods acquired in the lands he might discover; he and his heirs were to hold the titles of Admiral of the Ocean Sea and viceroy of such lands. He was provided with two ships of the caravel type, the *Niña* and the *Pinta*, procured by Martín Alonso Pinzón of the port city of Palos; the round-bellied neotype *Santa Maria* was chartered from its owner by Columbus. For his efforts in raising money and crews numbering ninety men in all, mostly from Palos, and for his skill in commanding the *Pinta*, Pinzón would later claim a share in the credit and glory of Columbus' discoveries. The two smaller vessels were about fifty feet long, and the *Santa Maria* was about eighty-two feet long. They were equipped for any contingency with weapons, a translator of Hebrew and Arabic to deal with Marco Polo's Kublai Khan if found, and goods to sell for gold.

The first voyage of Columbus left Palos on August 3, 1492. After a stopover at Spain's Canary Islands, the tiny fleet began its ocean trek on September 6. Constantly favorable trade winds caused the sailors to despair at ever gaining a wind to aid their return home. The southwesterly flights of birds persuaded Columbus to accept Pinzón's advice to change his course to the southwest. A *Niña* lookout was the first to sight land. Columbus named the land San Salvador, landed, and, thinking he had reached an outlying island of Japan, claimed it for Spain.

Japan, and Cathay itself, he thought, must be only ten days distant. The search brought him to what are modern Haiti and the Dominican Republic, which together he named Hispaniola (little Spain). The native Arawaks were

simple hunter-fishers who wore almost no clothes. Columbus was charmed
by their courtesy. The native Cubans were equally friendly to their future
enslavers. Arawak references to the *caniba* people (cannibals) and Cuban
allusions to gold in the interior at Cubanacam further conjured images of
Marco Polo's khan in Columbus' mind. Establishing the Hispaniola settlement of Navidad, the first in the New World, to organize gold-mining operations, Columbus departed for Spain before a favorable west wind, carrying
six Arawak captives and news of the discovery of tobacco.

Having lost Pinzón with the *Pinta*, which departed on November 21, and
the *Santa Maria*, on a reef on Christmas Day, 1492, Columbus had only the
Niña for his return. He suspected Pinzón of trying to precede him to the
khan, or to the sources of the gold, or back to Spain to claim the honor for
his own discoveries. Therefore, their meeting at sea on January 6, 1493,
precipitated a quarrel between the two captains. It was not until January 16
that the transatlantic return voyage commenced. Storms blew the *Niña* first
into the Portuguese Azores on February 18 and then into Lisbon on March 9,
causing King John II to charge Spain with illegal explorations of the African
coast and to claim Columbus' discoveries for Portugal. This litigation was
later settled in Spain's favor by the pope. Columbus' arrival in Palos on
March 14 and subsequent reception by Ferdinand and Isabella at Barcelona
at the end of April, accompanied by American natives in full ceremonial
dress, was the admiral's greatest moment.

The royal announcement of a second voyage was met with numerous volunteers. A fleet of seventeen ships and fifteen hundred men departed Cádiz
on September 25, 1493. On board were animals, seeds and plants, and tools
for the establishment of a colony. Among Columbus' discoveries were Do-
minica Island (spied on Sunday), the Virgin Islands, and Puerto Rico. He
found Navidad, however, destroyed by the natives and its settlers slain.
Farther east on the north coast of what is now the Dominican Republic, he
built the first European city in the New World, which he named Isabella.
Leaving his brother Diego in charge there, he himself led the exploration of
Cibao, the inland mountainous region of Hispaniola. There he founded the
fortress settlement of Santo Tomás. He had still not seen the khan, but Columbus did discover Jamaica on May 5, 1494.

Convinced that Cuba was indeed the Asiatic mainland, Columbus forced
his crew to sign an agreement to that effect. Back in Isabella, Columbus
found the settlers angry and the natives in rebellion. Diego had been inadequate to the task of governing. Columbus' response was to ship five hundred
natives to the slave market at Seville. Those who survived the journey,
however, were returned to Hispaniola by the monarchs, who may have had
in mind a more humane program of Christianization and agricultural exploitation for the colonies.

Columbus left Hispaniola again on March 10, 1496, leaving his brother Bartolomé to build a settlement at Santo Domingo. In the short space of four years since the coming of the Europeans, a flourishing native American population had been decimated by exploitation, massacre, disease, and famine. Charges of misgovernment and cruelty greeted his arrival in Cádiz on June 11.

For Columbus' third voyage in six ships there were no volunteers. Indeed, the two-hundred-man crew had to be shanghaied or bribed by release from prison. Departure was from Sanlúcar, near Cádiz, on May 30, 1498. Sailing a more southerly route, the fleet was becalmed eight days in unbearable heat. On July 31, Columbus named three-peaked Trinidad, and the next day the fleet first spied the South American mainland. The first Europeans landed in the Paria Peninsula of Venezuela on August 5. Noting the fresh water flowing from the Orinoco River and the pearls worn by the women, Columbus believed that this was one of the four rivers of the Garden of Eden.

Arriving to find violence and syphilis in Hispaniola, Columbus was returned to reality. He only came to terms with his rebellious governor, Francisco Roldán, by means of the infamous *repartimiento*, or distribution of native serfs among the settlers as laborers and miners. On August 23, 1500, Francisco de Bobadilla arrived, sent by Ferdinand to replace Columbus as viceroy. In response to the admiral's resistance, Bobadilla sent Columbus and Diego back to Spain in chains.

Yet Columbus won the sympathy of the royal couple. On May 9, 1502, with brother Bartolomé and son Fernando, age thirteen, Columbus left on his "high voyage" (*alto viaje*) to find a way through Hispaniola to the Indian Ocean and restore his reputation. He was specifically prohibited, however, from landing at Hispaniola, where Nicolás de Ovando now governed with twenty-five hundred men.

Fernando records Ovando's flotilla making for Spain, and ignoring Columbus' warnings of a storm at sea; twenty of twenty-four ships were lost. Fernando also relates the discovery of Martinique in the Lesser Antilles, the exploration of the coasts of Nicaragua and Costa Rica, and the acquisition of gold from the natives of Honduras. The Isthmus of Panama blocked all access to an "Indian Ocean." Ovando could not have known that he was only forty miles from the Pacific Ocean.

Columbus ultimately fared little better. His entry into the unexplored western Caribbean Sea cost him more than a year at sea and the loss of his ships to storm and sea worms. Ovando waited another year before extricating the marooned men from Saint Ann's Bay in June, 1504. Sick in body and mind but rich with gold and new maps, Columbus reached Sanlúcar on November 7, 1504. The queen would die on November 26. He only saw a disinterested Ferdinand the following spring at Segovia.

Summary

Christopher Columbus spent his last years in vain demands for his rights and titles under the original royal charter and back pay for his men. Nevertheless, his share of the wealth of the "Indies" allowed him to live comfortably. His son Diego did retain the titles of admiral and viceroy after a long litigation. Columbus' library fell to Fernando, who bequeathed it, as the Biblioteca Colombina, to the Cathedral of Seville, where it remains. Columbus' body was eventually buried in the Cathedral of Santo Domingo (Hispaniola), but its specific site is uncertain.

He believed himself guided by Providence and biblical prophecy in all of his undertakings, a faith that made him intolerant of opposition and capable of great brutality in the name of God. His instincts at sea were regarded by his sailors as divine. He found winds and currents and reckoned directions as if inspired. His achievements were immense. European economic and political power would leave the Mediterranean lands and focus forever on the Americas.

Bibliography

Colón, Fernando. *The Life of Admiral Christopher Columbus by His Son, Ferdinand.* Translated by Benjamin Keen. New Brunswick, N.J.: Rutgers University Press, 1959. An intimate and affectionate biography by Columbus' son. Fernando's book is the basis of all the extremely favorable accounts of Columbus' career.

Fuson, Robert H., trans. *The Log of Christopher Columbus.* Camden, Maine: International Marine Publishing, 1987. This translation is based on the abstract of Columbus' log made by Bartolomé de Las Casas, with additions from his *Historia de las Indias* (1875-1876) and from Fernando Columbus' history of the Columbus family.

Landström, Björn. *Columbus.* London: Allen & Unwin, 1967. Ample illustrations, especially maps and ship designs, are extremely useful for illuminating the background, life, and voyages of Columbus. This is an interestingly written biography.

Madariaga, Salvador de. *Christopher Columbus: Being the Life of the Very Magnificent Lord Don Cristóbal Colón.* New York: Macmillan, 1940. An engrossing biography of immense scholarship. Its extensive notes support a thorough discussion of debated Columbian issues. This book must be read by anyone serious about Columbus.

Morison, Samuel Eliot. *Admiral of the Ocean Sea.* Boston: Little, Brown, 1942. This is an eminently readable biography. Emphasizes Columbus as a seaman more than as an administrator. Does not stop at the "water's edge," as Morison claims other biographies do.

_____. *The European Discovery of America: The Southern Voyages* A.D. *1492-1616.* New York: Oxford University Press, 1974. Devotes eight chapters to Columbus, viewing him in the larger context of his southern voyages. This volume, by a lifelong student of Columbus, features photographs of coastlines as Columbus might have seen them. Includes forty-two pages of maps.

Paolucci, Anne, and Henry Paolucci, eds. *Columbus*. Flushing, N.Y.: Griffon House, 1988. One of the most recent books on Columbus, but does not add much in the way of new information.

Daniel C. Scavone

AUGUSTE COMTE

Born: January 19, 1798; Montpellier, France
Died: September 5, 1857; Paris, France
Areas of Achievement: Philosophy, sociology, historiography, and religion
Contribution: One of the greatest systematic thinkers of nineteenth century
France, Comte was the father of positivism, a philosophy which saw the
evolution of new ideas as the shaping force in history and regarded the
empirical method of science as the only valid basis of knowledge. Comte
sought to extend the method of science to the study of man, coining the
word "sociology." His later thought took a Romantic swing, emphasizing
the primacy of the feelings, glorifying religion in a secular guise, and
proposing a highly regulated social order.

Early Life

Isidore-Auguste-Marie-François-Xavier Comte, the eldest of four children, was born in the French university town of Montpellier on January 19,
1798. His father, Louis-Auguste Comte, was a tax official, a man of strict
habits and narrow interests; his mother, Félicité-Rosalie Boyer, twelve years
older than her husband, was a warm, emotional person who devoted her life
to her children. Both parents were devout Catholics and royalists.

Young Comte was near-sighted and small—his head and trunk seemed too
large for his limbs. He had an extraordinary memory, however, and proved
to be a brilliant student in the local lycée, winning prizes in Latin and mathematics, on occasion substituting for his teacher. At the age of fifteen, he was
admitted to the prestigious École Polytechnique in Paris. There his diligence
and acuteness led his awed classmates to nickname him "the philosopher."
Napoleon I had given this school, like Comte's lycée, a military tone and
discipline. Yet Comte, who at age fourteen had already rebelled against the
religion of his parents by becoming an atheist, was one of the most unruly
students at the school. Comte was a prominent spokesman for the students
when they supported Napoleon during his futile attempt to regain control of
France in 1815. Later, Comte was judged by authorities a ringleader of a
student effort to oust an unpopular professor, a conflict so heated that it
served as a pretext for temporarily closing the school. He was sent home and
was placed under police surveillance.

In 1817, Comte returned to Paris, studying independently and tutoring
students in mathematics to support himself. The possibility of an offer to
teach in a new American polytechnical school led Comte to immerse himself
in the writings of Thomas Paine and Benjamin Franklin, but the project was
not funded. Comte therefore became secretary to the exuberant social philosopher Henri Saint-Simon, borrowing the broad outlines of many of his own
later doctrines while writing essays and articles which appeared under Saint-

Simon's name. Comte served Saint-Simon for seven years, but was uncomfortable with the religious bent of Saint-Simon's late writings and believed that his social theory needed a more systematic theoretical foundation. A critical preface by Saint-Simon to an essay Comte published under his own name precipitated the end of the relationship in 1824.

By then, the headstrong Comte had dropped his first name, Isidore, in favor of Auguste; had fathered an illegitimate daughter, who would die at the age of nine, by an Italian woman; and was living with Caroline Massin, herself the offspring of an unmarried provincial actress, whom he had known for three years and would marry in 1825. He praised her kindness, grace, wit, and cheerful disposition; she had been sold by her debauched mother to a young lawyer when in her mid-teens and was by this time a registered prostitute. It was partly to help her get her name off of police rolls that he agreed to the marriage. Their union was marred by his seeming indifference to their straitened economic circumstances and her occasional disappearances. A final separation came in 1842. Nevertheless, she had provided needed support through the difficult period when he produced his most important work, the six-volume *Cours de philosophie positive* (1830-1842; course on positive philosophy). The most important part of this support came shortly after he had begun the series of seventy-two lectures out of which this book grew, when he had a nervous breakdown so severe that he was incapacitated for more than a year (1826-1827), was judged incurably insane by one physician, and attempted suicide.

Life's Work

Comte wanted to be a philosopher-prophet, like Francis Bacon, Nicolas Condorcet, or his mentor Saint-Simon. Living in an era scarred by deep social antagonisms and warring ideologies, he dreamed of creating a persuasive philosophical synthesis which could restore both spiritual and social order to European society. Such solid intellectual underpinning was lacking, he believed, in Saint-Simon's thought. Comte reasoned that if the method of science could be extended to every aspect of life, the intellectual unity which had characterized medieval Europe could be restored on a more lasting basis, and unity of thought would bring social order.

Comte interpreted the rise of science and its extension to the study of man in the context of a general theory of human intellectual development he borrowed, via Saint-Simon, from the eighteenth century economist and statesman Jacques Turgot. The "law of the three stages" held that as positive knowledge of nature gradually replaces earlier tendencies to attribute much in life to unseen powers, thought moves from a theological to a metaphysical stage, replacing imagined divinities with nonobservable abstractions. Yet they too fall to skepticism, and a scientific or positive outlook triumphs. For Comte, this concept constituted a general theory of history, accounting for institutional as well as intellectual development. Thus, he held that theological societies have military political systems; metaphysical societies have a juristic social organization; and positivist societies will have an industrial polity. A positivist approach to phenomena came first in the simple sciences, such as astronomy and physics, while metaphysical or even theological modes of thought linger where phenomena are more complex. Since sciences dealing with the latter must rest on the foundation of more general, simpler ones, of necessity new positive sciences emerged in the following order: mathematics, astronomy, physics, chemistry, biology, and sociology. Although the later volumes of the book contain many prescriptive judgments about the future needs of society which now would not be termed scientific, *Cours de philosophie positive* was a tour de force, a landmark in both philosophy and the historical study of science.

With its publication and the growth of his reputation, Comte secured academic posts at the Institut Laville and the École Polytechnique. His outspoken criticisms of some academicians at the school led to the rejection of his candidacy for a chair there. He retaliated by appealing to European public opinion through a bitter attack on his opponents in the preface of the last volume of *Cours de philosophie positive*, an action which brought his final break with Caroline and cost him his positions. His financial difficulties led admirers in both France and England (including John Stuart Mill, later a critic) to raise funds on his behalf.

Comte lived modestly in his last years. The most significant episode in this period was a passionate emotional relationship with a beautiful but unhappy and ill young woman, Clotilde de Vaux. He had known her only a year and a half when she died in the spring of 1846 from tuberculosis. Yet her memory absorbed him through his remaining years. He dedicated his late work to her, including a second monumental book, the four-volume *Système de politique positive* (1851-1854; *System of Positive Polity*, 1875-1877). He declared that it was she who had taught him the importance of feelings.

System of Positive Polity is a work which prophesies in great detail the future of Western society. Its vision is in part a realization of the plan of Comte's youth, but it reveals a remarkable shift in emphasis from reason and scientific understanding to the emotions. He had come to regard as futile his earlier dream of achieving intellectual unity through science. Now he made men's wants, that is, morality, the foundation for intellectual unity in positivism. The emphasis in this work had been presaged in his *Considerations sur le pouvoir spirituel* (1826; considerations on spiritual power), in which he wrote that the Catholic church, shorn of its supernaturalism, might provide an ideal structural model for positivist society. It was probably Comte's intense feelings for de Vaux that brought this hitherto inveterate rationalist to emphasize the heart above intelligence and knowledge, and to prescribe a cult of womanhood as the emotional center of his secular religion.

The object of worship in this system, which T. H. Huxley dubbed Catholicism minus Christianity, was humanity itself, past, present, and future. Scientist-priests were to control both religion and education, positivist in content, which would be the foundation of the new social order. Actual political power, Comte declared, would rest with bankers and industrialists, whom economic developments were already thrusting to the fore. They would, however, operate under the spiritual guidance of the priests. The new industrial working class, its morals strengthened by religion and examples of feminine virtue, would accept the dominion of the industrialists but also give full backing to the priests. The latter, as shapers of powerful public opinion, would ensure that the workers' interests were safeguarded.

Thus, Comte, who earlier had declared the intellect his lord, now saw the feelings, not reason, as the key to social unity. He contended that man has a benevolent instinct—coining the word "altruism" to describe it—but that it is weak unless nurtured by good institutions. This need provided Comte a rationale for dictating the features of his positivist utopia in obsessive detail, from career paths to private devotions, from indissoluble marriage and perpetual widowhood to the particular heroes of human progress who were to be honored on each day of the (thirteen-month) positivist calendar.

Summary

Like many in his age, including his German contemporary Georg Wilhelm Friedrich Hegel (whose complex philosophy paralleled Auguste Comte's in remarkable ways), Comte was a visionary, a self-proclaimed prophet for the ages who believed that he had unveiled profound truths with sweeping social implications. As was true of most other utopian visionaries, his concrete predictions were off the mark. Thus, while many were dazzled by the younger Comte's brilliance as an interpreter of the evolution of science and defender of its method in all realms of thought, the impact of his later writings was quite limited. Whereas a number of intellectuals, including Hippolyte-Adolphe Taine, Ernest Renan, and the logical positivists of the twentieth century, inherited his skepticism about nonempirical thinking, his religion of humanity was essentially stillborn, even though it championed the Humanism made popular by the Enlightenment. In emphasizing the limits of reason and the importance of emotions, he was at one with the Romantic movement, as were many other major writers of the nineteenth century. His sympathy for medieval institutions, if not medieval belief, was also widely shared by other intellectuals of his time, particularly in literature and art—it was the period of Walter Scott and Gothic revival, the period when the works of Dante (whom Comte much admired) were finally translated into English. Yet Comte's humorless preoccupation with order and perfection was not well suited to winning for him a broad and enthusiastic following. He antagonized onetime supporters such as Mill with his obsession with ordering—down to the level of minute details of thought and feeling, artistic creation, and religious devotion—the life of positivist society, for which he planned to be the high priest. His indifference to democracy and individual freedom separated him from the liberals of his day. His interest in old forms without old content alienated conservatives, and he had no interest in the growing nationalism which was to provide yet another basis for ideology in the decades which followed him. Yet, curiously, his thought had an affinity to a modern development for which he could have had little sympathy. In his obsession with uniformity and order, his vision of a society which sought to control every facet of man's intellectual and emotional life for social ends dictated by a small elite group, he was a precursor of the totalitarian movements of the twentieth century.

Bibliography

Comte, Auguste. *A General View of Positivism*. Translated by J. H. Bridges. New York: Speller, 1957. This book, written during the ferment of the Revolution of 1848 and published shortly after Comte founded the Positivist Society, is an excellent introduction to his later social philosophy. It relates his ideas to contemporaneous social developments.

Gould, F. J. *Auguste Comte*. London: Watts, 1920. This biography, though brief, provides a balanced survey of Comte's life and thought. It gives more attention than does the Sokoloff volume to those who comprised his intellectual circle and treats his ideas more fully. The curious positivist calendar is appended.

Lévy-Bruhl, Lucien. *The Philosophy of Auguste Comte*. Translated by Kathleen de Beaumont-Klein. New York: G. P. Putnam's Sons, 1903. A thorough and sympathetic treatment of Comte's thought by a highly regarded French scholar. Takes issue with Mill's contention that there are serious discrepancies between Comte's early and later writings.

Manuel, Frank. *The Prophets of Paris*. Cambridge, Mass.: Harvard University Press, 1961. This survey of a number of important French social philosophers devotes an illuminating chapter to Comte. The study provides a good perspective from which to assess Comte in relation to his intellectual milieu. Seen in the company of other visionaries, his detailed prescriptions are somewhat less puzzling.

Mill, John Stuart. *Auguste Comte and Positivism*. Ann Arbor: University of Michigan Press, 1961. First published in 1865, this critical assessment of Comte's ideas remains one of the most important books by an English author on Comte. Highly critical of Comte's later writings, it slights the elements of continuity they share with the rest of his work.

Sokoloff, Boris. *The "Mad" Philosopher, Auguste Comte*. New York: Vantage Press, 1961. A brief, readable biography which summarizes Comte's chief ideas while treating more fully the biographical context within which they developed. Gives more attention to his youth and his relationship with women than to his ties to other intellectuals.

R. Craig Philips

THE GREAT CONDÉ
Louis II de Bourbon, Prince de Condé

Born: September 8, 1621; Paris, France
Died: December 11, 1686; Fontainebleau, France
Area of Achievement: The military
Contribution: Condé played an important role in the struggle for royal absolutism, initially supporting the royal cause during the Fronde, then rebelling against the king. After reconciliation, he continued to serve as a successful and innovative military commander. He was part of the movement to abandon the old feudal levies in exchange for a tightly organized and highly trained and disciplined standing royal army. Condé was an expert tactician in the field.

Early Life

The Princes of Condé were members of the most important cadet branch of the ruling Bourbon family of France, descended through Duke Charles IV of Bourbon. Two sixteenth century ancestors were Huguenot leaders, but Henri I renounced Calvinism during the St. Bartholomew's Day Massacre of 1572 to save his life. The family continued to play important roles until the dethronement of Charles X in 1830, when Louis-Henri-Joseph committed suicide. The son of the above, Louis-Antoine-Henri, the Duke of Enghien, had been executed on Napoleon I's orders in 1804, ending the Condé line.

Louis II de Bourbon, the Duke of Enghien, a title the line's oldest male member held from birth, was a youth of such violent and moody temper that some questioned his sanity and his ability to function as an adult. By age twenty, however, he appeared to have outgrown the worst of these shortcomings, though he continued to be an extremely arrogant and undiplomatic individual, showing little tolerance for persons of lesser ability. Following the death of his father in 1646, he inherited the rank of "Premier Prince of the Blood," becoming the fourth Prince of Condé. As a young boy, he received a thorough education from the Jesuits at Bourges in central France and at the Royal Academy in Paris, where he was taught mathematics and horsemanship.

Though of high nobility, Louis, age twenty, had to enter into an unhappy marriage with the thirteen-year-old hunchbacked Claire-Clémence de Maillé-Brézé, a niece of Cardinal de Richelieu, Louis XIII's prime minister, in order to gain a military command. Richelieu believed him to be more trustworthy than most of the king's generals and named him commander in chief of an ill-trained and poorly disciplined French force on the Flemish frontier late in the Thirty Years' War. At this point, the emphasis in the Thirty Years' War had shifted from Germany to northeastern France. Louis, though he had no prior military experience or formal military training, immediately set about to train and instill discipline in his force, a task in which he was ably supported by two officers who had earlier served under King Gustavus II Adolphus of Sweden.

Life's Work

Condé won his first major victory in defeating a Spanish army that had besieged the border fortress of Rocroi, near Sedan, only five days after Louis XIV's accession to the throne. Rocroi, often considered the most important French victory of the seventeenth century, was won by the French cavalry, well supported by field artillery (though the French had only twelve, as opposed to twenty-eight Spanish guns), over the famous Spanish infantry, marking the beginning of the end of Spain's military prestige. Of the eighteen thousand Spanish infantry involved in the battle, eight thousand were killed and seven thousand captured (total Spanish casualties amounted to twenty-one thousand out of twenty-seven thousand men). French casualties numbered four thousand of about twenty-three thousand men engaged. The Spanish never again fielded infantry as good as the troops lost there. Condé continued to enhance his martial reputation during the last years of the Thirty Years' War, winning several significant victories in southwestern Germany. During this period, he served alongside his famous contemporary and sometime rival, Henri de La Tour d'Auvergne, Vicomte de Turenne.

It was during this period that the French army adopted the new tactics of concentrated fire and rapid movements. Condé became a master of these tactics, which supplemented Turenne's strategic ability. Condé was instrumental in furthering the new concepts of a rigidly disciplined and thoroughly trained army, as opposed to the old, poorly organized, and inadequately equipped and trained feudal levies. The old matchlock musket was replaced with the flintlock musket, and the formerly rather independent artillery was more fully integrated into the army, which was now composed of about 75 percent infantry, deemphasizing cavalry. Condé employed his rather mobile field artillery in a more concentrated fashion, following the example of Gustavus, providing more effective support for both infantry and cavalry. The number of camp followers, especially women, was substantially reduced, and the army became more national in makeup and spirit. Increasingly, the power and security of the state depended on the new royal standing army, which in France was carefully and strictly supervised by the war office, progressively replacing the formerly powerful feudal levies, largely controlled by the high nobles of the realm.

France emerged from the Thirty Years' War with the most powerful European army and with expanded borders, though the war with Spain continued until 1659. During the final phase of the Thirty Years' War, however, France faced a most serious internal challenge to royal power and national unity in the form of the Fronde (1648-1652).

The initial phase of the Fronde was supported primarily by the middle class and the *parlementaires* (judges and lawyers of the Paris law court), who were struggling to maintain traditional power distributions within government against the growth of royal absolutism. Condé, still serving in Germany until the Peace of Westphalia (October, 1648), which ended the Thirty Years' War, initially supported the royal cause. Following the peace in Germany, Cardinal Jules Mazarin, Richelieu's successor, fearing the power and following of the ambitious Condé, sent him first against Spain and then against the Spanish Netherlands. The war with Spain continued until 1659. Upon his return, Condé besieged rebellious Paris with an army of fifteen thousand and was instrumental in ending the first Fronde in the king's favor. As a result of disagreements with Mazarin, Condé fell into royal disfavor. Condé believed that he, not Mazarin, was the true savior of the king's power and demanded a greater role in government as well as high rewards. Condé was arrested in January, 1650, and imprisoned for about a year. Pressure from the noble party forced his release, but bitter disagreements continued, and Condé led the second Fronde, the Fronde of the Princes, believing that he should replace Mazarin as the king's chief minister. As a result of his undiplomatic arrogance and of his quarrel with Queen Anne of Austria, the widow of Louis XIII and regent for her young son Louis XIV, his opponents were able to maneuver him into open rebellion against Louis XIV, who had very recently been declared of age. At this time, the monopoly of military power had not yet fully shifted to royal hands, and the great nobles of the realm still held large estates with great wealth and their own powerful military forces. Condé raised an antiroyal army in southern France, while Turenne, who had briefly joined the Fronde, returned his loyalties to the Crown. The Fronde of the Princes, similar to the earlier Fronde, failed to gain popular support and brought France to the brink of anarchy. The frondeurs' goals were selfish and designed to benefit the aristocracy, rather than establish true constitutional government, in imitation of the English model, as frequently claimed. The frondeurs were also hindered in their struggle by their own, typically feudal inability to form a clear and lasting alliance, and by Condé's frequent shifts of allegiance and his lack of clear objectives. This was, in fact, the last serious attempt by the feudal aristocracy to halt the development of divine right royal absolutism. When Condé realized that power was slipping away from him, he fled to the Spanish Netherlands and for the next eight years served the Spanish. He served first in southern France and then in Flanders, though without notable success, partly because the Spanish never fully trusted him. Meanwhile Condé was sentenced in absentia to death for rebellion.

Following Condé's desertion, the Fronde came to an inglorious end. Louis XIV had broken the power of the *parlementaires* and of the nobles in general, and had firmly established royal absolutism. Condé and other rebels received a general amnesty following the Treaty of the Pyrenees in 1659. Condé regained all of his possessions and titles, though the king was initially reluctant to trust him fully. For the next few years, Condé lived at his estate of Chantilly about fifteen miles north of Paris and made it a center of the arts. Throughout his life, he had been a patron of the arts, and Chantilly attracted a literary circle that included Jean de La Fontaine, Molière, Jean Racine, and Jacques-Bénigne Bossuet. In 1667, when John II Casimir Vasa abdicated as King of Poland, Condé was advanced as his successor, a proposal which alarmed the Prussians in particular, and Louis was able to use this threat to keep Prussia out of the War of Devolution.

Condé returned to military service in 1668, when he led the French forces that captured Franche-Comté in a swift, two-week campaign. In 1672, in the war against Holland, he commanded the French forces in the Rhineland and the Netherlands. Following the death in battle of Turenne in July, 1675, Condé, now in overall command of the French forces, successfully defended Alsace against imperial forces. Later that year, ill with gout, he retired to Chantilly, where he spent his remaining years. He died in 1686, following a religious deathbed conversion, after a life without religion, in which he had rebelled against religious as well as worldly authority. He is at times described as an aggressive atheist, though he favored religious tolerance.

Summary

The Great Condé, along with Turenne, was among the most outstanding and innovative military commanders of the seventeenth century, though he, contrary to most of his contemporary military geniuses, had no formal military training or apprenticeship. He was an enterprising and daring tactician, who inspired his troops. Condé adopted military concepts, developed by Gustavus II Adolphus and by Oliver Cromwell, which emphasized mobility and the more flexible use of field artillery, especially in combination with cavalry. Condé employed these methods as early as the Battle of Rocroi, which resulted in a stunning victory over Spain's famous infantry. Following that battle, Condé was viewed as a model commander and teacher of these new concepts. During this period, however, strong fortifications increasingly dominated warfare, and it was in this latter area that Turenne's greater strategic skills, based on patience and planning, gained greater success and reputation. The reforms introduced by these two great captains were ably advanced by the Marquis de Louvois, one of France's greatest ministers of war, who held that office from 1677 to 1691.

Condé's role in the Fronde was designed to reverse the growth of royal absolutism and centralization of power in France and to preserve, or reestablish, traditional noble rights. His efforts failed, and he has to share in the blame for bringing France close to anarchy. His loyalty to the Crown, however, was firm and unchallenging following the amnesty of 1659.

Bibliography
Briggs, Robin. *Early Modern France, 1560-1715*. New York: Oxford University Press, 1977. A general introductory history with several charts, an index, a glossary, and a six-page annotated bibliography.
Montgomery of Alamein, Viscount. *A History of Warfare*. Cleveland: World Publishing, 1968. A general history of warfare, which places Condé and his times in a larger framework. Includes illustrations, maps, an index, and a short bibliography.
Ogg, David. *Europe in the Seventeenth Century*. 6th ed. London: Adam and Charles Black, 1952. A standard history, still of great value despite its age. Contains several maps, an index, and a ten-page bibliography.
Ranum, Orest. *Paris in the Age of Absolutism*. Bloomington: Indiana University Press, 1979. Chapter 10, entitled "The Frondeurs," is entirely devoted to the Fronde.
Wedgwood, C. V. *The Thirty Years' War*. New Haven, Conn.: Yale University Press, 1939. A standard history of the war. Despite its age this is an excellent treatment.

Frederick Dumin

ÉTIENNE BONNOT DE CONDILLAC

Born: September 30, 1714; Grenoble, France
Died: August 2, 1780; Château Flux, Beaugency, France
Area of Achievement: Philosophy
Contribution: In writings famed for precision, clarity, and persuasiveness,
  Condillac was the only major figure of the French Enlightenment to create
  a systematic theory of knowledge and exhibit a professional command of
  the issues of philosophy.

Early Life

Étienne Bonnot was born on September 30, 1714, at Grenoble, France,
the third son of Gabriel de Bonnot, Vicomte de Mably, a magistrate and
member of the *noblesse de la robe* in the Dauphiné provincial *parlement.*
The name Condillac, by which he would be known for the rest of his life,
was added in 1720, when his father bought the nearby estate and domain of
that name. As a child, his health was poor, his eyesight was bad, and he was
painfully shy. His education did not begin until after he was twelve, when a
local priest taught him the basics. His mother, about whom virtually nothing
is known, died when he was quite young, and his father died in 1727, when
he was thirteen.

After his father's death, he went to live with his eldest brother, Jean
Bonnot de Mably, a royal official in Lyons, but his personal situation does
not seem to have improved. His shy nature was apparently mistaken by his
brother and family for simplemindedness. Jean-Jacques Rousseau, who was
hired by Jean to tutor his children for a short time, was able to see what the
family had missed, and so began a long friendship.

Condillac's other brother, Gabriel Bonnot, had taken holy orders and styled
himself the Abbé de Mably. He, too, saw something in Condillac, and, a
few years later, Condillac went to Paris to live with Gabriel. Gabriel entered
Condillac first at Saint-Sulpice and then at the Sorbonne to study theology. By
1740, Condillac had completed the course of studies and was ordained a priest.

While he wore a cassock and called himself the Abbé de Condillac for the
rest of his life, it was reported that he only said mass once and otherwise
chose not to exercise the office. This was not unusual in France at that time.
Condillac was a man of pleasant but unremarkable appearance. His portrait
shows large, wide-set eyes, a high forehead, and a modest smile. Other
evidence indicates that he was of average height but slightly built. He wore
neither a beard nor a mustache and kept his hair long and curled in the
fashion of the day.

Life's Work

Condillac was twenty-six when he left the Sorbonne, and, under the sponsorship of his brother, was introduced to the social and literary life of Paris. He soon decided that his education was inadequate to move in that circle and began educating himself, reading the works of René Descartes, Gottfried Leibniz, Baruch Spinoza, and Nicolas de Malebranche. Sometime during this course of study, he developed a profound disapproval of their speculative systems of thought.

The English philosophers, whom he read next, were much more to his liking. Because he read no English, however, he had to rely on translations or someone's summary and commentary. John Locke's *An Essay Concerning Human Understanding*, published in 1690, had been translated into French in 1700 by Pierre Coste. It was this work that made the deepest impression on Condillac. He also read Voltaire's summary and commentary *Éléments de la philosophie de Newton* (1738; *The Elements of Sir Isaac Newton's Philosophy*, 1738), which also introduced him to the Idealism of Bishop George Berkeley's *A Treatise Concerning the Principles of Human Knowledge* (1710). He was also quite impressed with several works by Francis Bacon.

During these years, Condillac sometimes joined in the social life of the Paris salons, where he renewed his friendship with Rousseau, who introduced him to Denis Diderot. The three became good friends and met often. Later writings by both Rousseau and Diderot reflect Condillac's influence. Condillac does not seem to have made much of an impression on the other intellectuals at the salons, probably because of his acute shyness and timidity. Condillac, however, would make his reputation with the printed word.

In 1746, Condillac published his first book, *Essai sur l'origine des connaissances humaines* (*An Essay on the Origin of Human Understanding*, 1756), and his second, *Traité des systèmes* (treatise on systems), in 1749. These two books were very well received and brought Condillac recognition as a major philosopher. Shortly after publishing the second book, he was honored by election to membership in the Académie Royale des Sciences et Belles Lettres of Berlin.

What Condillac sought was a philosophy which was an exact science. He thought philosophy should be clear, precise, universal, and, above all, verifiable. *Essai sur l'origine des connaissances humaines* was a systematic elaboration of Locke's theory that all human knowledge was derived from two sources: the information received by the mind through the senses and the mind's ability to reflect upon that information and understand its meaning. It was a brilliant study, using only empirical evidence and a strictly logical methodology. Condillac's essay established empirical sensationism as the prevailing analysis of the working of the human mind for the Enlightenment.

His *Traité des systèmes* was a vigorous criticism of the metaphysical systems of Descartes, Leibniz, and others that were rationalistic and not empirical. He attempted to show that there was no empirical evidence for such ideas as Descartes' innate ideas or for Leibniz's monads, that these ideas were mere speculations without basis in fact. Condillac accused these philosophers of having used vague words that had no clear and precise meaning, thereby producing only confusion and misunderstanding.

In 1754, after some delay because of trouble with his eyes, Condillac published his most advanced work on the theory of empirical sensationism, *Traité des sensations* (*Condillac's Treatise on the Sensations*, 1930). To help illustrate the role of sensation in the acquisition of knowledge, he described what it would be like if a person were encased in marble and his mind had never received any sensory information, and, therefore, was completely blank. Condillac then imagined what would happen when the nose was uncovered and how the person's mind would react to a flood of olfactory information. All the person's perceptions, comparisons, memories, recognitions, and abstractions would consist only of odors. He then uncovered the other sense organs, one at a time, describing how the mind would react to the new data and correlate it with the data from the other sense organs. Condillac described how—when all senses were functioning together—these sense impressions produced pleasure and pain, and desires and aversions; he also described how all aspects of a person's mental life were derived from sensations.

After his first book on Locke's theory, he had discovered a problem which he attempted to correct in this work. Diderot had pointed it out to him. Locke had written about two sources of knowledge, sensory impressions and the reflection of the mind on these impressions. If sensation did not imprint knowledge directly on the mind but required the reflection of the mind, this meant that the mind was conscious of itself and its operations of thinking, doubting, reasoning, and willing. Condillac thought that this implied the existence of innate ideas, which he denied. In this book, he sought to avoid that issue by making language the means by which sensation passed into reflection to become knowledge. Language was the cause of the most complex operations of the mind, including attention, memory, imagination, and intuition. Since all language was learned, there could be no innate ideas.

In his *Treatise on the Sensations*, Condillac moved from being merely a student of Locke, having produced the most rigorous demonstration of sensationalist theory of his century. When it was pointed out that his work could be interpreted as advocating materialism and atheism, Condillac published two works in 1755 to refute the claim. In the brief *Dissertation sur la liberté*, and then in *Traité des animaux*, Condillac denied that animals were mere machines and possessed no spiritual soul. Condillac never agreed that his theories eliminated free will or the spiritual side of the human experience.

After 1754, Condillac's work was being discussed by intellectuals in other countries and by high officials of France. In 1758, he was invited to Parma to tutor the Duke of Parma's son, Ferdinand, who was a grandchild of the King and Queen of France. He remained there until January of 1767, during which time he wrote the impressive sixteen-volume *Cours d'études pour l'instruction du prince de Parme* (1775) for the young Ferdinand. The set included a grammar, a handbook of writing style, a book on the scientific method, an analysis of the psychology of thought, a philosophy of history, and history texts. In appreciation of his services, the duke obtained for Condillac the revenue of the Premonstratensian Abbey of Mureau for Condillac. This liberal income removed all personal financial worries for the rest of Condillac's life.

In 1768, Condillac, back in Paris, was elected to the Académie Française. He was asked to become tutor to the three sons of the dauphine, who included the future Kings Louis XVI, Louis XVIII, and Charles X, but he refused. Instead, he devoted himself to the publication of the *Cours d'études pour l'instruction du prince de Parme* and rarely attended the Académie or the salons. Condillac's criticisms of church politics had apparently earned for him the hostility of the Bishop of Parma, who delayed publication of the works. With the intervention of several of his philosophe friends, Condillac received permission to publish his books in Paris. In 1773, he left Paris for the peace and quiet of the château, where he remained for the rest of his life.

In 1776, Condillac published a book on political economy, *Le Commerce et le gouvernement considérés relativement l'un à l'autre*, in which he presented the novel idea that value was a matter of utility and not labor. That same year, he joined the Société Royale d'Agriculture d'Orléans. Condillac returned to Paris for a short visit each year; his last trip was in the summer of 1780. While there he fell ill and returned to Château Flux. When his condition worsened, he sent for a priest to reaffirm his Catholic faith. He died of a fever on the night of August 2, 1780, at the age of sixty-five.

Summary

Building on the work of Locke, Étienne Bonnot de Condillac contributed more to a synthesis of epistemology and psychology than did any other writer of philosophy of the Enlightenment. His method was empirical observation. His ideas and methodology inspired the philosophes, and reflections of his work are found throughout their works. The goal of the philosophes was to bring about a revolution in the way people thought and to end superstition, prejudice, and ignorance. They hoped to teach people to think clearly, rationally, and scientifically. The major theoretician behind this new way of thinking was Condillac. He established its epistemological foundations which he had derived with a methodology that he hoped would not only withstand criticism but also be applicable to all the fields of knowledge available to mankind.

Condillac's influence extended beyond his own time. Jeremy Bentham incorporated Condillac's concept of pleasure and pain as motivating forces into his philosophy of Utilitarianism. James Mill and John Stuart Mill also borrowed ideas from Condillac. His philosophy and methodology of history inspired a number of nineteenth and twentieth century historians in their attempts to make the writing of history scientific. The Enlightenment made important and productive contributions to philosophy and to a better understanding of how the human mind works. Condillac's work, which was central to the Enlightenment, is an important part, therefore, of the Western intellectual tradition.

The contrast between Condillac's work as a philosopher and his personal life makes his achievements remarkable. As a philosopher he was a stringent empiricist, but privately he was a devout Catholic. He believed that humans had souls without any empirical evidence to support such a belief. His ideas were among the most radical and progressive of his age, yet politically he was a conservative monarchist. As a philosopher his work concerned all the myriad sensations and experiences a person could have and how knowledge grew from them, but Condillac himself was virtually a one-dimensional person. He never married and was virtually a recluse who shunned contact with all but a very few people. He preferred the quiet and solitude of the countryside to the excitement of the city. With the few close friends he did have, he seems to have discussed only philosophical issues. For Condillac, philosophy was his life.

Bibliography

Cassirer, Ernst. *Philosophy of the Enlightenment.* Translated by Fritz A. C. Koelln and James P. Pettegrove. Princeton, N.J.: Princeton University Press, 1951. A brilliant and perceptive work of intellectual history. Cassirer presents no lengthy discussion of Condillac in any one place. Instead, he integrates his discussion of Condillac into topically arranged analyses, in which he reveals a fine appreciation for what is important and what is peripheral in Condillac's thought.

Gay, Peter. *The Enlightenment: An Interpretation.* 2 vols. New York: Alfred A. Knopf, 1966-1969. A lively and brilliant interpretation of the Enlightenment organized by topic. Less critical of the philosophes than some historians, but a gold mine of information.

_____. *The Party of Humanity: Essays in the French Enlightenment.* New York: W. W. Norton, 1971. A series of essays on various aspects of the Enlightenment by one of the period's most renowned historians. See especially the essay on "The Unity of the French Enlightenment."

Hazard, Paul. *The European Mind, 1680-1715.* Translated by J. Lewis May. Cleveland, Ohio: World Publishing, 1963. An interesting and well-respected treatment of the origins and early days of the Enlightenment. Often treats the philosophes with cynical amusement, which interferes with an appreciation of the book's positive qualities.

Knight, Isabel F. *The Geometric Spirit: The Abbé de Condillac and the*

French Enlightenment. New Haven, Conn.: Yale University Press, 1968. This is the closest there is to a biography of Condillac in English. Focuses primarily on Condillac's ideas concerning the origins of knowledge and gives little attention to his personal life. Perceptive in spots, but pedestrian in others.

Krieger, Leonard. *Kings and Philosophers, 1689-1789.* New York: W. W. Norton, 1970. An excellent, well-written history of the Enlightenment age. Explains how the Enlightenment was made possible, in part, by the political stability that resulted from the end of the Reformation wars and the rise of the centralized state, and how the ideas of the Enlightenment came into conflict with divine right monarchies and produced the French Revolution.

Woloch, Isser. *Eighteenth-Century Europe: Tradition and Progress, 1715-1789.* New York: W. W. Norton, 1982. One of the best general histories of the age with a good annotated bibliography. Recommended for the reader who needs an understanding of the whole age before concentrating on the intellectual history of Condillac and the Enlightenment.

Richard L. Hillard

MARQUIS DE CONDORCET

Born: September 17, 1743; Ribemont, France
Died: March 29, 1794; Bourg-la-Reine, France
Areas of Achievement: Sociology, education, and mathematics
Contribution: Condorcet's works synthesized the thinking of the philosophes of the Enlightenment. He spent his life promoting educational, political, social, and religious change in France.

Early Life

Marie-Jean-Antoine-Nicolas was born into the very old aristocratic family of Caritat, which took its title, Condorcet, from a town in Dauphiné. The Marquis de Condorcet spent his early years in pursuits typical of his class. He received his early education at the Jesuit school in Reims and then entered the Collège de Navarre in Paris. There he developed a lifelong commitment to science. In 1769, he was elected to the Academy of Sciences, followed by membership in the French Academy for his work in the science of statistics and the doctrine of probability. As a result of his reputation in mathematics, he was appointed inspector general of the mint in Paris.

While serving as inspector general, Condorcet met and married Sophie de Grouchy in 1786. Twenty years his junior and considered one of the great beauties of the day, Madame Grouchy presided over a salon of notable reputation, which attracted many of the leading personalities in Paris. There Condorcet conversed with people such as David Hume, the great British philosopher. At this time, Condorcet wrote the biographies, *Vie de M. Turgot* (1786; *The Life of M. Turgot*, 1787) and *Vie de Voltaire* (1789; *The Life of Voltaire*, 1790). These works reflected his appreciation for Anne-Robert-Jacques Turgot's Physiocratic economics and Voltaire's revolutionary religious and social theories. Condorcet had become a philosophe.

He also frequented the Baron d'Holbach's salon, the Café de l'Europe, where wide-ranging discussion included political and social reform, religion, education, science, and the arts. He wrote for Denis Diderot's *Encyclopédie: Ou, Dictionnaire raisonné des sciences, des arts, et des métiers* (1751-1772; *Encyclopedia*, 1965). While he respected Jean-Jacques Rousseau's work, it was Jean Le Rond d'Alembert's ideas that inflenced him most strongly. When the Marquis de Lafayette returned from his American success, it was with Condorcet that he conferred about the American Revolution and the future of France. Condorcet also knew Thomas Jefferson and Benjamin Franklin and thought that the United States was the place most likely to implement the ideals of the Enlightenment. Not surprisingly, when the French Revolution began, Condorcet repudiated all the religious and aristocratic ideals of his background and became one of the few philosophes actively involved in the Revolution.

Life's Work

Although he would not survive the Revolution, Condorcet is best remembered for the work that he produced during its first five years. On the eve of revolution, Condorcet and Emmanuel-Joseph Sieyès founded the '89 Club, a salon that became the meeting place for the politically moderate Girondists. Condorcet was elected as a representative from Paris to the Legislative Assembly. As secretary of this body, he wrote the address in 1791 which explained the Revolution to the European powers. The following year, he drafted the declaration that suspended the monarchy, disbanded the assembly, and called for a new government, the National Convention, to formulate a constitution for France. Though ultimately defeated in favor of the more radical proposal from the Jacobins, Condorcet's was the first of the constitutions presented to the convention. In this government, Condorcet represented the Department of Aisne.

Although the first person to declare for republican government, Condorcet voted against the execution of the king and queen. By 1793, his independent and moderate attitude and his enormous prestige made him dangerous to Robespierre, who was by then in control of the Revolution. When Condorcet objected to the arrest of his Girondist friends, Robespierre had him outlawed.

During these hectic but creative early years, Condorcet wrote his two most influential works. The first of these was his educational plan, submitted to the Legislative Assembly in 1792, which detailed a system for state education. It divided the proposed educational system into four parts: primary, secondary, higher, and adult education, all of which would be coeducational. All instruction would be based in free inquiry under the control of a corporation of scholars, independent of supervision by either the church or the state. The curriculum would be secular in emphasis. Primary education was to be free and compulsory for all children of the state. Characteristic of Jean-Jacques Rousseau's educational theory, students were to be allowed considerable freedom of choice in their curriculum, and administration would be minimal. The higher education component included a system of technical, medical, and teacher-training schools, which when finally implemented became the best in Europe. Condorcet assumed that all people would want and appreciate the opportunity to attend school and that they, like him, would recognize that only through education could the ideal of progress be attained. Although revolution and war prevented its immediate implementation, the plan became the basis of the education system ultimately adopted, not only by the French but also by other nations.

Equally influential was Condorcet's *Esquisse d'un tableau historique des progrès de l'espirit humain* (1795; *Sketch for a Historical Picture of the Progress of the Human Mind*, 1955), written just before his death in 1794. In this work, Condorcet analyzed all human history, past, present, and future; he used history to find evidence to justify his confidence that human progress was inevitable. The work is particularly significant, as it synthesized the major strains of Enlightenment thought and the goals of the French Revolution. It reflects the extent of Condorcet's optimism.

Condorcet divided the history of man into ten epochs, eight in the past, the ninth in his own age, and the tenth in the future. Up to the Middle Ages, Condorcet thought that mankind had made great progress. For example, the Greeks had opened the way for man's search for truth through the greatest of human inventions, philosophy. Then the Dark Ages fell, shrouded in superstition, ignorance, and clericism. Condorcet saw only the unintended development of precision in argumentation made by the Scholastics and the contributions to poetry, nobility of spirit, and individual freedom made by Dante in *La divina commedia* (c. 1320; *The Divine Comedy*, 1802) as worthy contributions of this epoch.

The fourteenth and fifteenth centuries brought renewed light to human understanding. Witness the development of the printing press, the tool that reawakened the mind of man, creating, according to Condorcet, "cultural revolution." The ninth epoch was his own, in which the Revolution would destroy old ideas and institutions, thus paving the way for the tenth epoch, in which perfect man would live in a perfect civilization.

All this progress was possible because science had revealed the secrets of nature and technology, which would relieve man of labor so that he might use his free time for self-improvement. Although Condorcet conceded that the intellectuals would dominate paternalistically until all people had the benefit of education, he believed that once educated, each individual would use his time constructively. The improvement of the individual would lead to social and political progress, stop exploitation, and produce true equality. Condorcet recognized that this process was not an easy one and that often there were periods when things seemed bleak, but he firmly believed that the spirit and reason of man would prevail, that perfectibility of man and society was inevitable. He believed in the unity of all knowledge and in the continuity of progress. He thought that this was the consummate lesson of human history.

Summary

As the youngest of the philosophes, Marquis de Condorcet embodied the principles of the Enlightenment. He represented the moderate Girondist position in the French Revolution. Thus, he voted against the execution of the king, while still being one of the first revolutionaries to promote republicanism. He worked hard in several capacities to achieve the goals of the Revolution. He was the leading educational theorist of the Revolution and the creator of a secular education system that became the model for many state systems established during the nineteenth and twentieth centuries. Condorcet insisted that education and science were crucial to social progress and human perfectibility. His theory of history particularly influenced Auguste Comte and the development of sociology.

Outlawed with other Girondists during the Reign of Terror, Condorcet went into hiding. He spent the last weeks of his life writing the *Sketch for a Historical Picture of the Progress of the Human Mind*, which he is said to have been holding in his hands when he died. On March 24, believing that his hiding place had been discovered, Condorcet fled Paris and hid in the countryside for three days. On March 27, he wandered into the village of Clamart, where he was captured and taken to the prison in Bourg-la-Reine to await execution. Whether by poison or from exhaustion, Condorcet was found dead in his cell two days later. Despite this dismal death, Condorcet never lost his faith in the Revolution or his optimism about the progress of the human spirit.

Bibliography

Becker, Carl. *The Heavenly City of the Eighteenth Century Philosophers*. New Haven, Conn.: Yale University Press, 1932. Reprinted many times and readily available, this provocative and brilliantly insightful essay has stimulated much research about the nature and influence of Enlightenment thinkers, including Condorcet. Any study of Enlightenment thinkers should begin with a reading of this book.

Bury, J. B. *The Idea of Progress: An Inquiry into Its Origins and Growth*. New York: Macmillan, 1920, 2d ed. 1932. This now-classic work on the idea of progress as the basic characteristic of Enlightenment thought contains an excellent analysis of Condorcet's role in the development of this idea.

Condorcet, Marquis de. *Sketch for a Historical Picture of the Progress of the Human Mind*. Translated by June Barraclough with an introduction by Stuart Hampshire. New York: Noonday Press, 1955. This is an excellent translation of Condorcet's best-known work, which strongly influenced the work of Auguste Comte and the development of sociology.

Durant, Will, and Ariel Durant. *The Age of Voltaire*. New York: Simon & Schuster, 1965. This intelligent, urbane, highly readable, and readily available account of the Enlightenment contains excellent insights into the role and contributions of Condorcet.

Gay, Peter. *The Party of Humanity: Essays in the French Enlightenment*. New York: Alfred A. Knopf, 1964. This stylistically excellent, soundly researched book is a brilliant synthesis of the various threads of Enlightenment thought. It clearly illustrates the environment that produced Condorcet as well as his contributions to the revolutionary quality of his age.

Lovejoy, Arthur O. *The Great Chain of Being: A Study of the History of an Idea*. Cambridge, Mass.: Harvard University Press, 1936. This standard work details the history of the ideas of natural law and progress.

Martin, Kingsley. *French Liberal Thought in the Eighteenth Century: A Study of Political Ideas from Bayle to Condorcet*. New York: Harper & Row, 1963. Based almost exclusively upon primary sources, this book remains the best analysis of the development of liberal thought in the eighteenth century. As such, it describes Condorcet's contributions, particularly his theories of history, social progress, and human perfectibility.

Shapiro, J. Salwyn. *Condorcet and the Rise of Liberalism*. New York: Harcourt, Brace, 1934. This biography is a thorough study of Condorcet and his contributions to the tradition of liberal thought in Western society.

Shirley F. Fredricks

NICOLAUS COPERNICUS

Born: February 19, 1473; Thorn (Toruń), Prussia
Died: May 24, 1543; Frauenburg (Frombork), Prussia
Area of Achievement: Astronomy
Contribution: Copernicus discarded the Ptolemaic system and introduced the theory that the planets, including the earth, revolve around the sun. He defended the right of learned men to discuss scientific theories, even when they differ from currently accepted beliefs and contradict religious dogma.

Early Life

Nicolaus Copernicus' family origins and the commercial interests of his hometown, Thorn (modern Toruń), reflect the dual claim which Germans and Poles alike have upon him. His father, Mikołaj (Nicolaus) Kopernik, was an immigrant from Kraków who married a daughter of a prominent burgher family, Barbara Watzenrode, and, like other Thorn merchants, prospered from the exchange of Hanseatic goods for the wheat, cattle, and other produce of Poland. Thorn burghers were subjects of the Polish king, but Polish tradition allowed associated lands such as Prussia to govern themselves autonomously. Consequently, they made their political wishes felt through their representatives in the Prussian diet rather than directly to the king.

Had Mikołaj not died in 1483, his sons, Andreas and Nicolaus, would probably have entered upon careers in commerce. The guardianship, however, fell to their uncle, Bishop Lucas Watzenrode of Ermland (Warmia), who was best able to provide for them a future in church administration. A university education being indispensable to holding church offices, Bishop Lucas sent the boys to study first in Kraków, then in Italy. Nicolaus not only became a master of mathematics and astronomy but also acquired knowledge of medicine, painting, and Greek. Upon his return to Prussia in 1503, Nicolaus followed the contemporary practice of Latinizing his name, Copernicus, and became one of the canons in the Ermland cathedral chapter. As his uncle's physician, assistant, and heir apparent, Copernicus was present during inspection tours, provincial diets, and royal audiences. For several years he managed the diocese efficiently but without enthusiasm—his uncle was a hard taskmaster who lacked a sense of humor. Eventually, Copernicus announced that his interests in astronomy were greater than his ambition to become a bishop. From that time on, like most of the other canons, he lived according to clerical rules but remained a simple administrator who had no thought of becoming a priest.

The first of several portraits made during his lifetime show Copernicus to have been a dark, handsome man dressed in simple but elegant clothing, with nothing of either the cleric or the dandy about him. He was so utterly unremarkable in other respects that few anecdotes about him exist, leaving relatively little information about his personal life and intellectual development. Yet two facts stand out. First, Copernicus was a Humanist whose closest friends and associates were poets and polemists. His translation of an ancient author, Theophilactus Symocatta, from Greek into Latin was the first such publication in the Kingdom of Poland, and he dedicated the work to his humanistically trained uncle, Bishop Lucas. Later Copernicus used Humanist arguments to defend his astronomical theories. Second, Copernicus must be seen as a bureaucrat whose busy life made it difficult for him to make the observations of the heavens on which his mathematical calculations were based. At one time or another, he was a medical doctor, an astrologer, a mapmaker, an administrator of episcopal lands, a diplomat, a garrison commander in wartime, an economic theorist, an adviser to the Prussian diet, and a guardian to numerous nieces and nephews.

Life's Work

About 1507, Copernicus seems to have become persuaded that the Ptolemaic system (which asserted that the earth was the center of the universe) was incorrect. From that point on, he spent every spare moment trying to demonstrate the correctness of his insight that the sun was the center of the planetary movements (the solar system).

His first description of his theory, the *Commentariolus* (1514; English translation, 1939), circulated among his friends for many years. Eventually, it came to the ears of Cardinal Schönberg, who wrote a letter asking Copernicus to publish a fuller account. This letter was ultimately published in *De revolutionibus orbium coelestium* (1543; *On the Revolutions of the Celestial Spheres*, 1939) as a proof that high officials in the papal curia approved of scholars' discussing the existence of a solar system. Copernicus made no answer. Instead, he asked his bishop to assign him light duties at some parish center where he could make his observations and concentrate on mathematical calculations. This request was difficult to grant, because Copernicus was known to be one of the more capable diocesan administrators.

For several years his work was interrupted by war. In 1520, the last grandmaster of the Teutonic Order, Albrecht of Brandenburg, made a final effort to reestablish his religious order as ruler of all Prussia. Copernicus led the defense of Allenstein (Olsztyn) and participated in the peace negotiations. In 1525, Albrecht, defeated at every turn, secularized the Teutonic Order in Prussia and became a Protestant vassal of the King of Poland. This brought about an immediate improvement of Albrecht's relationship to the rest of Prussia. Albrecht later called on Copernicus' services as physician, and, in 1551, he published a volume of Copernicus' astrological observations.

Copernicus labored for several years to restore order to the war-ravaged Ermland finances. He advised the Prussian diet to reform the monetary system, explaining that since everyone was hoarding good coins and paying taxes with debased coins, the income of the diet was being reduced significantly. Having expounded this early version of English financier Sir Thomas Gresham's law, he recommended that all coins be called in and new ones issued. The diet, aware that it did not have the bullion to mint a sufficient number of full-weight coins, took no action. There were other, more pressing problems: politics and religion.

The spread of Lutheran reforms through Poland was halted by royal action, but not before many cities and some prominent nobles had become Protestant. The ensuing era was filled with strident debate as fanatics on both sides denounced their opponents and demanded that all parties commit themselves to what they perceived as a struggle against ultimate evil. Copernicus sought to avoid this controversy but could not. When Ermland Bishop Johann Dantiscus sought to rid himself of all canons who gave any appearance of Protestant leanings, his eye fell on Copernicus, whose friends were corresponding with prominent Protestants and who, moreover, had as his housekeeper a young woman with children. Copernicus responded that his housekeeper was a widowed relative who could have no interest in a man as aged as he, but he argued in vain. He dismissed his housekeeper and watched as his friends went into exile. His health failing, Copernicus was indeed isolated from friends and family.

In 1539, a Lutheran mathematician at Wittenberg, Georg Joachim Rheticus, made a special journey to Frauenburg to visit Copernicus. Finding him ill and without prospect of publishing the manuscript he had completed at great labor, Rheticus extended his stay to three months so that he could personally copy the manuscript. He then arranged for the publication of *Narratio prima de libris revolutionum* (1540; *The First Account*, 1939) in Danzig and for the publication of the mathematical section in Nuremberg in 1542. Unable to supervise the printing of the theoretical section personally, Rheticus gave that task to another Protestant scholar, Andreas Osiander of Wittenberg.

Osiander was at a loss as to how to proceed. He saw that Copernicus had not been able to prove his case mathematically. Indeed, it would have been difficult for him to do so without inventing calculus (which was later created by Gottfreid Wilhelm Leibniz and Sir Isaac Newton independently of each other for the very purpose of calculating the elliptical orbits of the planets). Consequently, Copernicus had defended his ideas by demonstrating that Ptolemy's was not the only ancient theory describing the universe; indeed, there were ancient philosophers who believed that the sun was the center of a solar system. Moreover, he had argued that free inquiry into science was as necessary as freedom to write literature or produce fine art. In this respect, Copernicus was presenting his case to Renaissance Humanists, especially to the well-educated pope to whom he dedicated his book, as a test of free thought. Osiander, who perceived that the Catholic world was hostile to all innovations and was equally well aware of the debates raging in the Protestant world over biblical inerrancy, saw that Copernicus was treading on dangerous ground by suggesting an alternate view of the universe than the one presented in Scripture. Consequently, there was a real danger that the theory would be rejected entirely without having been read. To minimize that possibility, he wrote an unauthorized introduction which readers assumed was by Copernicus. This stated that the solar system was merely a hypothesis, a way of seeing the universe which avoided some of the problems of the Ptolemaic system. This led to much confusion and angered Copernicus considerably when he saw the page proofs. Copernicus, however, was too weak and ill to do anything about it. With a justice that is all too rare in this world, a copy of *On the Revolutions of the Celestial Spheres* arrived in time for him to know that his life's work was to survive.

Summary

Nicolaus Copernicus' theory was not immediately accepted, and not because of the controversies of the Reformation alone—although they made it dangerous for any scientist to suggest that the biblical descriptions of the heavens were incorrect. Copernicus' idealistic belief that God would create only perfectly circular planetary orbits made it impossible for him to prove his assertions mathematically. Nevertheless, Copernicus' theory was the only one to offer astronomers a way out of a Ptolemaic system of interlocking rings, which was becoming impossibly complex. His insights undermined the intellectual pretensions of astrology and set astronomy on a firm foundation of observation and mathematics.

Although Copernicus' defense of the freedom of inquiry was less important in the struggle against religious dogmatism than later demonstrations of the existence of the solar system, Copernicus became a symbol of the isolated and despised scientist who triumphs over all efforts by religious fundamentalists to silence him.

Bibliography

Armitage, Angus. *Sun, Stand Thou Still: The Life and Works of Copernicus, the Astronomer.* New York: Henry Schuman, 1947. The best-known of many biographies, its explanation of the conceptual problems facing Copernicus is easily followed by any sophisticated reader.

Beer, Arthur. *Copernicus Yesterday and Today.* Elmsford, N.Y.: Pergamon Press, 1975. A collection of useful essays which were delivered during the Copernicus celebration.

Copernicus, Nicolaus. *Three Copernican Treatises: The Commentariolus of*

Copernicus, The Letter Against Werner, The Narratio Prima of Rheticus. Edited and translated by Edward Rosen. New York: Columbia University Press, 1939. This timeless translation of basic documents relating to Copernicus' achievement is accompanied by an extensive learned commentary. Rosen demonstrates that Copernicus put forward a "hypothesis" rather than a "theory" out of a fear of arousing opposition from religious fundamentalists rather than from any doubt that he was right.

Kesten, Hermann. *Copernicus and His World.* New York: Roy Publishers, 1945. This literate biography deals with Copernicus' contemporaries as much as with the astronomer himself. Kesten presents Copernicus as a warrior in the contest between science and religion. He concludes with chapters on Bruno, Tycho Brahe, Kepler, and Galileo.

Rusinek, Michat. *The Land of Nicholas Copernicus.* Translated by A. T. Jordan. New York: Twayne, 1973. The text is relatively sparse, but the pictures and subtitles are unequaled in quality. The author traces the life of the astronomer through photographs of cities, castles, and personal possessions.

Stachiewicz, Wanda M. *Copernicus and the Changing World.* New York: Polish Institute, 1973. The four hundredth anniversary of Copernicus' birth brought forth a plethora of publications. This one is unique.

William Urban

ARCANGELO CORELLI

Born: February 17, 1653; Fusignano, Italy
Died: January 8, 1713; Rome, Italy
Area of Achievement: Music
Contribution: Corelli was one of the most significant violin virtuosos of the late Baroque period. He composed sonatas and concertos for string instruments, which became famous throughout Europe for their pedagogical and musical value.

Early Life
Arcangelo Corelli was born in Fusignano, a small village midway between Bologna and Ravenna. Corelli became the only accomplished musician in a family of wealthy landowners who generally preferred other professions, such as medicine and law. The high social status of the wealthy Corelli family definitely helped Corelli as he matured musically during his early years. He received his first music lessons from a priest in the nearby town of Faenza; other music lessons followed at Lugo. Since his early teachers and their qualifications are unknown, these music lessons could have been devoted to the rudiments of music rather than to violin playing, as has often been assumed. In 1666, Corelli moved to Bologna, one of the most important centers for instrumental music in seventeenth century Europe. From his studies in Bologna, he acquired an excellent violin technique and a knowledge of improvisation. It is likely that his teachers included some of the most significant Bolognese musicians of the day (Giovanni Benvenuti, Leonardo Brugnoli, and B. G. Laurenti). Corelli's improvement on the violin is attested by the fact that he was admitted as a member of Bologna's Accademia Filarmonica in 1670. Nothing is known of his activities between 1670 and 1675; he may have left Bologna for another Italian town in 1670, but he probably did not arrive in Rome until 1675, the year in which he began his career as a professional violinist.

Life's Work
Beginning in 1675, Corelli rapidly became one of the most important violinists in Rome. He performed for various local church functions, including the Lenten oratorios in the church patronized by Cardinal Pamphili. In 1679, Corelli became chamber musician to Queen Christina of Sweden, who hosted well-known musical gatherings at her palace in Rome. Two significant events of the year 1684 indicate his growing stature as a violinist: He was accepted as a member of the prestigious Congregazione dei Virtuosi di Santa Cecilia, and he began to play every Sunday for musical functions at Cardinal Pamphili's palace.

Corelli formally entered the service of Cardinal Pamphili as his music master on July 9, 1687. Three years later, when Cardinal Pamphili moved to Bologna, Corelli became first violinist and music director to the young Cardinal Pietro Ottoboni, nephew of Pope Alexander VIII. At Cardinal Ottoboni's palace, concerts were normally held every Monday evening. Corelli was thus an important part of Roman musical life, an accomplished violinist patronized by two wealthy Roman church officials, and a musician whose talents were esteemed so highly that he served as music director to these officials and was allowed to take up residence in their respective palaces.

While his reputation was increasing during the last two decades of the seventeenth century, Corelli published four books of trio sonatas for two violins and continuo (1681, 1685, 1689, 1694). Each of these books consists of twelve sonatas, distributed equally between major and minor keys. The first and third books of these publications belong to the more contrapuntal and learned church type of sonata, while the second and fourth books belong to the lighter and more dancelike chamber type of sonata. While Corelli's church and chamber sonatas can still be distinguished from one another, one of Corelli's major achievements was the intermingling of church and chamber styles to the point where his church sonatas begin to acquire some dancelike traits, while his chamber sonatas became more contrapuntal.

More than half of Corelli's church trio sonatas have four movements that alternate between slow and fast tempos. The opening slow movements all achieve variety by the use of several standard devices (motion in parallel thirds, close points of imitation, dissonances at cadential preparations, and chains of suspensions). The second movements are quicker, with three-part imitation between the two violins and bass. Usually the third movements are in a slower meter, which suggests the influence of the saraband dance. The inclusion of dance elements in these church sonatas is seen most clearly in the fast finales, which are reminiscent of a gigue in compound meter or another type of dance in a quick triple meter. The finales often juxtapose imitative sections with homophonic sections, and some finales have the binary form associated with dance pieces.

Corelli's chamber trio sonatas may have three or four movements. In those sonatas that open with slow preludi, the influence of the church sonata is evident in their use of through-composed form, active bass lines, and interweaving polyphonic lines. In addition to the polyphony of the preludi, these dance movements occasionally show church sonata influence by having sections that begin with imitation. The prevailing dancelike style is retained, however, through the use of the following stylistic features: movements in binary form, sections where the two violins move in similar rhythms and/or parallel thirds, an active bass part with two sustained violin parts, and a dominant first violin part over a slower-moving second violin part and bass line. Despite the intermingling of church and chamber sonatas in Corelli's sonatas, all these devices tend to make his chamber sonatas lighter and less complex than his church sonatas.

Corelli's most famous work is his fifth book of sonatas (1700), written for solo violin and continuo. Six of these sonatas are church sonatas, while five are chamber sonatas (the final piece is a set of variations). The church sonatas have five rather than four movements. Their opening slow movements have an active dialogue between violin and bass, and their quick second movements incorporate two melodic lines within the solo violin part to create a three-part imitative texture. Of the third and fourth movements, one will be slow and tuneful, while the other will be a virtuosic fast movement, using rapid scales and arpeggios. The finales will often show the influence of a quick dance, such as the gavotte or the gigue. The chamber sonatas have either four or five movements and open with the usual slow, contrapuntal preludi. They also have one interior slow movement and fast movements that are based on the rhythms of the allemanda, gavotte, or gigue. Their lighter, dancelike style is shown in the use of two-part rather than three-part imitation, the predilection for binary forms, and the frequent dominance of either the violin or bass part over the other. In all the sonatas in this fifth book, the presence of only one violin part leads Corelli to compose movements that are much more virtuosic, movements that became well known throughout the eighteenth century for both their musical and pedagogical value.

During his later years, Corelli was admitted to the Arcadian Academy, the most exclusive society in Italy. Since he published no more books of sonatas after 1700, his later years must have been devoted to his concertos, which were published posthumously in 1714. These may have been partially revised from earlier works, but the overall style suggests that they were primarily late creations. In general, Corelli's concertos are not innovative because they use the forms and textures of his trio sonatas. They are, however, significant for their mingling of church and chamber styles, for their increased tendency toward homophonic writing, and for their virtuosic display.

Corelli did not perform in public during the last few years of his life. After a period of failing health, he died on January 8, 1713. He was buried in the Pantheon, where his concertos were performed annually for some years to commemorate the anniversary of his death.

Summary

Arcangelo Corelli's great reputation has created considerable disagreement over his personality, the attribution of additional works to him, and the performance of his music. Despite his fame and wealth, Corelli, many biographers claim, was a courteous, modest, and mild-tempered man; other biographers claim that he was more passionate and aggressive. Of the many manuscripts and prints that contain additional music attributed to him, only a few have sonatas that may actually have been composed by Corelli (a trumpet sonata, four solo sonatas, and eight trio sonatas have been included in the new edition of Corelli's works, although the authenticity of at least four of these pieces is in doubt). His solo sonatas are found in numerous manuscripts and prints with many ornaments added, and although these ornaments differ considerably, many sources claim that they are based on Corelli's own performances.

Corelli had a tremendous impact on his contemporaries and eighteenth century successors. By the end of the eighteenth century, his various books of sonatas had been reprinted more than one hundred times. Some sonatas were arranged for other instruments or as concertos for strings. Many composers wrote works dedicated to Corelli or wrote original pieces that adopted many of his stylistic features. His music influenced composers in Italy (Antonio Vivaldi), France (François Couperin), Germany (Johann Sebastian Bach), and other European countries. Eighteenth century violin methods were based on his principles and recommended the daily study of his music for didactic purposes. He was the most outstanding violin teacher of his day, and many of his students had successful careers in Germany, France, and England (Francesco Geminiani, Michele Mascitti, and others). The tremendous impact of Corelli's music stems from a number of factors—the mixture of church and chamber styles, the balance between contrapuntal and homophonic textures, the clear-cut sense of tonality, and the tendency toward thematic unity. Because of these stylistic features, his music became the basis for all other late Baroque sonatas and was widely disseminated during the eighteenth century.

Bibliography

Deas, Stewart. "Arcangelo Corelli." *Music and Letters* 34 (January, 1953): 1-10. A good summary of Corelli's early life and his years in Rome. Discusses various anecdotes, taking the viewpoint that they suggest a modest, mild-tempered man. The general description of Corelli's works indicates some prejudice against his chamber sonatas and emphasizes his sense of balance and proportion.

Libby, Dennis. "Interrelationships in Corelli." *Journal of the American Musicological Society* 26 (Summer, 1973): 263-287. A detailed, valuable study of Corelli's style that stresses his overall sense of harmonic progression and tonality, and his tendency toward thematic unity within and between movements. Concludes by challenging the common view that Corelli was a mild-tempered person.

Marx, Hans Joachim. "Some Corelli Attributions Assessed." *Musical Quarterly* 56 (January, 1970): 88-98. Discusses five manuscripts that have works attributed to Corelli, noting that these pieces are by other composers. Also lists ten manuscripts and three prints with works attributed to Corelli, saying that only one or two of these sources may contain authentic works.

_____. "Some Unknown Embellishments of Corelli's Violin Sonatas." *Musical Quarterly* 61 (January, 1975): 65-76. Discusses some embellished versions of Corelli's solo sonatas, suggesting that some of them may have a didactic as well as an artistic purpose. Concludes with a valuable list of sources that have embellished versions of Corelli's opus five sonatas.

Pincherle, Marc. *Corelli: His Life, His Work*. Translated by Hubert Russell. New York: W. W. Norton, 1956. The most detailed account of Corelli's life and work. The biographical part is somewhat romanticized, but the description of Corelli's works and influence is thorough. Includes a valuable bibliography of the various seventeenth and eighteenth century editions and arrangements of Corelli's sonatas and concertos.

Talbot, Michael. "Arcangelo Corelli." In *The New Grove Italian Baroque Masters*, by Denis Arnold et al. New York: W. W. Norton, 1984. An objective summary of Corelli's life, style, and influence. Focuses mostly on known biographical details but also includes useful information on Corelli's influence and style, without discussing specific works in detail. Includes a brief list of Corelli's known and probable works, and an excellent bibliography.

John O. Robison

PIERRE CORNEILLE

Born: June 6, 1606; Rouen, France
Died: September 30, 1684; Paris, France
Areas of Achievement: Theater and drama
Contribution: Corneille wrote or collaborated on more than thirty plays during a career spanning forty-five years. His masterpiece, *The Cid*, is the first classical tragedy in French. His work dominated the French stage during the first half of the seventeenth century and helped to define the character of classical theater.

Early Life

Although Pierre Corneille wrote the first French classical tragedy and established the classical theater in France, relatively few details of his personal life are known. Born in Rouen, France, to provincial bourgeois parents, Corneille enjoyed the pleasures afforded by a stable family life. His Jesuit education, with its emphasis on the Latin classics and on the importance of the role of free will in man's search for a moral life, profoundly affected the dramatist's later works. In 1622, following his father's example, he chose to study law and was admitted to the bar in 1624. Timid by temperament, Corneille lacked the verbal eloquence and aggressiveness required for success in the legal profession. In 1641, he married Marie Lampérière; they had six children. Throughout his life, Corneille preferred the pleasures of an uncomplicated, provincial family life to the preciosity of Paris literary salons. As portraits of him in later life reveal, he was attractive and physically robust.

Corneille's early literary career began with the production of *Mélite: Ou, Les Fausses Lettres* (1630; English translation, 1776) when he was in his early twenties. After this early success, Corneille produced four comedies in quick succession: *La Veuve: Ou, Le Traître trahi* (1631; the widow), *La Suivante* (1633; the waiting-maid), *La Place royale: Ou, L'Amoreux extravagant* (1634; the royal square), and *L'Illusion comique* (1636; the comic illusion). At about this time Cardinal de Richelieu, the great minister of Louis XIII, engaged Corneille and four other dramatists, known collectively as "the five authors," to write plays for the royal court. Corneille found the restrictions of the collaboration oppressive and soon abandoned the group.

Life's Work

In 1636-1637, Corneille produced his masterpiece, *Le Cid* (*The Cid*, 1637). The play is based in part on a historical Spanish character, Rodrigo de Bivar (1040?-1099). As the play opens, Chimène, daughter of Don Gomez, learns of her father's approval of her marriage to Rodrigue, the Cid. Simultaneously, Rodrigue's father, Don Diègue, engages in an argument with Don Gomez and in the course of the argument Don Gomez strikes Don Diègue. Following the code of the times, Don Diègue demands that his son avenge his disgrace. Rodrigue is thus caught in a conflict between his love for Chimène and his duty to defend the honor of his family. By resolving to fulfill his family duty by killing Don Gomez, Rodrigue announces the fundamental tension which will resonate throughout all Corneille's great tragedies: the eternal human struggle to balance personal sentiment with duty to family and society.

Chimène's dilemma is equal to that of Rodrigue: How can she accept marriage to the man who has slain her father? Like Rodrigue, she chooses to uphold her family's honor and implores the king Don Fernando for vengeance. Ultimately, she confesses her love, and the king decrees that Rodrigue shall lead his armies in battle for a year while Chimène mourns her father's death; then the two shall be married. The dramatic power of the play resides in Corneille's skillful manipulation of the conflict of honor and love.

Despite its popular success, the play angered many of the conservative critics of the day. The ensuing stormy Quarrel of the Ancients and Moderns lasted for nearly a year, and it was officially resolved at the request of Richelieu by the forty *doctes* (learned men) of the newly formed French Academy. The largely negative judgment of the Academy dealt Corneille a severe blow. Although the Academy quibbled with some of Corneille's versification and with his laxity in strictly maintaining the classical Unities of time, place, and action, the central issue involved a rather academic determination of what was tragic, thus establishing those elements which could be properly included in a tragedy and those which could not.

The classicists, or ancients, of the Academy supported the Aristotelian distinction between *le vrai* (the real) and *le vraisemblance* (having the simple appearance of the real, or the verisimilar). History, the *doctes* maintained, is full of true events which conflict with common moral decency and thus are not the proper basis of art. Thus from the *doctes'* perspective, Chimène's marriage to her father's killer, though based in fact, was morally reprehensible and consequently an improper use of the real.

After receiving the Academy's judgment, Corneille did not produce another play for three years. Despite the distress which the debate caused Corneille, it resulted in the establishment of a clearer sense of the definition of tragedy and comedy, thus setting the stage for the creation of the mature masterworks of Corneille himself as well as those of Jean Racine and Molière later in the century.

Corneille's three-year silence ended in May, 1640, with the presentation of his second tragedy, *Horace* (English translation, 1656), quickly followed by two more tragedies, *Cinna: Ou, La Clémence d'Auguste* (1641; *Cinna*, 1713) and *Polyeucte* (1642; English translation, 1655). Corneille's reputation largely rests on these three great works and on *The Cid*.

Horace continues the theme first broached in *The Cid*. Horace must ultimately choose between his duty to Rome and his love for his wife and family. Despite the grandeur of the subject, Corneille's strict adherence to the unities, partly in response to the Academy's earlier critiques, attenuates the potential power of the work. *Cinna*, a political tragedy, and *Polyeucte*, a religious tragedy, both based on Roman sources, definitively established Corneille's literary reputation. *Cinna* has often been argued to be Corneille's finest play after *The Cid*, principally because of its strict faithfulness to classical form and the depiction of the slow evolution of Augustus' character from apparent tyrant to magnanimous hero. The language of the play, however, does not equal that of *The Cid*, often bordering on the grandiloquent. The weakness of plot and absence of fully developed characters have also evoked criticism.

In contrast with *Cinna*, *Polyeucte* incorporates a relatively complex plot with equally complex relationships between pagan and Christian characters of third century Rome. Polyeucte, recently converted to Christianity, is imprisoned and then killed for having destroyed pagan idols at a public sacrifice. As a result of Polyeucte's martyrdom, his wife, Pauline, and her weak father, Felix, who had ordered Polyeucte's death, convert to Christianity. The beauty of the play lies largely in the touching relationship of Polyeucte and Pauline, as the latter comes to realize her true love for her husband. The noted French poet/critic Charles-Pierre Péguy discovered in *Polyeucte* Corneille's most eloquent poetic voice, a triumphant evocation of the heroic and mystical registers of the human spirit.

Between 1643 and 1650, Corneille produced seven tragedies and three comedies with varying degrees of success. The works of this period, while always reflecting Corneille's genius for invention and versification, suffer from an absence of human interest, overuse of mechanical *coups de théâtre*, complicated intrigues, and mistaken identities—all techniques more typical of the later melodrama than of classical theater. The singular success of these years was his election to the French Academy in 1647.

Corneille's last triumph, *Nicomède* (1651; English translation, 1671), was followed by the complete disaster of *Pertharite, roi des Lombards* (1651). The public's absolute rejection of this last work sent Corneille into a seven-year retirement from the theater. From 1652 until 1659, he published a thirteen-thousand-line verse translation of the *Imitation de Jésus-Christ* (1652-1656) and completed *Discours de l'utilité et des parties du poème dramatique* (1660; *On the Uses and Elements of Dramatic Poetry*, 1947) and a series of critical evaluations of his plays. Between 1659 and 1674, when he produced his final tragedy, *Suréna* (1675), Corneille wrote six more tragedies and four comedies, works which he viewed as "the last spark of a fire about to die out." Having moved his family from Rouen to Paris in 1662, in order to secure his seat in the Academy, he died there in 1684.

Summary

Although Pierre Corneille's reputation among the larger public continues to rest on the four great tragedies written between 1636 and 1642, modern scholarship suggests that both his early comedies and late tragedies, taken in context and viewed as a whole, reveal a continuous movement toward experimentation, on both poetic and thematic levels. Such works as the early *L'Illusion comique* and the late *Suréna* testify to the dramatist's persistent attempts to dazzle his public with innovative responses to old dilemmas. Often going against the grain of established literary conventions of the times, Corneille's genius for invention led him both to great success and to total failure.

Corneille's great tragic personages, the grandeur of his style, and his relentless focus on the conflict between passion and moral obligations to society have established his place in world literature. What defines man's dignity in the Corneillian universe is the human freedom to choose. Corneille succeeded in presenting this conflict in a style marked by forcefulness, clarity, lyricism, and dignity. Thus Racine's words, pronounced before the Academy shortly after Corneille's death, are as accurate in their assessment of Corneille's work today as they were in 1684: "You know in what condition was the French stage when he began his work. Such disorder! such irregularity! No taste, no knowledge of the real beauties of the theater. . . . In this chaos . . . [Corneille] against the bad taste of the century, . . . inspired by an extraordinary genius, . . . put reason on stage. . . ."

Bibliography

Abraham, Claude. *Pierre Corneille*. Boston: Twayne, 1972. Written for the general reader, Abraham's book is the most accessible introduction to Corneille's principal works and to the times in which he created them. All French text has been translated into English.

Corneille, Pierre. *Le Cid*. Translated by Vincent J. Chang. Newark: University of Delaware Press, 1987. In addition to the most faithful English translation of *The Cid*, the text includes five elegantly written chapters on Corneille's life and times and an analysis of the play. Chang directs his work toward the non-French-speaking reader, distilling the best of French and English scholarship into seventy-five tightly argued pages.

_____. *Le Cid*. Edited with an introduction, notes, and variants by Peter H. Nurse. New York: Basil Blackwell, 1988. Edited by one of the foremost Corneillian scholars, this edition provides one of the most complete introductions to Corneille's masterpiece. Designed for the serious student, the text contains all the variants of the 1682 edition of *The Cid*.

Mallison, G. J. *The Comedies of Corneille: Experiments in the Comic*. Manchester, England: Manchester University Press, 1984. Copiously documented with extracts from the French texts, this volume seeks first to define comedy in its seventeenth century context and then to evaluate Corneille's concept of the genre in this light.

Nelson, Robert J. *Corneille, His Heroes and Their Worlds*. Philadelphia: University of Pennsylvania Press, 1963. The standard critical text dealing with the complex composition of Corneille's heroes, written by one of the most eminent Corneillian scholars. For the young scholar there is no better introduction to Corneille's plays. Detailed and reasoned analysis of all works is complemented by a vivid picture of the seventeenth century literary world.

Pocock, Gordon. *Corneille and Racine: Problems of Tragic Form*. New York: Cambridge University Press, 1973. Pocock's work is among the most readable scholarly studies centering on the contrasts between Racine and Corneille. The first ten chapters are devoted exclusively to an analysis of Corneille's principal works and his inventive versification. Although citations are in the original French, the author's lucid argument is accessible to the serious reader.

William C. Griffin

CORREGGIO
Antonio Allegri

Born: c. 1489; Correggio, Duchy of Modena
Died: c. March 5, 1534; Correggio, Duchy of Modena
Area of Achievement: Art
Contribution: Correggio executed frescoes and paintings of religious and mythological subjects that demonstrate his skills as one of the greatest masters of the High Renaissance. Correggio's innovations in composition, expressiveness, and particularly in the illusionistic foreshortening of figures seen from below (*di sotto in su*) were to have a tremendous influence on later Baroque painters.

Early Life
Antonio Allegri was born in the town from which his name is taken, Correggio, Italy. The date of his birth to Pellegrino Allegri and Bernardina Ormani has been debated. The year was once thought to have been 1494 because artist-biographer Giorgio Vasari stated that Correggio died at the age of forty; however, most scholars now place his birth nearer to the year 1489. Correggio's uncle, Lorenzo Allegri, was a painter, under whom he may have studied. The apprenticeship is unclear, however, as are many details of his life because of the absence of documents. While the story that he was Bianchi Ferrari's pupil in Modena is plausible, Mantua is a more important place for Correggio's formative career. Some work there has recently been attributed to him, and the strong influence of both Andrea Mantegna and Lorenzo Costa on Correggio's work between 1510 and 1518 argues strongly for his presence in nearby Mantua around that time. Influences from Dosso Dossi in nearby Ferrara are also likely.

Yet by far the greatest formative influence on Correggio was Rome. The evidence is stylistic, based especially on paintings in the cupola of S. Giovanni Evangelista. There is a blend of antique classicism; Raphael's *Stanza della Segnatura* (1508-1511) and the Sistine Chapel ceiling by Michelangelo are evident. Generous borrowings from Leonardo da Vinci suggest that he may also have traveled to Milan.

While no known description of the artist exists, it has been proposed that the Saint Anthony of Padua in the *Madonna and Child with Saint Francis* in Dresden is a self-portrait. Half smiling, he appears there as having been graceful and decidedly shy or withdrawn, as Vasari described him.

Life's Work
With the varied impressions made upon Correggio, including Florentine cultural stimuli, one might assume Correggio to have been merely eclectic. Yet the opposite is true. His handling of figure, space, and color was accom-

plished with fluid, sensual harmony. Even the classical references are never dry or academic and appear with the graceful casualness that suggests intimate familiarity.

The earliest documentary evidence for a painting, the *Madonna of Saint Francis*, is the contract made on August 30, 1514. References to Leonardo da Vinci and Raphael may indicate that the Rome visit had already been made. Earlier than this, but firmly attributed to Correggio, are *Christ Taking Leave of His Mother* (1514-1517) and two pictures of the *Marriage of Saint Catherine* (1510-1514), which show the strong influence of Costa and Mantegna. Other works attributed to Correggio from the period prior to 1518 include *The Holy Family with the Infant Saint John the Baptist, Adoration of the Magi, Judith*, and *Nativity*. The atmospheric effects in landscape from the *Nativity* and the *Adoration of the Magi* suggest a Venetian origin by way of Ferrara; the latter also indicates familiarity with the protomannerism of Emilia such as is seen in the works of Dosso Dossi.

In 1518, Correggio was summoned to Parma to decorate the suite of Giovanna da Piacenza, abbess of the convent of S. Paolo. As no sightseers were admitted to the room for two centuries, the first detailed account of the work was not published until 1794. It is the artist's first major work in fresco. The largely decorative treatment of the vault, with a network of reeds carrying festoons of fruit pierced by ovals through which putti glance downward, is largely Mantegnesque. The bands of reeds terminate in illusionistic, monochromatic lunettes that reflect extensive familiarity with the antique. A figure of Diana moves across the great hood of the chimney, glowing with soft flesh tones. The total effect is rich, harmonious, and enchanting.

By 1520, Correggio was at work on the decoration of the church of S. Giovanni Evangelista in Parma. The dome frescoes came first, then the half-dome of the apse, followed by frescoes on the underarches of the dome. He provided drawings for the nave frieze, executing a small portion of it which was finished by Francesco Mario Rondani and others. While he was in Parma, on November 3, 1522, Correggio signed a contract for the decoration of the choir and dome of the Cathedral of Parma. This year was the turning point in his career. Commissions for work began pouring in from various places. It is speculated that enough of the frescoes in S. Giovanni Evangelista were completed to have astonished Italy and created his fame.

The subject of the fresco in the dome of S. Giovanni Evangelista is the Vision of Saint John on Patmos, showing the risen Christ in the center surrounded by the glow of rich, luminous light. Cherubim surround this light, with the other apostles lining the base of the dome. There is a soaring effect, and illusionism, which was to impress later Baroque artists. It is evident that an audacious imagination was at work. The sculptural effect of the figures against the neutral background recall Raphael and Michelangelo. The atmospheric effect is the result of contact with Leonardo, the latest

Venetians, and the swirling, last scenes by Michelangelo in the Sistine Chapel. The coloration and the sinuous soft form of Raphael's *Triumph of Galatea* (1511-1513) are present, but the overall effect is uniquely Correggio's, with his harmonious, fluid forms.

The ceiling painting in the Cathedral of Parma is a logical consequence of the preceding dome and can be seen as the culmination of Correggio's artistry and as his most imaginative and creative effort. The *Assumption of the Virgin* (1526-1530) is an exciting celestial vision with great illusionistic depth of space. It is filled with the fluid, energetic movements of frolicking angels on soft masses of clouds amid a golden, mysterious glow of light. Throughout there is a festive gladness and a sensual exaltation. The virtuosity of illusionism plus the intertwining and piling up of figures is a tour de force unequaled before the seventeenth century.

During the period of his work at Parma, Correggio executed many other single paintings, plus altarpieces and mythological scenes. He did two paintings for the private chapel of the Del Bono family around 1524. The new elements are to be present in the remainder of the artist's works. The two paintings, now in Parma's Galleria Nazionale, *The Deposition* and *The Martyrdom of Four Saints*, are both very emotional, exhibiting a bolder color, a stronger, more direct source of light, and the use of relative clarity to give attention to the focal points. In addition, there is a decided "mannerism," shown in the flattening of space, choice of color, and prominent use of hands for expression. Among the notable paintings executed during the early to mid-1520's are the *Madonna of Saint Jerome*, "La Notte," or *Adoration of the Shepherds*, with its brilliant illumination amid the darkness, and the *Holy Family with Saint Francis*.

Correggio executed several mythological and allegorical paintings for Federigo II Gonzaga, the Duke of Mantua, which are among the most delightful and popular of his works. These include the *School of Love* and its pendant, *Venus, Cupid, and Satyr*, both of which may have been executed in the 1520's. The four great *Loves of Jupiter* were done in the 1530's and a second series of *Loves of Jupiter* were under way when Correggio died. The *Danae*, *Leda*, *Io*, and *Ganymede* were given by Federigo to Holy Roman Emperor Charles V. All contain nudes executed with great subtlety and grace. The figures are monumental but softened by atmospheric shadows, sensual poses, and rich flesh tones.

Summary

The works attributed to Correggio constitute a prodigious oeuvre. Had he lived past his forty odd years, Correggio probably would have revolutionized art. As it is, his stature is only now coming to be appreciated. The illusionistic space of Correggio's domes, with its antecedents in Mantegna's ceiling in Mantua, masterfully anticipated the artists of Baroque decoration from the

Carracci family and Guercino to Giovanni Lanfranco and Baciccia. The lessons of strength and drawing that Correggio learned from Raphael and Michelangelo were softened by the Venetian atmosphere and the shadows and smiles of Leonardo. In his own time, Parmigianino was profoundly influenced by Correggio when he worked by his side in Parma. Correggio in turn absorbed the lessons of the mannerists to a certain degree. The final outcome is a confusion about the exact position of Correggio's place in history. His art escapes easy labeling.

Correggio's abilities were to be greatly admired in the eighteenth century, the period of the discovery of his frescoes in San Paolo and the publication of documents by Girolamo Tiraboschi such as *Notizie de'pittori, scultori, incisori e architetti natii degli stati del serenissimo duca di Modena* (1786), as well as a history by Correggio's greatest admirer, Anton Raphael Mengs. Correggio's importance was eclipsed in the nineteenth century, and only recently have scholars seen his tremendous impact on artists from the later sixteenth and seventeenth centuries, from Baroccio, even Gian Lorenzo Bernini and the Carracci family, to a host of other lesser known artists. Correggio evoked the true grandeur of Renaissance classicism but indicated a new direction that was profoundly to affect art for centuries.

Bibliography

The Age of Correggio and the Carracci: Emilian Painting of the Sixteenth and Seventeenth Centuries. Washington, D.C.: National Gallery of Art, 1986. A beautifully produced catalog of more than two hundred Emilian paintings of the sixteenth and seventeenth centuries, organized and written by dozens of scholars for the exhibition appearing at the National Gallery of Art, Washington, the Metropolitan Museum of Art, New York, and the Pinacoteca Nazionale, Bologna. With beautiful illustrations, many in color, this is the most extensive treatment of the effects of Correggio on later sixteenth and seventeeth century art.

Gould, Cecil. *The Paintings of Correggio.* Ithaca, N.Y.: Cornell University Press, 1976. The most comprehensive, definitive, and up-to-date assessment of Correggio's paintings. It is well illustrated and includes documents and a helpful catalog of all surviving pictures including a discussion of attributions.

Longhi, Roberto. *Il Correggio e la Camera di San Paolo a Parma.* Genoa: Siglaeffe, 1956. Fundamental for the whole of Correggio's work as well as related matters of historiography.

Popham, Arthur E. *Correggio's Drawings.* London: Oxford University Press, 1957. A very valuable and well-illustrated treatment of the known drawings. Includes a discussion of drawings of questionable attribution.

Quintavalle, Augusta A. *La 'opera completa del Correggio.* Milan: Rizzoli Editore, 1970. With an introduction by Alberto Bevilacqua, this cursory study includes numerous illustrations and documentary material.

Vito Battaglia, Silvia de. *Correggio, Bibliografia*. Rome: Arti grafiche F. Lli Palombi, 1934. This standard work has collected all the documents and bibliographical references prior to 1934, and, while very reliable, it omits some references that are not art-historical.

Sharon Hill

HERNÁN CORTÉS

Born: 1485; Medellín, Extremadura, Spain
Died: December 2, 1547; Castilleja de la Cuesta, near Seville, Spain
Areas of Achievement: Exploration and the military
Contribution: Cortés skillfully led a small band of Spaniards and numerous Indian allies to the heart of the Aztec capital of Tenochtitlán (later Mexico City), and within two years he boldly conquered the powerful Aztec Empire. His most lasting contribution has been to western exploration and conquest of the New World.

Early Life

Hernán Cortés came from a Spanish region, Extremadura, where so many of the New World conquistadors originated. Although Cortés was born into a Spanish noble (Hidalgo) family, his parents—Martín Cortés de Monroy, an infantry captain, and Catalina Pizarro Altamirano—were of limited means. At the age of fourteen, Hernán was sent to school in Salamanca to prepare for a career in law. Cortés soon abandoned his studies and decided to follow in his father's footsteps and join the Spanish army, serving in Naples. In 1504, at the age of nineteen, hamstrung by what he perceived as limited possibilities in the Old World, the restless youth, like so many of his class, decided to board a ship bound for the Spanish Indies.

In many ways, the impressionable Cortés was a product of his times. Renaissance Spain was undergoing tremendous ferment during the last decades of the fifteenth century. For more than seven centuries, Spanish Catholics had fought an epic struggle against Islamic Moors called the *reconquista* (reconquest), and in 1492, under the recently unified leadership of Ferdinand of Aragon and Isabella of Castille, the Moors' final stronghold, Granada, fell. The *reconquista* markedly influenced succeeding generations of Iberians: It united Spain's divided kingdoms and regions into a strong nation-state with a powerful army; it rallied the country together under the banner of Catholicism—the young nation would embrace the faith with such religious fervor that it would take on the responsibility of defender of the Church throughout Europe and the New World; and it opened up economic possibilities for those Hidalgos who fought for the Crown and were rewarded for their efforts. Militarism, the rise of a Spanish national identity, the Catholic faith, and the seemingly unlimited potential for personal aggrandizement imbued succeeding generations of Hidalgos with a sense of commitment, purpose, and service to their Crown.

In the same year that Granada fell, Christopher Columbus discovered the New World, opening new military, religious, and economic possibilities for the expansion-minded Spanish state and for ambitious Hidalgos such as Cortés. Cortés secured a position as a notary on the island of Santo Domingo in the Caribbean and was given a small grant of Indians who provided labor and commodity tribute (*encomienda*). For six years, Cortés profited from his Indians, but once again he grew restless. In 1511, he joined Diego Velázquez's military conquest of Cuba, serving as a clerk to the treasurer. Rewarded by the conquistador Velázquez, who subsequently became governor of the island, Cortés was rewarded with another *encomienda* in Cuba and a government position. In Santiago de Baracoa, Cuba, Cortés attended to his bureaucratic duties, became a prominent local merchant, raised cattle, and had his *encomienda* Indians mine gold.

Life's Work

Just when it appeared that Cortés would settle down and tend to his thriving business concerns, reports began filtering back to Cuba from advance scouting expeditions of a fabulous Aztec Empire on the Caribbean mainland. In 1519, Governor Velázquez commissioned the thirty-four-year-old Cortés to lead an expedition to the Mexican mainland. As Cortés outfitted his expedition with men, ships, and provisions, Velázquez had second thoughts about Cortés' arrogant, pretentious manner. Fearing that he could not control his ambitious commander, Velázquez ordered the commission revoked. When Cortés learned that the governor planned to rescind his orders, he quickly set sail from Cuba on February 18, 1519, with 550 Spaniards, several Cuban Indians and black slaves, a few small cannons, sixteen horses, several mastiff dogs, and eleven small ships.

Cortés' two-year assault on the heavily populated Aztec Empire, against almost insurmountable odds, was one of the most formidable challenges of the age of exploration and conquest. Driven by the traits shared by all *reconquista* Hidalgos—religious zeal, dedication to the Crown, and a healthy lust for glory and gold—Cortés, both in his personal correspondence and in his riveting speeches to his men, evinced a single-minded obsession: to conquer the Aztecs or die trying. Chroniclers describe the conquistador as a man of average height, pale complexion, and a muscular frame. The standard that he carried into battle was particularly appropriate; fashioned of black velvet, embroidered with gold, with a red cross laced with blue-and-white flames, its motto was emblazoned in Latin: "Friends, let us follow the Cross; and under this sign, if we have faith, we shall conquer." From the moment the expedition landed off the coast of Yucatán until the final assault on the Aztec capital of Tenochtitlán in 1521, Cortés stayed true to that motto and never considered retreating or compromising.

Although the enemy enjoyed an overwhelming numerical superiority—the population of Tenochtitlán has been estimated at eighty thousand, in 1519— Cortés was able to take advantage of a number of favorable factors. First, Cortés shrewdly perceived that many of the Indian subject provinces chafed under and bitterly resented Aztec rule. The Spanish invasion signified—to

Indians such as the Tlaxcalans and later the Tarascans—a fortuitous opportunity to ally themselves with the foreign invaders, to overturn onerous Aztec tribute and to regain their independence. These subject populations not only provided Cortés with literally thousands of warriors but also complicated matters politically for the Aztec emperor Montezuma II. The emperor, who was coronated in 1503, had squelched serious rebellions throughout his reign. Yet, after more than a century of Aztec imperial rule, subject provinces who had provided commodity tribute and human sacrifice victims to the Aztecs on an unprecedented scale saw hope in an alliance with the Spaniards.

Cortés also benefited from the Aztecs' fatalistic religious vision. The Aztecs believed that the world had been destroyed and reborn by the gods on four separate occasions. Every fifty-two years, the cycle of destruction was at risk and the world might be destroyed. Cortés arrived in Mexico in the fateful fifty-second year (*ce atl*). Moreover, the Spanish at first were believed by the Indians to be gods, or at least, messengers of the gods. Native myth told of a light-skinned, bearded god, Quetzalcóatl, who believed in love, compassion, and mercy, and who forbade human sacrifice, practiced oral confession, baptism, and ascetic denial. This god, according to myth, had left the Valley of Mexico centuries before, vowing one day to return to reclaim his kingdom. The Christianity espoused by the Europeans almost surreally approximated the Quetzalcóatl cult. Montezuma, a devout philosophical and religious thinker in his own right, at times appeared almost mesmerized by the religious implications of the Spanish expedition.

Cortés did little to discourage the natives' religious uncertainties. The Spanish possessed the technological advantages of Spanish steel, muskets, crossbows, and armor. In addition, Cortés used psychological ploys to startle unsuspecting Aztec emissaries at propitious moments. From the deafening noise of the Spaniards' small cannons to the judicious use of the horses and menacing dogs—two animals which the Indians had never seen before—Cortés created an aura of invincibility around his troops that fortified his Indian allies, created indecision in the minds of the Aztec leadership, and bolstered the confidence of his soldiers.

Yet Cortés faced daunting odds. His expedition had lost its legal sanction from Velázquez, and he was perilously close to becoming an outlaw in the eyes of the Crown. Cortés, however, feigned ignorance of the revoked commission and founded a settlement on the coast of Mexico, La Villa Rica de la Vera Cruz (later Veracruz), claiming all the lands that he conquered for the King of Spain, Charles V. He shrewdly dispatched a ship to Spain with a letter to the king professing his loyalty to the Crown. Still, Cortés faced serious problems from Velázquez supporters in his midst.

Time and again on his climb up to Tenochtitlán, the Spanish commander demonstrated his uncanny ability to act decisively before the Aztecs and their allies could react. For example, at Cholula, the last major city on Cortés' route to the Aztec capital, the Spanish learned that they were about to be ambushed by an Aztec army. Cortés ordered a preemptive strike and massacred more than six thousand Indian warriors. (An Indian version of the conquest denies the ambush and characterizes Cortés' massacre as premeditated.) From that point on no serious attempts were made by the Aztecs to stop Cortés' advance on Tenochtitlán.

Another bold move was the decision to put Montezuma under house arrest while the Spanish stayed in the capital. As "guests" of the emperor Cortés and his troops could ensure that Montezuma was not organizing an uprising. The decision to rule through the emperor bought the Spanish valuable time.

When the Aztecs revolted on July 1, 1520 (called *la noche triste*—the sad night—by the Spanish), Cortés was forced to abandon Tenochtitlán. Bernal Díaz relates that 860 Spaniards died during the battle. Despite this overwhelming defeat, Cortés rallied his armed forces, convinced more than 100,000 native allies to join his cause, and launched a tactically brilliant land and naval invasion of Tenochtitlán less than a year later. Cortés' devotion to this cause was too much for the Indians, who by this time had been decimated by smallpox infection and were dying by the thousands in Tenochtitlán. On August 13, 1521, after fierce hand-to-hand combat in the capital, the last Aztec emperor, Cuauhtémoc, surrendered.

Cortés proved to be an able administrator of the colony, which he renamed New Spain. Charles V, facing troubles from nobles in Spain, was understandably reluctant to let conquistadors such as Cortés become too powerful. Royal officials replaced Cortés soon after the conquest, and Cortés returned to Spain to argue his case before the king. Although Cortés never became governor of New Spain, he was allowed to choose twenty-two towns of *encomienda* Indians (approximately twenty-three thousand Indians). Cortés chose the richest settlements in the colony. Moreover, he was named captain-general and awarded the title of Marqués del Valle de Oaxaca. While at the royal court, Cortés married the daughter of a count, further ingratiating himself with the Spanish aristocracy. He returned to New Spain in 1530 and lived there for ten years, where he introduced new European crops and products, looked for silver and gold mines, and encouraged exploration. Cortés' wealth and status made him a target of crown officials who distrusted his independent demeanor and feared his political contacts with the nobility in Spain. His last few years were spent in frustration in Spain. In 1547, he fell ill and died at his estate, Castilleja de la Cuesta, just outside Seville. According to his wishes his bones were moved to Mexico in 1556.

Summary

More than any other conquistador, Hernán Cortés embodied the characteristics of the group of fearless men who, imbued with the heady ideals of the *reconquista*, forged a massive Spanish Empire in the New World. Committed to service to the Crown, convinced that their cause was noble and just, comforted by the belief that they brought Christianity and civilization to barbarian peoples, and clearly motivated by material gain and glory, Cortés and his fellow conquistadors, at times ruthlessly and at times diplomatically, conquered the numerically superior Indians during the early sixteenth century. Unlike other conquistadors, however, Cortés had a strong commitment to the religious conversion of the natives. Moreover, he demonstrated himself to be an able and fair administrator in the first years after the conquest; again, a trait not shared by many conquerors. Although Cortés was denied the political post that he thought he deserved, he became one of the wealthiest men in the empire.

Interestingly, Cortés is today viewed unsympathetically in the land that he conquered. Ever since the Mexican Revolution (1911-1920), the pre-Columbian accomplishments of the Aztec, Maya, and Teotihuacán Indians have been lionized, while the "civilizing" efforts of Cortés and the Spanish have been lambasted by Mexican intellectuals. This view represents a complete turnabout for the historical legacy of the conquistadors, since prior to the revolution Spanish virtues were lauded while their defects were minimized. A black legend has been appropriated for Cortés as a symbol of all rapacious Spaniards. Postrevolutionary histories emphasize his ruthlessness, his defilement of Indian women, culture, and customs, and his single-minded obsession with the destruction of the Aztec Empire. Perhaps in the future a more balanced interpretation will prevail.

Bibliography

Cortés, Hernán. *Letters from Mexico*. Edited and translated by A. R. Pagden, with an introduction by J. H. Elliott. New York: Grossman, 1971. Self-serving letters written in the heat of battle by the conquistador, which detail conditions in Mexico during the conquest and give insight into the character of Cortés.

Díaz del Castillo, Bernal. *The True History of the Conquest of New Spain, 1517-1521*. Translated by Alfred Percival Maudslay, with an introduction by Irving Leonard. New York: Farrar, Straus & Giroux, 1966. A classic, riveting, first-person narrative of the conquest recollected by Díaz in his old age. Although Díaz believed that he was never given his just due—he was rewarded with a paltry *encomienda* in the hostile backlands of Guatemala—his account is relatively balanced. His descriptions of the Spanish entry to Tenochtitlán and the great Aztec market at Tlateloco are stunning.

León-Portilla, Miguel, ed. *The Broken Spears: The Aztec Account of the Conquest of Mexico*. Translated by Lysander Kemp. Boston: Beacon Press, 1962. A compilation of Aztec and early missionary sources that offers a much-needed corrective to the Spanish versions of the conquest. Although these sympathetic "native" sources are as biased as the Spanish accounts they reject, this is an evocative portrayal of the Indian defeat. Some of the Aztec poetry included is powerful and moving and gives readers a sense of the psychological loss felt by the natives.

Padden, R. C. *The Hummingbird and the Hawk: Conquest and Sovereignty in the Valley of Mexico, 1503-1541.* Columbus: Ohio State University Press, 1967. A provocative account of the conquest that emphasizes Cortés' religious zeal and the fundamental importance of human sacrifice to the Aztec faith. Nowhere else in the literature are Cortés' religious motivations portrayed so prominently. Good bibliography of the secondary literature included.

Prescott, William H. *History of the Conquest of Mexico.* New York: Bantam Books, 1964. A standard mid-nineteenth century, secondary narrative of the conquest which relies heavily on Spanish chroniclers. Extraordinarily detailed account of the background, motivations, and battles of the conquest.

White, Jon M. *Cortés and the Downfall of the Aztec Empire: A Study in a Conflict of Cultures.* New York: St. Martin's Press, 1971. A psychological and analytical portrait of Cortés and Montezuma that places both leaders in their religious and cultural milieu.

Allen Wells

FRANÇOIS COUPERIN

Born: November 10, 1668; Paris, France
Died: September 11, 1733; Paris, France
Area of Achievement: Music
Contribution: Couperin was the chief representative of French musical classicism in the waning years of the reign of Louis XIV and the regency which followed.

Early Life

François Couperin was the most famous member of a family of musicians sufficiently long-lived and well known that they constituted a musical dynasty much like the Bach family in Germany, to whom they have frequently been compared. The prominence of François within this group was acknowledged by the unofficial title "Le Grand," a sobriquet well established by the late eighteenth century and probably in use as early as 1710.

Couperin's early musical training and first professional experience centered on the organ at the Church of St. Gervaise, where his uncle, Louis Couperin, had served as organist, as had his father, Charles Couperin, since 1661. Charles died in 1679, and his son's musical training was continued by Jacques Thomelin, himself a famous organist, who became a second father to François. The young Couperin's talents were such that the council of St. Gervaise determined that he should inherit his father's position when he became eighteen, although they engaged Michel-Richard de Lalande as principal organist for the interim period. In 1685, the council extended to François an annual stipend of three hundred livres until a formal contract could be issued, an act which, considering Lalande's many other activities, suggests that the seventeen-year-old Couperin may have been assuming the role of organist in all but name for several years. He continued to occupy the organist's house of St. Gervaise and in 1689 married Marie-Anne Ansault. His spouse was to bear him four children, two of whom became prominent musicians in their own right, and also brought to Couperin contacts in the business world which would later become advantageous for some of his publishing ventures.

Life's Work

In 1690, Couperin obtained a royal privilege to print and sell his music, which led to the publication of the *Pièces d'orgues consistantes en deux messes: Messe pour les paroisses et messe pour les couvents*, two organ masses which represent his first published work and his only known compositions for this instrument. He was active as an organist for most of his life, and in 1693 he gained entry to the court of Louis XIV through a royal appointment as one of four court organists, each responsible for organ music in the royal court and chapel for one quarter of the year.

At about the same time, he was at work on several trio sonatas (two violins and continuo), some of which were later incorporated into the set entitled *Les Nations* (1726). These sonatas, conceived around 1693, reflect Couperin's awareness of the difference between French and Italian styles, his enduring admiration for Arcangelo Corelli, the quintessential composer of the Italian Baroque, and presumably the introduction into France of that genre which, for many, typifies Baroque instrumental chamber music.

Couperin's appointment as a court organist brought him into contact with the aristocracy; he subsequently became harpsichord instructor to many noble families and in 1694 was appointed Maître de Clavecin des Enfants de France. He took advantage of an edict by Louis XIV offering ennoblement to any person in respectable employment who could pay for it. About 1702, he was further honored as Chevalier de l'Ordre du Lateran. Such titular recognition must have been important to him, for upon his ennoblement he fashioned a family coat of arms, and the Lateran Cross is prominently displayed in the famous portrait by Andre Boüys by which Couperin generally is known.

Between 1693 and the king's death in 1715, Couperin established himself as the leading French composer. The esteem in which he was held is documented by the number of musical works dedicated to him at that time. He continued as organist at court and at St. Gervaise and was firmly established as the foremost teacher of harpsichord and organ.

His first book of harpsichord pieces, an accumulation of works written over a period of several years—and the literature by which he is best known in the modern era—was published in 1713. Couperin had for some time been assisting Jean-Henri d'Anglebert, the king's harpsichordist, in his duties at court, and when D'Anglebert withdrew because of ill health, Couperin officially replaced him in 1717. His second book of harpsichord pieces appeared at this time; it was no doubt his increasing responsibilities as harpsichord teacher that led to his famous treatise *L'Art de toucher le clavecin* (1716, 1717). This work, essentially pedagogical, endures as one of the most influential treatises on performance practice of the eighteenth century. Most keyboard tutors of the period concentrate on the realization of a figured bass and in that context offer instruction in the rudiments of harmony for the keyboard player. Couperin addresses performance itself, treating fingering, ornamentation, and style of performance to a degree uncommon until after mid-century.

Book 3 of Couperin's harpsichord pieces (1722) contained as a supplement the *Concerts royaux*, a series of trio-sonata movements written for two upper-range instruments (violin, flute, oboe) and continuo (keyboard plus viola da gamba or bassoon). *Les Goûts-réunis* (1724) continued in much the same vein; the varied movements represent a juxtaposition of French and

Italian styles more than any inherent blending or unification.

The two trio-sonata sets *Le Parnasse: Ou, L'Apothéose de Corelli* (1724) and *Concert instrumental sous le titre d'apothéose composé à la mémoire immortelle de l'incomparable Monsieur de Lully* (1725) are tributes to the composers Couperin regarded as defining his musical world. Titles to individual movements are quasi-programmatic in their reference to these composers and to their place among the gods and scenes of classic mythology, presumably their rightful place in Couperin's view. *Les Nations*, written almost thirty years prior to its publication, was Couperin's first effort in this type of instrumental chamber music. It is probable that many of the other collections published in the 1720's also had been written and performed at an earlier time, as references to such works appeared in some concerts during 1714 and 1715.

The *Pièces de violes avec la basse chifrée* (1728) are among Couperin's last works. They consist of two suites for solo bass viola da gamba and continuo (harpsichord and a second bass gamba).

The fourth book of harpsichord pieces (1730) was Couperin's last publication. In the preface to this volume, he referred to the illness which had been sapping his strength for some time, and the variety of pieces included here suggests less concern for consistency than in most of his earlier collections of instrumental music for any medium.

Very little substantive information exists concerning the composer's last years. He was buried in the Church of St. Joseph, a dependency of the parish of St. Eustache. Shortly before his death, he had obtained a new privilege for ten years to cover further publication of his works. Obviously there remained works awaiting publication, or he had further plans for new compositions, or both. Couperin's family did not pursue the project and, as no manuscripts of Couperin are known to remain, it is probable that a substantial body of music was irretrievably lost.

Summary

François Couperin's music was very much a reflection of the social milieu from which it emerged. There was much that was frivolous in the reign of Louis XIV; there was also an element of order which was imitated throughout the Western world. It is possible to hear Couperin's music and note only the care and attention given to ornamentation for the purpose of achieving a given effect; underlying the thin texture and careful decoration, however, one finds a technical control and artistic balance equal to that achieved in any age. Couperin expressed musically the conflict in the *grand siècle* between personal passion and self-control.

He claimed priority in introducing the sonata to France. He recognized and defined for his contemporaries the differences between French and Italian style and, in some of his instrumental chamber music, he achieved a balance, if not a synthesis, between those styles. In his four books of harpsi-chord pieces, the individual dance movements were organized into *ordres*, a grouping by key rather than by a stereotypical plan of dance movements. Here Couperin broke away from the literalness of choreography, both in the musical patterns of these works and in their sequence. They represent musi-cal conceptions far more than stylized dance pieces.

Couperin devoted much of his effort to teaching, an involvement reflected in his published treatise on playing the harpsichord. Couperin's advice and established procedure in teaching children to play the instrument before they were taught to read printed music anticipated by more than two centuries developments in instrumental teaching in Japan which have gained so much favor in the musical community of the last half of the twentieth century.

Bibliography

Abraham, Gerald, ed. *The New Oxford History of Music*. Vol. 6, *Concert Music, 1630-1750*. New York: Oxford University Press, 1986. Of Cou-perin's music only that for solo harpsichord receives more than passing mention, but here one finds a substantive exploration of the four books of harpsichord pieces, marked by some historical background and a sensitive description of many individual works.

Anthony, James R. *French Baroque Music: From Beaujoyeulx to Rameau*. New York: W. W. Norton, 1974. One of the most important studies of French music available. The author treats Couperin within his collective study of the various genres, forms, and idioms to which he contributed. The stylistic analysis of many of Couperin's important works is among the best, both in the treatment of individual works and in the exploration of their social context.

Brunold, Paul. *François Couperin*. Translated by J. B. Hanson. Monaco: Lyrebird Press, 1949. The substance of this text derives from an examina-tion of archival material generated during Couperin's life. His composi-tions are described in a cursory manner, but a collection of portraits, a reproduction of the only known signature of the composer, and the re-liance on primary sources make this an important source for any study of Couperin.

Bukofzer, Manfred F. *Music in the Baroque Era from Monteverdi to Bach*. New York: W. W. Norton, 1947. This popular study of Baroque music examines Couperin and his musical works in the context of his time and musical milieu. Offers a broad description of Couperin's works, encom-passing those for organ and chamber music as well as the better known harpsichord pieces.

Higginbottom, Edward. "François Couperin." In *The New Grove French Baroque Masters: Lully, Charpentier, Lalande, Couperin, Rameau*. Edited by James R. Anthony et al. New York: W. W. Norton, 1986. Based upon

Higginbottom's article in *The New Grove Dictionary of Music and Musicians* (1980). Couperin's life and works are addressed in two separate chapters. The author offers plausible explanations for some of the titles Couperin gave to his smaller works. The summary of style shows Couperin achieving a firm balance between a strong personal element and objective control in his music, particularly in his harpsichord works. Contains a comprehensive list of works and a bibliography.

Mellers, Wilfred. *François Couperin and the French Classical Tradition.* London: Denis Dobson, 1950. The principal English-language study of Couperin since its first appearance in the mid-twentieth century. Contains three chapters addressing the artistic environment of Couperin's years in Paris, taste during the *grand siècle*, and an overview of music, the court, and the theater during Couperin's life. Includes a sweeping study of Couperin's oeuvre, seven valuable appendices, a list of works, and a useful bibliography.

Newman, William S. *The Sonata in the Baroque Era*. Chapel Hill: University of North Carolina Press, 1959, rev. ed. 1966. As the title suggests, this work treats only Couperin's works known as sonatas, but that in effect encompasses the majority of his chamber music. The text offers a concise description of these works with thorough documentation.

Tunley, David. *Couperin*. London: British Broadcasting Corporation, 1982. There is no significant attempt here at biography. The author examines the prevailing musical scene in which Couperin worked and then discusses the works by genre. A good overview, liberally illustrated with musical examples.

Douglas A. Lee

GUSTAVE COURBET

Born: June 10, 1819; Ornans, France
Died: December 31, 1877; La Tour-de-Peilz, Switzerland
Area of Achievement: Art
Contribution: Courbet contributed to the formation of modern art by liberating subject matter and style from academic dogma. The most profound aspects of his contribution are the influences his works have had upon the subsequent analysis of realism.

Early Life

Gustave Courbet was born at Ornans, a town in the scenic Loue River valley of Franche-Comté in eastern France. There, his father, Eléonor Régis Stanislaus Courbet, was a prosperous landowner, whose ancestral home was in the neighboring village of Flagey. Gustave's mother, Suzanne Sylvie Oudot, came from a similar economic background of landed proprietors in Ornans. It was in the Ornans home of his grandfather, Jean-Antoine Oudot, a veteran of the French Revolution, that Gustave was born.

Courbet's early life and studies prior to his 1839 arrival in Paris at age twenty had provided him with valuable skills. The young artist's tutelage under Père Beau at Ornans followed his first years of school in 1831 at the *petit seminaire.* It was there that Courbet began to paint from nature. Subsequently, while attending the Collège Royal at Besançon (after autumn, 1837), Maître Flajoulot's emphasis on painting from the live model added another aspect of current artistic training to Courbet's abilities.

During this period, Courbet acquired a deep and lasting appreciation for the cultural heritage and rugged beauty of his native Franche-Comté. This region did not formally become a part of France until 1678 because of a long and complex history of geographical and political factors. The tradition of independence emanating from his native province played an important role in the formation of Courbet's character and notably influenced his attitudes toward formal training and academies.

In Paris, Courbet studied briefly with a minor painter. A greater source of inspiration was discovered at the Louvre, where Courbet diligently copied Dutch, Flemish, Venetian, and Spanish masters. Also significant were the friends he established in Paris: Alexandre Schanne, who became a character in Henri Murger's *Scènes de la vie de bohème* (1847-1849), the painter François Bonvin, and later, the writers Charles Baudelaire and Champfleury.

The decade of the 1840's proved to be a very important one for Courbet, in which his prodigious talent and originality became recognized. His first salon successes were *Self-Portrait with a Black Dog* (1844) and *The Guitarist* (1845). The artist's handsome features and vigorous physicality are evident in other numerous self-portraits of this period. With the *After Dinner at*

Ornans (1849), for which he received a gold medal at the Salon of 1849, Courbet had developed an artistic formula for elevating and monumentalizing common subjects that led to his first truly revolutionary works: *The Stonebreakers* (1849) and *The Burial at Ornans* (1849).

Life's Work

The Revolution of 1848 had occurred during the first crucial decade of Courbet's mature formation. Growing discontent with the failure of Louis-Philippe's government to incorporate democratic reform or acknowledge socialist ideas had led to this uprising which had a direct impact on Courbet's art. Courbet emerged as a pictorial advocate of a new, more democratic aesthetic. *The Stonebreakers*, which appeared at the Salon of 1850-1851, depicted a young boy and an old man laboring side by side to repair a road. Courbet was, in fact, depicting a form of public service (*corvée*) that was customary in rural France; yet the Parisian audience found his large-scale, unidealized figures to be offensive, and even threatening, as they harbored connotations of peasant uprising or violence. Courbet's realist manifesto, *The Burial at Ornans*, also exhibited at the Salon of 1850-1851, recorded a funeral in his native town. Again, Parisians were provoked by a scene which did not depict a known historical event or idealize its characters. Courbet had glorified the idea that the peasantry and rural bourgeoisie were worthy of the serious artistic treatment usually reserved for aristocratic subject matter and concerns. Courbet's works thus threatened established Parisian social and aesthetic values.

Courbet had entered the decade of the 1850's as an artist with strong political associations, which were subsequently incorporated into his total philosophy, as is evident in a statement from the period: "I am not only a socialist, but a democrat and a republican; in short, I am in favor of the whole revolution, and above all I am a realist."

The ability of an artwork to shock its viewers was used by Courbet in major salon submissions from this time onward to draw attention to his name and artistic message. Courbet was thus a subject of great controversy; yet, whether in praise or criticism, there was widespread acknowledgment of the impact of his style. Two works, *Young Ladies of the Village* (1851) and *The Bathers* (1853), demonstrate how Courbet's art had begun to interact with salon criticism. The first painting portrayed his three sisters in a rural setting bestowing a charitable gift upon a young shepherdess. Even Courbet was surprised when the honest depiction was mocked for its ugliness, as he had thought it dignified, even gracious. Courbet decidedly responded in the Salon of 1853 by creating a depiction of woman that was more truly a mockery of the sort his critics espoused. *The Bathers* depicted two very corpulent and egotistical women decadently bathing in the pool of a wooded glade. The very decadence of the women became his prime focus. Thus, a new aspect of Courbet's works developed, which may be termed the painted caricature.

By the mid-1850's, Courbet had entered into politics of a different kind which formalized his new conception of the artist's role as activist and showman. Partly in reaction to the amount of negative criticism that he inevitably generated, and partly out of his own entrepreneurial desire to make his painting more profitable, he established his own exhibition independent of the combined Salon and World Exhibition of 1855. For this occasion, he conceived of a large canvas, *The Painter's Studio: A Real Allegory of Seven Years of My Artistic Life* (1854-1855), in which Courbet depicts himself in the act of painting. He paints amid two groups, one composed of supportive patrons and the other composed of a puzzling assemblage of diverse characters and types that Courbet claimed to have seen in his travels. This huge work has had numerous interpretations and remains problematic, yet quite clearly it is an essential revelation of Courbet, as he sees himself in the process of creating, which is quite necessarily an act and role that he revolutionized.

Also beginning around 1855, Courbet envisioned a serial approach for his art, thus incorporating past works with future endeavors to create entire cycles of related paintings which would compare and contrast different aspects of society. The idea is said to have come from the novels of Honoré de Balzac; its relevance is exemplified in Courbet's works between the years 1855 and 1866.

In 1861, Courbet began to experience a strange mixture of acclaim and adversity. His *Fighting Stags* (1861) was widely admired, and there was even rumor of an official state purchase and Courbet's decoration with the highest honors. Yet, in the end, he only received a second-class medal—a great affront to an artist who had painted what many considered to be the best work in the salon.

This blow caused Courbet to break forever with the praised and accepted aesthetics of his time, as dictated by the salon. His reaction was deliberately to insult taste and sensibility in his salon submissions of 1863, 1864, and 1868. Yet, in the intervening year 1866, he reversed this trend and awed the critics with a new and fantasy-inspired image, *Woman with a Parrot*. Again, there was rumor of governmental purchase and Courbet's decoration. It did not come and was clearly meant to reprimand Courbet's past condemnation of accepted taste. A final reconciliation with the salon came in 1870, when he submitted two beautiful seascapes painted at Étretat in 1869, *The Stormy Sea* and *Cliffs at Étretat After the Storm*. Finally, the critics were filled with enthusiasm. Courbet had become a popular and briefly unproblematic artist.

Courbet's subsequent nomination for the Legion of Honor in June, 1870, caused a sensation; however, the painter held firm to his socialist principles and declined the award. With the outbreak of the Franco-Prussian War in July, Courbet was elected chairman of the arts commission, responsible for the protection of artworks in and around Paris. The duties of this position ultimately cast political overtones upon Courbet as the leader of a large and active group.

Courbet was transformed into a political scapegoat and held responsible for the destruction of the Vendôme Column. The subsequent trials, imprisonment, and exorbitant fines threatened to ruin Courbet and ultimately forced his exile to Switzerland, where he died four years later, a celebrated, but saddened, artist.

Summary

Throughout his life, Gustave Courbet maintained a spirit of Fourierist political optimism. Though his paintings were often conceived to provoke confrontation, he nevertheless believed that through a liberated artistic manifesto man could ultimately derive a philosophy of social harmony. These ideas had become formalized in Courbet's early maturity and were perpetuated by the artist's relations with his greatest patron, Alfred Bruyas, and with the social philosopher Pierre-Joseph Proudhon. Through their encouragement and support, Courbet was able to assess his role and the nature of his art: "To know in order to be able to create, that was my idea. To be in a position to translate the customs, the ideas, the appearance of my epoch, according to my own estimation; to be not only a painter, but a man as well; in short, to create living art—this is my goal." Courbet had set these ideas down in paint as early as 1849 with *The Burial at Ornans*. That the message of Courbet's art was clear to his contemporaries is demonstrated by the 1851 commentary of Paul Sabatier:

> Since the shipwreck of the *Medusa*, . . . nothing as original has been made among us. The clothes, the heads, have a solidity, a variety of tone and a firmness of drawing that is half Venetian, half Spanish; it is close to Zurbarán and to Titian. . . . It was not an easy thing to give dignity . . . to all these modern clothes. . . .

Courbet's late seascapes and somber still lifes are unique pictorial expressions. They represent his most poetic statements, in which the sheer physicality of paint invigorates the expressive power of the work. Courbet's influence on modern art is documented by subsequent generations of avant-garde artists who studied and even collected his works, notably Puvis de Chavannes, Henri Matisse, André Dunoyer de Segonzac, and Pablo Picasso.

Bibliography

Chu, Petra ten Doesschate, ed. *Courbet in Perspective*. Englewood Cliffs, N.J.: Prentice-Hall, 1977. Part of the Artists in Perspective series. Art historical essays from the nineteenth and twentieth centuries. A very useful gathering and translation of important contemporary accounts of Courbet's life and art, including contextual and stylistic essays.

Clark, Timothy J. *Image of the People: Gustave Courbet and the 1848 Revolution*. Princeton, N.J.: Princeton University Press, 1982. The most detailed analysis of Courbet's life and art between 1848 and 1851. Clark's approach, which is both Marxist and structuralist, sheds light on the social and political situations of the Second Republic and the simultaneous developments in Courbet's art—which became strikingly appropriate pictorial representations of these underlying social tensions.

Faunce, Sarah, and Linda Nochlin. *Courbet Reconsidered*. New Haven, Conn.: Yale University Press, 1988. A comprehensive, well-illustrated exhibition catalog composed of six essays and 101 entries. Topics addressed are critical and historical summary of Courbet's oeuvre, reinterpretation of *The Painter's Studio*, gender studies in Courbet, contextual art history, and America's response to Courbet.

Lindsay, Jack. *Gustave Courbet: His Life and Art*. New York: Harper & Row, 1973. A comprehensive biography which incorporates most of the literature available at the time of publication. Includes eighty-nine black-and-white illustrations and an extensive bibliography.

Mack, Gerstle. *Gustave Courbet*. New York: Alfred A. Knopf, 1951. Reprint. Westport, Conn.: Greenwood Press, 1970. The first monograph in English, which is primarily based on the first substantial French biography and its nineteenth century sources by Georges Riat, *Gustave Courbet peintre* (1906).

Nochlin, Linda. *Gustave Courbet: A Study of Style and Society*. New York: Garland, 1976. A sophisticated analysis of the origins of Courbet's style by one of the foremost authorities on the artist. Select bibliography and 121 black-and-white illustrations.

Rubin, James Henry. *Realism and Social Vision in Courbet and Proudhon*. Princeton, N.J.: Princeton University Press, 1980. Rubin considers Courbet's art, particularly *The Painter's Studio*, in relation to the theories of Proudhon, a contemporary and acquaintance of Courbet, to compare and contrast the doctrines of both enigmatic figures.

Toussaint, Hélène, et al. *Gustave Courbet, 1819-1877*. Paris: Musées Nationaux, 1977. The largest retrospective of Courbet's work in the twentieth century. The 1977/1978 catalog is a well-illustrated and scholarly monograph, with new interpretive breakthroughs made possible by sophisticated laboratory analysis at the Louvre. Essays include an introduction by Alan Bowness, an authoritative biography by Marie-Thérèse de Forges, and catalog entries and reinterpretive analysis of *The Painter's Studio* by Hélène Toussaint.

Claudette R. Mainzer

PÊRO DA COVILHÃ

Born: c. 1447; Covilhã, Beira, Portugal
Died: After 1526; Abyssinia (modern Ethiopia)
Areas of Achievement: Exploration, geography, and diplomacy
Contribution: Covilhã was the first Portuguese to visit India, one of the first Europeans to travel extensively in Arabia, the first to visit Sofala in southern Mozambique, and an unwilling resident of Abyssinia for at least thirty-three years. His report on his travels in India, Arabia, and along the coasts of India, Arabia, the Red Sea, and East Africa may have aided and influenced the course of Portuguese penetration of India and East Africa, and his residence in Abyssinia was critical in the opening of diplomatic relations between its emperor and Portugal.

Early Life

Pêro da Covilhã was born of humble parents in the town of Covilhã in Beira Baixa, about fifty miles from Coimbra and thirty from the Spanish border, around 1447. In his teens, Covilhã served the Duke of Medina-Sidonia in Spain, the head of the greatest of Castilian grandee families, the Guzmans. Their entourage was later to include both Christopher Columbus and Juan Ponce de León. While he was in Spain, Covilhã learned to fight and, more important, to rely on his wits; he also learned to speak both Spanish and Arabic fluently.

Covilhã returned to Portugal in 1474 and entered the service of Afonso V. In his years with Afonso, he gained distinction as a soldier in Afonso's campaign to enforce the claim of his wife, Juana, "La Beltraneja," daughter of Henry IV of Castile, to its throne against her aunt, Isabella the Catholic. Covilhã also visited France and Burgundy with the king in an unsuccessful attempt to gain aid from Louis XI and Charles the Bold.

When Afonso died in 1481, Covilhã continued in royal service under his successor, John II, holding the official position of squire of the royal guard. King John used Covilhã as a spy and diplomatic agent both in Spain, where there was a dangerous colony of rebellious Portuguese nobles living in exile, and in Morocco, where the Portuguese had captured Ceuta in 1415 and had been active ever since. On one of his trips to Morocco, Covilhã apparently used the purchase of horses as a cover for espionage and secret diplomacy.

Covilhã's proven resourcefulness, willingness to travel, courage, loyalty to the Crown, experience as a spy, and knowledge of Arabic were almost certainly the reasons why John and his successor, Manuel I, chose him for a mission that would take the rest of his life and secure for him a shadowy but significant place in the history of the Age of Exploration.

Life's Work

In May of 1487, John ordered Covilhã, about forty years old and recently married, and an Arabic-speaking Canarian, Afonso de Paiva, to carry out two exceedingly difficult missions: to gather information on India and the navigation and ports of the Indian Ocean, and to visit and establish contact with Prester John, the legendary Emperor of Abyssinia. Traveling by way of Valencia, Barcelona, Naples, and Rhodes, Covilhã and Paiva began their Eastern travels disguised as merchants buying honey in Alexandria to sell farther east. Since neither was ever challenged, it may be assumed that both Paiva and Covilhã had dark hair and complexions and spoke perfect Arabic. Both contracted fever in Alexandria and nearly died. The local authorities confiscated their cargo, anticipating their deaths, but indemnified them when they recovered, which allowed them to buy new trade goods. After this illness at the beginning of his travels, Covilhã was to remain healthy for the remainder of his life.

From Alexandria, they first went to Cairo and from there to Tor, on the Sinai Peninsula at the northern end of the Red Sea. From Tor they sailed down the Red Sea to Aden, where they parted company, agreeing to meet in Cairo in 1490. Paiva left for Abyssinia, but it is uncertain whether he ever reached the court of the emperor. The only fact known about his travels is that he died in Cairo, before Covilhã returned for their rendezvous.

Covilhã sailed from Aden to Cannanore on the west coast of India, disguised as an Arab merchant. From Cannanore, he went to Calicut, the major port for ships embarking westward with cinnamon, pepper, cloves, silk, pearls, gems, and other valuable Oriental products. From Calicut, he sailed, probably in early 1489, to Goa, then primarily a port for shipping horses. Impressed with the site, Covilhã apparently suggested it as a very promising center for Portuguese trade and occupation in his lost report to the Crown. Leaving India, he sailed to Hormuz, then the richest city on the Indian Ocean. From Hormuz, he continued his travels in the Indian Ocean, sailing down the west coast of Africa, arriving at Sofala in Mozambique at about the time that Bartolomeu Dias reached the Great Fish River on the east coast of South Africa. While on the African coast, Covilhã heard of the Isle of the Moon (Madagascar), which he also recommended as a potential Portuguese port of call or base. From Sofala, Covilhã returned to Cairo for his rendezvous with Paiva, stopping at Mozambique, Kilwa, Mombasa, and Malindi on the way.

In his travels, Covilhã had gathered priceless information, not only about trade, bases, and ports of call but also about the monsoons and their use by Arab and Chinese ships in the Indian Ocean. He had sailed from Aden to India on the summer monsoon of 1488 and had left for Hormuz and Arabia on the fall monsoon, shipping in both voyages as a passenger on merchant ships, which took advantage of the prevailing winds. This Arab practice of sailing with the monsoons was to become equally standard for Europeans sailing to India, starting with Vasco da Gama.

Arriving in Cairo in late 1490, Covilhã learned that Paiva had died and had left no account of his travels after they had parted company in Aden more than two years before. In Cairo, he met two Jewish agents sent by John II to find him, Rabbi Abraham of Beja and Joseph of Lamego, a shoemaker. They brought him new instructions from the Crown—that the mission to Abyssinia was essential and that Covilhã should finish it. Joseph of Lamego would take Covilhã's letters back to Portugal, but Covilhã and Rabbi Abraham would visit Hormuz; from Hormuz Covilhã would go to Abyssinia alone.

There is some doubt as to whether the Crown ever received the reports from Covilhã, which have never been found, although the majority of authorities believe that Lamego did return with them to Portugal and that copies were furnished to da Gama. Since many Portuguese records were destroyed in the Lisbon earthquake of 1755, it seems unlikely that they ever will be found. It is also possible that the reports carried by Lamego were lost in transit or even that Lamego never returned to Portugal. Even if the king never received any reports from Lamego, his successor, Manuel I, doubtless received some kind of oral report on Covilhã's eastern travels from Rabbi Abraham after his return from Hormuz.

Rabbi Abraham and Covilhã sailed together to Hormuz, where they parted company. Before he left for Abyssinia, Covilhã made a daring side trip; he visited Jidda, Mecca, and Medina. From Medina, he journeyed by caravan to Syria, hearing mass at the Convent of Saint Catherine on Mount Sinai. From Syria, he continued his travels, finally arriving at the court of the Emperor of Abyssinia in early 1494. There his travels ended.

Three successive neguses would not allow Covilhã to return to Portugal, although they sent an Abyssinian priest to Portugal as an envoy in 1510. Covilhã was granted lands and made an adviser and confidant of the royal family. He married an Abyssinian, by whom he had several children. He was not the only long-term honored captive. Other Europeans detained in Abyssinia included another Portuguese, two Catalans, a Basque, a German, a Greek, a Venetian, and eleven Genoese, mostly captives who had escaped from the Turks.

In 1520, Covilhã emerged from obscurity to play a crucial role in opening diplomatic relations between Portugal and Abyssinia. After many vicissitudes, a diplomatic expedition sent by the Portuguese from India led by Rodrigo de Lima arrived at the court of the reigning emperor, Lebna Dengel Dawit (David). Covilhã was able to assist the embassy through his knowledge of the language, country, and court. After a long stay in Abyssinia, the embassy was successful, finally returning to Portugal by way of Massawa and Goa in 1527. Covilhã did not return with the party but sent in his place a son, who died on the journey. Father Francisco Alvares, the chaplain of the embassy, published a memoir of the Lima mission, *Verdadeira informação das terras do Preste João das Indias* (1540; *The Prester John of the Indies: A True Relation of the Lands of the Prester John, Being the Narrative of the Portuguese Embassy to Ethiopia in 1520,* 1961), which is the principal source of both the mission and the career of Covilhã.

Nothing is known of the last years of Covilhã's life. He was still living when the Lima mission left Abyssinia in 1526, but he had died before the military expedition led by Estevão da Gama to assist the Abyssinians against an invasion by Islamic Somalis arrived in late 1541.

Summary

The effect of Pêro da Covilhã is extremely difficult to assess. No writings by him are known to exist, although the authenticity of his travels has never been questioned. If his accounts reached Lisbon in time to be of use to Vasco da Gama, then he is one of the most significant travelers in history; if not, then he is of secondary importance. His assistance to the Lima expedition is unquestionable, so it can safely be said that his place in history in helping to open diplomatic relations with the empire of Abyssinia is secure.

By any standard, Covilhã ranks with Marco Polo, Álvar Nuñez Cabeza de Vaca, and Sir Richard Burton as one of history's great wanderers. Traveling alone in hostile country—the Muslim world—he ran far greater risks than did Burton or Polo. Moreover, as a secret agent, Covilhã could anticipate only a pension and a title if he succeeded. These were ample rewards but hardly those which a successful sixteenth century conquistador or a nineteenth century explorer and travel writer might have received. Covilhã's travels seem an expression of a personal sense of duty to the Crown and of the spirit of adventure that was characteristic of the Renaissance.

Bibliography

Alvares, Francisco. *The Prester John of the Indies: A True Relation of the Lands of the Prester John, Being the Narrative of the Portuguese Embassy to Ethiopia in 1520.* Edited and revised by C. F. Beckingham and G. W. B. Huntingford. Translated by Lord Stanley of Alderley. Cambridge, England: Cambridge University Press, 1961. This is the fullest account of Covilhã and the source for most writings on him. Alvares, generally considered a very reliable source, came to know Covilhã well, and liked and admired him. Internal evidence indicates that the manuscript for *The Prester John of the Indies* was begun while Alvares was still in Abyssinia.

Diffie, Bailey W., and George D. Winius. *Foundations of the Portuguese Empire, 1415-1580.* Minneapolis: University of Minnesota Press, 1977. Diffie and Winius give an adequate description of Covilhã's travels, although they do not mention his trip to Mecca, Jidda, and Medina. They believe that news of Covilhã's travels did not reach Portugal before da

Gama sailed, basing their judgment on errors that da Gama made in India, which a knowledge of Covilhã's travels would have prevented.

Hale, John R. *The Age of Exploration.* New York: Time, 1966. Like Diffie and Winius, Hale omits Covilhã's side trip to Mecca but believes that Covilhã's message to the king did arrive before da Gama left.

Landström, Björn. *The Quest for India.* Garden City, N.Y.: Doubleday, 1964. Translated by Michael Phillips and Hugh Stubbs. Contains one of the fullest accounts of Covilhã's Eastern travels but very little about his stay in Abyssinia and its significance.

Parry, J. H. *The Age of Reconnaissance.* Cleveland: World Publishing, 1963. Parry gives a complete and sympathetic sketch of Covilhã's Asian travels but says virtually nothing about his stay in Abyssinia.

Penrose, Boies. *Travel and Discovery in the Renaissance, 1420-1620.* Cambridge, Mass.: Harvard University Press, 1955. Penrose writes an account much like Landstrom's—full on Covilhã's Asian travels, weaker on his Abyssinian years.

Prestage, Edgar. *The Portuguese Pioneers.* London: A. & C. Black, 1933. Prestage's work is the fullest of all on Covilhã's African years and very good on his Asian travels. He also devotes more space to showing his significance than any other author except Beckingham.

Sanceau, Elaine. *The Land of Prester John: A Chronicle of Portuguese Exploration.* New York: Alfred A. Knopf, 1944. Sanceau provides what is both the fullest and most readable of all accounts of Covilhã's career. Writing for a popular audience, Sanceau says little on the significance of Covilhã's travels but compensates her readers with a very complete view of his life in Abyssinia.

John Gardner